Disney

INF IN ITY

PRIMA Official Game Guide

Written by:
Howard Grossman & Michael Knight

FREE Mobile Version

Go to **www.primagames.com/code**

and enter this code:

c26j-prgv-2kax-5ebq

- Complete DIGITAL VERSION of the strategy guide.

- RESPONSIVE DESIGN optimizes your view for any size screen.

- ACCESS your eGuide from your PC, tablet, or ANY WEB-ENABLED DEVICE!

STILL HAVE QUESTIONS?
Post them to "Your Questions & Answers" on PrimaGames.com

Disney INFINITY

TABLE OF CONTENTS

Game Basics

BASICS

SEARCHING

Looking for missions is an easy process, since all Mission Givers for Main or Side Missions have a blue exclamation mark over their head and generate a blue beacon. After a mission is started the Mission Giver will have a blue question mark over them until the quest is completed. Challenges also give off a beacon as long as you have the correct character for that Challenge. Initially the beacon is yellow to represent the first level of difficulty, which is easy. As you complete a challenge the beacon will change to orange for medium and red for hard. When all three levels of difficulty are completed it will turn grey.

A lot of the guesswork is taken out of searching due to the green compass arrow built into the game. When in doubt, go into the mission log and make sure to activate a mission to get the helpful arrow to appear.

SHOW ME THE MONEY

A lot of the destructible environment as well as enemies will drop coins, however you must actually run over the coins to collect them. It is easy to overlook this fact, so make sure not to miss out. If you are running low on funds, try completing some challenges on the higher levels or simply find a spot with a lot of destructible objects to smash and let them regenerate so you can do it again.

MOVES/MOVEMENT

PEOPLE

There are a large number of characters to play with in this game, and fortunately they all move in a similar fashion. You use one stick to move and the other to look around for all human and super-human characters. You also use the same buttons to jump, block, dodge, and activate the character's "powers", however each character from a Play Set is unique and has his or her own powers and methods of attack. They do all share a few common movements that are essential to platforming, as explained here.

DOUBLE JUMP

The first common technique is the double jump, and while it is easy to do, there is more to it than merely pressing a button twice. Double jumps will allow you to jump higher, but they can also allow you to jump longer. The second jump can be done to extend the distance you cover, allowing you to jump across far ledges and buildings.

CLIMBING

Most of the platforming in the game will include plenty of climbing. This skill is easy to perform, but it can be tricky to know where you can actually climb. Always look for a ledge, edge, or ridge that has a yellow glow, which indicates you can grab on to it. Once you are hanging, there are a lot of options including jumping up or over to another grapple point, jumping down or off the structure, or following the hand hold to maneuver around the edge. Holding on to an edge and running or moving hand-over-hand is an important technique to get to through some tricky spots.

There are also other objects that can be climbed in various Play Sets such as poles, ropes, and drain pipes. These objects aren't highlighted in yellow all the time, but their narrow shape should give you a good idea that they are something to try out.

DODGE/CHARGE/ROLL

Several characters have the ability to move in a quick fashion that can be used for defense or offense. A roll is a great way to dodge an attack (by holding block and pressing the control stick) and to maneuver when there is a lot of action on screen at once. Also available is a charge move (done by pressing the normal attack button) that can be used to cover ground quickly or simply to move faster or to avoid a bad situation. There are also characters like the ones from Monsters University that can use a charging move to break objects or stun enemies.

VEHICLES

CARS

All vehicles move by using one stick to steer and the other to look around, and they all use the triggers to accelerate and brake/reverse. Cars can jump and, as you might guess, the faster it goes the farther it jumps—this is especially true when you hit a ramp. This is where two important features come in: drifting and turbo.

DRIFTING

Drifting is the process of holding both triggers while driving into a turn or even a circle. This maneuver is great for getting around corners when you are at top speeds, but more importantly it builds up the turbo meter. More turbo means more speed. Drift in any race or situation where you need to store up that potential boost.

TURBO

There is a meter under your vehicle that indicates how many bars of turbo you have.

When you do a stunt or drift, the meter in one bar will fill until it is yellow, which means you can activate that boost. After one bar is yellow, the next gauge will start to fill and continue the process. Once all segments of the meter are yellow, you are wasting an effort to build turbo and should use a boost as soon as possible. To activate the turbo is a simple flick of the control stick and your vehicle will shoot flames showing you are boosting. Obviously it can be dangerous to boost at a turn, but a drift can help control that speed. A turbo assist is great any time you are in a straightaway, a close race to the finish, or when you want to hit a ramp at top speed to maximize your air time for stunts or tricks.

STUNTS/TRICKS

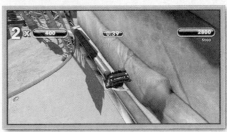

Probably the coolest thing about cars, besides high-speed driving, is the tricks you can pull off. After leaping in the air, pushing the right stick up, down, left, or right will trigger front or back flips, spins, or barrel rolls. Doing two of the same motions while in the air is considered a double trick. However, if you push in two different directions, the stunt is considered a combo and earns even more points. If you get enough height and speed, it is possible to pull off a triple combo for really big points. The key to chaining moves is to immediately flip the control stick when you are airborne and quickly press another direction as that move completes to perform the next trick.

BIKES

Two wheelers can perform stunts and tricks similar to cars, but they don't have a turbo gauge. Generally bikes are pretty slow, but to get a boost you need to do a trick that gives the bike a blue trail as it speeds along. This speed trail shows that the bike is going at top speed and it is the perfect time for hitting ramps to get big air and do tricks. A cool feature of bikes is that they can grind on rails and even build up a blue speed burst while doing so. One down side to bikes is that they are somewhat fragile. If you don't land well after even a short jump, that bike will break apart and you have to wait for it to reform.

GAME BASICS

CHARACTERS

POWER DISCS

PLAY SETS

TOY BOX

TOY BOX COLLECTION

ACHIEVEMENTS

MOUNTS

There are several unique animals to ride in the Play Sets, mostly in Lone Ranger. You can expect to find a bunch of horses, an elephant, and other critters in the Play Sets and Toy Box. Horses can run (accelerate) and turn, as they stand on their back legs and neigh, but they don't do stunts. However, unlike other rides, you can shoot while on horseback. That speed while shooting is a big advantage. As you might guess, an elephant doesn't run, but it can stomp and charge. Animal companions may not be as fast as other forms of transportation, but they are very fun to ride around and bring a lot of variety traveling throughout the worlds.

SHIPS

Found in the Pirates Play Set, ships are essential to the pirate theme and come in two types. There is a small dinghy, which is a tiny boat, but it still packs a cannon that can wipe out enemies and remove debris. The big ship is where you really get to act as a captain to customize, steer, and battle your boat on the open seas, however. Visually the ship can be customized like many buildings or NPCs, but the exciting part is changing the type of cannons it can fire and the type of power-ups it uses. These options make your ship the terror of the seas to anyone foolish enough to cross your path. It is literally a blast to sink other ships, especially when you can change views to see things from another angle and manually fire the final cannon to send them to the locker.

FLIGHT

A few special methods allow a player to fly through the world, and some even come with weapons. It is pretty thrilling to fly over an entire map, but remember that these are not fighting jets and most modes of air travel are not very fast. These vehicles move in a similar way to others, but there is the added element of controlling elevation by going higher and lower.

UNIQUE

There are many other modes of transportation that are unique to each Play Set and can appear in the Toy Box, such as the Hover Board and Glide Pack. Their special functionality determines how they are controlled and what they can do. These add a new experience in game play and can take a while to master.

COMBAT

Conflict is an essential part of any game, and in *Disney Infinity* it can take place on land, air, or sea. Each character has his or her own attacks, but these are further enhanced by Tools, Packs, and Vehicles. There are tons of variations, but here are a few tips to keep in mind when battling your way to victory.

ON FOOT

Characters like The Incredibles have unique superpowers that give them a big advantage in hand-to-hand combat, but most characters share some common moves. One move that is not very obvious is the ground slam, where a character jumps and attacks. This is useful when surrounded by enemies as it lifts your character out of danger for a second and delivers an attack with a small area of effect. On the other end of the spectrum is the defensive ability to block with a simple button press. This is often overlooked as players try to overpower enemies with combos, but it is probably one of the best options in a fight. Most attacks can be blocked, and while this doesn't get you any closer to defeating your enemy, it can set your enemy up to drop his or her guard. By blocking or absorbing an attack, it can create an opening for you to counter or avoid getting knocked out of range. This is a fallback move, so whenever you are not sure what to do in battle—block!

CARS

There are lots of options for vehicular combat, especially with the cars that have built-in guns. Also, vehicles from the Cars Play Set have a large variety of weapons including machine guns, mines,

GAME BASICS

CHARACTERS

POWER DISCS

PLAY SETS

TOY BOX

TOY BOX COLLECTION

ACHIEVEMENTS

and missiles that only appear after they are unlocked from side missions and purchased. All of these weapons are great for knocking the competition out of a race or destroying objects. Even without weapons, there is an overlooked ability for Cars characters to bump into other vehicles and knock them off balance. This isn't as powerful as a full-out weapon attack, but a hard hit could give the edge in a race.

SHOOTING

Numerous types of projectiles range from Toilet Paper Launchers to Tomahawks, but they are controlled in the same way. Gun-like toys can be fired from the hip and shot in the general direction the character is pointing. With enough firing of the toy, it will spread enough ammo to take out most targets. However, if you need precision, you can enter a zoomed in mode where you can place the aiming cursor over what you want to hit. The important thing to remember is that while the gun is locked in one position, you can still run and gun, allowing you to move quickly with the gun focused on a single point. This technique comes in handy when trying to shoot specific targets during Challenges. The Lone Ranger features some special projectile properties, because the shots all ricochet off of a target. Essentially a single shot can bounce and hit many targets, opening up lots of tricky shooting.

BIG GUNS

Many of the larger guns like the Gattling guns and cannons will change the perspective to first person. These powerful weapons can cover great distance, but they must be adjusted for height to lob and launch ammunition to reach the targets. Cannons are extremely damaging, but they track and move very slowly and have a slower rate of fire than most other guns. These are best for large and tough targets, otherwise use a Gattling gun to shoot lots of ammunition to track smaller and quicker targets.

ON THE OPEN SEAS

Your main ship from the Pirates Play Set has several types of cannons to take out enemies. There is a lot of strategy in choosing what type of cannon due to their firing rate, range, and damage capabilities. Another factor is whether you fire the guns from the helm, shoot the side cannons from a few views, or if you want to manually use the cannon to personally target and fire away on ships. The other important option is that the Broadside cannons can fire a single shot if you press the fire button quickly. But if it is held to charge the cannons, several of them will fire at the same time. All of these options depend on the type and amount of ships that you are battling, but in a large sea battle it is probably best to stick to the helm and blast with full cannon fire when you can hit with all your cannons.

In addition to the variety of cannons, there are many power-ups that can speed up your ship, turn the sea against foes, and even summon

the Kraken. Only a single power-up can be active at one time and each has a charge/recharge time before it can be used. These powerful weapons can quickly sink a single ship and can effectively turn the tide of battle.

FINISH THEM

Many enemies will fall down after taking some damage, but that doesn't mean they are defeated. A lot of them can be hit while they are down or trying to get up, so make sure to finish off a single enemy. Quickly switching enemies is a good tactic when you are surrounded, but it is always a good idea to reduce the number of foes you face as soon as possible.

MISSION TYPES

Each Play Set has a variety of missions to keep you busy. There are missions that tell a story or provide optional side quests, and even repeatable missions. A blue exclamation mark over a character denotes that he or she has a mission to discuss with you. Also, the character sends out a blue beacon above that can be seen from far away.

MAIN MISSIONS

These are the primary quests where you will encounter many familiar characters from that Play Set's world. The story missions are considered Main Missions, as they complete an adventure centered around each unique world. All of the Main Missions combine to tell a complete tale from start to finish, although the story can have several branching elements. This means that there can be several Main Missions going on at any given moment, but the main story leads to the same conclusion.

SIDE MISSIONS

Side Missions are usually optional tasks that can be done to enhance the journey. Beyond the obvious fun of completing them, there are often rewards that make it well worth your time to go through each one. These missions can be as quick as a single action or extend throughout the entire adventure. Like the Main Missions, these are given by someone with a blue exclamation mark and are sometimes extra missions given by primary characters, or new missions from general NPCs.

"HIDDEN" MISSIONS

These special type of Alert Missions are almost hidden because they are not explicitly listed in the mission log. These are not necessarily intended to be "secrets", and they may pop up as a message on screen, but they're easy to overlook or forget about. This includes missions such as the pennant collection in Monsters University and locating very elusive totems in Lone Ranger.

ALERT MISSIONS

Many of these missions are repeatable short quests that can appear at various times in an adventure. Generally they are simple tasks, like taking out some enemies or towing a car.

CHALLENGE MISSIONS

Challenges are unlocked as you complete certain tasks or missions in the Play Sets. They give off a yellow beacon, but the beacon will not appear if you are not using the specific character required. If you don't have that character active, the Challenge location is just a flat circle on the ground with that character's picture on it. Most of the missions are meant for all characters of that Play Set, but several are specific to a character. These can be played many times and have three levels of difficulty: easy, medium, and hard. They are a great diversion from the main story or perfect places to hone your skills for multiplayer games.

TOOLS AND PACKS

Each Play Set has its own unique Tools and Packs, but they are all equipped the same way. Except for vehicles from the Cars Play Set, everyone can equip one Tool and one Pack at a time. The Tools are held in the character's hand (which would be tough for a car!) and the Packs are something the character wears on its back (or, in the case of Cars, somewhere on their chassis). These can be set up with a quick swap on the directional pad to toggle them on and off. While you will generally want to use these awesome upgrades, you have to be aware that it will replace the default functionality of a button press. For example, when one of The Incredibles has the Hover Board active, he or she cannot use a regular attack. Ultimately the extra power of the Tools and Packs will replace your common moves, but being able to toggle back and forth with a quick swap is essential to rounded gameplay.

DECORATE/CUSTOMIZE

Inside each Play Set you can change the appearance of buildings and NPCs to customize that world. These are strictly visual changes, but they can alter the way an entire city looks and feels.

LEVELING UP

As characters earn Sparks, they will go up in level and be awarded a Spin in the Toy Box Vault. Leveling doesn't affect the character's attributes, and is strictly used to build up Spins to earn more precious toys from the Toy Box.

COLLECTIBLES

One of the main functions of the Play Set is to unlock content for the Toy Box. Each Play Set has red and green capsules that can unlock items in the Play Set and Toy Box. There are also Chests and a Vault that can be unlocked by specific characters to unlock exclusive content from that world into the Play Set. Check out the collectibles maps and info at the end of each Play Set to find any customization you are looking for.

PLAY SET COMPLETION

Disney Infinity does not have a completion meter or percentage for each Play Set. It is meant to be enjoyed to whatever extent the player wants. However for those looking to go the extra distance and complete as much of the game as possible, there are several ways to keep you busy for a long time. The Gold Star missions and achievement/trophies are an obvious goal to shoot for, but to really finish a Play Set means completing all of the following tasks:

- Main and Side Missions
- Challenges completed on all difficulties
- All capsules collected (red and green)
- All Gold Star missions done
- All Toy Store toys unlocked and purchased
- All Chests and Vaults opened

GAME BASICS

CHARACTERS

POWER DISCS

PLAY SETS

TOY BOX

TOY BOX COLLECTION

ACHIEVEMENTS

MONSTERS UNIVERSITY

SULLEY

Fearless and Fur-ocious:
He's the big monster around campus.

Biography

The big, lovable future scarer is in training at the Monsters University Play Set. Bust a few cycling moves across campus, set up traps for unsuspecting monsters, and avoid lectures.

Favorite Toys

TP Launcher
Effortlessly wrap a tree, vehicle, or anything else in a blanket of TP. Or just use it to annoy a rival security guard.

Bike
Sulley loves to pull off showy stuns and wheel around campus. Just don't mention how funny he looks on the under-sized bike.

Toy Box Adventure: Sulley's Paintball Brawl

Use those big ol' hairy arms to take out as many paintballers as possible before time runs out.

NOTE

Available in the Disney Infinity Starter Pack.

MIKE

*An eye for studying.
He might be green,
but he's scary keen.*

Biography

Join the campus clown in the Monsters University Play Set. Use a megaphone to scare rival monsters, study being sneaky, or just let Mike perform his signature jig.

Favorite Toys

TP Launcher

For a small green ball, Mike is pretty accurate with the TP Launcher. Enjoy some radical campus redecoration with TP.

Bike

Perfectly sized for someone double Mike's height and all the funnier for it. Mike is also pretty handy with 360-degree cartwheels and hanging flips (whatever those are).

Toy Box Adventure: Mike's Scare Pig Dash

Get Mike to grab as many pickups as time allows. The yellow is worth the least, red is the most, and orange is in the middle.

NOTE

Character sold separately.

RANDY

*Sneak and Scare.
Having fun was never so creepy.*

Biography

When it comes to creeping into the rival campus for some scare-worthy sabotage, Randy is the sneakiest in the Monsters University Play Set.

Favorite Toys

Hand Prank

Get Randy to set up the perfect angle so a giant foam hand shoots out at any unsuspecting victim inspecting the message board, and catapults them into the air.

Prank Boxing Glove

It's just an innocent telephone box—until Randy gets to it and sets up a giant boxing glove that sucker punches anyone who goes to use it.

Toy Box Adventure: Randy's Scavenger Hunt

Randy is in his element sneaking past the enemies and gathering as many of the collectibles as possible before time runs out.

NOTE

Character sold separately.

GAME BASICS

CHARACTERS

POWER DISCS

PLAY SETS

TOY BOX

TOY BOX COLLECTION

ACHIEVEMENTS

THE INCREDIBLES

MR. INCREDIBLE

He's a super dad.
Just don't get on his wrong side.

Biography

Dedicated to saving the world, Mr. Incredible uses his super strength and super combo attacks to vanquish Syndrome!

Favorite Toys

Mr. Incredible Sports Car

Its retro, sleek design and purring engine make this the perfect vehicle for any super dad. It can really go too, if you put your foot down.

Glider

He might be barrel-chested, but with a glider, Mr. Incredible floats like leaves on the breeze. A nice way to get down from a skyscraper.

Toy Box Adventure: Mr. Incredible, the Hero

Embark on a super adventure to destroy the domes and rescue the townsfolk before time runs out!

NOTE

Available in the Disney Infinity Starter Pack.

GAME BASICS

CHARACTERS

POWER DISCS

PLAY SETS

TOY BOX

TOY BOX COLLECTION

ACHIEVEMENTS

MRS. INCREDIBLE

*Stretch your imagination.
Flexible, fast, and fun.*

Biography

With her super-stretch skills, Mrs. Incredible can whip across town, yank objects closer, and swing up buildings. Evil-doers beware!

Favorite Toys

Hover Board

A zippy little way for Mrs. Incredible to navigate the metropolis, the Hover Board is great for flipping and dropping in on annoying baddies.

Incredicar

Whether it's picking up the kids, doing a grocery run, or chasing down the most evil wrongdoers in the city, this car is the perfect mom-mobile.

Toy Box Adventure: Mrs. Incredible's Grab It

Use her long arm of the law to pick up and return NPCs to the park, or get more points bringing criminals to the police station.

NOTE

Character sold separately.

THE INCREDIBLES

DASH

Can you keep up? Small but super speedy.

Biography

Play The Incredibles Play Set as the fastest kid on the block, Dash. Don't just fight the dreaded the enemy, run circles around them with your superhuman speed.

Favorite Toys

Helicopter
Drop Dash into a Helicopter and get a birds-eye view of your mission or just get to the top of buildings super quick.

Hover Board
Dash owns the concept of air surfing. He's turned it into an art form.

Toy Box Adventure: Dash's Data Dart

Speed around in a blur to avoid the red and blue balls while gathering the collectibles.

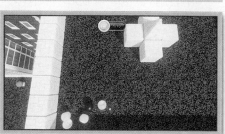

NOTE

Character sold separately.

VIOLET

Shield yourself. Sometimes defense is the best attack.

Biography

Violet has done her fair share of protecting, and her plasma shield is perfect for the job in The Incredibles Play Set. Her power of invisibility also comes in handy for avoiding trouble.

Favorite Toys

Helicopter
Getting in and out of this helicopter can get Violet out of a sticky situation. Have her hover above trouble spots so she can plan her method of attack.

Glider
She's graceful like no other, but with a glider on her back, Violet is a quiet and fearsome opponent in any Toy Box environment.

Toy Box Adventure: Violet's Stealth Mission

Use Violet's super agility to gather as many of the collectables as possible while avoiding the spotlights.

NOTE

Character sold separately.

GAME BASICS

CHARACTERS

POWER DISCS

PLAY SETS

TOY BOX

TOY BOX COLLECTION

ACHIEVEMENTS

SYNDROME

An evil mastermind.
Scheming is his game.

Biography

He's the flame-haired fanboy and self-appointed nemesis in The Incredibles Play Set. Join Syndrome in his campaign to take over the city and put The Incredibles in danger's way. What happens is up to you!

Favorite Toys

Glider

An evil mastermind likes to explain his plan in a long monologue. Why not do it as you are gracefully swooping down from above?

Zero Point Energy

The super static trick Syndrome has hidden up his sleeve. Use it to effortlessly pick up adversaries, objects, and even vehicles, and throw them around like playthings.

Toy Box Adventure: Syndrome's Sorting Sprint

Get up to no good by picking up and throwing NPCs to the surrounding rooftops. Hit a bullseye to get bonus points.

NOTE

Character sold separately.

PIRATES OF THE CARIBBEAN

CAPTAIN JACK SPARROW

The people's pirate.
Infinite play, pillage, and plunder.

Biography

Join Captain Jack Sparrow in an epic adventure of pirates, treasures, and sea battles. Lead him on his merry and slightly unbalanced way across the Pirates of the Caribbean Play Set. Savvy?

Favorite Toys

Sword

Captain Jack Sparrow's cutting edge skills come to life in a sword battle. Score points with every hit on your opponent.

Pirate Bomb

Captain Jack Sparrow loves throwing in a witty line, but how about a bomb? Land it near an opponent to score damage points.

Toy Box Adventure: Sparrow's Flight

Captain Jack Sparrow's bounty-grabbing adventure challenges you to gather as many of the collectibles as possible before time runs out.

NOTE

Available in the Disney Infinity Starter Pack.

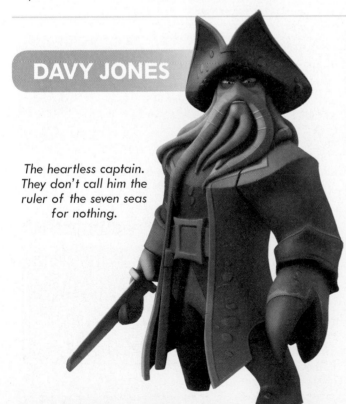

BARBOSSA

*The undead pirate.
Play by the Code.*

Favorite Toys

Sword

Barbossa is quick to draw his sword and scores points easily with his fast technique.

Pirate Bomb

Keep your bomb for a shock and awe attack. While your opponent is recovering, swoop in with your sword.

Toy Box Adventure: Barbossa's Blockade

Defeat enemies and gather the collectibles they drop. Take what you can before time expires and give nothing back!

NOTE

Character sold separately.

Biography

He's a master swordsman and a powerful character to wield. Barbossa is the much-feared, mutinous ex-first-mate of Captain Jack Sparrow and fun to play in the Pirates of the Caribbean Play Set.

DAVY JONES

*The heartless captain.
They don't call him the
ruler of the seven seas
for nothing.*

Favorite Toys

Sword

Davy Jones is a graceful swordsman despite being undead. Draw your sword and rack up those points ya filthy landlubbers!

Flintlock

The classic pirate pistol helps Davy Jones pick off his prey. Use the target to fire at your opponent, scoring points for each hit.

Toy Box Adventure: Davy Jones Collects Souls

Shiver me timbers! Davy Jones's adventure will have ya defeating enemies and collectin' as many treasures as possible before time expires!

NOTE

Character sold separately.

Biography

The demon of the deep, Davy Jones is feared by all who sail the seven seas. Beware of the sword-fighting feats and writhing tentacles of the Pirates of the Caribbean villain.

GAME BASICS
CHARACTERS
POWER DISCS
PLAY SETS
TOY BOX
TOY BOX COLLECTION
ACHIEVEMENTS

CARS

LIGHTNING MCQUEEN

*Buckle up.
He's pure fun on wheels.*

Biography

Whatever the task, Lightning McQueen is quick to react. Whether he's jumping a canyon, trailblazing through the desert, or towing another character in the Cars Play Set, nothing slows him down.

Favorite Toys

Tow Chain

This accessory is a lot of fun. Lightning can tow things while zooming around corners with maximum torque.

Tow-able Wrecking Ball

Combine super fast driving speed and the heavy momentum of a huge iron ball and you have destruction derby guaranteed.

Toy Box Adventure: Lightning's High Jinks

Zoom off to gather as many of the collectibles as possible before time runs out. Each color pickup is worth different points. Yellow is the least, red is the most, and orange is in the middle.

> NOTE
>
> Available in the Cars Play Set.

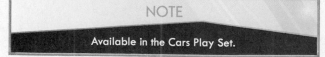

MATER

*Keep on truckin'.
No tow is too far for this rusty hero.*

Biography

Don't judge a book by its cover. Mater might be a bit rusty, but he's also got power under his hood. He's built for towing too, so he's one of the more helpful vehicles in the Cars Play Set!

Favorite Toy

Monster Truck Tires

Mater has a goofy smile whatever the ride, but with Monster Truck Tires underneath he'll chew up any asphalt you throw at him.

Toy Box Adventure: Mater's Tow-Go

Take the good-hearted local yokel on a mission to tow as many of the stranded Tourist Cars to their destinations as possible before time runs out.

> NOTE
>
> Character sold separately.

GAME BASICS

CHARACTERS

POWER DISCS

PLAY SETS

TOY BOX

TOY BOX COLLECTION

ACHIEVEMENTS

HOLLEY

Smooth agent.
Disarmingly charming.

Biography

Holley Shiftwell is as sharp and smart as she looks. Trained for any terrain, take Holley for a spin and she'll make even the hardest corners in the Cars Play Set feel like child's play.

Favorite Toys

Machine Gun

Every good spy has some decent kit. This rapid-fire machine gun is Holley's tool of the trade and is great for taking down those hit points in one spray.

Tow-able Ramp

Sometimes a spy has to edge her way into the trickiest places. This tow-able ramp is great for all-areas access.

Toy Box Adventure: Holley's C.H.R.O.M.E. Training

Enjoy a classic spy mission to destroy as many of the enemy targets as possible before time runs out, gathering new weapons as you go.

NOTE

Available in the Cars Play Set.

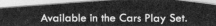

FRANCESCO

The open-wheeled champ.
With the horsepower to prove it.

Biography

Top European racer Francesco thinks he's the hottest thing since wheels were invented. With his high-speed racing and gadgetry, the sleek Italian car is Lightning's chief rival. Francesco can zip around the Cars Play Set and still have enough juice for showing off afterwards.

Favorite Toys

Machine Gun

If he's not outrunning you, he's outgunning you. On Francesco's hood, this machine gun becomes a super-reactive weapon.

Missile

While you are taking those hairpin bends like a madman, why not fire a missile towards an obstruction, opponent, or building just for kicks?

Toy Box Adventure: Francesco's Fracas

Take this Mediterranean motor around the track to complete three laps as quickly as possible.

NOTE

Character sold separately.

THE LONE RANGER

THE LONE RANGER

*Masking for trouble.
Outlaws won't catch
themselves.*

Biography

There's never a dull moment playing the smart-shooting, masked man of justice. Even with the odds stacked against you, you can use your climbing, riding, and bullet-ricocheting skills to win in the Lone Ranger Play Set.

Favorite Toys

Jupiter Train

The Lone Ranger can custom build a train and use it to help you transfer objects to specific locations and control the railroad.

TNT Pack

Blow walls, blockades, and annoyances sky high with this powerful pack of explosives. Then make sure you enjoy one of those "cool guy walks away from explosions" moments.

Toy Box Adventure: Ranger's Riff-Raff Run-In

Ride 'em to take out as many enemies as possible before the time runs out. Enemies on horseback are worth more points.

NOTE

Available in the Lone Ranger Play Set.

TONTO

*Brave at heart.
Play the spiritual warrior.*

Biography

He's the intelligent, Tomahawk-throwing partner of the Lone Ranger and always fun to play. Tonto is excellent on a horse, a feared adversary, and quite stylish with his crow headgear.

Favorite Toys

Elephant

Tonto's trusted steed has a long memory and an even longer nose. Great in a battle charge and a lot of fun to ride.

Stagecoach

The Wild West wouldn't be complete without a stagecoach and Tonto loves to out-flank an opponent in his.

Toy Box Adventure: Tonto's Spirit Sight

Get your moccasins movin' to collect as many of the pickups as possible before time runs out.

NOTE

Available in the Lone Ranger Play Set.

THE NIGHTMARE BEFORE CHRISTMAS

GAME BASICS

CHARACTERS

POWER DISCS

PLAY SETS

TOY BOX

TOY BOX COLLECTION

ACHIEVEMENTS

JACK SKELLINGTON

Funny bones.
Halloween with laughter.

Biography

Boo! Jack Skellington is up to his spooktacular Halloween tricks! Bone up on the action as the creepy King of Halloween uses jack-o-lanterns, screams, and screeches to scare off rivals. How terrifying do you feel?

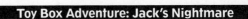

Favorite Toy

Jack-O-Lanterns

A curious mixture of lighting and the macabre.

Toy Box Adventure: Jack's Nightmare

There's only one rule to this adventure: Survive as long as possible. Well, at least stay in one piece. (We know Jack is immortal.)

NOTE

Character sold separately.

TOY STORY IN SPACE

BUZZ LIGHTYEAR

To infinity and beyond.
Gravity cannot hold him.

Biography

Power up with Buzz Lightyear and prepare to defend the galaxy! With his hard-hitting shoulder charge and jetpack, there's nothing and no one this Space Ranger can't blast to infinity and beyond. 3-2-1. Blast off!

Favorite Toys

Astro Blaster

It works! He is a fully powered Space Ranger in *Disney Infinity*.

Buzz Lightyear's Jetpack

If you want to go "beyond" you need the wings to do the job. 3-2-1. Takeoff!

Toy Box Adventure: Buzz Lightyear, Save Me!

The townspeople are in trouble! They're stranded on meters out in space and only Buzz can help. Rescue them before time runs out.

NOTE

Available in the Toy Story Play Set.

WOODY

GAME BASICS

CHARACTERS

POWER DISCS

PLAY SETS

TOY BOX

TOY BOX COLLECTION

ACHIEVEMENTS

Sheriff of toys.
Rustle up some fun.

Favorite Toy

Bullseye
What cowboy is complete without his hopalong?

Toy Box Adventure: Woody's Round Up

Complete three laps around the track as fast as possible in this gallop of epic proportions.

Biography

He's the good-natured toy cowboy who has a heart of gold and the courage of an explorer. On top of this, his shoulder charge knocks villains through the air with ease.

NOTE
Character sold separately.

JESSIE

Tomboy toy.
With a sunny personality.

Favorite Toy

Goo Shrinker
Shoot goo at Jessie's opponent and watch them shrink.

Toy Box Adventure: Jessie's Critter Corral

Those critters keep scattering. It's your job to pick up as many as you can and return them to the goal.

Biography

Yee haw! Saddle up with Jessie and harness her shoulder charge for some fast-moving action. When it comes to rounding up villains, this bold and brash gal doesn't know the meaning of the word "whoa!"

NOTE
Available in the Toy Story Play Set.

TANGLED

RAPUNZEL

Let your hair down.
She's a lot of fun.

Biography

She might be blonde and have luxurious, (really) long hair but she's nobody's fool. She's a dreamer, but Rapunzel reacts pretty quickly in a fight. Just ask her cast iron skillet which she uses to ward off any thug.

Favorite Toy

Cast Iron Skillet

Where Rapunzel gets her strength from to lift this thing, let alone swing it about, escapes us.

Toy Box Adventure: Rapunzel's Rail Ride

Rapunzel's beautifully illuminated adventure challenges you to collect all the lanterns before time runs out.

NOTE
Character sold separately.

WRECK-IT RALPH

WRECK-IT RALPH

Biography

Like knocking down stuff? Then Wreck-It Ralph is the character for you. Enjoy smashing the competition along with anything else that's in the way. Just clench those huge fists and pound up some brick dust!

Favorite Toy

Wreck-It Ralph's Cherry Bomb

Boom boom, gonna shake the room. Sort of what happens when you chuck a Cherry Bomb.

Toy Box Adventure: Ralph's Wreck'n Wrangle

While you're smashing, grab as many of the collectibles as possible before the clock ticks out. If there's one left.

> **NOTE**
> Character sold separately.

Bring the roof down. We mean literally.

VANELLOPE

*Track burning tomboy.
And the heart of a princess.*

Favorite Toys

Vanellope's Cherry Bomb

Boom boom, gonna shake the room. Sort of what happens when you chuck a Cherry Bomb.

Vanellope's Candy Cart

Watch the Glitch in motion in this multicolored and very zippy vehicle.

Toy Box Adventure: Vanellope's Sweet Ride

Burn around the track three times as quick as you can. (Which is pretty quick, we imagine.)

> **NOTE**
> Character sold separately.

Biography

Vanellope, also known as the Glitch, is hard-coded for speed. She's also agile and can teleport glitch style through any adventure. She's also no stranger to competition, so she'll always put up a fight.

GAME BASICS

CHARACTERS

POWER DISCS

PLAY SETS

TOY BOX

TOY BOX COLLECTION

ACHIEVEMENTS

FROZEN

ANNA

She's a free spirit who will capture your heart.

Biography

Anna's warm and caring character will melt any heart. Her courage is boundless and she's always ready with climbing hook and shovel swing to tackle whatever icy mountain or monster snowman gets in her way.

Favorite Toys

Shovel Swing
We had to look this one up, but basically you can dig with it and it doubles as quite the weapon. Especially in Anna's dainty but dangerous hands.

Climbing Hook
Duh, it's for, like, climbing. Scale the icy heights with this handy tool, but don't look down.

Toy Box Adventure: Anna's Chilling Challenge

Gather as many collectibles as possible before time runs out and things get frosty.

> ### NOTE
> Character sold separately.

ELSA

Snow Business. Meet the sub-zero star.

Biography

Elsa is the Snow Queen and quite a powerful character to have fun with. She's also strikingly beautiful, so if she doesn't freeze your world first, she'll definitely charm it with her presence.

Favorite Toy

Freeze Ball
This ball of ice packs a punch and Elsa's got plenty more where it came from.

Toy Box Adventure: Elsa's Snowy Slingshot

Use your slingshot to hit yellow targets for one point or red targets for five.

> ### NOTE
> Character sold separately.

FANTASIA

GAME BASICS

CHARACTERS

POWER DISCS

PLAY SETS

TOY BOX

TOY BOX COLLECTION

ACHIEVEMENTS

SORCERER'S APPRENTICE MICKEY MOUSE

Laugh before you leap.
Mickey always looks on the bright side.

Biography

He's the icon that hardly needs an introduction. Mickey is a naturally adventurous character, so *Disney Infinity* is a dream come true for him! He's an eternal optimist, regardless of the crazy worlds he will find along the way.

Favorite Toy

Mickey's Jalopy

It's cute to look at. That is until it burns past you and you realize that Mickey owned you.

Mickey's Broom

There's always a magic broom handy for Mickey's devastatingly-cute projectile attack.

Toy Box Adventure: Mickey's Magical Escape

Brooms have surrounded the castle and it's up to Mickey to find a way out.

> NOTE
>
> Character sold separately.

AGENT P

Vanquish evil...
or just look cool. Your decision.

Biography

Agent P is a platypus that is unflappable under pressure. This is partly due to his secret agent training and partly due to the fact that he can throw his fedora with devastating accuracy.

Favorite Toy

Flying Fedora

Is it a bird? Is it a plane? No, it's a fabulously fashionable flying accessory coming right at you.

Toy Box Adventure: Agent P & The Infinity-Inator

Dr. Doofenshmirtz has trapped Perry in the Infinity-inator! Survive the twisted games it creates and search for collectibles.

NOTE

Character sold separately.

GAME BASICS

CHARACTERS

POWER DISCS

PLAY SETS

TOY BOX

TOY BOX COLLECTION

ACHIEVEMENTS

His brand new project involves pinball and you.

PHINEAS

Biography

Phineas is part kid, part inventor, and all around a fun character. Let him drop some science on any enemy with his handy Baseball Shooter.

Favorite Toy

Water Slide

Phineas' slide is like a rail that he can use to grind down. This is a cool way to get from A to B.

Baseball Shooter

If you want to ensure your opponents get three strikes, this is the way to do it.

Toy Box Adventure: Phineas' Pinball Mania

It's a giant Pinball Table! Phineas has to keep the balls moving and enemies at bay with his Creativi-Toys.

NOTE

Character sold separately.

Power Discs

Disney Infinity Play Sets and Toy Box Worlds can be modified or customized through the use of Power Discs. These interactive discs are placed on the Disney Infinity Base to power up characters, grant unique abilities, customize the world, and provide exclusive toys. There are two distinct types of Power Discs: a circular disc and hexagonal-shaped disc. Circular Power Discs grant your character special power-ups that can be used in the Play Sets as well as in the Toy Box. Hexagonal Power Discs, on the other hand, unlock special gadgets, vehicles or mounts, and themes to help you personalize the Toy Box even more. By combining different Power Discs, you can get even more unique results.

Power Discs are sold in blind packs of two, and it is a mystery which ones you will receive. Furthermore, some Power Discs are rare (having a lower chance to be in each pack)—they have a special orange border to denote their rarity. The mystery of what is in each blind pack makes Power Discs very collectible and provides a great opportunity for people to swap them to try to collect them all.

> ## NOTE
>
> There were 20 Power Discs released in Series 1 when the game first premiered on August 18, 2013. On November 19, 2013, another 20 Power Discs were released as part of the Series 2 rollout. In Spring 2014, the Series 3 collection will be released with 17 more Power Discs.

MAGICBAND AND THE DISNEY DRAGON

In addition to the collectible Power Discs, there is one other special item you can acquire to bring something new to the Toy Box. An RFID wristband known as a MagicBand (available at Walt Disney World) can be placed on the hexagonal section of the Infinity Portal to unlock the Dragon Gate Toy Box item. Once the Dragon Gate is placed in your Toy Box, a dragon inspired by New Fantasyland will fly around your Toy Box. In addition, after waiting a short but random length of time longer, three green toy capsules will appear. The first contains the Dragon's Keep, which is fantasy-filled Toy Box items for the Disney Dragon. The second capsule holds the Dragon's Flight Sky, which is an exclusive Sky Theme for the Disney Dragon to soar through. The last green capsule has the Dragon's Domain, which is a Terrain Theme filled with surfaces and objects inspired by the Disney Dragon.

DISC TYPES

GAME BASICS

CHARACTERS

POWER DISCS

PLAY SETS

TOY BOX

TOY BOX COLLECTION

ACHIEVEMENTS

ABILITIES: CIRCULAR POWER DISCS

Usage: Placed underneath the character on the Disney Infinity Base.

Ability discs are circular red discs that grant special power-ups that can be used in the Play Sets and in the Toy Box. These provide special perks but do not change the look of the character or world in any way. When these discs are first placed under a character, or If you swap characters, a message will pop up on-screen stating what powers you have equipped. You can place two of these discs under a character (for a maximum of four discs between two characters) to get unique combo perks or you can stack two of the same disc on top of each other to multiply its effect!

TOYS: HEXAGONAL POWER DISCS

Usage: Placed in the hexagonal slot on the Disney Infinity Base.

Toy discs are hexagonal discs that unlock gadgets, weapons, vehicles, and more in the Toy Box. However, these toys will only appear when the hexagonal disc is on the Disney Infinity Base. Remove the disc from the base and the unlocked item goes away.

CUSTOMIZATION: HEXAGONAL POWER DISCS

Usage: Placed in the hexagonal slot on the Disney Infinity Base.

These discs provide numerous ways to personalize the atmosphere of the Toy Box. Customization discs come in two types: one that alters the Sky Theme and another that alters the Toy Box's textures. Changing the Sky Theme alters the sky background and music to match the theme of the disc. The texture disc changes the land and terrain to create a new visual theme.

COLLECTION AND TRADE EVENTS

The very nature of purchasing Power Discs in a blind bag leaves them a big mystery, and that makes them collectible. The common discs have about a 5% chance of appearing in the foil bag while the rare discs only have about a 2% chance of showing up. There are some tricks to try to feel the foil packaging to get an idea of the type of disc you could be getting (circular or hexagonal), but you still can't guess exactly what is inside. You can find specific Power Discs in a secondhand marketplace, but the best way to collect them is to swap with friends. If you don't have a community to trade with, look for retail swap events where you can meet new people and try to complete your collection.

RELEASE WAVES

SERIES 1

These were available to purchase at launch on August 18, 2013, and one is included with the Starter Kit.

This set includes four Ability discs, five Toy discs, and eight Customization discs. There are also three rare Toy discs.

- Disc 1 Ability: Bolt's Super Strength
- Disc 2 Ability: Fix-It Felix's Repair Power
- Disc 3 Ability: C.H.R.O.M.E. Armor Shield
- Disc 4 Ability: Pieces of Eight
- Disc 5 Toys: Mickey's Car
- Disc 6 Toys: Cinderella's Coach
- Disc 7 Toys: Kahn
- Disc 8 Toys: Stitch's Blaster
- Disc 9 Toys: Carl Fredricksen's Cane
- Disc 10 Customization: Sugar Rush Sky
- Disc 11 Customization: King Candy's Dessert Toppings
- Disc 12 Customization: Alice's Wonderland
- Disc 13 Customization: Tulgey Wood
- Disc 14 Customization: Marlin's Reef
- Disc 15 Customization: Nemo's Seascape
- Disc 16 Customization: Rapunzel's Kingdom
- Disc 17 Customization: Rapunzel's Birthday Sky
- Disc 18 Toys (Rare): Dumbo the Flying Elephant
- Disc 19 Toys (Rare): Astro Blasters Space Cruiser
- Disc 20 Toys (Rare): Abu the Elephant

SERIES 2

On November 19, 2013, Series 2 was released featuring five Ability discs, six Toy discs, and six Customization discs. There were also three rare Toy discs.

- Disc 1 Ability: Ralph's Power of Destruction
- Disc 2 Ability: Dr. Doofenshmirtz's Damage-Inator!
- Disc 3 Ability: Electro-Charge
- Disc 4 Ability: Star Command Shield
- Disc 5 Ability: User Control
- Disc 6 Toys: Pizza Planet Delivery Truck
- Disc 7 Toys: Maximus
- Disc 8 Toys: Headless Horseman's Horse
- Disc 9 Toys: Flamingo Croquet Mallet
- Disc 10 Toys: Hangin' Ten Stitch with Surfboard
- Disc 11 Toys: Mike's New Car
- Disc 12 Customization: Frozen Flourish
- Disc 13 Customization: Chill in the Air
- Disc 14 Customization: New Holland Skyline
- Disc 15 Customization: Victor's Experiments
- Disc 16 Customization: Halloweentown Sky
- Disc 17 Customization: Jack's Scary Decorations
- Disc 18 Toys (Rare): Captain Hook's Ship
- Disc 19 Toys (Rare): The Electric Mayhem Bus
- Disc 20 Toys (Rare): Condor Wing Glider

SERIES 3

In Spring 2014, the final series was released, featuring four Ability discs, nine Toy discs, and four Customization discs. There is one rare disc in this series (WALL-E's Fire Extinguisher), and this series also features the discs from the Phineas and Ferb Toy Box pack.

- Disc 1 Ability: Chernabog's Power
- Disc 2 Ability: Rapunzel's Healing
- Disc 3 Ability: Violet's Force Field
- Disc 4 Ability: Mickey's Sorcerer Hat
- Disc 5 Toys: Cruella De Vil's Car
- Disc 6 Toys: Disney Parks Parking Lot Tram
- Disc 7 Toys: Calico Helicopter
- Disc 8 Toys: Phillipe
- Disc 9 Toys: Tantor
- Disc 10 Toys: Dragon Firework Cannon
- Disc 11 Toys (Rare): WALL-E's Fire Extinguisher
- Disc 12 Toys: Toy Story Mania Blaster
- Disc 13 Toys: Angus
- Disc 14 Customization: WALL-E's Collection
- Disc 15 Customization: Buy 'N' Large Atmosphere
- Disc 16 Customization: Tri-State Area Terrain
- Disc 17 Customization: Danville Sky

POWER DISC COMBOS

Circular Power Discs allow you to use special power-ups that can be used in the Play Sets and Toy Box Worlds. To combine the Disney Infinity Power Discs, simply stack one Power Disc on top of another and place these underneath the Disney Infinity character. You can place two of these discs under a character (for a maximum of four between two characters) to get unique combo perks, such as Spark Shield when combining the C.H.R.O.M.E. Armor Shield and Pieces of Eight Power Discs. Also, you can stack two of the same disc together to multiply its effect!

OVERPOWERING STRENGTH

Provides an additional 2% Sparks from defeating enemies

Bolt's Super Strength + Pieces of Eight

IMPROVED SPARK SHIELD

Converts 3% of damage taken into Sparks

Star Command Shield + Pieces of Eight

LIGHTNING SHIELD

Reflects 5% damage back to the attacker

Bolt's Super Strength + Electro-Charge

HEROES UNITED

Increases pickup range by 50%

Violet's Force Field + Bolt's Super Strength

SPARK SHIELD

Converts 2% of damage taken into Sparks

C.H.R.O.M.E. Armor Shield + Pieces of Eight

IMPROVED REGEN BUFF

Provides 3% health regeneration

Electro-Charge + Pieces of Eight

MEGA SPARK SHIELD

Provides an additional 4% Sparks from defeating enemies

Violet's Force Field + Pieces of Eight

GIRL POWER

Increases damage by 5%

Violet's Force Field + Rapunzel's Healing Power

REGEN BUFF

Provides 2% health regeneration

Fix-It Felix's Repair Power + Pieces of Eight

NICELANDERS UNITE!

Boost experience rate by 5%

Ralph's Power of Destruction + Fix-It Felix's Repair Power

OVERWHELMING STRENGTH

Provides an additional 4% Sparks from defeating enemies

Chernabog's Power + Pieces of Eight

VICTORIOUS TRIUMPH

Increases health by 5%

Chernabog's Power + Mickey's Sorcerer Hat

C.H.R.O.M.E. GRAPPLE HOOK

Increases range for picking up objects by 2%

User Control + C.H.R.O.M.E. Armor Shield

FIX IT WITH SCIENCE

Provides 5% health regeneration

Fix-It Felix's Repair Power + Dr. Doofenshmirtz's Damage-Inator!

MEGA REGEN BUFF

Provides 4% health regeneration

Rapunzel's Healing + Pieces of Eight

GAME BASICS

CHARACTERS

POWER DISCS

PLAY SETS

TOY BOX

TOY BOX COLLECTION

ACHIEVEMENTS

POWER DISCS

⭐ ABILITIES: CIRCULAR POWER DISCS

BOLT'S SUPER STRENGTH

Got It? ✅
Series 1
Category: Damage
Rarity: Common

When you have this Power Disc under your character, your character has a 2% chance of inflicting 2% additional damage in both melee and ranged combat. This is cumulative, so if you have two of these discs, you have a 4% chance of inflicting more damage. This is useful in the Play Sets and the Toy Box—especially when you are facing lots of enemies.

FIX-IT FELIX'S REPAIR POWER

Got It? ✅
Series 1
Category: Health
Rarity: Common

Put this under your character and you get a 25% chance of receiving 25% more health, which can help keep you in the battle longer. Again, these are cumulative, so you have an even better chance to get health by stacking two of these Power Discs under your character.

C.H.R.O.M.E. ARMOR SHIELD

Got It? ✅
Series 1
Category: Armor
Rarity: Common

While this Power Disc is placed under your character, you have a 3% chance of receiving 4 seconds of invulnerability. Stack two of these so you get a 6% chance for invulnerability.

PIECES OF EIGHT

Got It? ✅
Series 1
Category: Economy
Rarity: Common

When you are playing in the Play Sets, you need to collect loot or others tokens of the local economy to purchase new tools and toys. Therefore, put one of these Power Discs under your character to get a 2% chance to collect an extra 25 units of loot. If you stack a second one, the greater your chance of getting this bonus.

RALPH'S POWER OF DESTRUCTION

Got It? ✅
Series 2
Category: Damage
Rarity: Common

Summon the destructive power of Wreck-It Ralph for a chance to deal 3% extra damage.

DR. DOOFENSHMIRTZ'S DAMAGE-INATOR!

Got It? ✅
Series 2
Category: Damage
Rarity: Common

Dr. Doofenshmirtz is at it again with a brand new Inator invention, which has a chance to deal 3% extra damage.

ELECTRO-CHARGE

Got It? ✅
Series 2
Category: Health
Rarity: Common

Young Victor Frankenstein has mastered an electrical method to grant 33% more health.

STAR COMMAND SHIELD

Got It? ✅
Series 2
Category: Armor
Rarity: Common

A good Space Ranger never leaves home without some extra protection, like this trusty shield that blocks 3% damage.

USER CONTROL

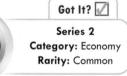

Got It? ✅
Series 2
Category: Economy
Rarity: Common

Summon the power of a User to gain experience at a 2% faster rate.

CHERNABOG'S POWER

Got It? ✅
Series 3
Category: Damage
Rarity: Common

A representation of pure evil from *Fantasia*, you can summon the demonic power of this villain to do 3% more damage.

RAPUNZEL'S HEALING

Got It? ✅
Series 3
Category: Health
Rarity: Common

The magic of Rapunzel's hair does more than make her blonde locks continue to grow. Her golden hair has healing properties that can give a character 40% more health.

VIOLET'S FORCE FIELD

Got It? ✅
Series 3
Category: Armor
Rarity: Common

The quiet daughter of the Incredibles can not only turn invisible, she can also generate a force field that can reduce damage by 3%.

MICKEY'S SORCERER HAT

Got It? ✅
Series 3
Category: Economy
Rarity: Common

The infamous and iconic hat from the The Sorcerer's Apprentice allows characters to gain experience at a 2% faster rate.

TOYS: HEXAGONAL POWER DISCS

MICKEY'S CAR

Got It? ☑
Series 1
Category: Vehicle
Rarity: Common

While in the Toy Box, put this on the pad and Mickey's Car will appear. Drive it around in the Toy Box and even use it for racing.

STITCH'S BLASTER

Got It? ☑
Series 1
Category: Weapon
Rarity: Common

Experiment 626 has left behind his blaster. Place this Power Disc on the pad and you can use it to attack your enemies at a distance.

ASTRO BLASTERS SPACE CRUISER

Got It? ☑
Series 1
Category: Vehicle
Rarity: Rare

This vehicle looks like the ride vehicles in the Buzz Lightyear's Astroblasters ride at the Disney theme parks. It stays on the ground, but has a built-in blaster.

CINDERELLA'S COACH

Got It? ☑
Series 1
Category: Vehicle
Rarity: Common

Want to travel and race in style? This Power Disc makes Cinderella's Coach appear in the Toy Box.

CARL FREDRICKSEN'S CANE

Got It? ☑
Series 1
Category: Weapon
Rarity: Common

Not only does this keep Mr. Fredricksen from falling over, it can also be used to whack enemies. Just pop this Power Disc onto the pad to get this item added to your Tools/Pack collection.

ABU THE ELEPHANT

Got It? ☑
Series 1
Category: Mount
Rarity: Rare

Remember when Genie changed Abu the Monkey into an elephant for Prince Ali's entrance into Agrabah? Now he can carry your character around a Toy Box World.

KAHN

Got It? ☑
Series 1
Category: Mount
Rarity: Common

Kahn carried Mulan into battle. Now this noble steed can take you for a ride.

DUMBO THE FLYING ELEPHANT

Got It? ☑
Series 1
Category: Helicopter
Rarity: Rare

Dumbo the Flying Elephant from the Disney theme parks spawns in the Toy Box when you use this Power Disc. Use it to fly around the world.

PIZZA PLANET DELIVERY TRUCK

Got It? ☑
Series 2
Category: Vehicle
Rarity: Common

This elusive truck has appeared in numerous Pixar movies including *Toy Story*. Drive this iconic vehicle in the Toy Box.

MAXIMUS

Got It? ☑

Series 2
Category: Mount
Rarity: Common

This steed is tough, but with a big heart. He instantly falls for Rapunzel and even becomes friend with his former nemesis Flynn Rider.

HANGIN' TEN STITCH WITH SURFBOARD

Got It? ☑

Series 2
Category: Hoverboard
Rarity: Common

Jump on this hover surfboard to move around quickly as Stitch goes along for the ride up in front.

THE ELECTRIC MAYHEM BUS

Got It? ☑

Series 2
Category: Vehicle
Rarity: Rare

With this you can drive the famous bus The Muppets used to go on their many adventures.

HEADLESS HORSEMAN'S HORSE

Got It? ☑

Series 2
Category: Mount
Rarity: Common

The very sight of the horse of the Headless Horseman is enough to give anyone a real nightmare.

MIKE'S NEW CAR

Got It? ☑

Series 2
Category: Vehicle
Rarity: Common

Take Mike Wazowski's vehicle out for a spin.

CONDOR WING GLIDER

Got It? ☑

Series 2
Category: Helicopter
Rarity: Rare

Based on the film *Condorman* you can become a soaring superhero, like the film's comic illustrator, when you activate this glider.

FLAMINGO CROQUET MALLET

Got It? ☑

Series 2
Category: Weapon
Rarity: Common

Use this toy for a quick game against the Queen of Hearts or as a combat club.

CAPTAIN HOOK'S SHIP

Got It? ☑

Series 2
Category: Helicopter
Rarity: Rare

Ahoy, this ain't no mere seafaring vessel. This special ship can fly!

CRUELLA DE VIL'S CAR

Got It? ☑

Series 3
Category: Vehicle
Rarity: Common

Jump in the villain's car from *101 Dalmatians* to chase after friends and foes.

DISNEY PARKS PARKING LOT TRAM

Got It? ☑

Series 3
Category: Vehicle
Rarity: Common

This vehicle can bring back fond memories of a trip to the Disney Parks. It provides the great comedic value of driving around a parking lot tram, especially when challenging fancy racecars.

TANTOR

Got It? ☑

Series 3
Category: Mount
Rarity: Common

Tantor often seems to be timid and even cowardly. However, the gentle elephant has a deep bond with his friends and is often inspired to acts of bravery.

TOY STORY MANIA BLASTER

Got It? ☑

Series 3
Category: Weapon
Rarity: Common

This toy originates from the Toy Story Midway Mania ride in Disney Parks. Unlike the Goo Guns from the Toy Story Play Set, this is a weapon designed to damage opponents.

CALICO HELICOPTER

Got It? ☑

Series 3
Category: Vehicle
Rarity: Common

The cunning and merciless villain from *Bolt* is always surrounded by cats and is a master strategist. Take control of Dr. Calico's helicopter, which is fully equipped with rockets to rain fire from above.

ANGUS

Got It? ☑

Series 3
Category: Mount
Rarity: Common

The beautiful black Clydesdale from *Brave* is fiercely loyal to Merida. Although he can be stubborn at times, his strong bond to his owner allows him to be coaxed into almost anything.

WALL-E'S FIRE EXTINGUISHER

Got It? ☑

Series 3
Category: Prop
Rarity: Rare

A rare toy inspired by a classic scene from *WALL-E*, it allows characters to use the propulsion from a fire extinguisher to hover in the air.

PHILLIPE

Got It? ☑

Series 3
Category: Mount
Rarity: Common

The loyal horse from *Beauty and the Beast* is the trusty companion and only mode of transportation for Belle and her father Maurice. The horse is loyal, but has been known to get spooked easily.

DRAGON FIREWORK CANNON

Got It? ☑

Series 3
Category: Weapon
Rarity: Common

This cannon from *Mulan* originated in ancient China and precedes modern guns as one of the first projectile-launching weapons.

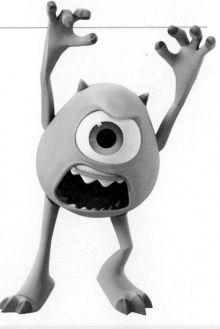

GAME BASICS

CHARACTERS

POWER DISCS

PLAY SETS

TOY BOX

TOY BOX COLLECTION

ACHIEVEMENTS

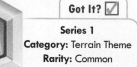

CUSTOMIZING: HEXAGONAL POWER DISCS

KING CANDY'S DESSERT TOPPINGS

Got It? ☑

Series 1
Category: Terrain Theme
Rarity: Common

While in a Toy Box, place this Power Disc on the pad to change the theme of the ground and themed terrain to that of the Sugar Rush video game in *Wreck-It Ralph*.

TULGEY WOOD

Got It? ☑

Series 1
Category: Sky Theme
Rarity: Common

Change the Sky Theme and music in your Toy Box World to that of *Alice in Wonderland*.

RAPUNZEL'S KINGDOM

Got It? ☑

Series 1
Category: Terrain Theme
Rarity: Common

The texture and terrain take on a theme from the movie *Tangled* with this Power Disc.

SUGAR RUSH SKY

Got It? ☑

Series 1
Category: Sky Theme
Rarity: Common

This Power Disc changes the Sky Theme of your Toy Box World to Sugar Rush, and also includes the music of this theme.

ALICE'S WONDERLAND

Got It? ☑

Series 1
Category: Terrain Theme
Rarity: Common

Theme the land and terrain of your Toy Box World to that of Wonderland.

RAPUNZEL'S BIRTHDAY SKY

Got It? ☑

Series 1
Category: Sky Theme
Rarity: Common

Lanterns fill the night Sky Theme as you listen to music from *Tangled* when you use this Power Disc.

NEW HOLLAND SKYLINE

Got It? ☑

Series 2
Category: Sky Theme
Rarity: Common

The Sky Theme becomes a gray cloudy scene with a full moon, tombstones, and the Holland windmill straight out of *Frankenweenie*.

FROZEN FLOURISH

Got It? ☑

Series 2
Category: Terrain Theme
Rarity: Common

Make the terrain a winter wonderland inspired by *Frozen* with this icy Terrain Theme.

NEMO'S SEASCAPE

Got It? ☑

Series 1
Category: Sky Theme
Rarity: Common

The Sky Theme changes to a watery atmosphere when you use this Power Disc.

HALLOWEENTOWN SKY

Got It? ☑

Series 2
Category: Sky Theme
Rarity: Common

The Sky Theme takes on the spooky appearance of *The Nightmare Before Christmas* including the infamous Spiral Hill and yellow moon.

CHILL IN THE AIR

Got It? ☑

Series 2
Category: Sky Theme
Rarity: Common

Change the Sky Theme to chilly snow-covered hills and trees inspired by *Frozen*.

MARLIN'S REEF

Got It? ☑

Series 1
Category: Terrain Theme
Rarity: Common

This Power Disc makes the land look like the bottom of the ocean and changes the terrain to an aquatic look.

JACK'S SCARY DECORATIONS

Got It? ☑

Series 2
Category: Terrain Theme
Rarity: Common

Turn the Toy Box into Halloweentown with the theme and Terrain Theme from *The Nightmare Before Christmas*.

VICTOR'S EXPERIMENTS

Got It? ☑

Series 2
Category: Terrain Theme
Rarity: Common

Give the Toy Box a grey monochrome theme filled with textures from *Frankenweenie*.

GAME BASICS

CHARACTERS

POWER DISCS

PLAY SETS

TOY BOX

TOY BOX COLLECTION

ACHIEVEMENTS

WALL-E'S COLLECTION

Got It? ☑

Series 3
Category: Terrain Theme
Rarity: Common

Transform the Toy Box into the desolate wasteland that the Earth has become due to consumerism and neglect.

BUY 'N' LARGE ATMOSPHERE

Got It? ☑

Series 3
Category: Sky Theme
Rarity: Common

The Sky Theme becomes a swirling dustbowl filled with empty buildings that are mere husks of their former glory. The most notable thing in the barren horizon are the numerous Buy 'N' Large signs.

TRI-STATE AREA TERRAIN

Got It? ☑

Series 3
Category: Terrain Theme
Rarity: Common

A simple and subtle texture, along with a few gadgets, that is reminiscent of summertime when Phineas and Ferb create their incredible inventions.

DANVILLE SKY

Got It? ☑

Series 3
Category: Sky Theme
Rarity: Common

Turn the Sky Theme into the backdrop of Phineas and Ferb's Tri-State Area. One of their greatest projects, a giant roller coaster, can be seen off in the distance. In addition, you can spot the iconic building of Doofenshmirtz Evil Incorporated, the lair of Agent P's nemesis.

Type	Name	Series	Category	Rarity	In-Game Effect
Ability (Circle)	User Control	2	Experience	Common	Character gains experience at a 2% faster rate
Ability (Circle)	Chernabog's Power	3	Damage	Common	Character does 3% more damage
Ability (Circle)	Rapunzel's Healing	3	Health	Common	Character has 40% more health
Ability (Circle)	Violet's Force Field	3	Armor	Common	Character receives 3% less damage
Ability (Circle)	Mickey's Sorcerer Hat	3	Experience	Common	Character gains experience at a 2% faster rate
Customization (Hexagonal)	Alice's Wonderland	1	Terrain Theme	Common	Make the Toy Box themed to *Alice In Wonderland*
Customization (Hexagonal)	Chill in the Air	2	Sky Theme	Common	Make the Sky Theme in the Toy Box themed to *Frozen*
Customization (Hexagonal)	Frozen Flourish	2	Terrain Theme	Common	Make all of the terrain objects in the Toy Box themed to *Frozen*
Customization (Hexagonal)	Halloweentown Sky	2	Sky Theme	Common	Make the Sky Theme in the Toy Box themed to *The Nightmare Before Christmas*
Customization (Hexagonal)	Jack's Scary Decorations	2	Terrain Theme	Common	Make all of the terrain objects in the Toy Box themed to *The Nightmare Before Christmas*
Customization (Hexagonal)	King Candy's Dessert Toppings	1	Terrain Theme	Common	Make all of the terrain objects in the Toy Box themed to Sugar Rush from *Wreck-It Ralph*
Customization (Hexagonal)	Marlin's Reef	1	Terrain Theme	Common	Make all of the terrain objects in the Toy Box themed to *Finding Nemo*
Customization (Hexagonal)	Nemo's Seascape	1	Sky Theme	Common	Make the Sky Theme in the Toy Box themed to *Finding Nemo*
Customization (Hexagonal)	New Holland Skyline	2	Sky Theme	Common	Make the Sky Theme in the Toy Box themed to *Frankenweenie*
Customization (Hexagonal)	Rapunzel's Birthday Sky	1	Sky Theme	Common	Make the Sky Theme in the Toy Box themed to *Tangled*
Customization (Hexagonal)	Rapunzel's Kingdom	1	Terrain Theme	Common	Make all of the terrain objects in the Toy Box themed to *Tangled*
Customization (Hexagonal)	Tulgey Wood	1	Sky Theme	Common	Make the Toy Box themed to *Alice In Wonderland*

Type	Name	Series	Category	Rarity	In-Game Effect
Customization (Hexagonal)	Victor's Experiments	2	Terrain Theme	Common	Make all of the terrain objects in the Toy Box themed to *Frankenweenie*
Customization (Hexagonal)	Sugar Rush Sky	1	Sky Theme	Common	Make the Sky Theme in the Toy Box themed to Sugar Rush from *Wreck-It Ralph*
Customization (Hexagonal)	WALL-E's Collection	3	Terrain Theme	Common	Make the terrain objects in the Toy Box themed to *WALL-E*
Customization (Hexagonal)	Buy 'N' Large Atmosphere	3	Sky Theme	Common	Make the Sky Theme in the Toy Box themed to *WALL-E*
Customization (Hexagonal)	Tri-State Area Terrain	3	Terrain Theme	Common	Make all of the terrain objects in the Toy Box themed to *Phineas and Ferb*
Customization (Hexagonal)	Danville Sky	3	Sky Theme	Common	Make the Sky Theme in the Toy Box themed to *Phineas and Ferb*
Toy (Hexagonal)	Abu the Elephant	1	Mount	Rare	Spawn the elephant version of Abu inside the Toy Box
Toy (Hexagonal)	Buzz Lightyear's Astro Blaster Ride	1	Vehicle	Rare	Spawn the Astro Blaster vehicle from the Buzz Lightyear attraction in the Disney Parks
Toy (Hexagonal)	Captain Hook's Ship	2	Helicopter	Rare	Spawn a flying airship themed after Captain Hook's ship
Toy (Hexagonal)	Carl Fredricksen's Cane	1	Weapon	Common	Spawn Carl's walker from *Up*
Toy (Hexagonal)	Cinderella's Coach	1	Vehicle	Common	Spawn Cinderella's Coach in the Toy Box
Toy (Hexagonal)	Condor Wing Glider	2	Glider	Rare	Spawn a glider pack that is wings ala *Condorman*
Toy (Hexagonal)	Dumbo the Flying Elephant	1	Helicopter	Rare	Spawn the Dumbo ride from the Disney Parks inside the Toy Box
Toy (Hexagonal)	Flamingo Croquet Mallet	2	Weapon	Common	Spawn a flamingo croquet mallet from *Alice in Wonderland*
Toy (Hexagonal)	Hangin' Ten Stitch with Surfboard	2	Hoverboard	Common	Spawn a surfboard that hovers with Stitch on the front of it
Toy (Hexagonal)	Headless Horseman's Horse	2	Mount	Common	Spawn the Headless Horseman's Horse in the Toy Box
Toy (Hexagonal)	Kahn	1	Mount	Common	Spawn Kahn the horse from *Mulan* in the Toy Box
Toy (Hexagonal)	Maximus	2	Mount	Common	Spawn Maximus from *Tangled* in the Toy Box
Toy (Hexagonal)	Mickey's Car	1	Vehicle	Common	Spawn Mickey's Car in the Toy Box
Toy (Hexagonal)	Mike's New Car	2	Vehicle	Common	Spawn Mike Wazowski's vehicle from *Monsters Inc.* in the Toy Box
Toy (Hexagonal)	Pizza Planet Delivery Truck	2	Vehicle	Common	Spawn the Pizza Planet Truck from *Toy Story* in the Toy Box
Toy (Hexagonal)	Stitch's Blaster	1	Weapon	Common	Spawn Stitch's Blaster from *Lilo and Stitch*
Toy (Hexagonal)	The Electric Mayhem Bus	2	Vehicle	Rare	Spawn The Electric Mayhem Bus from *The Muppets* inside the Toy Box
Toy (Hexagonal)	Cruella De Vil's Car	3	Vehicle	Common	Spawn Cruella's car from *101 Dalmatians* inside the Toy Box
Toy (Hexagonal)	Disney Parks Parking Lot Tram	3	Vehicle	Common	Spawn a Parking Lot Tram from the Disney Parks in the Toy Box
Toy (Hexagonal)	Calico Helicopter	3	Helicopter	Common	Spawn a helicopter from *Bolt* in the Toy Box
Toy (Hexagonal)	Phillipe	3	Mount	Common	Spawn the horse Phillipe from *Beauty and the Beast* in the Toy Box
Toy (Hexagonal)	Tantor	3	Mount	Common	Spawn the elephant Tantor in the Toy Box
Toy (Hexagonal)	Dragon Firework Cannon	3	Weapon	Common	Spawn a firework cannon from *Mulan* in the Toy Box
Toy (Hexagonal)	WALL-E's Fire Extinguisher	3	Prop	Rare	Spawn the fire extinguisher from *WALL-E*
Toy (Hexagonal)	Toy Story Mania Blaster	3	Weapon	Common	Spawn a blaster themed to Midway Mania from the Disney Parks
Toy (Hexagonal)	Angus	3	Mount	Common	Spawn Angus from *Brave* in the Toy Box

GAME BASICS

CHARACTERS

POWER DISCS

PLAY SETS

TOY BOX

TOY BOX COLLECTION

ACHIEVEMENTS

Toy Story in Space

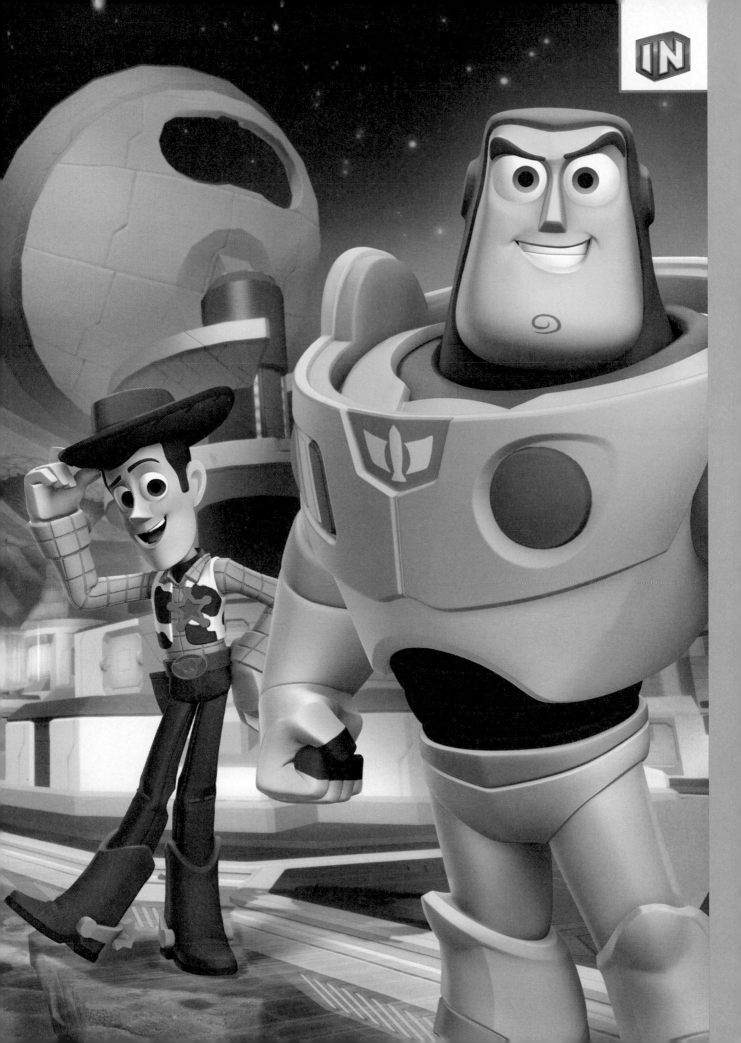

SAVE THE ALIENS AND BUILD A BASE

Teleporter

6

4

5

1

Entrance to
Goo Valley

Teleporter

Shield
Generator Tower

2

Star Command
Delivery Platform

8

Alien Village

3

City

Crystal Cave

10

Teleporter

7

Teleporter

Waterfalls

9

Canyons

Teleporter

Teleporter

CHALLENGES

1. Cliffside Collect
2. Here Comes the Cavalry!
3. Woody's Ramblin' Race
4. Blasters Away
5. Horsey Headache
6. Rocket Booster Blast
7. Buzz Lightyear's River Run
8. River Hoppin'
9. Jetpack Knack
10. Jessie's Roundup

⭐ POWER THE TOWER

Mission Giver: Rex (automatic)
Type: Locate
Rewards: 25 Crystals / 100 Sparks
Wii Rewards: 25 Crystals / 50 Sparks

Upon beaming down to the planet's surface, you and the rest of the inhabitants are assaulted by a barrage of volcanic debris. The only way to keep the Aliens safe is to activate the Shield Generator. This is a three-part mission, and when you accept the quest, the green compass arrow will guide you to jump across and up a few ledges to reach the Shield Generator.

At the base of the Shield Generator, pick up each of the two batteries and toss them into the bottom of the tower, which has an image of a battery.

The Shield Generator will fully extend and become operational when the batteries are inserted. The only task left to complete is to ride the elevator up to the top of the tower and push the IN button to activate the shield.

Each set of floor pads assembles by itself once you get to the top of the Construct-O-Lot and push the red button. To get to the shiny red button, jump up the floating floor pads. The first set of pads is very straightforward and a few jumps will get you to the top quickly. Each time you attempt to assemble another building lot, the pads will be placed in an increasingly difficult arrangement to navigate. Jump on the shiny red button on the top of the Construct-O-Lot and watch the floor assemble automatically to complete each set.

BUILD-A-LOT

Mission Giver: Hamm
Type: Platforming
Rewards: 100 Crystals / 100 Sparks
Wii Rewards: 100 Crystals / 50 Sparks

Now that the inhabitants are safe from falling debris, it is time to build a fully operational space station on this new planet. This is a lot easier than it sounds as it just requires creating a building lot for Rex by constructing a level area with floor pads. Rex will automatically beam down the floor pads, but they are scattered all over the place. To set up the floor pads, you first need to power the Construct-O-Lot with a battery. Using the compass, locate the battery and throw it into the empty battery slot.

NOTE

When the first set of floor pads has been placed, a teleporter will be installed at the far edge of the new flooring. This is a handy tool to beam down to the planet's surface, especially later in the game when all of the caverns below are covered with floor pads. Likewise, the matching teleporter below can be used to instantly warp back up to the City.

Wii NOTE

Delivery Platform not available for Wii.

New Toy Unlocked: Delivery Platform

GAME BASICS

CHARACTERS

POWER DISCS

PLAY SETS

TOY BOX

TOY BOX COLLECTION

ACHIEVEMENTS

PLATFORM PURCHASE

Mission Giver: Hamm
Type: Locate
Reward: 50 Crystals

In other words, all toys must be delivered to this special platform. Fortunately, you just unlocked this toy in the last mission and you can enter the Toy Store to buy it for a mere 25 crystals.

Wii NOTE

Mission not available for Wii.

Star Command protocol requires all interplanetary shipments to be made to an official Star Command Delivery Platform.

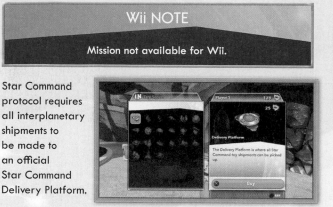

Wii NOTE

The Delivery Platform does not appear in the Wii version.

ALIEN ISSUES

VOLCANO VANISH

Mission Giver: Alien
Type: Locate
Rewards: 50 Crystals / 100 Sparks
Wii Rewards: 50 Crystals / 50 Sparks

One of the Aliens was lost during the violent volcanic eruption and you must find him. Use the compass to track the missing Alien and start the hunt, leaping up the nearby ledges to get to the higher plateau.

From this higher vantage point you should easily spot the missing Alien. Double jump to the floating platform, pick up the little green guy, and return him to the mission-giving Alien.

TAKE ME UP

Wii NOTE

Mission only available on Wii.

Mission Giver: Alien Tourist
Type: Sightseeing
Wii Reward: 50 Crystals

This mission is basically a tutorial on using the teleporter pads. Pick up the Alien and use the nearby teleporter to take it to the top level of the City.

Wii NOTE

The missing Alien is inside a cavern to the right of the Shield Generator.

New Challenge Available: **Cliffside Collect**

There are a lot of Alien retrieval and escort missions, and as the story progresses they become increasingly difficult. If you run into trouble, get to the highest spot you can to scout for a beacon or green arrow.

SIDE MISSION

CRYSTAL SMASH AND BASH

Mission Giver: Alien
Type: Locate
Rewards: 25 Crystals / 50 Sparks
Wii Reward: 25 Crystals

This is a simple mission designed to enforce the fact that the blue crystals break into smaller pieces that are used as currency to buy toys. Use the shoulder charge or ball toss to smash into three clusters of crystals to complete the lesson.

DRESS FOR SUCCESS

DRESS UP

Mission Giver: Rex
Type: Locate / Purchase / Customize
Rewards: 100 Crystals / 100 Sparks

Wii NOTE

Mission not available for Wii.

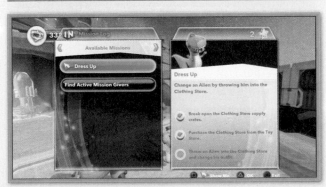

Poor Rex can't seem to tell the Aliens apart and he is getting really confused. Do him a favor and build the Clothing Store so the Aliens can wear different uniforms and costumes to help Rex distinguish one from another. This is a three-step process that involves breaking the supply creates, buying the Clothing Store, and changing an Alien's outfit. The first step of locating the supply crates takes place in the next mission, Clothing Store Crate Crash.

CLOTHING STORE CRATE CRASH

Mission Giver: Alien Mechanic
Type: Purchase
Rewards: 25 Crystals / 50 Sparks
Wii Rewards: 50 Crystals / 50 Sparks

The goal is simply to break five Clothing Store supply crates to earn that toy. Luckily, they are all clustered together near the Star Command Delivery Platform (in front of the Shield Generator) and can be smashed without too much searching.

New Toy Unlocked: Clothing Store

Wii NOTE

When the Clothing Store is built, Slinky Dog will beam down to the planet.

DRESS UP (CONTINUED)

Go into the Toy Store and buy the Clothing Store.

Pick up any Alien and throw it into the Clothing Store's orange spinning doors to change the Alien's appearance. Any single change to the Alien's body or head will do the trick.

SIDE MISSION: ALIEN FUN TIME

CAPSULE COLLECTION

Mission Giver: Alien
Type: Purchase
Rewards: 25 Crystals / 50 Sparks

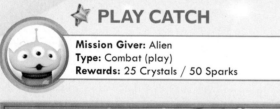

By the time you get this mission available, you may have already completed the tasks for it. Simply collect a few capsules to meet the Alien's request.

⭐ PLAY CATCH

Mission Giver: Alien
Type: Combat (play)
Rewards: 25 Crystals / 50 Sparks

An excited little Alien with a mitt wants to catch a ball. Equip the Softball in Packs and Tools and throw him a fast ball. He's wide open!

SIDE MISSION: ALIEN COSTUME CRAZE

> **NOTE**
>
> Each of the following side missions is unlocked after completing the previous one plus one other mission of any type.
>
> These missions are not available for Wii.

NEW HAT PLEASE

Mission Giver: Alien
Type: Purchase
Rewards: 50 Crystals / 100 Sparks

The same green guy that told you about the importance of capsule collecting wants a new hat. I guess he was hinting that he wants you to find lots of capsules so he can try out some new looks. This time around he wants a cowboy hat just like Woody's. The hat you need is located in a red capsule in a cavern near the clear Toy Store Icon. To get to the capsule you can smash the wall on either side of the cavern or climb up top and drop down through the breakable section on the roof. Once you find the hat, toss the Alien into the Clothing Store and place the hat on his head.

CRYSTALLIZE MY CRANIUM

Mission Giver: Alien
Type: Customize
Rewards: 50 Crystals / 50 Sparks

This little green guy is looking for a crystal hat, but first you must find the red capsule that has the hat he is looking for. The compass will guide you towards the red capsule, which is in the clifftops to the right of the Shield Generator. If you have trouble finding it, look for the little rocket house behind a trio ot trees. Grab the capsule to collect the Gem Hat and toss the Alien into the Clothing Store to give him the headgear he desires.

DINO-MYTE DRESSER

Mission Giver: Alien
Type: Customize
Rewards: 50 Crystals / 100 Sparks

Raar! This little fellow wants to be a dinosaur. To help him achieve his goal you must locate two red capsules to make him look like Rex. Both are located on the rocky formations in the Waterfall area with the Rex Outfit on the left and the Rex Cap on the right.

Go to the edge of the City and jump across to a rocky range that has the Woody Chest. Look to the right to find the red capsule with the Rex Cap on the second floating rock.

After collecting the cap, return to the previous ridge and jump up to the top. From there, leap down to the grassy ledge and make your way up a series of rocky hand holds to reach an unrelated red capsule that holds a Pricklepants Cap.

Finally, ascend to the top of this rocky formation and go out on the ledge to collect the Rex Outfit. Return to the City and toss the little green guy into the Clothing Store to give him the Rex Cap and Outfit.

PLEASE BUG ME

Mission Giver: Alien
Type: Customize
Rewards: 100 Crystals / 100 Sparks

This Alien wants to get in touch with his inner bug. To help him out, find the red capsule at the very back wall to the left of the Waterfall. However, to get to the capsule you must perform a ground pound to break the barrier to reveal the item below. Collect the Twitch Cap and return to toss the Alien into the Clothing Store to alter his headgear.

GAME BASICS

CHARACTERS

POWER DISCS

PLAY SETS

TOY BOX

TOY BOX COLLECTION

ACHIEVEMENTS

THE CRYSTAL CAVERN

Mission Giver: Hamm
Type: Customize
Rewards: 50 Crystals / 100 Sparks
Wii Rewards: 50 Crystals / 50 Sparks

Hamm has his ear to the ground and the word going around town is that an Alien found a unique cave full of crystals. Use the compass to go in back of the Shield Generator and leap up a pair of ledges.

Continue to jump up another larger formation and leap into the Waterfall area to the left.

The cave you are looking for is above you to the right of the Waterfall with a red capsule in front of the entrance. Jump up to the cave and smash all the crystals to collect a decent amount of crystals without too much effort. If you are desperate for a few crystals

to purchase a toy, this is good spot to visit as the room will regenerate over time. Make sure to smash the golden-colored cluster of crystals in the back that provide ten times the number of regular ones.

BULLSEYE EARNS HIS RANK

NOTE

Bullseye unlocks after completing twelve missions. When the trusty steed is purchased, three challenges will be unlocked.

New Toy Unlocked: Bullseye

New Challenges Available: Bullseye's Roundup, Bullseye Games, Here Comes the Cavalry

SOMETHIN' TO PROVE

Mission Giver: Slinky Dog
Type: Fetch
Rewards: 100 Crystals / 100 Sparks
Wii Rewards: 100 Crystals / 50 Sparks

This is the first riding mission you can try right after purchasing Bullseye and it is pretty straightforward to complete in the 45 second time limit. There are two crates to collect and return to the green target circle, and both of them are in a straight line. The first is out to the east of the Shield Generator. Grab it and return in a straight line going west to drop it off.

Continue due west towards the Alien Village and grab the next crate. Spin around and head straight back to place it in the green target zone.

NOTE

When you buy Bullseye from the Toy Store it unlocks a new toy, Jessie Alien. After you purchase the Jessie Alien it will appear on the Star Command Delivery Platform along with two red capsules, one on each side of the platform. These two capsules contain the Jessie Outfit and Jessie Hat to dress up other Aliens like Jessie. This also unlocks several new Bullseye missions.

 New Toy Unlocked: Jessie Alien

HORSEBACK SUPPLY RUN

 Mission Giver: Jessie Alien
Type: Fetch
Rewards: 250 Crystals / 100 Sparks

Like the previous Bullseye mission you must collect small supply crates and return them to the green target before time runs out. There is 1 minute and 30 seconds on the clock. That should be plenty of time if you remember to sprint with Bullseye instead of trotting along at a slower pace. The first crate is on the Shield Generator and a short ride on the lift plate will take you there in a jiffy.

The next one is on a ledge. The challenge here is that Bullseye can't climb. To get to this crate you need to pass by it and go all the way to a ramp near the Alien Village. Follow that path to the

edge of the cliff and make sure to grab the crate before leaping down.

The final crate is out in the Waterfall area and it will take a few tricky jumps to get to it. Be patient and slowly leap to each rocky formation to grab the crate. During this crate retrieval keep in mind that Bullseye can double jump like regular characters. Jump back to the City and be sure to drop the last crate in the green circle. If you toss the crate or drop it out of the green ring it will not count.

WII HORSEBACK SUPPLY RUN

Wii Reward: 50 Crystals

Wii NOTE

The Wii version of the Horseback Supply Run mission has significantly different locations for the crates and occurs much later in the game. To complete this mission the Teleporter Dish must be built in order to warp around the outskirts of the City.

Go to the teleporter at the Teleporter Dish and use it to warp to the first spot on the ledge near the entrance to Goo Valley.

When you arrive, use the teleporter again to warp to the next location in the cliffside near the Shield Generator.

Drop down the ledge to the right and go down one more ledge to find the first crate near a small stream.

Perform the same double teleport warp to return to the same spot as before. Instead of dropping down the leftmost ridge, follow the edge of the rocky terrain farther out near the Character Vault and look down to the side to find the second crate.

Once again, repeat the double teleport trip, but this time go to the left. From here drop down two ledges to make your way next to the Challenge beacon to grab and retrieve the third crate.

New Toy Unlocked: Buzz Lightyear Alien

Wii NOTE

Two more side missions (Jessie's Town and Giddy Up!) can be completed when Jessie and Bullseye are purchased, but they require that the Decoration Shop and Hospital are built.

GIVE THE CITY A MAKEOVER

PAINT THE TOWN NEW

Mission Giver: Rex
Type: Customize
Rewards: 100 Crystals / 100 Sparks
Wii Rewards: 100 Crystals / 50 Sparks

Rex is not impressed with Star Command's design style and wants to paint the town quite literally. Customize any building by changing its wall to make the dino happy.

SIDE MISSION

COLOR REQUIRED

Mission Giver: Alien (near Alien Village)
Type: Customize
Rewards: 50 Crystals / 100 Sparks
Wii Reward: 50 Crystals

The little green guy wants to see a "cool" building. All you have to do is change the wall, trim, and accent of any building to make it hip enough for the Alien.

BATTERY NEEDS

Mission Giver: Slinky Dog
Type: Customize
Rewards: 100 Crystals / 100 Sparks
Wii Rewards: 100 Crystals / 50 Sparks

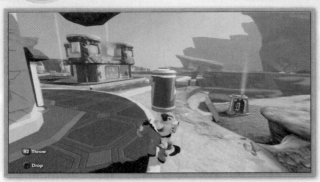

It's time to expand your base, which means you need to place more floor pads on the planet's surface. Use the compass to find a battery to power the Construct-O-Lot. It is easy to locate the portable power cell as it is in plain sight to the left of the Shield Generator. Grab the battery, turn around, and it is a straight trip to the base of the Construct-O-Lot.

Getting to the top of this tower is a bit more difficult than last time. Start by jumping up the ledges that lead to the crystal cave and leap to the first floor pad. The rest of the floating pads are easy to navigate, and when you make it to the top, jump on the big red button.

An Alien crash lands after flying into the cliff at this point.

REPORT FOR DUTY AT THE COMBAT SIMULATOR

NOTE

The crate crashing missions are unlocked sequentially one after the other. Each time you complete one, a new toy with the crates' name will become available in the Toy Store. However, you don't need to purchase the toy to go on to the next crate crashing mission. Several of these can be completed now, but the last few will require a special toy you will unlock in Goo Valley.

COMBAT CRATE CRASH

Mission Giver: Alien Mechanic
Type: Destroy
Rewards: 50 Crystals / 100 Sparks
Wii Rewards: 50 Crystals / 50 Sparks

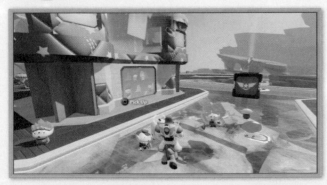

To get the next toy you need to smash five Combat Simulator supply crates. The first is right next to the Clothing Store.

The next one is below the floor pads that you have been assembling to expand the City. Drop down into the ravine and smash the crate below.

After breaking that crate, turn around and head in the opposite direction to find the third crate across several small gaps. Toss a ball at the

crate to easily break it without any fancy jumping maneuvers.

GAME BASICS

CHARACTERS

POWER DISCS

PLAY SETS

TOY BOX

TOY BOX COLLECTION

ACHIEVEMENTS

The fourth is in a tricky spot on this lower level of the planet. Use the compass to locate the hidden crate that is close by a stream.

The last crate is just around the corner from number four in an alcove at the base of the stream.

New Toy Unlocked: Combat Simulator

GET A COMBAT SIMULATOR

Wii NOTE
Mission only available on Wii.

Mission Giver: Slinky Dog
Type: Purchase
Wii Rewards: 100 Crystals / 50 Sparks

The Slinky Dog wants you to try out his Combat Simulator but first you must buy it at the Toy Store. Purchase the toy to complete the mission.

ENTER THE SIMULATOR

Mission Giver: Slinky Dog
Type: Destroy
Rewards: 25 Crystals / 100 Sparks

After buying the Combat Simulator in the Toy Store, speak to Slinky Dog to begin your combat training. Run over to the newly built simulator and use the teleporter to warp into the depths of the building to begin the fun.

Once inside the installation, you want to take the lift down to the ready room to begin the simulations. However, there are a few items to grab before you begin your training. To the right, on top of a stack of crates, is the Buzz Lightyear Chest. On the opposite side to the left is a green capsule high in the air. To reach this prize, you need to leap onto the stacks of crates and make a long double jump to get the Toy Story Space Track Set Toy Pack 3.

STAR COMMAND BLASTER QUALIFICATION

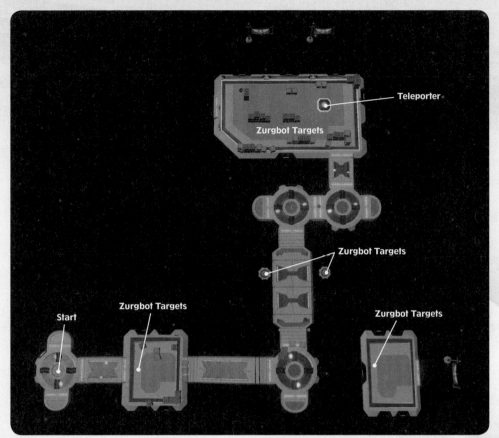

Mission Giver: Zurg Hologram
Type: Combat
Rewards: 100 Crystals / 250 Sparks
Wii Rewards: 250 Crystals / 100 Sparks

Talk to the Zurg Hologram to activate the first training area behind him and use the teleporter to warp to the new map.

The initial training session is all about aiming. Initially three Zurgbot targets will appear across from you and all you need to do is hit them with a fast ball.

Follow the path ahead and use a shoulder charge to smash through a set of breakable light blue crates.

The route will lead along an inclined ramp and a barrier will prevent you from proceeding until you hit the three moving Zurgbot targets. Take time to zoom in on each and toss the ball to hit the targets.

The next test is designed to teach you how to aim above you. There are two Zurgbot targets on each side and they are easy to hit if you stop, zoom in, and take your time to aim.

Continue to the final area where you need to hit any of the five targets. There is no danger or time limit to complete this task, which makes this a great chance to practice your aiming skills.

When all five targets have been hit, go across to their location to smash some orange crates. Pick up the red capsule with the Star Cadet Helmet 2 and finally use the warp pad to go back to the briefing room.

 **New Toy Unlocked: Star Command Blaster**

NOTE

In order to try out the next simulation mission you must return to the City and buy the Star Command Blaster. When you have this slick new toy, return to the Combat Simulator and go back to the ready room to confront the Zurg Hologram to try your first official combat mission.

New Challenge Available: Blast Away

⭐ SIMULATION 1: NO CHANCE

Mission Giver: Zurg Hologram
Type: Combat
Rewards: 500 Crystals / 500 Sparks
Wii Rewards: 500 Crystals / 500 Sparks

It is very satisfying to unload the blaster on the Zurgbots, but don't get overzealous. Keep your distance and use the gun's superior range to take out the enemies from as far away as you can.

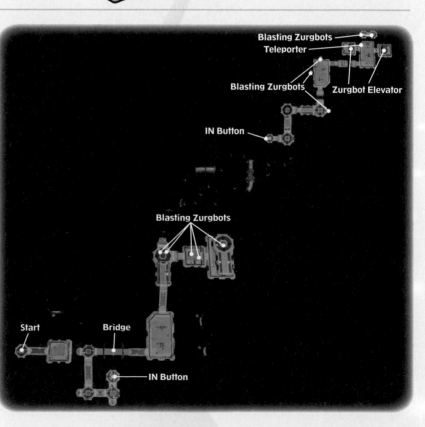

Blasting Zurgbots
Teleporter
Blasting Zurgbots
Zurgbot Elevator
IN Button
Blasting Zurgbots
Start
Bridge
IN Button

When the first group is dispatched, go down to the ramp to the right and wipe out all the Zurgbots in order to get to the large IN button that will activate a bridge. Be on the lookout in this area for a red capsule with the Star Cadet Outfit 2 behind some blue crates.

The large IN switch will create a new route, so backtrack to the location of this new route. Of course, as soon the bridge has been activated more Zurgbots will attack.

Enter the large rectangle section, and if you don't keep your distance be prepared to get rushed by Zurgbots. This isn't necessarily a bad thing as you can use a ground pound attack to hit several at one time if they surround you.

Head up the next ramp to encounter red Zurgbots that have dual blasters. Keep an eye on your green shield bar below your 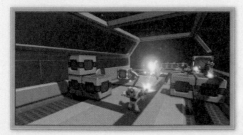 character and hide behind the heavy gray crates if you need to recharge your shields. The best tactic to deal with this type of robot is to shoot and dodge.

Behind this robot duo is a rail you can use to go to the next section, but turn to the right and take out a big group of firing Zurgbots to get to the green capsule with Toy Story Decorations Toy Pack 3 all the way in the back.

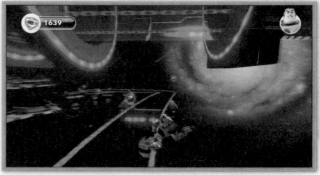

Return to the rail and jump on it to perform a rail slide. While grinding on this rail you cannot only jump straight up, but you can even leap from one rail to another.

At the bottom of the rail, step on the large IN button to rotate a platform into place.

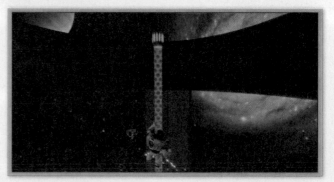

Cross this platform and waste a few Zurgbots to allow you access to a blue rope that will take you to the top of this structure.

GAME BASICS

CHARACTERS

POWER DISCS

PLAY SETS

TOY BOX

TOY BOX COLLECTION

ACHIEVEMENTS

Follow this topside path in an L shape. Along the way, collect the red capsule with a Mechanic Outfit next to a Zurgbot firing from a hovering platform.

Continue to the next section to wipe out the mace-wielding Zurgbots from a distance while behind the safety of gray crates. The goal

is to destroy the blue Zurgbots while avoiding fire from the red one in the back of the area. When all of the robots are reduced to junk, the barrier will drop, allowing access to the final section.

To complete this simulation you need to take down twelve Zurgbots; luckily they are released in waves and don't all attack at once. Initially

there only will be blue Zurgbots, which can be shot from a distance or tackled with a shoulder charge or ground pound.

However, the last wave includes two red Zurgbots in the back of the area. Keep out of range of their blaster attacks until you can wipe out all

the blue ones. When the red Zurgbots are all that remains, close in on them to shoot while dodging side to side.

When the coast is clear, search behind one of the large Zurgbot elevators to find a red capsule with the Mechanic Hat and use the warp pad to return to the ready room.

SIMULATION 2: IF YOU DARE

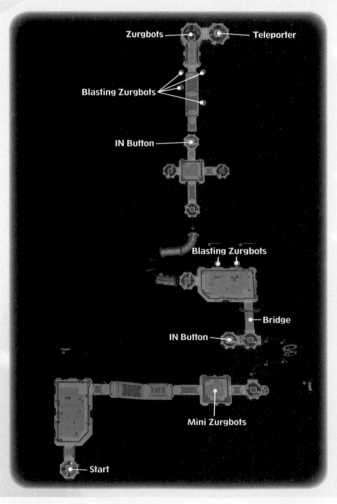

Mission Giver: Zurg Hologram
Type: Combat
Rewards: 50 Crystals / 500 Sparks
Wii Rewards: 500 Crystals / 500 Sparks

There is a new enemy to contend with right from the start. The new foe is a mini blue Zurgbot, which is faster and generally

appears in larger groups. Although they might be more numerous than their big brothers, they are weaker, which makes them a great target for the ground pound attack.

Follow the path past a lone red Zurgbot in a tunnel and prepare for a slew of tiny robots to attack in the next section. Don't

rush in. Just stay back and keep firing until they have all run into your blaster fire. When they are all gone, follow the path to the rail and look for a red capsule with the Space Suit Blaster behind some crates.

Go for a short rail slide and shoot up the crates in front of you to reveal an ambushing Zurgbot and a IN switch you need to activate.

Continue past the extended blue bridge and wipe out all the Mini Zurgbots and the duo of red Zurgbots on floating platforms to lower the barrier in this section. Also, be sure to collect the red capsule with a Space Suit Outfit in this section.

Rail slide through a series of rings and tunnels to get to the next area filled with little and big blue Zurgbots. Destroy the robots and make a quick detour to the right to get the red capsule with a Space Suit Helmet. To get to the next section, step on the IN button to lower the raised walkway.

This next area will be pretty rough as it is filled with four firing Zurgbots as well as the mini blue ones. Keep your distance from the red ones while you pick apart the small robots with blaster fire. To bring down the firing foe, use the gray crates for cover, peek out to fire a few shots, and then dodge back to safety.

To finish this level, there are eight more Zurgbots to destroy. As soon as you go past the raised barrier and enter the small tunnel several robots will arrive from below. Backtrack a bit to get some distance from the blue Zurgbots and fire like mad to take them all out. Before you hop on the teleporter make sure to grab the green capsule next to it that has the Toy Story Decorations Toy Pack 2.

GAME BASICS · CHARACTERS · POWER DISCS · PLAY SETS · TOY BOX · TOY BOX COLLECTION · ACHIEVEMENTS

SIMULATION 3: INEVITABLE DESTRUCTION

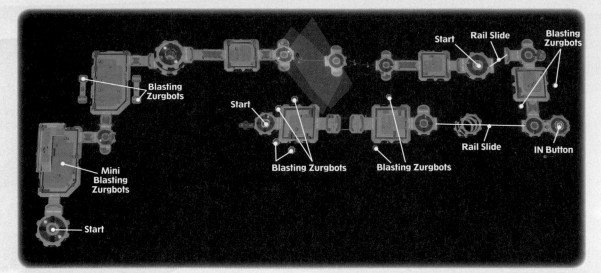

Mission Giver: Zurg Hologram
Type: Combat
Rewards: 500 Crystals / 500 Sparks
Wii Rewards: 1,000 Crystals / 500 Sparks

The new addition to this stage is small red Zurgbots that can fire just like their bigger models. Step into the first section and instead of staying back, charge in and attack with shoulder charge and ground pound attacks. It's not worth keeping your distance when the enemy's weapons significantly outnumber yours. Destroying all the robots will drop the barrier next to a red capsule that has Mechanic Tools.

Climb the blue rope to the top tier and continue down the path to face an onslaught of mini red Zurgbots and their bigger brothers. It is going to be really hard to dodge all the incoming blaster fire, but avoid the temptation of running in and getting surrounded by gunfire. In the next small section straight ahead, there is a red capsule with the Army Wall textures hiding behind some gray crates.

The next section is going to be tough due to numerous red Zurgbots firing upon you from floating platforms. Eliminate as many threats in the open area as you can and switch your focus to wiping out the shooting Zurgbots. If you end up taking too much damage in the center of this section retreat until your shields have regenerated.

Hop on the nearby rail to slide down and make sure to shoot the Zurgbot waiting for you at the platform. Rail slide down again while continually shooting to hit the pair of red Zurgbots on the bottom.

In the next section, an ambush of mini firing robots and big blue ones will attack. Shoot like crazy to destroy them or use the shoulder charge to knock some of them over the edge.

Step on another IN switch to extend a winding rail and hop on for a ride.

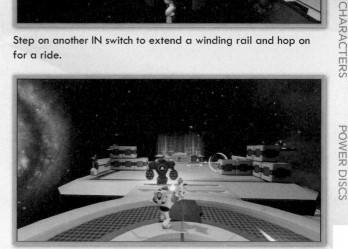

After the battle, step on the IN switch to lower the walkway above you. Run straight ahead to the next area and look behind the gray crates to find the Toy Story Space Track Set Toy Pack 4 in a green capsule.

The rail ends at a big battle area with a barrier that requires all robots to be destroyed. Keep a safe distance and shoot all the robots you can before closing in to take out the pair of red ones on floating platforms.

The final area is just ahead, and you must defeat twelve Zurgbots. Use the crates for cover as much as possible while shooting as many enemies as you can. As the number of enemies thins, charge towards the red Zurgbots on one side and take them out fast to avoid getting caught in crossfire.

The adjacent area is full of red and blue Zurgbots. Hold your ground and fire away from this spot instead of charging in. Make sure to hit the two red robots on the floating platforms as soon as you get a break in the action.

> ### NOTE
>
> There are still three more simulation missions to experience, but you will have to wait until you return from Goo Valley. At the end of this mission in the Wii version you will get the automatic mission Need you in Town. This mission simply reminds you to return to the City.

GAME BASICS

CHARACTERS

POWER DISCS

PLAY SETS

TOY BOX

TOY BOX COLLECTION

ACHIEVEMENTS

BUILD THE HATCHERY

HATCHERY CRATE CRASH

Mission Giver: Alien Mechanic
Type: Destroy
Rewards: 50 Crystals / 100 Sparks
Wii Rewards: 50 Crystals / 50 Sparks

Return to the Alien Mechanic to continue the crate smashing fun. This time the goal is to bust open five Hatchery supply crates. The first four are pretty close together at the edge of the budding colony leading to the Waterfall area. All four of these can be hit with a well-placed toss of your ball. Break the first one on the right and follow the edge while in a zoomed-in mode to target and hit the other three.

The final crate is a lot more tricky to tackle. To hit this last crate, leap across the deadly water to the location of the leftmost crate and jump up the small rock formation. From the edge of this rocky platform zoom in on the last crate and aim a bit high to lob a ball that will land on this final crate.

Wii NOTE

The Hatchery crates are not located at the Waterfall area. Instead they are found close to the Shield Generator.

The first is due south of the Shield Generator, across a narrow gap.

The second one is below the floor pads you are assembling right next to the teleporter. Smash this crate and use the teleporter to go back top side.

The last three are close together just east of the Shield Generator. All three can be taken out with a shot from a projectile.

New Toy Unlocked: Hatchery

NOTE

When the Hatchery is built, a new side mission (Egg Spotted!) will be unlocked. This side mission is off the beaten path and will be covered right before entering Goo Valley.

BUILD A HOSPITAL

HOSPITAL CRATE CRASH

Mission Giver: Alien Mechanic
Type: Destroy
Rewards: 50 Crystals / 100 Sparks
Wii Rewards: 50 Crystals / 50 Sparks

The Alien Mechanic will beam in the Hospital supply crates and you must smash all five. Start the search by jumping up to the plateau to the right of the Shield Generator.

Climb up a series of ledges to the left to get to the next crate near a red capsule with a Dolly Outfit.

Follow the ledge around to a breakable wall that hides the third crate. Bust open the wall and make sure to smash the gold crystals in the back of the little cave.

Wii NOTE

There is no breakable wall and cave in the Wii version. The crate is merely at the end of this ledge.

Continue to walk around the ledge past the breakable wall and look down to find the fourth crate.

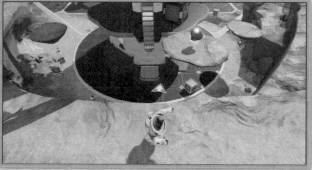

The last crate is nearby on the back of the Shield Generator Tower. Jump down to a small floating ledge and collect the red capsule with the Chunk Helmet. Jump over to the crate and simply toss a ball to smash it.

Wii NOTE

This crate is not on a ledge in the air, but is on the ground in back of the Shield Generator.

🔲 New Toy Unlocked: Hospital

ALIEN MEDICINE

This mission requires completion of Hospital Crate Crash and purchase of the Hospital.

Mission Giver: Alien
Type: Fetch
Rewards: 50 Crystals / 100 Sparks
Wii Rewards: 200 Crystals / 50 Sparks

An unlucky or reckless Alien flew right into the side of a cliff. Jump up the ledge to talk to unconscious Alien's friend. His buddy needs a Hospital, but you have to buy it from the Toy Store first. If it is already built, pick up the unconscious Alien and toss him into the Hospital.

There are still several additional crate missions left, but there are more pressing matters due to Hamm's exportations. Also, some of the upcoming crates are scattered in the Canyons and will require some new toys to get to them.

SOMETHING IS WRONG WITH THE VOLCANO

YOU FLOOR ME

Mission Giver: Slinky Dog
Type: Platforming
Rewards: 100 Crystals / 100 Sparks
Wii Rewards: 100 Crystals / 50 Sparks

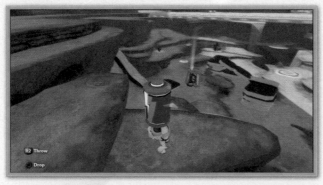

Unlocking all those buildings from the crate crashing mission leaves you plenty of options to expand your City. However, you will need to get more "floor space" to put all these structures. Talk to Slink about constructing a third building lot by assembling more floor pads. The goal is the same as the previous mission—you simply need to get the battery and toss it into the base of the Construct-O-Lot.

Leap up the staircase of floor panels, but this time around several of them will rotate in mid air. Jump on the moving panels and ride them to

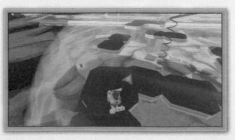

the stationery one across the way to continue your trek to the top and that big red button.

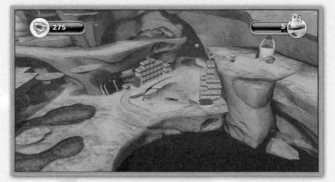

The planet's volcano just doesn't know when to quit! All of the pent up underground pressure is causing the surface to split and to start filling up with goo. Hamm is the resident geology expert (due to his extensive reading of Andy's textbook) and he takes on the mission to explore the new fissure leading to Goo Valley.

After a brief exploration of the volcano issue, Hamm reports back that it is worse than he thought, and he will need some help. There are still a lot of other missions you can complete, but this volcano issue sounds serious. Plus, you get to visit a whole new area with several really cool new toys! Go towards the entrance of Goo Valley where the surface collapsed to give Hamm a hand.

SIDE MISSIONS: BEFORE YOU GOO TO THE VALLEY

GAME BASICS

CHARACTERS

POWER DISCS

PLAY SETS

TOY BOX

TOY BOX COLLECTION

ACHIEVEMENTS

NOTE

On the way to Goo Valley there are a few more extra side missions you can take care of right next to the entrance of Goo Valley. Both of these are on a high ridge to the right of the entrance to Goo Valley. It will be a lot easier to get to this spot later, but if you want you can take care of them now. You can get up to this spot if you climb the cluster of crates under the ridge or if you follow the rocky edge on the right side of the Shield Generator.

Side Missions not available for Wii.

EGG SPOTTED!

Mission Giver: Slinky Dog
Type: Fetch
Rewards: 50 Crystals / 100 Sparks

SPORE SEARCH

Mission Giver: Twitch (Bug) Alien
Type: Fetch
Rewards: 50 Crystals / 50 Sparks

When the Hatchery Is built, talk to Slink to get this mission. Carefully navigate the crates near the right ridge and locate the red egg with a white circle. Pick up the precious cargo and return it to the blue pad at the Hatchery.

Speak to the Alien dressed in a green bug costume to get the mission to gather pollen from the Spore Plants. The mission requires ten spores and fortunately there are two clusters of plants on this ridge. Bust open a group of Spore Plants and reveal the tiny pink spores. Collect as many as you can and go to the other group or simply wait for the plants to regenerate.

When the egg has been placed, press the big IN button on the Hatchery to activate the machine and hatch the egg. Your reward

is releasing a brand new critter to inhabit the planet and live among the Aliens.

GO TO GOO VALLEY

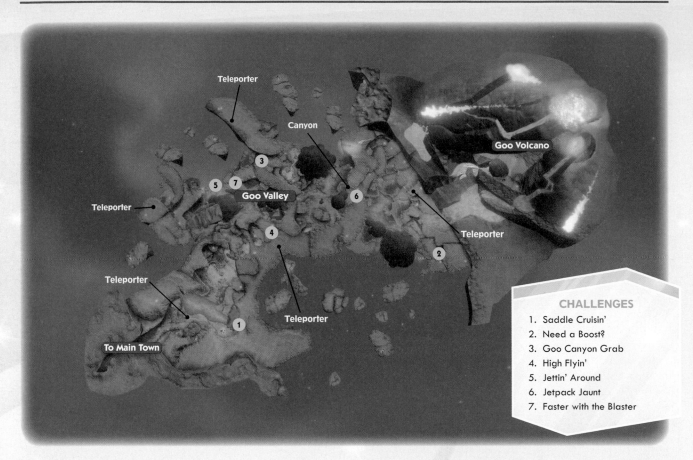

CHALLENGES
1. Saddle Cruisin'
2. Need a Boost?
3. Goo Canyon Grab
4. High Flyin'
5. Jettin' Around
6. Jetpack Jaunt
7. Faster with the Blaster

HAMMY RENDEZVOUS

Mission Giver: Alien
Type: Platforming
Rewards: 200 Crystals / 100 Sparks
Wii Rewards: 500 Crystals / 50 Sparks

The slotted pig needs help. At the volcano.

Hamm needs a hand dealing with the new discovery he has made at the volcano. Go down into the sunken surface and jump up the ledges to follow the cavern to enter Goo Valley.

SIDE MISSION

Wii NOTE

Side Mission not available for Wii.

SPORE SAMPLES

Mission Giver: Alien
Type: Collecting
Rewards: 50 Crystals / 50 Sparks

The Alien wants to further study spores. Oblige the little green guy by smashing ten of them. There is a pair of Spore Plants next to this Alien

and a few single plants at the far ends of the cavern. Smash them in a circuit returning to each one as it regenerates.

FOLLOW HAMM TO THE VOLCANO

THE GOO SIDE OF THE MOON

Mission Giver: Hamm
Type: Platforming
Rewards: 200 Crystals / 100 Sparks
Wii Rewards: 50 Crystals / 50 Sparks

The green compass arrow will help guide you to the top of the volcano. Hamm will help lead you by rocket boosting ahead of you—who says pigs can't fly! If you get lost and backtrack Hamm will always keep pace with you to show you the next spot you are supposed to reach. You're free to explore this area as much as you want, but it will be easier once you complete the next task and get a few new toys.

There are plenty of interesting geological features of Goo Valley and your first encounter will be with a river of Purple Goo. These shallow streams of goo won't hurt you, and the purple version will shrink you. Becoming tiny can be very useful to sneak into small spaces like the little alcove with a red capsule containing the Pricklepants Wall.

Cross the Purple Goo and the next pool you encounter is filled with Green Goo that has the opposite effect, enlarging you about three

times your normal size. The size increase from Green Goo can allow you to reach higher ledges you couldn't reach in your normal size. Continue to follow Hamm by climbing up a high ledge you can't reach in your normal state.

Jump down a series of ledges and you will spot Hamm near the purple pool below. Hamm will quickly leap to a ledge to the left and you have to figure out how to follow him up that high ledge.

The Purple Goo won't help as it will make you smaller and there is no green stream to bathe in. The important lesson you will quickly learn is that the glowing fruit from the trees has the same properties as the corresponding colored goo. Pick up a Green Goo fruit and toss it at the pumpkin-like thing at the bottom of that high ledge. The orange spotted species will get large and make the perfect stepping stone to reach the hand hold above.

Follow the pig by leaping across a series of ledges over a purple stream of goo.

Hamm will boost up on a high ledge, leaving you to figure out how to get up there. Pick up the pumpkin-like critter and place it in the

depression in the dirt under the ledge. Grab a nearby Green Goo fruit and hit the pumpkin critter to make it large enough to jump on and reach the ledge above.

GAME BASICS
CHARACTERS
POWER DISCS
PLAY SETS
TOY BOX
TOY BOX COLLECTION
ACHIEVEMENTS

NAVIGATE GOO VALLEY CANYON

To continue to follow Hamm, you will need to grab the orange critter on the floating ledge to give you a boost to reach the next ledge.

Once again you will need the nearby pumpkin inhabitant. Place it in the divot under the ledge where Hamm is taunting you. There is a series of ledges that prevent you from simply carrying the orange creature. The best option is to grab a Purple Goo fruit and shrink the creature to make it small enough to carry and jump with.

Wait for the pumpkin creature to return to full size and jump on it to be able to leap to the ledge above.

Jump across a few rocky ridges to follow Hamm. To reach him on the next ledge you will need to do a bit of work to get the next orange stepstool.

Go to the left past a purple stream and leap up a series of ledges to move hand over hand around the mountainside.

Pick up your familiar orange friend and carry it over two purple streams to the bottom of the ledge. Use the nearby Green Goo fruit to bump up its size and leap up the ledge to continue your journey to the base of the volcano.

The next section to conquer is a series of Purple Goo waterfalls. The method to get past these falling goo waterfalls is to leap up to the highest ledge and jump across the first waterfall. Jump up to the next hand hold and leap across the second waterfall.

Drop down to the ledge below and follow it around to a ladder of ledges going up to the base of the volcano. There is also a gap in the wall to the right that can be used to get to the top using a wall jump technique.

⭐ PLANETARY PLUMBER

Mission Giver: Hamm
Type: Platforming
Wii Rewards: 200 Crystals / 50 Sparks

The Goo is draining into the center of the planet. If you don't plug the volcano's flow, the pressure is going to cause the whole planet to split apart. To plug the drain you need to push several large columns of rock into the hole. Start your journey by jumping down to the ledge below and climbing up and around a large pillar of rock.

At the top of the large pillar is a blue section of rock that can be destroyed with a shoulder charge. Breaking this first pillar will loosen the huge rock above.

Leap across a narrow gap and wall jump up to the next breakable blue rock formation. Reduce this rock to rubble and leap towards the waterfall of Green Goo.

Using the lowest hand hold, leap across the falling ooze to the left.

Continue climbing the cliff's face up and to the left until you get to even ground. There is a huge section of blue rock nearby, but you can't break it in your normal form.

Take a quick dip in the Green Goo nearby to go large and return to smash that blue column of rock.

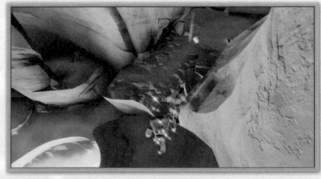

This should plug up the whirlpool below, but now you have to get out of there before the volcano collapses around you. Jump back down to where you started where Hamm is eagerly awaiting your return.

GAME BASICS
CHARACTERS
POWER DISCS
PLAY SETS
TOY BOX
TOY BOX COLLECTION
ACHIEVEMENTS

The planet is saved and with the volcano finally put out of commission for good the force field is no longer necessary. Your reward is a jetpack that makes getting around blast. Make sure to buy this in the Toy Store and equip it to one of your quick selections. Since his task is completed, Hamm will return to the City, but don't follow him yet. There are a lot of side missions to explore in Goo Valley.

New Toy Unlocked: Buzz Lightyear's Jetpack

New Toy Unlocked: Goo Valley Teleporters

TIP

Both of these toys are unlocked after completing Planetary Plumber, but you might have guessed from the little commercial that the jetpack is a very important toy. The teleporters are a tool for getting around Goo Valley, but with the jetpack you can navigate any area. If your funds are low, make sure to buy the jetpack first because it will unlock several other missions in this region.

New Toy Unlocked: Buzz Lightyear Alien

NOTE

Don't forget that buying the jetpack (or rocket booster) doesn't give you instant access to it. You must go back to the City and pick it up on the Delivery Platform. It may seem like a lot of backtracking for one item, but it is an awesome toy that makes traversing Goo Valley a blast. After you pick up the new toy, return to Goo Valley to explore with style. As an added bonus, as soon as you pick up the jetpack the Buzz Lightyear Alien toy will become unlocked.

New Challenges Available: Goo Valley Grab, Racing Champion (requires Bullseye), Goo Valley Astro Blaster Master (requires Blaster), Astro Blaster Boss (requires Blaster), Jet and Grab (requires Jetpack), Master of the Jetpack (requires Jetpack), Goo Valley Jet 'n' Grab (requires Jetpack)

SIDE MISSIONS: ALIEN RESCUE

DISRUPTIVE ERUPTION

Mission Giver: Alien
Type: Rescue
Rewards: 50 Crystals / 75 Sparks
Wii Rewards: 50 Crystals / 3 Sparks

The volcano has wreaked havoc in Goo Valley, leaving lots of Aliens lost or stranded. Help this green guy by returning it to its friend. To get his buddy back, follow the edge close to where his friend is trapped and leap up to a higher ridge. Perform a long double jump to make it to the hovering platform to pick up the Alien and leap to return it where the compass indicates.

FRIENDLY RECOVERY

Mission Giver: Alien
Type: Rescue
Rewards: 50 Crystals / 75 Sparks
Wii Rewards: 50 Crystals / 3 Sparks

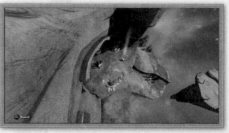

This Alien's friend is in trouble, but luckily the guy that needs rescuing is really close. Simply look to the right to notice his pal stuck on a high rocky mantle. There is a short and a long route to perform the rescue. If you have the rocket booster, you can zip up to get the green guy and drop back down to return to his buddy.

However, this mission doesn't require any additional toys to complete if you want to take a slightly longer route. Just up the hill from this mission giver is a series of ledges you can take to go up to a long curving edge. Grip onto the hand hold and follow it as it wraps around the stony column right next to the lost Alien.

ALIEN LIBERATION

Mission Giver: Alien
Type: Rescue
Rewards: 50 Crystals / 75 Sparks
Wii Rewards: 50 Crystals / 3 Sparks

Of course finding the Alien isn't the goal; it is rescuing the green guy. Pick up the Alien and go around the long way to jump across a series of floating platforms.

Another lost Alien needs to be found and it is just beyond that towering wall riddled with holes where you get the mission. The quickest rescue method is to rocket boost up and over the wall to find the lost green guy and boost him back over to his pal.

> ### NOTE
> When you complete any three missions after buying and picking up the jetpack, a new toy will become available.

 New Toy Unlocked: Star Command Boost Pack

New Challenges Available: Goo Valley Rocket Roundup (requires Rocket Booster) and Blaster Ribbon Booster (requires Rocket Booster)

Still, if you haven't bought any of the new toys in Goo Valley, you can still save the little guy. Go around this large wall to the right and take a quick dip in the purple pool. Now that you are tiny, you can sneak through a hole in the wall to get to the lost Alien.

SIDE MISSIONS: JETPACK JOYRIDE

> ### NOTE
> These side missions require Buzz Lightyear's Jetpack.

VOLCANIC RESCUE

Mission Giver: Alien
Type: Rescue
Rewards: 50 Crystals / 75 Sparks
Wii Rewards: 50 Crystals / 3 Sparks

The Alien's lost friend requires your assistance. It is a clear path to find his friend on a large floating rocky crag.

Use the jetpack to fly over to the lost Alien, but make sure to turn off the jetpack to allow enough room to land from all the momentum you've built up. Pick up the lost guy and zoom back to his pal.

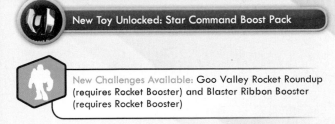

GAME BASICS

CHARACTERS

POWER DISCS

PLAY SETS

TOY BOX

TOY BOX COLLECTION

ACHIEVEMENTS

WEARY TRAVELLER

Mission Giver: Alien Tourist
Type: Transport
Rewards: 50 Crystals / 75 Sparks
Wii Rewards: 50 Crystals / 3 Sparks

Follow the edge of the cliff to get as close as possible and use the rocket booster to leap up high to safely make it to the rocking landing. The jetpack can also be used to get to this spot but it is a lot harder to time the landing.

Look for the tourist on a large boulder in the middle of Goo Valley. He wants to go out to one of the rocky platforms floating in space.

SIDE MISSIONS: GIVING THE ALIENS A BOOST

> **NOTE**
>
> These side missions require the Star Command Boost Pack.

ALIEN RESCUE, VOLCANO STYLE!

Mission Giver: Alien
Type: Rescue
Rewards: 50 Crystals / 75 Sparks
Wii Rewards: 50 Crystals / 3 Sparks

THREE EYES, TWO LAZY LEGS

Mission Giver: Alien Tourist
Type: Transport
Rewards: 50 Crystals / 75 Sparks
Wii Rewards: 50 Crystals / 3 Sparks

This lost Alien is really far out in space on a tiny chuck of rock.

While it might be possible to jump off the edge of the cliff and fly over with the jetpack, trying to nail that landing is really rough.

An easier path involves flying over to the rocky platform to the left of the target and rocket boosting up.

Pick up the tourist and rocket boost over the nearby ridge.

The small ledge the Alien wants to get to will require using the rocket booster next to a cluster of purple trees.

To get to the ledge above, move out towards the edge of the platform to rocket boost and hit the booster again to keep your height as you hover towards the ledge.

GOO EXPERIMENTS

NOTE

These missions require the completion of Research Crate Crash in the Waterfall area. However, to complete that mission you will need the jetpack you earned in Goo Valley or the Teleporter Dish. Complete that crate crash mission and return to Goo Valley to finish of these final missions.

FIELD ASSISTANT

Mission Giver: Hamm
Type: Locate
Wii Rewards: 100 Crystals / 3 Sparks

NOTE

Hamm needs some help with his Goo research. Help him track down his field researchers and give them a hand with their experiments. This mission is automatically completed when the following four side missions have been done.

Wii NOTE

To complete this mission on the Wii you must find the first scientist, which also gives you The Big Stink mission. The green guy is hiding behind a blue breakable that you must fly to or jump up on the pumpkin critter to reach.

GREEN GOO GROW MISSIONS

THE BIG STINK

Mission Giver: Alien Scientist
Type: Locate
Rewards: 100 Crystals / 100 Sparks
Wii Rewards: 100 Crystals / 3 Sparks

The little scientist wants you to Goo yourself large and ground pound a Stink Spore. The compass will guide you to the Stink Spore target and luckily there is a stream of Green Goo nearby. Take a quick dip and hurry over to pound the spore.

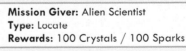 SWIMMING IN GREEN

Wii NOTE

Mission not available on Wii.

Mission Giver: Alien Scientist
Type: Locate
Rewards: 100 Crystals / 100 Sparks

NOTE

The same scientific Alien as before is really hung up on Green Goo. He wants to take a dip in the Green Goo, for science. Pick up the experimental guy and toss him into the nearby pool.

Completing these two missions is the first requirement to unlock the Goo Grower.

GAME BASICS

CHARACTERS

POWER DISCS

PLAY SETS

TOY BOX

TOY BOX COLLECTION

ACHIEVEMENTS

PURPLE GOO SHRINK MISSIONS

THE LITTLE STINK

Mission Giver: Alien
Type: Locate
Rewards: 100 Crystals / 100 Sparks
Wii Rewards: 100 Crystals / 3 Sparks

You need to shrink a Stink Spore and give it a good ground pound. The Stink Spore is next to a small pool of Green Goo on a ledge and the closest Purple Goo fruit is off in the distance. This is a great time to use the jetpack to zoom straight across to the tree to pick up the fruit. Grab the Purple Goo fruit beneath the tree and zoom back to hit the Stink Spore with the fruit to shrink it.

Use the ground pound move when the Stink Spore is small to complete the Alien's request.

⭐ TINY TREE

Mission Giver: Alien
Type: Locate
Rewards: 100 Crystals / 100 Sparks
Wii Rewards: 100 Crystals / 3 Sparks

The next experiment requires shrinking a Goo fruit tree.

Go back to the same spot you got the Purple Goo fruit for The Little Stink and drop down to the green tree to hit it with the fruit and reduce its size.

LOST RESEARCHERS

Wii NOTE

This mission is only available for Wii.

Mission Giver: Hamm
Type: Locate
Wii Rewards: 100 Crystals / 3 Sparks

Use the compass to go to a large breakable wall with a Stink Spore and little green pool to the left. Smash the blue wall to reveal the Alien Scientist that will give you the Tiny Tree mission.

NOTE

Completing these two missions is the first requirement to unlock the Goo Shrinker.

MEET UP WITH SLINKY DOG

Mission Giver: Slinky Dog
Type: Locate
Rewards: 50 Crystals / 50 Sparks

NOTE

After thoroughly exploring Goo Valley and completing all available side missions, return to the City and speak to Slinky Dog.

SLINKY DOG'S SPECIAL MISSIONS

GAME BASICS

CHARACTERS

POWER DISCS

PLAY SETS

TOY BOX

TOY BOX COLLECTION

ACHIEVEMENTS

NOTE

Slinky Dog summons you from Goo Valley. When you return to the Main Town, speak to him to receive a series of several missions.

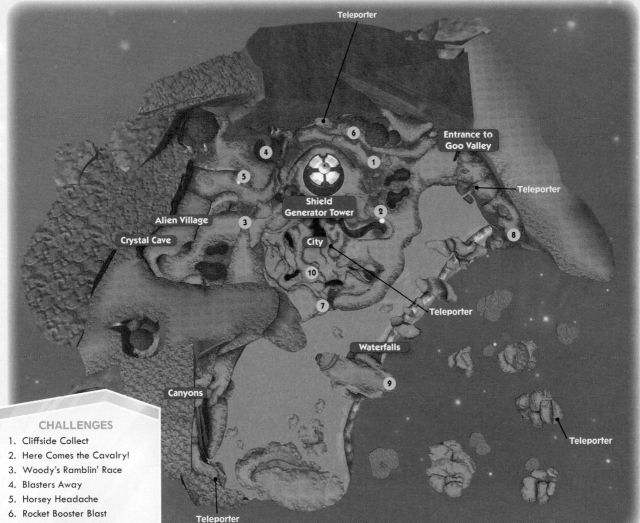

Teleporter

6

Entrance to Goo Valley

4

1

Teleporter

5

2

Shield Generator Tower

Alien Village

3

8

Crystal Cave

City

10

Teleporter

7

Teleporter

Waterfalls

9

Canyons

Teleporter

Teleporter

CHALLENGES

1. Cliffside Collect
2. Here Comes the Cavalry!
3. Woody's Ramblin' Race
4. Blasters Away
5. Horsey Headache
6. Rocket Booster Blast
7. Buzz Lightyear's River Run
8. River Hoppin'
9. Jetpack Knack
10. Jessie's Roundup

NOTE

Upon returning to the Main Town several new Challenges will be available if you bought the toys from Goo Valley.

CHANGING WALLS

Wii NOTE

Mission not available for Wii.

 New Challenges Available: Jetpack Pickup (requires jetpack), Jetpack Jive (requires jetpack), Rocket Booster Blast (requires rocket booster), River Rocket (requires rocket booster)

 Mission Giver: Slinky Dog
Type: Customize
Rewards: 50 Crystals / 100 Sparks

The pup thinks the Shield Generator will look a lot better with some new color. Simply go to the base of the tower and customize it with any new wall paint.

⭐ CERTIFIABLY QUACKED

Wii NOTE

Mission not available for Wii.

NOTE

Requires completion of Alien Medicine.

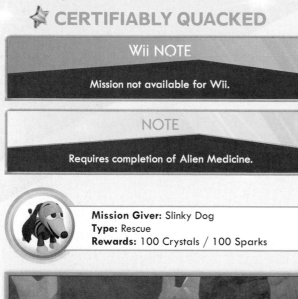

Mission Giver: Slinky Dog
Type: Rescue
Rewards: 100 Crystals / 100 Sparks

Slinky Dog has a medical mission for you that requires bringing two sick Aliens to the Hospital. To find the first, follow the compass up the large ridge to the west of the Shield Generator. Return this green guy for medical attention and look for the next patient.

The second sick Alien is to the east on a high ledge near the entrance to Goo Valley. Return this Alien and you will be well on your way to becoming a Star Command Medic.

New Toy Unlocked: Medicine Ball

⭐ FINAL FLOOR

Mission Giver: Slinky Dog
Type: Customize
Rewards: 100 Crystals / 100 Sparks
Wii Rewards: 100 Crystals / 50 Sparks

Before you complete the rest of the crate crashing missions you should complete the fourth building lot. Grab the last battery and toss it a short distance into the Construct-O-Lot.

There are now two series of rotating floor pads to negotiate. Hop on the moving panels and ride them to stationary pads that are slightly higher up. At the top of the towering pads, jump on the button to complete the last building lot.

SIDE MISSION: SARGE IS IN CHARGE

> **NOTE**
>
> These side missions become available when two buildings have been placed. The Sarge Alien can be found to the west of the Shield Generator near the back rocky wall by a little rocket house. These missions are not available for Wii.

Use a drop kick move to boot the green guy across the gap towards his pal.

STUCK AND OUTTA LUCK

Mission Giver: Sarge Alien
Type: Rescue
Rewards: 50 Crystals / 50 Sparks
Wii Reward: 50 Crystals

TOWER WITH TEAM POWER

Mission Giver: Sarge Alien
Type: Rescue
Rewards: 50 Crystals / 50 Sparks
Wii Reward: 50 Crystals

The Sarge costumed Alien wants to go the Great Tower (Shield Generator) to greet his friends arriving from home. Pick up the Alien and jump down to the ground level, then ride the elevator on the Shield Generator all the way to the top.

An Alien near the Horsey Headache Challenge needs your help to save his friend who is stuck. Follow the compass and perform a simple double jump to get to a plateau and reach his buddy.

DECORATE THE CITY

DECORATION CRATE CRASH

Mission Giver: Alien Mechanic
Type: Destroy
Rewards: 50 Crystals / 100 Sparks
Wii Rewards: 50 Crystals / 50 Sparks

Go all the way into the Alien Village, to the back wall near the Character Vault, to find the second one.

It's time to break some more crates to earn a new toy. Start out by going west to the Alien Village and break the first one near the huge blue breakable wall.

GAME BASICS · CHARACTERS · POWER DISCS · PLAY SETS · TOY BOX · TOY BOX COLLECTION · ACHIEVEMENTS

The third one is in a small alcove on the way back to the City. Leap up two ledges and turn to the right to find this crate.

The next two are actually above the third one and can be accessed by leaping up the ridge to the right.

Wii NOTE

Decoration Center crates are in different locations as follows.

The first is behind the Shield Generator near the little waterfall.

To the right of the waterfall is another crate on a ledge.

Leap up to the ledge that held the crate to find the third one in a crystal-filled cave.

The next one is in a little alcove up by the teleporter pad, but if you can't warp there just climb the series of ledges.

Drop down from this high ledge and make your way to the entrance of Goo Valley to find the last one amongst the trees.

🔹 New Toy Unlocked: Decoration Center

DECORATE THE TOWN

Wii NOTE
Mission not available for Wii.

Mission Giver: Rex
Type: Customize
Rewards: 200 Crystals / 100 Sparks

Rex found some great decorations in the Toy Store and he wants you to put one up in front of a building. Go to any open decorating spot, marked by the little gray nubs, and place any decoration item you have collected thus far.

SIDE MISSION

DECORATION INTRODUCTION

Wii NOTE
Mission not available for Wii.

Mission Giver: Rex
Type: Customize
Rewards: 50 Crystals / 100 Sparks

An Alien thinks the City needs an army base. You don't really want to go down that road and you can make the Alien happy by putting up a military-looking decoration. The Canon Bunker

capsule is at the edge of a platform outside of the cave loaded with crystals that you visited when you completed the mission The Crystal Cavern.

SIDE MISSION: ALIEN COWGIRL

JESSIE'S TOWN

Wii NOTE
Mission not available for Wii.

Mission Giver: Jessie Alien
Type: Customize
Rewards: 250 Crystals / 100 Sparks

This Jessie lookalike wants to give the town a western theme. In order to give the place a wild west makeover you will need to collect a few items to place one decoration and customize three buildings. The first thing to get is the Jessie Wall collectible in a red capsule at the top of the Hospital. Ride up the grey lift in back of the IN button to go to the roof and climb the antenna to reach this high capsule.

To place a western decoration, go to the right side of the entrance of Goo Valley and jump up to the cliff above. There is a red capsule

with Snake In My Boot in a shallow hole towards the far end of this ridge.

GAME BASICS

CHARACTERS

POWER DISCS

PLAY SETS

TOY BOX

TOY BOX COLLECTION

ACHIEVEMENTS

GIDDY UP!

Mission Giver: Jessie Alien
Type: Fetch
Rewards: 250 Crystals / 100 Sparks
Wii Reward: 50 Crystals

There is 1 minute and 30 seconds on the timer to gather three small crates and return them to the green circle in town. The first is out in the Waterfall area by the Woody Chest.

Look for the second one in the little cave to the right of Shield Generator just past the breakable wall.

The last one is all the way west by the Alien Village.

Wii NOTE

You have 2 minutes and 30 seconds to complete this mission and the crates are in the following positions around the City ....and the crates are illustrated in the pictures above.

SIDE MISSION: ALIEN COSTUME CAPERS

Wii NOTE

Missions are not available for Wii.

THE PRICKLEPANTS

Mission Giver: Alien
Type: Customize
Rewards: 100 Crystals / 100 Sparks

Make this Alien look like his thespian hedgehog friend Mr. Pricklepants by dressing him in lederhosen. To do this you need to collect two capsules. The first one should have been collected during the Combat Crate Crash mission. If not, follow the stream on the lower part of the planet to a small alcove that has the Pricklepants Outfit.

To find the hat, you have to jump out to the rocks in the Waterfall area and leap over to a big formation that has the Pricklepants Cap on a grassy ledge.

UNIFORM DECISION

Mission Giver: Alien
Type: Customize
Rewards: 100 Crystals / 100 Sparks

Change this Alien to look like our favorite green army man, Sarge. The red capsule with the Sarge Helmet is located at the far edge of town over a small purple pool, near the Buzz Lightyear Challenge.

Go to the Alien Village to find the Sarge Outfit hovering over a pool of water.

Finally, you have to get the Sarge Prop, which is in a red capsule at the top of a tall stack of crates to the right of the entrance of Goo Valley.

CUTE COSTUMES

Mission Giver: Alien
Type: Customize
Rewards: 200 Crystals / 150 Sparks

This time around you must dress up two Aliens to look like a rag doll (Dolly) and a pink bear (Lotso). Start out by collecting the Dolly Hair capsule that is next to the Shield Generator and can be grabbed by leaping off of a ledge.

The Dolly Outfit should have been collected during the Hospital Crate Crash mission. If you missed it, look behind the Shield Generator on a high ledge with a hidden cave.

To gather the Lotso costume, go to the back of a tree near the Sarge Alien to find the Lotso Outfit.

The head gear for this costume is a lot harder to locate. The Lotso Cap is at the edge of the City between two rock segments. Look down from this spot to see a tiny floating rock with the red capsule on it.

SIDE MISSION: DECORATE THE TOWN

Wii NOTE

Missions are not available for Wii.

SIGNATURE STYLE

Mission Giver: Alien
Type: Customize
Rewards: 100 Crystals / 100 Sparks

Simply customize any building's wall, trim, and accent with any color you want!

DOLL UP THE PLACE

Mission Giver: Alien
Type: Customize
Rewards: 100 Crystals / 100 Sparks

The goal is to color a building like a rag doll, so you need to find the Dolly Wall paint and customize a building with it. The capsule with the Dolly Wall can be found on a ledge to the left of the Shield Generator.

DINO DECORATING

Mission Giver: Alien
Type: Customize
Rewards: 100 Crystals / 100 Sparks

This Alien wants to decorate the City with pretty dinosaur eggs. Find the capsule with the Dinosaur Eggs, which is located in back of the Horsey Headache Challenge near the Alien rocket house. Place the decoration anywhere in the City to make the Alien happy.

BUILD THE TELEPORTER DISH

SAVE YOUR FEET, BUY A TELEPORTER

Mission Giver: Rex
Type: Purchase
Rewards: 200 Crystals / 100 Sparks

This mission prompts you to get the Teleport Dish, but you must complete the next mission (Teleporter Dish Crate Crash) to unlock the toy. Once the building is available, go into the Toy Store and buy the Teleporter Dish.

TELEPORTER DISH CRATE CRASH

Mission Giver: Alien Mechanic
Type: Destroy
Rewards: 50 Crystals / 100 Sparks
Wii Rewards: 50 Crystals / 50 Sparks

It's crate crashing time again. Most are pretty easy to locate, except for one tricky crate. To find the first two, go to the high ridge just east of the Shield Tower that is to the right of the Challenge beacon. On this plateau is a crate to the right of the rocket house. The second one is even closer to the rocket house, but on a ledge up above.

The next crate is a little difficult to find and requires a lot of ledge leaping. After breaking the two previous crates, jump up to the thin ledge and move hand over hand while leaping up around the large rocky column.

At the end of this ledge, jump up two levels and work your way back in the opposite direction, to the left, until you are over the lip of a cave that is below. Drop down and enter the cavern to smash the troublesome crate.

Go back out where you first leapt up to those ledges and follow the curving path toward the entrance of Goo Valley. The fourth crate is in plain sight on this route. Across a few floating platforms on the right side of the Goo Valley entrance is the last crate.

Wii NOTE

Teleporter Dish crates are in different locations as follows.

The first set of crates is still east of the Shield Generator, but on that high ledge are three crates in a triangular arrangement.

The next two crates are also close together above the previous trio. The rocket booster will make it really easy to reach these high crates.

New Toy Unlocked: Teleporter Dish

TELEPORTATION MADE FUN AND EASY

 The Teleporter Dish has a special teleport pad in front of it that can take you to several hard-to-reach locations of the Main Town. Press the big IN button to change the image on the screen and use the pad to zip off to the corresponding location.

 There are four different destinations you can warp to based on the image above the button. Here are the images and locations you will be teleported to.

 The image on the screen of the Waterfall will take you to a high chunk of rock way out in the Waterfall area.

 Look for the image of a semicircle to teleport in the mountains behind the Shield Generator.

The image of a long ledge will warp you all the way out to the edge of the Canyon.

 The final screen image shows a little rocket house, allowing you to teleport to the right ridge by the entrance to Goo Valley.

Wii NOTE

In the Wii version the teleport will initially take you to one spot, but if you use that pad it will take you to another location instead of warping you right back. You can perform two consecutive teleports to check out all possible warping locations. The order of teleportation is to the right ridge near Goo Valley and then high up in the mountains in back of the Shield Generator.

BUILD THE RESEARCH STATION

RESEARCH STATION CRATE CRASH

NOTE

This crate crash is one of the toughest as it extends the range of exploration into the Canyon. In fact, it will require the teleporter at the Teleporter Dish or the jetpack/rocket booster from Goo Valley.

Mission Giver: Alien Mechanic
Type: Destroy
Rewards: 100 Crystals / 100 Sparks
Wii Rewards: 50 Crystals / 50 Sparks

The first is out in the Waterfall area and it would be easy to boost or fly to get to it, but if you want, you can reach it with a long toss of a ball from an accessible platform near the edge of the waterfall.

The rest are located in the Canyon, so either fly over with the jetpack or use the teleporter to warp to the Canyon.

On a tall rocky ledge is the second crate, which can be accessed by jumping up the pillars next to it.

To the left of those stony pillars is another crate on top of a rocky archway in a somewhat hidden part of the Canyon.

The next crate is near the far wall near the Alien and rocket house. Jump across two small platforms towards the little green guy and follow the nearby stream behind the waterfall to get to the crate near the blue egg.

For the last one, backtrack to the teleporter and drop down to the area below near the water's edge. The large rocky mesa next door holds the last crate on the bottom.

GAME BASICS · CHARACTERS · POWER DISCS · PLAY SETS · TOY BOX · TOY BOX COLLECTION · ACHIEVEMENTS

Wii NOTE

Research Station crates are in different locations as follows.

Go to the western edge of the City near the waterfall to find the first one.

Make a quick right turn following the mountainside to find the next one.

The third is in the stream to the west of the Shield Generator. If you have the rocket booster it will make it a short trip, otherwise you need to leap up like you have many times before.

Your next target is the crate on the large slanted slab of rock.

Finally, follow the rocky wall or fly to the left to reach the last crate.

 New Toy Unlocked: Research Station

NOTE

When this mission is completed, several new missions will unlock at Goo Valley. Make sure to head back there to complete the rest of that area as soon as you can.

SIDE MISSION DIVERSIONS

SECRET OF THE CLOTHING STORE

Wii NOTE

Mission not available for Wii.

Mission Giver: Alien
Type: Platforming
Rewards: 100 Crystals / 100 Sparks

The mission is pretty straightforward: find the secret area on the Clothing store. Climb the dark-colored area of the building to get to the roof and leap on top of the three cylindrical peaks.

Each time you get to the top of these little towers, the light on it will turn blue showing you have activated it. When all three lights are blue, a red capsule with the Stinky Pete Hat will appear and the mission will be completed.

BULLSEYE CAVES IN

Mission Giver: Alien
Type: Platforming
Rewards: 100 Crystals / 100 Sparks
Wii Reward: 100 Crystals

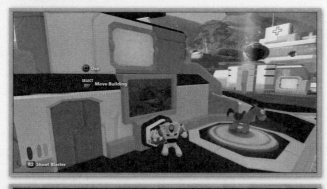

The tough part about this mission is getting Bullseye high up in the mountains since the horse can't climb. However, with the Teleporter Dish completed you can warp to this spot in an instant. Press the IN button to show the image on the screen below and zip to the cavern in the mountains.

ROCKET BOOSTER RIDE

Mission Giver: Twitch Alien
Type: Platforming
Rewards: 100 Crystals / 100 Sparks
Wii Reward: 50 Crystals

The Alien on the right ridge to the entrance of Goo Valley wants to go high into the sky. Pick up the little guy and use the rocket booster to jump through nine green rings.

Wii NOTE

This Alien in the Canyon wants to jump up through three green rings.

BUILD THE HERO MONUMENT

HEROES CRATE CRASH

> **NOTE**
>
> This crate crash requires the use of the teleporter at the Teleporter Dish.

Mission Giver: Alien Mechanic
Type: Destroy
Rewards: 200 Crystals / 100 Sparks
Wii Rewards: 50 Crystals / 50 Sparks

The first crate is in the Waterfall area on a floating chunk of rock in back of the Woody Chest. Leap towards the chest and jump up to the top of this section to get a view of this crate that can be hit with a shot from the blaster.

Use the teleporter pad to zip out to the Waterfall area and the second crate is within shooting range.

Jump down to a ledge with a light blue egg and make your way across the floating rocky platforms to find the third crate near a red

capsule with the Horseshoe Accent. Without the jetpack or rocket booster, this would be a one-way trip as it is impossible to get back to the City from this remote spot.

From the same ledge with the light blue egg, go towards the City, and this time look down to find the fourth crate. You can simply shoot it from this lofty spot.

After hitting crate four, jump down to the adjacent platform near the red capsules. This next crate can be tricky to spot, but if you look in the gap of this rocky section you should see it below next to the Doctor Outfit.

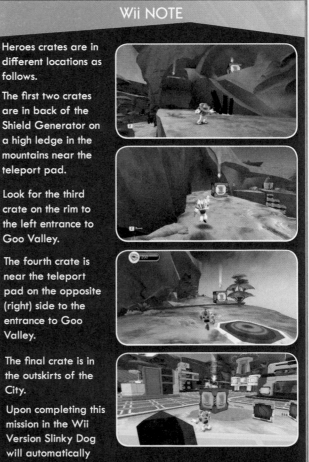

> ## Wii NOTE
>
> Heroes crates are in different locations as follows.
>
> The first two crates are in back of the Shield Generator on a high ledge in the mountains near the teleport pad.
>
> Look for the third crate on the rim to the left entrance to Goo Valley.
>
> The fourth crate is near the teleport pad on the opposite (right) side to the entrance to Goo Valley.
>
> The final crate is in the outskirts of the City.
>
> Upon completing this mission in the Wii Version Slinky Dog will automatically give your the mission Head to Water Fall Cove.

 New Toy Unlocked: Monument of Heroes

SIDE MISSION: ALIEN DRESS UP

GAME BASICS

CHARACTERS

POWER DISCS

PLAY SETS

TOY BOX

TOY BOX COLLECTION

ACHIEVEMENTS

Wii NOTE

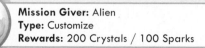

Missions not available for Wii.

TRIXIE TRAPPINGS

Mission Giver: Alien
Type: Customize
Rewards: 200 Crystals / 100 Sparks

An Alien is convinced that decorating a building to look like a blue dinosaur will make the town strong. To do this you will find the Trixie Wall paint and customize a building. To get the Trixie Wall, go up to the ledge to the right of the Shield Generator and walk to the back near a rocket-shaped house. Look for the breakable ground and perform a ground pound to break into the cave below.

This cave hides several goodies including a light blue egg, Jessie Chest, and two red capsules.

Take a quick dip in the Purple Goo to shrink down in order to pass through the small opening on the upper ridge. In order to exit this cave, you need to go through the small exit that is blocked by the red capsule with the Trixie Wall.

COMPLIMENTARY COLORS

Mission Giver: Alien
Type: Customize
Rewards: 200 Crystals / 100 Sparks

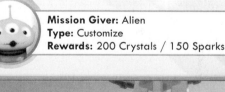

The goal this time around is to customize a building with the Woody Wall paint. Woody's Wall is hard to find amongst the red capsules scattered in the Waterfall area. It is next to the teleporter in the Waterfall area on a large rocky ledge. The easiest way to get it is to warp to the higher spot in the Waterfall area and jump down to it.

ROCK 'N' CLOWN COSTUMES

Mission Giver: Alien
Type: Customize
Rewards: 200 Crystals / 150 Sparks

This dress-up mission wants to turn the Aliens into a rock man (Chunk) and a clown (Chuckles). The Chunk Helmet is right behind the Shield Generator on a floating platform.

To find the rest of the rock man costume, fly out to a rock formation in the Waterfall area that has the Buzz Lightyear Chest. In a grassy nook is the Pricklepants Cap right at the edge of the water.

The clown suit is located along the rocky pillar on the ridge to the left of the entrance to Goo Valley. Move hand over hand along the ledge and drop down to get the Chuckles Outfit.

Chuckles Hair is hard to notice and harder to obtain. Go out to the Canyon and if you look high into the sky there is a red capsule. The only way to pick up this tough collectible is by using the rocket booster.

EPIC ANIMAL COSTUMES

Mission Giver: Alien
Type: Customize
Rewards: 100 Crystals / 100 Sparks

The last two Aliens to play dress up want to look like Trixie and Buttercup. To find the Trixie Cap, search out in the Waterfall area close to the Canyon.

After collecting the dinosaur cap you can make a short trip to the the Trixie Outfit. The capsule you need is hovering just above the water between

the gap of the Canyon and the area with a large slated rock on top. You can try to fly to collect this tricky outfit or simply walk off the end and fall into the water.

The Buttercup Outfit is high up on the Shield Generator. Take the elevator to the top and go to the back of the tower. Drop off of the edge

to land on the platform with the red capsule.

The Buttercup Cap is tough to find as it is high in the sky out in the Waterfall area. Get to a high vantage point and use the jetpack to fly out

over the water. The height of the capsule may be tricky and it will require you to deactivate and reactive the jetpack to slightly lower your altitude.

A SHEPHERD'S THREADS

Mission Giver: Twitch Alien
Type: Customize
Rewards: 50 Crystals / 100 Sparks
Wii Rewards: 50 Crystals

The Alien wants to look like a shepherd and requires a decoration to give him a new look. You should already have the Bo Peep's Crook item required as it is hanging near a ledge in back of the Shield Generator that you have probably climbed several times in your adventures.

SIDE MISSIONS: BUTTERCUP ALIEN

A FRIEND IN NEED

 Mission Giver: Buttercup Alien
Type: Rescue
Rewards: 50 Crystals / 100 Sparks
Wii Reward: 50 Crystals

The little unicorn-costumed Alien has an injured friend that needs help. Use the compass to drop all the way to the lowest level of the Canyon and find a little cave with a breakable blue wall.

Bust through the wall and grab the unconscious Alien. The tricky part is flying or teleporting back to the City to toss the hurt little guy into the Hospital.

JETPACK WATERFALLS

 Mission Giver: Buttercup Alien
Type: Platforming
Rewards: 100 Crystals / 100 Sparks
Wii Reward: 50 Crystals

The waterfalls call to the unicorn-costumed Alien. Pick him up and take him for a jetpack joyride through ten green hoops. The tough part is that the jetpack can't change altitude so you must stop and fly at different heights to reach all ten rings.

Wii NOTE

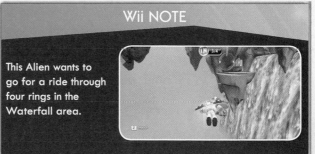

This Alien wants to go for a ride through four rings in the Waterfall area.

ALIEN'S NEW CLOTHES

Wii NOTE

Mission not available for Wii.

 Mission Giver: Buttercup Alien
Type: Customize
Rewards: 100 Crystals / 100 Sparks

Simply pick up the unicorn-dressed Alien, use the nearby teleporter, and toss it into the Clothing Store to give it a makeover.

SIDE MISSIONS: REX ALIEN

COLLECTING SPORES

Wii NOTE

Mission not available for Wii.

Mission Giver: Rex Alien
Type: Rescue
Rewards: 50 Crystals / 50 Sparks

Gather pollen by breaking ten Spore Plants. Search around the Canyon to break as many pods as you can to collect all the pollen the Alien needs.

BULLSEYE JOYRIDE

Mission Giver: Rex Alien
Type: Rescue
Rewards: 100 Crystals / 100 Sparks
Wii Reward: 50 Crystals

This Alien wants to gallop on a horse and feel the wind. Summon Bullseye, pick up the green guy, and run through ten green rings to give the Alien a thrill.

UNFOUND FRIEND

Mission Giver: Rex Alien
Type: Rescue
Rewards: 50 Crystals / 100 Sparks
Wii Reward: 50 Crystals

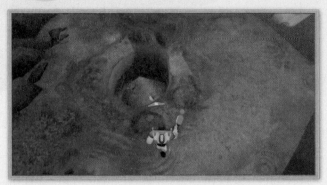

An Alien got lost out in the Canyon. Use the compass to track the unconscious guy that is down a hole near a cluster of Spore Plants and take the injured fella to the Hospital.

Wii NOTE

The injured Alien is on top of a plateau across from the teleport pad at the Canyon.

COLLECT THE PRIMAL GOO

NOTE

Exact locations of Goo globs may differ on Wii. Also, the Green Goo globs are located in the Waterfall area while the Purple Goo globs are in the Canyon.

These are the second set of required missions to unlock the Goo Shrinker and Goo Grower.

THE PURPLE PRIMAL GOO

Mission Giver: Alien (Waterfall)
Type: Locate
Rewards: 500 Crystals / 100 Sparks
Wii Rewards: 750 Crystals / 100 Sparks

Several members of Hamm's Alien research team have been studying the effects of goo to see if they can use it to defend their colony. Help out their efforts by collecting twenty globs of Purple Goo. It can be tricky to find all twenty of these, but the compass arrow will always point you in the right direction. To make this task a lot easier, make sure you have the jetpack and the rocket booster. Below are the locations of all the pretty piles of Purple Goo scattered around the Canyon.

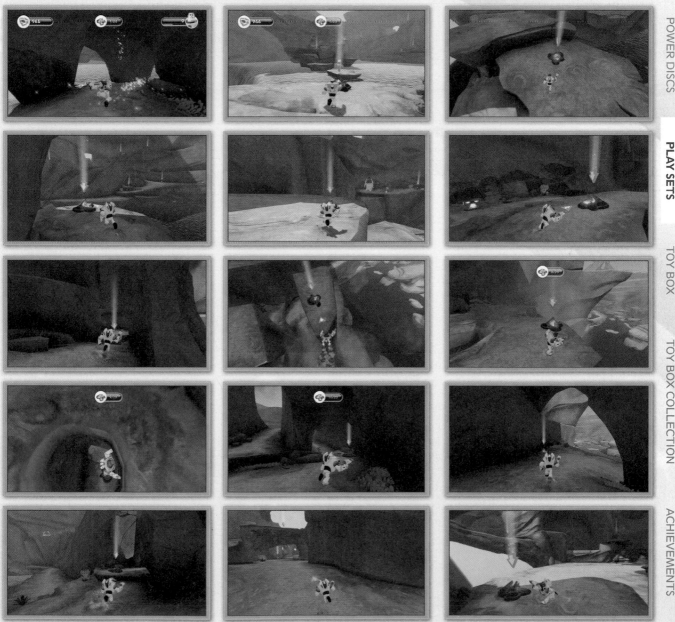

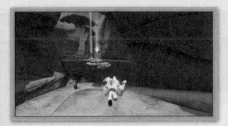

New Toy Unlocked: Goo Shrinker

THE PRIMAL GREEN GOO

Mission Giver: Alien (Waterfall)
Type: Locate
Rewards: 500 Crystals / 100 Sparks
Wii Rewards: 750 Crystals / 100 Sparks

Green Goo has been spotted near the City and you must to help out the goo researchers by collecting twenty globs. These globs will take a bit of patience to collect as they are strewn around hard-to-reach parts of the Waterfall area.

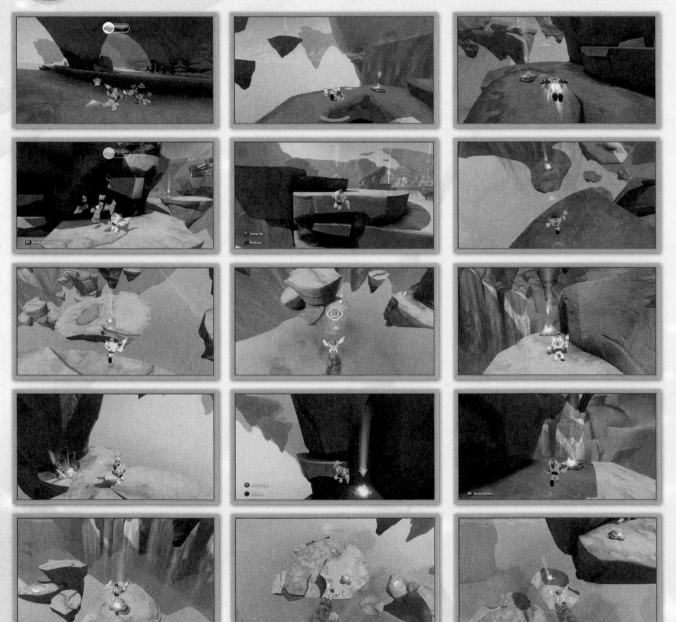

 New Toy Unlocked: Goo Grower

GOO GUN SIDE MISSIONS

Wii NOTE

These missions are not available on Wii and require both the Goo Grower and Goo Shrinker.

THE ACCIDENTAL GIANT

Mission Giver: Hamm
Type: Sightseeing
Rewards: 50 Crystals / 50 Sparks

TINY PROBLEMS

Mission Giver: Hamm
Type: Sightseeing
Rewards: 50 Crystals / 50 Sparks

Another one of Hamm's assistants got into some Green Goo this time and needs to be turned back to normal. The accident took place in the same location as the other goo incident, so go out towards the Alien Village and use the Goo Shrinker to stop the giant Alien from stomping around.

A Research Alien got shrunk and Hamm can't seem to find it. Go out to the Alien Village and shoot the little guy with the Goo Grower until he returns to full size.

GAME BASICS

CHARACTERS

POWER DISCS

PLAY SETS

TOY BOX

TOY BOX COLLECTION

ACHIEVEMENTS

SIDE MISSIONS: BUZZ LIGHTYEAR ALIEN

NOTE

These missions require buying the Buzz Lightyear Alien and will rely on the jetpack and rocket booster. Each subsequent mission will be unlocked after you complete the previous mission in this list plus one additional mission.

CRATE CLAIM

Mission Giver: Buzz Lightyear Alien
Type: Fetch
Rewards: 250 Crystals / 100 Sparks
Wii Reward: 50 Crystals

With just a little over a minute on the clock you have to really fly (literally) to complete this task on time. The first crate is easy enough to collect as it is nearby at the top of the depression leading to Goo Valley.

Little crate number two is on a ledge to the west of the Shield Generator. You can't get to it directly, so fly towards it, but pass by it to get to a pair of ledges that you can jump up to. Grab the crate quickly and fly back to the green target drop spot.

The final crate is out at the Waterfall area. Do a double jump off the edge of the City and fly over to collect and return the crate.

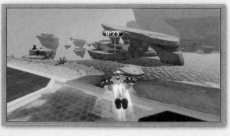

Wii NOTE

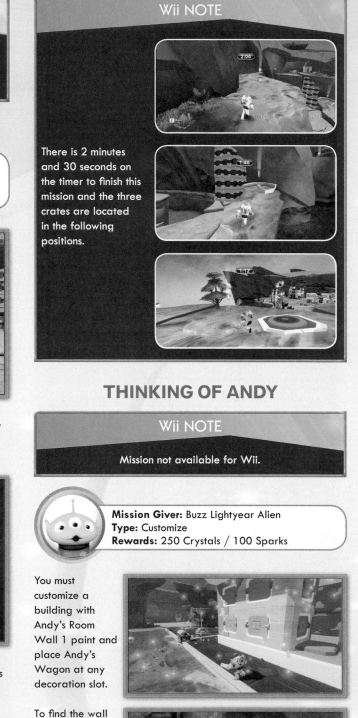

There is 2 minutes and 30 seconds on the timer to finish this mission and the three crates are located in the following positions.

THINKING OF ANDY

Wii NOTE

Mission not available for Wii.

Mission Giver: Buzz Lightyear Alien
Type: Customize
Rewards: 250 Crystals / 100 Sparks

You must customize a building with Andy's Room Wall 1 paint and place Andy's Wagon at any decoration slot.

To find the wall paint, get the red capsule at the top of the little waterfall west of the Shield Generator.

The wagon you require is on a tall stack of crates to the left of the entrance to Goo Valley.

SPEEDY DELIVERY

Mission Giver: Buzz Lightyear Alien
Type: Sight Fetch
Rewards: 250 Crystals / 100 Sparks
Wii Reward: 100 Crystals

This is by far the toughest crate challenge in the game. If you make a mistake just abort and restart. Also, make sure to use the jetpack to move around the City as fast as possible as you will need every second in this 1 minute and 30 second challenge! Fly out to the edge of the water and use the rocket booster to leap to the first crate in the Waterfall area.

Leap off the edge of the City and fly towards the Canyon to collect the next crate. Make sure to land slightly to the left to bump into a ridge that

will stop you quickly and safely.

The last crate is a long way out in the Waterfall area and time will be really tight. Leap off the City's edge again over the water and fly directly out to the tiny floating rock. Make sure to land to the right to break your momentum. Pick up the crate and blaze a trail flying all the way back to the green drop circle to make it just in time.

Wii NOTE

You have 3 minutes to finish this mission and the three crates are located in the following positions.

GAME BASICS

CHARACTERS

POWER DISCS

PLAY SETS

TOY BOX

TOY BOX COLLECTION

ACHIEVEMENTS

SIDE MISSIONS: ALIEN TOURIST CITY

HELP ME GET THERE

Mission Giver: Tourist Alien
Type: Sightseeing
Rewards: 50 Crystals / 100 Sparks
Wii Reward: 50 Crystals

The little green guy and his camera wish to travel and take photos. It's a simple enough request to honor—well at least it starts out

that way on the first mission. Look for the tourist in the cave next to the Shield Generator right by the Toy Store icon.

Pick up the Alien and follow the compass to take it to the edge of the City near a purple pool.

TAKE ME THERE

Mission Giver: Tourist Alien
Type: Sightseeing
Rewards: 50 Crystals / 100 Sparks
Wii Reward: 50 Crystals

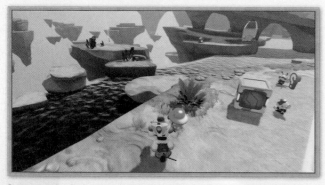

Return to the little cave by the Toy Store icon to find the tourist that wants to further explore the planet. Assist the green guy by taking him out to the Waterfall area. Go out to the edge of the City and follow the compass to double jump across the water to take the Alien sightseeing.

ALIEN TAXI

Mission Giver: Tourist Alien
Type: Sightseeing
Rewards: 50 Crystals / 100 Sparks
Wii Reward: 50 Crystals

The tourist wants to take a picture of a great view. Scoop him up and go to the Teleporter Dish to use the pad to warp to the high ridge to the right of the entrance to Goo Valley. To warp to this spot make sure to press the big IN button until you see the following image on the screen (with the little rocket house).

Wii NOTE

The tourist's destination is on a high ledge in the Canyon near the hole that goes to a small cave.

UNDER THE CITY

Mission Giver: Tourist Alien
Type: Sightseeing
Rewards: 100 Crystals / 100 Sparks

The Alien wants to go somewhere it can observe the goo. Pick it up and use the teleporter in the center of the City to go below the surface to check out the goo pools.

A VIEW FROM ABOVE

Mission Giver: Tourist Alien
Type: Sightseeing
Rewards: 50 Crystals / 100 Sparks
Wii Reward: 50 Crystals

Take the tourist to the top of the large slanted slab of rock near the Canyon.

NEW VIEWPOINT

Mission Giver: Tourist Alien
Type: Sightseeing
Rewards: 100 Crystals / 100 Sparks
Wii Reward: 100 Crystals

Get the tourist on the top of the mountain to the right of the Shield Generator.

The tourist's destination is out in the Waterfall area near the River Hoppin' Challenge.

GAME BASICS

CHARACTERS

POWER DISCS

PLAY SETS

TOY BOX

TOY BOX COLLECTION

ACHIEVEMENTS

SIDE MISSIONS: LOTSO RESCUE

FRIEND BY THE FALLS

Mission Giver: Buttercup Alien
Type: Rescue
Rewards: 50 Crystals
Wii Reward: 50 Crystals

An Alien is stranded out in the Waterfall area. Jump in the air to get some height and use the jetpack to fly out to the remote location to get the Alien.

Climb up to rescue the green guy and fly back to his friend.

Wii NOTE

The lost Alien is located on the following floating rock.

THE LOST LONER

Mission Giver: Lotso Alien
Type: Rescue
Rewards: 50 Crystals / 100 Sparks
Wii Reward: 50 Crystals

Look for another lost Alien in the Waterfall area behind a big blue breakable wall. Pick up the injured Alien and take him to the Hospital.

BOOSTER DOWN

Mission Giver: Lotso Alien
Type: Rescue
Rewards: 100 Crystals / 100 Sparks
Wii Reward: 100 Crystals

Another Alien is stranded out in the Waterwall area. Use the jetpack to fly out to get the little green guy and boost up to a higher vantage point to fly back and return him to his friend.

Wii NOTE

The stranded Alien is located next to the Canyon.

IN A FIX

Mission Giver: Lotso Alien
Type: Rescue
Rewards: 100 Crystals / 100 Sparks
Wii Reward: 100 Crystals

The lost Alien is in a lower section of the Waterfall area that is a bit tricky to get to. Start out by flying towards the Alien and run into the large rocky pillar behind it. Pick up the Alien and either boost all the way up in line with the City or zip across to the teleport pad to make it a quick trip.

Wii NOTE

This lost Alien is located in this spot in the Waterfall area.

GAME BASICS

CHARACTERS

POWER DISCS

PLAY SETS

TOY BOX

TOY BOX COLLECTION

ACHIEVEMENTS

COMPLETE THE COMBAT SIMULATIONS

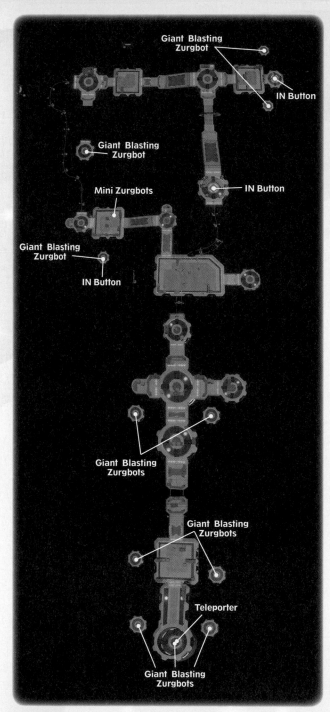

Giant Blasting Zurgbot

IN Button

Giant Blasting Zurgbot

Mini Zurgbots

IN Button

Giant Blasting Zurgbot

IN Button

Giant Blasting Zurgbots

Giant Blasting Zurgbots

Teleporter

Giant Blasting Zurgbots

SIMULATION 4: UNFATHOMABLE

Mission Giver: Zurg Hologram
Type: Combat
Rewards: 750 Crystals / 500 Sparks
Wii Rewards: 1,000 Crystals / 500 Sparks

At the start of this simulation is a Giant Blasting Zurgbot accompanied by several blue ones. This huge red robot shoots a large energy sphere that might be slow, but it can go through objects to hit you. Luckily this big projectile is slow enough to easily to dodge. Shoot up the blue bots and outmaneuver the energy balls to wipe out this group.

Before you head down the ramp to the next batch of robots, look for a red capsule with the Zurg Wall behind some blue crates. Continue down the ramp to confront several Mini Zurgbots. The shoulder charge or ground pound attack can deal with them very well.

The real challenge here is the big red Zurgbot on the floating platform that shoots large projectiles. Keep in mind that your blaster fire's a lot faster than the Giant Blasting Zurgbots and you can stand your ground in a one-on-one battle.

Before you jump on the rail for a curving ride, take out the Giant Blasting Zurgbot.

Go for a fun rail slide and in the next section look to the left crates to find the red capsule with the Ray Zapper. The section just up ahead has a pair of the Giant Blasting Zurgbots. Stay back to take them out from a distance and let your blaster's superior firing rate do its job.

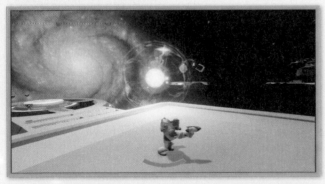

Continue past this spot to battle another pair of big reds to get to the large IN button.

Cross the extended blue bridge and step on the next IN button to go for a rail slide to the final area.

Take on a mixed group of big and little Blasting Zurgbots and make sure to look for the green capsule with Toy Story Decorations Toy Pack 1 behind gray crates.

To complete the final battle you must destroy ten robots of various types. The biggest threats are the Giant Blasting Zurgbots, because although they fire slowly, the large energy spheres can make it hard to battle their brethren. The last three enemies are a trio of big red Zurgbots. It can be easy to get overwhelmed if the screen is filled with huge projectiles, so take out one at a time. The robot in the middle is the easiest to take out and should be your first target. When it is gone, shoot and move to keep the Zurgbots guessing. Keep in mind that their elevated position will require you to jump up on the crates or leap into the air to hit them. If you are quick at zipping in and out of the zoomed-in mode you can target each one and overwhelm them with blaster fire.

⭐ SIMULATION 5: ULTIMATE DOWNFALL

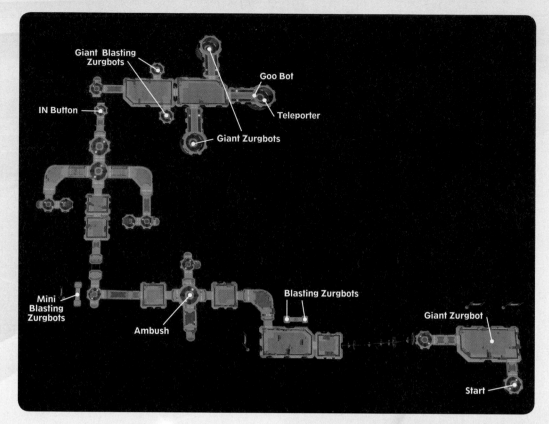

Mission Giver: Zurg Hologram
Type: Combat
Rewards: 750 Crystals / 500 Sparks
Wii Rewards: 1,000 Crystals / 500 Sparks

Rail slide to the next long area filled with red and blue bots. Beat up the blue bots and keep your distance to fire blaster shots at the Zurgbots that are trying to shoot you. Whenever you get into a battle of mixed Zurgbots like this, use a shoot and move tactic to avoid getting pinned down. When the reinforcements arrive it will include a Giant Zurgbot. Back up and fire away from a safe place to destroy this robot and avoid laser fire.

A super-sized blue Zurgbot makes its appearance. It is a tough robot to deal with up close due to its own form of the ground pound where it slams its huge mace-like fists into the floor. The good news is that like its other blue brothers, it has no long-range attack and can safely be dealt with if you can get some distance.

A small group of blue Mini Zurgbots have to be destroyed in the adjacent area to lower the barrier. You can unleash your blaster, but it is  a lot more fun to get physical with the little blue bots.

The next area is an ambush! A blue Giant Zurgbot will appear in front and in back while Giant Blasting Zurgbots pop up on each side. Standing in the center of this four-way attack is not a great idea. Charge in any direction to remove the threat and get some space to wipe out the rest of the robots on your own terms. When the coast is clear, check the right side near some crates to find a red capsule with the Zurg Cap.

Go up the inclined ramp and wipe out the firing Zurgbots from a safe distance.

The next section has several big bots, and the real threat comes from the Blasting Zurgbots on the floating platforms. Don't race into the mess of robots. Fire from a distance until you get a chance to focus on each red Zurgbot on the sides. Move up to the adjacent section to wipe out some blue bots and go down the side route to the right to find a red capsule with the Zurg Outfit.

Step on the nearby IN button to lower the next section of the level and stay back when you are about to go into the next battle. Take out as many robots as possible in this section and let them come to you.

When the blue barrier drops, step into the next section and look to the left for the green capsule with the Toy Story Space Track Set Toy Pack 5. Immediately backtrack a bit to get some space to deal with the giant blue bots at a safe distance.

The final section has a new and very deadly robot in the back: Goo Bot. Not only can this robot shoot Purple Goo to shrink you, it also uses a sort of chain lighting maneuver to create more Zurgbots! Needless to say, it is always a top priority target as it can continue to spawn an endless robot army.

GAME BASICS

CHARACTERS

POWER DISCS

PLAY SETS

TOY BOX

TOY BOX COLLECTION

ACHIEVEMENTS

⭐ SIMULATION 6: NO SURVIVAL

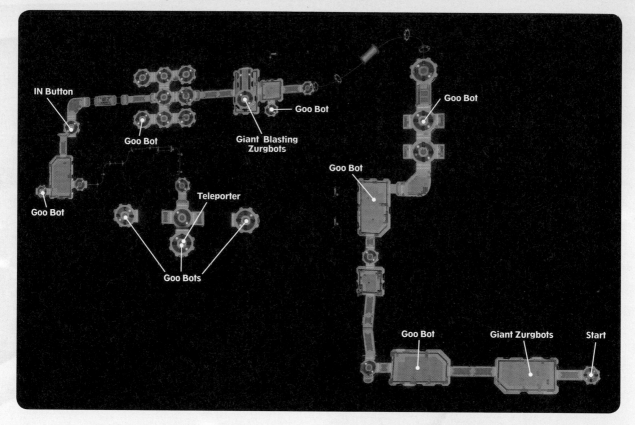

NOTE

The final simulation requires completion of the Collect the Primal Goo missions and six buildings being built.

Mission Giver: Zurg Hologram
Type: Combat
Rewards: 1,000 Crystals
Wii Rewards: 1,000 Crystals / 500 Sparks

The next section features the Goo Bot that keeps spawning blue Zurgbots. It might seem like a good idea to just stand back and keep firing away as the blue bots come to you. However, it is more efficient to charge the Goo Bot and take it out to prevent it from continuing to create more targets.

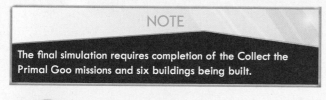

The next combat section has a few Mini Zurgbots that can safely be dealt with from a distance. Wipe out the robots and grab the red capsule

on top of the gray crates to the left to find the Zurg Minion Helmet.

The final simulation is really going to test your combat skills. It starts out with a trio of giant robots. Keep your distance and fire away.

In the next part there is a Goo Bot in the back and several red Zurgbots guarding it with gunfire. Shoot the Blasting Zurgbots at a distance while trying to dodge and charge in to directly tackle the Goo Bot.

Fight your way to the next section and battle another Goo Bot to lower the blue barrier. To deal with this Goo Bot just run in and unleash your blaster to destroy it as fast as you can.

Go for a rail slide through several rings to get to the next spot with lots of robots. There is a Goo Bot on the side, but the other big problem is the Giant Blasting Zurgbot on the upper section. There are two choices here: if you are quick, you can run in and waste the Goo Bot, or you can stay back and zoom in on the red Zurgbot to take it out first.

The next section has a barrier and you must destroy all the robots. Get close to the Goo Bot and fire away to stop it from producing a robot army, then clean up the rest of the bots. If you feel like you are getting pinned down, use the open circular-like paths to get to a safe distance. Make sure to check out the cluster of crates on the side that has a red capsule with the Zurg Accent.

Go to the large IN button to lower the track above and jump into another group of robots. Stand your ground in the center and blast the Goo Bot while trying to avoid the robot fire.

Jump on the next IN button to extend the rail on the opposite side of the area. Go for a rail ride to the final battle full of Goo Bots.

Wii NOTE

Upon completion of the final simulation in the Wii version, an automatic mission Come Back to Town will remind you to go back to the City.

GAME BASICS

CHARACTERS

POWER DISCS

PLAY SETS

TOY BOX

TOY BOX COLLECTION

ACHIEVEMENTS

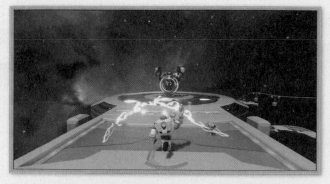

There are three round areas and each has a Goo Bot that will summon robots to challenge you. Run down each of these paths and charge the Goo Bot to stop its robot production.

⭐ DEFEAT ZURG!

Mission Giver: Slinky Dog
Type: Combat
Rewards: 1,000 Crystals / 1,000 Sparks
Wii Rewards: 1,000 Crystals / 50 Sparks

After completing the final combat simulation, the City is under attack by an enormous Emperor Zurg. The only way to battle this giant is to turn the Shield Generator into a Goo Cannon.

You must take the batteries back from the Zurgbots and insert them into the Shield Generator at the tower's base. The first battery is out in the Waterfall area, and that area is now filled with Zurgbots.

The Giant Zurgbots that surround the battery make it hard to acquire the power cell, but you must battle them up close. Clear out the first few and destroy any neighboring Zurgbots.

Once you pick up the battery the task is not over as you still need to return it to the tower. The battery is too large to fly or boost with, so your obvious option is to get to the teleporter below. However if you want to make it really easy, you could just shoot the battery with the Goo Shrinker to make it small enough to carry.

Toss the battery to the ledge below with the big Blasting bot and leap down to destroy the bot. Pick up the battery and step into the Green Goo to become large enough to boost and fly while holding the power cell, then make a long boosting leap to the teleporter pad.

Warp back to the City and place the first of two batteries at the base of the tower.

The second battery is in the Canyon, so fly or teleport out there and use the compass to locate it. You should expect that area to be filled with Zurgbots, so ready your blaster to wipe them all out.

Collect the battery near the back wall and shrink it down to size to make it easy to carry on your way back to the City.

Place the final battery in the base of the tower, take the elevator to the top, and press the IN button to fire the Goo Cannon.

Wii NOTE

The batteries are in different locations as follows.

The first one is at the edge of the City near two little rocket houses.

The second battery is at the far edge of the City on the opposite side near the large mountainous wall.

GAME BASICS

CHARACTERS

POWER DISCS

PLAY SETS

TOY BOX

TOY BOX COLLECTION

ACHIEVEMENTS

ALIEN EASTER EGG HUNT

When you build the Hatchery, you are introduced to egg gathering by completing the mission Egg Spotted. The hatched egg will introduce a new species into the wild, and you can find the new critters in the Play Set as soon as they hatch. However, that mission was only the beginning of your inter-species introduction. There are actually thirteen colored eggs to find throughout the Main Town and Goo Valley. Below is the location of all the hidden eggs. Make sure to check out the collectibles map for each location.

Main Town

Got It?		Egg Appearance	Location	Creature Inside Egg
✓	E1	Turquoise with purple spots and purple center	Under the breakable floor behind the Rocket Booster Blast challenge pad.	Nostrilloid
✓	E2	Blue with light blue rings and yellow center	Behind and to the left of the Blasters Away challenge pad.	Gummboid
✓	E3	Pink with blue spots and light blue center	At the far end of the forest with the Sarge Alien to the left of the tower.	Boomeroid
✓	E4	Red-orange with yellow center	On the cliffs by the house to the right, just above the Goo Valley entrance hole.	Snoutoid
✓	E5	Red with darker red streaks and light blue center	In the high cave to the left of the Goo Valley entrance.	Snailian
✓	E6	Light blue with light blue center	Down the hole at the top of the cliff to the right of the Canyon entrance.	Pinchoid
✓	E7	Blue with etchings and light blue center	Behind the waterfall cave at the very end of Jetpack Canyon.	Twitchoid
✓	E8	Light blue with a large white center	At the lowest level of the tallest giant floating space rock outside the Main Town.	Unicoid
✓	E9	Purple with blue spots and purple circle	Through the small cave hole on the cliff to the left above the Goo Valley entrance hole.	Rabbitoid

Goo Valley

Got It?		Egg Appearance	Location	Creature Inside Egg
✓	E10	Pink with purple spots and pink center	Follow the ledge hang at the bottom of the area to the immediate left of the third valley.	Octoid
✓	E11	Light green with blue stripes and blue circle	On the floating space rock at the far end of the second valley.	Leafoid
✓	E12	Dark purple with light blue center	Inside the small cave at the end of the purple puddle in the second valley area.	Quackoid
✓	E13	Light green with large purple circle	Underneath the breakable floor in the high town portion.	Wedgoid

GAME BASICS

CHARACTERS

POWER DISCS

PLAY SETS

TOY BOX

TOY BOX COLLECTION

ACHIEVEMENTS

COLLECTIBLES

Main Town

CRYSTAL CAVE

JESSIE 2

E5

E3 32 60

E2 1

WOODY 1

10

E9

56

ENTRANCE TO GOO VALLEY

20

22

25

68 12

2 74

E4

44

13 7 75

59 5

51

E1

64

15

21

8

19 28

27

9

47

73

TOWER

ALIEN VILLAGE

37

CITY

38

36

40

62

35

43

START HERE

16

39

WOODY 2

E7

3

42

31

JESSIE 1

WATERFALLS

34

BUZZ 1

48 49

55 67

54 17

14

E6

E8

63 24

71

6

69

70

CANYONS

46

18

11

53

26

57

72

58

Combat Simulation 0

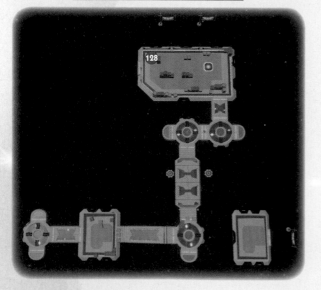

128

Combat Simulation 1

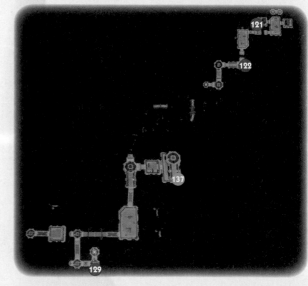

121

122

137

129

Combat Simulation 2

Combat Simulation 3

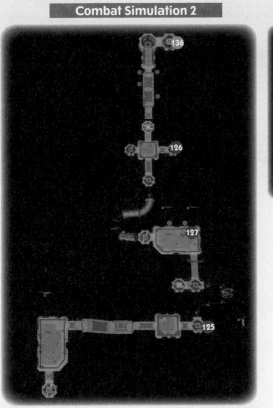

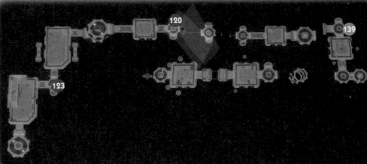

🔴 Red Capsules – Main Town

Got It?	#	Unlockable Item	Zone	Location
✓	1	Andy's Room Wall 1	Main Town	Above the waterfall behind and to the right of the Blasters Away challenge pad.
✓	2	Andy's Wagon	Main Town	On the pile of crates to the left of the Goo Valley entrance hole.
✓	3	Bo Peep Bonnet	Main Town	Above the waterfall cave at the end of Jetpack Canyon.
✓	4	Bo Peep Outfit	Main Town	On top of the Monument of Heroes.
✓	5	Bo Peep's Crook	Main Town	On the ledge hang behind the Cliffside Collect challenge pad.
✓	6	Buttercup Cap	Main Town	High in the sky between the two large rock plateaus above the water islands outside of the town.
✓	7	Buttercup Outfit	Main Town	At the platform around the middle of the Tower.
✓	8	Buzz Helmet	Main Town	Around the Delivery Platform after buying the Buzz Lightyear Alien from the Toy Store.
✓	9	Buzz Outfit	Main Town	Around the Delivery Platform after buying the Buzz Lightyear Alien from the Toy Store.
✓	10	Cannon Bunker	Main Town	On the tip of the cliff near the cave entrance to the left of the Tower before the forest.
✓	11	Chuckles Hair	Main Town	High above the alien house right at the entrance to Jetpack Canyon.
✓	12	Chuckles Outfit	Main Town	Drop down from a ledge hang above and to the left of the Goo Valley entrance hole.
✓	13	Chunk Helmet	Main Town	On a small floating island behind the Tower.
✓	14	Chunk Outfit	Main Town	The bottom of the island in the water with the alien house.
✓	15	Dinosaur Eggs	Main Town	Floating in the air near the alien house to the left of the Horsey Headache challenge pad.
✓	16	Doctor Bag	Main Town	Under town in the tunnel near the Jessie challenge pad.
✓	17	Doctor Outfit	Main Town	At the base of the wall jump area at the back of the large floating space rock nearest the teleporter rock.
✓	18	Doctor's Stethoscope	Main Town	On the first ledge after entering the big Jetpack Canyon cave.
✓	19	Dolly Hair	Main Town	Off the edge of the cliff with the Cliffside Collect challenge pad.
✓	20	Dolly Outfit	Main Town	Near the high cave entrance directly behind the Tower.
✓	21	Dolly Wall	Main Town	Cliff to the left of the Tower above the first Slinky Dog battery.
✓	22	Flagpole	Main Town	Slightly over the edge outside the high cave entrance directly behind the Tower.
✓	23	Flowerbed 1	Main Town	Unlocked after buying the Decoration Center.
✓	24	Flowerbed 2	Main Town	At the back of the cave down the hole at the top of the cliff to the right of the Jetpack Canyon entrance.
✓	25	Gem Hat	Main Town	Between the trees near the Rocket Booster Blast challenge pad.
✓	26	Horseshoes Accent	Main Town	At the back middle of the large floating space rock nearest Jetpack Canyon.
✓	27	Jessie Hat	Main Town	Around the Delivery Platform after buying the Jessie Alien from the Toy Store.

GAME BASICS · CHARACTERS · POWER DISCS · PLAY SETS · TOY BOX · TOY BOX COLLECTION · ACHIEVEMENTS

Got It?	#	Unlockable Item	Zone	Location
✓	28	Jessie Outfit	Main Town	Around the Delivery Platform after buying the Jessie Alien from the Toy Store.
✓	29	Jessie Wall	Main Town	Above the Hospital building.
✓	30	Key to the City	Main Town	In front of the Shield Tower after all buildings have been built.
✓	31	Lotso Cap	Main Town	At the end of the large drainage tunnel underneath the Main Town.
✓	32	Lotso Outfit	Main Town	Behind a large tree at the end of the forest with the army alien to the left of the Tower.
✓	33	Monument to Zurg's Defeat	Main Town	In front of the Shield Tower after beating Zurg.
✓	34	Plush Flowers	Main Town	Just above the water to the right of the entrance to Jetpack Canyon.
✓	35	Pricklepants Cap	Main Town	At the back of the tall island near the waterfall at the back of town.
✓	36	Pricklepants Outfit	Main Town	Under town inside the small drainage tunnel.
✓	37	Researcher Goggles	Main Town	High in the air between two ledges near the alien houses to the left of the Tower.
✓	38	Rex Accent	Main Town	Under town further down the tunnel near the Jessie challenge pad.
✓	39	Rex Cap	Main Town	On a small island near the waterfall at the back of town.
✓	40	Rex Outfit	Main Town	At the tip of the tall island by the waterfall outside of town.
✓	41	Rex Wall	Main Town	Above the Combat Simulator building.
✓	42	Sarge Helmet	Main Town	In the Shrink Goo puddle at the back of the town.
✓	43	Sarge Outfit	Main Town	Middle of alien houses in front of the Infinity Vault to the left of the Tower.
✓	44	Sarge Prop	Main Town	On the pile of crates to the right of the Goo Valley entrance hole.
✓	45	Sheriff's Badge	Main Town	On top of the Decoration Center.
✓	47	Snake In My Boot	Main Town	In a shallow hole around the cliffs by the flowers at the right of the Goo Valley entrance hole.
✓	48	Star-letts Hair 1	Main Town	On the large floating space rock closest to the bottom, with the teleporter pad.
✓	49	Star-letts Hair 2	Main Town	Above the large floating space rock closest to the Main Town area.
✓	50	Star-letts Outfit 1	Main Town	Inside the satellite dish atop the Teleporter building.
✓	51	Star-letts Outfit 2	Main Town	In the Shrink Goo under the breakable floor behind the Rocket Booster Blast challenge pad.
✓	52	Stinky Pete Hat	Main Town	Press the three buttons on top of the Clothing Shop.
✓	53	Tourist Camera	Main Town	On the small floating space rock at the far right closest to the waterfall.
✓	54	Tourist Hat	Main Town	Near the gold crystal at the bottom of a large floating space rock outside of the Main Town.
✓	55	Tourist Outfit	Main Town	On the small floating space rock above the one with the teleporter outside of the Main Town.
✓	56	Trixie Accent	Main Town	Through the small cave door to the left above the entrance hole to Goo Valley.
✓	57	Trixie Cap	Main Town	On a cliff underneath the large flat plateau rock on the way to Jetpack Canyon.
✓	58	Trixie Outfit	Main Town	Just above the water in the gap behind the large flat plateau rock on the way to Jetpack Canyon.
✓	59	Trixie Wall	Main Town	Behind small cave hole under the breakable floor behind the Rocket Booster Blast challenge pad.
✓	60	Twitch Cap	Main Town	Inside a hole at the end of the forest with the army alien to the left of the Tower.
✓	61	Volcano Trophy	Main Town	At the first stop of the Tower's entrance, after completing the "Planetary Plumber" mission.
✓	62	Water Fountain	Main Town	Underneath the tall island by the waterfall outside of town.
✓	63	Wood Trim	Main Town	When dropping down again to leave the cave down the hole at the top of the cliff to the right of the Jetpack Canyon entrance.
✓	64	Woody Hat	Main Town	Inside the cave with breakable walls to the right of the Tower.
✓	65	Woody Holster	Main Town	Above the Hatchery building.
✓	66	Woody Outfit	Main Town	On top of the Research Station.
✓	67	Woody Wall	Main Town	At the top of the large floating space rock nearest the teleporter rock.
✓	68	Woody's Roundup Critters	Main Town	Jump between ledge hangs high above the cliff to the left and above the Goo Valley entrance hole.
✓	69	Zurg Statue	Main Town	On the cliffs to the right above the Jetpack Canyon entrance.

🪣 Green Capsules – Main Town

Got It?	#	Unlockable Item	Zone	Location
✓	46	Shield Tower	Main Town	On a small floating space rock near the base of the waterfall outside and to the right of the Main Town.
✓	70	Toy Story Alien Townsperson Toy Pack 1	Main Town	At the end of the first large area after entering the big Jetpack Canyon cave.
✓	71	Toy Story Alien Townsperson Toy Pack 2	Main Town	In a cave at the base of the large landmass across the water from Jetpack Canyon.
✓	72	Toy Story Alien Townsperson Toy Pack 3	Main Town	In a cave underneath the large flat plateau rock on the way to Jetpack Canyon.
✓	73	Toy Story Alien Townsperson Toy Pack 4	Main Town	On a hangable ledge under the alien crash location.
✓	74	Toy Story Alien Townsperson Toy Pack 5	Main Town	On a floating rock above the Goo Valley entrance hole.
✓	75	Toy Story Alien Townsperson Toy Pack 6	Main Town	On a floating rock just outside the middle platform of the Tower.

Infinity Chests/Vault – Main Town

Got It?	#	Unlockable Item	Zone	Location
✓	Jessie1	Jessie Chest 1	Main Town	Behind the waterfall cave at the end of Jetpack Canyon.
✓	Jessie2	Jessie Chest 1	Main Town	Under the breakable floor behind the Rocket Booster Blast challenge pad.
✓	Buzz1	Buzz Chest 1	Main Town	Island in the water with the alien house.
✓	Woody1	Woody Chest 1	Main Town	By the waterfall to the right of the Blasters Away challenge pad.
✓	Woody2	Woody Chest 2	Main Town	On the medium-sized island by the waterfall at the rear of town.
✓	Vault	Master Avatar Vault	Main Town	At the end of the alien houses to the left of the Tower.

Goo Valley

Red Capsules - Goo Valley

Got It?	#	Unlockable Item	Zone	Location
✓	76	Army Accent	Goo Valley	Above the first green grow puddle.
✓	77	Bullseye Cap	Goo Valley	Behind the pumpkin-like creature near the end of the third valley area.
✓	78	Bullseye Outfit	Goo Valley	Small cave near the bottom of the Purple Goo river in the third valley.
✓	79	Buttercup Face	Goo Valley	Between ledge hangs when going to the area with the pumpkin-like creature by the volcano entrance.
✓	80	Chuckles Face	Goo Valley	Behind the breakable wall behind the pumpkin-like creature by the volcano entrance.
✓	81	Dark Carbon Trim	Goo Valley	Inside the large breakable wall cave to the right of the cliff above the first Green Goo puddle.
✓	82	Dolly Accent	Goo Valley	Behind the breakable wall at far back right of the volcano entrance's valley.
✓	83	Dolly's Sunflowers	Goo Valley	Inside the small cave along the right wall after climbing up from the second valley.
✓	84	Gem Outfit	Goo Valley	On a ledge high above the left side of the second valley area.
✓	85	Hamm Cap	Goo Valley	Slightly in the air in the Goo Valley town, on the cliff closest to the volcano.
✓	86	Hamm Outfit	Goo Valley	Between ledge hangs just under the volcano entrance.
✓	87	Jessie Felt Accent	Goo Valley	High in the air between two high ledges between the second and third valley areas.
✓	88	Jetpack	Goo Valley	On a low floating rock past the volcano valley, towards the Goo Valley town.
✓	89	Light Carbon Trim	Goo Valley	On a ledge high above the left side of the first valley area.

Combat Simulation 4

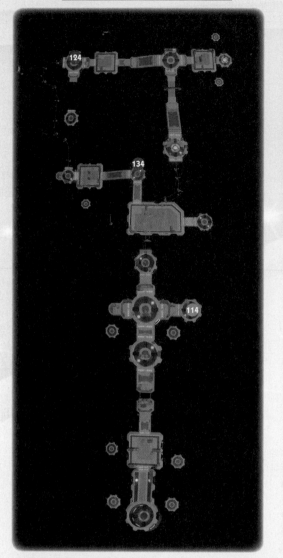

Combat Simulation 5

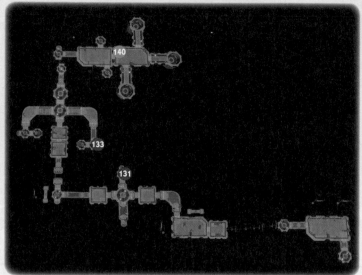

Combat Simulation 6

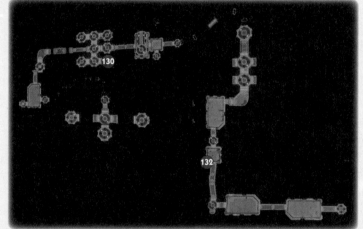

Got It?	#	Unlockable Item	Zone	Location
✓	90	Lotso Accent	Goo Valley	Behind the large tree to the right after climbing up the wall to leave the third valley.
✓	91	Lotso Staff	Goo Valley	At the end of the ledge hang area after turning left immediately after entering the third valley.
✓	92	Lotso Wall	Goo Valley	Behind the large breakable wall to the left when first entering the third valley.
✓	93	Painter Hat	Goo Valley	On a floating space rock beyond the left side of the third valley area.
✓	94	Painter Item	Goo Valley	Between the trees in the purple puddle in the second valley area
✓	95	Painter Outfit	Goo Valley	Floating high in space at the left side of the Goo Valley town, when facing it from the volcano.
✓	96	Pixar Lamp	Goo Valley	Floating rock above the right side of the beginning of Goo Valley.
✓	97	Plush Hearts	Goo Valley	Inside the small cave at the end of the purple puddle in the second valley area.
✓	98	Pricklepants Accent	Goo Valley	Floating in space far past the left side of the second valley area.
✓	99	Pricklepants Wall	Goo Valley	Inside a small cave at the left side of the first purple shrink puddle.
✓	100	Puppet Theatre	Goo Valley	Floating rock hovering over space outside of the second valley area.
✓	101	Researcher Outfit	Goo Valley	At the far end of the cliff just under the volcano entrance.
✓	102	Slinky Cap	Goo Valley	Breakable wall at the upper left of the second valley area.
✓	103	Slinky Outfit	Goo Valley	Large breakable wall cave to the left of the first green puddle.
✓	104	Stinky Pete Outfit	Goo Valley	Underneath a floating space rock beyond the left side of the third valley area.
✓	105	Stinky Pete Pick Axe	Goo Valley	At the right end of the cliff when facing the volcano entrance.
✓	106	Stretch Cap	Goo Valley	Ledge above the pumpkin-like creature to the immediate left of entering Goo Valley.
✓	107	Stretch Outfit	Goo Valley	Follow the ledge hang at the bottom of the area to the immediate left of the third valley.
✓	108	Twitch Outfit	Goo Valley	Underneath the purple waterfall at the very bottom of the volcano entrance.

Got It?	#	Unlockable Item	Zone	Location
✓	109	Wheezy Cap	Goo Valley	In the third valley between the shrink scientist and his Stink Spore.
✓	110	Wheezy Microphone	Goo Valley	Past the edge of the purple waterfall at the base of the volcano entrance's valley.
✓	111	Wheezy Outfit	Goo Valley	The beginning of the ledge hang at the bottom of the area to the immediate left of the third valley.
✓	112	Woody Accent	Goo Valley	Above the ledge to the right of the second mandatory pumpkin-like creature.

🗿 Green Capsules – Goo Valley

Got It?	#	Unlockable Item	Zone	Location
✓	113	Toy Story Alien Critter Toy Pack 1	Goo Valley	At the edge of a high ledge between the third and fourth valley areas.
✓	114	Toy Story Alien Critter Toy Pack 2	Goo Valley	High above the left wall at the entrance to Goo Valley.
✓	115	Toy Story Alien Critter Toy Pack 3	Goo Valley	On a ledge high above the left side of the second valley area.
✓	116	Toy Story Alien Townsperson Toy Pack 7	Goo Valley	Breakable wall at the left side after climbing up from the second valley.
✓	117	Toy Story Breakable Toy Pack	Goo Valley	To the left of the volcano's entrance.
✓	118	Toy Story Space Track Set Toy Pack 1	Goo Valley	On the floating rock between the volcano entrance and the Goo Valley town.
✓	119	Toy Story Space Track Set Toy Pack 2	Goo Valley	Pass through the small hole inside the breakable wall at the end of the third valley.

🗄 Infinity Chests/Vault – Goo Valley

Got It?	#	Unlockable Item	Zone	Location
✓	Jessie3	Jessie Chest 3	Goo Valley	At the end of the valley to the right of the second mandatory pumpkin-like creature.
✓	Buzz2	Buzz Chest 2	Goo Valley	Breakable wall cave to the right of the first purple shrink puddle.
✓	Woody3	Woody Chest 3	Goo Valley	At the first wide-area opening in the cave from Main Town to Goo Valley.

🗿 Red Capsules – Combat Simulator

Got It?	#	Unlockable Item	Zone	Location
✓	120	Army Wall	Combat Simulator	Behind the crates to the left of the first zip line in Combat Simulator 3.
✓	121	Mechanic Hat	Combat Simulator	Behind the robot room at the left near the teleporter at the end of Combat Simulator 1.
✓	122	Mechanic Outfit	Combat Simulator	Behind the crates before the first turn after climbing up the first pipe climb in Combat Simulator 1.
✓	123	Mechanic Tools	Combat Simulator	Behind the crates directly ahead when leaving the first arena area in Combat Simulator 3.
✓	124	Ray Zapper	Combat Simulator	On the crates to the left after going down the first zip line in Combat Simulator 4.
✓	125	Space Suit Blaster	Combat Simulator	Behind the crates right before the first zip line in Combat Simulator 2.
✓	126	Space Suit Helmet	Combat Simulator	On top of the crate stack to the right after the second zip line in Combat Simulator 2.
✓	127	Space Suit Outfit	Combat Simulator	Behind the crates in the arena room before the second zip line in Combat Simulator 2.
✓	128	Star Cadet Helmet 2	Combat Simulator	Behind the crates to the left of the final platform in Star Command Blaster Qualification.
✓	129	Star Cadet Outfit 2	Combat Simulator	Behind the crates to the right near the first ground button in Combat Simulator 1.
✓	130	Zurg Accent	Combat Simulator	Behind crates down the left path at the second area after the zip line in Combat Simulator 6.
✓	131	Zurg Cap	Combat Simulator	Behind the crates down the right path in the ambush room before the first ascending slope in Combat Simulator 5.
✓	132	Zurg Minion Helmet	Combat Simulator	To the left after going up the first ascending ramp in Combat Simulator 6.
✓	133	Zurg Outfit	Combat Simulator	Behind the crates at the end of the right path in the fight area before the elevator in Combat Simulator 5.
✓	134	Zurg Wall	Combat Simulator	Behind the crates directly ahead after leaving the first arena area in Combat Simulator 4.

🗿 Green Capsules – Combat Simulator

Got It?	#	Unlockable Item	Zone	Location
✓	135	Toy Story Decorations Toy Pack 1	Combat Simulator	Behind the crates to the left after going down the second zip line in Combat Simulator 4.
✓	136	Toy Story Decorations Toy Pack 2	Combat Simulator	Behind the stack of crates behind the end teleporter in Combat Simulator 2.
✓	137	Toy Story Decorations Toy Pack 3	Combat Simulator	Behind the crates at the left in the area to the right before the first zip line in Combat Simulator 1.
✓	138	Toy Story Space Track Set Toy Pack 3	Combat Simulator	Near the ceiling to the left before the main elevator.
✓	139	Toy Story Space Track Set Toy Pack 4	Combat Simulator	Behind the crates directly ahead after ascending the first elevator in Combat Simulator 3.
✓	140	Toy Story Space Track Set Toy Pack 5	Combat Simulator	To the left at the beginning of the Goo Bot fight at the end of Combat Simulator 5.

🗄 Infinity Chests/Vault – Combat Simulator

Got It?	#	Unlockable Item	Zone	Location
✓	Buzz3	Buzz Chest 3	Combat Simulator	On the crates in the ready room, to the right before the elevator.

⭐ Toy Story in Space Gold Stars

Got It?	#	Type	Star Names	Star Description
✓	1	Challenge	Bring It On!	Complete 10 Challenges on Medium
✓	2	Challenge	Easy Does It!	Complete 10 Challenges on Easy
✓	3	Challenge	No Problem!	Complete 10 Challenges on Hard
✓	4	Collectibles	Capsule Collection	Collect 100 capsules
✓	5	Customize	City Style	Place 15 decorations
✓	6	Customize	Remodeling Master	Apply 30 building customizations
✓	7	Customize	Trend Setter	Apply 50 alien customizations
✓	8	Easter Egg	Break Away	Destroy 10 rare (gold) gem clusters
✓	9	Easter Egg	Hatchery Mastery	Hatch 10 eggs
✓	10	Easter Egg	Master Healer	Heal 6 injured aliens
✓	11	Mission	Battle Ready	Complete "Simulation 6: No Survival"
✓	12	Mission	Catch the Fever	Complete "Play Catch"
✓	13	Mission	Doctor Certified	Complete "Certifiably Quacked"
✓	14	Mission	Egg Hunt	Complete "Egg Spotted!"
✓	15	Mission	Friends with Horns	Complete "Epic Animal Costumes"
✓	16	Mission	Green Bath	Complete "Swimming in Green"
✓	17	Mission	Happy Little Tree	Complete "Tiny Tree"
✓	18	Mission	Helpful Citizen	Complete "Under the City"
✓	19	Mission	Hero of Help	Complete "Alien Medicine"
✓	20	Mission	Horse Run	Complete "Giddy Up!"
✓	21	Mission	Lost and Found	Complete "Volcano Vanish"
✓	22	Mission	Lots Came Together!	Complete "Final Floor"
✓	23	Mission	Powers Up	Complete "Power the Tower"
✓	24	Mission	The Battle Begins!	Complete "Simulation 1: No Chance"
✓	25	Mission	The Goo Volcano	Complete "Planetary Plumber"
✓	26	Mission	The Great Defender	Complete "Defeat Zurg!"
✓	27	Mission	The Great Retrieval	Complete "Speedy Delivery"
✓	28	Mission	Ultimate Achiever	Complete 100 missions
✓	29	Purchase	Absolutely All	Buy every toy in the Toy Store
✓	30	Purchase	All Buildings Built	Build all eight buildings

Toy Story in Space Toy List

Got It?	Toys	Toy type	Unlock Conditions	Toy Box Export	Commercial
✓	Alien Horse	Mount	Buy all 8 buildings, or 20 missions after buying Bullseye.	Yes	Yes
✓	Bullseye	Mount	Complete 12 missions.	Yes	Yes
✓	Buzz Lightyear Alien	NPC	Immediately after buying the Jetpack.	Yes	No
✓	Buzz Lightyear's Jetpack	Vehicle	Complete the "Planetary Plumber" mission.	Yes	Yes
✓	Clothing Store	Building	Complete the "Clothing Store Crate Crash" mission.	Yes	Yes
✓	Combat Simulator	Building	Complete the "Combat Crate Crash" mission.	Yes	Yes
✓	Decoration Center	Building	Complete the "Decoration Crate Crash" mission.	Yes	Yes
✓	Delivery Platform	Unique	Complete the "Build-A-Lot" mission.	Yes	No
✓	Goo Grower	Held Item	Complete "The Primal Green Goo" and "Swimming in Green".	Yes	Yes
✓	Goo Shrinker	Held Item	Complete "The Purple Primal Goo" and "Tiny Tree".	Yes	Yes

Got It?	Toys	Toy type	Unlock Conditions	Toy Box Export	Commercial
✓	Goo Valley Teleporters	Unique	Complete the "Planetary Plumber" mission.	No	No
✓	Hatchery	Building	Complete the "Hatchery Crate Crash" mission.	Yes	Yes
✓	Hospital	Building	Complete the "Hospital Crate Crash" mission.	Yes	No
✓	Jessie Alien	NPC	Immediately after buying Bullseye.	Yes	No
✓	Medicine Ball	Held Item	Complete "Certifiably Quacked".	Yes	Yes
✓	Mega Pixar Ball	Held Item	Complete 30 missions.	Yes	Yes
✓	Monument of Heroes	Building	Complete the "Heroes Crate Crash" mission.	Yes	No
✓	Research Station	Building	Complete the "Research Station Crate Crash" mission.	Yes	No
✓	Star Command Blaster	Held Item	Complete the "Star Command Blaster Qualification" mission.	Yes	Yes
✓	Star Command Boost Pack	Vehicle	Complete 3 missions after buying the Jetpack.	Yes	Yes
✓	Teleporter Dish	Building	Complete the "Teleporter Dish Crate Crash" mission.	Yes	No

Toy Story in Space Challenges

Main Town

Got It?	Name	Location	Description	Toy Required	Character	Easy	Medium	Hard
✓	Cliffside Collect	Cliff to the right of the Tower.	Collect as many Challenge Orbs as you can before your time runs out.	N/A	Any	20 orbs in 1:10	40 orbs in 1:10	60 orbs in 1:10
✓	Here Comes the Cavalry!	Right next to the Delivery Platform.	Pass through all the race gates before your time runs out.	Bullseye	Any	6 gates in :40	6 gates in :30	6 gates in :20
✓	Woody's Ramblin' Race	To the left of the Tower before the alien houses.	Get Woody and Bullseye through all the race gates before your time runs out.	Bullseye	Woody	8 gates in 1:10	8 gates in :50	8 gates in :30
✓	Blasters Away	By the waterfall on the cliffs to the left of the Tower.	Break open as many targets as you can before your time runs out.	Star Command Blaster	Any	25 targets 1:30	40 targets 1:30	50 targets 1:30
✓	Horsey Headache	On the cliff overlooking the alien houses to the left of the Tower.	Break open as many targets as you can before your time runs out.	Alien Horse	Any	20 targets in :50	25 targets in :50	40 targets in :50
✓	Rocket Booster Blast	On the cliff above the Cliffside Collect pad.	Collect as many Challenge Orbs as you can before your time runs out.	Star Command Booster Pack	Any	25 orbs in 1:10	40 orbs in 1:10	58 orbs in 1:10
✓	Buzz Lightyear's River Run	Near the water and shrink goo at the back of town.	Fly Buzz Lightyear through all the gates before the time runs out.	Jetpack	Buzz	11 orbs in 1:30	11 orbs in 1:10	11 orbs in 1:00
✓	River Hoppin'	At the cliffs to the very far right near the flowers.	Collect as many Challenge Orbs as you can before your time runs out.	Star Command Booster Pack	Any	30 orbs in 1:00	40 orbs in 1:00	45 orbs in 1:00
✓	Jetpack Knack	The Island with the alien house in the water area.	Collect as many Challenge Orbs as you can before your time runs out.	Jetpack	Any	40 orbs in 1:10	60 orbs in 1:10	90 orbs in 1:10
✓	Jessie's Roundup	Underneath the Main Town.	With Jessie and Bullseye, collect the Challenge Orbs before your time runs out.	Bullseye	Jessie	30 orbs in 1:00	45 orbs in 1:00	60 orbs in 1:00

Goo Valley

Got It?	Name	Location	Description	Toy Required	Character	Easy	Medium	Hard
✓	Saddle Cruisin'	At the end of Goo Valley Town, close to the cave back to Main Town.	Collect as many Challenge Orbs as you can before your time runs out.	Bullseye	Any	20 orbs in 1:05	30 orbs in 1:05	40 orbs in 1:05
✓	Need a Boost?	To the right of Goo Volcano's entrance.	Collect as many Challenge Orbs as you can before your time runs out.	Star Command Booster Pack	Any	20 orbs in 1:10	30 orbs in 1:10	40 orbs in 1:10
✓	Goo Canyon Grab	Between the second and third Goo Valley valleys.	Collect as many Challenge Orbs as you can before your time runs out.	N/A	Any	20 orbs in 1:05	30 orbs in 1:05	40 orbs in 1:05
✓	High Flyin'	Next to the houses in the Goo Valley Town.	Collect as many Challenge Orbs as you can before your time runs out.	Jetpack	Any	20 orbs in :40	30 orbs in :40	40 orbs in :40
✓	Jettin' Around	By the Purple Goo waterfall in the second valley.	Collect as many Challenge Orbs as you can before your time runs out.	Jetpack	Any	20 orbs in :55	30 orbs in :55	40 orbs in :55
✓	Jetpack Jaunt	Between the third and fourth valley areas.	Pass through all the race gates before your time runs out.	Jetpack	Any	15 gates in :50	15 gates in :40	15 gates in :35
✓	Faster with the Blaster	Near the end of the second valley.	Break open as many targets as you can before your time runs out.	Blaster	Any	20 targets in 1:40	30 targets in 1:40	40 targets in 1:40

GAME BASICS | CHARACTERS | POWER DISCS | **PLAY SETS** | TOY BOX | TOY BOX COLLECTION | ACHIEVEMENTS

TOY STORY IN SPACE Wii PLAY SET OVERVIEW

			MAIN TOWN		
Mission Giver	**Mission Type**	**Mission Name**	**Mission Objective**	**Unlocks**	**Page #**
Automatic/Rex	Main	Power the Tower	Get to the tower, insert the tower's batteries, and press the button on top of the tower.		46
Hamm	Main	Build-A-Lot	Insert the battery, climb to the top, and press the button.		47
NPC	Side	Crystal Smash and Bash	Break three blue crystals near the city.		49
NPC	Main	Volcano Vanish	Find the Alien who is stuck on the floating rock platform above the cave.		48
Tourist Alien	Side	Take Me Up	Take the Alien to the designated location.		48
Alien Mechanic	Main	Clothing Store Crate Crash	Break five crates.	Clothing Store	49
Hamm	Main	The Crystal Cavern	Reach the cave indicated.		52
Rex	Side	Paint the Town New	Customize the wall of any building.		54
Slinky Dog	Main	Battery Needs	Insert the battery and press the button at the top.		55
Alien Mechanic	Main	Combat Crate Crash	Break five crates.	Combat Simulator	55
Slinky Dog	Main	Get a Combat Simulator	Purchase the Combat Simulator.		56
NPC	Side	Color Required	Customize any building's wall, accent, and trim.		54
NPC	Side	Stuck and Outta Luck	Rescue the stranded Alien.		79
NPC	Side	Tower with Team Power	Take the Alien to the top of the tower.		79
Tourist Alien	Side	Help Me Get There	Take the Alien to the compass location.		100
Tourist Alien	Side	Take Me There	Take the Alien to the compass location.		100
Slinky Dog	Main	Enter the Simulator	Enter the Combat Simulator.		56

			COMBAT SIMULATOR		
Mission Giver	**Mission Type**	**Mission Name**	**Mission Objective**	**Unlocks**	**Page #**
Zurg Hologram	Main	Star Command Blaster Qualification	Complete the challenge in the teleporter.	Star Command Blaster	56
Zurg Hologram	Main	Simulation 1: No Chance	Complete the challenge in the teleporter.		58
Zurg Hologram	Main	Simulation 2: If You Dare	Complete the challenge in the teleporter.		60
Zurg Hologram	Main	Simulation 3:Inevitable Destruction	Complete the challenge in the teleporter.		62

			MAIN TOWN		
Mission Giver	**Mission Type**	**Mission Name**	**Mission Objective**	**Unlocks**	**Page #**
Slinky Dog	Main	Need You in Town	Return from Combat Simulator		62
Slinky Dog	Main	You Floor Me	Insert the battery and press the button at the top.	Goo Valley	66
Alien Mechanic	Main	Hospital Crate Crash	Break five crates.	Hospital	65
NPC	Side	Alien Medicine	Build a Hospital and take the Alien to it.	Medicine Ball	66
Slinky Dog	Side	Somethin' to Prove	Bring two objects to the designated spot.		52
NPC	Side	Bullseye Joyride	Pick up the alien while riding Bullseye and take him through a series of hoops.		94
Alien Mechanic	Main	Hatchery Crate Crash	Break five crates.	Hatchery	64
NPC	Main	Hammy Rendezvous	Meet Hamm in Goo Valley.		68

			GOO VALLEY		
Mission Giver	**Mission Type**	**Mission Name**	**Mission Objective**	**Unlocks**	**Page #**
Hamm	Main	Goo Side of the Moon	Follow Hamm to the erupting volcano.		69
Hamm	Main	Planetary Plumber	Break the pillars around the volcano.	Goo Valley Teleporters, Jetpack	71
Hamm	Main	Field Assistant	Complete "The Big Stink", "The Little Stink", "Tiny Tree", "The Purple Primal Goo", and "The Primal Green Goo".		75
NPC	Main	The Big Stink	Grow yourself large and then ground pound a Spore Plant.		75
NPC	Main	Tiny Tree	Shrink a Goo Fruit tree.		76
NPC	Main	The Little Stink	Jump on a small, shrunken Spore Plant.		76
NPC	Side	Disruptive Eruption	Rescue the Alien and take him back to the town.		72
NPC	Side	Volcanic Rescue	Rescue the Alien and take him back to the mission giver.		73
NPC	Side	Alien Liberation	Rescue the Alien and take him back to the mission giver.		73
NPC	Side	Weary Traveller	Take the Alien to the designated location.		74
NPC	Side	Friendly Recovery	Rescue the Alien and take him back to the mission giver.		72
NPC	Side	Three Eyes, Two Lazy Legs	Take the Alien to the designated location.		74
NPC	Side	Alien Rescue, Volcano Style!	Rescue the Alien and take him back to the mission giver.		74
Slinky Dog	Main	Meet Up with Slinky	Return from Goo Valley and stand near Slinky.		76

GAME BASICS

CHARACTERS

POWER DISCS

PLAY SETS

TOY BOX

TOY BOX COLLECTION

ACHIEVEMENTS

> ## Wii NOTE
>
> The Wii version of this Play Set has a different mission order than listed in the walkthrough. The Wii Overview represents the unique flow of missions, in the order they would appear, for the Wii version.

MAIN TOWN					
Mission Giver	**Mission Type**	**Mission Name**	**Mission Objective**	**Unlocks**	**Page #**
Alien Mechanic	Main	Teleporter Dish Crate Crash	Break five crates.	Teleporter Dish	85
Rex	Side	Save Your Feet, Buy a Teleporter	Purchase the teleporter building.		85
NPC	Side	Bullseye Caves In	Ride Bullseye to the high cave.		89
Alien Jessie	Side	Giddy Up!	Deliver three crates around town to the target area.		82
Alien Jessie	Side	Horseback Supply Run	Deliver crates around town to the target area.		53
Slinky Dog	Main	Final Floor	Insert the battery and press the button at the top.		78
Alien Mechanic	Main	Decoration Crate Crash	Break five crates.	Decoration Center	80
Alien Mechanic	Main	Research Crate Crash	Break five crates.	Research Station	87
Alien Mechanic	Main	Heroes Crate Crash	Break five crates.	Monument of Heroes	90
Alien Buzz	Side	Crate Claim	Deliver crates around town to the target area.		98
Alien Buzz	Side	Speedy Delivery	Deliver crates around town to the target area.		99

WATERFALL/CANYON					
Mission Giver	**Mission Type**	**Mission Name**	**Mission Objective**	**Unlocks**	**Page #**
NPC	Main	The Primal Green Goo	Collect twenty globs of Green Goo.	Goo Grower	96
NPC	Main	The Purple Primal Goo	Collect twenty globs of Purple Goo.	Goo Shrinker	95
Alien Tourist	Side	Alien Taxi	Take the Alien to the compass location.		100
NPC	Side	Unfound Friend	Rescue the Alien and take him to the Hospital.		94
NPC	Side	A View From Above	Take the Alien to the compass location.		101
NPC	Side	A Friend in Need	Rescue the Alien and take him to the Hospital.		93
NPC	Side	New Viewpoint	Take the Alien to the high cliffs to the left of the Goo Valley entrance.		101
NPC	Side	Friend by the Falls	Rescue the stranded Alien and bring him back to the mission giver.		102
NPC	Side	Booster Down	Pick up the Alien and return him to the mission giver.		103
NPC	Side	Jetpack Waterfalls	Fly the Alien through the hoops.		93
NPC	Side	The Lost Loner	Rescue the Alien and take him to the Hospital.		102
NPC	Side	Rocket Booster Ride	Pick up the Alien and return him to the mission giver.		89
NPC	Side	In A Fix	Pick up the Alien and return him to the mission giver.		103

COMBAT SIMULATOR					
Mission Giver	**Mission Type**	**Mission Name**	**Mission Objective**	**Unlocks**	**Page #**
Zurg Hologram	Main	Simulation 4: Unfathomable	Complete the challenge in the teleporter.		104
Zurg Hologram	Main	Simulation 5: Ultimate Downfall	Complete the challenge in the teleporter.		106
Zurg Hologram	Main	Simulation 6: No Survival	Complete the challenge in the teleporter.		108

MAIN TOWN					
Mission Giver	**Mission Type**	**Mission Name**	**Mission Objective**	**Unlocks**	**Page #**
Slinky Dog	Main	Defeat Zurg!	Insert the batteries into the tower, then press the button at the top.		110

WII COLLECTIBLES

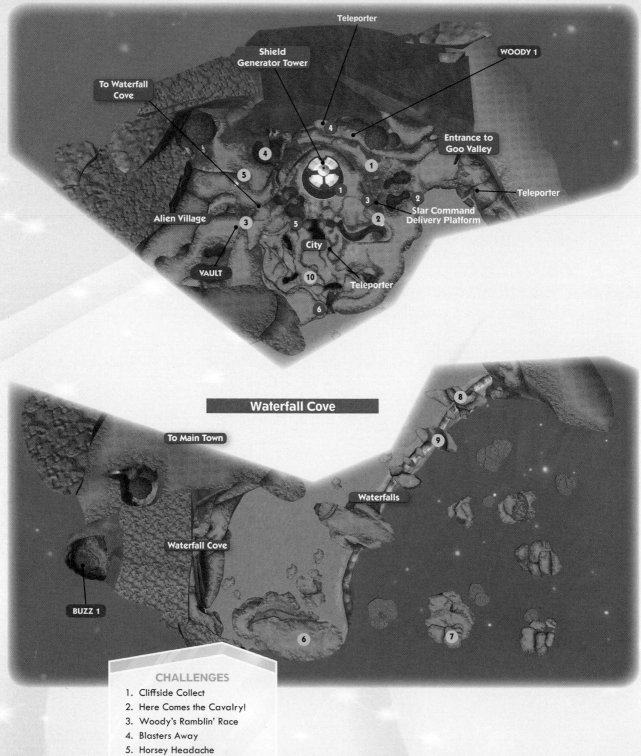

Main Town

Teleporter

Shield
Generator Tower

WOODY 1

To Waterfall
Cove

4

Entrance to
Goo Valley

4

1

Teleporter

5

1

3

2

Alien Village

3

2

Star Command
Delivery Platform

5

2

City

VAULT

10

Teleporter

6

Waterfall Cove

8

To Main Town

9

Waterfalls

Waterfall Cove

BUZZ 1

6

7

CHALLENGES

1. Cliffside Collect
2. Here Comes the Cavalry!
3. Woody's Ramblin' Race
4. Blasters Away
5. Horsey Headache
6. Rocket Booster Blast
7. Buzz Lightyear's River Run
8. River Hoppin'
9. Jetpack Knack
10. Jessie's Roundup

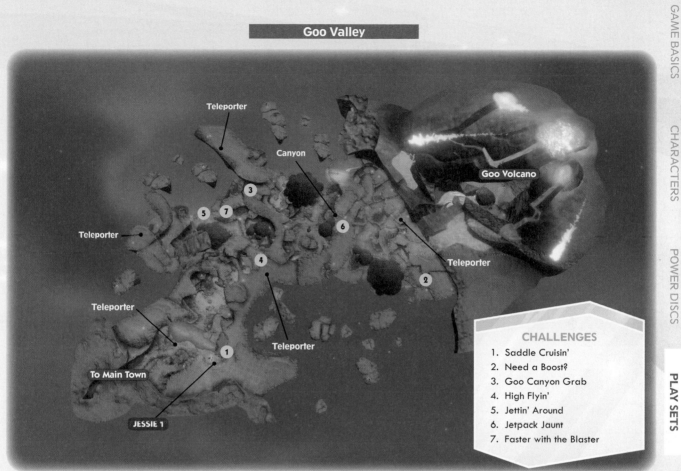

Goo Valley

Teleporter

Canyon

Goo Volcano

Teleporter

Teleporter

Teleporter

Teleporter

To Main Town

JESSIE 1

CHALLENGES

1. Saddle Cruisin'
2. Need a Boost?
3. Goo Canyon Grab
4. High Flyin'
5. Jettin' Around
6. Jetpack Jaunt
7. Faster with the Blaster

Red Capsules

Got It?	#	Unlockable Item	Zone	Location
✓	1	Rex Wall	Main Town	To the right of the Shield Generator Tower.
✓	2	Horseshoe Accent	Main Town	To the right just before the crater leading to Goo Valley.
✓	3	Dark Carbon Trim	Main Town	Just beyond the edge of the ridge with the Cliffside Collect Challenge.
✓	4	Cowhide Wall	Main Town	Near the teleporter in the high cave in back of the Tower.
✓	5	Wood Trim	Main Town	Small ledge near the stream to the left of the Tower.
✓	6	Rex Accent	Main Town	At the end of the City to the left, near the water's edge.

Infinity Chests/Vault

Got It?	#	Unlockable Item	Zone	Location
✓	Buzz1	Buzz Chest 1	Waterfall Cove	In an open grassy area in the west of the Canyon.
✓	Jessie1	Jessie Chest 1	Goo Valley	In a small cave behind a breakable blue wall near that is to the right of the entrance and at the end of the Purple Goo pool.
✓	Woody1	Woody Chest 1	Main Town	On the cliff to the right in back of the Shield Generator.
✓	Vault	Master Avatar Vault	Main Town	Due west from the City next to Woody's Ramblin' Race Challenge.

GAME BASICS

CHARACTERS

POWER DISCS

PLAY SETS

TOY BOX

TOY BOX COLLECTION

ACHIEVEMENTS

Toy Story in Space University Challenges

Main Town

Got It?	Name	Location	Description	Toy Required
✓	Rocket Booster Blast	Top of large rock next to the Canyon.	Collect as many Challenge Orbs as you can before your time runs out.	Rocket Booster
✓	Cliffside Collect	Cliff to the right of the Tower.	Collect as many Challenge Orbs as you can before your time runs out.	N/A
✓	Woody's Ramblin' Race	To the left of the Tower before the alien houses.	Get Woody and Bullseye through all the race gates before your time runs out.	Bullseye
✓	Blasters Away	By the waterfall on the cliffs to the left of the Tower.	Break open as many targets as you can before your time runs out.	Star Command Blaster
✓	Jetpack Knack	Small island in the Waterfall section.	Collect as many Challenge Orbs as you can before your time runs out.	Jetpack
✓	Buzz Lightyear's River Run	Large floating rock in the Waterfall section.	Pass through all Challenge gates before time runs out.	Jetpack
✓	River Hoppin'	Small island in the Waterfall section.	Collect as many Challenge Orbs as you can before your time runs out.	Rocket Booster
✓	Jessie's Roundup	Underneath the Main Town.	With Bullseye, collect the Challenge Orbs before your time runs out.	Bullseye

Goo Valley

Got It?	Name	Location	Description	Toy Required
✓	Saddle Cruisin'	At the end of Goo Valley Town, close to cave back to Main Town.	Collect as many Challenge Orbs as you can before your time runs out.	Bullseye
✓	Need a Boost?	To the right of Goo Volcano's entrance.	Collect as many Challenge Orbs as you can before your time runs out.	Rocket Booster
✓	Goo Canyon Grab	Between the second and third Goo Valley valleys.	Collect as many Challenge Orbs as you can before your time runs out.	N/A
✓	High Flyin'	Next to the houses in the Goo Valley Town.	Collect as many Challenge Orbs as you can before your time runs out.	Jetpack
✓	Jettin' Around	By the Purple Goo waterfall in the second valley.	Collect as many Challenge Orbs as you can before your time runs out.	Jetpack
✓	Jetpack Jaunt	Between the third and fourth valley areas.	Pass through all the race gates before your time runs out.	Jetpack
✓	Faster with the Blaster	Near the end of the second valley.	Break open as many targets as you can before your time runs out.	Blaster
✓	Blue Ribbon Booster	Top level near end of first valley by teleporter.	Collect as many Challenge Orbs as you can before your time runs out.	Rocket Booster

⭐ Toy Story in Space University Gold Stars

Got It?	#	Type	Name	Description
✓	1	Challenge	Small Steps	Master any challenge on the "Easy" level.
✓	2	Customize	Remodeling Master	Apply 30 building customizations.
✓	3	Easter Egg	Break Away	Find and break 25 Gems.
✓	4	Mission	Goo Research	Unlock both of the Goo Guns.
✓	5	Mission	Hero of Help	Complete "Alien Medicine".
✓	6	Mission	Hi-Yo, Bullseye!	Ride horseback to collect the necessary supplies.
✓	7	Mission	Horse Run	Complete "Giddy Up!".
✓	8	Mission	Lots Came Together!	Complete "Final Floor".
✓	9	Mission	Major Achiever	Complete 50 missions.

Got It?	#	Type	Name	Description
✓	10	Mission	Minor Achiever	Complete 25 missions.
✓	11	Mission	Powers Up	Complete "Power the Tower".
✓	12	Mission	The Great Defender	Complete "Defeat Zurg!".
✓	13	Mission	The Great Retrieval	Complete "Speedy Delivery".
✓	14	Mission	Ultimate Achiever	Complete 75 missions.
✓	15	Purchase	Absolutely All	Buy every toy in the Toy Store.
✓	16	Purchase	All Buildings Built	Build all 8 buildings.

Toy Story in Space Toy List

Got It?	Toys	Toy type	Unlock Conditions	Toy Box Export	Commercial
✓	Alien Horse	Mount	Buy all 8 buildings, or 20 missions after buying Bullseye.	Yes	Yes
✓	Bullseye	Mount	Complete 12 missions.	Yes	Yes
✓	Buzz Lightyear Alien	NPC	Immediately after buying the Jetpack.	Yes	No
✓	Buzz Lightyear's Jetpack	Vehicle	Complete the "Planetary Plumber" mission.	Yes	Yes
✓	Clothing Store	Building	Complete the "Clothing Store Crate Crash" mission.	Yes	Yes
✓	Combat Simulator	Building	Complete the "Combat Crate Crash" mission.	Yes	Yes
✓	Decoration Center	Building	Complete the "Decoration Crate Crash" mission.	Yes	Yes
✓	Goo Grower	Held Item	Complete the "Primal Green Goo" and "Swimming in Green" missions.	Yes	Yes
✓	Goo Shrinker	Held Item	Complete the "Purple Primal Goo" and "Tiny Tree" missions.	Yes	Yes
✓	Hatchery	Building	Complete the "Hatchery Crate Crash" mission.	Yes	Yes
✓	Hospital	Building	Complete the "Hospital Crate Crash" mission.	Yes	No
✓	Jessie Alien	NPC	Immediately after buying Bullseye.	Yes	No
✓	Medicine Ball	Held Item	Complete "Certifiably Quacked".	Yes	Yes
✓	Mega Pixar Ball	Held Item	Complete 30 missions.	Yes	Yes
✓	Monument of Heroes	Building	Complete the "Heroes Crate Crash" mission.	Yes	No
✓	Research Station	Building	Complete the "Research Crate Crash" mission.	Yes	No
✓	Star Command Blaster	Held Item	Complete the "Star Command Blaster Qualification" mission.	Yes	Yes
✓	Star Command Boost Pack	Vehicle	Complete 3 missions after buying the Jetpack.	Yes	Yes
✓	Teleporter Dish	Building	Complete the "Teleporter Crate Crash" mission.	Yes	No

GAME BASICS

CHARACTERS

POWER DISCS

PLAY SETS

TOY BOX

TOY BOX COLLECTION

ACHIEVEMENTS

Monsters University

M.U. SCARING 101

M.U. Campus

- Grounds Keeper
- Clock Tower
- To Paintball Area
- Spikey Blue Monster
- Bike Stunts
- Art
- Library
- Purple Monster
- Start Here
- Scare Hall
- Registration Hall
- University Hall
- Dorm
- Squishy
- Bike Path
- Student Union
- Deliveries
- Yellow Monster
- Red Winged Monster
- Tunnel to Fear Tech
- Tunnel to Frat Row

CHALLENGES

1. Classroom Run
2. Campus Collector
3. Campus Collector Bike
4. Sulley's Campus Collector
5. Squeal and Steal

CAMPUS CLEAN UP

Mission Giver: Squishy
Type: Destroy
Rewards: 25 Coins / 20 Sparks

Welcome to M.U.! Unfortunately the rival school, Fear Tech, has really made a mess of the campus. Show off your M.U. spirit and remove the Fear Tech standees littering the school grounds. Follow the compass to locate and shoulder charge each of the five standees. They are all located around the fountain in the center of campus.

SCARE SIMULATOR

Mission Giver: Squishy
Type: Scare
Rewards: 50 Coins / 25 Sparks

Locate Squishy near the fountain and talk to him to learn about a mission to practice your scaring skills. Several scare simulation dummies are on loan from the School of Scaring to practice surprising the Fear Tech students. Simply walk up to each dummy and press the scare button to frighten all three of them. It is pretty obvious if you're successful as the dummies will let out a loud cry when frightened.

SNEAK PEEK

Mission Giver: Squishy
Type: Scare
Rewards: 200 Coins / 50 Sparks

Find Squishy again and learn about an advanced scaring skill.

The Poloski Sneak and Scream is a great technique to get the drop on Fear Tech students that are more aware of their surroundings than the simulation dummies. The goal of this mission is to learn to slowly sneak up on a target and scare the wits out of them (in this case four of them). The best scares are the ones that nobody sees coming, so you must creep quietly without being seen

to scare the really tough students. Next to the first advanced dummy is a blue capsule that will demonstrate the technique. It should be obvious which direction the dummy is facing, but you must note the red field around that dummy that represents its field of awareness. As you get close to this red area you must hold the sneak button to silently approach the target. If the dummy see/hears you, it will sound an alarm and you must get out of its field of view for it to reset. If you get caught, just circle around the back of the dummy and wait for the siren to stop.

SIDE MISSIONS AT M.U.

DOOMED DORM

Mission Giver: Yellow Monster
Type: Platforming
Rewards: 200 Coins / 25 Sparks

Fear Tech totally pranked the dorms and you have to get rid of the large banners before someone sees them. Climb up the front of the dorm using the small light-colored ledges and unhook the edge of the banner.

GAME BASICS

CHARACTERS

POWER DISCS

PLAY SETS

TOY BOX

TOY BOX COLLECTION

ACHIEVEMENTS

Drop down a bit to a horizontal ledge and go up to the other side to unhook the other side of the banner. Remove both banners by unhooking all four corners.

BACKPACK BACKTRACK

Mission Giver: Purple Monster
Type: Collect
Rewards: 200 Coins / 80 Sparks

The poor purple monster had a bunch of Fear-It-Week tokens, but they fell through a hole in its backpack.

A LAND OF HANDS

Mission Giver: Blue Monster
Type: Collect
Rewards: 100 Coins / 35 Sparks

There are a bunch of Foam Hands all over campus. Fear Tech may think they are number one, but that is probably just how high they can count. Use the compass to find all eight orange hands, located mostly at the front of the buildings.

⭐ CLOTHES MAKE THE MONSTER

Mission Giver: Art
Type: Customize
Rewards: 100 Coins / 25 Sparks

Fear Tech put their logos on some of the M.U. students and Art is really upset about the mismatched students. Pick them up and toss them into the Student Union building to give them some M.U. blue. Grab the light blue monster right in front of the Student Union and toss it inside to change its hat. You can simply remove its hat or change its hair or horns as long as the Fear Tech item is gone.

AMBUSH THE BUSH

Mission Giver: Purple Monster
Type: Scare
Rewards: 200 Coins / 30 Sparks

A student from Fear Tech is attempting to deface your campus by putting up a poster. Creep up on the student behind the bush, using a slow stealthy walk, to get close and scare it back to its school.

CLEAN UP AND GO ON THE OFFENSIVE

STUDENT AID

Mission Giver: Squishy
Type: Platforming
Rewards: 200 Coins / 30 Sparks

Fear Tech has wrapped several of the statues of the School of Scaring in toilet paper and it is bringing down morale. Use your powerful scare skills to blow the toilet paper off of three statues.

Visit Squishy to hear about one of M.U.'s students getting pranked by Fear Tech. The poor monster was tied up in toilet paper and left on the roof of the library. The library is the red building to the west, and the easiest way to climb the building is with a little boost from a monster in the grass. Scare the blue protruding eyeball to reveal a big monster below that will provide a handy platform.

Leap on top of the platform and climb the drain pipe nearby to get to the roof.

Locate the poor student and scare it to break its paper bonds and free it from its trap.

REMOVE THE ROLLS

Mission Giver: Squishy
Type: Scare
Rewards: 100 Coins / 35 Sparks

Squishy has another mission for you and it is a somewhat dirty job.

ROLL OUT

Mission Giver: Squishy
Type: Buy
Rewards: 50 Coins / 25 Sparks

Enough cleaning up after Fear Tech! It's time to take the challenge back to them and put their school on the defensive. Squishy had the M.U. mechanics develop a Toilet Paper Launcher to turn the tables on Fear Tech. Go to the Toy Store menu and buy the awesome toy for 300 coins.

Wait for the monster mail delivery and go to the drop off spot to open the slightly wet box to claim your hot new toy!

New Toy Unlocked: Toilet Paper Launcher

THE ROAD TO FEAR TECH

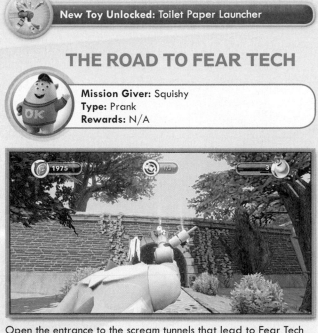
Mission Giver: Squishy
Type: Prank
Rewards: N/A

Open the entrance to the scream tunnels that lead to Fear Tech by shooting the three targets above the gate with the Toilet Paper Launcher.

New Toy Unlocked: Beastly Bike

NOTE

Buy and pick up the bike as soon as possible. It is the fastest mode of transportation (until the end) and it makes it a lot more fun going from place to place.

New Challenges Available: Campus Collector, Campus Collector Bike

FIND A FRIEND

Mission Giver: Squishy
Type: Locate
Rewards: 100 Coins / 10 Sparks

Locate the M.U. student at the Fear Teach end of the scream tunnels. Get the new bike you just unlocked as it will make moving through the tunnels go a lot faster. Ride through the tunnel and pick up the walkie-talkie as you locate the student.

SIDE MISSION

CARD COUNTER

Mission Giver: Red Winged Monster
Type: Collect
Rewards: 100 Coins / 30 Sparks

A monster was bullied by one of the guys from Fear Tech and had all of its collectable Scare Cards knocked out of its tentacles. There are seven cards to locate, mostly around Registration Hall.

PRANK FEAR TECH

Fear Tech

CHALLENGES
1. Fear Tech Collector
2. Fear Tech Cyclist
3. Randy's Rampage

Archie's Pen

Sports Statue

Scare School

Pink Dotted Monster

Botanical

Yellow Horned Monster

Dorms

3

Library

Science

1

2

Door Design School

Tunnel to M.U.

Red Monster

Health & Phys. Ed.

Don

Blue Winged Student

Randy

GAME BASICS

CHARACTERS

POWER DISCS

PLAY SETS

TOY BOX

TOY BOX COLLECTION

ACHIEVEMENTS

REVENGE GROWS ON TREES

Mission Giver: Green Monster with Purple Hat
Type: Prank
Rewards: 250 Coins / 35 Sparks

Now that you have infiltrated Fear Tech, the first objective is to T.P. four trees in the center of their campus.

New Challenges Available: Randy's Rampage, Fear Tech Cyclist, Fear Tech Collector

New Toy Unlocked: Bat-Winged Pest Bush

BAT-WINGED BUSH BATTLE

Mission Giver: Blue Monster
Type: Collect
Rewards: 100 Coins / 30 Sparks

Show some school pride by scaring away the bat-winged pests that keep perching around campus. Follow the compass to a bat-filled bush and let out a roar.

STATUE UPGRADE

Mission Giver: Don
Type: Prank
Rewards: 250 Coins / 35 Sparks
Wii Rewards: 300 Coins / 35 Sparks

Don is impressed with your T.P. Launcher and suggests you try it out on two of Fear Tech's statues. Unlike the trees, the statues are guarded by Fear Tech security. If they see you, the screen will turn red around the edges and the guard will pursue you. It is not too difficult to run away when they spot you, so you can let the alarm state cool off. It is possible to try to fight off the guard, but it is really not worth the hassle when you can just get out of the immediate area and let things cool off.

If you like to run and gun, it is possible to shoot the statues while being chased, but if you get hit too many times you get sent into a "locked room". The blue capsule in the room will show you how to escape by jumping over the vent and attacking to slam down and break through it.

Sneak up on the first statue and shoot it twice quickly before the guard can catch you.

The second statue can be tricky because there is not as much cover nearby. Watch the guard's movement and sneak in to fire the first shot. If you get caught, circle around quickly and fire off one more shot to wrap up the mission.

ABOVE AND BEYOND

Mission Giver: Squishy (radio)
Type: Locate
Rewards: 100 Coins / 25 Sparks

There is a hidden M.U. student at Fear Tech—use the compass to find that student. Climb up the drain pipe on the side of the School of Scaring to get to the roof to locate the student.

A BANNER DAY

Mission Giver: Yellow Horned Monster
Type: Platforming
Rewards: 100 Coins / 35 Sparks
Wii Rewards: 250 Coins / 35 Sparks

Climb up the nearby flagpole and unfurl a surprise banner that reads M.U. Rocks!

A VIEW OF BLUE

Mission Giver: Red Antenna Monster
Type: Platforming
Rewards: 200 Coins / 30 Sparks

Inspired by the first flag you unfurled, this monster wants you to paint the campus blue with two more flags. To get to the first flag, climb up the Science building ledge and scare the guard to knock it out.

GARGOYLE PAPER CAPER

Mission Giver: Pink Dotted Monster
Type: Prank
Rewards: 300 Coins / 45 Sparks

This student really hates the gargoyle statues on the Fear Tech buildings. Do it a favor by wrapping six of them in T.P. and let Fear Tech know what you think of their architectural style. The first gargoyle statue is on the Science building right behind the student requesting the mission and is an easy shot.

The second one is on the opposite side of the building, so jump across to the adjacent building and walk around the ledge to shoot it.

The third one is just across the other section of the building, which can be accessed by walking on top of a large connecting sky bridge. Jump over to the other section and go up to the third tier to shoot the statue.

Simply follow this ledge around the building to locate number four.

Leap back to the School of Botany rooftop and head toward the Scare School to spot the next gargoyle from the corner of the rooftop.

The last one is on the other side of the front of the Scare School and you will need to scale the Library to get to it. Go to the corner and jump up on the ledge to get a clear shot at it.

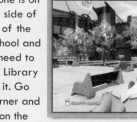

Leap up the door behind that monster to get to the second ledge. Follow the narrow ledge around the building and go up to the third tier to finally reach the flag.

Leap off the flagpole to snag the orange pennant and make your way to Door Design School. Scale the building using the dark-colored trim that leads to a narrow ledge you can climb around.

Follow the dark ledge around the building to another set of climbable ledges to make it to the roof. This flagpole is guarded and it is up to you if you want to sneak up and scare the guard or make a run for the flag.

A LESSON IN PRIDE

Mission Giver: Blue Winged Monster
Type: Platforming
Rewards: 200 Coins / 30 Sparks

Know what this campus needs? More M.U. blue! Earn major tokens by putting up four M.U. banners on their Door Design School and Dorms. Climb up to the roof of the Door Design School and grind across the yellow wire to drop the first banner.

GAME BASICS

CHARACTERS

POWER DISCS

PLAY SETS

TOY BOX

TOY BOX COLLECTION

ACHIEVEMENTS

Jump across to the rooftop of the Library and grind across another yellow cable to unfurl the second banner.

The last two are both hung across lines on the School of Botany Building, however there are students guarding the rooftops, which makes it really tricky to get to the banners. The goal of course is to scare the guards and casually coast across the yellow wires, but if you get caught, make a run for it and quickly zip to the other side.

TREES A CROWD

Mission Giver: Yellow Horned Monster
Type: Prank
Rewards: 200 Coins / 30 Sparks

The hidden student on the roof that gave you the first flagpole mission wants to really stick it to Fear Tech by T.P.ing five of their trees.

It sounds simple but you must avoid the patrolling students to hit the trees. Use the compass to locate three groups of three trees between the School of Botany and Scare School buildings. The other two are just past the trio of trees near the edge of campus. The patrolling student will not make it easy to shoot any of these groups. There are two obvious choices here. The first is to shoot as many trees as possible and run around the School of Botany building to attack the rest from the other side. This is a hit-and-run approach that keeps the guard chasing you while you target the trees.

The other safer option is to sneak up on the guard and scare it to put it out of commission. It can be tough to get the drop on the guard, but once the guard is knocked out you should be able to tag all the trees you need.

TERRI AND TERRY ARE MISSING

TERRIFYING TECHNIQUES

Mission Giver: Randy
Type: Scare
Rewards: 200 Coins / 30 Sparks

Terri and Terry have gone missing, but there is a student nearby who knows where Fear Tech is keeping them. That student is really fast, but if you can sneak up on it and scare it really good it should be knocked off guard long enough to tell you where they have taken Terri and Terry.

VERY SCARY FOR TERRI AND TERRY

Mission Giver: Randy
Type: Scare
Rewards: 300 Coins / 40 Sparks

Randy has found the student that knows where Terri and Terry are. Sneak up on the student and scare that monster so it will tell you where they are. This student is very aware of its surroundings and is partially invisible, which makes it hard to locate. Lurk around the back of the School of Botany building and wait for your target to turn and show its back so you can sneak up on it.

SIDE MISSIONS

FEAR TECH CHECK

Mission Giver: Red Antenna Monster
Type: Scare
Rewards: 300 Coins / 25 Sparks

The Fear Tech student body is getting suspicious and it is up to you to scare two of them so they don't start having funny ideas. Find the first student that is mostly invisible near the Library and give it a good scare.

The second student is not far away from the Library and can be snuck up upon by dropping between the bushes near the Fear Tech statue. Make sure not to get too close to the bushes as your target passes or the student will notice you. Also, you must sneak up on the student slowly or it will hear your footsteps.

POSTER PAINTS

Mission Giver: Purple Monster
Type: Prank
Rewards: 1,000 Coins / 100 Sparks

A purple monster wants to redecorate the Fear Tech recruitment posters with your handy paintball gun. There are 20 of these and it will not be easy to find them all. It might be tempting to ride around on the bike to scan for them, but you are better off going on foot and using the shoulder charge to dash around. Tackle this chore by searching the perimeter of campus, checking in between buildings, and finally searching the rooftops. Here are shots of all 20 for easy reference!

GAME BASICS

CHARACTERS

POWER DISCS

PLAY SETS

TOY BOX

TOY BOX COLLECTION

ACHIEVEMENTS

ALERT MISSION:
FEAR TECH PENNANT COLLECTION

Mission Giver: Automatic
Type: Platforming
Rewards: 1,000 Coins / 350 Sparks

While completing the previous side mission make sure to collect all the orange Fear Tech pennants. There are 20 of these hidden on their campus. If you can find all of them you will unlock the Sludge Balloon.

See page 158 for the location of all pennants.

New Toy Unlocked: Fear Tech's Sludge Balloon

RETURN TO M.U. TO HATCH A PLAN

TALK TO DON

Mission Giver: Squishy (radio)
Type: Locate
Rewards: 100 Coins / 20 Sparks

The last monster you scared at Fear Tech gave up the info that Terri and Terry are being held at M.U. in the Clock Tower. Go back through the scream tunnel to look for your friend. However, upon your return it seems that Fear Tech students are running around M.U. like they own the place. Don has some ideas how to catch them so you can question them about your frat brother. Use the compass to find Don and find out what his plan is all about.

New Toy Unlocked: Paintball Gun

NOTE

Once the gun is purchased, a round red-winged monster will mention the Paintball Arena. It is a completely optional area that will be covered at the end of this section.

PRACTICALLY JOKING

Mission Giver: Don
Type: Buy
Rewards: 100 Coins / 30 Sparks

Don was a master prankster in his day and the Toy Store recently got a shipment of new joke items. Buy the sweet Give 'em a Hand Launcher and set it up where Don has indicated.

New Toy Unlocked: Give 'em a Hand Launcher

NOTE

If you have not already received the message, a light blue spiked monster will tell you to go check out Frat Row. This is a completely optional section that will be covered at the end of the story missions.

ALERT MISSION: **REPAIR THE FOUNTAIN**

Mission Giver: None
Type: Scare/Platforming
Rewards: 100 Coins / 10 Sparks

Use your scare power on the M.U. fountain to clear it of toilet paper.

Several more complicated clean-up missions become available at M.U. These include Repair the Library, University Hall, Registration Hall, and Dorm. These missions involve platforming around each building and removing posters, banners, or toilet paper. They are completely optional but they can be quite challenging and fun.

NOTE

In the Wii version of the game, this is a regular mission given by an NPC and not an alert mission.

ALERT MISSION: **DARE TO SCARE**

Mission Giver: None
Type: Scare
Rewards: 250 Coins / 25 Sparks

Get rid of three Fear Tech students roaming around M.U.

BIKE SIDE MISSIONS

TAKE A BIKE

Mission Giver: Light Blue Monster
Type: Riding
Rewards: 100 Coins / 35 Sparks

The spiky-headed light blue monster by the bike stunt area has another challenge for you. Pass through all twenty gates in a leisurely ride around campus.

REJECT THE TECH

Mission Giver: Light Blue Monster
Type: Customize
Rewards: 200 Coins / 35 Sparks

Some Fear Tech goons force M.U. students to wear their school logo. Use the compass to locate the green monster with the Fear Tech hat and foam hand. Take the monster to the Student Union to remove the accessories or replace them with M.U. gear.

The next student you need to customize is a dark blue monster right in front of the Student Union. Toss this student into the stand

and get rid of the pennant and hat it is wearing.

RESCUE TERRI AND TERRY AT THE CLOCK TOWER

SPRING FORWARD

Mission Giver: Squishy
Type: Prank
Rewards: 200 Coins / 30 Sparks

Locate Squishy to find out that the entire section of campus with the Clock Tower is closed for renovation. You must find a way to launch yourself over the gate to get in and look for your friend. Use the newly acquired Joke Launcher and place it near Squishy to catapult yourself over the closed Clock Tower gate. Make sure to rotate it so that the yellow arrow points towards the gate.

New Toy Unlocked: Morning Edition Launcher

TIME FOR A RESCUE

Mission Giver: Squishy
Type: Platforming
Rewards: 750 Coins / 50 Sparks

Time to climb the Clock Tower to look for Terri and Terry. Start by scaring an underground monster to make a ledge pop up to allow access to the wooden walkway.

Follow the wooden planks and leap up a series of light grey ledges to get to the corner piece. Travel around this corner section until you reach a wooden platform.

Follow this around the tower again to another section where you can climb up the red bricks to reach a higher ledge of more wooden scaffolding.

Leap up the large corner edges of the tower to a yellow pipe that will take you right next to the face of the clock. Jump up a few more ledges to get to the window at the top.

Once inside the top of the tower climb the black metal ladder to find Terri and Terry!

New Toy Unlocked: School Colors Ender

⭐ SECRET OF THE SCARE

Mission Giver: Groundskeeper
(Dark Grey Monster with Rake)
Type: Scare
Rewards: 100 Coins / 30 Sparks

Talk to the Groundskeeper to learn how to open the gates to the main campus.

Follow the compass to find the monument and roar at its lighted eye target to activate its hidden features that open the gates as well as enable two other switches on University Hall.

New Toy Unlocked: Scream Energy Launcher

New Challenge Available: Classroom Run

CLOCK TOWER SIDE MISSIONS

TIME FOR A CHANGE

Mission Giver: Art
Type: Platforming
Rewards: 300 Coins / 25 Sparks

After taking care of the Fear Tech banners for Art, he wants you to remove them from the Clock Tower as well. In addition, you need to remove the poster placed by Fear Tech. Start by scaring up a platform to climb up to the wooden plank and bring down the first poster.

Follow the wooden walkway to the next poster and scare it down.

Work your way around the corner ledges to find the third one on a red brick wall.

Climb the red brick ledge from the third one to get to a bit of scaffolding that hides another.

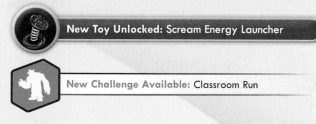

Drop back down and go around the corners to the other red brick wall to climb up to the next tier and find the fifth poster.

The last two targets are the ones holding up the banner. Jump up to the top as you did before and release the banner.

GAME BASICS · CHARACTERS · POWER DISCS · **PLAY SETS** · TOY BOX · TOY BOX COLLECTION · ACHIEVEMENTS

TECH TOCK

Mission Giver: Art
Type: Scare
Rewards: 300 Coins / 10 Sparks

Three Fear Tech goons are hanging around on the M.U. campus at the Clock Tower. Sneak up on all of them to send them back to their school with a valuable lesson.

 New Toy Unlocked: Breaking News Ender

ALERT MISSION: CAMPUS PENNANT COLLECTION

Mission Giver: Automatic
Type: Platforming
Rewards: 1,000 Coins / 350 Sparks / Glow Urchin

This mission officially begins when you collect the first M.U. pennant, but it can't be completed until the Clock Tower area is unlocked. You must find 20 blue pennants throughout the M.U. campus to earn the Glow Urchin toy. They are scattered all over campus and the trickiest ones are on little ledges on the rooftops of buildings.

See page 157 for the location of all pennants.

New Toy Unlocked: Glow Urchin

THE ULTIMATE PLAN

⭐ SECRET MEETING

Mission Giver: Squishy
Type: Locate
Rewards: 200 Coins / 20 Sparks

Terry and Terri collected some new info before they were locked up. Go meet Don on the roof of University Hall (a secret place where Fear Tech can't hear you). Locate the glowing eye switch and roar into it to activate a platform.

Leap up the grey ledges and scoot around the top one to get to the roof and meet Don.

New Toy Unlocked: Cracklin' Backpack

SIDE MISSIONS

THIS IS THE ENDER

Mission Giver: Yellow Monster
Type: Prank
Rewards: 200 Coins / 35 Sparks

This is a simple request from the yellow monster—it just wants to see a Joke Ender in a specific spot. Locate the area with the compass and place the School Colors Ender you received from saving Terri and Terry. Remember that you can't trigger the joke and must be patient until a student tries it out.

⭐ A PEACEFUL BALANCE

Mission Giver: Art
Type: Prank
Rewards: 300 Coins / 25 Sparks

Art's meditative state is disrupted by the Fear Tech "decorations" hanging from the School of Scaring. You need to take them down, but getting to the top of the school will not be that obvious. At the side of the school look for the eye switch and roar to make the walls move outward. The two narrow walls allow you to wall jump to the roof.

Walk along the edge of the green roof and step on the two supports holding up the first banner.

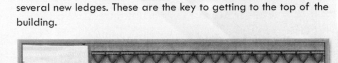

On the left side of the building is another eye switch that creates several new ledges. These are the key to getting to the top of the building.

Climb up the lower ledges at the corner and jump across to the left to get a littler higher. Then jump back right to the top corner section that leads around the edge to a green drain pipe leading to the roof.

Jump along the roof and go to the edge to take down all three supports to drop the second banner.

From the corner where you climbed up to the roof, jump to the green section and head to the peak of this vaulted roof to drop the final banner.

New Toy Unlocked: Pile it on Ender

TERRI AND TERRY'S NIGHTTIME CAPERS

⭐ DORM PARTY!

Mission Giver: Terri and Terry
Type: Prank/Scare
Rewards: 300 Coins / 35 Sparks

It seems that Terri and Terry are up for a little revenge shenanigans involving fireworks blasting into six Fear Tech dorms. They are hanging out at the scream tunnel connecting to M.U. When you accept the mission night will fall and the patrolling guards will break out their flashlights. Quickly make your way to the dorms near the parking lot and sneak up to scare the guard out cold. Equip the backpack and toss fireworks into the windows to get the first two rooms.

Go around the corner to the edge of campus to spot more rooms, but be careful of the guard.

Hide in the passage below street level to easily sneak up on the guard and deliver a shocking scare. With the guard sleeping the

night away, quickly launch fireworks in the remaining four rooms to finish the mission.

HOUSE PARTY!

Mission Giver: Terri and Terry
Type: Prank
Rewards: 300 Coins / 40 Sparks

Fear Tech students are occupied on Frat Row causing trouble. This is a great time to do some M.U. decorations on the School of Botany. Night falls once again and it's time to sneak up on the guards at the rear of the building. Once the guard is disabled it should be a piece of cake to toss fireworks into several of the rooms. Three are located near the corner of the building.

The other two are a lot tougher to tackle because two guards nearly overlap at your target destination. Scare the somewhat invisible guard that passes right by the two windows and quickly toss the fireworks before the other guard gets close.

New Toy Unlocked: Incoming Call Ender

DECORATION CELEBRATION

Mission Giver: Terri and Terry
Type: Prank
Rewards: 500 Coins / 30 Sparks

Fear Tech has had enough fireworks to give them a thrill. Now it's time to add a bit of decorations to their School of Scaring. Make your way to the rooftop and drop down behind a Fear Tech guard to scare them and release the M.U. banner.

The next banner is at the front of the school and must be reached by going to the top of the spiked roof. There is a thin beam you can cross that will connect right where the banner is hanging.

The last banner is on the rooftop to the left (from the front of the school). Wait for the guard to turn around and jump down to sneak up and scare him good. Drop the last banner in the corner next to the gargoyle you T.P.ed earlier.

New Toy Unlocked: Scream Tunnel Sludge Ender

DON'S PRANK SIDE MISSIONS

NOTE

All jokes must be performed on students, so you must help one start off a combo or just be patient. The best place on Fear Tech to set up combos is in front of the Health and Phys. Ed building.

DOUBLE TROUBLE

Mission Giver: Don
Type: Prank
Rewards: 300 Coins / 30 Sparks

The latest tally on the scoreboard still has Fear Tech in the lead. Don suggests setting up a double Joke Launcher to rack up lots of points. The goal is to chain two Joke Launchers together on Fear Tech's campus, and the location will be important to make it a lot easier to pull off. In front of the Phys. Ed. building are several spots to customize jokes. Place two Joke Launchers like the Scream Energy Launcher and aim them at each other for a double combo that is actually an infinite loop.

New Toy Unlocked: Leafing So Soon? Launcher

PRANKS FOR EVERYTHING

Mission Giver: Don
Type: Prank/Scare
Rewards: 500 Coins / 35 Sparks

The last joke worked so well that Don starting thinking of another combo linking them with an Ender for a great finale. The objective is to use two Joke Launchers with a Joke Ender for a big chained prank combo. The Launchers should already be in place from the previous mission, and all you need to do is add an Ender. Make sure the second Launcher points towards the Ender, and if you test it be sure to replace the Ender if it gets smashed.

 New Toy Unlocked: Vender Ender

TRIPLE TROUBLE

Mission Giver: Don
Type: Prank/Scare
Rewards: 500 Coins / 45 Sparks

To rake in tons of tokens for Fear-It Week, Don wants to pull off a triple Launcher. Return to the same spot as before and replace the Ender with a Launcher to make a quick triple combo.

 New Toy Unlocked: Vender Machine Launcher

CAPTURE THE SCARE PIG

⭐ FOOTBALL WRAPPER

Mission Giver: Randy
Type: Prank/Scare
Rewards: 250 Coins / 50 Sparks

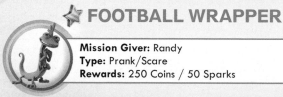

Randy needs a diversion to distract the Fear Tech students to find out where they are keeping the Scare Pig. Fear Tech is so proud of their athletics program that the best way to get their attention is to toilet paper their Sports Statue (the football monument). This is another nighttime mission, and it will take three shots to cover the statue. Fear Tech's best sprinters guard that statue on the night shift and it is very likely they will chase you down after a single shot.

It is not worth trying to scare all the guards into submission, and if you do get caught the statue keeps the amount of T.P. (number of hits) it already had on it. Sneak in and fire off shots as you circle around it.

 **New Toy Unlocked:** Fly Swatter Launcher

⭐ KEY TO SUCCESS

Mission Giver: Randy
Type: Scare
Rewards: 750 Coins / 50 Sparks

Archie the Scare Pig has been located at his pen and he is currently out for feeding time. The guard watching over Archie is tough, but you need to scare him to get the keys to unlock the pen. Wait for the guard to pass by and follow it around the pen, slowly creeping up on it until you are close enough to deliver a good scare.

⭐ RACE TO VICTORY

Mission Giver: Randy
Type: Riding
Rewards: 1,000 Coins / 100 Sparks

While Squishy and the others work to open the gate, use Archie to smash through Fear Tech's mascot statues. That'll really rile them up!

Randy shows up in front of the pen to help out, but the mascot snatching is not going to be that easy because the pen was rigged with an alarm and the guards are coming quick. Your only chance is to hop on the Scare Pig and make a break for the scare tunnel to go back to the M.U. campus.

You need to buy the others some time to open the gates. Hop on Archie and smash through seven mascot statues to keep Fear Tech busy.

The first one is right in front of the pen and a quick jump should allow you to get over the ledge and plow right through it.

The next statue is straight ahead, so make the little piggy sprint and crash through it.

As you turn the corner next to the parking lot a guard will probably notice you, but Archie is super fast and you can continue to the next statue without much fear of getting hit.

The fourth statue is right next to the last one and a well-placed jump should take it out easily.

Swerve to the left and make a sharp turn to run directly into statue number five. If the guard in the parking area is giving you a lot of trouble, just circle around the lot a bit and it won't be able to match Archie's pace.

Continue all the way down the edge of the Fear Tech campus and turn right to find statue number six.

The last statue is towards the center of campus by the School of Botany.

After breaking the last mascot statue, the gates will finally be opened and all you have to do is ride Archie through the scream tunnel back to M.U.

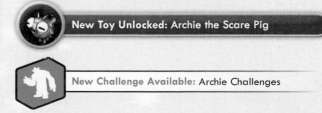

New Toy Unlocked: Archie the Scare Pig

New Challenge Available: Archie Challenges

GAME BASICS

CHARACTERS

POWER DISCS

PLAY SETS

TOY BOX

TOY BOX COLLECTION

ACHIEVEMENTS

Frat Row

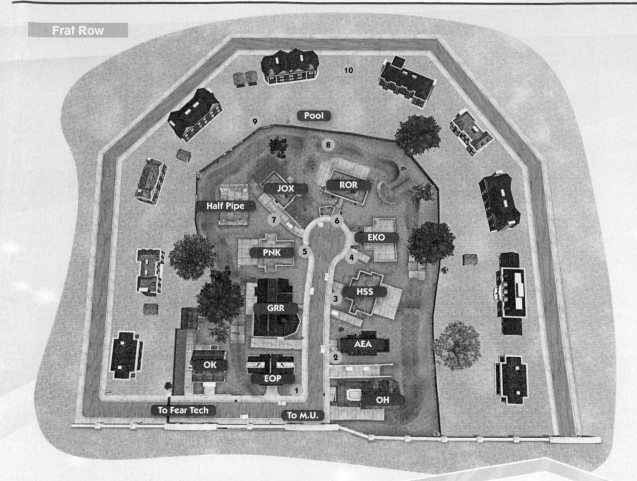

CHALLENGES

1. Mike's Mayhem
2. Timed Swine
3. Wheels and Thrills
4. Frat Row Round Up
5. Wild Wheels
6. Paint the Frat Collector
7. Paintball Ruckus
8. Round the Row
9. Bike Hop and Pop
10. Crazy Frat Stunts

NOTE

All of the events on Frat Row are side missions, but they unlock many items and gold stars.

ALERT MISSION: OK PENNANT COLLECTION

Mission Giver: Automatic
Type: Platforming
Rewards: 1,000 Coins / 350 Sparks

Similar to the previous areas there is a somewhat hidden mission to collect 20 OK pennants at Frat Row. Complete all the Main Missions first to fill out the Row with buildings and ramps that will make it a lot easier to collect the pennants.

See page 159 for the location of all pennants.

New Toy Unlocked: Tiny Terror

⭐ GO TO THE ROW

Mission Giver: Light Blue Spiky Monster
Type: Locate
Rewards: 50 Coins / 10 Sparks

Go outside the gates of M.U. to find the tunnel to Frat Row.

FRAT ROW FIX UP

TRASH FROM THE BASH

Mission Giver: Blue Winged Monster
Type: Destroy
Rewards: 250 Coins / 30 Sparks

The frat boys were so excited about Fear-It Week that they threw a party, but left trash all over the place. Use the compass to help clean up by running into five trash piles. The bike will make the task a lot faster, but they are all pretty close and a quick shoulder charge will do the job just as well.

⭐ FRAT HOUSE MAKEOVER

Mission Giver: Brown Four-Armed Monster
Type: Customize
Rewards: 100 Coins / 30 Sparks

They are giving out Fear-It Week tokens for the best of Frat Row. Try to earn some precious coins by decorating the OK House, which is right by the monster.

New Toy Unlocked: Bike Park Table Top

REBUILD THE ROW

ROR ON A WIRE

Mission Giver: Light Green Monster
Type: Platforming
Rewards: 250 Coins / 35 Sparks

ROR House had a wild party and put up banners all over the row. You need to slide across the wires to remove the banners and clean up the row.

The first part can be accomplished by climbing the nearby light pole and sliding on the wire to remove both banners.

The other two banners can be reached by climbing the OH House and sliding across the power line.

New Toy Unlocked: PNK House

THINK PNK

Mission Giver: Yellow Dotted Monster
Type: Buy/Build
Rewards: 100 Coins / 20 Sparks

Go into the Toy Store and buy the PNK House.

 **New Challenge Available:** Wild Wheels

GAME BASICS

CHARACTERS

POWER DISCS

PLAY SETS

TOY BOX

TOY BOX COLLECTION

ACHIEVEMENTS

ROOFTOP DROP

Mission Giver: Yellow Monster
Type: Platforming
Rewards: 100 Coins / 30 Sparks

The GRR guys had a party on their roof and it was off the hook, however one guy is afraid to climb down. Climb up the pole near the GRR House and slide across to the roof to pick up the student. Provide a little encouragement by picking it up and tossing it from the roof.

New Toy Unlocked: Sweet Bike Jump

BAT'S A PROBLEM

Mission Giver: Green Monster
Type: Scare
Rewards: 250 Coins / 35 Sparks

Frat Row is overrun with an infestation of bat-winged pests. Use the compass to track them down and scare them away. The first group is on the porch of GRR, another is at OH House, the third is on the roof of EOP, and the last is in the back of AEA.

HSS STORY

Mission Giver: Green Monster
Type: Destroy
Rewards: 100 Coins / 20 Sparks

Remove the crates from the HSS area to make room for their house.

New Toy Unlocked: HSS House

HSS HOUSE HUNCH

Mission Giver: Green Monster
Type: Buy/Build
Rewards: 100 Coins / 20 Sparks

Go into the Toy Store and buy the HSS House.

New Toy Unlocked: Bike Park Berm

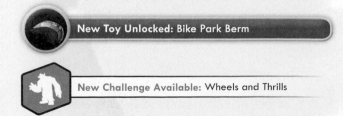

New Challenge Available: Wheels and Thrills

JOX BOXES

Mission Giver: Yellow Dotted Monster
Type: Destroy
Rewards: 100 Coins / 20 Sparks

Smash through the JOX crates to make their house look awesome. There are four crates to smash in the open lot at the back of the row.

New Toy Unlocked: JOX House

WHERE'S THE JOX HOUSE

Mission Giver: Yellow Dotted Monster
Type: Buy/Build
Rewards: 100 Coins / 20 Sparks

Go into the Toy Store and buy the JOX House.

New Toy Unlocked: Bike Park Half Pipe

New Challenge Available: Paintball Ruckus

A FRESH LOOK

Mission Giver: Purple Monster
Type: Combat
Rewards: 100 Coins / 20 Sparks

Too many freshmen are hanging out at the EKO lot. Find the four youngsters and clear them out by throwing them off the lot.

New Toy Unlocked: EKO House

IS THERE AN EKO?

Mission Giver: Purple Monster
Type: Buy/Build
Rewards: 100 Coins / 20 Sparks

Go into the Toy Store and buy the EKO House.

New Toy Unlocked: Roaring Ramp

New Challenge Available: Frat Row Round-Up

CRATE BIG ROR

Mission Giver: Aqua Dotted Monster
Type: Destroy
Rewards: 100 Coins / 20 Sparks

Before ROR can move in you need to smash those crates!

LET THE ROR OUT

New Toy Unlocked: ROR House

Mission Giver: Aqua Dotted Monster
Type: Buy/Build
Rewards: 100 Coins / 20 Sparks

Go into the Toy Store and buy the ROR House.

GAME BASICS

CHARACTERS

POWER DISCS

PLAY SETS

TOY BOX

TOY BOX COLLECTION

ACHIEVEMENTS

 New Toy Unlocked: Bike Park Dual Pool

 New Challenges Available: Round the Row, Paint the Frat Collector, Bike Hop and Pop & Crazy Frat Stunts. (Bike Hop and Pop & Crazy Frat Stunts require the purchase of the "Dual Pool")

NOTE

Buying all the Frat Houses unlocks the Terrifying Two-Wheeler (Sulley's Bike).

 New Toy Unlocked: Terrifying Two-Wheeler

FUN AT FRAT ROW

SCALE THE WALLS

 Mission Giver: Red Monster
Type: Customize
Rewards: 100 Coins / 25 Sparks
Wii Rewards: 250 Coins / 25 Sparks

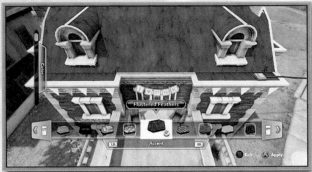

PNK House is looking pretty good, but adding a few touches would really make it shine. Customize the house with any single decoration.

HOMEWORK HERO

 **Mission Giver:** Blue Dotted Monster
Type: Riding/Collect
Rewards: 500 Coins / 50 Sparks
Wii Rewards: 1,000 Coins / 350 Sparks

The student's scream homework isn't going well. It needs you to collect ten scream cans by performing tricks on the bike. Before you can even hope to collect all the cans, make sure you buy all the bike park items from the Toy Store—the ramps are essential to reach many of the cans. One of the first ones starts from a straight path leading to a large group. A good jump will claim the can.

Continue straight ahead, jump to the balcony, and hit the ramp, pulling to the right to claim another can.

Two more cans can be picked up on the roof of the Frat House by jumping up the dirt ramp and riding along the wooden plank. Continue riding on the balcony and leap off the edge to grab the second one.

To take a break from all the stunts and trick jumps, follow the dirt path to a large mound to easily reach a can.

NOTE

In order to collect all the scream cans and complete the mission, you need to buy all the Bike Ramps.

The last four are above the halfpipe and will require a good boost of speed to get enough height. It can be really tricky trying to reach without running off the track. Line up under the canisters in a very straight line, back up, and build up some speed while keeping your wheels straight so you can cleanly hit the cans.

Grab an easy-to-reach can by JOX House using the dirt mound right underneath it.

PAINTBALL COMPETITION

The Sewers

M.U. Ready Room

4

Entrance

3

Mission Giver

2

1

FT Ready Room

Paintball Area

CHALLENGES

1. Paintball Press
2. Scream Tunnel Collector
3. Paintball Panic
4. Paintball Party

TUNNEL OF PAINT

Mission Giver: Red Winged Monster
Type: Locate
Rewards: 100 Coins / 20 Sparks

NOTE

All of the events in the Paintball Arena are optional Side Missions, and they require the purchase of the Paintball Gun.

Locate the Paintball Arena.

HAVE A PAINTBALL!

Mission Giver: Blue Striped Monster
Type: Paintball Match
Rewards: 100 Coins / 25 Sparks

Compete in the first paintball challenge. This is a 1-minute timed event to take down three challengers. Since this is the first event, it will be pretty easy. Just run towards the back of the room and take out the targets. If you have trouble spotting them, look for the red arrow over their heads.

New Challenge Available: Paintball Panic

PAINT BY NUMBERS

Mission Giver: Blue Striped Monster
Type: Paintball Match
Rewards: 100 Coins / 30 Sparks

Paintball is a numbers game that earns Fear-It-Week tokens for the school that defeats the opposing students. Get ready for round two in order to win more tokens. Again there is a 1-minute time limit, but you won't have to run around looking for Fear Tech students as they will charge you. Seek cover quickly and pick them off from behind a wall. There are six students to deal with and you have to go to the offensive to quickly track down any monsters hiding behind walls.

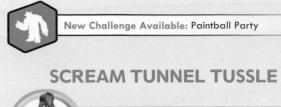

New Challenge Available: Paintball Party

SCREAM TUNNEL TUSSLE

Mission Giver: Blue Striped Monster
Type: Paintball Match
Rewards: 200 Coins / 30 Sparks

Round 3 starts with 1 minute on the clock and there are now eight students to take down. This round introduces the stationary paintball cannon, which is great to wipe out enemies at a distance. Jump on the big gun right in front of your starting position and blast your targets as they run towards you. Make sure to check the sides to make sure none are hiding out.

New Challenge Available: Paintball Press

THE COLOR OF SUCCESS

Mission Giver: Blue Striped Monster
Type: Paintball Match
Rewards: 300 Coins / 35 Sparks

This is the final competition and the last chance to really wipe out Fear Tech. There is an extra 15 seconds on the clock and you will probably need it to defeat all ten students. The cannon was a viable option last mission, but it is not going to get you through the entire thing. The enemies are a lot better at hiding behind the small walls and there are too many to stay stationary. Use the shoulder charge to cover ground quickly as well as to bump into the enemy and stun them.

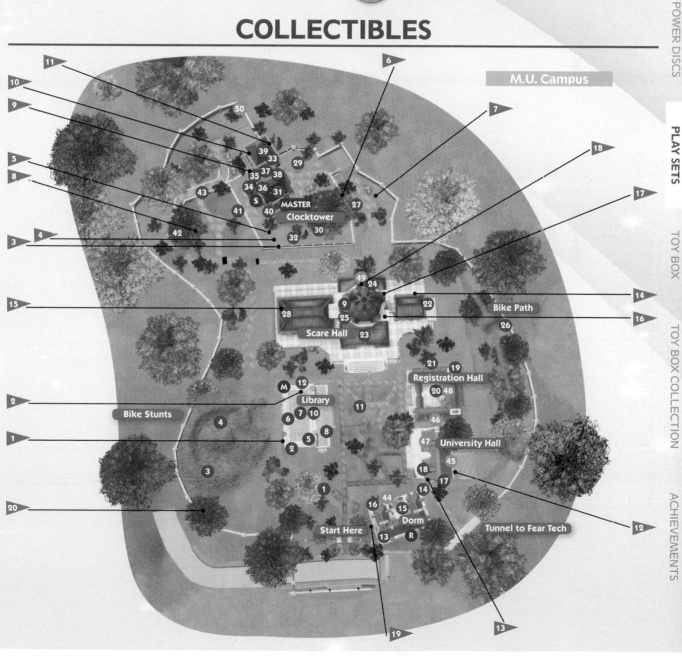

Many of your foes will take cover behind walls and even duck under the low walls making them hard to hit.

Take out targets with a few quick shots and try not to empty your gun tracking them down. Run and gun to get in close and avoid wasting shots chasing them only to leave you empty with a somewhat long load time.

New Challenge Available: Scream Tunnel Collector

New Toy Unlocked: Slithering Cycle

GAME BASICS · CHARACTERS · POWER DISCS · PLAY SETS · TOY BOX · TOY BOX COLLECTION · ACHIEVEMENTS

COLLECTIBLES

M.U. Campus

Fear Tech

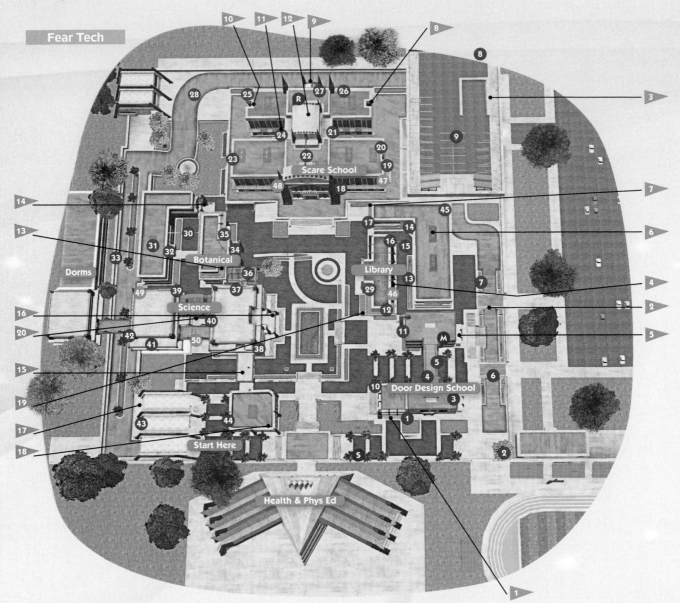

🔴 Red Capsules

Got It?	#	Unlockable Item	Zone	Location
✓	1	Monstrous	M.U. Campus	On the path to the left entering M.U. Campus.
✓	2	Dreamy 'Do	M.U. Campus	On the side of the Library nearest the main entrance to M.U. Campus.
✓	3	Frightening Feathers	M.U. Campus	On the hill at the back of the Bike Stunt area.
✓	4	Warts and Stripes	M.U. Campus	On the far end of the Bike Stunt area.
✓	5	Old Couch	M.U. Campus	On the roof ledge of the Library nearest the entrance to M.U. Campus.
✓	6	Leaf Pile	M.U. Campus	On the roof ledge of the Library nearest the Bike Stunt area.
✓	7	Mike Accent	M.U. Campus	On the roof of the Library.
✓	8	Sneaky Spikes	M.U. Campus	On the upper tentacles that come out of the Library after roaring at the door.
✓	9	Frosty Feathers	M.U. Campus	Inside the secret room in the roof of Scare Hall.
✓	10	The Cooler	M.U. Campus	On the roof ledge of the front of the Library.
✓	11	Glam Gazer	M.U. Campus	In the center of the quad in M.U. Campus.
✓	12	Wee Waggy Wings	M.U. Campus	On the gutter pipe on the far side of the Library near Scare Hall.
✓	13	Scraggly Strands	M.U. Campus	On the corner of the roof of the Dorm nearest the main entrance to M.U. Campus.
✓	14	Loathsome Lights	M.U. Campus	On the corner of the roof of the Dorm nearest the University Hall.
✓	15	Uni-fin	M.U. Campus	Right above the front door to the Dorm.
✓	16	Dungeon Stone	M.U. Campus	On the front corner of the roof of the Dorm nearest the main entrance to M.U. Campus.

Frat Row

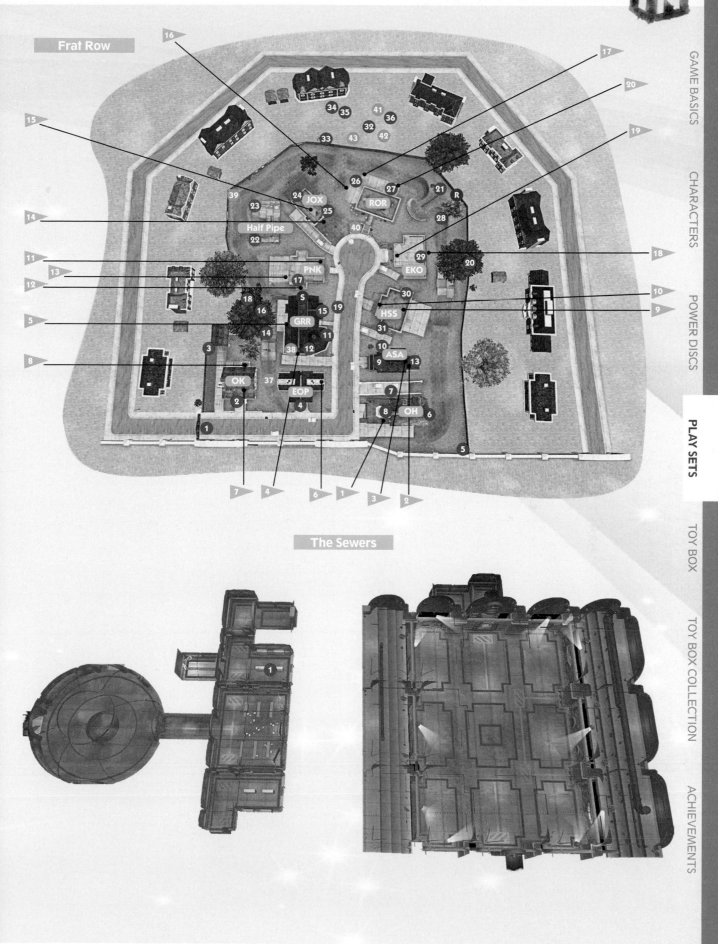

The Sewers

GAME BASICS

CHARACTERS

POWER DISCS

PLAY SETS

TOY BOX

TOY BOX COLLECTION

ACHIEVEMENTS

MU Campus Pennants

Fear Tech Pennants

GAME BASICS

CHARACTERS

POWER DISCS

PLAY SETS

TOY BOX

TOY BOX COLLECTION

ACHIEVEMENTS

Frat Row Pennants

Got It?	#	Unlockable Item	Zone	Location
✓	17	Longhorns	M.U. Campus	On the chimney of the University Hall.
✓	18	Ghastly Grooves	M.U. Campus	On the front ledge of the University Hall.
✓	19	Plated Tail	M.U. Campus	On the roof of Registration Hall.
✓	20	Freakish Fan	M.U. Campus	On the ledge above the front door of Registration Hall.
✓	21	Sulley Walls	M.U. Campus	On the small ledge at the end of Registration Hall.
✓	22	M.U. Pennant Pride	M.U. Campus	In between the walls on the side of Scare Hall near the Bike Path.
✓	23	Wall Scaler	M.U. Campus	On the roof to the front of Scare Hall.
✓	24	M.U. Hat	M.U. Campus	In the tunnel at the rear of Scare Hall.
✓	25	Newsstand	M.U. Campus	On the ledge on the left wing of Scare Hall.
✓	26	Fishy Accent	M.U. Campus	In the trees along the Bike Path.
✓	27	Terrible Teeth	M.U. Campus	On the little fountain directly behind Scare Hall leading to the Clock Tower.
✓	28	Funny Flappers	M.U. Campus	In between the rooftops on the far left side of Scare Hall near the tunnel to the Paintball Area.
✓	29	Beasty Beanpole	M.U. Campus	In the yard in right side of the Clock Tower.
✓	30	Polka Dot Panic	M.U. Campus	In the yard in front of the Clock Tower.
✓	31	Alarming Arms	M.U. Campus	On the ledge at the front Base of the Clock Tower.
✓	32	Four Fanged	M.U. Campus	In the air near the fence facing Scare Hall.
✓	33	Stripe Accent	M.U. Campus	On the chain-linked scaffolding at the side of the Clock Tower.
✓	34	Randy Scales Wall	M.U. Campus	On the left ledge of the Clock Tower.
✓	35	Curly South-Pointing Horns	M.U. Campus	On the path going up to the Clock Tower.
✓	36	Slippery Slug	M.U. Campus	On the wooden suspended platform on the Clock Tower.
✓	37	Scowling Brown	M.U. Campus	Inside the little room at the top of the Clock Tower.
✓	38	Creepy Comb-Over	M.U. Campus	At the top of the Clock Tower facing M.U. Campus.
✓	39	JOX House Walls	M.U. Campus	At the top of the Clock Tower facing away from M.U. Campus.
✓	40	Three's the Charm	M.U. Campus	On the scaffolding at the back of the Clock Tower.
✓	41	Scary 'Stache	M.U. Campus	On the ledge to the left of the Clock Tower by statue.
✓	42	Shocking Shrimp	M.U. Campus	In the middle of the circular sitting area by the statue.
✓	43	Triclops	M.U. Campus	On the railing of the bridge near the statue.

Green Capsules

Got It?	#	Unlockable Item	Zone	Location
✓	44	Monstery Metal	M.U. Campus	On the roof of the Dorm facing the quad.
✓	45	Monsters University Student Pack 1	M.U. Campus	On the back of the roof of University Hall.
✓	46	Monsters University Student Pack 4	M.U. Campus	On the gutter pipe between University Hall and Registration Hall.
✓	47	Monsters University Decoration Pack 1	M.U. Campus	On the front of the roof of University Hall.
✓	48	Monsters University Paintball Arena Pack 1	M.U. Campus	On the roof of Registration Hall.
✓	49	Monsters University Decoration Pack 2	M.U. Campus	On the back of the roof of Scare Hall.
✓	50	Creeping Concrete	M.U. Campus	In the very back of the Clock Tower area along the wall.

Infinity Chests/Vault

Got It?	#	Unlockable Item	Zone	Location
✓	S	Sulley Chest 1	M.U. Campus	On the wooden suspended platform on the Clock Tower.
✓	M	Mike Wazowski Chest 1	M.U. Campus	On the roof of the Library.
✓	R	Randy Chest 1	M.U. Campus	On the roof of the Dorm.
✓	Master	Monsters Avatar Vault - Reward 1	M.U. Campus	At the base of the Clock Tower.

Red Capsules

Got It?	#	Unlockable Item	Zone	Location
✓	1	Beastly Clothes	Frat Row	By the entrance to Fear Tech.
✓	2	Fancy Scales	Frat Row	On the roof of the OK House.
✓	3	Shrieking Shingles	Frat Row	On top of the EOP House.
✓	4	Freakish Flagstone	Frat Row	In front of the garage to the OK House.
✓	5	Grim Grandma Gauze	Frat Row	In the far back corner past the OH House.
✓	6	Double Fringe Fangs	Frat Row	On the back wall of the OH House.
✓	7	Spooky Spikes	Frat Row	On the driveway of the OH House.

Got It?	#	Unlockable Item	Zone	Location
✓	8	Flustered Feathers	Frat Row	On the balcony of the OH House.
✓	9	Terrible Toupee	Frat Row	On top of the AEA House.
✓	10	Beautiful Buck	Frat Row	On the wire next to the AEA House.
✓	11	OK Frat Pennant	Frat Row	On the patio of the GRR House.
✓	12	Pokey Posterior	Frat Row	On the roof of the GRR House.
✓	13	Crabby Accent	Frat Row	On the back balcony of the AEA House.
✓	14	Slick Spike	Frat Row	On the cables that are behind the GRR House.
✓	15	Shiver Shingles	Frat Row	On the roof of the GRR House.
✓	16	Savage Scales	Frat Row	Behind the GRR House by the fence.
✓	17	Roarin' Reptile	Frat Row	On the roof of the PNK House.
✓	18	Hair-Raising Horns	Frat Row	Along the fence behind the PNK House.
✓	19	Bat Trap	Frat Row	On top of the car on the main road.
✓	20	Long Southward Pointers	Frat Row	By the tree along the Bike Trail.
✓	21	Scary Scales	Frat Row	In the back between the ROR House and EKO House.
✓	22	Snake Accent	Frat Row	On top of the Half Pipe.
✓	23	OK Frat Wall	Frat Row	On top of the Half Pipe.
✓	24	PNK House Walls	Frat Row	On the back roof of the JOX House.
✓	25	Wild Wood Shingles	Frat Row	On the front roof of the JOX House.
✓	26	Double Trouble Dorsal	Frat Row	On the back of the ROR House.
✓	27	Monster Muscles	Frat Row	On the back of the ROR House.
✓	28	Scaring Manual	Frat Row	On the cable above the Bike Trail.
✓	29	Stubby Buddy	Frat Row	On top of the EKO House.
✓	30	Tenticlegs	Frat Row	On top of the chimney of the HSS House.
✓	31	Janitor's Rake	Frat Row	On top of the HSS House.
✓	32	Morbidly Medium	Frat Row	In the center of the Pool.
✓	33	Scary Cinnamon	Frat Row	Along the fence by the Pool.
✓	34	Goofy Goggles	Frat Row	Along the back part of the fence by the Pool.
✓	35	Fishy Accent	Frat Row	In the back side of the Pool.
✓	36	Diclops	Frat Row	By the trash can by the fence around the Pool.

🎩 Green Capsules

Got It?	#	Unlockable Item	Zone	Location
✓	37	Monsters University Building Pack 2	Frat Row	On the wire to the left of the EOP House.
✓	38	Monsters University Building Pack 3	Frat Row	On the patio of the GRR House.
✓	39	Monsters University Building Pack 1	Frat Row	Along the fence by the Half Pipe.
✓	40	Creepy Concrete Accent	Frat Row	On the wire going from JOX House to EKO House.
✓	41	Monsters University Student Pack 3	Frat Row	In the air at the back of the Pool.
✓	42	Monsters University Paintball Cannon	Frat Row	In the air at the front of the Pool.
✓	43	Monsters University Decoration Pack 4	Frat Row	In the air at the front of the Pool.

🎁 Infinity Chests/Vault

Got It?	#	Unlockable Item	Zone	Location
✓	R	Randy Chest 3	Frat Row	At the end of the Bike Trail.
✓	S	Sulley Chest 3	Frat Row	On top of the GRR House.

🎩 Red Capsules

Got It?	#	Unlockable Item	Zone	Location
✓	1	Mop Top	Fear Tech	On the wall of the Door Design School.
✓	2	Fancy Fangs	Fear Tech	In the corner of the wall past the Door Design School.
✓	3	Fear It Flags	Fear Tech	On the side platform of the Door Design School.
✓	4	Creepy Craters	Fear Tech	On the connecting beam of the Door Design School.
✓	5	Batty Wings	Fear Tech	On the wire above the Door Design School.
✓	6	Vending Machine	Fear Tech	On the ground along the pathway.
✓	7	Horrifying Hide	Fear Tech	On top of the hedge along the pathway.
✓	8	Scream Tunnel Cover	Fear Tech	In the back corner of the wall behind the Library.

Got It?	#	Unlockable Item	Zone	Location
✓	9	Creepy Campus Colors	Fear Tech	On top of a car in the parking lot behind the Library.
✓	10	Hulking	Fear Tech	On the front wall of the Door Design School.
✓	11	Polite Pucker	Fear Tech	On the front wall of the Door Design School.
✓	12	HSS House Walls	Fear Tech	On the roof of the Library.
✓	13	Sticker Walls	Fear Tech	In between the Library and the building behind it by the hedges.
✓	14	Petrifying Paths	Fear Tech	In the corner of the wall between the Library and the building behind it.
✓	15	Spikey Seat	Fear Tech	On the wire between the Library and the building behind it.
✓	16	Jumpy Gel	Fear Tech	On the back side of the Library wall.
✓	17	Buggy Antennas	Fear Tech	On the ledge of the dorms closest to Scare School.
✓	18	Daffy Dots	Fear Tech	On the front ledge of Scare School.
✓	19	Night Gliders	Fear Tech	On the side of Scare School up the spider wall.
✓	20	Tentacles Times Two	Fear Tech	On the roof of Scare School by the sunroof.
✓	21	Barbeque Grill	Fear Tech	On the side of Scare School along the inside wall.
✓	22	Curvy Creepers	Fear Tech	At the very top of Scare School on the crossbeam.
✓	23	Roundish Rascal	Fear Tech	On the side of Scare School up the spider wall.
✓	24	Triple Trouble	Fear Tech	On the side of Scare School along the inside wall.
✓	25	Tentacle Wall	Fear Tech	On the back ledge of Scare School.
✓	26	Foot Locker	Fear Tech	On the back ledge of Scare School.
✓	27	Lanky Limbs	Fear Tech	On the pipe at the back of Scare School.
✓	28	Eyeclops	Fear Tech	On the rail right in front of Archie's Pen.
✓	29	Woeful Wagger	Fear Tech	On the wall in the front of the Library.
✓	30	Crazy Kisser	Fear Tech	On the rail to the Botanical Building.
✓	31	Monster Movers	Fear Tech	On the sun roof of the building behind the Botanical Building.
✓	32	Shriveled Sponge	Fear Tech	On the ledge behind the Botanical Building.
✓	33	Scare Squares	Fear Tech	On the walkway by the Dorms.
✓	34	Foam Finger	Fear Tech	Above the main entrance to the Botanical Building.
✓	35	Eerie Earrings	Fear Tech	Up the spider wall in the front of the Botanical Building.
✓	36	Dire Spires	Fear Tech	On the glass cover next to the Botanical Building.
✓	37	Gargoyle Wings	Fear Tech	On the ledge of the Science Building.
✓	38	Crazy Coif	Fear Tech	On the ledge of the Science Building.
✓	39	Quadropods	Fear Tech	On the ledge of the Science Building.
✓	40	Pretty Peepers	Fear Tech	On the ledge of the Science Building in between the two connectors.
✓	41	Fur-ocious	Fear Tech	On the ledge of the building on the left from the tunnel to M.U.
✓	42	Teensy Weensy Terror	Fear Tech	On the ledge of the building on the left from the tunnel to M.U.
✓	43	Yucko Stucco	Fear Tech	On the ledge of the building on the left from the tunnel to M.U.
✓	44	Knobby Knobs	Fear Tech	On the ledge of the building on the right from the tunnel to M.U.
✓	45	Curly South-Pointing Horns	Fear Tech	On the roof of the building behind the Library.

🗑 Green Capsules

Got It?	#	Unlockable Item	Zone	Location
✓	46	Monsters University Decoration Pack 3	Fear Tech	On the back wall of the Library.
✓	47	Monsters University Paintball Arena Pack 2	Fear Tech	On the statue at the front of Scare School.
✓	48	Monsters University Critter Pack 1	Fear Tech	On the front ledge of Scare School.
✓	49	Monsters University Student Pack 2	Fear Tech	On the ledge of the Science Building.
✓	50	Monsters University Critter Pack 2	Fear Tech	On the railing of the catwalk on the Science Building.

📦 Infinity Chests/Vault

Got It?	#	Unlockable Item	Zone	Location
✓	M	Mike Wazowski Chest 2	Fear Tech	On the roof of the Door Design School.
✓	R	Randy Chest 2	Fear Tech	On the very top part of the roof on Scare School.
✓	S	Sulley Chest 2	Fear Tech	Right in front of the Health & Phys. Ed. Building.

🗑 Red Capsules

Got It?	#	Unlockable Item	Zone	Location
✓	1	Lurking Lampshade	Paintball Area/Sewers	In the locker room.

Monsters University Gold Stars

Got It?	#	Type	Star Names	Star Description
✓	1	Challenge	Combination Lock	Perform a two-stunt combo on the bike.
✓	2	Easter Egg	Student Switch	Change the appearance of a student.
✓	3	Mission	Buttoned Up	Use a building button to transform a building.
✓	4	Mission	Frat Go	Go to Frat Row.
✓	5	Mission	Remodeller	Customize a Frat Row building.
✓	6	Mission	Just Joking	Place a Prank Object.
✓	7	Mission	Scared Silly	Scare a targeted Fear Tech student.
✓	8	Mission	Save the Twins	Rescue Terri and Terry from their place of captivity.
✓	9	Mission	Exchange Student	Go to Fear Tech.
✓	10	Purchases	Painter	Purchase the Paintball Gun.
✓	11	Mission	Sneaks and Hi-Jinks	Go to Fear Tech at night.
✓	12	Mission	Gold Pedal	Perform 25 stunts on the bike.
✓	13	Mission	Reform School	Repair the School of Scaring.
✓	14	Mission	Get Along, Little Hoggy	Ride Archie through the tunnels to Monsters University.
✓	15	Challenge	The Completist	Complete 15 missions in the Monsters University Play Set.
✓	16	Mission	Paint Master	Complete all Paintball Challenges at any level of difficulty.
✓	17	Easter Egg	The Collector	Find 25 Red Capsules in the Play Set.
✓	18	Mission	Big Monster on Campus	Complete one Activity using the "Hard" difficulty setting.
✓	19	Challenge	Bike Master	Complete all Bike Challenges at any level of difficulty.
✓	20	Challenge	Frat Master	Complete all Frat Row Challenges at any level of difficulty.
✓	21	Mission	Football Wrapper	Cover Fear Tech's sports statue with T.P.
✓	22	Easter Egg	Batty Bush	Scare the bat-winged pests 15 times.
✓	23	Easter Egg	Six Tricks	Create a six Prank Object combo.
✓	24	Easter Egg	Pranks for Nothing	Activate a Prank Object on 25 students.
✓	25	Easter Egg	Monster Modifier	Change the appearance of 10 students.
✓	26	Purchases	Pedal Power	Purchase a bike.
✓	27	Purchases	Jokester	Purchase every Prank Object.
✓	28	Purchases	Leader of the Pack	Purchase the Cracklin' Backpack.
✓	29	Purchases	On a Roll	Purchase the Toilet Paper Launcher.
✓	30	Purchases	Frat Row Pro	Purchase every Frat Row building.

Monsters University Toy List

Got It?	Toys	Toy Box Export	Toy Type	Commercial	Got It?	Toys	Toy Box Export	Toy Type	Commercial
✓	Terrifying Two-Wheeler	Yes	Vehicle/Mount	No	✓	Morning Edition Launcher	Yes	Unique	No
✓	Slithering Cycle	Yes	Vehicle/Mount	No	✓	Vending Machine Launcher	Yes	Unique	No
✓	Tiny Terror	Yes	Vehicle/Mount	No	✓	Leafing So Soon? Launcher	Yes	Unique	No
✓	Beastly Bike	Yes	Vehicle/Mount	Yes	✓	Fly Swatter Launcher	Yes	Unique	No
✓	Archie the Scare Pig	Yes	Vehicle/Mount	Yes	✓	Vender Ender	Yes	Unique	No
✓	Paintball Cannon	Yes	Prop	No	✓	Breaking News Ender	Yes	Unique	No
✓	Roarin' Ramp	Yes	Unique	No	✓	School Colors Ender	Yes	Unique	Yes
✓	Bike Park Dual Pool	Yes	Unique	No	✓	Have a Nice Trip Launcher	Yes	Unique	No
✓	Bike Park Half Pipe	Yes	Unique	No	✓	Scream Tunnel Sludge Ender	Yes	Unique	No
✓	Bike Park Berm	Yes	Unique	No	✓	Pile It On Ender	Yes	Unique	No
✓	Bike Park Table Top	Yes	Unique	No	✓	Incoming Call Ender	Yes	Unique	Yes
✓	Sweet Bike Jump	Yes	Unique	No	✓	Paintball Gun	Yes	Held Item	Yes
✓	PNK House	Yes	Building	No	✓	Toilet Paper Launcher	Yes	Held Item	Yes
✓	JOX House	Yes	Building	No	✓	Cracklin' Backpack	Yes	Held Item	Yes
✓	HSS House	Yes	Building	No	✓	Glow Urchin	Yes	Held Item	Yes
✓	EKO House	Yes	Building	No	✓	Bat-Winged Pest Bush	Yes	Held Item	No
✓	ROR House	Yes	Building	No	✓	Sludge Balloon	No	Held Item	No
✓	Give 'em a Hand Launcher	Yes	Unique	Yes					
✓	Scream Energy Launcher	Yes	Unique	No					

Monsters University Challenges

Got It?	Name	Location	Description	Character	Easy	Medium	Hard
✓	Classroom Run	Clock Tower Area	Gather as many collectibles as you can before time runs out.	Any	10 targets in 1:30	20 targets in 1:30	35 targets in 1:30
✓	Fear Tech Collector	Fear Tech below School of Science	Gather as many collectibles as you can before time runs out.	Any	20 targets in 1:00	35 targets in 1:00	48 targets in 1:00
✓	Randy's Rampage	Fear Tech between Library buildings	Break as many collectibles as you can as Randy before the time runs out.	Randy	10 targets in 1:30	20 targets in 1:30	30 targets in 1:30
✓	Fear Tech Cyclist	Fear Tech in front of Health & Phys. Ed. Building	Gather as many collectibles as you can before time runs out.	Any	10 targets in 1:30	10 targets in 1:15	10 targets in 1:00
✓	Paintball Ruckus	Frat Row Alcove	Defeat Fear Tech students in a Paintball competition.	Any	4 targets in 0:50	8 targets in 0:50	12 targets in 0:50
✓	Wheels and Thrills	Frat Row Alcove	Gather as many collectibles as you can before time runs out.	Any	20 targets in 1:30	35 targets in 1:30	50 targets in 1:30
✓	Wild Wheels	Frat Row Alcove	Pass through all the gates before time runs out.	Any	8 checkpoints in 1:00	8 checkpoints in 0:50	8 checkpoints in 0:40
✓	Paint the Frat Collector	Frat Row Alcove	Defeat Fear Tech students in a Paintball competition.	Any	25 targets in 1:20	35 targets in 1:20	45 targets in 1:20
✓	Frat Row Round-Up	Frat Row Alcove	Break as many collectibles as you can before the time runs out.	Any	20 targets in 0:50	30 targets in 0:50	40 targets in 0:50
✓	Round the Row	Frat Row Alcove	Pass through all the gates before time runs out.	Any	10 checkpoints in 1:10	10 checkpoints in 1:00	10 checkpoints in 0:50
✓	Mike's Mayhem	Frat Row Entrance	Gather as many collectibles as you can as Mike before time runs out.	Mike	15 targets in 1:30	30 targets in 1:30	42 targets in 1:30
✓	Timed Swine	Frat Row Entrance	Gather as many collectibles as you can before time runs out.	Any	20 targets in 1:00	40 targets in 1:00	60 targets in 1:00
✓	Crazy Frat Stunts	Frat Row Pool	Do bike tricks to reach the score goal before time runs out.	Any	3000 points in 1:00	6000 points in 1:00	10000 points in 1:00
✓	Bike Hop and Pop	Frat Row Pool	Gather as many collectibles as you can before time runs out.	Any	20 targets in 1:30	35 targets in 1:30	50 targets in 1:30
✓	Campus Collector Bike	M.U. Campus Bike Stunt area	Gather as many collectibles as you can before time runs out.	Any	25 targets in 1:20	35 targets in 1:20	45 targets in 1:20
✓	Campus Collector	M.U. Campus in front of the Library	Gather as many collectibles as you can before time runs out.	Any	12 targets in 2:00	25 targets in 2:00	50 targets in 2:00
✓	Squeal and Steal	M.U. Campus near Clock Tower	Gather as many collectibles as you can before time runs out.	Any	20 targets in 1:00	30 targets in 1:00	40 targets in 1:00
✓	Sulley's Campus Collector	M.U. Campus near University Hall	Gather as many collectibles as you canas Sulley before time runs out.	Sulley	5 targets in 0:40	10 targets in 0:40	15 targets in 0:40
✓	Scream Tunnel Collector	Paintball Arena	Break as many collectibles as you can before the time runs out.	Any	10 targets in 0:45	20 targets in 0:45	30 targets in 0:45
✓	Paintball Press	Paintball Arena	Defeat Fear Tech students in a Paintball competition.	Any	4 enemies in 1:00	8 enemies in 1:00	10 enemies in 1:00
✓	Paintball Panic	Paintball Arena	Defeat Fear Tech students in a Paintball competition.	Any	4 enemies in 1:00	8 enemies in 1:00	10 enemies in 1:00
✓	Paintball Party	Paintball Arena	Defeat Fear Tech students in a Paintball competition.	Any	4 enemies in 1:00	8 enemies in 1:00	10 enemies in 1:00

WII COLLECTIBLES

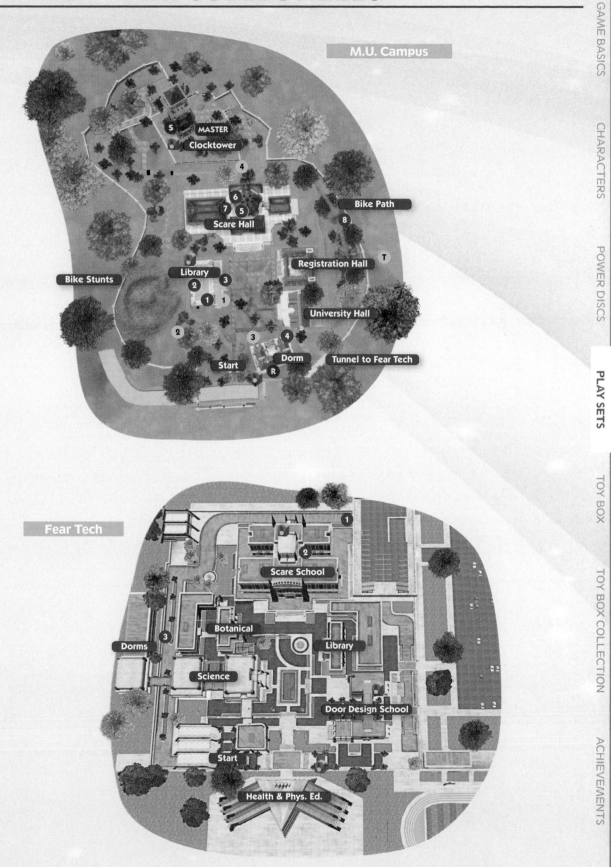

M.U. Campus

MASTER
Clocktower
Scare Hall
Bike Path
Library
Registration Hall
Bike Stunts
University Hall
Start
Dorm
Tunnel to Fear Tech

Fear Tech

Scare School
Botanical
Dorms
Library
Science
Door Design School
Start
Health & Phys. Ed.

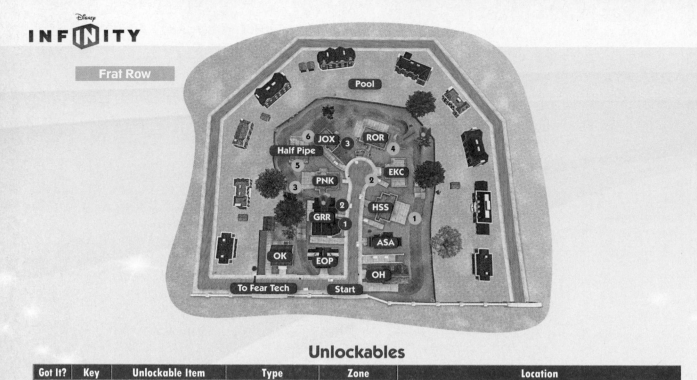

Unlockables

Got It?	Key	Unlockable Item	Type	Zone	Location
				MU Main	
✓	1	Old Couch	Red Capsule	MU	On the roof ledge of the Library nearest the entrance to MU Campus.
✓	2	Leaf Pile	Red Capsule	MU	On the roof ledge of the Library nearest the Bike Stunt area.
✓	3	The Cooler	Red Capsule	MU	On the roof ledge of the front of the Library.
✓	4	Loathesome Lights	Red Capsule	MU	On the corner of the roof of the Dorm nearest the University Hall.
✓	5	Newsstand	Red Capsule	MU	On the ledge on the left wing of Scare Hall.
✓	6	Phone Booth	Red Capsule	MU	On the ledge on the left wing of Scare Hall.
✓	7	Vending Machine	Red Capsule	MU	Inside the walkway in Scare Hall.
✓	8	Fishy Accent	Red Capsule	MU	In the trees long the bike path.
✓	S	Sulley Chest	Avatar Chest	MU	On the wooden suspended platform on the Clock Tower.
✓	M	Mike Wazowski Chest	Avatar Chest	MU	Top ledge from the roof, in the northwest corner of the Library.
✓	R	Randy Chest	Avatar Chest	MU	On the roof of the Dorm.
✓	Master	Monsters Avatar Vault - Reward 1	Avatar Vault	MU	At the base of the Clock Tower.
				Frat Row	
✓	1	OK Frat Pennant	Red Capsule	Frat Row	On the patio of the GRR House.
✓	2	Shiver Shingles	Red Capsule	Frat Row	On the roof of the GRR House.
✓	3	Wild Wood Shingles	Red Capsule	Frat Row	On the front roof of the JOX House.
				Fear Tech	
✓	1	Scream Tunnel Cover	Red Capsule	Fear Tech	In the back corner of the wall behind the Library.
✓	2	Barbeque Grill	Red Capsule	Fear Tech	On the side of Scare School along the inside wall.
✓	3	Scare Squares	Red Capsule	Fear Tech	On the walkway by the Dorms.

Monsters University Challenges

Got It?	#	Name	Location
✓	1	Campus Collector	M.U. Campus
✓	2	Campus Collector Bike	M.U. Campus
✓	3	Sulley's Campus Collector	M.U. Campus
✓	4	Squeal and Steal	M.U. Campus

Got It?	#	Name	Location
✓	1	Wheels and Thrills	Frat Row
✓	2	Frat Row Roundup	Frat Row
✓	3	Wild Wheels	Frat Row
✓	4	Paint the Frat Collector	Frat Row
✓	5	Round the Row	Frat Row
✓	6	Stunt Challenge	Frat Row

⭐ Monsters University Gold Stars

Got It?	#	Type	Name	Description
✓	1	Challenge	Combination Lock	Perform a two-stunt combo on the bike.
✓	3	Mission	Buttoned Up	Use a building button to transform a building.
✓	4	Mission	Frat Go	Go to Frat Row.
✓	5	Mission	Remodeller	Customize a Frat Row building.
✓	6	Mission	Just Joking	Place a Prank Object.
✓	7	Mission	Scared Silly	Scare a targeted Fear Tech student.
✓	8	Mission	Save the Twins	Rescue Terri and Terry from captivity.
✓	9	Mission	Exchange Student	Go to Fear Tech.
✓	10	Purchases	Painter	Purchase the Paintball Gun.
✓	11	Mission	Sneaks and Hi-Jinks	Go to Fear Tech at night.
✓	12	Mission	Gold Pedal	Perform 25 stunts on the bike.
✓	13	Mission	Reform School	Repair the School of Scaring.
✓	14	Mission	Get Along, Little Hoggy	Ride Archie through the tunnels to Monsters University.
✓	15	Challenge	The Completist	Complete 15 missions in the Monsters University Play Set.
✓	16	Mission	Paint Master	Complete all Paintball Challenges at any level of difficulty.
✓	17	Easter Egg	The Collector	Find 25 Red and Green Capsules in the Play Set.
✓	18	Mission	Big Monster on Campus	Complete one Activity using the "Hard" difficulty setting.
✓	19	Challenge	Frat Master	Complete all Frat Row Challenges at any level of difficulty.
✓	20	Mission	Football Master	Cover Fear Tech's sports statue with T.P.
✓	21	Easter Egg	Batty Bush	Scare the bush bats 15 times.
✓	22	Easter Egg	Six Tricks	Create a six Prank Object combo.
✓	23	Easter Egg	Pranks for Nothing	Activate a Prank Object on 25 students.
✓	24	Purchases	Pedal Power	Purchase a bike.
✓	25	Purchases	Jokester	Purchase every Prank Object.
✓	26	Purchases	Leader of the Pack	Purchase the Cracklin' Backpack.
✓	27	Purchases	On a Roll	Purchase the Toilet Paper Launcher.
✓	28	Purchases	Frat Row Pro	Purchase every Frat Row building.
✓	29	Challenge	Hog Heaven	Complete the Archie challenge at any level of difficulty.

Monsters University Toy List

Got It?	Toys	Toy Type	Commercial
✓	Terrifying Two-Wheeler	Vehicle/Mount	No
✓	Slithering Cycle	Vehicle/Mount	No
✓	Tiny Terror	Vehicle/Mount	No
✓	Beastly Bike	Vehicle/Mount	Yes
✓	Archie the Scare Pig	Vehicle/Mount	Yes
✓	Paintball Cannon	Prop	No
✓	Roarin' Ramp	Unique	No
✓	Bike Park Dual Pool	Unique	No
✓	Bike Park Half Pipe	Unique	No
✓	Bike Park Berm	Unique	No
✓	Bike Park Table Top	Unique	No
✓	Sweet Bike Jump	Unique	No
✓	PNK House	Building	No
✓	JOX House	Building	No
✓	HSS House	Building	No
✓	EKO House	Building	No
✓	ROR House	Building	No
✓	Give 'em a Hand Launcher	Unique	Yes
✓	Phone Booth Launcher	Unique	No
✓	Scream Energy Launcher	Unique	No
✓	Morning Edition Launcher	Unique	No
✓	Vending Machine Launcher	Unique	No
✓	Leaving So Soon? Launcher	Unique	No
✓	Glow Urchin Launcher	Unique	No
✓	Fly Swatter Launcher	Unique	No
✓	Vending Ender	Unique	No
✓	Breaking News Ender	Unique	No
✓	School Colors Ender	Unique	Yes
✓	Have a Nice Trip Ender	Unique	No
✓	Scream Tunnel Sludge Ender	Unique	No
✓	Pile It On Ender	Unique	No
✓	Incoming Call Ender	Unique	Yes
✓	Paintball Gun	Held Item	Yes
✓	Toilet Paper Launcher	Held Item	Yes
✓	Cracklin' Backpack	Held Item	Yes
✓	Glow Urchin	Held Item	Yes
✓	Bat-Winged Pest Bush	Held Item	No
✓	Sludge Balloon	Held Item	No

The Incredibles

Three notorious criminals apprehended by The Incredibles are about to be sent off to a maximum security prison. However, Syndrome shows up and frees the villains! The arch enemy of The Incredibles sends the heroic family flying off in the distance as he unleashes a horde of robots on the city.

SEARCH AND RESCUE ON THE DOCKS

Hoarder Chest

Hoarder Chest

Hoarder Chest

Hoarder Chest

⭐ WHERE THERE'S SMOKE

Mission Giver: Edna
Type: Combat/Platforming
Rewards: N/A
Wii Rewards: 500 Coins

Follow the green compass arrow, jumping up on the demolished building and avoiding the flames. Continue to rush through the flaming wreckage and grab on to the ledge above that is highlighted with a yellow tint.

Attack the water tower on the roof of the building to knock it over and douse the flames.

Follow the path of the toppled tower toward the gas trucks, but that route will become blocked when the trucks explode. Turn to the left towards a tower that has two brown crates that can be jumped over.

Climb the pole to the top of the metal tower and double jump across the moving crates and stack of cargo boxes to get to the tower on the other side.

Run down the metal stairs to confront four attacking robots unleashed by Syndrome. Each of your targets is highlighted by a red arrow. A few simple attacks should take care of each one. However, look out for the rocket-launching robot on the ship that can blast you from a distance. Block its rockets if you can't outrun them, and make that robot your top target.

 New Toy Unlocked: Mr. Incredible's Sports Car

CLEAN UP SYNDROME'S MESS

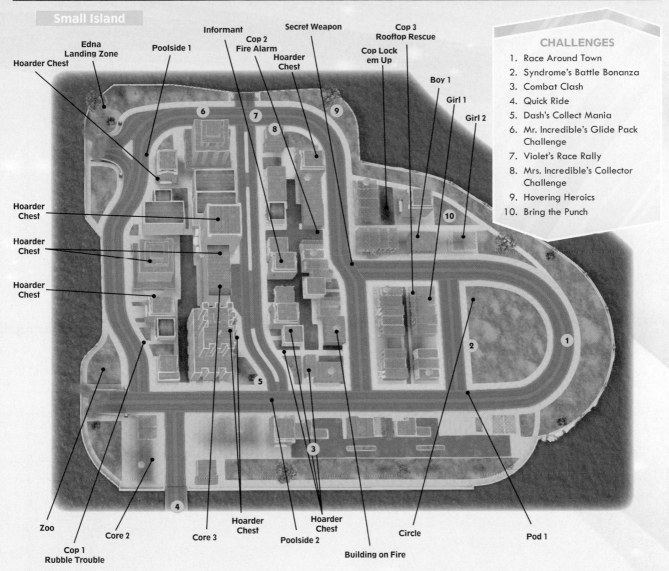

Small Island

Hoarder Chest
Edna Landing Zone
Poolside 1
Informant
Cop 2 Fire Alarm
Secret Weapon
Hoarder Chest
Cop 3 Rooftop Rescue
Cop Lock em Up
Boy 1
Girl 1
Girl 2

Hoarder Chest
Hoarder Chest
Hoarder Chest

Zoo
Cop 1 Rubble Trouble
Core 2
Core 3
Hoarder Chest
Poolside 2
Hoarder Chest
Building on Fire
Circle
Pod 1

CHALLENGES

1. Race Around Town
2. Syndrome's Battle Bonanza
3. Combat Clash
4. Quick Ride
5. Dash's Collect Mania
6. Mr. Incredible's Glide Pack Challenge
7. Violet's Race Rally
8. Mrs. Incredible's Collector Challenge
9. Hovering Heroics
10. Bring the Punch

DAMAGE ASSESSMENT

Mission Giver: Edna
Type: Buy/Locate
Rewards: 300 Coins / 50 Sparks
Wii Rewards: 250 Coins / 50 Sparks

NOTE

This is a three-part mission assisting cops, each with unique tasks to help the city.

Wii NOTE

In the Wii version, you must first complete the "Fire Alarm" mission before you can do Damage Assessment.

Edna is on her way, but Syndrome has destroyed all the bridges. Local law enforcement needs your help, but first you need to get the sports car to travel around the city. Go into the Toy Store to buy Mr. Incredible's Sports Car and someone will be nice enough to drop off your car. Jump into the driver's seat and follow the compass to find the first officer trying to deal with the damage from the Omnidroids.

New Challenges Available: Violet's Race Rally, Syndrome's Battle Bonanza, Dash's Collect Mania, Collect Crazy, Mrs. Incredible's Collector Challenge, Glide 'n' Grab, Mr. Incredible's Glide Pack Challenge, Hover Board Hustle, Hovering Heroics, Speed Battle, Blast From Above, Eat My Dust.

Side tabs: GAME BASICS · CHARACTERS · POWER DISCS · PLAY SETS · TOY BOX · TOY BOX COLLECTION · ACHIEVEMENTS

RUBBLE TROUBLE

Mission Giver: Policeman
Type: Fetch
Rewards: 100 Coins / 25 Sparks
Wii Rewards: 250 Coins / 25 Sparks

The officer mentions that several citizens are trapped under debris. Use the compass to find the six trapped people and smash the debris to set them free.

FIRE ALARM!

Mission Giver: Policeman
Type: Platforming
Rewards: 100 Coins / 25 Sparks

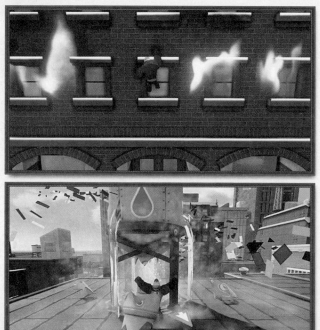

A historic building was set on fire by a couple of Syndrome's robots. Use the compass to find the burning building and wipe out the Omnidroids that started the fire. The most obvious path to the top is the yellow highlighted ledges in the front of the building. Use them to quickly climb to the top and smash the water tower to put out the fire.

ROOFTOP RESCUE

Mission Giver: Policeman
Type: Platforming
Rewards: 100 Coins / 25 Sparks
Wii Rewards: 250 Coins / 25 Sparks

There are three people trapped on rooftops. It's up to you to get up there and take them to safety. The first boy is trapped on the building right in front of the policeman, and the building is easy to climb. The task really isn't to save the boy as much as it is to get him into the circle of yellow blockades. This can be done with one well-aimed toss of the lad—don't worry, this is a superhero city and everyone is very durable. Knock down the big blue billboard on the roof, pick the boy up, and try your best at tossing him into the circle below. If you miss, you will need to jump down and toss him until he is safely in the circle.

Climb to the next building and fling the girl into the safety of the circle below.

Finally, climb back up the red building where you saved the boy, jump across the billboard that was knocked over earlier, and toss the last girl in the ring below.

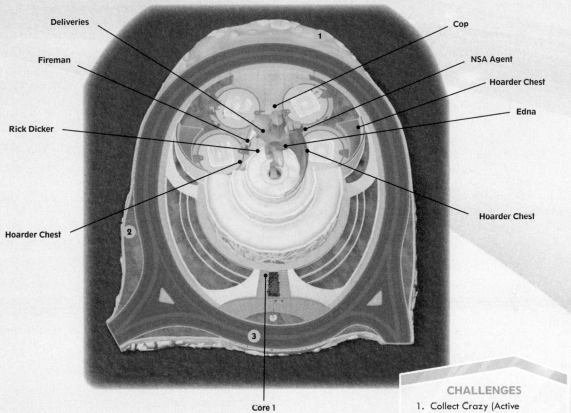

REACTIVATE THE HEADQUARTERS

Deliveries

Fireman

Rick Dicker

Hoarder Chest

Cop

NSA Agent

Hoarder Chest

Edna

Hoarder Chest

Core 1

GAME BASICS

CHARACTERS

POWER DISCS

PLAY SETS

TOY BOX

TOY BOX COLLECTION

ACHIEVEMENTS

CHALLENGES

1. Collect Crazy (Active Lifestyle Mission)
2. Romp Around Town
3. Blast From Above

EDNA ARRIVES

Mission Giver: Policeman
Type: Combat
Rewards: 500 Coins / 200 Sparks

To find it you will need to climb up the adjacent building and jump across to take it on.

Edna has almost arrived, but the Omidroids have swarmed the landing zone. Follow the red arrows to Edna's arrival spot and destroy all five robots. One of them is on the roof.

⭐ THE SECRET OF HEROES ISLAND

Mission Giver: Edna
Type: Buy/Build
Rewards: 500 Coins / 100 Sparks

To reactivate the hidden base of operations, the bridge must be repaired. Go in to the Toy Store and buy the bridge for 100 coins.

New Toy Unlocked: Downtown Express Bridge

Make your way across the bridge and run towards the Hall of Heroes. When you arrive, Edna will give you a clue about how to unlock the HQ. Take special note of the triangular buttons that appear when she mentions the mural. Climb the side of the building and work your way around it to the golden buttons. Press both of them to reactivate the HQ.

Climb to the top of the HQ using the ledges that are on the top tier. At the very top, near the statue, step on the platform in the center to reopen the HQ.

New Toy Unlocked: Training Facility

New Toy Unlocked: SuperMax Prison

NOTE

When the HQ is back up and running, three mission paths become available: Training, Prisoner Capture, and Tech Research. The first two are initiated by purchasing the Training Facility and SuperMax Prison respectively, and the last unlocks when those buildings are both bought.

TRAINING MISSIONS

ROOM TO BREATHE

Mission Giver: Edna
Type: Buy/Build
Rewards: N/A
Wii Rewards: 100 Coins

To reach your full potential, you need to buy the National Supers Agency Training Facility from the Toy Store. Enter the Toy Store menu to buy it for 500 coins and place it on one of the four open areas in the HQ.

 New Toy Unlocked: Purple Truck

SHAPE UP!

Mission Giver: Edna
Type: Fetch
Rewards: 100 Coins / 50 Sparks
Wii Rewards: 250 Coins / 50 Sparks

Edna informs you that your fighting skills are so last season, but the newly built Training Facility can get you up to snuff. Pick up the Sensei in the center of the HQ and take him to the Training Facility to begin your lessons.

> ### NOTE
>
> The first training mission illustrates how to use the super attack. This is a unique attack for each of The Incredibles and Syndrome, so there are five gold star missions available if you have all of the characters for this Play Set.

SENSEI MISSIONS

> ### NOTE
>
> These are unique missions for each character to teach them their super move. Only the current character has to complete his or her mission to proceed, but if you want to use the super move for another character in this Play Set, return to the Sensei to learn it.

⭐ THE POWER WITHIN

Mission Giver: Sensei
Type: Training
Rewards: 100 Coins / 100 Sparks
Wii Rewards: 250 Coins / 100 Sparks

The first lesson for Mr. Incredible to defeat Omidroids is to call upon your strength. Learn to use the Super Ground Pound by pressing the super attack button. This is a great attack for crowd control as it damages all enemies in its path.

⭐ FANTASTIC ELASTIC

Mission Giver: Sensei
Type: Training
Rewards: 100 Coins / 100 Sparks
Wii Rewards: 250 Coins / 100 Sparks

Mrs. Incredible can use her Elasti-Hand move to pull herself to an Omnidroid and get past its blocking defenses. This is a very important part of her attacking arsenal to break through an Omnidroid's block state.

GAME BASICS · CHARACTERS · POWER DISCS · PLAY SETS · TOY BOX · TOY BOX COLLECTION · ACHIEVEMENTS

⭐ VANISHING ACT

Mission Giver: Sensei
Type: Training
Rewards: 100 Coins / 100 Sparks
Wii Rewards: 250 Coins / 100 Sparks

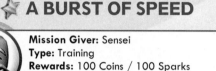

Using invisibility, Violet can avoid detection from enemies or make enemies that are aware of her lose sight of her. Use her power of invisibility to drop out of sight from the Omnidroid and sneak up to attack it.

⭐ A BURST OF SPEED

Mission Giver: Sensei
Type: Training
Rewards: 100 Coins / 100 Sparks
Wii Rewards: 250 Coins / 100 Sparks

Dash's super speed can deal high damage to a single Omnidroid, breaking through its block state. Use his fast attack to become a mobile weapon as well as a method to travel around the city quickly.

⭐ ZERO POINT POWER SURGE

Mission Giver: Sensei
Type: Training
Rewards: 100 Coins / 100 Sparks
Wii Rewards: 250 Coins / 100 Sparks

The Zero Point Energy tool can freeze Omnidroids and lift them overhead so they can be tossed around like toys. Throwing the Omnidroids deals high damage to them or others that they smash into.

 New Toy Unlocked: Glide Pack

> **NOTE**
>
> After buying the Glide Pack, go through the tutorial on how to equip Packs and Tools.

LEARNING TO GLIDE

Mission Giver: Edna
Type: Training
Rewards: 100 Coins / 100 Sparks
Wii Rewards: 250 Coins / 100 Sparks

Take the elevator to the top of the HQ and open the blue capsule to learn how to glide. Fly through all the green rings and dive bomb down to the circle of yellow gates below.

TRAINING SIDE MISSIONS

UPPERCUT AFICIONADO

Mission Giver: Sensei
Type: Training
Rewards: 100 Coins / 50 Sparks
Wii Rewards: 250 Coins / 50 Sparks

After the initial lesson, which is different for each character, continue to speak to the Sensei to learn all of the other combat techniques. The next move to master is the uppercut combo. The first part can be done by pressing and holding the attack button to launch the enemy and yourself into the air. While airborne press attack again to perform the second part of the combo. Do the combo three times to prove you have mastered the move.

HANDLING A CROWD

Mission Giver: Sensei
Type: Training
Rewards: 100 Coins / 50 Sparks
Wii Rewards: 250 Coins / 50 Sparks

Switch between the targets using (LS) and pressing (Y).

This is a simple but effective lesson about quickly switching between targets. Simply flick the movement stick in the direction of an enemy to target and attack it. This is a very useful technique when fighting groups of enemies that surround you.

DODGE

Mission Giver: Sensei
Type: Training
Rewards: 100 Coins / 50 Sparks
Wii Rewards: 250 Coins / 50 Sparks

Move (LS) in a direction and press (⊙) to dodge out of the way of an attack.

Combat is not simply about fighting and blocking. Sometimes the best maneuver is to dodge an attack entirely. Move the directional stick while pressing the same button to block in order to dive out of the way. This can be done while running or blocking.

 New Challenge Available: Collect Crazy

⭐ ACTIVE LIFESTYLE

Mission Giver: Sensei
Type: Collect
Rewards: N/A

There are opportunities to master your skills all over this city. Find the Collect Crazy challenge and complete it.

Complete the Collect Crazy activity located around the back side of the HQ.

COLLECTOR CHALLENGE

Mission Giver: Sensei
Type: Collect
Rewards: 25 Coins

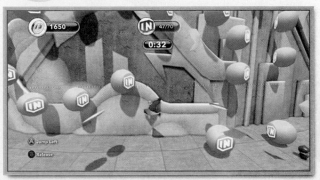

Collecting enough balls shouldn't be too hard if you start in a big cluster and keep moving in one direction to clear out all of them at that level. Jump up to the next climbable ledge and pick up the balls, following them to the next set.

GAME BASICS

CHARACTERS

POWER DISCS

PLAY SETS

TOY BOX

TOY BOX COLLECTION

ACHIEVEMENTS

PRISONER CAPTURE MISSIONS

NO ESCAPE

Mission Giver: Rick Dicker
Type: Buy/Build
Rewards: 100 Coins / 25 Sparks
Wii Rewards: 250 Coins / 25 Sparks

Buy the SuperMax Prison in the Toy Store to house criminals and open several missions to apprehend the villains that Syndrome set free.

New Toy Unlocked: Ice Cream Truck

New Toy Unlocked: Newspaper Stand

⭐ ANIMAL PANDEMONIUM!

Mission Giver: Fireman at HQ
Type: Fetch
Rewards: 100 Coins / 200 Sparks

A devious droid has released the animals from the local zoo. You need to help round them up and toss them back into the zoo. Head towards the zoo and use the compass to locate all six animals including a panda, giraffe, lion, elephant, monkey, and penguin.

LOCK 'EM UP

Mission Giver: Policeman
Type: Locate
Rewards: 100 Coins / 100 Sparks

A local policeman wants to see every crook and criminal locked up behind bars. Look for the criminals that are dressed in black-and-white-striped clothes. Luckily the first one is right next to the officer.

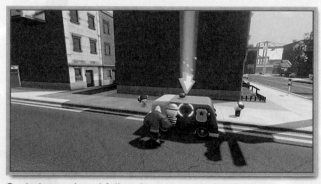

Grab the crook and follow the compass to a police van to toss the villain inside. Track down all five crooks to clean up the streets of Metroville.

THE HOARDER PURSUIT AND CAPTURE

HIDE AND SEEK

Mission Giver: Rick Dicker
Type: Locate
Rewards: 100 Coins

Now that the prison is built, it is time to bring in the villains Syndrome unleashed on the city. The first target is The Hoarder, who has been sighted at the docks. Use the compass to make your way there to check it out. It is a long walk back to the city, so look for a blue sign with a car on it to summon a vehicle.

When you arrive at the designated spot at the docks, The Hoarder shows up and traps a cop with the mysterious UFO device he is riding. This machine fails to work on your character and The Hoarder is apprehended by the police.

⭐ FIND ALL

Mission Giver: Rick Dicker
Type: Locate
Rewards: N/A

Find and destroy all of The Hoarder's traps around the city. This is a very tough mission to complete. Smash the traps as you find them, but wait for the helicopter before you really scour the city. Releasing the hostages will uncover several new superheroes that can be recruited at the HQ to join you in combat.

TIGHT SPACES

Mission Giver: Rick Dicker (radio)
Type: Platforming
Rewards: 250 Coins / 50 Sparks
Wii Rewards: 500 Coins / 50 Sparks

Before The Hoarder can be prosecuted, you must smash his traps to release all the hostages. Use the compass to locate and rescue five citizens scattered around the pier. The last person you save will join your cause and go to the HQ, ready to fight with you when he is recruited.

New Toy Unlocked: Forklift

Wii NOTE

In the Wii version, the Hoarder's traps are located around Small Island and not around the Pier. Also, Rick Dicker gives you a side mission called No More Traps.

⭐ PRISONER DELIVERY

Mission Giver: Rick Dicker (radio)
Type: Escort
Rewards: 500 Coins / 200 Sparks
Wii Rewards: 100 Coins / 200 Sparks

With The Hoarder in custody, it's time to transport the villain to the SuperMax Prison at HQ. Escort the paddy wagon to headquarters as you defend against Syndrome's attacks.

Keep an eye on the paddy wagon's yellow bar to see how much damage it is taking—if it is completely depleted your mission will fail.

The goal is to keep the Omnidroids from damaging the paddy wagon. But keep your guard up—Syndrome's forces will do everything they can to prevent the truck from reaching HQ. Enlist the aid of the local police by smashing the yellow barricades. This will not only open a clear route for the truck, but the cops will attack the robots and distract them.

Remember that the paddy wagon can't move if there is anything blocking it. That includes robots, barricades, and even chucks of road debris. Try to stay a little ahead of the truck to keep the path clear and eliminate any robots in front of it.

Once the truck finally makes it to HQ, grab The Hoarder and toss him into the prison to lock him up once and for all.

 New Toy Unlocked: Pink Family Car

New Challenges Available: Quick Ride, Romp Around Town

NOTE

Completion of this mission lowers the bridges to allow access to the Big island, however there is a lot more to do on the Small island. At this point it is probably best to follow the Tech Missions until you get the Hover Board.

SNORING GLORIA'S PODS

FIND SNORING GLORIA

Mission Giver: Rick Dicker
Type: Locate
Rewards: N/A
Wii Rewards: 100 Coins

The next villain has been spotted in the city. Use the compass to track down Snoring Gloria. She unleashes a mutated version of her plants that puts citizens to sleep. The only way to destroy the large pod is to take out the smaller ones first.

RISE AND SHINE

Mission Giver: Rick Dicker
Type: Destroy
Rewards: 500 Coins / 100 Sparks
Wii Rewards: 100 Coins / 25 Sparks

You must destroy two groups of pods (six smaller and two larger ones), and luckily the first group of pods appears right in front of you. Follow the red arrow to one of the smaller pods on the grass and destroy it. Each time one of the smaller pods is eliminated, the vine leading to the large pod will disappear and the larger pod will lose some of its leafy defenses.

The other two smaller pods are on the rooftops. Use the red arrow to find them, but if you have trouble locating their exact position, follow the green vines coming out of the large pod for a clue. Go after pod number two by climbing a light-colored building with plenty of ledges to help you climb up.

The last little pod of this group can easily been seen from the roof where you took on the second one. Jump down to the street and climb up the blue front of the building to reach the last one.

Finally, jump down to the street and take out the defenseless large pod amongst the outcropping of little blue sleep-inducing pods.

Track the next group using the red arrows to locate the second group of pods just down the street. Tackle the first smaller pod by climbing a dark stone facade next to a light blue one. Smash the pod on the roof and jump across to the air conditioners and pipe leading to the roof of the next one.

The last smaller pod is across the street on a roof near a water tower. Glide across to the building or jump down to the street to climb up the front of it.

> **NOTE**
>
> This building can catch fire but it is easily put out by knocking over the water tower on the roof. In the Wii version, the building does not catch fire.

New Toy Unlocked: Edna's Costume Shop

> **NOTE**
>
> Sprawling Sleep Pods is open at this point, but it takes place on the Big island. It might be worthwhile to wait for the Tech Mission path to catch up.

⭐ SPRAWLING SLEEP PODS

Mission Giver: Rick Dicker
Type: Destroy
Rewards: 100 Coins / 200 Sparks

Snoring Gloria has placed her sleep-inducing plants all over the city. Track them down and destroy them all! The larger pods only have two smaller support pods this time, but you must destroy five large pods to complete the mission.

Pods Set 1

The first set of pods is just across the bridge and is not very challenging. The smaller pods are not very high up, so it will be quick work to wipe them all out.

Pods Set 2

You can find the next set of pods by using the red arrow to go across the docks. The first small pod is right on the street and can be taken out by slamming into it with the Hover Board.

The second small pod is on a rooftop of a dark-colored building with green windows. This place may light on fire, but there is a handy water tower on the roof to handle the blaze.

The last smaller pod is on the roof of the brown building next door, but it is not possible to climb that structure to get to the roof. Go to the roof where you met Mirage and glide over to the dark building to wall jump to the ledge. From here, glide down to the pod, smash it, and leap to the street below to wipe out the large pod.

Pods Set 3

Follow the red arrow to the next set of pods and climb a light tan building using a pipe to get to the first small pod.

Leap down to the street and smash the smaller pod out in the open.

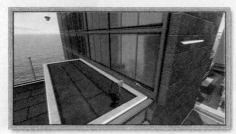

The last little pod of this group is on top of a dark grey building. Climb the building next to it with the blue windows. Jump around and to the side of the dark building to catch on to a yellow ledge and climb up. Leap to a pipe to the right to get to the roof and smash the last little pod. Finish off the big pod below and head just up the street to the next group.

Pods Set 4

Take out the first smaller pod on the ground level next to the large one.

Follow the vine leading up a light-colored building and climb the building next to it to get to the roof. Knock over a blue-backed billboard and destroy the second pod on the adjacent roof.

The third pod with the long vine going up the side of the light-colored building has to be climbed from the opposite side of that vine. Leap up to the rooftops and jump across to the scaffolding under the sunny billboard. Use the pipe on the left to make it to the roof and remove that third little pod.

Pods Set 5

The last group is by the bridge leading to HQ. Wipe out the pod on the street.

Climb the building with the light blue windows and the vine on it to get to the roof and smash the pod.

The last one is a bit tricky as the red arrow can point down from this roof when the pod is really high above on the next rooftop.

Jump across to a platform with a horizontal pipe and grind on it to the front under a billboard. Continue to go around the building, grinding on another pipe and finally climbing to the roof to destroy the last pod.

EDNA'S SHOP MISSIONS

A SHOP OF HER OWN

Mission Giver: Edna
Type: Buy/Build
Rewards: 100 Coins / 25 Sparks

In order for Edna to create her new masterpieces, she needs her workshop that is unlocked after completing the Rise and Shine mission. Simply go into the Toy Box to buy and place the building once you have completed that mission.

New Toy Unlocked: Orange Car

NOTE

The completion of Edna's Costume Shop will prevent Syndrome's Zero Point Energy weapon from working on you. That is some impressive fabric she is using!

WITNESS PROTECTION

Mission Giver: Edna
Type: Customize
Rewards: 100 Coins / 50 Sparks

Someone hanging around HQ thinks that Syndrome is after him. Pick the man up and throw him into Edna's Costume Shop to change his appearance.

WHICH WITNESS?

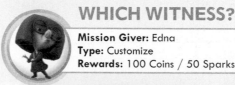

Mission Giver: Edna
Type: Customize
Rewards: 100 Coins / 50 Sparks

Syndrome has targeted one of your agency's undercover operatives. Use the compass to find the man, dressed as a construction worker, and bring him to Edna's Costume Shop for a makeover.

TECH RESEARCH MISSIONS

IT'S A SECRET

Mission Giver: NSA Agent
(suit and glasses guy at HQ)
Type: Locate
Rewards: 100 Coins / 50 Sparks

Using the compass, locate the tall building and climb up to the rooftop of the light tan building next to it. Leap onto the air conditioner and double jump up to the next air conditioner to gain access to a pipe leading to the roof of the building next door.

There is an informant in the city that you need to meet. She knows a contact inside Syndrome's organization who is willing to defect to the side of the good guys. Use the compass to find the female informant, but it is not safe to talk in the open. Follow her up to the roof and grind across two power lines to a safe area.

The mysterious defector can't speak in the city. She will meet you back at HQ.

New Toy Unlocked: HQ Research Station

The defector is waiting on a nearby rooftop on a very tall building.

NOTE

The Glide Pack and Learning to Glide missions will be unlocked if the Sensei missions were not completed.

NOTE

Three new Mayor Side Missions are now unlocked.

MAYOR SIDE MISSIONS

YACHT PARTY

Mission Giver: Cop
Type: Platforming
Rewards: 100 Coins / 50 Sparks

The mission will automatically warp you to a rooftop at the dock with the Mayor nearby. The goal is to pick up the Mayor and get him to the boat in 30 seconds. There is a blue capsule nearby that will demonstrate how to dive bomb and swoop to gain more distance and height from gliding.

A cop across from the docks will inform you that the Mayor is late for a fund-raising event and needs you to get him there fast.

The concept behind swooping is to use the speed of diving down to ricochet you back up, allowing you to go further than simply slowly gliding downward.

MAYOR MENACE

Mission Giver: Mayor
Type: Platforming
Rewards: 100 Coins / 50 Sparks

The Mayor is roaming the streets in dire straits. He has to get home before his wife or he will be in big trouble. Without asking any questions, you need to use the Glide Pack to quickly get him to his house in 45 seconds. The actual mission begins on a ledge with the Mayor's house off in the distance. The only way to get to the Mayor's house first is by gliding and swooping twice. Double jump off the ledge to get some height and swoop as you approach the two light-colored vent shafts.

After that swoop, continue gliding for a bit until you are close to his house. Do one last swoop just as you go over the street and zip up to safely land on the roof.

MAYOR OF THE SKIES

Mission Giver: Mayor
Type: Platforming
Rewards: 100 Coins / 50 Sparks

For the last time, the Mayor needs your help to meet someone for lunch because he is running late... again. How this guy ever got elected is a mystery. Still, as a hero it is your job to help all of the citizens of Metroville. You have 30 seconds to complete this mission, but it is a lot easier than the previous one. The same method of double swooping should be used, but it is a lot harder to find the target.

There is a lot more room for error on this mission and you can land on the roof or even in the alley and still have enough time to run to the target circle.

GADGETS GALORE

Mission Giver: Mirage
Type: Buy/Build
Rewards: 100 Coins

> NOTE
>
> Requires completion of the Tight Spaces mission.

Mirage managed to smuggle out some data on Syndrome's newest tech he is using, but she needs a Research Station to access it. Go into the Toy Store menu to buy it and then place the station.

GAME BASICS

CHARACTERS

POWER DISCS

PLAY SETS

TOY BOX

TOY BOX COLLECTION

ACHIEVEMENTS

SUPER RECRUITS

Mission Giver: Policeman
Type: Locate
Rewards: 100 Coins / 25 Sparks

A policeman at the HQ mentions that there is a Super at the HQ waiting to help in combat. After freeing the last hostage from The Hoarder's trap in mission Tight Spaces, the little hero will appear at the HQ near the elevator to the top. Speak to the little blue hero and recruit him to help you battle the bad guys.

> **NOTE**
>
> You must be close to the HQ to activate this mission.

EMERGENCY AT HEADQUARTERS

Mission Giver: Edna (radio)
Type: Combat
Rewards: 300 Coins / 100 Sparks
Wii Rewards: 250 Coins / 100 Sparks

The Omnidroids are invading the new headquarters. Follow the red arrows to their location and destroy them all! Keep your cool when fighting the big attack wave and jump from foe to foe as you learned from your Sensei. Whenever possible, pound on the robots and then pick them up to right before they explode to toss them at others and damage multiple Omnidroids in a single shot. This is going to be a long and difficult battle, so take your time and try to eliminate them one at a time.

 New Toy Unlocked: Ambulance

> **NOTE**
>
> Completing this mission unlocks the second round of the Sensei's missions.

SENSEI SIDE MISSIONS

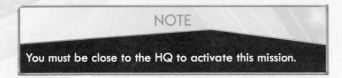

THROWING THINGS

Mission Giver: Sensei
Type: Training
Rewards: 100 Coins / 50 Sparks
Wii Rewards: 250 Coins / 50 Sparks

Pick up the green car and hurl it at the Omnidroid. Throwing things at enemies is a great way to take out groups of robots rapidly.

> **NOTE**
>
> This mission is for Mr. Incredible only.

MUSCLE MEMORY

Mission Giver: Sensei
Type: Training
Rewards: 100 Coins / 50 Sparks
Wii Rewards: 250 Coins / 50 Sparks

Mr. Incredible's super power is his super strength. This allows him to lift heavy objects and throw them—including Omidroids. Lift the holographic Omnidroid and toss it at the group of robots.

GAME BASICS

CHARACTERS

POWER DISCS

PLAY SETS

TOY BOX

TOY BOX COLLECTION

ACHIEVEMENTS

⭐ SCIENCE TO THE RESCUE

Mission Giver: Mirage
Type: Fetch/Combat
Rewards: N/A
Wii Rewards: 100 Coins / 25 Sparks

A Science Agent has a powerful weapon secretly placed in the city. Take him there and protect the weapon to buy him enough time to activate the device. Pick up the green-haired agent and hop into a car to hightail it to the weapon.

Throw the scientist into the machine to get him to work activating the device, which will trigger several waves of Omnidroids. The goal is to wipe out the robots quickly before they can damage the weapon. Stay close to the weapon to keep an eye on it and try to wipe out the opposition as quickly as possible by attacking and tossing the Omnidroids into each other.

The first wave has three Omnidroids that will be easy to handle but the next has six: three on each side of the weapon. The third wave has five foes, but it features the upgraded robots with rocket launchers and flamethrowers. Grab one of the two deadly robots and toss it at the trio of basic Omnidroids.

After that last wave the secret weapon will activate, but it needs some time to prepare to launch. Continue to protect the device and keep an eye on its yellow energy bar to make sure it doesn't get destroyed.

New Toy Unlocked: Hover Board

THE SKY HAS FALLEN

Mission Giver: Mirage (radio)
Type: Fetch
Rewards: 350 Coins / 100 Sparks
Wii Rewards: 250 Coins / 25 Sparks

The weapon worked and now Mirage wants the data core from one of the fallen Omnidroid's spawners to analyze it.

Follow the compass just up the street to confront several robots around the core. Pick up the core and quickly make your way back to the HQ to place it on the scanner in front of the Research Station.

New Toy Unlocked: Grey Utility Truck

New Challenge Available: Defeat Omnidroids 2

TECH RESEARCH PART 2

Big Island

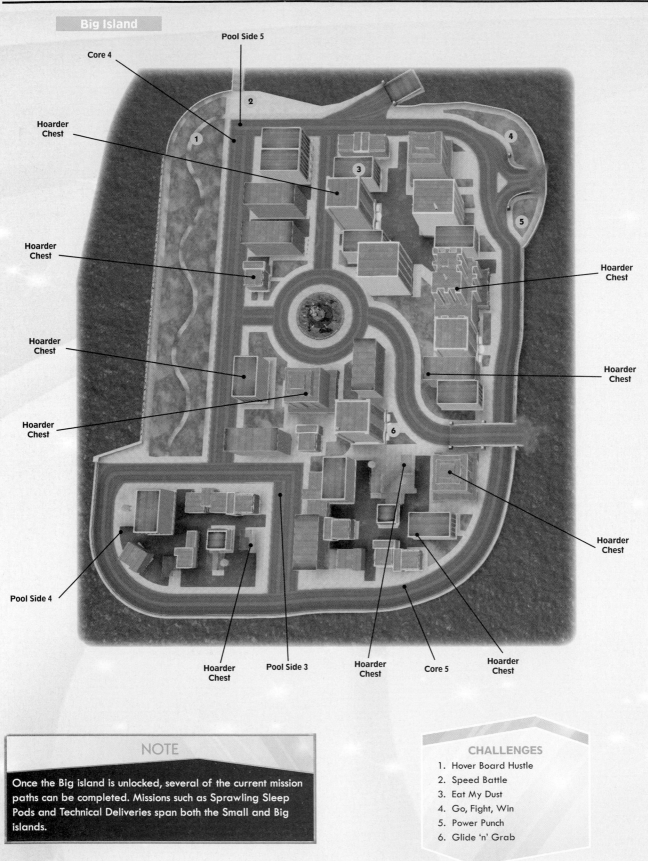

Pool Side 5

Core 4

Hoarder Chest

Hoarder Chest

Hoarder Chest

Hoarder Chest

Hoarder Chest

Hoarder Chest

Hoarder Chest

Hoarder Chest

Hoarder Chest

Pool Side 4

Hoarder Chest

Pool Side 3

Hoarder Chest

Core 5

Hoarder Chest

NOTE

Once the Big island is unlocked, several of the current mission paths can be completed. Missions such as Sprawling Sleep Pods and Technical Deliveries span both the Small and Big islands.

CHALLENGES

1. Hover Board Hustle
2. Speed Battle
3. Eat My Dust
4. Go, Fight, Win
5. Power Punch
6. Glide 'n' Grab

TECHNICAL DELIVERIES

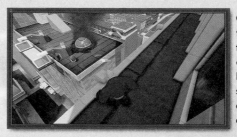

Glide or hover from the ledge to reach the adjacent building with a scaffolding and collect the tricky core.

> ## NOTE
>
> This mission requires the Glide Pack or Hover Board to get to some objectives.

 Mission Giver: Mirage (radio)
Type: Fetch
Rewards: 350 Coins / 100 Sparks

> ## NOTE
>
> The next two cores require access to the Big Island.

Thanks to the new weapon there are deactivated Omnidroid sky spawners all over the city. Track down five of them, smash them open, and return the cores to be scanned at the Research Station. The first one can be found right by the HQ. Take the elevator to the top and use the compass to drop down two levels to find it.

The fourth core is easy to find but the area is usually swarming with Omnidroids. Smash open the sky spawner and return the core to the Research Station.

The next core is on the roof of a building near the water across from the docks.

The final core is located on the Big Island on the roof of a building adorned with blue glass windows; it is near the water's edge and close to a bridge. Expect to deal with lots of Omnidroids to obtain this core.

Return to the rooftop where you met Mirage. Knock over the large blue-backed billboard to create a launching pad. From this spot, the goal is to hover or glide across the street below to the building to the left.

HOVERING HEROES

 Mission Giver: Mirage
Type: Buy
Rewards: 100 Coins / 25 Sparks

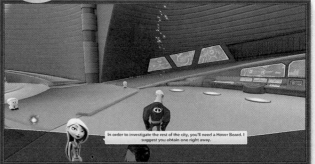

When you land, use the wall jump ability to bounce between two narrow sections of the building and gain access to the upper ledge.

This mission is a reminder to get the Hover Board. If it is already purchased the mission will instantly be completed.

GAME BASICS

CHARACTERS

POWER DISCS

PLAY SETS

TOY BOX

TOY BOX COLLECTION

ACHIEVEMENTS

MAYOR SIDE MISSION

CRASH LANDING

Mission Giver: Edna (radio)
Type: Training
Rewards: 500 Coins / 100 Sparks
Wii Rewards: 500 Coins / 25 Sparks

NOTE

Requires purchase of the Hover Board.

ISLAND GETAWAY

Mission Giver: Policeman
Type: Escort
Rewards: 100 Coins / 100 Sparks

Speak to the cop near the small pier to help escort the Mayor to the luau on his private island. This is a one-minute timed mission, so you need to act quickly. The situation can get complicated very quickly as one of Baron Von Ruthless's bombs conveniently arrives at that moment, turning the Mayor and other citizens into monsters. Look for the green arrow over the Mayor monster, attack him to change him back, and pick him up to get out of there fast.

Activate the Hover Board and drive off the pier, making sure to go over the red buoys. The Hover Board can't go over water for long, but going over the red floating objects resets the amount of time it can hover.

Something crash landed on the Big Island. Follow the compass to check it out. That "something" turns out to be a Tank Omnidroid that is bigger, tougher, and more powerful than its robot cousins. Its large metal claws will crush you if you are too close and not active enough to avoid them. But its main weapon is a long, powerful red laser. Circle around the large robot and dodge whenever necessary. The goal is to become a moving target to avoid its laser while providing a chance to attack from the side or back. Throwing objects at it can be effective, but the range of its laser can make that a bit of a challenge. There will be plenty more of these from now on, so take your time and learn how to hit and run.

 **New Toy Unlocked:** School Bus

SIDE MISSION
PROTECTIVE MEASURES

Mission Giver: Edna
Type: Escort/Combat
Rewards: 100 Coins / 200 Sparks

Toss all ten of the criminals into the paddy wagon and protect it as it drives towards the HQ. Pick up the first criminal in the black-and-white stripes to get the wagon moving.

Make sure to smash the barricades to get some much needed help from the cops. Not only do you have to protect the wagon from the Omnidroids, but you have to collect the roaming criminals at the same time. The police can be a great distraction to keep the Omnidroids busy while you collect the men in stripes.

Don't spend too much time trying to clear out every robot because they keep on coming. Get the criminals into the paddy wagon and clear

its path, including rasing the barrier on the bridge by pushing the large IN button.

SENSEI SIDE MISSION — FINAL LESSON

STRAIGHT AHEAD

Mission Giver: Sensei
Type: Training
Rewards: 100 Coins / 100 Sparks

Your training has come along nicely and it's time to learn an advanced technique from the Sensei.

This maneuver is a two-hit combo performed by pressing and briefly holding the attack button to launch the enemy in the air, and then pressing attack again to dash in and hit them as they land.

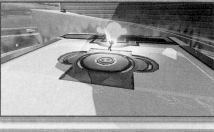

NOTE

This final training mission uses the same button commands for each character in the Play Set, but how they perform the move is unique to each character's personality.

STRANDED WITNESS

Mission Giver: Edna
Type: Fetch/Customize
Rewards: 100 Coins / 50 Sparks

An informant is hiding out on a deserted island, but it's time to bring him to the costume shop and give him a new disguise. Use the compass to find the area, but it will not be that easy to get there, unless you wait until you have the helicopter. It is possible to get to the island using the Hover Board from the small nearby pier.

Right sidebar: GAME BASICS | CHARACTERS | POWER DISCS | PLAY SETS | TOY BOX | TOY BOX COLLECTION | ACHIEVEMENTS

If you time it just right and leap at the end you can make it to the island before you sink. The truly tough part is trying to get back to that small nearby pier with the informant. This will require a very well-timed jump to land on the pier before you run out of hover power.

The other route is actually part of a challenge and uses the red buoys to keep you hovering along. This can be a little tough at first, since you need to navigate several of them in a wide arch, but it is good option if the other path is too frustrating. Once the informant is back at HQ, give him a makeover to complete the mission.

BARON VON RUTHLESS PURSUIT

RUTHLESS DISCOVERY

Mission Giver: Rick Dicker
Type: Locate
Rewards: 100 Coins / 100 Sparks
Wii Rewards: N/A

Baron Von Ruthless has been spotted in the city. Track him down using the compass, but don't expect him to stand still. The Baron will quickly move to several key locations and you must follow him. The first spot to track him is on a building with brown brick bands and light-colored squares. Climb the pipe to make it to the rooftops.

From here, climb up the side of the billboard to make your way to the very top of the roof.

The hunt continues on a rooftop in the distance. This is a great spot to use the Hover Board to quickly travel from roof to roof.

Next, climb up a few vent shafts on that roof and slide across the black wire to another building. Make your way up to the top of the roof to finally find the Baron.

BOMB SCARE

Mission Giver: Rick Dicker (radio)
Type: Locate
Rewards: 100 Coins / 50 Sparks
Wii Rewards: 100 Coins / 25 Sparks

Baron Von Ruthless is living up to his namesake by placing a bomb that transforms citizens into monsters. If you just finished Ruthless Discovery, you can simply jump from the rooftop and land right next to the bomb. Take out any Omnidroids in the area and pick up the bomb to carry it near the water's edge. The only way to destroy the Baron's bombs are to immerse them in water. This fact will be very important in later missions.

Wii NOTE

In the Wii version, there is a mission called "Clean Up Crew" after this mission.

BOMBS GALORE

Mission Giver: Rick Dicker (radio)
Type: Locate
Rewards: 500 Coins / 100 Sparks
Wii Rewards: 500 Coins / 25 Sparks

The bombs will infect any citizen that gets close to the toxic fumes, turning them into green hulking monsters. To make matters worse, Omnidroids will swarm the scene, making it tough to carry the bombs to the fountain.

You didn't think with a name like Baron Von Ruthless that he would settle for placing a single bomb, did you? He has upped the ante and placed four of them around the fountain on the Big Island. Use the compass to track them down and toss them into the fountain to destroy them.

If you start to get overwhelmed, toss the bomb in the direction of the fountain and clear out any nearby threats to make it easier to get the bomb under water without getting harassed.

New Toy Unlocked: The Incredicar

Wii NOTE

In the Wii version, there is a mission called "Waterworks" after this mission.

PRISONER CAPTURE MISSIONS PART 2
SNORING GLORIA CAPTURE

FOUNTAIN OF TROUBLE

Mission Giver: Rick Dicker
Type: Locate
Rewards: 100 Coins

Snoring Gloria has been spotted in the city near the fountain located on the larger island. Track her down with the compass and capture her.

New Toy Unlocked: Green Sports Car

PATH TO JUSTICE

Mission Giver: Rick Dicker (radio)
Type: Locate
Rewards: 2,000 Coins / 200 Sparks

Snoring Gloria is in custody but needs to be transported to the prison. This is a simple mission, because you only need to locate the paddy wagon to complete it.

GAME BASICS · CHARACTERS · POWER DISCS · PLAY SETS · TOY BOX · TOY BOX COLLECTION · ACHIEVEMENTS

⭐ ESCORTING GLORIA

Mission Giver: Policeman
Type: Locate
Rewards: N/A
Wii Rewards: 25 Coins

and worse yet the bombs will transform the citizens of Metroville into green monsters. A few quick attacks will return the citizens to normal, but try to ignore them when bombs are present and focus on getting rid of the bombs causing all the problems.

Gloria is securely in the wagon, and it's time to escort it and her to the HQ to throw her in the clink. However, this trip has an added complication—Baron Von Ruthless has placed bombs along the way. Follow the wagon and pick up the first bomb to chuck it into the fountain. The bombs must be disposed of in water to destroy them.

Battle a group of Omidroids on the bridge and follow the wagon around HQ. There are still plenty of bombs to dispose of as well as tough Omnidroids to deal with. Try to stay a little ahead of the wagon to quickly grab the bombs and toss them in the water. Even this close to the HQ there are lots of citizens that can get affected, making it difficult to protect the wagon.

Once the wagon finally makes it to the HQ, pick up Gloria and toss her into the SuperMax Prison.

The paddy wagon won't move while there are bombs around it,

New Toy Unlocked: The Incredicopter

BARON VON RUTHLESS CAPTURE

HIDEOUT DISCOVERY

Mission Giver: Rick Dicker
Type: Combat
Rewards: 100 Coins / 100 Sparks
Wii Rewards: 100 Coins / 25 Sparks

Buy The Incredicopter to blast him and change him and his hulking monsters back to normal. Get in the copter and get familiar with the controls before following the red arrows. Look for the five green monsters with a red arrow above them. You may have to fly pretty low to locate some of these targets.

Baron Von Ruthless has transformed himself into a monster and it will require heavy airborne firepower to change him back.

After the fourth target has been hit, Baron Von Ruthless will transform into a monster near the fountain. Blast him to turn him back to normal and destroy the Omnidroids in the area before landing The Incredicopter.

BARON VON RUTHLESS TRANSFORMED

Mission Giver: Cop
Type: Combat
Rewards: 2,000 Coins / 200 Sparks
Wii Rewards: 1,000 Coins

You know the drill: escort the paddy wagon back to HQ, keeping it safe from Syndrome's attacks. The twist to this mission is that you can and should use The Incredicopter to provide support from above. Keep the wagon in sight at all times and destroy the Omnidroids in the surrounding area. Also, make sure to take out the barricades and enlist the help of the local police.

Throw the final villain in prison to put an end to Syndrome's evil distraction.

 New Toy Unlocked: Zero Point Energy Gauntlet

ALL OUT ATTACK

Mission Giver: NSA Agent
Type: Combat
Rewards: 100 Coins / 200 Sparks

Omnidroids are attacking all over the city. It's time to put that new helicopter to use! This is a timed mission that requires you to destroy 32 Omnidroids in seven minutes. While the Omnidroids are in groups, they are generally small groups and they are strewn through the Big and Small Islands as well as the HQ towards the end of the mission.

What makes the mission difficult is the distance they cover as well as the different altitudes. Some are way up on the rooftops while others are hiding amongst the streets and alleyways. Changing altitude is a slow process, so avoiding going too high or low in search of your targets.

DEFEAT SYNDROME

⭐ ZERO POINT POWER UP

Mission Giver: Mirage
Type: Buy/Combat
Rewards: 100 Coins / 50 Sparks
Wii Rewards: 100 Coins

Thanks to all your valiant efforts, the secrets to Syndrome's Zero Point Energy weapon have been unlocked. Buy it at the Toy Store and get ready to put it to the test. Syndrome drops off several Omnidroids for target practice for your new toy. Get out of the middle of the group, quickly target one of the robots, and hurl it into the group of other droids. You can expect a lot of laser fire from these massive Omnidroids. The best thing you can do is get in back of them and toss them around to split them up. Don't bother trying to attack them. Just pick them up and toss them around as fast as you can.

⭐ THE FINAL SHOWDOWN

Mission Giver: Cop
Type: Combat
Rewards: 2,500 Coins / 300 Sparks
Wii Rewards: 1,000 Coins / 25 Sparks

The cop at the HQ thinks it's about time to take on Syndrome directly. Use the compass to track him down for a final confrontation. He is on top of a building that can be tricky to climb. Climb up to the rooftop near the building he is on and jump across to the scaffolding with the sunny billboard.

Slide across the black wire to the other scaffolding and climb the brown stone ledges on the light-colored building.

On the rooftop use the Hover Board to make it to the other side to find Syndrome.

ROUND 1

The first round against Syndrome starts out slow. He tosses purple energy balls that explode with a sizeable area of effect. To deal with this attack, continue running back and forth on the rooftop so he can't get a bead on you.

He will also drop two robots on the roof, but this is actually a good thing. Pick one up with your Zero Point Energy Gauntlet and hurl it at him!

ROUND 2

Syndrome will still toss the exploding spheres and drop a pair of droids on your side of the roof, but he has a trio of rocket-launching Omnidroids on his side that make it impossible to hit him until they are gone. Between Syndrome's attacks and the rocket barrage, it is very tough to have a chance to pick up one of the robots to throw at Syndrome. Remember that both of these attacks can be blocked as well as dodged.

Timing is everything during this battle and it takes practice and experience to know when you have a clean opportunity to toss one of the droids. The good news is that as you destroy the rocket-shooting robots on his side it becomes easier to launch your robots.

ROUND 3

For the final round, Syndrome calls in two laser-shooting Omnidroid Tanks. Luckily they are not as fast at firing their beams as the rocket Omnidroid Tanks were at shooting you. However, what they lose in speed they more than make up for in durability as it takes several hits from your robots to take out those laser-shooting tanks. Dodge the beams by racing back and forth, but make sure to have plenty of room to roll in either direction.

The most threatening attacks are the lasers, but there is a slight pause between when one Omnidroid finishes and the other fires. Use this delay as the prime time to toss one of your robots at them. Of course, Syndrome may throw one of his energy balls at that moment, but there is a good chance the robot you are holding would block it. It is important to note that you can use the robots on your side as a shield to some extent, but you are better off tossing them as soon as you get a chance.

When all of Syndrome's Omnidroid Tanks are gone, toss one last robot at him to finish him off.

GAME BASICS

CHARACTERS

POWER DISCS

PLAY SETS

TOY BOX

TOY BOX COLLECTION

ACHIEVEMENTS

COLLECTIBLES

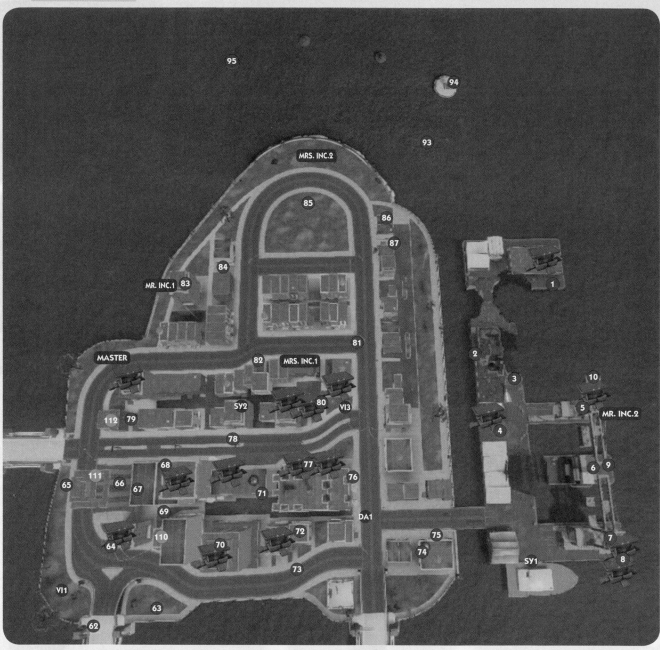

🔴 Red Capsules

Got It?	#	Unlockable Item	Zone	Location
✓	1	Fancy Suit	Metroville Docks	On the building directly to the left at the start.
✓	2	Ice Cream Cone	Metroville Docks	Around the right side of the building in front of the start.
✓	3	Boy Hero Body	Metroville Docks	Around the left side of the first building on fire.
✓	4	Surgeon Hair	Metroville Docks	Hiding behind the crates in the main area of the Big Docks.
✓	5	Surgeon Body	Metroville Docks	At the end of the dock under the first crane to the left.
✓	6	Mad Scientist Hair	Metroville Docks	On the back side of the stack of cargo crates.

HQ

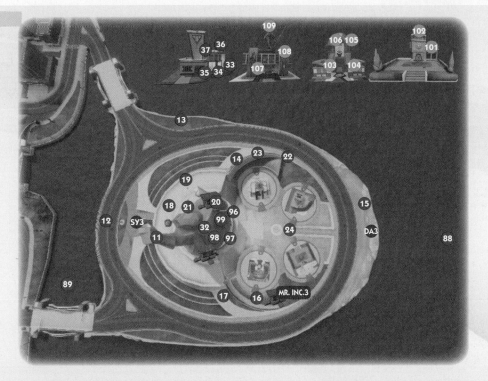

Big Island

GAME BASICS

CHARACTERS

POWER DISCS

PLAY SETS

TOY BOX

TOY BOX COLLECTION

ACHIEVEMENTS

Got It?	#	Unlockable Item	Zone	Location
✓	7	Chauffeur Head	Metroville Docks	At the end of the dock under the second crane to the left.
✓	8	Construction Foreman Body	Metroville Docks	On the top of the crane that is nearest the boat.
✓	9	Police Chief Body	Metroville Docks	In the air in between the two cranes.
✓	10	Dark Dress	Metroville Docks	On the top of the crane that is nearest the starting position.
✓	11	Cute Dress	Metroville NSA HQ	On the right side of the wall at the base of the statue.
✓	12	Medical Bag	Metroville NSA HQ	At the very top of the flagpole by the HQ.
✓	13	Boy Outfit	Metroville NSA HQ	On the grass near the bridge leading to the Big Island.
✓	14	Vest Outfit	Metroville NSA HQ	On the thin strip of grass to the left side of the HQ building.
✓	15	Grey Hair	Metroville NSA HQ	Behind the HQ building on the dirt.
✓	16	Old Lady Head	Metroville NSA HQ	Behind the HQ building to the right.
✓	17	Coffee Mug	Metroville NSA HQ	On the thin strip of grass to the right side of the HQ building.
✓	18	Bald	Metroville NSA HQ	On the first tier of the HQ building in front of the statue.
✓	19	Suit and Pocket Watch	Metroville NSA HQ	On the second tier of the HQ building in front of the statue.
✓	20	Jackhammer	Metroville NSA HQ	On the third tier of the HQ building at the feet of the statue.
✓	21	Syndrome Walls	Metroville NSA HQ	In the air by the fist of the statue.
✓	22	Mad Scientist	Metroville NSA HQ	On the right side of the wall after opening the HQ.
✓	23	Businessman Hair	Metroville NSA HQ	On the right side of the wall after opening the HQ.
✓	24	Cute Face	Metroville NSA HQ	In the air above the HQ.
✓	25	Fireman Head	Metroville Big Island	On the side of the building on the ledge facing HQ Island.
✓	26	Female Happy Face	Metroville Big Island	On the ledge in front of the billboard.
✓	27	Pink Nurse Hair	Metroville Big Island	On the building with the air vents jutting out facing HQ Island.
✓	28	Construction Foreman Head	Metroville Big Island	On the knocked down railing that over looks the fountain.
✓	29	Special Ops Body	Metroville Big Island	On the center billboard ledge by the fountain.
✓	30	Underminer Walls	Metroville Big Island	In the grass along the pathway that goes along the waterline.
✓	31	Construction Helmet	Metroville Big Island	On the power line near the fountain.
✓	32	Policeman Face	Metroville NSA HQ	Behind the elevator in the HQ.
✓	33	Mr. Incredible Captures The Hoarder	Metroville NSA HQ	In front of the Super Max Prison.
✓	34	Snoring Gloria	Metroville NSA HQ	In front of the Super Max Prison.
✓	35	Baron Von Ruthless	Metroville NSA HQ	In front of the Super Max Prison.
✓	36	Syndrome	Metroville NSA HQ	On top of the Super Max Prison.
✓	37	The Hoarder	Metroville NSA HQ	On top of the Super Max Prison.
✓	38	Nurse Outfit	Metroville Big Island	On the ledge near the billboard facing the fountain.
✓	39	Superhero Walls	Metroville Big Island	At the top of the fountain in the Big Island.
✓	40	Tiled Walls	Metroville Big Island	On the dock that is on the same side as HQ Island.
✓	41	Superhero Accent	Metroville Big Island	In the grass along the pathway that goes along the waterline.
✓	42	Boy Hero Hair	Metroville Big Island	On the window washing ledge facing away from the fountain.
✓	43	Underminer Trim	Metroville Big Island	At the top of the building that views the entire length of the curved pathway.
✓	44	Boy Hero Head	Metroville Big Island	On the roof of the building next to the road.

Got It?	#	Unlockable Item	Zone	Location
✓	45	Masked Criminal Face	Metroville Big Island	On the ledge in front of the billboard facing away from the Big Docks.
✓	46	Businesswoman Head	Metroville Big Island	In the air atop of the skyscraper with elevators that is near the fountain.
✓	47	Happy Guy Face	Metroville Big Island	On the knocked down railing that is by the skyscraper near the fountain.
✓	48	Lavender Dress	Metroville Big Island	On the roof of the building at the bend of the road that leads to the Small Island.
✓	49	Villain Hair	Metroville Big Island	On the roof ledge of the building at the bend of the road that leads to the Small Island.
✓	50	Aviator Hair	Metroville Big Island	On the side of the building near the end of the Island on the same side as the Big Docks.
✓	51	Underminer Accent	Metroville Big Island	Off the side of the tall building near the end of the Island on the same side as the Big Docks.
✓	52	Executive Head	Metroville Big Island	On the billboard ledge that is facing the water.
✓	53	Fireman Uniform	Metroville Big Island	On the edge of the building at the bend near the bridge to the Small Island.
✓	54	Power Suit	Metroville Big Island	On a power line connecting two buildings facing the Big Docks.
✓	55	Mayor Head	Metroville Big Island	On the edge of the building with elevators at the bend near the bridge to the Small Island.
✓	56	Business Dress	Metroville Big Island	At the very top of the skyscraper nearest the bridge to the Small Island.
✓	57	Hair and Glasses	Metroville Big Island	In the air off the pipe jump that is right next to the bridge leading to the Small Island.
✓	58	Stubbly Head	Metroville Big Island	On a ledge of the building at the bend of the road facing the fountain.
✓	59	Surfer Dude Hair	Metroville Big Island	On the roof of the building in between both bridges leading to the Small Island.
✓	60	Syndrome Accent	Metroville Big Island	On the knocked down railing that is at the top of the skyscraper near the bridge to Small Island.
✓	61	Mayor Hair	Metroville Big Island	Under the bridge leading to the Small Island.
✓	62	Surfboard	Metroville Small Island	Under the bridge leading to the Big Island.
✓	63	Business Casual	Metroville Small Island	To the left of the bridge leading to the Big Island.
✓	64	Face with Makeup	Metroville Small Island	On the roof of the building closest to the bridge leading to the Big Island.
✓	65	Grey Suit	Metroville Small Island	On the roof of the building closest to the bridge leading to HQ Island.
✓	66	Brushed Metal Trim	Metroville Small Island	In between two buildings along the road that leads directly to HQ Island
✓	67	Monocle and Mustache	Metroville Small Island	High up in the air next to the skyscraper near the bridge leading to HQ Island.
✓	68	Combat Trainer Head	Metroville Small Island	On the roof of the highest building along the road to HQ Island.
✓	69	Fireman Axe	Metroville Small Island	In the air off of the roof ramp between the buildings that are nested inside the two streets.
✓	70	Happy Gentleman Face	Metroville Small Island	On the upper ledge of the skyscraper that is along the road to the Big Island.
✓	71	Executive Hair	Metroville Small Island	On the window washing ledge facing the Big Island.
✓	72	Mad Scientist Body	Metroville Small Island	On the roof of the building right across from the zoo.
✓	73	Happy Lady Face	Metroville Small Island	In the air in between the zoo and the building across it.
✓	74	Chauffeur Body	Metroville Small Island	On the building with the water tower that is nearest the Big Docks.
✓	75	Fancy Handbag	Metroville Small Island	On the wall of the building with the water tower that is nearest the Big Docks.
✓	76	Combat Trainer Sword	Metroville Small Island	High up the spider wall running up the skyscraper facing the Big Docks.
✓	77	Spiked Hair and Glasses	Metroville Small Island	High up the spider wall running up the skyscraper facing the Park.
✓	78	Combat Trainer Body	Metroville Small Island	Off the antenna that is over the road that goes straight to HQ Island.
✓	79	Chauffeur Hat	Metroville Small Island	On the building closest to the bridge leading to HQ Island.
✓	80	Scientist Suit	Metroville Small Island	Near the air vent coming from the building.
✓	81	Villain Face	Metroville Small Island	Floating on the power line that is parallel to the main street headed to the Park.
✓	82	Villain Costume	Metroville Small Island	On the power line directly across from the other power line.

GAME BASICS

CHARACTERS

POWER DISCS

PLAY SETS

TOY BOX

TOY BOX COLLECTION

ACHIEVEMENTS

Got It?	#	Unlockable Item	Zone	Location
✓	83	Fireman Face	Metroville Small Island	On the roof of the building by the Park that is facing HQ Island.
✓	84	Businessman Face	Metroville Small Island	On the roof of the building nearest the Park.
✓	85	Summer Outfit	Metroville Small Island	On the ground in the middle of the Park.
✓	86	Combat Trainer Hair	Metroville Small Island	On the roof of the building to the right of the Park.
✓	87	Pig Tails	Metroville Small Island	On the ground in between two buildings to the right of the Park.
✓	88	Dark Hair and Round Glasses	Metroville NSA HQ	Out on the water behind HQ Island.
✓	89	Policeman Hair	Metroville NSA HQ	Out on the water by the bridge to the Small Island.
✓	90	Hair and Pearls	Metroville Big Island	On the water past the dock that is on the same side as HQ Island.
✓	91	Frozone Wall	Metroville Big Island	On the water past the tiny island that is near the Big Island.
✓	92	Combed Hair	Metroville Big Island	On the tiny island past the Big Island at the top of the radio tower.
✓	93	Brown Hairdo	Metroville Big Island	On the water in between the Park and the tiny island.
✓	94	Mayor Outfit	Metroville Big Island	On the tiny island behind the radio tower.
✓	95	Briefcase	Metroville Small Island	On the far left red dinghy past the Park.
✓	96	Syndrome	Metroville NSA HQ	At the base of the HQ building.
✓	97	Mr. and Mrs. Incredible	Metroville NSA HQ	At the base of the HQ building.
✓	98	Violet	Metroville NSA HQ	At the base of the HQ building.
✓	99	Dash	Metroville NSA HQ	At the base of the HQ building.

🗑 Green Capsules

Got It?	#	Unlockable Item	Zone	Location
✓	100	Metroville Townsperson Toy Pack 1	Metroville NSA HQ	At the very top of the Super Max Prison.
✓	101	Metroville Building Toy Pack 2	Metroville NSA HQ	On top of the Training Facility.
✓	102	Metroville Building Toy Pack 3	Metroville NSA HQ	On top of the Training Facility.
✓	103	Metroville Zoo Toy Pack	Metroville NSA HQ	On the Research Facility.
✓	104	Metroville Building Toy Pack 1	Metroville NSA HQ	On the Research Facility.
✓	105	Villain Toy Pack	Metroville NSA HQ	On the Research Facility.
✓	106	Hero Toy Pack	Metroville NSA HQ	On the Research Facility.
✓	107	Townsperson Toy Pack 1	Metroville NSA HQ	On Edna's Costume Shop.
✓	108	Townsperson Toy Pack 2	Metroville NSA HQ	On Edna's Costume Shop.
✓	109	Townsperson Toy Pack 3	Metroville NSA HQ	On Edna's Costume Shop.
✓	110	Metroville Decorations Toy Pack 5	Metroville Small Island	On a ledge of the building facing HQ Island near the bridge to the Big Island.
✓	111	Metroville Decorations Toy Pack 3	Metroville Small Island	On a ledge of the building near the bridge to HQ Island.
✓	112	Metroville Decorations Toy Pack 4	Metroville Small Island	On a ledge of the building near the bridge to HQ Island.
✓	113	Metroville Decorations Toy Pack 2	Metroville Big Island	On the roof of the skyscraper in between the two bridges to the Small Island.
✓	114	Metroville Decorations Toy Pack 1	Metroville Big Island	On the roof top of the building across from the billboard near the fountain.
✓	115	Metroville Plants Toy Pack	Metroville Big Island	On the building directly at the end of the curved walkway near the water.
✓	116	Metroville Decorations Toy Pack 6	Metroville Big Island	On the ledge in front of the billboard near the bridge to HQ Island.
✓	117	Metroville Building Toy Pack 4	Metroville Big Island	On the dock that is on the same side as HQ Island.

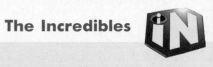

Infinity Chests/Vault

Got It?	#	Unlockable Item	Zone	Location
✓	DA1	Dash Chest 1	Metroville Small Island	At the base of the building directly in front of the street to the Big Docks.
✓	DA2	Dash Chest 2	Metroville Big Island	On the grass near the curved walkway by the fountain.
✓	DA3	Dash Chest 3	Metroville NSA HQ	At the back of the HQ building past the road.
✓	Master	Incredibles Avatar Vault - Reward 1	Metroville Small Island	On the roof of the building near the bend in the road headed to HQ Island.
✓	MR. INC.1	Mr. Incredible Chest 1	Metroville Small Island	At the base of the building near the pathway to the bridge heading to HQ Island.
✓	MR. INC.2	Mr. Incredible Chest 2	Metroville Docks	On the second level of the first crane.
✓	MR. INC.3	Mr. Incredible Chest 3	Metroville NSA HQ	On the left side of the HQ base.
✓	MRS. INC.1	Mrs. Incredible Chest 1	Metroville Small Island	On top of the building on the street headed to HQ Island with the water tower.
✓	MRS. INC.2	Mrs. Incredible Chest 2	Metroville Small Island	In the grass area by the Park.
✓	MRS. INC.3	Mrs. Incredible Chest 3	Metroville Big Island	By the bridge nearest HQ Island going to the Small Island.
✓	SY1	Syndrome Chest 1	Metroville Docks	On top of the boat in the Big Docks.
✓	SY2	Syndrome Chest 2	Metroville Small Island	On the top of the building with the white antenna.
✓	SY3	Syndrome Chest 3	Metroville NSA HQ	At the base of the stairs to the front of the statue.
✓	VI1	Violet Chest 1	Metroville Big Island	In front of the fountain.
✓	VI2	Violet Chest 2	Metroville Small Island	In the grass near the bridge headed to HQ Island.
✓	VI3	Violet Chest 3	Metroville Small Island	On the ground near the intersection.

The Incredibles Gold Stars

Got It?	#	Type	Star Names	Star Description
✓	1	Mission	Where There's Smoke...	Complete this mission.
✓	2	Mission	The Secret of Heroes Island	Complete this mission.
✓	3	Mission	Prisoner Delivery	Complete this mission.
✓	4	Mission	No More Traps	Complete this mission.
✓	5	Mission	Active Lifestyle	Complete this mission.
✓	6	Mission	Animal Pandemonium!	Complete this mission.
✓	7	Mission	Sprawling Sleep Pods	Complete this mission.
✓	8	Mission	Science to the Rescue	Complete this mission.
✓	9	Mission	The Power Within — Mr. Incredible	Complete this mission with Mr. Incredilble.
✓	10	Mission	Fantastic Elastic — Mrs. Incredible	Complete this mission with Mrs. Incredilble.
✓	11	Mission	A Burst of Speed — Dash	Complete this mission with Dash.
✓	12	Mission	Vanishing Act — Violet	Complete this mission with Violet.
✓	13	Mission	Zero Point Power Surge — Syndrome	Complete this mission with Syndrome.
✓	14	Mission	Crash Landing	Complete this mission.
✓	15	Mission	Escorting Gloria	Complete this mission.
✓	16	Mission	Baron Von Ruthless Transformed	Complete this mission.
✓	17	Mission	Technical Support	Complete this mission.
✓	18	Mission	The Final Showdown	Complete this mission.

GAME BASICS
CHARACTERS
POWER DISCS
PLAY SETS
TOY BOX
TOY BOX COLLECTION
ACHIEVEMENTS

Got It?	#	Type	Star Names	Star Description
✓	19	Collectibles	A Headache for the Hoarder	Find and break open 10 The Hoarder chests.
✓	20	Collectibles	Trap Springer	Find and break open 20 The Hoarder chests.
✓	21	Collectibles	Deliver 3 Tech Pieces	Find and deliver three tech objects to the Tech building.
✓	22	Collectibles	Find 50 red capsules	Find 50 Red Capsules.
✓	23	Challenge	Up for the Challenge	Complete ten Challenges on any difficulty.
✓	24	Challenge	Super Challenge	Complete every Challenge on any difficulty.
✓	25	Combat	Your Own Worst Enemy	Defeat an Omnidroid using another Omnidroid.
✓	26	Combat	Zero Point Hero	Defeat an Omnidroid using Zero Point Energy.
✓	27	Combat	Heavy Landing	Damage multiple Omnidroids with a single Glide Pack Dive Bomb.
✓	28	Combat	Chopper Dropper	Defeat multiple Omnidroids using a single Helicopter Bomb.
✓	29	Combat	Pulse Power	Hit multiple Omnidroids with a single EMP shot from The Incredicar.
✓	30	Combat	Omnidriod Destroyer	Destroy 50 Omnidroids.

The Incredibles Toy List

Got It?	Toys	Toy Box Export	Toy Type	Commercial
✓	Bridge 1	Yes	Unique	Yes
✓	Super Max Prison	Yes	Building	Yes
✓	Glide Pack	Yes	Prop	Yes
✓	Tech Building	Yes	Building	Yes
✓	Training Facility	Yes	Building	Yes
✓	Hover Board	Yes	Prop	Yes
✓	Edna's Costume Shop	Yes	Building	Yes
✓	Bridge 2	Yes	Unique	No
✓	Bridge 3	Yes	Unique	No
✓	Bridge 4	Yes	Unique	No
✓	Incredicar	Yes	Vehicle/Mount	Yes
✓	Townspeople Newspaper Stand	Yes	Unique	Yes
✓	Hot Dog Stand	Yes	Unique	Yes
✓	Orange Car	Yes	Unique	No
✓	Bus	Yes	Unique	No
✓	Green Sports Car	Yes	Unique	No
✓	Grey Diesel	Yes	Unique	No
✓	Pink Car	Yes	Unique	No
✓	Ambulance	Yes	Unique	No
✓	Health Upgrade 1	No	Unique	Yes
✓	Health Upgrade 2	No	Unique	Yes
✓	Incredicopter	Yes	Vehicle/Mount	Yes
✓	Mr. Incredible's Sports Car	Yes	Vehicle/Mount	Yes
✓	Zero Point Energy Toy	Yes	Held Item	Yes

Got It?	Toys	Toy Box Export	Toy Type	Commercial
✓	Townspeople #1	Yes	Townsperson	Yes
✓	Townspeople #2	Yes	Townsperson	No
✓	Townspeople #3	Yes	Townsperson	No
✓	Townspeople #4	Yes	Townsperson	No
✓	Townspeople #5	Yes	Townsperson	No
✓	SH Townspeople 1	Yes	Unique	No
✓	SH Townspeople 2	Yes	Unique	No
✓	SH Townspeople 3	Yes	Unique	No
✓	SH Townspeople 4	Yes	Unique	No
✓	Mirage	No	Mission Giver	No
✓	Sensei Townspeople	Yes	Mission Giver	No
✓	SH Townspeople 5	Yes	Unique	No
✓	Super Strength Gloves	No	Held Item	Yes
✓	Sticky Hand	No	Held Item	Yes
✓	Dash Speed Boots	No	Held Item	Yes
✓	Violet Invisibility Toy	No	Held Item	Yes
✓	Townspeople Forklift	No	Unique	No
✓	Purple Truck	No	Unique	No
✓	Ice Cream truck	No	Unique	No
✓	Super Ground Pound	Yes	Unique	No
✓	Sticky Hand Ability	Yes	Unique	No
✓	Super Speed Ability	Yes	Unique	No
✓	Invisibility Ability	Yes	Unique	No
✓	Zero-Point Energy Ability	Yes	Unique	No

The Incredibles Challenges

Got It?	Name	Location	Description	Character	Requirements		
					Easy	Medium	Hard
✓	Quick Ride	Next to the toy store	Pass through all the Challenge Gates before the time runs out.	Any	12 checkpoints in 1:00	12 checkpoints in 0:50	12 checkpoints in 0:45
✓	Violet's Race Rally	Near the bridge leading to the HQ	Pass through all the Challenge Gates as Violet before the time runs out.	Violet	11 checkpoints in 1:00	11 checkpoints in 0:50	11 checkpoints in 0:40
✓	Hovering Heroics	Near the bridge leading to the HQ	Using the Hover Board, pass through all the Challenge Gates before the time runs out.	Any-Hover Board	14 checkpoints in 0:55	14 checkpoints in 0:50	14 checkpoints in 0:45
✓	Mrs. Incredible's Collector Challenge	Near the bridge leading to the HQ	Collect as many orbs as possible as Mrs. Incredible before the time runs out.	Mrs. Incredible	20 targets in 1:10	30 targets in 1:10	40 targets in 1:10
✓	Bring the Punch	Just outside of the park going towards HQ	Defeat all the enemies before the time runs out.	Any	5 enemies in 2:00	10 enemies in 2:00	15 enemies in 2:00
✓	Syndrome's Battle Bonanza	Park	Defeat all the enemies as Syndrome before the time runs out.	Syndrome	5 enemies in 1:30	10 enemies in 2:00	10 enemies in 2:00
✓	Race Around Town	Park	Pass through all the Challenge Gates before the time runs out.	Any	8 checkpoints in 0:50	8 checkpoints in 0:35	8 checkpoints in 0:30
✓	Combat Clash	By the Park closer to the docks	Defeat all the enemies before the time runs out.	Any	2 enemies in 2:30	4 enemies in 2:30	6 enemies in 2:30
✓	Dash's Collect Mania	Main Street	Gather as many collectibles as you can as Dash before the time runs out.	Dash	20 targets in 0:50	30 targets in 0:50	40 targets in 0:50
✓	Mr. Incredible's Glide Pack Challenge	Near the bridge leading to the HQ	Gather as many collectibles as you can as Mr. Incredible and using the Glide Pack before the time runs out.	Mr. Incredible-Glide Pack	70 targets in 1:15	80 targets in 1:15	90 targets in 1:15
✓	Collect Crazy	In back of the HQ	Collect as many orbs as possible before the time runs out.	Any	70 targets in 1:15	80 targets in 1:15	90 targets in 1:15
✓	Romp Around Town	In the back of the HQ	Pass through all the Challenge Gates before the time runs out.	Any	70 targets in 1:15	80 targets in 1:15	90 targets in 1:15
✓	Blast From Above	On the other side of the road in front of the HQ	Use The Incredicopter to defeat all the enemies before time runs out.	Any-The Incredicopter	70 targets in 1:15	80 targets in 1:15	90 targets in 1:15
✓	Power Punch	Near the bridge to the Small Island	Use the Glide Pack or Hover Board to defeat all of the enemies before time runs out.	Any-Glide Pack or Hover Board	10 enemies in 3:00	14 enemies in 3:00	16 enemies in 3:00
✓	Go, Fight, Win	Near the bridge to the Small Island	Defeat the enemies before time runs out.	Any	5 enemies in 1:50	10 enemies in 1:50	15 enemies in 1:50
✓	Eat My Dust	On a rooftop	Use The Incredicopter to go through all the Challenge Gates before the time runs out.	Any-Incredicopter	16 checkpoints in 1:40	16 checkpoints in 1:30	16 checkpoints in 1:10
✓	Hover Board Hustle	Near the path extending to the water	Pass through all the Challenge Gates using the Hover Board before the time runs out.	Any-Hover Board	18 checkpoints in 1:25	18 checkpoints in 1:15	18 checkpoints in 1:10
✓	Speed Battle	Near the path extending to the water	Use The Incredicar to defeat all the enemies before time runs out.	Any-Incredicar	12 enemies in 1:00	24 enemies in 1:00	34 enemies in 1:00
✓	Glide 'n' Grab	Near the bridge leading to the Small Island near the docks	Gather as many collectibles as you can using the Glide Pack before your time runs out.	Any-Glide Pack	30 targets in 0:50	45 targets in 0:50	70 targets in 0:50

GAME BASICS CHARACTERS POWER DISCS PLAY SETS TOY BOX TOY BOX COLLECTION ACHIEVEMENTS

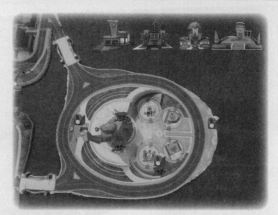

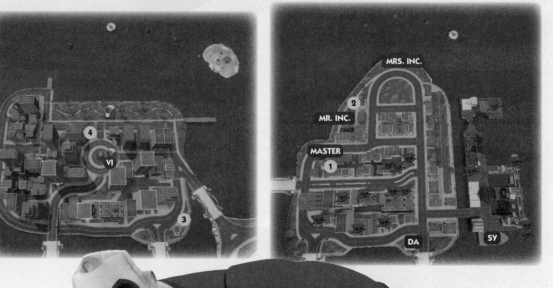

Unlockables

Got It?	Key	Unlockable Item	Type	Zone	Location
✓	DA	Dash Chest	Avatar Chest	Metroville Small Island	By the bridge near the Big Docks.
✓	Master	Incredibles Avatar Vault - Reward 1	Avatar Vault	Metroville Small Island	On the roof of the building near the bend in the road headed to HQ Island.
✓	MR. INC.	Mr. Incredible Chest	Avatar Chest	Metroville Small Island	At the base of the building near the pathway to the bridge heading to HQ Island.
✓	MRS. INC.	Mrs. Incredible Chest	Avatar Chest	Metroville Small Island	In the grass area by the park.
✓	SY	Syndrome Chest	Avatar Chest	Metroville Docks	On top of the boat in the Big Docks.
✓	VI	Violet Chest	Avatar Chest	Metroville Big Island	In front of the fountain.

Incredibles Challenges

Got It?	#	Name	Location
✓	1	Collect Crazy	Small Island
✓	2	Bring the Punch	Small Island

Got It?	#	Name	Location
✓	3	Go, Fight, Win	Big Island
✓	4	Dash's Collect Mania	Big Island

⭐ Incredibles Gold Stars

Got It?	#	Type	Name	Description
✓	1	Mission	The Secret of Heroes Island	Use the Toy Store to purchase the bridge to Heroes Park. Then open the HQ.
✓	2	Mission	Prisoner Delivery	Defend the armored paddy wagon from Syndrome's Omnidroids.
✓	3	Mission	Handling a Crowd	Complete this mission.
✓	4	Mission	Room to Breathe	Buy the Training Facility.
✓	5	Mission	Clean Streets	Buy the Super Max Prison.
✓	6	Mission	Secret Shopper	Buy Edna's Costume Shop.
✓	7	Mission	It's a Secret	Use the Compass to find the Informant.
✓	8	Mission	Bomb Squad	Find and destroy Baron von Ruthless' bombs.
✓	9	Mission	Science to the Rescue	Complete this mission.
✓	10	Mission	The Power Within — Mr. Incredible	Complete this mission with Mr. Incredilble.

Got It?	#	Type	Name	Description
✓	11	Mission	Fantastic Elastic — Mrs. Incredible	Complete this mission with Mrs. Incredilble.
✓	12	Mission	A Burst of Speed — Dash	Complete this mission with Dash.
✓	13	Mission	Vanishing Act — Violet	Complete this mission with Violet.
✓	14	Mission	Zero Point Power Surge — Syndrome	Complete this mission with Syndrome.
✓	15	Mission	Crash Landing	Complete this mission.
✓	16	Mission	Escorting Gloria	Complete this mission.
✓	17	Mission	Precious Parts	Take the Omnidroid data core to the HQ Research Station to be scanned.
✓	18	Mission	Technical Deliveries	Take all the Omnidroid data cores to the HQ Research Station.
✓	19	Mission	The Final Showdown	Complete this mission.

The Incredibles Toy List

Got It?	Toys	Toy Type	Commercial
✓	Downtown Express Bridge	Unique	No
✓	Super Max Prison	Building	Yes
✓	Glide Pack	Prop	Yes
✓	Training Facility	Building	Yes
✓	HQ Research Station	Building	Yes

Got It?	Toys	Toy Type	Commercial
✓	Hover Board	Prop	Yes
✓	Edna's Costume Shop	Building	Yes
✓	Incredicopter	Vehicle/Mount	Yes
✓	Mr. Incredible's Sports Car	Vehicle/Mount	Yes
✓	Zero Point Energy Toy	Held Item	Yes

GAME BASICS

CHARACTERS

POWER DISCS

PLAY SETS

TOY BOX

TOY BOX COLLECTION

ACHIEVEMENTS

Pirates of the Caribbean

RESCUE GIBBS AND THE MAP

Treasure Map Clock Tower Lady Navigator

3

2

1

Treasure

Mr. Gibbs Deliveries Dock

CHALLENGES

1. Buccaneer Break
2. Brawl at the Bay
3. Buccaneer Bay Ballyhoo

DOCK AND COVER

Mission Giver: Automatic
Type: Sailing
Rewards: 50 Coins / 100 Sparks
Wii Rewards: 50 Coins / 100 Sparks

Row the dinghy through town and find a safe place to dock.
Simply follow the green compass arrow and you can't miss it.

WE KNOW WHERE GIBBS BE!

Mission Giver: Pintel and Ragetti
Type: Combat
Rewards: 50 Coins / 100 Sparks

Smash through the crates with your sword and speak to Pintel and Ragetti. They know where Mr. Gibbs is (in jail), and he is critical if you ever hope to sail on a boat larger than that dinghy. Follow the men and take aim with your Flintlock Pistol to shoot open the gate.

 Keeping following the men until you run into an ambush. There are three enemies to deal with, but some quick swordplay will wipe them all out while Pintel and Ragetti work on unlocking the next gate.

⭐ RESCUE MASTER GIBBS!

Mission Giver: Pintel and Ragetti (automatic)
Type: Platforming
Rewards: 50 Coins / 100 Sparks
Wii Rewards: 250 Coins / 100 Sparks

Mr. Gibbs is being held in the fort's prison tower. Run through the open gate and follow the compass up several staircases.

 Wait for the convenient cannonball that blows away the debris blocking your path, and shoot the lock to open a gate.

 Keep climbing the stairs while wiping out small waves of enemies until you finally get to the tower that Mr. Gibbs is being held in. Climb up the metal ledges near the blue tutorial capsule and work your way up and to the left around the trestle.

Finally, drop down over the doorway and shoot open the lock on the door to set Mr. Gibbs free. Make sure to run inside the cell to grab the Vengeance Mid Hull capsule that is needed for a side mission.

THE MAP'S HIDING PLACE

Mission Giver: Mr. Gibbs (automatic)
Type: Platforming
Rewards: 50 Coins / 100 Sparks

Davy Jones is looking for the map, but luckily only Mr. Gibbs knows where it is at. Follow Mr. Gibbs and the green compass arrows to slide down a long rail.

GAME BASICS
CHARACTERS
POWER DISCS
PLAY SETS
TOY BOX
TOY BOX COLLECTION
ACHIEVEMENTS

The map is hidden in a cave above Mr. Gibbs' location. To get there, grab on to the thin edges in the mountainside and leap up to the cave.

Unfortunately, you are a bit slow retrieving the map and Maccus, a hammerhead-looking beast, grabs the map for Davy Jones. Grab the red capsule that holds the Vengeance Front Hull next to the mapless chest.

SLEW OF SIDE MISSIONS

⭐ I WANTS TO BE A NAVIGATOR

Mission Giver: Educated Townsperson
Type: Customize
Rewards: 50 Coins / 50 Sparks

A well-educated man has studied the stars and maps and is ready to join a crew as a navigator. The only problem is he doesn't look the part. Not far from the man is a shop, next to a blue tutorial capsule, that can change people's appearance. However, before he can truly look like a navigator you need the proper customizations. The navigator's hats and body pieces are located near the Challenge beacon. One is under an awning near a lamppost and the other is next to the staircase. The last piece of this puzzle is just around the corner of the customizing shop. Pick the man up and throw him into the shop to change is body, head, and hat into a navigator.

TREASURE OUTSIDE OF TOWN

Mission Giver: Pintel and Ragetti
Type: Locate
Rewards: 200 Coins / 50 Sparks

There's a treasure hidden just outside of town and a quick pan of the camera gives you a clue. Use the compass to track the treasure near an archway on the beach.

HEAVY SLEEPER

Mission Giver: Pirate Townsperson (Man 1)
Type: Delivery/Fetch
Rewards: 50 Coins / 50 Sparks

A lazy pirate complains about not wanting to do anything, but at least he is kind enough to offer the cure to his dilemma. He says the only way to motive him is to toss him in the water. Oblige the man by picking him up and throwing him into the water.

RID US O' THEM CRATES!

Mission Giver: Pirate Townsperson (Man 1)
Type: Destroy
Rewards: 50 Coins / 50 Sparks

The lazy townsperson was true to his word and a quick dunk brought him back with another mission. The man is upset about the East India Trading Company trying to set up port in his town. He wants you to destroy all five EITC crates. The closest one is right next to a red capsule with the Vengeance Rear Hull.

The next one is on a balcony in back of the building where you just smashed the first crate.

Slide across a rail to the top of a building with a red capsule that has the Vengeance Sails. Leap down to the thatched roof and jump to the balcony to find the third crate.

Go over the nearby bridge with the red smoldering wreckage and leap down the side to find the fourth one.

This final one is a short distance away at the edge of a water wheel.

YE OWN QUEST

Mission Giver: Pirate Townsperson (Man 2)
Type: Locate
Rewards: 50 Coins / 50 Sparks

If the last treasure wasn't exciting enough, now there is a special treasure with your very face on it. This treasure is actually a Vault/Chest but you don't have to open it, just get close. It is by the blue tutorial capsule.

TREASURE ON THE TRUSSES

Mission Giver: Pirate Townsperson (Man 2)
Type: Locate
Rewards: 50 Coins / 50 Sparks

One of the men rebuilding the fort mentioned that he saw treasure in the scaffolding. The chest you are looking for is near your ship and is not too far off. Jump down from your location and leap around the blockade on the stairs. Climb up the wooden scaffolding to locate the pirate chest.

GAME BASICS

CHARACTERS

POWER DISCS

PLAY SETS

TOY BOX

TOY BOX COLLECTION

ACHIEVEMENTS

TIME HAS STOPPED

Mission Giver: Pirate Townsperson (Woman)
Type: Locate
Rewards: 50 Coins / 50 Sparks

Davy Jones destroyed the clock tower, and for some reason this woman wants to see it but can't get there. Pick her up like a human taxi and carry her there.

TIME FOR VENGEANCE

Mission Giver: Pirate Townsperson (Woman)
Type: Locate
Rewards: 50 Coins / 50 Sparks

After seeing the clock tower, the woman mentions that if you collect all five parts of the ship *Vengeance* from red capsules, you can customize your own ship to look just like it. At this point you should have four parts, and the last one is by your ship. Climb up a pole to reach a high platform and rail slide across to find the Vengeance Theme on the other side.

GET A SHIP AND SET SAIL

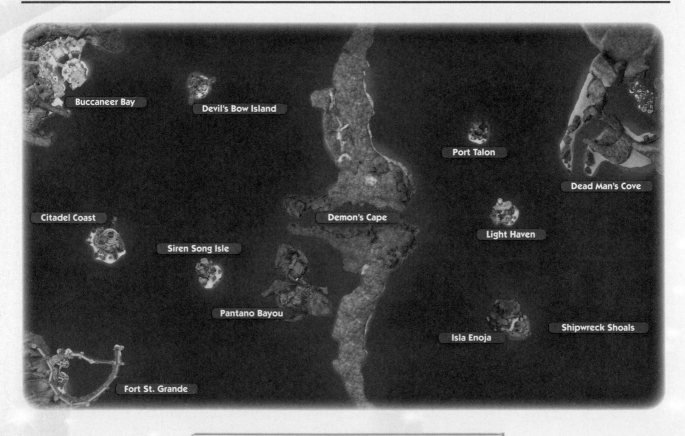

> ## NOTE
>
> If you are having trouble getting your bearings on the open sea, climb all the way to the top of the crow's nest and you can locate islands and land masses.

⭐ A CAPTAIN NEEDS A SHIP!

Mission Giver: Mr. Gibbs (automatic)
Type: Buy
Rewards: 50 Coins / 100 Sparks

The only way to go after the treasure without the map is to speak to Tia Dalma who knows the route. Of course to visit her will require a ship and the money to pay for it. Go into the Toy Store and buy the ship as long as you have 600 coins to spare.

To actually get the ship in the water, you must pick it up from the delivery platform that can be found using the compass. Shoot open the locked gate and go pick up your pirate package.

🏴 **New Challenges Available:** Brawl at the Bay (Barbossa), Buccaneer Bay Ballyhoo

 New Toy Unlocked: Player's Pirate Ship

Wii NOTE

In the Wii version, the ship automatically appears at the dock once purchased. There is no delivery platform.

BLAST YE OUT O' THE COVE!

Mission Giver: Mr. Gibbs (automatic)
Type: Ship Combat
Reward: 50 Coins

This is your first time on a big ship and you need to pay attention to all the tutorials to really master controlling the vessel and using its many views. Once you get the hang of it, get to the task at hand. There is a bunch of debris blocking your ship from leaving the cove. Open fire with the cannons to clear a way out.

WHAT'S OUR HEADING?

Mission Giver: Mr. Gibbs (automatic)
Type: Sailing
Reward: 200 Coins

Set a course to visit Tia Dalma. She is the only person who can help you get your hands on the treasure before Davy Jones. She lives on an island called Pantano Bayou, which is right across from Buccaneer Bay, and the compass will guide you there. However, you can't dock until the attacking pirates have been sunk.

SHIP UPGRADE SIDE MISSIONS

NOTE

Upgrades to your ship will happen automatically after you pick up the pirate package. However, new cannons must be swapped out with current ones at each station to take advantage of their unique abilities. Also, cannons can fire a single shot by pressing the attack button but if you hold that button you can charge up the attack and the cannons will fire several shots at once.

NEW CANNONS

LONG RANGE CANNONS, A MUST!

Mission Giver: Crew (Headband)
Type: Buy
Reward: 50 Sparks

One of the crew points out that far away ships would be a lot easier to hit if you bought the Long Range Cannon. The man is right; the increased range is very helpful for firing on ships that are normally too far away and can't fire back. This is a great upgrade and is well worth the coins. Go into the Toy Store and buy it as soon as you can afford to. After buying the cannon, you have to open the package and actually have to swap the cannon by going close to it and pressing the button to flip it to the next cannon.

New Toy Unlocked: Long Range Cannon

GET YE A FLAMETHROWING CANNON

Mission Giver: Crew (Headband)
Type: Buy
Reward: 50 Sparks

Buy the Flamethrower Cannon and shoot flaming fury at anyone unwise enough to get within range.

 New Toy Unlocked: Flamethrower Cannon

THEY SAYS YER A RAT, SIR!

Mission Giver: Crew (Headband)
Type: Buy
Rewards: 1,000 Coins / 50 Sparks
Wii Rewards: 750 Coins / 50 Sparks

Some braggart pirates told your crew that they could easily shoot your vessel out of the sea. Follow the compass to locate the braggart pirates and prepare to take on three waves of assault ships. This is a very rough battle and the only good news is that your ship will recover in between battles. The first wave has five ships.

⭐ AIN'T NO CANNON LIKE THE TRIPLE SHOT!

Mission Giver: Crew (Headband)
Type: Buy
Reward: 50 Sparks

Triple Shot Cannons are not just three cannons shooting at once, the cannons alternate shots, essentially giving you rapid-fire machine-gun-like firepower.

 **New Toy Unlocked:** Triple Shot Cannon

UPGRADE YOUR FIREPOWER

HIT THEM WITH ANOTHER BROADSIDE!

 Mission Giver: Crew (Bald with eye patch)
Type: Buy
Reward: 50 Sparks

The bigger ships will be easier to take on with more Broadside Cannons. Essentially this can double your fire and is a must for any real pirate that expects to survive on the high seas.

 New Toy Unlocked: Extra Broadside Cannons

MORE GUNPOWER!

 **Mission Giver:** Crew (Bald with eye patch)
Type: Buy
Reward: 50 Sparks

The Blunderbuss is an upgraded gun that packs a big wallop. A single shot from this weapon can send enemies flying into the air.

 **New Toy Unlocked:** Blunderbuss

UPGRADE YOUR SHIP

A BETTER RUDDER, CAP'N

 Mission Giver: Crew (Hat and beard)
Type: Buy
Reward: 50 Sparks

A new rudder will allow the ship to turn faster in battle and the increased maneuverability will help position your ship to maximize your firepower.

 New Toy Unlocked: Rudder

A NEW HELM, SIR!

Mission Giver: Crew (Hat and beard)
Type: Buy
Reward: 50 Sparks

Get a new helm to move fast and stay quick while turning the ship.

 New Toy Unlocked: Helm

GAME BASICS · CHARACTERS · POWER DISCS · **PLAY SETS** · TOY BOX · TOY BOX COLLECTION · ACHIEVEMENTS

WE NEED US SOME FISH!

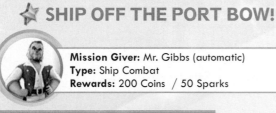

Mission Giver: Crew (Hat and beard)
Type: Buy
Reward: 50 Sparks

New Toy Unlocked: Fisherman

A member of the crew intelligently points out that the sea is full of fish and it makes sense to get a fisherman onboard to catch them for the crew. Go into the Toy Store to buy the Fisherman.

SHIP COMBAT SIDE MISSION

⭐ SHIP OFF THE PORT BOW!

Mission Giver: Mr. Gibbs (automatic)
Type: Ship Combat
Rewards: 200 Coins / 50 Sparks

Upon entering the open seas you will almost immediately be drawn into your first naval battle.

Hopefully you had enough coins to upgrade your cannons or buy the long-range version. Even without any upgrades this won't be a tough battle if you can circle around the ships and blast them in the front while you unload with your Broadside Cannons. There is one wave of three ships and you will know the battle is won when you hear Mr. Gibbs bellow, "Patch her up lads".

MASTS AT THE READY

Mission Giver: Mr. Gibbs (automatic)
Type: Buy
Reward: 50 Sparks

Purchase the Foremast Sail from the Toy Store to increase the speed of your ship.

New Toy Unlocked: Foremast Sail

SHIP CUSTOMIZING MISSIONS

⭐ A FACELIFT FOR THE SHIP!

Mission Giver: Crew (Big hair)
Type: Buy
Rewards: 500 Coins / 50 Sparks

A member of the crew is itching to get the ship a new look. He suggests that as you travel, pick up new pieces to make the boat look ship-shape. Change the appearance of the ship by going to the delivery area on the boat and selecting Customize. As you gain more pieces from capsules, you will be able to make additional alterations to your ship. You should have several themes available at this point. Change to any one of them to complete the mission.

ONE SHIP, MANY FACES

Mission Giver: Crew (Big hair)
Type: Buy
Rewards: 1,000 Coins / 50 Sparks

This guy must have been an interior decorator before becoming a pirate. He wants you to collect more pieces to develop more looks for the ship. To meet the requirements of this mission you need to collect five different complete themes, which will require you to visit many of the small islands. Check out the collectibles map and data at the end of the chapter to find all of the pieces.

DARKEN THE SAILS

Mission Giver: Crew (Big hair)
Type: Buy
Rewards: 1,000 Coins / 50 Sparks

This final makeover for the ship is to collect all the black ship pieces to turn it dark. Check out the collectibles map and data at the end of the chapter to find all of the pieces.

PANTANO BAYOU

CHALLENGES
1. Shootin' Up the Swamp
2. Pantano Bayou Dash

Statue Piece 3 · Dock · Pads · Statue Puzzle · Kraken's Bane · Dock

Dinghy · Dock · Statue Piece 2 · Dock · Statue Piece 1 · Stinky Man · Tia Dalma · Button · Cave

GAME BASICS · CHARACTERS · POWER DISCS · PLAY SETS · TOY BOX · TOY BOX COLLECTION · ACHIEVEMENTS

 FIND TIA DALMA

Mission Giver: Mr. Gibbs
Type: Locate
Rewards: 50 Coins / 100 Sparks
Wii Rewards: 100 Coins / 100 Sparks

Use the dinghy to sail up the river of the bayou to find Tia Dalma's home. Use the onboard cannon to shoot any of the nasty bomb-tossing turtles and floating debris.

Dock the ship and take out a tougher pair of enemies that can block. Rather than get into a battle of attrition, block their attack and counter with a combo.

Continue to follow the compass and climb up the wooden ladder to find Tia Dalma.

 HELP ME AN' I HELP YOU

Mission Giver: Tia Dalma
Type: Platforming
Rewards: 200 Coins / 100 Sparks

Tia tells you the importance of the map and finding the five pieces of the Kraken's Bane. However, before she tells you where to look for them she has a statue that needs fixing and you're just the pirate for the job. Jump down from her treetop dwelling and leap across a small gap.

Leap up to a thin edge on a rock wall and follow it all the way around to the left. Jump down to encounter the Stinky Man and follow the path up several plateaus.

Eventually you will find the wooden ladder that leads to the first piece of the statue—the head. Wipe out the turtle guard and grab the head, which will teleport to its proper place next to the ladder leading up to Tia Dalma.

Slide down the nearby yellow rope that places you right where the statue will reside. From here, the second piece is in the same direction as the docks, but up a narrow ramp instead.

Follow the compass to cross two small bridges and leap up a series of ledges to find the second piece of the statue—a skull-like hunk of stone.

Run around the corner of the tree to find a rope that you can slide down to reach a stone structure in the middle of the swamp. Climb up the stony ruins and use the rail slide technique once more to reach the final piece. Take note of the nearby gate with a bomb symbol on it. You can't open these types of doors yet, but on your return trip you will have the ability to do so.

The statue will re-form near the base of the ladder to Tia Dalma. Go back to her now that it has been restored and learn about the five pieces of the Kraken's Bane.

SIDE MISSION

HE SMELLS OF FETID CHUM

Mission Giver: Stinky Man (Man in hat)
Type: Fetch
Rewards: 50 Coins / 50 Sparks

A man has been fishing for days on end and smells like low tide on a hot day. Pick him up and toss him in the swamp to clean him off.

THE FIRST PIECE OF THE KRAKEN'S BANE

⭐ DE FIRST PIECE O' DE BANE

Mission Giver: Tia Dalma
Type: Platforming
Reward: None

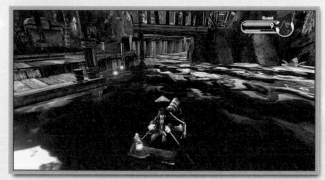

The five pieces of the Kraken's Bane is your only hope to defeat Davy Jones. Now that Tia Dalma is satisfied with your efforts, she tells you that the first piece is located in the ruins and the compass will guide you there. Jump down from her tree house and hop back in the dinghy. Tia has raised a water gate that grants access to the ruins and it's time to row, row, row your boat to check them out.

As you sail through the bayou, shoot the floating debris and blow up the bomb-chucking turtles as you go.

Dock the boat and go up the ramp or the nearby ladder to the ridge above. There is a lady here offering the Missin' Me Sister side mission as well as a gate that requires pressing a hidden button to gain access.

GAME BASICS

CHARACTERS

POWER DISCS

PLAY SETS

TOY BOX

TOY BOX COLLECTION

ACHIEVEMENTS

Drop the lady off by her sister and climb the snake rope near the gate right next to the blue tutorial capsule. At the top of that ridge is an IN button that opens the gate below. There is a bunch of booty in the little cave you just unlocked as well as the El Caleuche Rear Hull.

Welcome to your first puzzle! There is a large statue in the center of this area that must be rotated into the proper position to get to the piece of the Bane at the top. Standing on the pads placed around this statue will rotate its sections. To solve the puzzle, you have to notice which sections move as you step on each pad.

The pad in front of the statue rotates the top two segments counterclockwise 90 degrees.

Back on the trail of the first Bane piece, go into the temple ruins and wipe out several swordsmen and a bomb-throwing turtle. You are safe from the bombs as long as you stay under the roof of the ruins and that is a great spot to wipe out the swordsmen. When they are gone, block any incoming explosives until you wall jump up to the turtle and take it down.

Jump up a few ledges and slide across a line to get to the second pad that spins the entire statue counterclockwise.

The third pad on the left (from where you first entered) rotates the bottom two segments counterclockwise 90 degrees.

Now that you know how the pads move the statue, the first objective is to line up the statue so all the faces are aligned. This can be done by getting two pieces correct and then spinning those two in order to line up with the third. Start by trying to line up the bottom and middle pieces by repeatedly stepping on the center pad.

Run down a long ramp and break out the Flintlock Pistol to shoot a few enemies in the distance. The gun is a great weapon at long range, but you have to be pretty quick on the draw or the swordsman will charge you and cut you down. There is another bombable lock you can't open in this area, but continue your journey under the ruins.

With the bottom two pieces aligned, go to the pad on the left and turn both of these pieces until they line up with the top.

After all pieces are lined up, go to the pad on the right across the wire and keep turning it until the entire statue is in the correct position.

The spherical top of the statue will blow apart, revealing the first piece of the Kraken's Bane. The faces of the statue will act as ledges you can climb to reach it.

New Toy Unlocked: Atlas Blade

New Challenge Available: Pantano Bayou Dash

SIDE MISSION

MISSIN' ME SISTER

Mission Giver: Female Townsperson (Woman with hair net)
Type: Fetch
Rewards: 50 Coins / 50 Sparks

The woman is in dire straits because her sister needs her and apparently she has lost the ability to walk. She needs you to pick her up and carry her to her sister near the docks. It's a short trip and all you need to do is hoist her overhead and drop off the edge near the ladder to find her sister.

DERE ARE MORE PIECES!

Mission Giver: Tia Dalma (automatic)
Type: Locate
Reward: 100 Sparks

Ride the wires all the way down to the dock area where Tia Dalma awaits you. The next piece of the Bane is at Fort St. Grande on the other side of Demon's Cape. The rocks blocking the entrance to the Demon's Cape will crumble into the sea to allow passage into the mysterious area.

A metal gate will open allowing you to leave.

NOTE

This opens two mission paths that send you in search of the rest of the pieces of the Kraken's Bane. One path takes you to Fort St. Grande (It's At Fort St. Grande!) and the other leads through Demon's Cape (Demon's Cape Sounds Invitin'), which has two more missions.

Wii NOTE

In the Wii version, Demon's Cape is not present. Therefore, you do no sail through it and the missions at Demons Cape are not available.

TIA DALMA SIDE MISSIONS

LOST ME SOME LIGHT

Mission Giver: Tia Dalma
Type: Fetch
Rewards: 200 Coins / 50 Sparks

The Ore of Light is a powerful metal that glows. Tia Dalma wants your help collecting five pieces that are located around her hut. Jump up on the top of her house to collect the first and leap down for the second.

The third one is on the tip of a branch and the fourth is near the right side of the house.

The final one is on a little platform on a branch above the tree house.

DIS' SWAMP IS A MESS!

Mission Giver: Tia Dalma
Type: Destroy
Rewards: 200 Coins / 50 Sparks

Clean up all the wreckage littering the island and Tia Dalma will give you a reward. Go back to the dinghy and follow the compass to navigate the swamps and shoot six piles of debris.

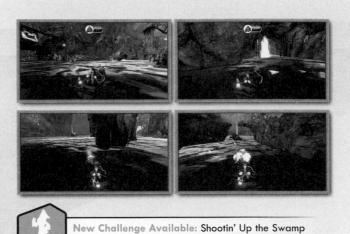

 New Challenge Available: Shootin' Up the Swamp

YOU WAN' MAGIC? SO DO I

Mission Giver: Tia Dalma
Type: Locate
Rewards: 500 Coins / 50 Sparks

Tia Dalma's Magic Rune is on a small island, but you can't get there yet.

This mission leads to Port Talon Island. Tia Dalma will greet you at the entrance to a cave, and when you blow up the fiery mess in the middle and open the chest, the gates will slam closed. There are three pirates to take down if you want to leave this cave with the Magic Rune.

GAME BASICS

CHARACTERS

POWER DISCS

PLAY SETS

TOY BOX

TOY BOX COLLECTION

ACHIEVEMENTS

NOTE

This next mission unlocks when you return to Pantano Bayou and speak to Tia Dalma after collecting the rune she requested.

⭐ RID ME O' DEM PIRATES!

Mission Giver: Tia Dalma
Type: Ship Combat
Rewards: 1,000 Coins / 50 Sparks

After completing that rune fetching mission, return to Tia Dalma for one last side mission. Several pirate ships have swarmed Pantano Bayou and she needs you to get rid of them.

There are three waves of ships to deal with and it is a good idea to move out a bit further to create some distance and let the range of your cannons keep them at bay. Also, don't forget to use your power-up items you earned from other missions. They can easily wipe out one ship while you focus your guns on another.

Wii NOTE

In the Wii version, there are three side missions you must complete before this misson. They are "Lost Me Some Light", "Dis' Swamp is a Mess", and "You Wan' Magic? So do I.

FORT ST. GRANDE

Crate Side Missions

2nd Piece of Kraken's Bane

Fort

CHALLENGES
1. Gatherin' Grande
2. Rally on the Fort

IT'S AT FORT ST. GRANDE!

Mission Giver: Tia Dalma
Type: Locate
Rewards: 200 Coins / 100 Sparks

This mission will be completed when you get close to Fort St. Grande.

SEND THEM TO THE DEPTHS!

Mission Giver: Mr. Gibbs
Type: Combat
Reward: 500 Coins

Other ships are already circling Fort St. Grande and they happen to be Navy ships. If you can destroy them you can salvage the pieces to make your boat look like one from the Royal Navy. There are two waves of ships to destroy and it's best to keep moving to avoid taking too much damage in each wave. Wipe out the first wave of three ships and prepare for the next battle.

Wave two has only one ship to deal with, but it has a lot of Broadside Cannons.

GOIN' IN UNDER COVER

Mission Giver: Crew (Big hair)
Type: Customize
Rewards: 200 Coins / 100 Sparks

To sneak into Fort St. Grande and infiltrate it, make your boat look like a Royal Navy vessel by customizing it from the ship menu and selecting the Royal Naval Theme Pack. Dock at the fort under cover and disembark to complete the mission.

WE BE IN THE NAVY NOW

Mission Giver: Pirates (automatic)
Type: Locate/Combat
Rewards: 200 Coins / 100 Sparks

When you set foot on land, a mission will automatically appear to get to the top of the fort. Even though your ship is camouflaged, your character is not. It is probably a good idea to avoid the naval townspeople and go around the ledges to the left.

Take the long way around to the fort by following the outside perimeter close to the city wall and climbing up a rickety-looking ladder.

Continue the journey to the top of the fort, climbing another ladder. Davy Jones' crew will assault the city. Jump up on some crates and climb a ladder up the side of a small tower to reach a ledge at the top of the fort.

DEFEND THE FORT!

Mission Giver: Pirates (automatic)
Type: Combat
Reward: 100 Sparks
Wii Rewards: 500 Coins / 100 Sparks

At the top of the fort, Davy Jones' men will greet you with swords. There is a new enemy with extra armor along with a pair of swordsmen. Try to knock the swordsmen off the ledge you are on or wipe them out quickly to deal with the new enemy that is the real threat. This new oyster-looking foe has a very long sword that adds to its range when using its leaping attack. Don't take any chances with this tough enemy—simply block and wait for it to attack, then counterattack with a three-hit combo.

Go inside the fort tower and leap up the wooden support beams and binding rope to make it to the top next to an IN button.

Hit the button to open the gate and continue your ascension, climbing a wooden structure to reach the very top of the fort.

Waiting for you on the top of the fort is Maccus, the one who stole the map back in Buccaneer Bay. Block and wait for Maccus to stop attacking—Maccus can strike three times in a row—before you counterstrike with a two-hit combo of your own.

Maccus' other attack is a rolling move that ends with the hammerhead leaping out at the end. If you can dodge this move, Maccus is very vulnerable to strikes on his back while he is stunned.

⭐ SECOND PIECE O' THE KRAKEN'S BANE

Mission Giver: Tia Dalma (automatic)
Type: Combat
Rewards: 2,000 Coins / 250 Sparks

Make your way back down using the rail slide technique several times and confront Maccus once again. He won't do the rolling attack here, but he has a new trick that consists of shooting you at close range. Block this attack as well as his sword swipes and resort to countering.

After taking enough damage, you can make a break for the ladder nearby and finally find the chest with the second piece of the Kraken's Bane. At the end of the mission is another ship upgrade that is a great buy for making travel quicker on the open seas.

GAME BASICS

CHARACTERS

POWER DISCS

PLAY SETS

TOY BOX

TOY BOX COLLECTION

ACHIEVEMENTS

New Toy Unlocked: Speed Burst

As soon as you set sail from Fort St. Grande, expect the Royal Navy to engage you in ship-to-ship combat. There are only a few ships to deal with, and if you'd rather not fight use the Speed Burst to run away.

New Challenges Available: Gatherin' Grande and Rally on the Fort

SIDE MISSION

FIGHTIN' FISH FOR THE FORT

Mission Giver: Generic Pirate man and woman - Automatic after returning to the fort after getting the Kraken pieces from Dead Man's Cove and Shipwreck Shoals
Type: Combat
Reward: 500 Coins / 50 Sparks

Head up to the top tier of the fort to battle Davy Jones's crew. There are a lot of fishmen to deal with and it is a good idea to block to prevent being overwhelmed. Wipe them out one at a time to even the odds.

JOURNEY TO DEMON'S CAPE

⭐ DEMON'S CAPE SOUNDS INVITIN'

Mission Giver: Tia Dalma
Type: Locate
Rewards: 500 Coins / 100 Sparks

As soon as you emerge from the Demon's Cape, a bunch of pirates will attack. Circle around the ship and try to avoid lining up side by side. Hit the enemy at the front of their ship where they have fewer cannons.

Set sail through the dark and mysterious passage on Demon's Cape. After sailing through the entrance it will automatically put you on the other side of the sea.

New Toy Unlocked: Mizzen Mast Sail

NOTE

There are two paths to take after going through the Demon's Cape and each one holds a piece of the Kraken's Bane. Head out to Dead Man's Cove (Off to Dead Man's Cove!) or the Shipwreck Shoals (Da Next Piece Awaits Ye).

FIND THE SHIPWRECK SHOALS

DA NEXT PIECE AWAITS YE

Mission Giver: Tia Dalma
Type: Buy
Rewards: 500 Coins / 100 Sparks

After sailing through the Demon's Cape, make your way to the Shipwreck Shoals to find the next piece of the Kraken's Bane.

WHO NEEDS VOODOO? YOU DO

Mission Giver: Tia Dalma
Type: Buy
Rewards: 100 Sparks

Set sail through the dark and mysterious passage on Demon's Cape. After sailing through the entrance, it will automatically put you on the other side of the sea. Tia Dalma will chime in about a very special type of cannon that can be purchased. This is not an optional upgrade, and is required in order to protect Tia Dalma as she pulls the wreckage from the sea.

Buy the cannon, open the package, and make sure those cannons are active for the next mission. The only way to take down the ghostly sunken ships is with the Voodoo Cannon.

New Toy Unlocked: Voodoo Cannon

⭐ KEEP THE SEA WITCH SAFE

Mission Giver: Tia Dalma
Type: Buy
Rewards: 1,000 Coins / 100 Sparks

Blast the attacking sunken ships so Tia Dalma can get the piece of the Kraken's Bane. There are nine ships to sink, so don't expect a quick battle to get the next piece. For a real thrill, man one of the Voodoo Cannons yourself and shoot ghostly skulls at the enemy ships.

NOTE

Tia Dalma will raise a sunken shipwrecked island right out of the sea, but it won't stay for long. Search the island for the next piece of the Kraken's Bane quickly.

The pieces for the Sunken Ship Theme are located on this island, and you need to make sure you collect them all before you leave.

GAME BASICS

CHARACTERS

POWER DISCS

PLAY SETS

TOY BOX

TOY BOX COLLECTION

ACHIEVEMENTS

FIND THE NEXT PIECE ON SHIPWRECK SHOALS

Tia Dalma

Piece of the
Kraken's Bane

CHALLENGES

1. Scurry on the Shipwreck

ON THE SHIP O' THE DEAD

Mission Giver: Mr. Gibbs
Type: Locate
Rewards: 200 Coins / 100 Sparks

The sunken ship island will only last for a short time. Disembark your ship and search the outlining area of the island for capsules before you make your way to the main path.

⭐ BANE FROM BENEATH

Mission Giver: Mr. Gibbs
Type: Platforming
Rewards: 2,000 Coins / 250 Sparks

Leap up a few ledges and climb up the ropes to the top tier. At the top, make sure to grab the Sunken Ship Theme in a capsule to the left.

Go up a few more ledges and use the Blunderbuss to blow away some pirates. Look out for the bomb-tossing turtle that has as much range with its bombs as you have with your gun.

Leap up another web of ropes and climb hand over hand to collect the Sunken Shipwreck Rear Hull from a red capsule. Leap up the ledge to find  the chest with the next piece of the Kraken's Bane.

 Opening the chest allows you to collect Calypso's Rage, which is one of several power-ups that can be placed on the ship to provide a new feature. This one allows you to create a storm that turns the sea against your enemy.

New Toy Unlocked: Calypso's Rage

BACK TO ME SHIP!

Mission Giver: Mr. Gibbs
Type: Platforming
Rewards: 200 Coins / 100 Sparks

Grabbing the Kraken's Bane will trigger the island to slowly start to sink, and it's time to get out of there fast. Slide down a few wooden poles to get off the sinking island, but only after you have all five pieces of the Sunken Ship Theme.

 Even though most of the island will sink, the challenge Scurry on the Shipwreck will still be available.

GAME BASICS   CHARACTERS   POWER DISCS   **PLAY SETS**   TOY BOX   TOY BOX COLLECTION   ACHIEVEMENTS

DEAD MAN'S COVE

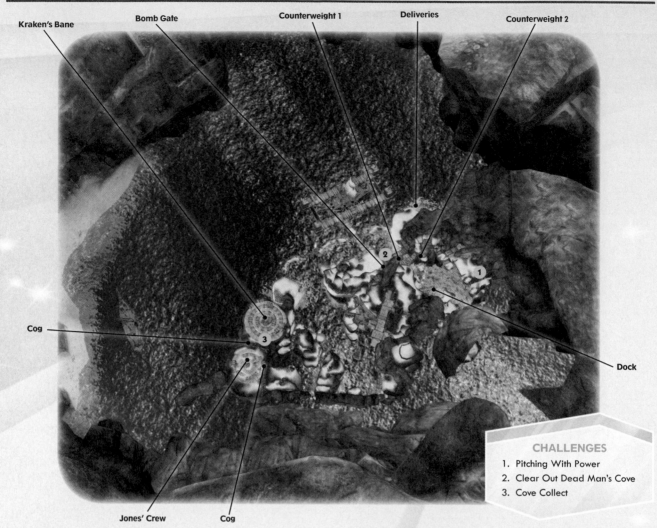

Kraken's Bane
Bomb Gate
Counterweight 1
Deliveries
Counterweight 2
Cog
Dock
Jones' Crew
Cog

CHALLENGES
1. Pitching With Power
2. Clear Out Dead Man's Cove
3. Cove Collect

OFF TO DEAD MAN'S COVE!

Mission Giver: Tia Dalma (automatic)
Type: Locate
Rewards: 500 Coins / 100 Sparks
Wii Rewards: 200 Coins / 100 Sparks

Another piece of the Kraken's Bane is at Dead Man's Cove. You must pass through the Demon's Cape to get there and sail deep inside the cover to find this island.

NOTE

In the Wii version, you do not sail through Demon's Cape to get to Dead Man's Cove.

BLASTING IS THE ONLY WAY!

Mission Giver: Pintel and Ragetti
Type: Buy
Reward: 200 Coins

Remember those locks with the bomb symbol on them? Well you can finally open them once you purchase and pick up the Pirate Bomb.

Equip your new tool and teach that locked gate a lesson for trying to keep you out. Blow it up with a bomb, and remember to go back to the

other places you might have been shut out from.

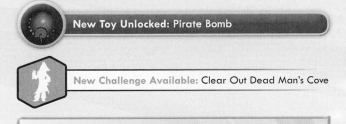

New Toy Unlocked: Pirate Bomb

New Challenge Available: Clear Out Dead Man's Cove

NOTE

In the Wii version, the bombs automatically appear in your pack/tools after purchase.

KNOCK REALLY HARD. SAVVY?

Mission Giver: Pintel and Ragetti
Type: Buy
Rewards: 200 Coins / 100 Sparks

First Counterweight

To get around at the cove, and the other side of the island, you need a boat. But there isn't one waiting for you as there was back at the Bayou. Follow the compass to the docks, but you need to remove the counterweights to allow passage. The first step is to go through a long tunnel until you emerge back out in the sunlight.

The only way to get past these junk-filled areas is to use the Pirate Bomb to blow up the mess. The red color in the junk heap is dead giveaway that it can be blown up.

The Pirate Bombs can also be used on the red somewhat-rusted-looking bars to destroy them and reveal a thin ledge in the rock.

Leap up the ledge when it is clear and jump up to the upper walkway. Follow the wooden road to the right and blow up the pile of junk, then blow up the gate with the bomb symbol around the corner.

Several of Jones' men will rush you, but this is a great chance to use the Pirate Bombs to blow them to smithereens before they even get close. The bombs are very powerful, but they follow a large arc that only makes them useful at a distance.

Continue through the gates the pirates came out of and toss a bomb to knock out the first counterweight.

Second Counterweight

Starting from the docks, run behind Pintel and Ragetti to go up a series of plateaus. Leap across a split in the path and slide down near the docks on the opposite side you started from.

A bunch of pirates will greet you, but if you stay on the higher ledge and drop bombs on them, they will never get a chance to touch you.

Run through the gate they came out of and leap up a ledge to a spot where you can blow up some cluttered junk on the right side.

When it is gone, go down that path and blast open a pair of bombable gates.

The gate to the left leads to the second counterweight that can be blown up to finally drop the blockade.

Return to the dock and get into the dinghy to row it through the newly opened passage.

Follow the compass and blast any enemies you see until you can park the boat at the next dock, which of course is full of enemies.

Leap up a series of ledges and destroy the clutter on the side of the rocky pillar. Jump to this pillar once it is clear and move along a ledge to the right.

Blow up a few piles of burning junk to clear a path. Remove the clutter on a rocky wall to allow you to climb along the ledge to the right.

Wipe out the infestation of pirates and perform a wall jump on the narrow passage to reach the top level near the fort.

UP TO THE RUINS

Mission Giver: Pintel and Ragetti
Type: Platform
Reward: 200 Coins

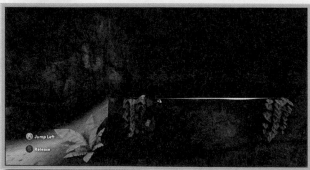

To get to the fort, blow up some rubble and use the ledge to the right to find the Cursed Theme Pack. Continue up the ramp where the debris once was.

FIGHTIN' THE FISH FACES

Mission Giver: Pintel and Ragetti
Type: Combat
Reward: 200 Coins

Davy Jones' crew is looking for the piece of the Kraken's Bane too. You have to fight them in the old ruined fort to beat them to it.

Pirates of the Caribbean

However, before you get into the fort, you have to open the door. This is a simple task considering the cog you need is right by you and a green arrow will hover over it. Pick up the old cog and place it near the others on the wall next to the IN button.

When the cog is in place, press the IN button and enter the circular arena for a big battle with Jones' men. Start out the fight by tossing some bombs at the enemies before the swordsmen charge you.

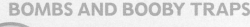

Continue to run and use bombs at long range for as long as you can, but the oyster-looking pirate will track you soon enough. Block its incoming attacks and counter, but only when you are safe from the bombing turtle nearby.

BOMBS AND BOOBY TRAPS

 Mission Giver: Pintel and Ragetti
Type: Combat
Rewards: 500 Coins / 100 Sparks

Find the cog to solve the gate puzzle and get to the piece of the Kraken's Bane. The cog is on a small platform. Pick it up and put it with the others on the wall. Push the IN button and open the gate.

 New Challenge Available: Pitching With Power

SCHOOLS OF FISH TO FIGHT

 Mission Giver: Pintel and Ragetti
Type: Combat
Rewards: 500 Coins / 100 Sparks

It's time to take down Maccus and several more of Jones' crew. When the gate is open, don't charge into the next area—instead let them come to you. Run away to get some distance and open fire with the Blunderbuss or Pirate Bombs. Try to do as much damage as possible from a distance so that you don't get overwhelmed by their superior numbers.

Maccus will be the last foe standing. Battle him the same way you have before by blocking and countering when he is done with his assault.

⭐ ANOTHER PIECE BE HERE

 Mission Giver: Pintel and Ragetti
Type: Combat
Rewards: 2,000 Coins / 250 Sparks

The goal is to get to the top of the moving platforms, but first you need to find another cog to get things moving—literally. Smash a bunch of crates by a red capsule to find the cog.

GAME BASICS · CHARACTERS · POWER DISCS · **PLAY SETS** · TOY BOX · TOY BOX COLLECTION · ACHIEVEMENTS

SIDE MISSION

FIND SOME SHINE!

Mission Giver: Tia Dalma (automatic)
Type: Locate
Rewards: 1,000 Coins / 50 Sparks

Getting to the top of the center pillar is not that difficult if you take your time and let the moving platforms line up. Jump on the lowest moving platform and wait for the next taller platform to get close enough to jump to.

One of the crew heard rumors that someone stashed treasure on Dead Man's Cove. There is only one chest to search for and it is in a circular area where you went to take care of one of the counterweights.

Near the top of the ascension you will get a break by jumping to a stationary ledge. Wait for the tallest moving platform and hop on board to get to the center and another piece of the Kraken's Bane.

As soon as you open the chest, the gates will lock and you must wipe out the trio of pirates to get out alive.

New Toy Unlocked: Phase Shift

New Challenge Available: Cove Collect

ALERT MISSION: HELPIN' OTHER PIRATES

Type: Locate
Rewards: 1,000 Coins / 100 Sparks

While sailing the open seas, you may come across other pirates under attack by the Royal Navy. This is a very long battle with several waves and it is best to have your favorite power-up in the set up before you get surrounded. Remember that the ship will repair over time. If you need to, get away from the heat of combat to take a break.

THE FINAL PIECE AT BUCCANEER BAY

Treasure

Map

Clocktower Lady

Navigator

Kraken's Bane

3

2

1

Treasure

Mr. Gibbs

Deliveries

Dock

CHALLENGES

1. Buccaneer Break
2. Brawl at the Bay
3. Buccaneer Bay Ballyhoo

TO BUCCANEER BAY WIT' YOU!

Mission Giver: Tia Dalma (automatic)
Type: Locate
Rewards: 500 Coins / 100 Sparks

Throw Pirate Bomb

Sail back to where it all started at Buccaneer Bay and speak to
Tia Dalma when you land.

GAME BASICS

CHARACTERS

POWER DISCS

PLAY SETS

TOY BOX

TOY BOX COLLECTION

ACHIEVEMENTS

LAST PIECE, MATEY

Mission Giver: Tia Dalma
Type: Combat
Rewards: 1,000 Coins / 250 Sparks

It's time to take the last piece of the Kraken's Bane, but you have to fight through all the fish men from Davy Jones to get it.

Wipe out the first batch of fish men with bombs or the Atlas blade. The turtles and oyster-looking fish men carry shields and the enemies are now better at blocking. Speaking of blocking, if you get surrounded, be patient and block, waiting for your chance to strike. Trying to attack and overpower superior numbers will not work and will become frustrating. Take out one enemy at a time, and when they are gone, blow up the debris on the bridge to clear a path.

The next big battle will take place where you had your first fight. There are more of Jones' crew to deal with, but Maccus joins them this time. Bombs do a lot of damage and are a great choice at a distance, but only if you can avoid the incoming fire from the turtles. Either block their bombs or dodge them and return with one of your own. It can be tough to fight fire with fire in this scenario and is only worth the effort if you can hit several enemies with a bomb. Otherwise, resort to your Blunderbuss for range attacks and keep Maccus at bay for as long as possible.

⭐ ALL TOGETHER!

Mission Giver: Tia Dalma (automatic)
Type: Locate
Rewards: 5,000 Coins / 1,000 Sparks

After the battle, the bell in the tower will crash to the ground and reveal the last hidden piece of the Kraken's Bane. Grab the final piece and get back to your ship.

DEFEAT DAVY JONES

⭐ BACK TO YOUR LOCKER, JONES!

Mission Giver: Mr. Gibbs
Type: Ship Combat
Rewards: 2,000 Coins / 250 Sparks

Now that you finally have the Kraken's Bane, it is time to take on Davy Jones. Make sure the Kraken's Bane is equipped on the ship as it will be essential to repel the monster while fighting Jones. This is a five-wave fight that will really test your sea savviness. Not only are there a lot of ships to deal with, but the Kraken can creep up at any time. The only thing in your favor is that the ship will recover in between waves.

Head out to sea in search of the *Flying Dutchman*. Try to maneuver away from its sides that have the most cannons, but make sure to keep firing as you circle around it.

The Kraken will attack throughout the sea battle, and this would normally send other pirates to the bottom of the ocean. However, with the Kraken's Bane equipped, you can zap the Kraken and send it back into the sea.

The *Flying Dutchman* can be sunk, but unlike normal ships it will pop right back out of the water. In fact, it has to be sunk several times to proceed to the next phase of the battle.

After taking enough damage, Jones will call in some reinforcements. There are four ships to sink in this wave, but they are relatively small. Keep firing on the enemies' ships while aiming for the front or back of their ships.

Mr. Gibbs will usually announce that the Kraken is coming by saying something like "Cap'n, it's the Kraken!" or "Sea Monster!" and at the end of this wave, it will launch a quick surprise attack.

NOTE

Most of the time Mr. Gibbs will alert you to a Kraken attack, but it can launch a sneak attack that is very hard to notice. Keep your eyes peeled and the Kraken's Bane charged. Failing to use the Bane in time is instant defeat!

Wave three is a fight with the *Flying Dutchman* again. Blast it at a distance if at all possible, and always move away from its Broadside Cannons.

The fourth attack wave has six ships to deal with and the goal is to avoid getting sandwiched between two enemy ships. Try to keep foes on one side (within range) and blast away.

The final wave is your last battle with the *Flying Dutchman*! The ship has a lot of health, but if you can get it out of position and expose the front of it to the full might of your cannons, it will go down without too much of a problem.

Defeating Jones will unlock the Kraken Hammer, allowing you to now summon the Kraken and sic it on enemies!

New Toy Unlocked: Kraken Hammer

GAME BASICS

CHARACTERS

POWER DISCS

PLAY SETS

TOY BOX

TOY BOX COLLECTION

ACHIEVEMENTS

COLLECTIBLES

Buccaneer Bay

Dead Man's Cove

Devil's Bow Island

Citadel Coast

Fort St. Grande

Isla Enoja

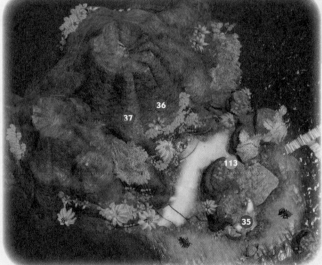

Port Talon

Light Haven

GAME BASICS

CHARACTERS

POWER DISCS

PLAY SETS

TOY BOX

TOY BOX COLLECTION

ACHIEVEMENTS

Pantano Bayou

Shipwreck Shoals 1

Shipwreck Shoals 2

Siren Song

🔴 Red Capsules

Got It?	#	Unlockable Item	Zone	Location
✓	1	Bayou Beauty's Hat	Buccaneer Bay	On the left side of the pathway at the start.
✓	2	Pirate Carpenter's Head	Buccaneer Bay	On the wall to the right after docking the dinghy.
✓	3	Bayou Beauty's Head	Buccaneer Bay	Near the third set of stairs leading up to the outer walls.
✓	4	Privateer's Head	Buccaneer Bay	Near the first set of stairs leading up to the outer walls.
✓	5	Pirate Carpenter's Hair	Buccaneer Bay	On the roof of the building near the gate requiring bombs.
✓	6	Black Hull Front	Buccaneer Bay	On the rope above the locked gate.
✓	7	Privateer's Hair	Buccaneer Bay	On the ground near the waterfalls.
✓	8	Navigator's Body	Buccaneer Bay	At the base of the stairs near the chapel.
✓	9	Navigator's Head	Buccaneer Bay	Behind the building near the waterfalls.
✓	10	Navigator's Hat	Buccaneer Bay	In front of the building with the water wheel.
✓	11	Vengeance Front Hull	Buccaneer Bay	At the back of the tunnel where the map was.
✓	12	Pirate Carpenter's Body	Buccaneer Bay	On the arch where the sand meets the stairs.
✓	13	Vengeance Rear Hull	Buccaneer Bay	In front of the building at the base of the stairs leading to the tower.
✓	14	Vengeance Sails	Buccaneer Bay	On top of the building at the base of the stairs leading to the tower.
✓	15	Bayou Beauty's Body	Buccaneer Bay	At the top of the front stairs leading to the tower.
✓	16	Dragon Woman's Body	Buccaneer Bay	In the building at the base of the stairs leading to the tower.
✓	17	Dragon Woman's Hat	Buccaneer Bay	On the back pathway up the tower facing the dock.
✓	18	Vengeance Theme Pack	Buccaneer Bay	On the wooden platform above the dock.
✓	19	Privateer's Body	Buccaneer Bay	On the back pathway up the tower.
✓	20	Dragon Woman's Head	Buccaneer Bay	On the front ledge halfway up the tower.
✓	21	Vengeance Mid Hull	Buccaneer Bay	Inside the cell at the top of the tower.
✓	22	Shen Zhou Mid Hull	Devil's Bow	Past the wooden gate near all the treasure chests.
✓	23	Shen Zhou Front Hull	Devil's Bow	On the ledge across from the steps.
✓	24	Gunner's Bandana	Citadel Coast	On top of the tower under the cage.
✓	25	Gunner's Head	Citadel Coast	On top of the tower under the cage.
✓	26	Shen Zhou Theme Pack	Citadel Coast	On the ledge under the tower.
✓	27	Shen Zhou Sails	Siren Song	Inside the cell in the wall by the docks.
✓	28	Gunner's Body	Siren Song	On the upper level of the rock formation on a platform near the dock.
✓	29	Shen Zhou Rear Hull	Siren Song	At the very top of the rock formation.
✓	30	Musician's Head	Port Talon	In front of the gate in the cave.
✓	31	Shivaji Theme Pack	Port Talon	Inside the cave near the treasure chests.
✓	32	Musician's Hat	Port Talon	On the wooden platform near the mouth of the cave.
✓	33	Shivaji Sails	Light Haven	Tucked along the wall near the cliff wall.
✓	34	Shivaji Rear Hull	Light Haven	On the side of the tower.
✓	35	Shivaji Mid Hull	Isla Enoja	On the platforms near the cannon.
✓	36	Shivaji Front Hull	Isla Enoja	On the wooden platform inside the cave.
✓	37	Musician's Body	Isla Enoja	Along the ridge near the waterfall inside the cave.
✓	38	El Caleuche Front Hull	Pantano Bayou	On the rock plateau near the dock.
✓	39	Fisherman's Body	Pantano Bayou	In front of the locked gate requiring bombs.
✓	40	Black Hull Rear	Pantano Bayou	Inside the cave past the locked gate requiring bombs.
✓	41	Bounty Hunter's Head	Pantano Bayou	On top of the wooden platform before the big bridge.
✓	42	Fisherman's Head	Pantano Bayou	On the cliff with the rope coming from the wooden platform.

Got It?	#	Unlockable Item	Zone	Location
✓	43	Bounty Hunter's Hair	Pantano Bayou	Right near the big bridge made of stone past the wooden platform.
✓	44	Bayou Raftman Head	Pantano Bayou	On the ladder leading up to the painted house.
✓	45	El Caleuche Sails	Pantano Bayou	Inside the little water cave with the cages.
✓	46	Bounty Hunter's Body	Pantano Bayou	On the rope above the second dock in the bayou.
✓	47	Bayou Raftman Body	Pantano Bayou	Up the ramp from the second dock and by the wall.
✓	48	El Caleuche Rear Hull	Pantano Bayou	Behind the gate that requires a button to open.
✓	49	Quartermaster's Head	Pantano Bayou	Up on the ledge near the button.
✓	50	Quartermaster's Body	Pantano Bayou	By the pillar holding up the stone platform.
✓	51	Bayou Rascal Head	Pantano Bayou	Tucked in the wall past the stone platform.
✓	52	El Caleuche Theme Pack	Pantano Bayou	In the air by the stacked stone blocks on top of the stone platform.
✓	53	Quartermaster's Eye Patch	Pantano Bayou	Tucked in the wall past the small wooden bridge.
✓	54	El Caleuche Mid Hull	Pantano Bayou	In the cell behind the gate requiring bombs.
✓	55	Bayou Raftman Hair	Pantano Bayou	By the left wall entering the big statue area.
✓	56	Fisherman's Hair	Pantano Bayou	On the left wall entering the big statue area.
✓	57	Bayou Rascal Body	Pantano Bayou	On the top of the platform in the big statue area.
✓	58	Bayou Rascal Hair	Pantano Bayou	On the rope leading from top of the platform in the big statue area.
✓	59	Royal Marine's Body	Fort St. Grande	Behind the building nearest the bridge but along the beach.
✓	60	Captain's Head	Fort St. Grande	On the roof of the building nearest the bridge but along the beach.
✓	61	Skeletal Theme Pack	Fort St. Grande	On the roof of the building nearest the bridge.
✓	62	Skeletal Rear Hull	Fort St. Grande	On the ledge with the tree nearest the bridge.
✓	63	Skeletal Front Hull	Fort St. Grande	Across the bridge at the end of the paved beachfront.
✓	64	Captain's Body	Fort St. Grande	On the ledge under the archway leading outside of the Fort walls.
✓	65	Skeletal Mid Hull	Fort St. Grande	On the wooden beam under the archway leading outside of the fort walls.
✓	66	Black Sails	Fort St. Grande	In the room inside the wall that is locked by a bomb gate.
✓	67	Captain's Hair	Fort St. Grande	In the window of the room inside the wall that is locked by a bomb gate.
✓	68	Lieutenant's Body	Fort St. Grande	On the wooden platform on the far side of the fort wall.
✓	69	Royal Marine's Hat	Fort St. Grande	On the rope from the tower past the fort wall.
✓	70	Lieutenant's Hair	Fort St. Grande	On the wooden platform near the gates on top of the wall.
✓	71	Royal Marine's Head	Fort St. Grande	Inside the tower at the top of the fort wall.
✓	72	Skeletal Sails	Fort St. Grande	On the rope leading away from the fort wall.
✓	73	Lieutenant's Head	Fort St. Grande	On the rope wrapping around the top of the tower.
✓	74	Sunken Shipwreck Mid Hull	Shipwreck Shoals	On the rock pathway in front of the dock.
✓	75	Sunken Shipwreck Theme Pack	Shipwreck Shoals	At the top of the wooden platform with the rope ladder.
✓	76	Sunken Shipwreck Front Hull	Shipwreck Shoals	On the platform surrounded by waterfalls.
✓	77	Sunken Shipwreck Sails	Shipwreck Shoals	On the broken mast connecting two waterfalls
✓	78	Sunken Shipwreck Rear Hull	Shipwreck Shoals	On the ledge at the top near the treasure.
✓	79	Swabbie's Bandanna	Dead Man's Cove	On the bridge by the dock.
✓	80	Lady Buccaneer's Bandana	Dead Man's Cove	Behind the two fences that require bombs.
✓	81	Lady Buccaneer's Body	Dead Man's Cove	On the rope connected to the dinghy dock directly past the bomb gate.
✓	82	Admiral's Daughter's Hair	Dead Man's Cove	Under the bridge directly in front of the ship dock.
✓	83	Pirate Lord's Body	Dead Man's Cove	On the water between all of the rock islands to the right of the ship dock.
✓	84	Cursed Sails	Dead Man's Cove	On the very top of the tallest rock islands to the right of the ship dock.
✓	85	Pirate Smithy's Head	Dead Man's Cove	On the fallen mast near the Skull Cave.

Got It?	#	Unlockable Item	Zone	Location
✓	86	Cursed Mid Hull	Dead Man's Cove	On the ledge inside Skull Cave.
✓	87	Pirate Smithy's Body	Dead Man's Cove	In the very back of Dead Man's Cove inside the gated cave.
✓	88	Pirate Smithy's Bandana	Dead Man's Cove	On the end of the elevated wooden platform on the near the fort.
✓	89	Admiral's Daughter's Head	Dead Man's Cove	Right on the beach in front of the dinghy dock.
✓	90	Cursed Theme Pack	Dead Man's Cove	On the wooden platform past the beach and wall climb.
✓	91	Swabbie's Body	Dead Man's Cove	At the edge of the pathway from the beach.
✓	92	Cursed Fore Hull	Dead Man's Cove	On the rope connecting the two big islands in Dead Man's Cove.
✓	93	Lady Buccaneer's Head	Dead Man's Cove	On the little island platform under the long rope connecting the two main islands.
✓	94	Pirate Lord's Hat	Dead Man's Cove	On the ledge near the back of the island by the two waterfalls.
✓	95	Cursed Rear Hull	Dead Man's Cove	On the dinghy dock near the back of the island by the two waterfalls.
✓	96	Black Theme Pack	Dead Man's Cove	Behind the rock near the back of the island by the two waterfalls.
✓	97	Swabbie's Head	Dead Man's Cove	Behind the bomb gate on the ledge near the entrance to the fort.
✓	98	Pirate Lord's Head	Dead Man's Cove	On a couple crates straight past the gate at the fort.
✓	99	Admiral's Daughter's Body	Dead Man's Cove	Past the second gate in the fort and to the left.
✓	100	Black Hull Mid	Dead Man's Cove	On the upper ledge of the moving platforms.
✓	101	Flying Dutchman Theme Pack	Buccaneer Bay (Return)	On the roof of the building at the base of the stairs leading to the tower.
✓	102	Flying Dutchman Mid Hull	Buccaneer Bay (Return)	On the back of the tower near the dock.
✓	103	Flying Dutchman Front Hull	Buccaneer Bay (Return)	By the stairs leading down to the beach.
✓	104	Flying Dutchman Sails	Buccaneer Bay (Return)	At the top of the stairs behind the water wheel near the waterfalls.
✓	105	Flying Dutchman Rear Hull	Buccaneer Bay (Return)	On the rope above the locked gate.

Green Capsules

Got It?	#	Unlockable Item	Zone	Location
✓	106	Pirates Decorations Toy Pack 2	Buccaneer Bay	Inside the chapel after returning.
✓	107	Pirates Crewman Toy Pack 2	Buccaneer Bay	On the rope above the dock.
✓	108	Pirates Town Set Toy Pack 1	Devil's Bow	On the ledge under the tower.
✓	109	Pirates Town Set Toy Pack 3	Citadel Coast	On the top of the steps by the dock.
✓	110	Pirates Town Set Toy Pack 4	Siren Song	On the uppermost part of the rock formation.
✓	111	Pirates Town Set Toy Pack 2	Port Talon	Behind the trees near the dock.
✓	112	Pirates Plants Toy Pack 1	Light Haven	At the base of the tower.
✓	113	Pirates Plants Toy Pack 2	Isla Enoja	In front of the entrance to the cave.
✓	114	Pirates Crewman Toy Pack 1	Pantano Bayou	On the far side of the docks.
✓	115	Pirates Townsperson Toy Pack 3	Pantano Bayou	To the right of the ramp by the second dock.
✓	116	Pirates Townsperson Toy Pack 2	Fort St. Grande	Behind the building nearest the bridge but along the beach.
✓	117	Pirates Townsperson Toy Pack 4	Fort St. Grande	Behind the crate leading to the tower at the top of the fort wall.
✓	118	Pirates Decorations Toy Pack 1	Shipwreck Shoals	On the rock pathway in front of the dock.
✓	119	Pirates Townsperson Toy Pack 1	Dead Man's Cove	On the far side of the bridge by the dock.

GAME BASICS

CHARACTERS

POWER DISCS

PLAY SETS

TOY BOX

TOY BOX COLLECTION

ACHIEVEMENTS

🗄 Infinity Chests/Vault

Got It?	#	Unlockable Item	Zone	Location
✓	DJ1	Davy Jones Chest 1	Buccaneer Bay	Near the docks on the same side as the delivery platform.
✓	DJ2	Davy Jones Chest 2	Pantano Bayou	On the ground right by the wooden house with paintings in it.
✓	DJ3	Davy Jones Chest 3	Dead Man's Cove	Next to the bridge.
✓	HB1	Hector Barbossa Chest 1	Buccaneer Bay	At the top of the stairs behind the water wheel near the waterfalls.
✓	HB2	Hector Barbossa Chest 2	Pantano Bayou	On the dock.
✓	HB3	Hector Barbossa Chest 3	Dead Man's Cove	On the ledge near the back of the island by the two waterfalls.
✓	JS1	Jack Sparrow Chest 1	Buccaneer Bay	Near the buildings in front of the tower.
✓	JS2	Jack Sparrow Chest 2	Pantano Bayou	Right by the second dock in the bayou.
✓	JS3	Jack Sparrow Chest 3	Dead Man's Cove	On the elevated wooden platform on the near the fort.
✓	MASTER	Pirates Avatar Vault - Reward 1	Buccaneer Bay	In the entryway near the chapel.

⭐ Pirates of the Caribbean Gold Stars

Got It?	#	Type	Star Names	Star Description
✓	1	Mission	Rescue Master Gibbs!	Complete "Rescue Master Gibbs!" mission.
✓	2	Mission	Buy Yerself a Ship!	Complete "A Captain Needs a Ship!" mission.
✓	3	Mission	That Be Demon's Cape	Complete "Demon's Cape Sounds Invitin'" mission.
✓	4	Mission	Find Tia Dalma	Complete "Find Tia Dalma" mission.
✓	5	Mission	Keep the Sea Witch Safe	Complete "Keep the Sea Witch Safe" mission.
✓	6	Mission	Darken the Sails!	Complete "Darken the Sails!" mission.
✓	7	Mission	De First Piece O' De Bane	Complete "De First Piece O' De Bane" mission.
✓	8	Mission	Second Piece o' the Kraken's Bane	Complete "Second Piece O' the Kraken's Bane" mission.
✓	9	Mission	Another Piece Be Here	Complete "Another Piece Be Here" mission.
✓	10	Mission	Bane From Beneath	Complete "Bane From Beneath" mission.
✓	11	Mission	Last Piece, Matey	Complete "All Together" mission.
✓	12	Mission	Ship Off the Port Bow!	Complete "Ship Off the Port Bow!" mission.
✓	13	Mission	Sink the Scurvy Rats.	Complete "Rid Me O' Dem Pirates!" mission.
✓	14	Mission	Man the Cannon!	Purchase all cannon abilities.
✓	15	Mission	Back To Your Locker, Jones!	Complete "Back to Your Locker, Jones!" mission.
✓	16	Challenge	Accomplished Pirate	Complete all Challenges.
✓	17	Easter Egg	Big Impact	Throw 100 Pirate Bombs.
✓	18	Easter Egg	Down to the Depths	Sink 30 ships.
✓	19	Easter Egg	Island Explorer	Visited all small islands.
✓	20	Easter Egg	Creatin' a Crew	Customize ten townspeople.
✓	21	Easter Egg	One Ship, Many Faces	Customize the ship five times.
✓	22	Easter Egg	Crow's Nest Climb	Climb to the crow's nest on your ship.
✓	23	Easter Egg	Pillage and Plunder	Break 100 crates or barrels.
✓	24	Easter Egg	There Be Gold, Mate	Find 10 treasure chests.
✓	25	Easter Egg	Salty Old Sailor	Sail for two hours total in your ship.
✓	26	Easter Egg	Small but Powerful	Defeat seven enemies in your dinghy.
✓	27	Easter Egg	Down Ye Goes!	Sink a ship using the deck cannon turret.
✓	28	Easter Egg	All Hands On Deck	Sail out of an island with your friend on the ship.
✓	29	Easter Egg	Own the Hammer	Buy Kraken Hammer.
✓	30	Purchases	Monarch of the Sea	Purchase all ship abilities.

Pirates of the Caribbean Toy List

Got It?	Toys	Toy Box Export	Toy Type	Commercial
✓	Fisherman	Yes	Crewman	No
✓	Blunderbuss	Yes	Held Item	Yes
✓	Atlas Sword	Yes	Prop	No
✓	Pirate Bomb	Yes	Held Item	Yes
✓	Calypso's Rage	No	Ship Ability	Yes
✓	Kraken Hammer	No	Ship Ability	Yes
✓	Phase Shift	No	Ship Ability	No
✓	Speed Burst	No	Ship Ability	No
✓	Extra Broadside Cannons	No	Ship Upgrade	No
✓	Flamethrower Cannon	Yes	Ship Upgrade	Yes

Got It?	Toys	Toy Box Export	Toy Type	Commercial
✓	Foremast Sail	No	Ship Upgrade	No
✓	Helm	No	Ship Upgrade	No
✓	Long Range Cannon	Yes	Ship Upgrade	Yes
✓	Mizzen Mast Sail	No	Ship Upgrade	Yes
✓	Rudder	No	Ship Upgrade	No
✓	Triple Shot Cannon	Yes	Ship Upgrade	Yes
✓	Voodoo Cannon	Yes	Ship Upgrade	Yes
✓	Player Pirate Ship	No	Vehicle/ Mount	Yes

Pirates of the Caribbean Challenges

Got It?	Name	Location	Description	Character	Requirements Easy	Requirements Medium	Requirements Hard
✓	Brawl at the Bay	Buccaneer Bay near bell tower	Defeat enemies as Barbossa before time runs out.	Barbossa	3 enemies in 3:00	6 enemies in 3:00	10 enemies in 3:00
✓	Buccaneer Bay Ballyhoo	Buccaneer Bay near customize shop	Gather as many collectibles as you can before time runs out.	Any	30 targets in 1:30	45 targets in 1:30	60 targets in 1:30
✓	Buccaneer Break	Buccaneer Bay upper embankment	Gather as many collectibles as you can before time runs out.	Any	20 targets in 1:30	35 targets in 1:30	50 targets in 1:30
✓	Gatherin' Grande	Fort. St. Grande beach plateau	Gather as many collectibles as you can as Davy Jones before time runs out.	Davy Jones	25 targets in 2:00	40 targets in 2:00	55 targets in 2:00
✓	Rally on the Fort	Fort. St. Grande near upper fort	Gather as many collectibles as you can before time runs out.	Any	30 targets in 2:15	50 targets in 2:15	70 targets in 2:15
✓	Pantano Bayou Dash	Pantano Bayou near temple ruins	Gather as many collectibles as you can before time runs out.	Any	40 targets in 1:30	50 targets in 1:30	60 targets in 1:30
✓	Shootin' up the Swamp	Pantano Bayou near dock by Tia Dalma	Gather as many collectibles as you can before time runs out.	Any	10 targets in 2:00	15 targets in 2:00	21 targets in 2:00
✓	Clear out Dead Man's Cove	Dead Man's Cove near your ship	Defeat enemies before time runs out.	Any	3 enemies in 3:00	6 enemies in 3:00	10 enemies in 3:00
✓	Cove Collect	Dead Man's Cove near moving platform puzzle	Gather as many collectibles as you can as Captain Jack Sparrow before time runs out.	Captain Jack Sparrow	10 targets in 3:00	15 targets in 3:00	20 targets in 3:00
✓	Pitching with Power!	Dead Man's Cove near counterweight	Gather as many collectibles as you can before time runs out.	Any	10 targets in 2:30	15 targets in 2:30	20 targets in 2:30
✓	Scurry on the Shipwreck	Shipwreck Shoals	Gather as many collectibles as you can before time runs out.	Any	25 targets in 2:00	50 targets in 2:00	70 targets in 2:30

GAME BASICS

CHARACTERS

POWER DISCS

PLAY SETS

TOY BOX

TOY BOX COLLECTION

ACHIEVEMENTS

WII COLLECTIBLES

Buccaneer Bay

Dead Man's Cove

GAME BASICS

CHARACTERS

POWER DISCS

PLAY SETS

TOY BOX

TOY BOX COLLECTION

ACHIEVEMENTS

Devil's Bow Island

Fort St. Grande

Light Haven

Isla Enoja

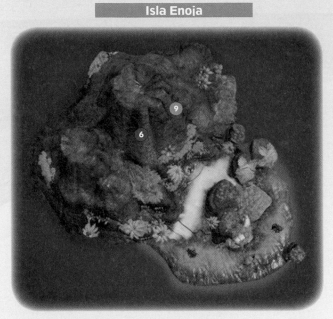

Pantano Bayou

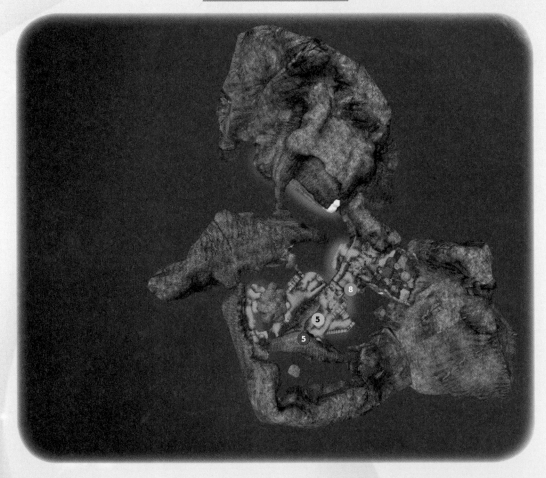

Unlockables

Got It?	Key	Unlockable Item	Type	Zone	Location
✓	1	Revenge Theme Pack (Vengeance Theme Pack)	Red Capsule	Buccaneer Bay	Near the first set of stairs leading up to the outer walls.
✓	2	Shivaji Theme Pack	Red Capsule	Fort St. Grande	On the roof of the building nearest the bridge.
✓	3	El Caleuche Theme Pack	Red Capsule	Light Haven	Climb to to the top of the tower and grind down the rope.
✓	4	Skeletal Theme Pack	Red Capsule	Devil's Bow	Past the wooden gate near all the treasure chests.
✓	5	Sunken Shipwreck Theme Pack	Red Capsule	Pantano Bayou	Behind the gate that requires a button to open.
✓	6	Cursed Theme Pack	Red Capsule	Isla Enoja	On the wooden platform inside the the cave.
✓	7	Pirates Town Set Toy Pack 1	Green Capsule	Devil's Bow	On the ledge under the tower.
✓	8	Pirates Town Set Toy Pack 3	Green Capsule	Pantano Bayou	To the right of the ramp by the second dock.
✓	9	Pirates Plants Toy Pack 2	Green Capsule	Isla Enoja	On the wooden platform inside the the cave.
✓	DJ	Davy Jones Chest	Avatar Chest	Buccaneer Bay	Near the docks.
✓	HB	Hector Barbossa Chest	Avatar Chest	Buccaneer Bay	At the top of the stairs behind the water wheel near the waterfalls.
✓	JS	Jack Sparrow Chest	Avatar Chest	Buccaneer Bay	Near the buildings in front of the tower.
✓	Master	Pirates Avatar Vault - Reward 1	Avatar Vault	Buccaneer Bay	In the entryway near the chapel.

Pirates of the Caribbean Challenges

Got It?	#	Name	Location
✓	1	Buccaneer Break	Buccaneer Bay
✓	2	Brawl at the Bay	Buccaneer Bay
✓	3	Bucaneer Bbay Ballyhoo	Buccaneer Bay

Got It?	#	Name	Location
✓	4	Pitching with Power	Dead Man's Cove
✓	5	Pantano Bay Dash	Pantano Bay
✓	6	Gatherin' Grande	Fort St. Grande

Pirates of the Caribbean Gold Stars

Got It?	#	Type	Name	Description
✓	1	Mission	Rescue Master Gibbs!	Complete "Rescue Master Gibbs!" mission.
✓	2	Mission	We Know Where Gibbs Be	Complete "We Know Where Gibbs Be!" mission.
✓	3	Mission	To Fort St. Grande	Get into Fort St. Grande.
✓	4	Mission	To Dead Man's Cove	Get into Dead Man's Cove.
✓	5	Mission	To Buccaneer Bay	Get back to Buccaneer Bay
✓	6	Mission	Buy Yerself a Ship!	Complete "A Captain Needs a Ship!" mission.
✓	7	Mission	Last Piece, Matey	Complete "Last Piece, Matey." mission.
✓	8	Mission	Sink the Scurvy Rats.	Complete "Rid Me O' Dem Pirates!" mission.
✓	9	Challenge	Help the Town	Complete all Buccaneer side missions.
✓	10	Challenge	Pirate Lord	Complete a Hard Challenge.
✓	11	Mission	Back To Your Locker, Jones!	Complete "Back to Your Locker, Jones!" mission.

Got It?	#	Type	Name	Description
✓	12	Easter Egg	Big Impact	Throw 100 Pirate Bombs.
✓	13	Easter Egg	Down to the Depths	Sink 30 ships.
✓	14	Easter Egg	Crow's Nest Climb	Climb to the crow's nest on your ship.
✓	15	Easter Egg	Pillage and Plunder	Break 100 crates or barrels.
✓	16	Easter Egg	There Be Gold, Mate	Find 20 treasure chests.
✓	17	Easter Egg	Salty Old Sailor	Sail for two hours total in your ship.
✓	18	Easter Egg	Small but Powerful	Defeat five enemies in your dinghy.
✓	19	Easter Egg	Down Ye Goes!	Sink a ship using the deck cannon turret.
✓	20	Easter Egg	Own the Hammer	Buy the Kraken Hammer.
✓	21	Purchases	Monarch of the Sea	Purchase all ship abilities.

Pirates of the Caribbean Toy List

Got It?	Toys	Toy Type	Commercial
✓	Blunderbuss	Held Item	Yes
✓	Atlas Sword	Prop	No
✓	Pirate Bomb Pack	Prop	Yes
✓	Calypso's Rage	Ship Ability	Yes
✓	Kraken Hammer	Ship Ability	Yes
✓	Phase Shift	Ship Ability	No
✓	Speed Burst	Ship Ability	No
✓	Extra Broadside Cannon	Ship Upgrade	No

Got It?	Toys	Toy Type	Commercial
✓	Flamethrower Cannon	Ship Upgrade	Yes
✓	Foremast Sail	Ship Upgrade	No
✓	Helm	Ship Upgrade	No
✓	Long Range Cannon	Ship Upgrade	Yes
✓	Rudder	Ship Upgrade	No
✓	Triple Shot Cannon	Ship Upgrade	Yes
✓	Player's Pirate Ship	Vehicle/Mount	Yes

Cars

WELCOME TO RADIATOR SPRINGS

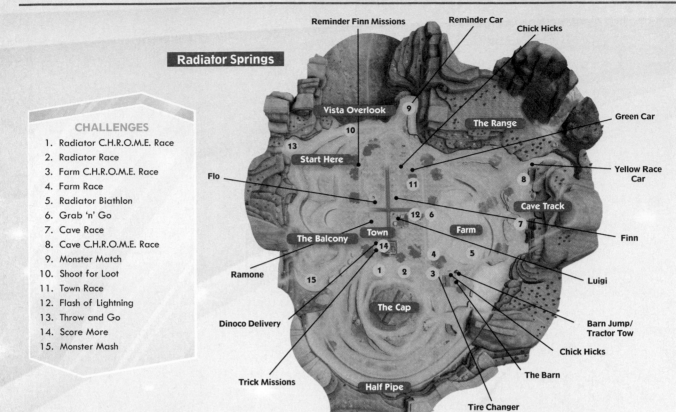

Radiator Springs

Reminder Finn Missions
Reminder Car
Chick Hicks
Vista Overlook
9
The Range
Green Car
10
13
Start Here
Yellow Race Car
Flo
8
11
Cave Track
12 6
Farm
7
Finn
The Balcony
Town
14
4
5
Luigi
Ramone
1 2 3
15
Barn Jump/ Tractor Tow
The Cap
Chick Hicks
Dinoco Delivery
The Barn
Trick Missions
Half Pipe
Tire Changer

CHALLENGES

1. Radiator C.H.R.O.M.E. Race
2. Radiator Race
3. Farm C.H.R.O.M.E. Race
4. Farm Race
5. Radiator Biathlon
6. Grab 'n' Go
7. Cave Race
8. Cave C.H.R.O.M.E. Race
9. Monster Match
10. Shoot for Loot
11. Town Race
12. Flash of Lightning
13. Throw and Go
14. Score More
15. Monster Mash

FIND LUIGI

Mission Giver: Luigi
Type: Locate
Rewards: 50 Coins / 25 Sparks
Wii Rewards: 100 Coins / 25 Sparks

This mission is designed to teach the basics of controlling the car by using the accelerator, working the brake/reverse, and learning to jump. Try out all of the basic driving abilities and follow the green compass arrow to find Luigi's shop.

CALIBRATE GPS

Mission Giver: Luigi
Type: Collect
Rewards: 50 Coins / 25 Sparks
Wii Rewards: 100 Coins / 25 Sparks

Use the built-in GPS system (green compass arrow) to collect all the green balls with a white arrow pointing up.

NOTE

WHAT'S NEXT?

At this point a lot of options become available. There are two main mission paths to choose from as well as numerous side quests. Each initial choice has a chain of events that will follow, but you can jump from one chain to another if you want. The most straightforward method to cover them all is to pick one path and continue until you unlock the new toys, such as the Turbo Level 1 or Tow Chain Level 2, and then switch to another branch.

Main Missions: Jump at Flo's and Meet Chick at The Barn

Side Quests: Clear the Race Track, Smash and Bash, Jump into The Barn

Wii NOTE

While several of the missions in the Wii version of Cars are similar, there are also some different missions and changes to the order of the missions. The Wii-specific maps are located at the end of the chapter and the overview at the beginning of this chapter helps you keep track of the flow of the missions and lists on what page you can find the walkthrough for each mission.

FLO'S MISSIONS

⭐ JUMP AT FLO'S

Mission Giver: Flo
Type: Trick/Stunt
Rewards: N/A
Wii Rewards: 300 Coins / 50 Sparks

Flo needs something flashy to draw attention to her Café. There is nothing like a fantastic jump to get folks to notice the place. In order to perform a leap of that level, Flo's place needs some big ramps. Each place at Radiator Springs can be adjusted into a more stunt-friendly area by pushing the large green buttons in their locations. Press the green button near the fuel stalls and get some distance to zoom up the canopies and perform an amazing jump.

Wii NOTE
Challenge not available for Wii.

New Challenge Available: Radiator Cap Race

⭐ BALES OF FIRE

Mission Giver: Flo
Type: Destroy/Combat
Rewards: 200 Coins / 100 Sparks
Wii Rewards: 500 Coins / 100 Sparks

A tractor with a bad case of backfire caught several hay bales on fire. They have to be smashed before the town burns to the ground.

There are seven bales that need to be bashed to bits and they are all located in a rough circle around The Barn at The Farm.

Wii NOTE
Challenge not available for Wii.

New Challenge Available: Grab n' Go

RESCUE RAMONE

Mission Giver: Flo
Type: Delivery (tow)
Rewards: 50 Coins / 50 Sparks
Wii Rewards: 100 Coins

Putting out the fires was pretty exciting, but Flo's pal Ramone missed all the action. She is worried about him and it is up to you to locate him. Follow the compass to find him stuck on a rocky ledge.

NOTE
At this point the most obvious choice is to complete the Tow Ramone mission, but you can leave him stranded and go back to Flo's to continue her other missions.

ALERT MISSION: OUT OF GAS

Mission Giver: Little Grey Car (blue picture in mission list)
Type: Delivery (tow)
Rewards: 50 Coins / 25 Sparks

This is a repeatable mission that will be unlocked at this point. A small car just outside of town has run out of gas. Activate your tow cable and drag the car back to Flo's to quickly get it back on the road.

CATCH A SPEEDER

Mission Giver: Flo
Type: Delivery (tow)
Rewards: 200 Coins / 100 Sparks
Wii Rewards: 200 Coins / 100 Sparks

Hot rods are tearing up the streets and scaring away Flo's customers. Somebody has to catch the reckless drivers and lock them up in Mater's Impound until they cool off. The hot heads are easy to spot by the red flashing light around them. Also, they are driving very fast and dangerously. It won't be that easy to stop the speeders. Follow behind one and stick with it until you can gain enough ground to get close enough to use the tow cable.

Once the speeder is apprehended, take it to the Impound to get it off the streets.

Wii NOTE

Sarge's Surplus Hut and Turbo Level 1 are not unlocked here for Wii.

New Toy Unlocked: Sarge's Surplus Hut

New Toy Unlocked: Turbo Level 1

Wii NOTE

When the Turbo is unlocked, Luigi will remind you to buy it. Once you acquire it, a new path of missions will unlock, starting with Drift Tutorial.

New Toy Unlocked (Wii): Fillmore's Organic Fuels

BUY SARGE'S HUT

Mission Giver: Flo
Type: Buy/Build
Rewards: 50 Coins / 25 Sparks
Wii Rewards: 100 Coins / 50 Sparks

The Sheriff is out of town as well as Sarge, the military vehicle that helps keep the town in line. Radiator Springs needs some law and order and the best way to solve that is to buy Sarge's Surplus Hut from the Toy Store. It costs 500 coins and you might not have that much to spend so early on. If you want it buy the building now, go smash some hay bales or complete a few more missions to save up. Once the building is placed, a new path of missions will become available at Sarge's place.

New Toy Unlocked (Wii): Sarge's Surplus Hut

POSTAL PROBLEM

Mission Giver: Flo
Type: Unique
Rewards: 250 Coins / 50 Sparks

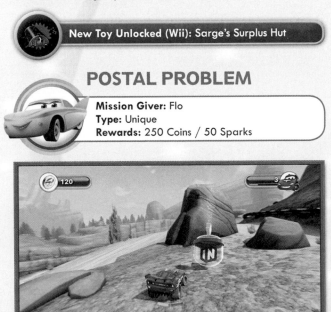

Flo's mailbox was knocked over by the speeders zipping around town. Help her find a new one by locating a red capsule with the object and place it on the spot indicated near the Café.

Follow the compass around The Cap and find the red capsule on a small ledge. Return to Flo's V8 Café and drive around to the back to locate the small grey nub where a Decorate message will appear. Go into the Decorate menu and select Flo's Mailbox to place it and complete the mission.

IN A JAM

Mission Giver: Flo
Type: Combat
Rewards: 200 Coins / 50 Sparks
Wii Rewards: 300 Coins / 100 Sparks

Flo's mail problems aren't over after her mailbox has been replaced. There is a big traffic jam in town and the mail can't get through. Smash through the cluster of cars to clear out the traffic jam at the four-way intersection.

NOTE

Radiator Springs Curios not unlocked here for Wii.

New Toy Unlocked: Radiator Springs Curios

⭐ COLLECTOR PLATES

Mission Giver: Flo
Type: Collect
Rewards: 250 Coins / 50 Sparks
Wii Rewards: 750 Coins / 100 Sparks

Some of the hot rods speeding around town stole fifteen license plates from Radiator Springs Curios. With the help of the compass, track down all fifteen plates that are spread around the outskirts of town and even hidden on ledges and behind hay bales.

New Toy Unlocked (Wii): Tow Chain 4

SIDE MISSIONS

CLEAR THE RACE TRACK

Mission Giver: Little Dark Grey Car (green picture by tree near Mater in mission list)
Type: Destroy
Rewards: 100 Coins / 50 Sparks

A little car northeast of town drove three hours to watch his friend race, but the roadway is all jammed up with debris. Follow the compass to the race track at the range and caves and drive along the track smashing ten piles of debris.

FIND A FRIEND TO RACE

Mission Giver: Little Dark Grey Car
(green picture in mission list)
Type: Locate
Rewards: 100 Coins / 25 Sparks

Return to the little car after clearing out the debris and he will mention that his friend is eager to race you. Use the compass to find his friend at the entrance to the caves.

CAVE RACE

Mission Giver: Yellow Race Car
Type: Race
Rewards: 50 Sparks

Now that the caves are clear to race, a sporty yellow car is waiting to meet you at the entrance to the caves. The car is very excited to race, but you must come in first place to complete the mission. This is a relatively short race requiring only two laps, but it's not easy. At the start of the race, rapidly press the accelerator to build up the turbo meter and launch from the start at full speed.

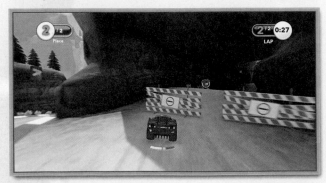

There is an alternate route through the caves that can give you an edge, but the real key to victory is drifting into the turns.

Make sure to drift into each large turn and fill that turbo meter as much as possible. As soon as you find a straight section of track, or an area you can navigate really well, hit the turbo for a much-needed speed boost.

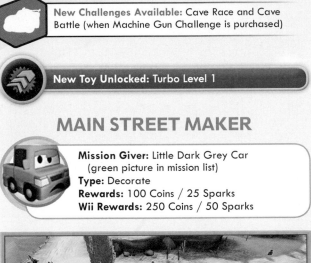

New Challenges Available: Cave Race and Cave Battle (when Machine Gun Challenge is purchased)

New Toy Unlocked: Turbo Level 1

MAIN STREET MAKER

Mission Giver: Little Dark Grey Car
(green picture in mission list)
Type: Decorate
Rewards: 100 Coins / 25 Sparks
Wii Rewards: 250 Coins / 50 Sparks

The town would attract a lot more tourists with a makeover. Go to any building in town and decorate it with at least one alteration to complete the mission.

New Toy Unlocked (Wii): Radiator Springs Curios

BUY RADIATOR SPRINGS CURIOS

Mission Giver: Little Blue Car
Type: Buy
Rewards: 100 Coins / 50 Sparks

Go to the Toy Store and purchase Radiator Springs Curios. This building costs 1,000 coins to purchase.

LUIGI'S MISSIONS

PURCHASE TURBO

Mission Giver: Luigi
    (at The Farm) (in Town in Wii)
Type: Buy
Rewards: 25 Coins / 25 Sparks
Wii Rewards: 100 Coins / 50 Sparks

This is pretty obvious—just go into the Toy Store to buy the Turbo. However, you still need to pick up the package that arrives on the Dinoco drop point. Make your way to the drop point and open the box to acquire the ability to use a turbo boost.

 New Toy Unlocked (Wii): Turbo Level 1

DRIFTING DRILL

Mission Giver: Luigi
Type: Tutorial
Rewards: 50 Coins / 25 Sparks
Wii Rewards: 100 Coins / 50 Sparks

Speak to Luigi to learn about drifting. All the famous race cars are doing it, and Fillmore's special fuel will build up your turbo power each time you do. A drift is performed by pressing the accelerator and brake at the same time while steering in the direction you want to go. A drift can be held as long as you like, but it is mainly used in turns. To complete the mission, perform a drift while following the arrows in a circle around Luigi. When the turbo meter is filled, the mission will be over.

 New Challenge Available: Radiator Cap Race

FIND GUIDO!

Mission Giver: Luigi
Type: Locate
Rewards: 50 Coins / 25 Sparks
Wii Rewards: 200 Coins / 50 Sparks

Guido likes playing tricks on Luigi, but now is not a great time. Luigi is preparing a new racetrack and needs Guido back ASAP. Follow the compass to find Guido at the Base of The Cap and bounce into the little blue jokester.

FIND LUIGI'S CRATES

Mission Giver: Luigi
Type: Collect
Rewards: 200 Coins / 50 Sparks
Wii Rewards: 300 Coins / 100 Sparks

Luigi has a big surprise for the town, but all the supplies have fallen off the helicopter that was supposed to deliver them. Use the compass to locate all three of the Dinoco crates around Radiator Springs and tow them back to Luigi.

Wii NOTE

Fillmore's Organic Fuels not unlocked here for Wii.

New Toy Unlocked: Fillmore's Organic Fuels

GAME BASICS | CHARACTERS | POWER DISCS | **PLAY SETS** | TOY BOX | TOY BOX COLLECTION | ACHIEVEMENTS

FOLLOW GUIDO'S BALLOONS

Mission Giver: Luigi
Type: Destroy
Rewards: 100 Coins / 25 Sparks

With the crates returned to Luigi, he can reveal the big surprise—a racing hub. Follow the compass to pass through the thirteen red balloons.

SIDE MISSIONS

SMASH AND BASH

Mission Giver: Yellow Car near The Barn
(blue picture in mission list)
Type: Destroy
Rewards: 100 Coins / 50 Sparks
Wii Rewards: 250 Coins / 50 Sparks

Smash through one of the fenced areas at The Farm and drive into fifteen hay bales to help clear the air for this poor highly allergic vehicle.

 **New Challenge Available:** Grab 'n' Go

 New Toy Unlocked (Wii): Missiles Challenge

 New Challenges Available: Battle Race in Radiator Springs and C.H.R.O.M.E.-athalon

STUNT PRACTICE

Mission Giver: Little Tan Car
(blue picture in mission list)
Type: Stunt/Trick
Rewards: 100 Coins / 50 Sparks
Wii Rewards: 250 Coins / 50 Sparks

Next to the Fire Station is a small car that is looking for someone to do air tricks. Simply follow the request from the little car to learn how to jump and perform a flat spin, barrel roll, front flip, and back flip. They are all simple moves that require a jump and a press of the control stick in one of four directions. This must be completed in 1 minute and 30 seconds.

PERFORM TRICKS

Mission Giver: Little Tan Car
(blue picture in mission list)
Type: Stunt/Trick
Rewards: 250 Coins / 50 Sparks
Wii Rewards: 500 Coins / 100 Sparks

Now that you know how to perform several tricks, the same car that gave you the quick tutorial wants to see three cool stunts done from a high place. This event has a 1 minute and 30 seconds time limit, but that shouldn't present any problems. Luckily the Fire Station right next to the little car has a ramp that is a great spot to do all three of these tricks. Drive up the hill opposite the Fire Station and hit the ramp with as much speed as possible. The first trick the little car wants to see is a double front flip, so hit the ramp and hold forward to flip twice in a row before landing. Next up is the barrel roll. That can be done by holding right on the stick. Finally, do a double back flip by holding back on the control stick.

Wii NOTE

Challenge not available for Wii.

 New Challenge Available: Town Race

JUMP INTO THE BARN

Mission Giver: Little Grey Car
(blue picture in mission list)
Type: Trick/Stunt
Rewards: 100 Coins / 50 Sparks
Wii Rewards: 250 Coins / 50 Sparks

A little car in front of The Barn heard that it was impossible to jump all the way through The Barn. To prove it wrong, press the button on the silo to drop the ramp and build up the turbo meter.

The jump will be easy if you can get enough speed when you hit the ramp, and a turbo boost will take care of that issue. Note that you don't need to jump through the entire barn, but merely get up to the top section and then you can drive through.

LITTLE BO BEEP

Mission Giver: Little Grey Car
(blue picture in mission list)
Type: Delivery (tow)
Rewards: 200 Coins / 50 Sparks
Wii Rewards: 300 Coins / 100 Sparks

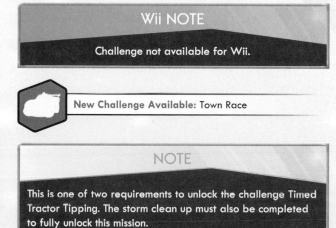

Speak to the car out front of The Barn again to find out about the missing tractors. Use the compass to locate three tractors and tow them back inside The Barn.

Wii NOTE

Challenge not available for Wii.

 New Challenge Available: Town Race

NOTE

This is one of two requirements to unlock the challenge Timed Tractor Tipping. The storm clean up must also be completed to fully unlock this mission.

FINN'S MISSIONS

NOTE

A small grey (blue picture in mission list) car in the northwest part of town will remind you to purchase the toys that Finn mentions. These missions don't have to be completed to purchase the toys, and if you buy them before speaking to the car, they will be automatically be completed when you talk to it.

SPY TRAINING

Mission Giver: Finn
Type: Tutorial
Rewards: 50 Coins / 50 Sparks
Wii Rewards: 250 Coins / 50 Sparks

Finn is on holiday and stopped by Radiator Springs to unwind. Sarge was nice enough to let him stay at his Surplus Hut while he is out. The news about the big race at Radiator Springs is attracting a lot of attention and C.H.R.O.M.E. has decided to activate you as an agent. There is a catch of course. You must prove you can handle their training regimen—the C.H.R.O.M.E.-athalon. The regimen turns out to be some basic ability tests including a jump, quick turn, and side bash (used to smash into cars when racing).

Wii NOTE

Missiles Challenge and the related challenges are not unlocked here for Wii.

New Toy Unlocked: Missiles Challenge

NOTE

Buying the Missiles Challenge unlocks the following challenges.

New Challenge Available: Battle Race in Radiator Springs and C.H.R.O.M.E.-athalon

New Toy Unlocked (Wii): Ramone's House of Body Art

ALERT MISSION: SPEEDER

Mission Giver: Little Grey Car (blue picture in mission list)
Type: Delivery (tow)
Rewards: 50 Coins / 25 Sparks

This is a repeatable mission that will be unlocked at this point. Chase down the speeding car with a red flashing light and tow it to Mater's Impound.

FINN AT THE FARM (WII ONLY)

Mission Giver: Little Blue Car
Type: Locate
Wii Rewards: 100 Coins / 50 Sparks

Finn is waiting for you at The Farm with a top secret mission. Head to the cave that takes you to The Farm.

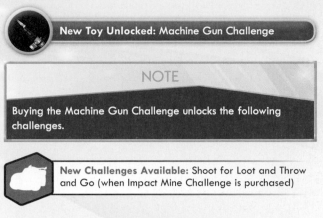

TRACTOR TIPPING

Mission Giver: Finn
Type: Combat
Rewards: 100 Coins / 25 Sparks
Wii Rewards: 100 Coins / 25 Sparks

New Toy Unlocked: Machine Gun Challenge

NOTE

Buying the Machine Gun Challenge unlocks the following challenges.

New Challenges Available: Shoot for Loot and Throw and Go (when Impact Mine Challenge is purchased)

There Is some suspicious activity around town and Finn suggests that you brush up on your stealth skills by surprising five tractors. Go to the fenced farm area and sneak up on the tractors. Get in close and honk the horn to scare the hapless tractors and cause them to tip over.

CHICK HICKS' MISSIONS

MEET CHICK AT THE BARN

Mission Giver: Chick (near Mater's Impound)
Type: Locate
Rewards: 25 Coins / 25 Sparks

Chick wants to race you to The Barn, but it's not really a race. Take your time to get there and follow the green arrow to find him out front.

DRIVE TO THE FARM (WII ONLY)

Mission Giver: Little Blue Car
Type: Locate
Wii Rewards: 100 Coins / 50 Sparks

Follow the GPS system to a cave that takes you to The Farm. Once you arrive, you have completed this mission.

GAME BASICS

CHARACTERS

POWER DISCS

PLAY SETS

TOY BOX

TOY BOX COLLECTION

ACHIEVEMENTS

TAKE A PRACTICE LAP

Mission Giver: Chick (near The Barn)
Type: Race
Rewards: 50 Coins / 25 Sparks
Wii Rewards: 250 Coins / 50 Sparks

Chick is all about racing and he wants to challenge you to a spin around town. However, out of the pure generosity of his motor he will let you take a practice lap first, so you don't hurt yourself. There is no pressure on the practice lap around Radiator Springs, so take it easy and learn the course.

CHICK'S CHALLENGE

Mission Giver: Chick (near The Barn)
Type: Race
Rewards: 250 Coins / 100 Sparks
Wii Rewards: 500 Coins / 100 Sparks

Talk to Chick and get ready to race for real this time! Rev your engine to max out the turbo meter and take first place from the start of the race. However don't expect to hold that spot for the entire race. Chick is very aggressive and he may overtake the number one spot. Don't give up even if your car goes off the track or falls into second place. The race is meant to be close and with three laps there is a lot of opportunity to retake the lead. One good spot to use is the springing platform in front of Sarge's Surplus Hut. This tricky spot will hurl your vehicle into the air, allowing your car to cut across a bit of the track and gain an advantage.

Drift into every corner to fill the turbo meter and blaze across the field to cut off sections of track to gain a bit of an edge. Keep in mind that in general cars will always go faster on the track versus cutting corners in the grass or dirt. This race is very forgiving in terms of straying off course and there are a few alternate routes that can be taken as long as your car is close to the track.

Wii NOTE

Challenge and Turbo Level 1 not unlocked here for Wii.

New Challenges Available: Radiator Farm Race and Farm Battle (if Missile Challenge has been purchased)

New Toy Unlocked: Turbo Level 1

LUIGI IN TOWN (WII ONLY)

Mission Giver: Little Blue Car (at The Farm)
Type: Locate
Wii Rewards: 100 Coins / 50 Sparks

It is time to head back to the Town from The Farm to find Luigi. Drive back to the cave on the side of The Farm area to get back to the Town area.

RAMONE'S MISSIONS

GAME BASICS

CHARACTERS

POWER DISCS

PLAY SETS

TOY BOX

TOY BOX COLLECTION

ACHIEVEMENTS

NOTE

There is a small grey car in the far north, near a ramp leading up the rocky hills. This little vehicle will remind you to purchase the tow chain upgrades unlocked from Ramone's missions. These missions don't have to be completed to purchase the toys, and if you buy them before speaking to the car, they will be automatically be completed when you talk to it.

TOW RAMONE

Mission Giver: Flo (Ramone in Wii)
Type: Delivery (tow)
Rewards: 100 Coins / 50 Sparks
Wii Rewards: 250 Coins / 50 Sparks

Ramone is in a pretty embarrassing spot for a car—he ran out of gas! He was cruising around and completely lost track of his fuel level. Tow Mater may not be around, but any of the Cars characters can tow cars almost as well as the famous brown truck. Get near Ramone and activate the tow cable. Once he is hooked up, drive him back to Flo's for a fill-up.

2 New Toy Unlocked: Tow Chain Level 2

BUY RAMONE'S (WII ONLY)

Mission Giver: Flo
Type: Buy
Wii Rewards: 100 Coins / 50 Sparks

Go to the Toy Store and purchase Ramone's House of Body Art. This will set you back 750 coins. If you can't afford it now, you can always earn some coins and come back and complete this mission.

MISPLACED PAINT

Mission Giver: Ramone (near Flo's)
Type: Collect
Rewards: 200 Coins / 100 Sparks
Wii Rewards: 300 Coins / 100 Sparks

Ramone is trying out for a new reality show called Detail My Dents, but he is missing his premium paint cans. Use the compass to collect ten hidden paint cans. Collecting the cans is pretty obvious and won't require a lot of tricky leaps, but a few are on higher ledges.

Wii NOTE

These toys are not unlocked here for Wii.

3 New Toy Unlocked: Tow Chain Level 3

NOTE

Buy and collect Tow Chain Level 3 to unlock the following.

4 New Toy Unlocked: Tow Chain Level 4

New Toy Unlocked: Turbo Level 1

New Toy Unlocked: Ramone's House of Body Art

CORNY CONCOCTION

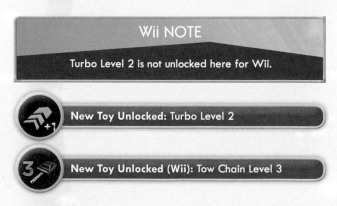

Mission Giver: Fillmore
Type: Collect
Rewards: 50 Sparks
Wii Rewards: 250 Coins / 50 Sparks

New Toy Unlocked (Wii): Cozy Cone Motel Hut

NEW PAINT JOB

Mission Giver: Ramone (near Flo's)
Type: Decorate
Rewards: 200 Coins / 100 Sparks

Detail My Dents features lots of tricked-out sedans. If Ramone wants to get on the show he has to give one of his customers a new custom color. Buy Ramone's House of Body Art and tow a car to the shop to decorate it with a new color.

FILLMORE'S MISSIONS

BUY FILLMORE'S (WII ONLY)

Mission Giver: Flo
Type: Buy/Build
Wii Rewards: 100 Coins / 50 Sparks

Flo's customers are asking for a taste of Fillmore's Organic Fuel. Since she can't find Fillmore anywhere, you need to purchase Fillmore's Organic Fuels from the Toy Store for 750 coins. You might not have that much to spend so early on. If you want to buy the building now, go smash some hay bales or complete a few more missions to save up. After building this structure, you can get some new missions from Fillmore.

Fillmore's organic fuels are awesome, but he is working on making the ultimate fuel that only requires one tank. The groovy van needs some new materials and asks your help to collect three corn for his new recipe. Follow the compass and use the tow cable to collect the corn.

When the corn is attached to your car, tow it back to Fillmore's and go to the back near several colorful barrels to drop it off in the mixer.

Wii NOTE

Turbo Level 2 is not unlocked here for Wii.

New Toy Unlocked: Turbo Level 2

New Toy Unlocked (Wii): Tow Chain Level 3

STUNTS AND RACING TRACKS

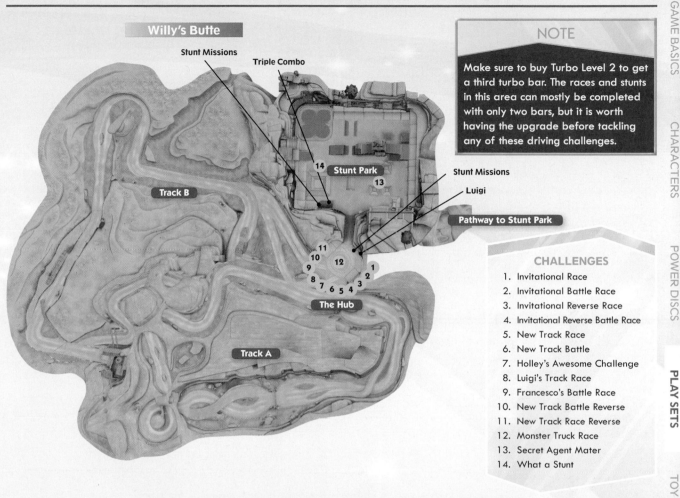

Willy's Butte

Stunt Missions
Triple Combo

14 **Stunt Park**
13

Stunt Missions
Luigi

Pathway to Stunt Park

Track B

11
10
9   12   1
8   2
7 6 5 4 3

The Hub

Track A

CHALLENGES

1. Invitational Race
2. Invitational Battle Race
3. Invitational Reverse Race
4. Invitational Reverse Battle Race
5. New Track Race
6. New Track Battle
7. Holley's Awesome Challenge
8. Luigi's Track Race
9. Francesco's Battle Race
10. New Track Battle Reverse
11. New Track Race Reverse
12. Monster Truck Race
13. Secret Agent Mater
14. What a Stunt

THE HUB (RACING MISSIONS)

TRACK TRASH TAKEDOWN

Mission Giver: Luigi (at The Hub)
Type: Destroy
Rewards: 100 Coins / 25 Sparks
Wii Rewards: 250 Coins / 50 Sparks

Luigi's new track is ready to go... well except for all the shipping crates littering the course. Take a practice lap on the new track and smash through all the trash.

RACE THE KING

Mission Giver: Dark Grey Car (green picture in mission list)
Type: Race
Rewards: 300 Coins / 75 Sparks

It seems that The King helped Luigi with the supplies for the track and now that it is finished he is looking for someone to race. Take up the challenge and try out the first real race on the new track. Start out with a full turbo boost and make sure to drift into each corner. This track is a lot more complex than previous ones and there are a lot more alternate routes as well as obstacles. While the obstacles are not that hard to avoid, hitting them will cost precious time. Avoid the orange-and-yellow barrels or they will explode and set you back a bit. Also, make sure to avoid or simply jump over the blue-and-white-striped rails.

Drifting and possibly doing tricks in the air can fill your turbo meter, but make sure to grab the fuel cans that can help top off your turbo quickly.

There are lots of options to take advantage of on this course, but don't expect them to simply be short cuts. Following the main track is faster than going through the dirt, but with a good boost you can cut off sections of the track and save time. Also, there are lots of traffic blockages with white-and-orange-striped planks. These can be smashed through to open a new route. However, taking an alternate path is not a guarantee that it is quicker than following the track.

What makes the optional paths attractive is when it has turbo cans! The tricky path to the left has a lot of turbo refilling cans, but if your turbo meter is already full it would be better off to use the boost on the long straightaway and cover more ground quickly and safely.

 New Toy Unlocked: Cozy Cone Motel

New Challenge Available: Race Track A Forward

SIDE MISSION

COZY CONE LAUNCH

Mission Giver: Yellow Car (blue picture in mission list)
Type: Delivery (tow)
Rewards: 200 Coins / 50 Sparks

This car on the outskirts of town wants to go to the Cozy Cone. Simply tow the vehicle to the Cozy Cone and toss it in.

LUIGI AND THE STUNT PARK (WII ONLY)

Mission Giver: Little Blue Car
Type: Locate
Wii Rewards: 200 Coins / 50 Sparks

Luigi is waiting for you at the Stunt Park. From the Town, drive to the cave leading to the Stunt Park to open new missions.

BALLOON POPPIN'

Mission Giver: Luigi
Type: Collect/Destroy
Rewards: 100 Coins / 25 Sparks
Wii Rewards: 500 Coins / 100 Sparks

Guido was up to his old tricks or he did a terrible job of placing the red balloons. Luigi wants you to pop all three. This won't require any special tricks—just line up beneath them on the ramps, turn around and get some distance, flip back around once more, and gun it to reach the balloons.

GAME BASICS

CHARACTERS

POWER DISCS

PLAY SETS

TOY BOX

TOY BOX COLLECTION

ACHIEVEMENTS

> **NOTE**
>
> Completing this mission opens the Stunt Park side missions.

 New Toy Unlocked: Impact Mine Challenge

New Challenge Available: Throw and Go (after purchasing Impact Mine Challenge)

RACE REVERSAL

 Mission Giver: Luigi
Type: Race
Rewards: 300 Coins / 75 Sparks
Wii Rewards: 750 Coins / 100 Sparks

Poor Luigi. It seems nobody is impressed with his track. He wants his track to be numero uno, not just "fine". Luigi has an idea rumbling under his hood to reverse the track to create The Backwards Track Race. This is the same track you raced The King, but driving on it backwards opens up some new options. It's important to note that you don't have to win the race; coming in second will still complete the mission.

There are several paths to take, but don't always be swayed by a bunch of turbo cans. The path might be tempting, but only if you can navigate it well. Otherwise it is best to stick to the track and drift to build up the turbo meter.

Dirt path shortcuts are great only if you have the speed (turbo boost) to make up for the rough surface that slows you down. Going through these areas without a boost can actually slow you down.

> **Wii NOTE**
>
> Challenges are not available for Wii.

New Challenges Available: Race Track A Reverse and Battle Race Track A (if Machine Gun Challenge was purchased)

> **NOTE**
>
> Carlos Veloso Arrives

A TRIP HOME (WII ONLY)

Mission Giver: Little Blue Car
Type: Locate
Wii Rewards: 100 Coins / 50 Sparks

It is now time to drive back to town. Leave the race track and make your way back to Radiator Springs.

RACE TRACK B

LUIGI AT THE NEW TRACK (WII ONLY)

Mission Giver: Little Blue Car
Type: Locate
Wii Rewards: 100 Coins / 50 Sparks

Luigi has created a new track and is waiting for you there. Go to the cave that leads to the Race Invitational Track.

LUIGI'S NEW TRACK B

Mission Giver: Luigi
Type: Race
Rewards: 300 Coins / 75 Sparks
Wii Rewards: 750 Coins / 100 Sparks

How does Luigi manage to get so many race tracks made in such a short time? There is a brand new track and it is attracting all the international racers. This is only a two-lap race, and even though you start out in first it is possible to retake the lead from almost any position. Collect the turbo fuel cans, but don't drive recklessly to get them. There are often several options, so pick the one that is most comfortable to navigate.

If you hit the ramp with enough speed, it will propel you to the top level. There are two large holes to drive around, but there are also several turbo boosting cans. Going to the top level is a gamble that only pays off if you can get the cans without crashing.

 New Toy Unlocked: Monster Truck Tires

New Challenges Available: Race Track B Forward, Battle Race Track B, and Monster Truck Race in Radiator Springs (if Monster Truck Tires were purchased)

NOTE

After completing the initial racing path and stunt missions it is time to return to Radiator Springs for a new event.

STUNT SIDE MISSION

STUNTED GROWTH

Mission Giver: Dark Grey Car
(green picture in mission list)
Type: Trick/Stunt
Rewards: 50 Sparks
Wii Rewards: 750 Coins / 100 Sparks

Perform enough tricks in the hub to earn at least 5,000 points before the 2 minute time limit expires. Drift in a circle and completely fill your turbo power, then hit one of the grey halfpipes at full speed to perform a double or triple trick. The method to rack up points fast is to quickly perform a trick and immediately after perform a different trick in another direction.

NOTE

Completing this mission opens the Stunt Park side missions.

STUNT PARK

RING ROUND UP

Mission Giver: Dark Grey Car
(green picture in mission list)
Type: Trick/Stunt
Rewards: 100 Coins / 25 Sparks
Wii Rewards: 750 Coins / 100 Sparks

To prove you are a master trickster, do a trick through fifteen rings around the Stunt Park in 3 minutes. In reality, you don't need to do a fancy trick through the rings as a simple jump will do the job. There should be plenty of time to go through all the rings as long as you don't chase them around the course. Each corner has several in close proximity and the best approach is to complete the rings in groups that are very close. There are more than fifteen rings on the track, so don't spend too much time trying to go through one if it's giving you trouble.

Wii NOTE

Super Pipe and challenge not unlocked here for Wii.

New Toy Unlocked: Super Pipe

New Challenge Available: Monster Truck Race Track B (after purchasing Monster Tires)

New Toy Unlocked (Wii): Full Pipe

PURCHASE FULL PIPE (WII ONLY)

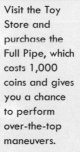

Mission Giver: Little Blue Car
Type: Buy
Wii Rewards: 100 Coins / 50 Sparks

Visit the Toy Store and purchase the Full Pipe, which costs 1,000 coins and gives you a chance to perform over-the-top maneuvers.

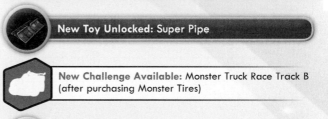

LEARN GRIND

Mission Giver: Dark Grey Car
(green picture in mission list)
Type: Tutorial
Rewards: 100 Coins / 25 Sparks
Wii Rewards: 500 Coins / 100 Sparks

The little car in the Stunt Park will teach you to grind on special rails after purchasing the Super Pipe. Drifting on the rails will allow the car to grind and build the turbo meter as well. Drive up the ramp to the right of the car and grind through the red balloons over the car.

 New Toy Unlocked (Wii): Super Pipe

PURCHASE SUPER PIPE
(WII ONLY)

Mission Giver: Little Blue Car
Type: Buy
Wii Rewards: 100 Coins / 50 Sparks

The Stunt Park needs a new stunt. Go to the Toy Store and purchase the Super Pipe that you just unlocked. For this cool stunt, you need to pay 1,000 coins. However, it is worth it.

PURCHASE SUPER RAMP
(WII ONLY)

Mission Giver: Little Blue Car
Type: Buy
Wii Rewards: 100 Coins / 50 Sparks

Go to the Toy Store and purchase the Super Ramp that was unlocked for you as you talked to the Little Blue Car. The Super Ramp costs 1,000 coins and is a thrill and a half.

DOUBLE TRICKS (WII ONLY)

Mission Giver: Little Blue Car
Type: Trick/Stunt
Wii Rewards: 750 Coins / 100 Sparks

This car wants to see some cool double combos. A double trick is performing the same trick twice while a double combo is doing two different tricks in a row. You must perform three combos that consist of a front flip and spin, spin and roll, and back and front flip combos.

 **New Toy Unlocked: Stunt Clover Pool**

PURCHASE CLOVER POOL (WII ONLY)

Mission Giver: Little Blue Car
Type: Buy
Wii Rewards: 100 Coins / 50 Sparks

Go to the Toy Store and purchase the Stunt Clover Pool. This stunt consists of four small pools and costs 1,000 coins. Use it to perform even more stunts.

GO TO FLO (WII ONLY)

Mission Giver: Little Blue Car
Type: Locate
Wii Rewards: 100 Coins / 50 Sparks

Flo is looking for you. Time to leave the Stunt Park and head back to Radiator Springs. Follow the GPS compass to the gates at the exit of the park.

DOUBLE COMBOS

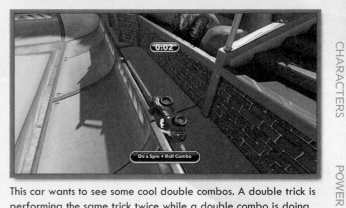

Mission Giver: Dark Grey Car
(green picture in mission list)
Type: Trick/Stunt
Rewards: 500 Coins / 100 Sparks
Wii Rewards: 1,000 Coins / 100 Sparks

This car wants to see some cool double combos. A double trick is performing the same trick twice while a double combo is doing two different tricks in a row. You have 2 minutes to perform three combos that consist of a front flip and spin, spin and roll, and back and front flip combos.

Wii NOTE

Super Ramp and challenge not unlocked here for Wii.

 New Toy Unlocked: Super Ramp

 New Challenge Available: Monster Truck Race Track B (after purchasing Monster Tires)

TRIPLE COMBOS

Mission Giver: Tan Car
(green picture in mission list)
Type: Trick/Stunt
Rewards: 750 Coins / 100 Sparks
Wii Rewards: 1,000 Coins / 100 Sparks

The other car in the Stunt Park wants to see if you can pull off three triple combos in 2 minutes. However, it gets to choose the tricks, and they are not simply doing the same trick three times. The first combo trick is a front flip, back flip, and front flip. The second combo is a barrel roll, front flip, and spin. The final combo series is a spin, barrel roll, and spin. To do the triple tricks make sure to drift until your turbo power is maximized.

GAME BASICS
CHARACTERS
POWER DISCS
PLAY SETS
TOY BOX
TOY BOX COLLECTION
ACHIEVEMENTS

 New Toy Unlocked: Stunt Clover Pool

 **New Challenge Available:** Extended Time Stunt (after purchasing Stunt Clover Pool, Super Pipe, and Full Pipe)

NOTE

After completing the racing path and stunt missions, it is time to return to Radiator Springs for a new event.

FILLMORE'S MISSIONS

FIND FILLMORE (WII ONLY)

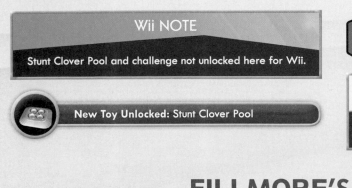

Mission Giver: Little Blue Car
Type: Locate
Wii Rewards: 100 Coins / 50 Sparks

Fillmore has some jobs for you. Head back to Radiator Springs to find out how you can help him.

TRICKY, TRICKY

Mission Giver: Fillmore
Type: Trick/Stunt
Rewards: 500 Coins / 100 Sparks

Stop in to check on your pal Fillmore to get an update on his new fuel formula. Apparently a famous stunt car wants to use the newly opened Stunt Park and it is up to you to do some tricks around town to get that stunt car's attention. The goal of this mission is to perform enough stunts to earn 3,000 points in 1 minute and 30 seconds. There are lots places to pull off stunts

in the town, but if you put Ramone's House of Body Art shop in the default spot it will have a ramp right next to Fillmore. With a decent amount of speed, it should be fairly easy to use that ramp to pull of double combos like a spin and barrel roll for 2 x 600 points.

 New Toy Unlocked: Full Pipe

 **New Challenges Available:** Radiator Stunt Score and Stunt Park Stunt Score + Extended Time Stunt [Mater Only] (after purchasing Full Pipe)

New Toy Unlocked (Wii): Turbo Levels 2

GOURD GATHERER

Mission Giver: Fillmore
Type: Collect
Rewards: 100 Sparks
Wii Rewards: 750 Coins / 100 Sparks

The last batch of fuel Fillmore was cooking up didn't quite meet his expectations. To get more zing he wants to try a new ingredient and is enlisting your help to collect three pumpkins. Follow the compass to tow back the pumpkin to the barrel mixer for his new brew.

GAME BASICS

CHARACTERS

POWER DISCS

PLAY SETS

TOY BOX

TOY BOX COLLECTION

ACHIEVEMENTS

TRACTOR RESCUE

Mission Giver: Fillmore
Type: Delivery (tow)
Rewards: 300 Coins / 100 Sparks

The tractors are scared of the storm and need to be towed back to The Barn. Drive by The Farm and use the tow cable to haul five of them safely in The Barn. This is a great time to use the multiple tow cables you bought to drag in several tractors at a time. When all five of them are safe the storm will subside.

SIDE MISSION

MONSTER MESS

Mission Giver: Dark Grey Car (blue picture in mission list)
Type: Destroy
Rewards: 300 Coins / 100 Sparks

Everyone loves a good monster truck smash-up! This car wants to see a bunch of broken trailers crushed with the Monster Tires. Equip the Monster Tires at the Tire Change Pad and hunt down the trailers with the compass.

 New Challenge Available: Monster Mash (after purchasing Monster Tires)

STORM DAMAGE

Mission Giver: Ramone
Type: Decorate
Rewards: 300 Coins / 100 Sparks

While you were taking care of the tractors, the storm caused a lot of damage to the town. Check in with Ramone to help repair and repaint four storm-damaged buildings: Flo's, the Fire Station, Luigi's Casa Della Tires, and Mater's Impound.

STANLEY'S TRAVELS

Mission Giver: Finn
Type: Delivery (tow)
Rewards: 300 Coins / 100 Sparks

The famous statue of Stanley in front of the Fire Station blew away in the storm. Use the compass to find the statue and tow it back to its rightful place in front of the Fire Station. When it is returned it will give the town a much needed morale boost after the storm's devastation.

WRONG TURN

Mission Giver: Finn
Type: Locate
Rewards: 500 Coins / 100 Sparks

The C.H.R.O.M.E. satellite is showing that five tourist cars are stuck in precarious spots around town, thanks to the storm. Use the compass to track down the cars to perform some search and rescue operations. Many of the cars are indeed stuck in tough spots that will require some tricky jumps. Make sure to build up enough speed when hitting the ramps and activate the tow cable as soon as you get close so you don't sail past the cars. Ultimately, the cars don't need to be towed anywhere and simply need to be touched.

SIDE MISSION

TIMED TRACTOR TIP

> **NOTE**
>
> Requires completion of the Little Bo Beep mission.

Mission Giver: Little Grey Car (Blue picture)
Type: Combat
Rewards: 300 Coins / 50 Sparks
Wii Rewards: 500 Coins / 100 Sparks

The little car in front of The Barn doesn't seem to have a lot of sympathy for the trauma the tractors went through after the storm. It wants you to try to tip five tractors in 1 minute. An easy way to meet this goal is simply to find one tractor and keep tipping it, by honking, as soon as it gets back on its wheels.

ON TRACK WITH LUIGI (WII ONLY)

Mission Giver: Little Blue Car (at The Farm)
Type: Locate
Wii Rewards: 100 Coins / 50 Sparks

Luigi is waiting for you at his new track. Go through the cave that takes you to Luigi's Race Track and meet up with Luigi to open some new racing missions.

NOTE

Storm Clean Up Completed

PAINT THE TOWN

Mission Giver: Flo
Type: Decorate
Rewards: 500 Coins / 100 Sparks
Wii Rewards: 500 Coins / 100 Sparks

Now that the storm has subsided and the town has been repaired, it's time to add a bit of "ka-chow" to show off to the other racers who they support. Customize three buildings using the Ka-chow! texture found in a red capsule.

READY TO RACE AT WILLY'S BUTTE

With the new Race Track B ready to go and the storm under control, the focus of the town shifts to racing. Many famous international racers are heading to Radiator Springs. One of the first famous cars to arrive is Shu Todoroki from Japan.

LUIGI'S READY TO RACE (WII ONLY)

Mission Giver: Little Blue Car
Type: Locate
Wii Rewards: 100 Coins / 50 Sparks

Luigi is waiting for you at the new track. Drive through the cave that leads to the Race Invitational Track to meet up with him.

DOUBLE BACK DASH

Mission Giver: Luigi
Type: Race
Rewards: 500 Coins / 100 Sparks
Wii Rewards: 1,000 Coins / 100 Sparks

Look for any spot to cut corners where you can avoid a decent amount of the track. However, make sure to drift into corners and use the speed of turbo on rough terrains.

A new reverse race track (Track B) is now open to celebrate the re-beautification of Radiator Springs. Compete in the new reverse race going up against Shu Todoroki and take the number one spot! This is a relatively short race with only two laps, so there is not a lot of time to get comfortable on the track. On your first attempt, just get familiar with the course and don't feel pressured to win. Once you have a good understanding of its alternate paths and turbo boosting areas it will be a lot easier to win.

The ramps are fun for a thrill, but they don't always provide an edge in racing. Soaring through the air is slower than using a turbo in a straightaway and landing might not put you in a good position to collect turbo cans.

A fully upgraded turbo will provide four bars of speed-boosting power. There is no reason to hold on to that race-winning speed for too long, but it is a good idea to save one meter towards the end. Often a last lap turbo boost at the end can be used to steal a victory in a come-from-behind photo finish.

Wii NOTE

This track is known as Race Invitational Track for Wii.

Wii NOTE

Challenges are not available for Wii.

New Challenges Available: Race Track B Reverse and Battle Race B Reverse (after purchasing Missile Challenge)

SIDE MISSION

FRANCESCO'S CHALLENGE

NOTE

This side mission requires completion of the Double Combos mission.

Mission Giver: Dark Grey Car Hub (blue picture in mission list)
Type: Race
Rewards: 750 Coins / 150 Sparks
Wii Rewards: 1,000 Coins / 100 Sparks

Francesco Bernoulli has arrived on the scene and he's set up a race with trick barrels scattered around the track. This race is between you and the Italian sports car. It is the same reverse course you just beat Shu Todoroki on, so it should be very familiar. This race is only two laps, but it is a lot more treacherous due to all the explosive red-and-yellow-striped barrels.

Avoid the main central path, as that is usually a prime spot for barrels. Also, be careful of ramps that can land you in a bad spot right in front of a group of explosive problems. Stick to the outside areas to collect turbo boosts and avoid the road hazards Francesco has left for you.

RADIATOR SPRINGS WRAP UP

FILLMORE'S ULTIMATE FUEL

Mission Giver: Fillmore
Type: Collect
Rewards: 300 Coins / 100 Sparks
Wii Rewards: 500 Coins / 100 Sparks

Fillmore thinks he finally figured out the ingredient he needs for the ultimate fuel. To make a hot organic fuel, he needs a hot organic vegetable like a spicy red pepper. Use the compass to round up three peppers. These are a lot harder to get a hold of than the corn and pumpkins. Some will require daring jumps and require you to activate the tow cable in mid-air to grab the hot veggies.

IMPOUND GO-ROUND

Mission Giver: Finn
Type: Delivery (tow)
Rewards: 300 Coins / 100 Sparks
Wii Rewards: 1,000 Coins / 100 Sparks

The vandals that were captured earlier have escaped from Mater's Impound. Bring them all back before they can do any damage to the town. Track down the hot rods and tow the five mischievous cars back to the Impound. If the hot rods are tough to capture, build up the turbo meter and use a boost on a straight stretch of road to overtake them.

THE FINAL RACE —
INTERNATIONAL RACE INVITATIONAL

RADIATOR SPRINGS INVITATIONAL

Mission Giver: Luigi
Type: Race
Rewards: 1,000 Coins / 100 Sparks

When six of the best racing cars in the world are competing in a five-lap race, you know it will be tough to win. The good and bad thing about this race is that any car can catch up to first place. There are enough variations from car crashes, vehicle bashing, and great drifting or turbo usage that almost any car can win from any position. This means don't give up hope if you fall several spots back. Simply try to always improve your position. The best thing about holding first place is that there are not a lot of distractions. When the track is open, there are lots of options to grab turbo boosting cans.

If the other racers start to pack together, look for alternate routes—not simply to lower your track time, but to break away from the bunch. The other racers are pretty adept at smashing into you, and that could easily cause a loss of one or two places. There are several sections like this plateau that can shave off a bit of time, but more importantly it can allow you a way to avoid the crowd.

Experience on the track is invaluable because it teaches when to use a turbo to maximize speed and when to coast a bit to slow down enough to grab turbo boosting cans. For example, it can be a good idea to boost when there is a long stretch of track, but hitting the top of the hill at top speed will send your car too high in the air, preventing you from being able to grab all the turbo cans as you land.

Of course drifting is important in this race and you use it whenever you can, but that doesn't mean holding it so that you slow down or crash. There are a few very tight turns such as this that requires heavy drifting to keep top speed in the turns. Right before this, spot another sharp turn and several turbo tanks. While it is good to max out the turbo meter, it is a waste to not use it whenever possible.

New Challenges Available: Race Track C Forward and Race Track C Reverse, Battle Race Track C Forward (after purchasing Machine Gun Challenge), Battle Race Track C Reverse (after purchasing Mine Challenge)

COLLECTIBLES

Radiator Springs

GAME BASICS

CHARACTERS

POWER DISCS

PLAY SETS

TOY BOX

TOY BOX COLLECTION

ACHIEVEMENTS

Willy's Butte

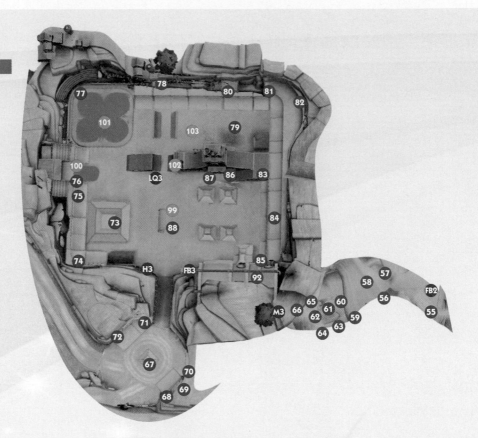

Red Capsules

Got It?	#	Unlockable Item	Zone	Location
✓	1	Fillmore Wall	Vista Overlook	On the Vista Overlook nearest the Old Road.
✓	2	Sheet Metal Trim	Old Road	Driving up the Old Road from the Vista Overlook on the right.
✓	3	Holley Purple Trim	Old Road	At the end of the rail nearest the Vista Overlook.
✓	4	Carbon Fiber Trim	Old Road	On the middle of the railing on the Old Road.
✓	5	Aqua Stucco	Old Road	At the end of the rail nearest the Balcony.
✓	6	Shingle Accent	Old Road	In the middle of the tunnel in the Old Road.
✓	7	Camouflage	Balcony	In the middle of the tunnel in the Balcony.
✓	8	Camera	Balcony	Floating at the peak of the ramp jump in the Balcony.
✓	9	Wood Accent	Balcony	At the top of the banked wall on the Balcony.
✓	10	Camo Accent	Balcony	In between the two ramps facing out on the Balcony.
✓	11	Gold Piston Cup	Balcony	On the lower part of the Balcony at the end of the railing.
✓	12	Top Hat	Old Road	At the edge of the Old Road facing the Town.
✓	13	Spare Parts Windmill	Balcony	On the island ramp jumps that lead to the Balcony.
✓	14	Crown	Balcony	On the top of the ramp that leads to the Balcony from the Town.
✓	15	Spiked Wheels	Range	At the Range nearest the Vista Overlook.
✓	16	Small Wheels	Range	On the ramp at the Range.
✓	17	Wind Chime	Range	Inside the tunnel at the Range.
✓	18	Colored Tires	Town	In between the Mater's Impound Lot and the Farm.
✓	19	Rusteze Baseball Hat	Cave Track	In between the Farm and the Cave Track main entrance.

Got It?	#	Unlockable Item	Zone	Location
✓	20	Guido at Work Sign	Cave Track	Along the ledge leading to the Cave Track from the Range.
✓	21	Tire Tree	Cave Track	On the ledge near the main front entrance of the Cave Track.
✓	22	Tiara	Cave Track	On the little ledge right by The Farm.
✓	23	Flower Quilt Accent	Cave Track	On the top of the rock near The Farm.
✓	24	Sheet Metal Accent	Cave Track	Near the turning sign at the back of the main entrance of the Cave Track.
✓	25	Italian Afro	Cave Track	Near the bottom entrance to the Cave Track nearest The Farm.
✓	26	Bow	Cave Track	On the right part of the main entrance to the Cave Track.
✓	27	Blue Flags	Cave Track	Off the ledge on the upper level of the Cave Track.
✓	28	Tank Treads	Cave Track	On the raised platform in the side of the wall on the upper level of the Cave Track.
✓	29	Stop Sign	Cave Track	On the larger island jump platform on the upper level of the Cave Track.
✓	30	Stickers	Cave Track	On the ledge across from the island jumps on the upper level of the Cave Track.
✓	31	Interstate Sign	Cave Track	Along the wall on the lower level of the Cave Track.
✓	32	Pizza Planet Rocket	Farm	In the air on the ramp jump behind The Farm.
✓	33	Holley Accent	Half Pipe Gulch	In the tunnel at Half Pipe.
✓	34	Tractor Wheels	Half Pipe Gulch	Up on the side of the wall at Half Pipe.
✓	35	Surfboard	Half Pipe Gulch	In the air on the ramp jump next to the tunnel in Half Pipe.
✓	36	Tractor Crossing Sign	Half Pipe Gulch	On the ledge near the tunnel in Half Pipe.
✓	37	Sports Car Topiary	Half Pipe Gulch	Under the ramp jump next to the tunnel in Half Pipe.
✓	38	Pink Camo	Half Pipe Gulch	On top of some barrels in Half Pipe.
✓	39	Shiny Wood Accent	Half Pipe Gulch	On top of the Half Pipe ledge near the tunnel.
✓	40	Tin	Half Pipe Gulch	On top of the Half Pipe ledge near the bend.
✓	41	Sandbag Barricade	Half Pipe Gulch	On top of the Half Pipe ledge near the bend.
✓	42	Pink Flamingo 1	Half Pipe Gulch	In the air on the ramp jump at the bend of Half Pipe.
✓	43	Red Mailbox	Half Pipe Gulch	Next to a rock near the opposite side of the tunnel in Half Pipe.
✓	44	Gas Hat	Cap	On the rail that is sticking out of the trail on The Cap.
✓	45	Cars Crossing Sign	Cap	On top of a rock at the front Base of The Cap.
✓	46	Holley's Wall	Cap	On the trail, nearest The Farm, leading up to the top of The Cap.
✓	47	Tree Camo	Cap	On The Cap under the "RS" letters.
✓	48	Mater Trim	Cap	On the trail, nearest the Balcony, leading up to the top of The Cap.
✓	49	Red Brick	Cap	On a lip nearest the Balcony of The Cap.
✓	50	Parking Meter	Cap	On the end of the rail at the very back side of The Cap.
✓	51	Sarge's Antique Cannon	Cap	On the middle of the rail at the very back side of The Cap.
✓	52	Holley's Hubcap Pinwheel	Cap	On the end of the rail at the very back side of The Cap.
✓	53	Basic Brick	Balcony	Underneath the Balcony nearest the Town.
✓	54	Mater Wall	Balcony	Underneath the Balcony nearest the island jumps.
✓	55	Beige Stucco	Pathway to Stunt Park	At the entrance to the Pathway to Stunt Park.
✓	56	Pink Flamingo 2	Pathway to Stunt Park	On the ramp to the left near the entrance to the Pathway to Stunt Park.

Got It?	#	Unlockable Item	Zone	Location
✓	57	Rusty Trim	Pathway to Stunt Park	On the ground to the right near the entrance to the Pathway to Stunt Park.
✓	58	Hangin' Tire	Pathway to Stunt Park	On the wall to the right near the entrance to the Pathway to Stunt Park.
✓	59	Baseball Hat	Pathway to Stunt Park	On the upper ledge on the left side of the Pathway to Stunt Park.
✓	60	Tire Tracks	Pathway to Stunt Park	Under the ramp jump in the Pathway to Stunt Park.
✓	61	Motorin' Topiary	Pathway to Stunt Park	In the air on the ramp jump in the Pathway to Stunt Park.
✓	62	Monster Wheels	Pathway to Stunt Park	On the wall past the jump in the Pathway to Stunt Park.
✓	63	Orange Cone	Pathway to Stunt Park	On the ledge to the left past the jump in the Pathway to Stunt Park.
✓	64	Mohawk	Pathway to Stunt Park	On the far side of the jump in the Pathway to Stunt Park.
✓	65	Grass Accent	Pathway to Stunt Park	Tucked in the bottom of the wall on landing part of the ramp.
✓	66	Gold Parking Meter	Pathway to Stunt Park	At the exit of the Pathway to Stunt Park.
✓	67	Wood Plank	Hub	In the middle of the Hub on the platform.
✓	68	Dinoco Feather Hat	Hub	On the right side of the ramp near the Pathway to Stunt Park.
✓	69	Blue Burnout	Hub	On the center of the ramp near the Pathway to Stunt Park.
✓	70	Wood Trim	Hub	On the left side of the ramp near the Pathway to Stunt Park.
✓	71	Highway Walls	Hub	On the ramp to the right near Stunt Park.
✓	72	Corrugated Wall	Hub	On the ramp to the left near Stunt Park.
✓	73	Mattress	Stunt Park	Inside the Square Pool to the left as you enter.
✓	74	Starting Gate Lights	Stunt Park	Above the 1/4 Pipe Turn.
✓	75	Concrete Accent	Stunt Park	On the rail leading to the top of the Cradle Pool.
✓	76	Yellow Flags	Stunt Park	Above the Cradle Pool.
✓	77	Wood Planks Accent	Stunt Park	At the back of the Clover Pool.
✓	78	Low Profile Wheels	Stunt Park	On the Mine Car Track.
✓	79	Rusty Wall	Stunt Park	On top of the four-way ramp in the back of Stunt Park.
✓	80	Dinoco Baseball Hat	Stunt Park	On the far side of the Mine Car Track.
✓	81	Tire Shrub	Stunt Park	On the upper part of the Bank Jump.
✓	82	White Stucco	Stunt Park	In the corner on the upper part of the Bank Jump.
✓	83	Tire Accent	Stunt Park	On the ramp leading to the Big Jump in Stunt Park.
✓	84	Announcer Speakers	Stunt Park	On the ledge for the 1/4 Pipe Edge.
✓	85	Winner's Circle	Stunt Park	In the corner of the 1/4 Pipe Edge.
✓	86	Checkered Flags	Stunt Park	In the circular tunnel inside the Big Jump Tower.
✓	87	Blue Mailbox	Stunt Park	In the square tunnel inside the Big Jump Tower.
✓	88	Checkerboard Trim	Stunt Park	Inside the Full Pipe.
✓	89	Thin Wheels	Farm	In a hay bale in The Farm.
✓	90	Traffic Cone	Farm	In a hay bale in The Farm.
✓	91	Red Firestone	Farm	In a hay bale in The Farm.
✓	92	Bronze Piston Cup	Stunt Park	Inside the wall tunnel to the right entering Stunt Park.
✓	93	Flo's Mailbox	Cap	On the back ledge of The Cap; appears only after Flo's Mission.

Green Capsules

Got It?	#	Unlockable Item	Zone	Location
✓	94	Radiator Springs Plants Toy Pack 1	Town	On the roof of Mater's Impound.
✓	95	Flo's V8 Café	Town	In the barn on the second level at the Farm.
✓	96	Radiator Springs Vehicle Toy Pack	Town	Inside the Court House in the Town.
✓	97	Tow Mater Impound Lot	Town	On top of Luigi's Building.
✓	98	Radiator Springs Plants Toy Pack 3	Town	Inside of Flo's Café.
✓	99	Radiator Springs Decoration Toy Pack 3	Stunt Park	On top of the Full Pipe at Stunt Park.
✓	100	Radiator Springs Decoration Toy Pack 4	Stunt Park	In the Cradle Pool at Stunt Park.
✓	101	Radiator Springs Courthouse	Stunt Park	In the Clover Pool at Stunt Park.
✓	102	Luigi's Casa Della Tires	Stunt Park	Off the Big Jump at Stunt Park.
✓	103	Radiator Springs Farmhouse	Stunt Park	In the air past the Quarter Pipe.
✓	104	Radiator Springs Decoration Toy Pack 2	Town	On top of Sarge's Building.
✓	105	Radiator Springs Plants Toy Pack 4	Town	On top of the Curios Building.
✓	106	Radiator Springs Decoration Toy Pack 1	Town	Inside Ramone's House of Body Art.
✓	107	Radiator Springs Plants Toy Pack 2	Town	Inside Fillmore's Building.
✓	108	Radiator Springs Critter Toy Pack	Town	On the roof of Cozy Cone.

Infinity Chests/Vault

Got It?	#	Unlockable Item	Zone	Location
✓	FB1	Francesco Bernoulli Chest 1	Town	By the tree behind Flo's building.
✓	FB2	Francesco Bernoulli Chest 2	Pathway to Stunt Park	At the entrance to the Pathway to Stunt Park.
✓	FB3	Francesco Bernoulli Chest 3	Stunt Park	Directly to the right exiting the Pathway to Stunt Park.
✓	H1	Holley Shiftwell Chest 1	Balcony	On the Balcony near the jumps.
✓	H2	Holley Shiftwell Chest 2	Stunt Park	Directly to the left exiting the Pathway to Stunt Park.
✓	H3	Holley Shiftwell Chest 3	Town	Near the road in front of The Farm.
✓	LQ1	Lightning McQueen Chest 1	Old Road	On the top part of the Old Road near the middle of railing.
✓	LQ2	Lightning McQueen Chest 2	Town	On the ground near the Balcony and Half Pipe.
✓	LQ3	Lightning McQueen Chest 3	Stunt Park	At the Base of the Big Jump.
✓	MASTER	Cars Avatar Vault - Reward 1	Balcony	Under the Balcony.
✓	M1	Mater Chest 1	Town	Right out front of Mater's Impound.
✓	M2	Mater Chest 2	Farm	Right in front of The Farm.
✓	M3	Mater Chest 3	Pathway to Stunt Park	Near the exit to the Pathway to Stunt Park.

GAME BASICS

CHARACTERS

POWER DISCS

PLAY SETS

TOY BOX

TOY BOX COLLECTION

ACHIEVEMENTS

⭐ Cars Gold Stars

Got It?	#	Type	Star Names	Star Description
✓	1	Mission	Blazin' Bales!	Bash through all the flaming hay bales.
✓	2	Mission	Finn's In	Purchase and place Sarge's Surplus Hut.
✓	3	Mission	Chick 'n' Farm	Win a race against Chick at The Farm.
✓	4	Mission	Tidyin' Town	Restore the town after the tornado.
✓	5	Mission	Race the King	Complete a race with "The King".
✓	6	Mission	Backtrack	Win a race on the backward version of Luigi's first track.
✓	7	Mission	Speedway Special	Win a race on Luigi's second track.
✓	8	Mission	Drivin' in Reverse	Win a race on the backward version of Luigi's second track.
✓	9	Mission	Higher Tires	Complete a Monster Truck race.
✓	10	Mission	Showstopper	Complete the "Jump at Flo's" mission.
✓	11	Mission	What a Stunt!	Complete the "Tricky, Tricky" mission.
✓	12	Mission	Trickster	Complete the "Triple Combos" mission.
✓	13	Mission	Ring-a-Ding	Complete the "Ring Round Up" mission.
✓	14	Mission	Our Town	Customize buildings in Radiator Springs.
✓	15	Mission	International Race Pro	Finish the Radiator Springs Invitational in First Place.
✓	16	Challenge	Monster Master	Complete two Monster Tire Events.
✓	17	Challenge	Best Battler	Win all Battle Race Challenges at any skill level.
✓	18	Challenge	Race Master	Win all Race Challenges at any skill level.
✓	19	Challenge	Lizzie's License Plates	Collect every license plate.
✓	20	Challenge	Kachow! Customizer	Collect 80 Red Capsules.
✓	21	Easter Egg	Trick Master	Perform 100 Air Tricks of any kind.
✓	22	Easter Egg	Paint Job Pro	Perform 50 customizations on tourist cars.
✓	23	Easter Egg	Decorator	Place ten decorations.
✓	24	Easter Egg	Never Miss a Trick	Complete every trick mission.
✓	25	Easter Egg	Speed Trap	Catch five speeders.
✓	26	Purchases	Builder	Place every building in the Play Set.
✓	27	Purchases	Tow Master	Purchase every tow chain upgrade.
✓	28	Purchases	Turbo Master	Purchase every turbo upgrade.
✓	29	Purchases	Stunt Master	Purchase every Stunt Park upgrade.
✓	30	Purchases	C.H.R.O.M.E. Agent	Purchase every Weapon Challenge.

Cars Toy List

Got It?	Toys	Toy Box Export	Toy Type	Commercial
✓	Traffic Truck	Yes	Townsperson	No
✓	Traffic Van	Yes	Townsperson	No
✓	Towable Wrecking Ball	Yes	Unique	No
✓	Towable Ramp	Yes	Unique	No
✓	Turbo Level 1	No	Unique	Yes
✓	Turbo Level 2	No	Unique	No
✓	Full Turbo	No	Unique	No
✓	Sarge's Surplus Hut	Yes	Building	Yes
✓	Fillmore's Organic Fuels	Yes	Building	Yes
✓	Ramone's House of Body Art	Yes	Building	Yes
✓	Radiator Springs Curios	Yes	Building	Yes

Got It?	Toys	Toy Box Export	Toy Type	Commercial
✓	Cozy Cone Motel	Yes	Building	Yes
✓	Tow Chain Level 2	No	Unique	Yes
✓	Tow Chain Level 3	No	Unique	No
✓	Tow Chain Level 4	No	Unique	No
✓	Machine Gun Challenge	Yes	Unique	Yes
✓	Missiles Challenge	Yes	Unique	Yes
✓	Impact Mine Challenge	Yes	Unique	Yes
✓	Monster Truck Tires	No	Unique	Yes
✓	Super Pipe	No	Building	Yes
✓	Super Ramp	No	Building	No
✓	Full Pipe	Yes	Building	No
✓	Stunt Clover Pool	Yes	Building	No

Cars Challenges

Got It?	Name	Location	Description	Character	Easy	Medium	Hard
✓	Holley's Awesome Challenge	Willy's Butte Hub	Take first place as Holley.	Holley	1st place in 3 laps	1st place in 3 laps	1st place in 3 laps
✓	Francesco's Battle Race	Willy's Butte Hub	Win first place in this Battle Race as Francesco Bernoulli.	Francesco	1st place in 3 laps	1st place in 3 laps	1st place in 3 laps
✓	Secret Agent Mater	Stunt Park	Perform tricks as Mater to achieve the point minimum before time runs out.	Mater	10,000 points in 4:20	15,000 points in 4:20	25,000 points in 4:20
✓	Monster Truck Race	Willy's Butte Hub	Compete in a Monster Truck Race with Monster Tires.	Any-Monster Tires	1st place in 3 laps	1st place in 3 laps	1st place in 3 laps
✓	Invitational Reverse Battle Race	Willy's Butte Hub	Use C.H.R.O.M.E. gadgets to defeat the other racers.	Any	1st place in 3 laps	1st place in 3 laps	1st place in 3 laps
✓	Invitational Reverse Race	Willy's Butte Hub	Finish the race in first place.	Any	1st place in 3 laps	1st place in 3 laps	1st place in 3 laps
✓	Invitational Race	Willy's Butte Hub	Finish the race in first place.	Any	1st place in 3 laps	1st place in 3 laps	1st place in 3 laps
✓	Luigi's Track Race	Willy's Butte Hub	Finish the race in first place.	Any	1st place in 3 laps	1st place in 3 laps	1st place in 3 laps
✓	New Track Battle Reverse	Willy's Butte Hub	Use C.H.R.O.M.E. gadgets to defeat the other racers.	Any	1st place in 3 laps	1st place in 3 laps	1st place in 3 laps
✓	New Track Race Reverse	Willy's Butte Hub	Finish the race in first place.	Any	1st place in 3 laps	1st place in 3 laps	1st place in 3 laps
✓	New Track Battle	Willy's Butte Hub	Use C.H.R.O.M.E. gadgets to defeat the other racers.	Any	1st place in 3 laps	1st place in 3 laps	1st place in 3 laps
✓	New Track Race	Willy's Butte Hub	Finish the race in first place.	Any	1st place in 3 laps	1st place in 3 laps	1st place in 3 laps
✓	Invitational Battle Race	Willy's Butte Hub	Use C.H.R.O.M.E. gadgets to defeat the other racers.	Any	1st place in 3 laps	1st place in 3 laps	1st place in 3 laps

Got It?	Name	Location	Description	Character	Requirements		
					Easy	Medium	Hard
✓	What a Stunt!	Stunt Park	Earn the minimum required points by performing tricks.	Any	7,500 points in 3:00	12,500 points in 3:00	16,500 points in 3:00
✓	Cave Race	On rock near the Range and Caves	Finish the race in first place to win.	Any	1st place in 3 laps	1st place in 3 laps	1st place in 3 laps
✓	Monster Match	Near the spawn point by the Toy Store	Pass through all checkpoints in time allowed using Monster Tires.	Any- Monster Tires	20 checkpoints in 2:00	20 checkpoints in 1:45	20 checkpoints in 1:30
✓	Shoot for Loot	Vista Overlook	Break as many collectibles as you can before the time runs out.	Any	10 targets in 1:30	15 targets in 1:30	21 targets in 1:30
✓	Farm Race	Near the Barn	Finish the race in first place to win.	Any	1st place in 3 laps	1st place in 3 laps	1st place in 3 laps
✓	Score More	In back of Flo's near the Balcony	Earn the minimum required points by performing tricks.	Any	5,000 points in 3:00	10,000 points in 3:00	15,000 points in 3:00
✓	Farm C.H.R.O.M.E. Race	Near the Barn	Use C.H.R.O.M.E. gadgets to defeat the other racers.	Any	1st place in 3 laps	1st place in 3 laps	1st place in 3 laps
✓	Grab 'n' Go	South section of The Farm	Gather as many collectibles as you can before time runs out.	Any	15 targets in 0:45	20 targets in 0:45	25 targets in 0:45
✓	Flash of Lightning	Between The Farm and Town	Lightning McQueen must win a battle race.	Lightning McQueen	1st place in 3 laps	1st place in 3 laps	1st place in 3 laps
✓	Radiator Race	In back of the Firehouse	Finish the race in first place.	Any	1st place in 3 laps	1st place in 3 laps	1st place in 3 laps
✓	Radiator C.H.R.O.M.E. Race	In back of the Firehouse	Use C.H.R.O.M.E. gadgets to defeat the other racers.	Any	1st place in 3 laps	1st place in 3 laps	1st place in 3 laps
✓	Radiator Biathlon	At The Farm	Break as many collectibles as you can before the time runs out.	Any	7 targets in 1:30	14 targets in 1:30	21 targets in 1:30
✓	Cave C.H.R.O.M.E. Race	On rock near the Range and Caves	Use C.H.R.O.M.E. gadgets to defeat the other racers.	Any	1st place in 3 laps	1st place in 3 laps	1st place in 3 laps
✓	Monster Smash	At the Balcony	Break as many collectibles as you can before the time runs out using Monster Tires.	Any- Monster Tires	15 targets in 0:45	20 targets in 0:45	24 targets in 0:45
✓	Town Race	Between The Farm and Town	Finish the race in first place to win.	Any	1st place in 3 laps	1st place in 3 laps	1st place in 3 laps
✓	Throw and Go	Near the Old Road	Break as many collectibles as you can before the time runs out.	Any	15 targets in 0:30	17 targets in 0:30	18 targets in 0:30

Wii NOTE

The Wii version of this Play Set has a different mission order than listed in the walkthrough. The Wii Overview represents the unique flow of missions, in the order they would appear, for the Wii version.

CARS Wii PLAY SET OVERVIEW

			RADIATOR SPRINGS		
Mission Giver	**Mission Type**	**Mission Name**	**Mission Objective**	**Unlocks**	**Page #**
Luigi	Main	Find Luigi	Locate Luigi by Flo's.		256
Luigi	Main	Calibrate GPS	Calibrate your GPS by locating the green markers placed around Radiator Springs.		256
Luigi	Main	Find Guido!	Find Guido at the base of The Cap.		261
Flo	Main	Jump at Flo's	Lower the ramp and perform a jump at Flo's.		257
Flo	Main	Rescue Ramone	Find Ramone near The Barn.		257
Ramone	Main	Tow Ramone	Tow Ramone to Flo's for gas.		267
NPC	Main	Drive to the Farm	Drive to the cavern that takes you to The Farm.		265

			FARM		
Mission Giver	**Mission Type**	**Mission Name**	**Mission Objective**	**Unlocks**	**Page #**
Chick Hicks	Main	Take a Practice Lap	Drive a lap around The Barn.		266
Chick Hicks	Main	Chick's Challenge	Complete a three-lap race against Chick.		266
NPC	Main	Jump Into the Barn	Use a ramp to jump up into The Barn.		263
NPC	Main	Little Bo Beep	Bring three tractors back to The Barn.	Monster Truck Tires	263
NPC	Main	Stunt Practice	Complete the four stunts.		262
NPC	Main	Luigi in Town	Drive to the cave that takes you back to town.		266

			RADIATOR SPRINGS		
Mission Giver	**Mission Type**	**Mission Name**	**Mission Objective**	**Unlocks**	**Page #**
Luigi	Main	Purchase Turbo	Go to the Toy Store and purchase Turbo.	Turbo Level 1	261
Luigi	Main	Drifting Drill	Learn and practice drifting.		261
Luigi	Main	Find Luigi's Crates	Locate and tow Luigi's three crates in Radiator Springs.		261
Flo	Main	In a Jam	Clear the intersection of the NPCs causing a traffic jam.		269
Flo	Main	Catch a Speeder	Catch a speeder and tow them to Mater's.	Fillmore's Organic Fuel	258
Flo	Main	Buy Fillmore's	Purchase Fillmore's Organic Fuels from the Toy Store.		268
Fillmore	Main	Corny Concoction	Collect three ears of corn for organic fuel.	Tow Chain Level 3	268
NPC	Main	Luigi and the Stunt Park	Drive to the cave leading to the Stunt Park.		270

			STUNT PARK		
Mission Giver	**Mission Type**	**Mission Name**	**Mission Objective**	**Unlocks**	**Page #**
Luigi	Main	Balloon Poppin'	Pop the Balloons!		270
Luigi	Main	Learn to Grind	Learn to grind along special edges to gain energy for the Turbo Meter.	Super Pipe	274
NPC	Main	Purchase Super Pipe	Go to the Toy Store and buy the Super Pipe.		274
NPC	Main	Stunted Growth	Perform stunts to score more than 5,000 points.	Unlock Stunt Park area	273
NPC	Main	Purchase Super Ramp	Buy Super Ramp.		274
NPC	Main	Perform Tricks	Complete three tricks from a high place.		263
NPC	Main	Ring Round Up	Collect the rings.	Unlock Full Pipe	273
NPC	Main	Purchase Full Pipe	Visit the Toy Store and purchase the Full Pipe.		273
NPC	Main	Double Tricks	Perform the same trick twice in a rom		274
NPC	Main	Purchase Clover Pool	Buy the Clover Pool from the Toy Store.		275
NPC	Side	Triple Combos	Perform a series of triple combos for the tourist car.		275
NPC	Main	Go to Flo	Drive to the gates that take you back to town and continue to Flo.		275

RADIATOR SPRINGS					
Mission Giver	**Mission Type**	**Mission Name**	**Mission Objective**	**Unlocks**	**Page #**
Flo	Main	Buy Sarge's Hut	Go to the Toy Store and buy Sarge's Hut.	Sarge's Surplus Hut	258
Finn McMissile	Main	Spy Training	Complete basic spy moves.	Ramone's House of Body Art	264
Finn McMissile	Main	Finn at the Farm	Head to the cave that takes you to The Farm.		264
FARM					
Mission Giver	**Mission Type**	**Mission Name**	**Mission Objective**	**Unlocks**	**Page #**
Finn McMissile	Main	Tractor Tipping	Tip over five tractors.	Machine Gun Challenge	265
NPC	Side	Smash and Bash	Destroy fifteen hay bales.	Missiles Challenge	262
NPC	Side	Timed Tractor Tip	Tip five tractors in 1 minute.		278
Flo	Side	Bales of Fire	Destroy the hay bales to stop the fire.	Impact Mine Challenge	257
NPC	Main	On Track with Luigi	Go through the cave that takes you to the race track.		279
TRACK A					
Mission Giver	**Mission Type**	**Mission Name**	**Mission Objective**	**Unlocks**	**Page #**
Luigi	Main	Track Trash Takedown	Race around the track and destroy the crates.		269
Luigi	Main	Race Reversal	Complete the race track in reverse.		271
NPC	Main	A Trip Home	Leave the track and return to town.		271
RADIATOR SPRINGS					
Mission Giver	**Mission Type**	**Mission Name**	**Mission Objective**	**Unlocks**	**Page #**
Flo	Main	Buy Ramone's	Purchase Ramone's House of Body Art from the Toy Store.		267
Ramone	Main	Misplaced Paint	Find all ten of Ramone's paint cans.	Cozy Cone Motel Hut	267
Ramone	Main	Main Street Maker	Customize a building.	Radiator Springs Curios	260
NPC	Main	Buy Radiator Springs Curios	Purchase Radiator Springs Curios from the Toy Store.		260
Flo	Main	Collector Plates	Find fifteen plates.	Tow Chain Level 4	269
Fillmore	Main	Gourd Gatherer	Find three pumpkins for fuel.		276
NPC	Main	Luigi at the New Track	Go to the cave that leads to the Race Invitational Track.		272
TRACK B					
Mission Giver	**Mission Type**	**Mission Name**	**Mission Objective**	**Unlocks**	**Page #**
Luigi	Main	Luigi's New Track B	Race in the new track Luigi has created.		272
NPC	Main	Find Fillmore	Return to town and drive to Fillmore.		276
RADIATOR SPRINGS					
Mission Giver	**Mission Type**	**Mission Name**	**Mission Objective**	**Unlocks**	**Page #**
Fillmore	Main	Tricky, Tricky	Complete tricks for 3,000 points.	Turbo level 2	276
Flo	Main	Paint the Town	Customize three buildings with "Kachow!"		279
Fillmore	Main	Fillmore's Ultimate Fuel	Round up the peppers and bring 'em back to Fillmore.		281
Finn McMissile	Main	Impound Go-Round	Tow the hot rods back to Mater's Impound Lot before they cause any more mischief.		281
NPC	Side	Double Combos	Perform a series of double combos.		275
NPC	Main	Luigi's Ready to Race	Go to the cave leading to the Race Invitational Track.		279
TRACK B					
Mission Giver	**Mission Type**	**Mission Name**	**Mission Objective**	**Unlocks**	**Page #**
Luigi	Main	Double Back Dash	Win the Reverse Track B race.		280
NPC	Side	Francesco's Challenge	Finish in first place in Francesco's Challenge.		281

WII COLLECTIBLES

Town

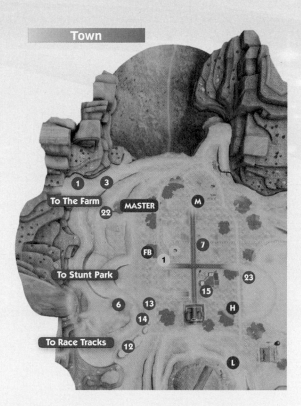

The Farm

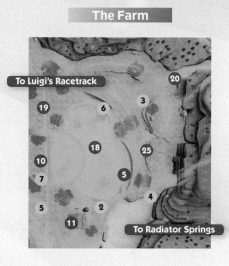

Stunt Park (Visit 1)

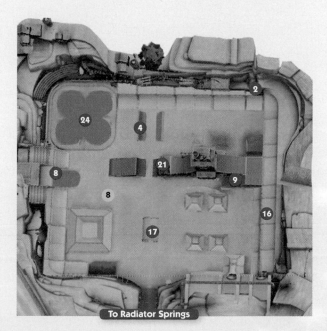

Track A (Visit 1)

Unlockables

Got It?	Key	Unlockable Item	Type	Zone	Location
✓	1	Fillmore Wall	Red Capsule	Town	On the Vista Overlook.
✓	2	Sheet Metal Trim	Red Capsule	Stunt Park	On top of corner wall.
✓	3	Holley Purple Trim	Red Capsule	Town	On ramp up to Vista Overlook.
✓	4	Aqua Stucco	Red Capsule	Stunt Park	On top of Half-Pipe.
✓	5	Wood Accent	Red Capsule	Farm	Next to fence on right side of Farm area.
✓	6	Camo Accent	Red Capsule	Town	In between the two ramps near the cliffs to the left of the town.
✓	7	Flower Quilt Accent	Red Capsule	Town	Near Flo's.
✓	8	Sheet Metal Accent	Red Capsule	Stunt Park	Over gap on left side of Stunt Park.
✓	9	Holley Accent	Red Capsule	Stunt Park	On ramp leading up to Super Ramp.
✓	10	Shiny Wood Trim	Red Capsule	Farm	On left side of Farm area.
✓	11	Tin	Red Capsule	Farm	Use Towable Ramp to jump up and get it next to race banner.
✓	12	Holley's Wall	Red Capsule	Town	On the last of the jumping plateaus to the left of the Town.
✓	13	Red Brick	Red Capsule	Town	To the left of the Fire Station.
✓	14	Basic Brick	Red Capsule	Town	To the left of the Fire Station.
✓	15	Beige Stucco	Red Capsule	Town	Near the Fire Station.
✓	16	Rusty Trim	Red Capsule	Stunt Park	At top of wall on right side of Stunt Park.
✓	17	Orange Cone	Red Capsule	Stunt Park	On top of Full Pipe.
✓	18	Grass Accent	Red Capsule	Farm	In the middle of the large field.
✓	19	Wood Plank	Red Capsule	Farm	At far end of area near cave to Luigi's Race Track.
✓	20	Wood Trim	Red Capsule	Farm	Up on high area in far right side of Farm area.
✓	21	Corrugated Wall	Red Capsule	Stunt Park	At end of Super Ramp.
✓	22	Concrete Accent	Red Capsule	Town	Near the cave leading to the Farm.
✓	23	Wood Planks Accent	Red Capsule	Town	To the right of the Town.
✓	24	Rusty Wall	Red Capsule	Stunt Park	At bottom of Stunt Clover Pool.
✓	25	White Stucco	Red Capsule	Farm	Off side of cliff on right side of Farm area.
✓	FB	Francesco Bernoulli Chest	Avatar Chest	Town	By the tree behind Flo's building.
✓	H	Holley Shiftwell Chest	Avatar Chest	Town	To the right of the Fire Station.
✓	L	Lightning McQueen Chest	Avatar Chest	Town	At the bottom right of the Town area.
✓	MASTER	Cars Avatar Vault - Reward 1	Avatar Vault	Town	Near the cave leading to the Farm.
✓	M	Mater Chest	Avatar Chest	Town	Right out front of Mater's Building.

Cars Challenges

Got It?	#	Name	Location
✓	1	What A Stunt!	Stunt Park (Visit 1)
✓	2	Secret Agent Mater	Stunt Park (Visit 1)
✓	3	Farm Race	Farm (Visit 2)
✓	4	Grab 'n' Go	Farm (Visit 2)
✓	5	Monster Match	Farm (Visit 2)
✓	6	Throw and Go	Farm (Visit 2)
✓	7	Radiator Biathlon	Farm (Visit 2)
✓	8	Shoot for Loot	Farm (Visit 2)
✓	9	Francesco's Battle Race	Track A (Visit 1)

Got It?	#	Name	Location
✓	10	Luigi's Track Race	Track A (Visit 1)
✓	11	Holley's Awesome Challenge	Track A (Visit 1)
✓	12	Score More	Radiator Springs (Visit 4)
✓	13	Monster Smash	Radiator Springs (Visit 4)
✓	14	New Track Race	Track B (Visit 1)
✓	15	New Track Battle	Track B (Visit 1)
✓	16	New Track Race Reverse	Track B (Visit 1)
✓	17	New Track Battle Reverse	Track B (Visit 1)
✓	18	Monster Truck Race	Track B (Visit 1)

Cars Gold Stars

Got It?	#	Type	Name	Description
✓	1	Mission	Blazin' Bales!	Bash through all the flaming hay bales.
✓	2	Mission	Catch a Speeder	Catch speeders and take them to Mater's.
✓	3	Mission	Chick 'n' Farm	Win a race against Chick at The Farm.
✓	4	Mission	Fillmore's Ultimate Fuel	Collect spicy red peppers for Fillmore.
✓	5	Mission	Race the King	Complete a race with "The King".
✓	6	Mission	Backtrack	Win a race on the backward version of Luigi's first track.
✓	7	Mission	Speedway Special	Win a race on Luigi's second track.
✓	8	Mission	Drivin' in Reverse	Win a race on the backward version of Luigi's second track.
✓	9	Mission	Showstopper	Complete the "Jump at Flo's" mission.
✓	10	Mission	Trickster	Complete the "Triple Combos" mission.
✓	11	Mission	Ring-a-Ding	Complete the "Ring Round Up" mission.
✓	12	Mission	Luigi and the Stunt Park	Go to the International Invitational Track.
✓	13	Mission	International Race Pro	Finish the Radiator Springs Invitational in First Place.

Got It?	#	Type	Name	Description
✓	14	Challenge	Monster Master	Complete two Monster Truck Events.
✓	15	Challenge	Best Battler	Win all Battle Race Challenges at any skill level.
✓	16	Challenge	Race Master	Win all Race Challenges at any skill level.
✓	17	Challenge	Lizzie's License Plates	Collect every license plate.
✓	18	Challenge	Kachow! Customizer	Collect 80 Red Capsules.
✓	19	Easter Egg	Trick Master	Perform 100 Air Tricks of any kind.
✓	20	Easter Egg	Never Miss a Trick	Complete every trick mission.
✓	21	Easter Egg	Speed Trap	Catch five speeders.
✓	22	Purchases	Builder	Place every building in the Play Set.
✓	23	Purchases	Tow Master	Purchase every tow chain upgrade.
✓	24	Purchases	Turbo Master	Purchase every turbo upgrade.
✓	25	Purchases	C.H.R.O.M.E. Agent	Purchase every Weapon Challenge.

Cars Toy List

Got It?	Toys	Toy Type	Commercial
✓	Traffic Truck	Townsperson	No
✓	Traffic Van	Townsperson	No
✓	Towable Wrecking Ball	Unique	No
✓	Towable Ramp	Unique	No
✓	Turbo Level 1	Unique	Yes
✓	Turbo Level 2	Unique	No
✓	Full Turbo	Unique	No
✓	Sarge's Surplus Hut	Building	Yes
✓	Fillmore's Organic Fuels	Building	Yes
✓	Ramone's House of Body Art	Building	Yes
✓	Radiator Springs Curios	Building	Yes
✓	Cozy Cone Motel	Building	No

Got It?	Toys	Toy Type	Commercial
✓	Tow Chain Level 2	Unique	Yes
✓	Tow Chain Level 3	Unique	No
✓	Tow Chain Level 4	Unique	No
✓	Machine Gun Challenges	Unique	Yes
✓	Missiles Challenge	Unique	Yes
✓	Impact Mine Challenge	Unique	Yes
✓	Monster Truck Tires	Unique	Yes
✓	Super Pipe	Building	Yes
✓	Super Ramp	Building	No
✓	Full Pipe	Building	No
✓	Stunt Clover Pool	Building	No

The Lone Ranger

CAVENDISH CHAOS IN COLBY

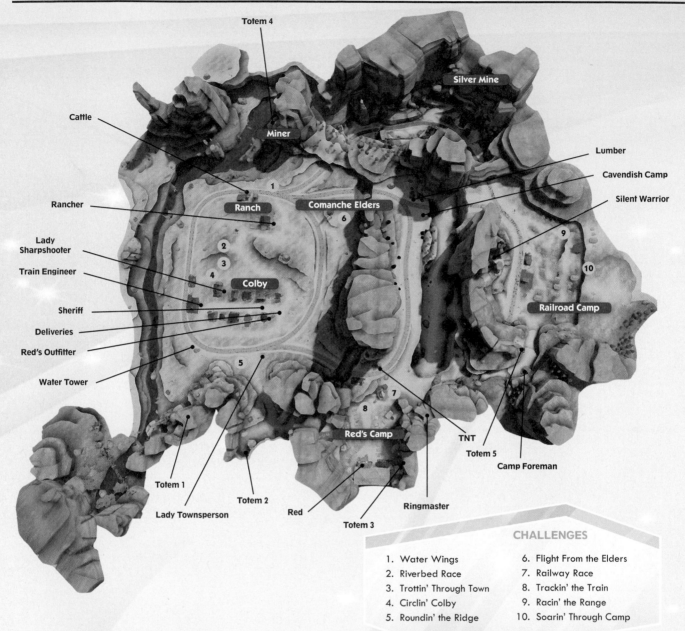

Totem 4

Silver Mine

Cattle

Miner

Lumber

Cavendish Camp

Rancher

Ranch

Comanche Elders

Silent Warrior

Lady Sharpshooter

Train Engineer

Colby

Railroad Camp

Sheriff

Deliveries

Red's Outfitter

Water Tower

Totem 1

Lady Townsperson

Totem 2

Red

Totem 3

Red's Camp

Ringmaster

TNT

Totem 5

Camp Foreman

CHALLENGES

1. Water Wings
2. Riverbed Race
3. Trottin' Through Town
4. Circlin' Colby
5. Roundin' the Ridge
6. Flight From the Elders
7. Railway Race
8. Trackin' the Train
9. Racin' the Range
10. Soarin' Through Camp

SAVIN' COLBY

Mission Giver: Automatic
Type: Combat
Reward: 500 Coins

Things move fast in the wild west. As soon as the mission starts you are under fire. Take down five members of the Cavendish Gang.

SOAKIN' THE SALOON

Mission Giver: Train Engineer
Type: Target Shooting
Reward: 100 Coins
Wii Reward: 25 Coins

The Saloon is on fire! Put it out by releasing a flood of water from the tower on the roof. Enter first-person-shooting mode to aim for the target on the water tower and put out the fire.

BUILDIN' RELATIONSHIPS

Mission Giver: Sheriff
Type: Build
Rewards: 250 Coins / 50 Sparks

The Cavendish Gang made a mess of Colby and you need to help repair the city. Run up to the destroyed structures and select Repair Building to fix and repair three of the buildings.

SIDE MISSION

TARGET PRACTICE

Mission Giver: Lady Sharpshooter
Type: Target Shooting
Rewards: 100 Coins / 20 Sparks

There is a lady in town that is obsessed with shooting skills. She will provide lots of sharpshooting side missions and the first is to literally hit the side of a barn. Take aim at the target on the side of the stable and open fire.

ROUNDIN' EM UP

Mission Giver: Train Engineer
Type: Fetch
Rewards: 250 Coins / 50 Sparks

Looks like some mules broke out of the corral during the initial chaos. Help the town out by searching for four stray mules and riding them back to the stable. Follow the compass to find two on each side of the town and round them up by jumping into the stable.

New Toy Unlocked: Silver

New Toy Unlocked: Scout

⭐ MOUNT UP

Mission Giver: Sheriff
Type: Buy
Rewards: 100 Coins / 20 Sparks

The Sheriff gives some good advice: buy a horse. Traveling around the west is tiring work and the only way to get around is on horseback. Go into the Toy Store and buy your first horse.

GAME BASICS / CHARACTERS / POWER DISCS / PLAY SETS / TOY BOX / TOY BOX COLLECTION / ACHIEVEMENTS

 New Challenges Available: Starts with Circling Colby and then unlocks in order as follows: Trottin' Through Town, Riverbed Race, Railway Race, Racin' the Range

TOWNSPERSON SIDE MISSIONS

MISSING HER MAN

Mission Giver: Lady Townsperson
Type: Destroy
Rewards: 250 Coins / 50 Sparks

A young woman is worried about her husband who went hunting in the hills near the telegraph lines. Get on your horse, which seems to be on the roof of the bank, and use the compass to track the husband.

Jump up the ledges and climb around a large rock structure to find the husband in a cave.

Pick up the man and get back on your horse to take him back to Colby to drop him off in front of his wife.

 **New Toy Unlocked:** Black Horse

DAMSEL IN THIS DRESS

Mission Giver: Lady Townsperson
Type: Customize
Rewards: 100 Coins / 20 Sparks

The poor lady's dress is ruined and she can't afford a new one. Pick her up and toss her into one of Red's traveling outfitters to change her dress.

GET THE TRAIN RUNNING

CLEARIN' THE RAILS

Mission Giver: Train Engineer
Type: Destroy/Combat
Rewards: 250 Coins / 50 Sparks

TRAININ' DAY

Mission Giver: Train Engineer
Type: Buy
Rewards: 100 Coins / 20 Sparks

The Cavendish Gang built blockades on the tracks to keep the trains from running. Use the compass to find the blockade and shoot the TNT by them to clear the tracks. You also have to deal with members of the gang that are patrolling the blockades. Take out the first blockade next to the water tower.

Now that the tracks are clear it's time to get a train. Go into the Toy Store and buy the Constitution Engine.

New Toy Unlocked: Constitution Engine

New Toy Unlocked: Target Package 1

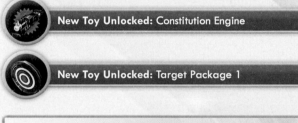

NOTE

There are two additional Alert Missions that can pop up as you go through this adventure. Save the Bank and Save the Camp are similar to the other alert missions in rewards and objective. Like the others, they involve ridding the world of several members of the Cavendish Gang.

Follow the tracks to locate the second group on the right of the train station and try to focus on hitting the TNT so the explosion wipes out a few of the Cavendish Gang.

The last blockade is on the left side of the train station and should be an easy shot after clearing out most of the guards.

RANCHER MISSIONS

RANCH HAND

Mission Giver: Sheriff
Type: Combat
Rewards: 500 Coins / 50 Sparks

There is trouble out at the ranch and you need to deal with those Cavendish boys to the keep the rancher safe. Follow the red arrows to ride out to the ranch and clear out the four punks.

 New Toy Unlocked: Box Car

LIBERATIN' THE TOWER

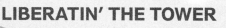

Mission Giver: Rancher
Type: Combat
Rewards: 250 Coins / 175 Sparks

The drought is taking its toll on the town and it seems the train hasn't been delivering any water. Check out the water tower and defeat the gang members that have surrounded the tower.

New Toy Unlocked: TNT Pack

SIDE MISSION
RUNNIN' THE MILL

Mission Giver: Rancher
Type: Target Shooting
Rewards: 100 Coins / 20 Sparks
Wii Rewards: 250 Coins / 20 Sparks

The windmill at the ranch is jammed, so go check it out! This is an easy one to take care of—just go to the windmill and shoot the target to get it moving again.

COMANCHE ELDERS SIDE MISSIONS

THUNDERING STALLION

Mission Giver: Comanche Elders
Type: Locate
Rewards: 250 Coins / 20 Sparks
Wii Rewards: 100 Coins / 20 Sparks

Speak to the Comanche Elders to find the Thundering Stallion and make contact. This mission can only be done at night, so make sure to try it whenever the sun goes down.

If you spot the ghostly spirit, sprint towards it and touch it before it runs away.

 New Toy Unlocked: Palomino

 New Toy Unlocked: Thundering Hooves Pack

CHASING THUNDER

Mission Giver: Comanche Elders
Type: Locate
Rewards: 250 Coins / 20 Sparks
Wii Rewards: 100 Coins / 20 Sparks

WAY OF THE WARRIOR

Mission Giver: Comanche Elders
Type: Locate
Rewards: 250 Coins / 50 Sparks
Wii Rewards: 100 Coins / 50 Sparks

The spirit horse still runs wild. Wait until nightfall and make contact with the Thundering Stallion around Colby.

After buying the Bridge to the Railroad Camp, the Comanche Elders tell you about a mysterious Silent Warrior that can fight by your side if he finds you worthy. Follow the compass past Red's Traveling Entertainments through a tunnel to reach the Railroad Camp.

 New Toy Unlocked: Chestnut Horse

⭐ THE THUNDERING HORSE

Mission Giver: Comanche Elders
Type: Locate
Rewards: 250 Coins / 50 Sparks
Wii Rewards: 100 Coins / 50 Sparks

Return to the Comanche Elders after meeting Red for the final trial of the Thundering Horse. For the last time, wait until night and make contact with the spirit horse around Colby or the temporary Cavendish Camp.

Catching the spirit horse for the third time pays off with a special pack that gives you additional "horsepower" by allowing you

to call upon the Thundering Stallion to stampede right through enemies.

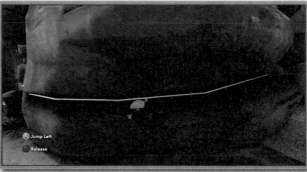

Ride toward the hills on the left and work your way up the rocky plateaus by jumping up a ledge and grabbing on to a thin edge of a boulder.

GAME BASICS

CHARACTERS

POWER DISCS

PLAY SETS

TOY BOX

TOY BOX COLLECTION

ACHIEVEMENTS

SHARPSHOOTING SIDE MISSIONS

RUNNIN' AND GUNNIN'

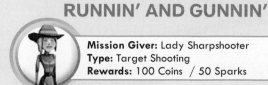

Mission Giver: Lady Sharpshooter
Type: Target Shooting
Rewards: 100 Coins / 50 Sparks

To get up to the higher level you need to remove the rubble by the wooden planks by shooting the dynamite buried in the debris. Climb up the first wooden ladder and shoot the next set of dynamite in the rock.

The little lady wants to see how fast you can knock out a bunch of targets in town. You only have 30 seconds to complete the task, but there are also only five targets on the main streets of Colby. On foot you might have to hustle, but on horseback you can trot along and take them out with well-placed zoomed-in shots.

AIMIN' TO RIDE

Mission Giver: Lady Sharpshooter
Type: Target Shooting
Rewards: 250 Coins / 50 Sparks

She wasn't that impressed with your previous performance and wants to witness how well you can shoot on horseback. Ride towards the five targets at a slow pace and keep firing as you move around the ranch.

New Toy Unlocked: Black Pinto

Leap across the long gap to land on the ledge with the Silent Warrior. It is well worth the trip to seek out the warrior, because he will grant you an extra set of fists to fight off enemies.

New Toy Unlocked: Silent Warrior Pack

TRAIN TIME

RARIN' TO GO

Mission Giver: Train Engineer
Type: Buy
Rewards: 100 Coins / 20 Sparks

The train engineer knows the rancher needs water but to make that kind of delivery you will need a way to transport water. Go into the Toy Store and buy the newly unlocked Water Car.

New Toy Unlocked: Water Car

RAILROAD SWITCH

Mission Giver: Train Engineer
Type: Customize
Rewards: 250 Coins / 50 Sparks

 To customize the train you need to signal the train to stop at the station by shooting the switch target. The switch will change the green-tipped bars to red ones and cause the train to stop at that station.

When the train has stopped, step into the circle next to the station to select Place Train Cars or Customize Train Cars. Add the Water Car you just bought to one of the empty slots called Flatbed Cars.

NOTE

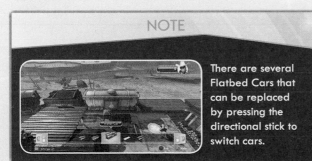

There are several Flatbed Cars that can be replaced by pressing the directional stick to switch cars.

⭐ ENDIN' THE DROUGHT

Mission Giver: Train Engineer
Type: Train Delivery
Rewards: 250 Coins / 175 Sparks

The train is ready to go, but the Water Car has to be filled before you can transport water from the water tower in Colby to the ranch. Shoot the switch to turn the gates back to green and quickly ride out to the water tower. Shoot the target to activate the tower and it will fill the Water Car. The train doesn't need to be babysat while it makes the delivery. Look for the message to pop up on screen to let you know it has done its job.

Any of the delivery towers (water, livestock, lumber, and TNT) will only produce one set of cargo each time the target is hit. That means you must shoot the target again after the train has picked up the load and dropped it off.

New Toy Unlocked: Cattle Car

TOWNSPERSON SIDE MISSION

SKIRTING THE ISSUE

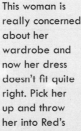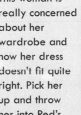

Mission Giver: Lady Townsperson
Type: Customize
Rewards: 100 Coins / 20 Sparks

This woman is really concerned about her wardrobe and now her dress doesn't fit quite right. Pick her up and throw her into Red's traveling outfitters to give her a new dress.

GAME BASICS CHARACTERS POWER DISCS PLAY SETS TOY BOX TOY BOX COLLECTION ACHIEVEMENTS

GETTING TNT

PATROLLIN' THE CANYON

Mission Giver: Sheriff
Type: Combat
Rewards: 250 Coins / 50 Sparks

Some of Cavendish's men have been spotted fleeing into the canyon. Follow the red arrows to hunt them down and wipe them out.

New Toy Unlocked: Dining Car

MININ' HIS BUSINESS

Mission Giver: Sheriff
Type: Combat
Rewards: 100 Coins / 20 Sparks
Wii Rewards: 250 Coins / 20 Sparks

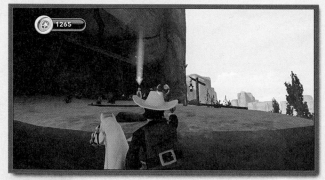

The Cavendish Gang is hiding out in a cave or cavern, but the problem is there is no way to get to them without a generous use of TNT. The old miner is know for stocking TNT and maybe he will give you some. Use the compass to find the miner on a ledge near a deep ravine.

New Toy Unlocked: Golden Horse

 SEEIN' RED

Mission Giver: Miner
Type: Combat
Rewards: 100 Coins / 50 Sparks

The miner would be happy to give you some TNT but the Cavendish Gang took all of it. Red Harrington might have some. She tends to have stuff that nobody else does. The bridge to get to Red's encampment costs 1,500 coins and if you don't have the money you might need to shoot around town or complete a few other missions. Follow the compass out to the encampment and head to the back to find Red.

New Toy Unlocked: Bridge to Red's

New Toy Unlocked: Target Package 2

CATTLE DRIVIN'

Mission Giver: Red
Type: Combat
Rewards: 250 Coins / 175 Sparks

If you want Red's TNT you'll have to do her a favor first. She is interested in cattle but is not about to do a cattle drive to bring them in. The only way to get cattle to Red is to bring them by train from the ranch. Ride out to the ranch and shoot the target to the cattle supply station.

Buy the Cattle Car if you haven't already and place it on the train, then just wait for it to pick up the cattle and deliver them to Red's camp.

New Toy Unlocked: TNT Car

CAVENDISH CLEAR OUT

BACK FOR MORE

Mission Giver: Rancher
Type: Locate
Rewards: 100 Coins / 20 Sparks
Wii Rewards: 250 Coins / 20 Sparks

The rancher hears a ruckus going on in Colby. Ride into town and check it out!

A HEAP A' TROUBLE

Mission Giver: Sheriff
Type: Combat
Rewards: 250 Coins / 50 Sparks

The Cavendish Gang blew up the jail and busted their men out. Take down all four bandits to clean up Colby.

New Toy Unlocked: Gatling Gun Car

REPAIR AND REFORM

Mission Giver: Sheriff
Type: Build
Rewards: 100 Coins / 20 Sparks

When the Cavendish boys broke their buddies out of jail they really wrecked the place. Go to the building that usually has the Sheriff sign on it and repair it.

New Toy Unlocked: Cannon Car

GATLING/CANNON SIDE MISSIONS

> **NOTE**
>
> Requires purchase of Cannon and Gatling Car or Combo Car.

TRAININ' YOUR SIGHTS

Mission Giver: Lady Sharpshooter
Type: Target Shooting
Rewards: 250 Coins / 50 Sparks
Wii Rewards: 100 Coins / 50 Sparks

It's time to up the ante on shooting and break out the big guns. Go to the train station and stop the train to equip it with the Gatling Gun Car. Shoot the switch to start the train again and hop on board to use one of the guns.

It takes a little while to get used to the big weapon, but keep your eyes on the green arrows and try to line up your shots before you get too close. Don't try to get all 20 targets in one trip by swinging from the left to the right. Concentrate on your accuracy and successfully hitting the targets instead of chasing where each one is located. Also, remember that the gun has great range and can be used to hit targets at significant distances.

New Toy Unlocked: Gatling Gun Targets

GAME BASICS

CHARACTERS

POWER DISCS

PLAY SETS

TOY BOX

TOY BOX COLLECTION

ACHIEVEMENTS

SHOOTIN' DOWN THE TRACK

Mission Giver: Lady Sharpshooter
Type: Target Shooting
Rewards: 250 Coins / 50 Sparks

Load a cannon on the train (or use the Combo Gun Car) and practice your making cannon fodder out of the green targets placed around the train tracks.

 New Toy Unlocked: Cannon Targets

AIMIN' HIGH

Mission Giver: Lady Sharpshooter
Type: Target Shooting
Rewards: 100 Coins / 50 Sparks

There is only one target to hit in this mission, but the trick is getting a clean shot at it. You need to get to the top of the hills and the journey begins by leaping up a few plateaus on the rocky mountainside.

Jump up to a thin yellow-highlighted ledge and run around the rock to the right.

Go through a small tunnel and climb the wooden planks to a ledge. Make your way up another set of planks and the target will be in plain sight next to the totem.

SIDE MISSION

FETCHIN' WATER

Mission Giver: Train Engineer
Type: Train Delivery
Rewards: 100 Coins / 50 Sparks

If you removed the Water Car, stop it at the station and replace it. Shoot the target at the water tower to reset it and let the train fill up and make the delivery.

SHERIFF MISSIONS

CLEARIN' THE LINES

Mission Giver: Sheriff
Type: Platforming
Rewards: 250 Coins / 175 Sparks

Turn to the left and leap up several more wooden planks to reach a totem.

The telegraph is down and the town is cut off from communications. The Sheriff asks you to check the wire to find out what is causing all the trouble. Follow the compass to find the problem on the lines—bird's nests are disrupting the signal. Shoot the first nest to clear the line and continue to follow it to find the next obstruction.

The second nest can be targeted from the ground and it is the last one that will be so easy to spot. Go to the edge of a stream and look way up into the sky to find the nest near the tracks.

Drop down to a plateau next to where you shot the nest and take aim at the target on the wooden bridge to bring down the nest. Double jump across it to find that last nest.

New Toy Unlocked: Combo Gun Car

The lines continue high up over the rocky mountains and it is time to get off the horse for some old-school platforming. Jump up the wooden planks and follow a ledge to the right to find another set of planks to climb to the top of a plateau. Search for the nest from this vantage point and shoot it down.

DISRUPTIN' THE BLAST

Mission Giver: Sheriff
Type: Platforming
Rewards: 250 Coins / 50 Sparks

Security must not be a top priority in Colby because there is dynamite all over town. In under 2 minutes you have to find all five bundles of dynamite before they blow. Run up the ramp in back of the Colby Rooming House and leap to the ledge to get to the roof and defuse the first one.

INFINITY

From the roof of the hotel, double jump across to the bank and continue up the street by leaping to the next rooftop with another stack of dynamite. It is a long jump but if you get on the ledge and double jump as you fly towards the building (for length not height), it is possible to grab the ledge and get to the roof of the jail.

Jump up to the awning of the General Merchandise store and take care of the dynamite.

The next bundle is across the way near the water tower. Leap off the roof of the General Merchandise store to land on a balcony of the saloon. Climb up to the roof and make one more leap to the next building to find another stash of dynamite.

The last batch is at the stable and doesn't require any fancy roof jumping—well the other's didn't either but it makes the mission a lot faster to complete. Jump up to the small roof in back near a pile of lumber and blow out the fuse on the dynamite dilemma.

New Toy Unlocked: The Jupiter

PURSUIN' THE POSSE

Mission Giver: Sheriff
Type: Combat
Rewards: 250 Coins / 50 Sparks

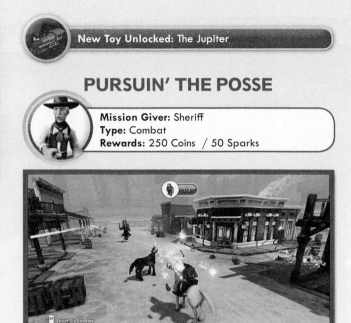

A bunch of thieves stole loads of silver from the town and are making a getaway on horseback. Run all three down right in town and shoot them quickly to avoid having to chase them around on horseback.

New Toy Unlocked: Brown Pinto

RANCHER AND NECKLACE SIDE MISSIONS

CHECKIN' IN

Mission Giver: Rancher
Type: Combat
Rewards: 100 Coins / 50 Sparks

The rancher heard an explosion coming from the hills beyond the train tracks. The spot he is referring to is where the miner hangs out. Make your way out to the hill and wipe out the three members of the Cavendish Gang that are laying siege to the miner's hideout.

STOLEN GOODS

Mission Giver: Rancher
Type: Fetch
Rewards: 100 Coins / 50 Sparks

Some men ran off with the rancher's wife's necklace. The jewelry is very sentimental because it's all the man has left to remember his wife. The only place they can pawn something like that is at Red's. It is time to pay her a visit.

AN HONEST TRADE

Mission Giver: Red
Type: Fetch
Rewards: 100 Coins / 50 Sparks

Red recalls a gentleman bringing her a trinket but she paid dearly for it. All you have to do is bring her something of significantly higher value and the necklace is yours. That doesn't sounds like a great deal, but you have to help the rancher! The only thing that will satisfy Red is some silver ore.

RED'S TRAVELING ENTERTAINMENT MISSIONS
RINGMASTER SIDE MISSIONS

THE GOLDEN SKUNK

Mission Giver: Ringmaster
Type: Fetch
Rewards: 100 Coins / 20 Sparks

The Ringmaster in Red's camp is looking for a golden skunk for his collection. Use the compass to find one outside of Colby and bring it back to him.

⭐ SEEIN' ELEPHANTS

Mission Giver: Ringmaster
Type: Buy
Rewards: 100 Coins / 20 Sparks

Most folks haven't seen an elephant and the Ringmaster thinks he can make a ton of money charging people to see it. This mission will unlock the elephant in the Toy Store and you simply need to buy it for the Ringmaster.

 New Toy Unlocked: Elephant

ARMADILLO ROUND-UP

Mission Giver: Ringmaster
Type: Fetch
Rewards: 100 Coins / 50 Sparks

How about a performing armadillo? Maybe that will get people's attention. Ride out next to the ranch to find another animal performer for the Ringmaster and bring it to him.

GAME BASICS
CHARACTERS
POWER DISCS
PLAY SETS
TOY BOX
TOY BOX COLLECTION
ACHIEVEMENTS

DEALING WITH BANDITS

CAVENDISH RETURNS

Mission Giver: Fortune Teller
Type: Combat
Rewards: 250 Coins / 50 Sparks

When visiting Red's camp stop by to speak with the fortune teller. She has an ominous message about Cavendish approaching Colby to seek revenge.

Ride back to Colby to confront Butch Cavendish and his gang. Open fire and light up the red arrow targets to wipe all five out.

ELEPHANT-BACK RIDIN'

Mission Giver: Red
Type: Combat
Rewards: 250 Coins / 50 Sparks

Cavendish's men snuck into the camp at night and made off with the elephant you gave the Ringmaster. Ride out near the temporary Cavendish Camp to locate the stolen elephant and wipe out the gang that took it.

Hop on the elephant and ride the slow-moving pachyderm all the way back to the corral at Red's Traveling Entertainments.

TRAMPLIN' THE CAMP

Mission Giver: Red
Type: Combat
Rewards: 250 Coins / 50 Sparks

The Cavendish Gang set up camp right near the railroad track so they can stop the trains and take all their supplies. To get back at them, take the elephant for a stroll through the Cavendish camp. You must return the elephant to the Ringmaster to complete the mission.

RAILROAD CAMP

TROMPIN' AROUND

Mission Giver: Ringmaster
Type: Platforming
Rewards: 250 Coins / 20 Sparks
Wii Rewards: 100 Coins / 20 Sparks

The Ringmaster's elephant has become restless and needs some exercise. He has set up a course of checkpoints (green arrows) that he wants you to run through with his cooped up pachyderm. They lead all the way to the Railroad Camp.

CHASIN' ELEPHANTS

Mission Giver: Red
Type: Combat/Fetch
Rewards: 250 Coins / 50 Sparks

That gang of bandits is really fixated on the elephant. They took him again and stole some of Red's money as well. You have 3 minutes and 20 seconds to track down the Cavendish Gang to get back Red's silver and reclaim the elephant. The red arrows will point you to the first bandit close to Red's.

Continue to the lumber station next to the temporary camp to wipe out the other two bandits. Hop on the elephant and take it back to the Ringmaster once again.

RINGMASTER SIDE MISSIONS, PART 2

RUNNIN' ROBBERS

Mission Giver: Ringmaster
Type: Combat
Rewards: 250 Coins / 50 Sparks

A bunch of thieves took the Ringmaster's money. Luckily they didn't get too far as they are lurking around just outside of the encampment. Hop on your horse and chase down the three thieves before they can get away. Make sure to return to the Ringmaster to return his stolen goods.

WILD HORSE ROUND-UP

Mission Giver: Ringmaster
Type: Fetch
Rewards: 100 Coins / 20 Sparks

It seems the rabbit you brought is a stubborn thing and this time the Ringmaster is looking for something he knows he can train—a wild horse. You have 1 minute and 20 seconds to follow the compass and retrieve a wild horse. Sprint out to the canyon and quickly change steeds to the black horse, then run all the way back to the Ringmaster.

REJECTED SKUNK

Mission Giver: Ringmaster
Type: Fetch
Rewards: 100 Coins / 50 Sparks

A golden skunk isn't drawing the crowds the Ringmaster hoped for—in fact it might be driving them away. Pick up the golden stinker and take it back to the desert where you found it.

RABBIT ROUND-UP

Mission Giver: Ringmaster
Type: Fetch
Rewards: 100 Coins / 50 Sparks
Wii Rewards: 100 Coins / 50 Sparks

Surprisingly or not, the armadillo you brought is untrainable. Now the Ringmaster wants a performing rabbit that is hanging out near the railroad tracks. Follow the compass to capture the bunny and see if the Ringmaster has better luck with this critter.

GAME BASICS

CHARACTERS

POWER DISCS

PLAY SETS

TOY BOX

TOY BOX COLLECTION

ACHIEVEMENTS

BRIDGE TO RAILROAD CAMP

⭐ BRIDGIN' THE GAP

Mission Giver: Train Engineer
Type: Buy
Rewards: 100 Coins / 50 Sparks

Go into the Toy Store and buy the Bridge to Railroad Camp to open up access to that area by train.

New Toy Unlocked: Bridge to Railroad Camp

RETAKIN' THE CAMP

Mission Giver: Camp Foreman
Type: Combat
Rewards: 500 Coins / 175 Sparks
Wii Rewards: 250 Coins / 175 Sparks

While you are out strolling with the elephant in the previous mission stop to talk to the Camp Foreman. The Cavendish Gang is attempting to stop the trains by shutting down the Railroad Camp. Fight them off before they destroy the whole encampment.

New Toy Unlocked: Lumber Car

LUMBERIN' ALONG

Mission Giver: Camp Foreman
Type: Buy
Rewards: 100 Coins / 50 Sparks

The Railroad Camp is low on supplies and could really use some lumber. Go to any train station and buy the Lumber Car if you haven't purchased it already. Shoot the switch to stop the train and load the Lumber Car on the train. Ride along the track to find the lumber station and shoot the target to restock it for delivery to the camp.

New Toy Unlocked: Target Package 3

THIRSTIN' FOR MORE

Mission Giver: Red
Type: Train Delivery
Rewards: 100 Coins / 50 Sparks

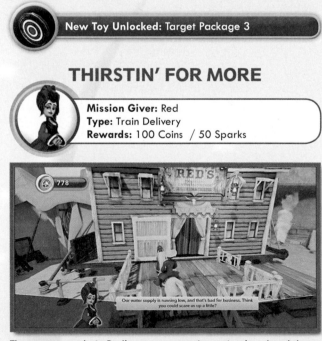

The water supply in Red's encampment is running low. Load the Water Car on the train and hit the target on the water tower to quench their thirst.

LUMBERIN' AWAY

Mission Giver: Red
Type: Train Delivery
Rewards: 100 Coins / 50 Sparks

Deliver lumber by train from the lumber station to Red's.

TRAIN DELIVERY SIDE MISSIONS

MOOVIN' 'EM IN

Mission Giver: Train Engineer
Type: Train Delivery
Rewards: 100 Coins / 50 Sparks

The Sheriff wants to deliver some livestock to Colby. Stop and load the train with the Cattle Car and make sure to shoot the target at the cattle supply station for the train to pick up and make the delivery.

⭐ BARRELIN' THROUGH

Mission Giver: Train Engineer
Type: Train Delivery
Rewards: 100 Coins / 50 Sparks

Buy and load the TNT Car onto the train. Ride out towards Red's and shoot the target on the TNT station. Wait for the train to pick up its load and deliver the TNT to the ranch.

WOOD IF YOU COULD

Mission Giver: Train Engineer
Type: Train Delivery
Rewards: 100 Coins / 50 Sparks

The rancher is doing some repairs on his property and needs some lumber. Make sure to load the Lumber Car on the train and shoot the target at the lumber station to reset and prepare a fresh bundle of lumber.

DYNAMITE DELIVERY

Mission Giver: Train Engineer
Type: Train Delivery
Rewards: 100 Coins / 50 Sparks

Deliver TNT by train from Red's to Colby.

TIMBER TRAIL

Mission Giver: Train Engineer
Type: Train Delivery
Rewards: 100 Coins / 50 Sparks

Some of the old buildings in Colby need fixing up. Transport some lumber to the town by placing the Lumber Car on the train and shooting the lumber station to refill its supply.

SUPPLY ERRANDS

CAMPIN' OUT

Mission Giver: Camp Foreman
Type: Train Delivery
Rewards: 100 Coins / 50 Sparks
Wii Rewards: 250 Coins / 50 Sparks

Climb up into the hills using the same path you traversed to find the Silent Warrior. Shoot the target on the bridge to lower it and double jump across to the ledge with the Gatling gun.

STRIKIN' CAMP

Mission Giver: Camp Foreman
Type: Combat
Rewards: 250 Coins / 50 Sparks

You didn't think you were going to climb all the way up by the Gatling gun just to drop off some supplies, did you? Put that ammunition to use and jump on the big gun to wipe out Cavendish's Gang below. It takes several shots to take down these tough bandits but the gun has infinite ammo so take your time.

NOTE

At this point the first flying mission can be completed if you buy the Crow Wing Pack. See the end of the chapter for how to unlock this awesome ability to fly.

SIDE MISSIONS

NIGHT WATCH

Mission Giver: Fortune Teller
Type: Combat
Rewards: 100 Coins / 50 Sparks
Wii Rewards: 250 Coins / 50 Sparks

After clearing out the Railroad Camp, the fortune teller will have a premonition that it's in danger. This is a shoot 'em up at the camp and there are five bandits that need to be cleared out.

HELPING THE HERD

Mission Giver: Red
Type: Train Delivery
Rewards: 100 Coins / 50 Sparks

Deliver cattle by train from the ranch to Red's.

DRINKIN' IT IN

Mission Giver: Camp Foreman
Type: Train Delivery
Rewards: 100 Coins / 50 Sparks

Transport water by train from the water tower in Colby to the Railroad Camp.

A BANG UP JOB

Mission Giver: Camp Foreman
Type: Train Delivery
Rewards: 100 Coins / 50 Sparks

Deliver TNT by train from Red's to the Railroad Camp.

CONFRONT BUTCH CAVENDISH

MINE BLAST

Mission Giver: Sheriff
Type: Train Delivery
Rewards: 1,000 Coins / 175 Sparks

Butch Cavendish and his men are holed up at the silver mine and it is time to take care of them once and for all. To do that you need to load up the TNT Car with plenty of explosive power and blow up the entrance to the silver mine. Make sure the TNT Car is placed on the train and the TNT station is ready to fill the car.

Then, make sure the track switch near the silver mine entrance is pointing towards the boarded-up entrance. It should switch when the TNT is loaded and the train is heading down that track.

Wii NOTE

In the Wii version of the mission, you must ride to the silver mine and use the Gatling guns and cannons to shoot targets to destroy the buildings and then defeat Butch Cavendish and three members of his gang.

GAME BASICS

CHARACTERS

POWER DISCS

PLAY SETS

TOY BOX

TOY BOX COLLECTION

ACHIEVEMENTS

NOWHERE TO HIDE

Mission Giver: Sheriff (automatic)
Type: Combat
Rewards: 1,000 Coins / 175 Sparks

Follow the train into the silver mine and climb up the hills to turn the Gatling guns and cannons on the Cavendish Gang.

The full description of the mission is very important to pay attention to. It clearly states to use the guns to destroy their hideout at the silver mine, not the bandits. In fact, the bandits will just keep regenerating no matter how many times you shoot them. It can take a while to figure that out if you jump early on the big guns and open fire. The real objective is to use the Gatling gun to take out the red targets around the small buildings and then switch to the cannon to hit the green target and finish it off. However, this doesn't mean you can ignore the bandits because they can still hit you and even wreck your Gatling gun, causing it to smoke or light on fire.

The first building to fall is the one on the bottom level in the center. After that is gone, wipe out a bunch of the bandits to trigger the next targets.

The other three buildings will sprout Gatling targets and can be taken out in any order. Try to hit the Gatling targets as quickly as possible to reveal the green cannon target and move on to the next.

Finally, when all four buildings are gone, take out any straggling bandits. To finish the job, there is one more cannon target to shoot in order to close the book on Butch Cavendish.

New Toy Unlocked: Thundering Stallion

SIDE MISSION WRAP UP

HELPIN' A STRANGER

Mission Giver: Rancher
Type: Locate
Rewards: 100 Coins / 50 Sparks

A friend of the rancher went out to the silver mine and hasn't returned. The rancher wants you to check the mine to see what happened to his friend. Ride out to the silver mine and look behind one of the small buildings on the ground level to find a whole group of people hiding out.

CATTLE CALL

Mission Giver: Camp Foreman
Type: Train Delivery
Rewards: 100 Coins / 50 Sparks

Deliver cattle by train from the cattle station near Colby to the Railroad Camp.

LUMBERIN' ABOUT

Mission Giver: Camp Foreman
Type: Train Delivery
Rewards: 100 Coins / 50 Sparks

Deliver lumber by train from the lumber station to the Railroad Camp.

MININ' FOR SILVER

Mission Giver: Camp Foreman
Type: Platforming
Rewards: 100 Coins / 50 Sparks

The foreman came across a secret cave high in the hills that is full with silver. He is happy to share the silver up there if you can get to it. Getting to the four spots where the silver is hidden will be easy if you can get the Crow Wing Pack, but it IS possible to get to all of them without it—it's just a lot harder!

Go to the silver mine area and enter the cave where you destroyed Cavendish's men and buildings. Follow the tracks until you emerge back outside and immediately look to your right to find the first batch of silver.

One of the stashes of silver is pretty easy to get to. This one is hidden in the far end of the mine and simply requires a few double jumps onto some ledges.

The third one can be found with some basic platforming. Jump up the narrow passage in the hills and shoot the dynamite to clear a thin ridge you can climb around.

Leap to another ledge in the giant rock and run onto the wooden platforms. Jump up to the ledge and get up to the top tier to find the third stash of silver.

This final stash is where flying would be really useful, yet it can be found on foot if you are careful. Start out by jumping on the slanted part of this building, jump down to the balcony, and run around the building.

This is where it gets tricky. Run around to the corner of the building near a large rock. Walk up to the corner of the very edge of this area (not on the boulder) and jump to the rock next to the roof.

Jump onto the chute and slowly walk all the way to the end of the line. It is very easy to fall off, so take your time!

Leap down to the roof below and slide down the long roof panel to a smaller section of roof right next to the tracks. Perform a long double jump to land on the track and follow it towards the green arrow.

When the track breaks up, carefully step along the remaining wooden beam to the left. Take it nice and slow until you can double jump to the other side of the track.

Finally, use one more long double jump to get to the last stash and clear the mission without the ability to fly.

DRY SPELL

Mission Giver: Fortune Teller
Type: Train Delivery
Rewards: 100 Coins / 175 Sparks

The last delivery mission is to compensate for an upcoming drought. The goal is to deliver water by train to all stations before the river bed runs dry. Keep resetting the water tower at Colby after each delivery until every station is watered.

CROW WING ABILITY

Mission Giver: Automatic
Type: Platforming
Rewards: 1,000 Coins / 50 Sparks

This is sort of a hidden mission that runs throughout the adventure. There are five special totems to find in the Play Set, and once you have encountered them all you will gain the ability to fly!

The first totem should have been found when searching for the nests during the Clearin' the Lines mission. Outside of Colby you can climb up some wooden planks on the side of the mountain and go up several more planks to a high ledge.

The second totem is easy to find but also easy to overlook. The canyon near Colby had some Cavendish boys lurking around, but you probably didn't go all the way around the fire into the small alcove where it hides.

The third totem is also easy to find but is out of sight at Red's Traveling Entertainments. Next to Red is a brown building that obscures this totem to the left of it.

The next one is NOT easy to find and your only clue is that you might have noticed the planks on the left side of the wall when visiting the miner. There are a series of ledges below that hide the fourth totem as well a few boulders that lead to a little island. The planks on the side near the miner can be used to climb down to the find the totem and get back up.

The last one is also hard to notice because it is really high up. Go to the Railroad Camp and climb to the area where you went to meet the Silent Warrior and used the Gatling gun. However, instead of climbing the wooden planks, run out towards the hills to the left.

Run as far as you can along this path to a notice a tower on a ridge and a series of wooden planks you can climb.

To get to the top of this tower you need to leap up the wooden structure by climbing up boards and moving around to the sides to continue your ascension. It is not a simple climb straight up. Expect to have to maneuver around the tower as you go higher. The prize at the top is the Crow Wing Pack.

The prize was certainly worth all the effort because the Crow Wing Pack grants the ability to turn into a crow and fly across the entire Play Set to collect all capsules.

New Toy Unlocked: Crow Wing Pack

NOTE

Buying this ability unlocks new challenges.

New Challenges Available: Flight From the Elders, Water Wings, Roundin' the Ridge, Trackin' the Train, and Soarin' Through Camp

Wii NOTE

In the Wii version, the Crow Wing Shrine is sitting on top of the train tunnel. You do not have to climb the scaffolding.

GAME BASICS

CHARACTERS

POWER DISCS

PLAY SETS

TOY BOX

TOY BOX COLLECTION

ACHIEVEMENTS

COLLECTIBLES

Red Capsules

Got It?	#	Unlockable Item	Zone	Location
✓	1	Rusty Water Car	Colby	On the side of the General Merchandise building.
✓	2	Mustache Face	Colby	Behind the Grand Colby Saloon.
✓	3	Metal Trim	Colby	On the roof of the Grand Colby Saloon.
✓	4	Cowgirl Hat	Colby	On the roof of the Bank.
✓	5	Plastic Water Car	Colby	On the top of the back staircase of the Colby Rooming House.
✓	6	Monocle and Top Hat	Colby	On the roof of J.R. Stein, Furniture and Undertaker.
✓	7	Corrugated Metal Lumber Car	Colby	On the roof of Samuel's Livery Stable.
✓	8	Rusty Engine Wheels	Colby	On the roof of the Colby train station.
✓	9	Huge Nose Face	Colby	Behind the boulder near the water tower right by the river.
✓	10	Plastic Trim	Colby	On the river right beside a big boulder.
✓	11	Painted Engine	Colby	At the base of the spire, near the waterfall.
✓	12	Plastic Engine	Colby	On the ledge leading up to the spire.
✓	13	White Trim	Colby	On the ladder leading up to the spire.
✓	14	Cowgirl Outfit	Colby	On the railroad tracks next to the spire.
✓	15	Patched Suit	Colby	On the ledge leading up to the spire.
✓	16	Plastic Tarp Lumber Car	Colby	On the rock steps behind J.R. Stein, Furniture and Undertaker.
✓	17	Plastic Wheels	Colby	On the right side of the canyon behind the Bank.
✓	18	Elderly Female Face	Colby	On the left side of the canyon behind the Bank.
✓	19	Rusted Metal Coal Car	Colby	Near the bridge coming up to Red's Camp.
✓	20	Rusty Wheels	Colby	Straight behind the landing zone.
✓	21	Dress and Apron	Colby	Behind the rocks near the Comanche Elders' Camp.
✓	22	Wooden Wheels	Colby	Across from the Colby train station and behind a boulder on the other side of the river.
✓	23	Camouflage Coal Car	Ranch	Behind the Ranch, near the rock and in front of the river.
✓	24	Standard Coal Car	Ranch	In the graveyard.
✓	25	Racecar Car	Ranch	In between the ranch house and the town.
✓	26	Buffalo Horn Headdress	Ranch	Between the water tower and the Barn.
✓	27	Suspenders	Ranch	On the ground near the Farmhouse.
✓	28	Big Nose Face	Ranch	On the roof of the Farmhouse.
✓	29	Worn Wood Car	Ranch	On the roof of the Farmhouse.
✓	30	Rusty Engine	Ranch	Behind the water tower near the river.
✓	31	Miner Attire	Ranch	Behind the barn, on the other side of the river.
✓	32	Wide Nose Face	Ranch	Behind the barn, on the other side of the river and near the top of the rocks.
✓	33	Smiling Female Face	Ranch	By a boulder across the railroad from the Comanche Elders' Camp.
✓	34	Comanche Warrior Attire	Comanche Elders	In front of the Comanche Elders' Camp.
✓	35	Comanche Warrior Face	Comanche Elders	In front of the Comanche Elders' Camp.

GAME BASICS

CHARACTERS

POWER DISCS

PLAY SETS

TOY BOX

TOY BOX COLLECTION

ACHIEVEMENTS

Got It?	#	Unlockable Item	Zone	Location
✓	36	Railroad Worker Attire	Comanche Elders	Near the tunnel to the Silver Mine.
✓	37	Rusty Trim	Comanche Elders	Behind the rock near the tunnel to the Silver Mine.
✓	38	Thick Mustache	Silver Mine	Near the entrance to the Silver Mine along the wall.
✓	39	Twisted Horned Mask	Silver Mine	In the air over the railroad.
✓	40	Goatee and Top Hat	Silver Mine	Along the wall, in between the boulders and across from Sleeping Man.
✓	41	Imp Mask and Cape	Silver Mine	On top of an old railroad track along the boulder wall.
✓	42	Checkered Shirt	Silver Mine	In the air near the boulder wall.
✓	43	Tuxedo	Silver Mine	Over a wooden platform near the mini tunnel.
✓	44	Racecar Engine Wheels	Silver Mine	Inside mini tunnel.
✓	45	Gypsy Attire	Silver Mine	Inside mini tunnel.
✓	46	Floral Water Car	Silver Mine	On the elevated railroad near the mini tunnel.
✓	47	Simple Suit	Silver Mine	Behind the wooden house near the boulder wall.
✓	48	Floral Lumber Car	Silver Mine	On top of the wooden platform with tracks leading to the mini tunnel.
✓	49	Plastic Coal Car	Silver Mine	On top of the wooden platform with tracks leading to the mini tunnel.
✓	50	Stone Wheels	Silver Mine	Tucked into the wall near the Silver Mine Entrance.
✓	51	Male Face 6	Silver Mine	Tucked into the wall near the Silver Mine Entrance.
✓	52	Shiny Wheels	Silver Mine	Inside the tunnel that is next to the Sleeping Man.
✓	53	Circus Water Car	Red's	On the roof of the lumber building.
✓	54	Floral Wheels	Red's	Near the top of the boulder near the railroad.
✓	55	Zebra Water Car	Red's	On the roof of the shack along the railroad tracks.
✓	56	Circus Lumber Car	Red's	In the air over the railroad.
✓	57	Skirt and Sash	Red's	On the ground near the bridge to the Railroad Camp.
✓	58	Metal Tile Trim	Red's	Near the top of the boulder near the railroad switcher.
✓	59	Bearded Woman	Red's	On the ground near the railroad switcher.
✓	60	Coiled Snake	Red's	At the top of the boulder near the railroad track.
✓	61	Bison Head	Red's	On the ground beside the little white house near the boulder.
✓	62	Zebra Coal Car	Red's	In the air by the bridge to Railroad Camp.
✓	63	Male Face 3	Red's	Inside the cave.
✓	64	Diamonds and Stripes	Red's	On the top of the wooden platform behind the wagons.
✓	65	Suspenders and Chaps	Red's	On the wooden platform under the elevated train tracks.
✓	66	Light Makeup Face 1	Red's	Behind the wooden house right near the entrance of Red's Camp.
✓	67	Merchant Suit	Red's	On the top of the boulder right near the entrance of Red's Camp.
✓	68	Frilly Dress and Corset	Red's	Behind the tents.
✓	69	Zebra Car	Red's	Inside the tent.
✓	70	Floral Coal Car	Red's	In the air over the tents.
✓	71	Beak Mask	Red's	Behind the tents.

Got It?	#	Unlockable Item	Zone	Location
✓	72	Leaf Mask	Red's	Beside the Palmistry and Psychic Readings.
✓	73	Circus Car	Red's	Inside the tent.
✓	74	Circus Trim	Red's	On top of the barrel freight of the train.
✓	75	Visor	Red's	On top of the boulder behind the Hall of Oddities.
✓	76	Shifty Eyed Face	Red's	Behind the tents that are near the Hall of Oddities.
✓	77	Circus Coal Car	Red's	In the tent near the Red's Traveling Entertainments.
✓	78	Male Face 2	Red's	In front of the Grand Colby Saloon.
✓	79	Light Makeup Face 3	Red's	On the ground near the elevated train tracks.
✓	80	Camouflage Car	Railroad Camp	To the side of the train tunnel.
✓	81	Painted Coal Car	Railroad Camp	To the side of the train tunnel.
✓	82	Carbon Fiber Wheels	Railroad Camp	In between the wagon and piles of wood.
✓	83	Camouflage Lumber Car	Railroad Camp	Behind the tents near the fenced off area by the hay.
✓	84	Carbon Fiber Trim	Railroad Camp	In between tents.
✓	85	Camouflage Water Car	Railroad Camp	Near the tents by the wagon and pile of wood.
✓	86	Beard and Hat	Railroad Camp	In between tents.
✓	87	Camouflage Engine	Railroad Camp	In front of the wooden house behind the tents.
✓	88	Opaque Trim	Railroad Camp	Behind the tent by the railroad tracks.
✓	89	Painted Lumber Car	Railroad Camp	Behind the rock near the railroad track.
✓	90	Striped Pants	Railroad Camp	Behind the tents.
✓	91	Racecar Engine	Railroad Camp	In front of the railroad station.
✓	92	Male Face 8	Railroad Camp	On top of the boulders across from the train station.
✓	93	Soldier Uniform	Railroad Camp	On top of boulders across from the train station near the Gatling gun.
✓	94	Male Face 1	Railroad Camp	Across from the train station, on top of the boulders and underneath the shed.
✓	95	Fine Vest Suit	Railroad Camp	Behind a tent across from the train station.
✓	96	Narrow Male Face	Railroad Camp	Across from the train station beside the rock.
✓	97	Soldier Hat	Railroad Camp	Across from the train station tucked away along the wall.
✓	98	Long-Nosed Mask	Railroad Camp	By the hole in the wall.
✓	99	Full Beard and Hat	Colby	In the air behind the Grand Colby Saloon.
✓	100	Bamboo Hat	Colby	In the air over the Sheriff building.
✓	101	Floral Engine	Red's	In the air near the bridge to the Railroad Camp.
✓	102	Decorative Hat	Red's	In the air over the river.
✓	103	Zebra Lumber Car	Red's	In the air over the bridge to the Railroad Camp near the lumber yard.
✓	104	Zebra Engine	Colby	In the air near the bridge to Red's Camp.
✓	105	Circus Engine	Red's	In the air near the bridge to Red's Camp.
✓	106	Painted Water Car	Railroad Camp	Behind the wooden house that is behind the tents.

GAME BASICS

CHARACTERS

POWER DISCS

PLAY SETS

TOY BOX

TOY BOX COLLECTION

ACHIEVEMENTS

Green Capsules

Got It?	#	Unlockable Item	Zone	Location
✓	107	Colby Jail House Siding	Railroad Camp	On the hill across from the train station.
✓	108	Colby Stone Wall	Railroad Camp	In the air near the bridge to Red's Camp.
✓	109	Colby Weathered Floorboard	Railroad Camp	Along the wall of the Railroad Camp near the entrance to the Silver Mine.
✓	110	Colby Buildings Toy Pack 4	Colby	Over the water tower that is on the roof of the Grand Colby Saloon.
✓	111	Colby Buildings Toy Pack 1	Colby	In the air behind the Colby Rooming House.
✓	112	Colby Buildings Toy Pack 3	Colby	Over the water tower in front of the spire.
✓	113	Colby General Store Siding	Colby	In the air by the water tower and spire.
✓	114	Colby Townsperson Toy Pack 1	Colby	On the ledge near the spire wall and near the waterfall.
✓	115	Colby Townsperson Toy Pack 2	Colby	At the top of the spire.
✓	116	Colby Townsperson Toy Pack 5	Colby	Behind the Sheriff building.
✓	117	Colby Bank Bricks	Colby	On the top of the rocks in the canyon behind the Bank.
✓	118	Colby Platform Floorboard	Ranch	Under the windmill.
✓	119	Colby Rooming House Siding	Ranch	On the far side of the river.
✓	120	Colby Train Station Siding	Ranch	On the side of the ranch house.
✓	121	Colby Stable Siding	Ranch	On the side of the ranch house.
✓	122	Colby Wash House Siding	Ranch	Near the ranch house and behind the wagon.
✓	123	Colby Buildings Toy Pack 2	Ranch	In the air behind the train station.
✓	124	Colby Saloon Siding	Ranch	In the air in between the ranch house and the cattle barn.
✓	125	Colby Townsperson Toy Pack 4	Ranch	On the island in the river across from the train station.
✓	126	Vertical Sliding Walls	Ranch	In the air over the river, past the island.
✓	127	Colby Townsperson Toy Pack 3	Ranch	On the shore, opposite from the island.
✓	128	Colby Floorboard	Comanche Elders	Behind a rock near the Comanche Elders.
✓	129	Colby Hardware Store Siding	Comanche Elders	In the air near the bridge to Red's Camp.
✓	130	Red's Wooden Floorboard	Silver Mine	On the ground near the entrance to the Silver Mine.
✓	131	Colby Worn Floorboard	Silver Mine	On the cliffside directly across from Sleeping Man.
✓	132	Colby Decorations Toy Pack 2	Silver Mine	On the cliffside directly across from Sleeping Man.
✓	133	Colby Large Floorboard	Silver Mine	In the air across from Sleeping Man.
✓	134	Colby Wooden Shingles	Silver Mine	Up the path on the cliffside.
✓	135	Colby Wooden Siding	Silver Mine	Tucked into the wall behind the dynamite.
✓	136	Colby Decorations Toy Pack 1	Silver Mine	On the elevated train track.
✓	137	Colby Wood Moulding	Silver Mine	In the air in between the entrance to the Silver Mine and the elevated train tracks.
✓	138	Colby Polished Floorboard	Silver Mine	In front of Sleeping Man.
✓	139	Colby Critter Toy Pack 1	Red's	On the roof of the red train.
✓	140	Colby Townsperson Toy Pack 7	Red's	Inside the tent beside the Grand Colby Saloon.

Got It?	#	Unlockable Item	Zone	Location
✓	141	Red's Wooden Siding	Red's	Beside the tent that is behind Red's Traveling Entertainments.
✓	142	Colby Townsperson Toy Pack 8	Red's	Inside the tent of the Hall of Oddities.
✓	143	Colby Large Wooden Siding	Red's	In the air behind the tents and near the elevated train track.
✓	144	Red's Bricks	Red's	On top of the tall boulder.
✓	145	Colby Store Vertical Siding	Red's	Along the wall near the tunnel.
✓	146	Colby Townsperson Toy Pack 6	Red's	Near the bridge to Railroad Camp.
✓	147	Colby Plants Toy Pack 1	Red's	Inside the tunnel to Railroad Camp.
✓	148	Colby Wooden Crate	Railroad Camp	In the hole in the wall.
✓	149	Colby Small Siding	Railroad Camp	Over the train tunnel and underneath the wooden platform.
✓	150	Colby Plants Toy Pack 2	Railroad Camp	In the corner of the Railroad Camp near the wooden house.

🎁 Infinity Chests/Vault

Got It?	#	Unlockable Item	Zone	Location
✓	LR1	Lone Ranger Chest 1	Ranch	In the cemetery.
✓	LR2	Lone Ranger Chest 2	Colby	At the base of the spire.
✓	LR3	Lone Ranger Chest 3	Railroad Camp	On the upper ledge across from the train station.
✓	Master	Lone Ranger Avatar Vault - Reward 1	Colby	Tucked into the wall inside the canyon behind the Bank.
✓	T1	Tonto Chest 1	Comanche Elders	On the ground near the Comanche Elders' Camp.
✓	T2	Tonto Chest 2	Red's	At the base of the tall boulder at Red's Camp.
✓	T3	Tonto Chest 3	Silver Mine	On the cliffside directly across from Sleeping Man.

⭐ Lone Ranger Gold Stars

Got It?	#	Type	Star Names	Star Description
✓	1	Mission	Horsing Around	Buy a horse.
✓	2	Mission	Delivery Training	Deliver supplies by train.
✓	3	Mission	Red's Traveling Entertainments	Get to Red's Traveling Entertainments.
✓	4	Mission	The Railroad Camp	Get to the Railroad Camp.
✓	5	Mission	Cavendish's Downfall	Defeat Butch Cavendish.
✓	6	Mission	No Ordinary Round-Up	Capture all of the mystical animals.
✓	7	Mission	All's Said and Done	Complete 50 missions.
✓	8	Challenge	Rough Rider	Attempt all Horse Racing Challenges.
✓	9	Challenge	Horse Master	Successfully complete the highest level of difficulty on all Horse Racing Challenges.
✓	10	Challenge	Winging It	Attempt all Crow Flight Challenges.
✓	11	Challenge	Flight Master	Successfully complete the highest level of difficulty on all Crow Flight Challenges.
✓	12	Easter Egg	Sharpshooter	Hit 20 shooting gallery targets.
✓	13	Easter Egg	Dead Eye	Hit 50 shooting gallery targets.
✓	14	Easter Egg	Gatling Gunner	Shoot 20 Gatling gun targets.

GAME BASICS

CHARACTERS

POWER DISCS

PLAY SETS

TOY BOX

TOY BOX COLLECTION

ACHIEVEMENTS

Got It?	#	Type	Star Names	Star Description
✓	15	Easter Egg	Cannon Master	Shoot 20 Cannon targets.
✓	16	Easter Egg	Tailor Made	Customize townspeople 20 times.
✓	17	Easter Egg	Gang Wrangler	Defeat 20 Cavendish Gang members.
✓	18	Easter Egg	Gang Wrangling Legend	Defeat 75 Cavendish Gang members.
✓	19	Easter Egg	All is Found	Collect 20 prize capsules.
✓	20	Easter Egg	Barrel Breaker	Break 200 barrels.
✓	21	Easter Egg	Track of All Trades	Deliver each resource at least one time.
✓	22	Easter Egg	Track Master	Deliver five resources by train.
✓	23	Easter Egg	Frequent Flyer	Fly as a crow 30 times.
✓	24	Easter Egg	Surprise Attack	Summon the Silent Warrior to defeat 20 enemies.
✓	25	Easter Egg	Dynamite Defeat	Defeat 20 enemies with dynamite from the TNT pack.
✓	26	Purchases	Trunk Space	Purchase the Elephant.
✓	27	Purchases	Railroad Tycoon	Purchase all of the Train Cars.
✓	28	Purchases	On Target	Purchase all of the Target Packages.
✓	29	Purchases	Hold Your Horses	Purchase every horse from the Toy Store.
✓	30	Purchases	The Completist	Purchase every toy from the Toy Store.

Lone Ranger Toy List

Got It?	Toys	Toy Box Export	Toy Type	Commercial
✓	Black Horse	Yes	Vehicle/Mount	No
✓	Black Pinto Horse	Yes	Vehicle/Mount	No
✓	Box Car	No	Vehicle/Mount	No
✓	Bridge to Railroad Camp	No	Unique	No
✓	Bridge to Red's	No	Unique	No
✓	Brown Pinto Horse	Yes	Vehicle/Mount	No
✓	Cannon Car	No	Vehicle/Mount	No
✓	Cannon Targets	No	Unique	No
✓	Cattle Car	No	Vehicle/Mount	Yes
✓	Chestnut Horse	Yes	Vehicle/Mount	No
✓	Constitution Engine	No	Vehicle/Mount	No
✓	Crow Wing Pack	Yes	Prop	Yes
✓	Elephant	Yes	Vehicle/Mount	Yes
✓	Gatling Gun Car	No	Vehicle/Mount	Yes
✓	Gatling Gun Targets	No	Unique	No
✓	Combo Gun Car	No	Vehicle/Mount	No

Got It?	Toys	Toy Box Export	Toy Type	Commercial
✓	Golden Horse	Yes	Vehicle/Mount	No
✓	Lumber Car	No	Vehicle/Mount	Yes
✓	Palomino	Yes	Vehicle/Mount	No
✓	Dining Car	No	Vehicle/Mount	No
✓	Scout	Yes	Vehicle/Mount	No
✓	Silent Warrior Pack	Yes	Prop	Yes
✓	Silver	Yes	Vehicle/Mount	Yes
✓	Target Package 1	No	Unique	No
✓	Target Package 2	No	Unique	No
✓	Target Package 3	No	Unique	No
✓	The Jupiter	No	Vehicle/Mount	No
✓	Thundering Hooves Pack	Yes	Prop	Yes
✓	Thundering Stallion	Yes	Vehicle/Mount	Yes
✓	TNT Car	No	Vehicle/Mount	Yes
✓	TNT Pack	Yes	Prop	Yes
✓	Water Car	No	Vehicle/Mount	Yes

Lone Ranger Challenges

Got It?	Name	Location	Description	Character	Requirements		
					Easy	Medium	Hard
✓	Circlin' Colby	Near Colby	Ride a horse through all the gates before the time runs out.	Any	7 gates in 1:00	7 gates in 0:45	7 gates in 0:35
✓	Trottin' Through Town	Near Colby	Ride a horse through all the gates before the time runs out.	Any	8 gates in 1:00	8 gates in 0:50	8 gates in 0:40
✓	Riverbed Race	Near Colby	Ride a horse through all the gates before the time runs out.	Any	9 gates in 1:10	9 gates in 0:55	9 gates in 0:45
✓	Railway Race	Near Red's	Ride as Lone Ranger through all the gates before the time runs out.	Lone Ranger	10 gates in 1:30	10 gates in 1:15	10 gates in 1:00
✓	Racin' the Range	Railroad Camp	Ride a horse through all the gates before the time runs out.	Any	12 gates in 2:00	12 gates in 1:45	12 gates in 1:30
✓	Flight from the Elders	Near Comanche Elders	Use the Crow Wing Pack to gather the collectibles before the time runs out.	Any	15 collectibles in 1:10	30 collectibles in 1:10	40 collectibles in 1:10
✓	Water Wings	Near Ranch	Use the Crow Wing Pack to gather the collectibles before the time runs out.	Any	15 collectibles in 1:10	30 collectibles in 1:10	40 collectibles in 1:10
✓	Roundin' the Ridge	Near Canyon by Colby	Use the Crow Wing Pack to gather the collectibles before the time runs out.	Any	20 collectibles in 1:10	35 collectibles in 1:10	50 collectibles in 1:10
✓	Trackin' the Train	Near Red's	Using Tonto and the Crow Wing Pack, gather the collectibles before time runs out.	Tonto	15 collectibles in 1:10	30 collectibles in 1:10	45 collectibles in 1:10
✓	Soarin' Through Camp	Near Railroad Camp	Use the Crow Wing Pack to gather the collectibles before the time runs out.	Any	20 collectibles in 1:00	35 collectibles in 1:00	45 collectibles in 1:00

GAME BASICS · CHARACTERS · POWER DISCS · PLAY SETS · TOY BOX · TOY BOX COLLECTION · ACHIEVEMENTS

Unlockables

Got It?	Key	Unlockable Item	Type	Zone	Location
✓	LR	Lone Ranger Chest 1	Avatar Chest	Ranch	In the cemetery.
✓	TO	Tonto Chest 1	Avatar Chest	Comanche Elders	On the ground near the Comanche Elders' Camp.
✓	MASTER	Lone Ranger Avatar Vault - Reward 1	Avatar Vault	Colby	Tucked into the wall inside the canyon behind the bank.

Lone Ranger Challenges

Got It?	#	Name	Location
✓	1	Circlin' Colby	Near train station
✓	2	Trottin' Through Town	Near train station
✓	3	Riverbed Race	Near train station

Got It?	#	Name	Location
✓	4	Final Race	Near Red's
✓	5	Flight from the Elders	Near Commanche Elders
✓	6	Water Wings	Near Red's

Lone Ranger Gold Stars

Got It?	#	Type	Name	Description
✓	1	Mission	Horsing Around	Buy a horse.
✓	2	Mission	Helping Hand	Help the Rancher.
✓	3	Mission	Red's Traveling Entertainments	Get to Red's Traveling Entertainments.
✓	4	Mission	All's Said and Done	Complete 20 missions.
✓	5	Challenge	Rough Rider	Complete all Colby Horse Racing Challenges.
✓	9	Easter Egg	Sharpshooter	Hit 20 shooting gallery targets.
✓	10	Easter Egg	Dead Eye	Hit 50 shooting gallery targets.
✓	11	Easter Egg	Marksman	Hit 250 shooting gallery targets.
✓	12	Easter Egg	Gatling Gunner	Shoot 20 Gatling gun targets.
✓	13	Easter Egg	Gang Wrangler	Defeat 10 Cavendish Gang members.
✓	14	Easter Egg	Gang Wrangler Master	Defeat 25 Cavendish Gang members.

Got It?	#	Type	Name	Description
✓	15	Easter Egg	Gang Wrangling Legend	Defeat 50 Cavendish Gang members.
✓	16	Easter Egg	All is Found	Collect 50 prize capsules.
✓	17	Easter Egg	Barrelling Through	Break 20 barrels.
✓	18	Easter Egg	Barrel Breaker	Break 200 barrels.
✓	19	Easter Egg	Frequent Flyer	Fly as a crow 30 times.
✓	20	Easter Egg	Surprise Attack	Summon the Silent Warrior to defeat 10 enemies.
✓	21	Easter Egg	Dynamite Defeat	Defeat 10 enemies with dynamite from the TNT pack.
✓	22	Purchases	On Target	Purchase all of the Target Packages.
✓	23	Purchases	Hold Your Horses	Purchase every horse from the Toy Store.
✓	24	Purchases	The Completist	Purchase every toy from the Toy Store.
✓	25	Purchases	Rolling Thunder	Purchase the Thundering Hooves Pack.

Lone Ranger Toy List

Got It?	Toys	Toy Type	Commercial
✓	Black Horse	Vehicle/Mount	No
✓	Black Pinto Horse	Vehicle/Mount	No
✓	Brown Pinto Horse	Vehicle/Mount	No
✓	Chestnut Horse	Vehicle/Mount	No
✓	Constitution Engine	Vehicle/Mount	No
✓	Crow Wing Pack	Prop	Yes
✓	Elephant	Vehicle/Mount	Yes
✓	Gatling Gun Targets	Unique	No
✓	Golden Horse	Vehicle/Mount	No
✓	Palomino	Vehicle/Mount	No

Got It?	Toys	Toy Type	Commercial
✓	Passenger Car	Vehicle/Mount	No
✓	Scout	Vehicle/Mount	No
✓	Silent Warrior Pack	Prop	Yes
✓	Silver	Vehicle/Mount	Yes
✓	Target Package 1	Unique	No
✓	Target Package 2	Unique	No
✓	Target Package 3	Unique	No
✓	Thundering Hooves Pack	Prop	Yes
✓	Thundering Stallion	Vehicle/Mount	Yes
✓	TNT Pack	Prop	Yes

Introduction to the Toy Box

Disney Infinity is a huge game with infinite possibilities. The Toy Box is a key feature of the game, and it can be somewhat daunting at first since there is so much to do. This part of the guide focuses entirely on the Toy Box, which encompasses all parts of *Disney Infinity* that are outside of the various Play Sets.

EXPLORING THE TOY BOX

After completing the introduction to the game, you find yourself in the Toy Box Launch. While you have several options, such as getting right into one of the Play Sets, it is a good idea to take some time and explore the Toy Box. In the center of this area is the Disney Castle. Select a character and place it on your Disney Infinity Base to get started.

THE DISNEY INFINITY HUB

When you first enter the Toy Box Launch, your character is standing in the middle of the Disney Infinity Hub. The Hub has four buttons that you activate by standing on them. Use them to access different areas of the game. The red button takes you to the Travel menu, where you can select from Mastery Adventures, Adventures, Prebuilt Toy Box Worlds, and the Play Set that you have placed on the Disney Infinity Base. In addition, you can also save your current Toy Box or load one you have previously saved. The yellow button opens the Disney Infinity Vault, where you can unlock new Toys to use in the Toy Box. The green button opens the Build Menu, where you can select Toys you have already unlocked. Finally, the purple button takes you to the Hall of Heroes.

> **NOTE**
>
> The current Toy Box will be saved automatically in a default save slot when you exit. However, it is a good idea to get in the habit of naming the Toy Box in which you are working and saving it regularly. If you don't and you open another Toy Box, it will save over the old opened one when you exit. You can have up to 100 Toy Box saves—as long as your gaming system has storage room.

TAKING A WALK

The best way to explore the Toy Box Launch is to take a walk. From the hub, start moving around the left side of the castle. There is a beam of light shining up into the sky in the distance. Walk towards the light.

You need to jump up onto a small ledge to get the Toy Box Blaster. This tool is now added to your inventory in the Tools/Pack menu. The Blaster comes in handy for fighting enemies. To select the Blaster, follow the directions on the screen to open the Tools/Pack menu. Here you can select items you have unlocked to use. You can even assign an item to one of two quick slots so you can quickly access it without having to open the menu. Once you have the Blaster selected, give it a try. By this time, there may be enemies spawning in the area.

Now that you have the Blaster, head over to the other side of the castle. There is another beam of light at the top of a slope. Climb the slope to find an Autopia Car. Hop in to give it a spin.

As soon as you climb into the Autopia Car, an entire track and landscape appears magically before you. Since you are already in the driver's seat, go ahead and take the car for a spin around the track and get a feel for driving. Then you can continue driving off the course and around the Toy Box to get where you want to go faster than by walking.

GATHERING SPARKS AND SPINS

There are several capsules in the Toy Box Launch. Blue capsules are Helps. Touch them to reveal tips or other information on playing the game. Green capsules contain either Sparks or Spins. Sparks are the experience in the game. Collect them to level up your characters. You can also get Sparks by breaking barrels, crates, and other objects, by defeating enemies, and by earning medals in the Adventures.

Spins are the way you unlock new toys for the Toy Box. There are lots of Spins in green capsules in the Toy Box Launch, but this is the only place where they are in capsules. You can also earn Spins by leveling up your characters and completing Adventures. Look around the

Toy Box to find as many Spins as you can. There are some inside and on top of the castle as well as hidden in groups of crates and barrels. For more information on using Spins to unlock Toys, see the Disney Infinity Vault section of the guide.

As you continue to explore the Toy Box Launch, you will run into some enemies. Use the Toy Box Blaster or just regular attacks to defeat them. Since you have the Autopia Car, you can also run into them at full speed. Continue destroying crates and fighting enemies as you explore the main land area of the Toy Box Launch. There are some more areas floating off in the air away from the main land, but don't worry about those now. Later, when you get air vehicles or have completed the Building Mastery Adventure, you will be able to get to those areas and find more green capsules.

WHAT TO DO NEXT

Now that you have experienced the basics of the Toy Box Launch, it is time to learn more about the Toy Box. It is also a good time to learn more about how to fight and drive, which you will need to know for not only the Toy Box, but also for the Play Sets. The best place to learn this is in the Mastery Adventures. So after collecting all the Sparks and Spins you can in the Toy Box Launch, head back to the Disney Infinity Hub to continue your training and learn how to Travel to different Toy Boxes and other aspects of the game.

> **TIP**
>
> It is a good idea to complete all of the Mastery Adventures before continuing on. Keep reading to find more information on these in the next section.

Travel

When you want to leave a Toy Box and go somewhere else, you can step on the red button at the Disney Infinity Hub or select Travel from the Pause menu. Either way, this takes you to the Travel menu where you can choose to try out Mastery Adventures, or other Adventures. You can also go to one of the Prebuilt Toy Box Worlds, or even save or load a Toy Box of your own. When you first begin *Disney Infinity*, it is a good idea to go through the Mastery Adventures to help you learn the ropes of not only playing the game, but using the many different features of the Toy Box.

MASTERY ADVENTURES

Think of the Mastery Adventures as tutorials for learning the ways to manipulate and build in the Toy Box, as well as how to play *Disney Infinity* whether you are in the Toy Box or one of the Play Sets. There are six different Mastery Adventures, but you only have access to three at the start. The other three are unlocked as you complete Building Mastery and then the other Mastery Adventures related to building in sequential order. Also be sure to do the Combat Mastery and Driving Mastery Adventures so you can learn the moves and mechanics of fighting and driving. Both of those come in handy throughout the game. Completing these two Mastery Adventures unlocks several Adventures, which are essentially challenges where you can put what you have learned to work.

BUILDING MASTERY

> There be no better way to build up your world than by goin' on a treasure hunt! Place pieces in your Toy Box to help get to the gold!

The Building Mastery Adventure is a brief tutorial on using the editor for building and manipulating the Toy Box. When the Adventure begins, you must help a Captain Hook townsperson find some treasure. Follow him to the highlighted area to continue.

Your fist task is to use the editor to place three trees. Follow the on-screen instructions to open the editor and then choose one of the trees. Select it and then position it where you want to place it. Repeat this process two more times with different trees so that there are three trees in total.

There is no way for Captain Hook to get up onto a higher level. Therefore, open the editor and select a Bluff. Line it up with the hillside so that it is within the blue box and place it. Now the Bluff can serve as a ramp for you and your friend to get up to the next area.

Once you get to the top of the level, you need to get across a gap. Bring up the editor and select the Super Cannon. Position it along the edge of the gap. However, since it is facing the wrong direction, you need to rotate it so it is facing across the gap. Once you have rotated the cannon, place it, walk into it, and launch yourself across the gap to the other side.

Continue to the next highlighted spot. You need to enter a cave, but there is no entry. Therefore, open the editor and place the Cave of Wonders at the indicated spot. You can then hop through the opening and enter the cave.

The bridge to the castle is missing a section. Bring up the editor and drop a Castle Bridge segment into position. Follow the on-screen directions to change the elevation of the bridge so that it lowers into the correct spot. You can also move the camera around to get a better view on your construction.

Follow the cave to the Treasure Grotto, however you find it is not in the correct place. Use your Magic Wand and select the Treasure Grotto. Then press the Move button. Now move the Treasure Grotto towards you so that it is adjacent to the block on which you are standing. Walk into the Treasure Grotto to complete the Adventure, earn a Spin you can use to unlock a toy from the Disney Infinity Vault, and receive a Mastery Star. This also unlocks the Dynamics Mastery and Creativi-Toy Mastery Part 1 Adventures.

COMBAT MASTERY

We'll pit you against the pros and teach you how to battle all the baddies in the Toy Box.

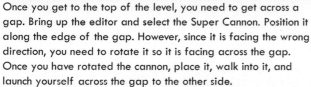

Your next task is to remove a Statue. Open up the Tools/Packs menu following the directions on the screen. Then scroll through your available tools to select the Magic Wand. Hold down the aim button to select the Statue. Finally press the delete button to send the Statue back to the inventory and get it out of your way.

The Combat Mastery Adventure is a great way to learn the different ways you can fight against enemies. To get started, walk up to the wooden doors and press the attack button to knock down the door that is.

Enter the training area and begin clearing out the crates and other objects by pressing the attack button. Then try using the alternate attack button to destroy several items in front of you. Finally, jump up into the air and then press the attack button to come down with a slam attack that can destroy several objects in the area around you.

Next you have to try getting a moving target. Follow after the Gaston townsperson and pick him up by pressing the action button. Then follow the directions on the screen to throw him out of the training area. In combat, picking up an enemy not only can cause damage to the enemy you pick up, but also to any enemies you throw that enemy at. Unfortunately, Gaston is not so easy to get rid of. Now that you have learned how to throw, follow the directions on the screen to kick Gaston out of the training area. During combat, you can pick up enemies and throw them for damage. You can also use them as a projectile and throw them into other enemies.

You are now ready for the battle arena. Gaston has put together a number of enemies to take you on. It starts off with a single Zurgbot. Rush forward and attack to destroy it. Then defeat two more that appear.

A Blaster appears in the middle of the area. Move over and pick it up—it will come in handy. Press the alternate attack button to fire the Blaster at enemies and hit them from longer range. Then, as they get close, finish them up with normal attacks. Gaston sends more and more enemies to attack. Defeat them all using a variety of attacks.

Now you have to knock Gaston into the arena. Take aim with the Blaster and fire at him. Once he is in the arena, he calls in a bunch of enemies. However, this time you get some allies to help you. Defeat all of the enemies to get the Mastery Star as well as a Spin. In addition, you also unlock three new Adventures—Sumo, Gladiator Arena, and Dome Defense.

DRIVING MASTERY

> Become a pro at driving and doing tricks with this driving Adventure.

One of the fun things to do in the Toy Box is racing. Complete this Mastery Adventure to earn a Mastery Star and a Spin, as well as to unlock five Adventures—Battle Race, Lap Race, Battle Race Reverse, Lap Race Reverse, and Off Road. At the start, you learn the basics of driving. Press the accelerator button to start driving and steer through the first couple of turns.

Now you need to drift through the next three turns. Follow the directions on the screen. As you drift, your car builds up energy that you can then use to activate turbo. Drifting can take some practice and, for these turns, you don't want to drift through the entire turn.

As soon as you hit the straightaway, activate the turbo for a burst of speed. Do this through the next two straightaways as well. Try hitting the jumps while using turbo to get some extra air.

There is more to the Toy Box than just driving around on tracks. You can also do stunts. In the next part of the Adventure, you must get 10 collectibles. These are yellow balloon-like spheres that you break by running into them. The driving arena is filled with ramps and other obstacles. While jumping in the air, follow the directions on the screen to do different tricks. Landing a trick builds up energy, just like drifting.

Try driving up the halfpipe ramps. When you get to the top and into the air, your car will automatically rotate and come back down. This is a good time to pull off a trick as well. Play around as you try different tricks while you finish getting all of the collectibles to complete the Driving Mastery Adventure.

DYNAMICS MASTERY

Learn how and what the Physics Blocks can do in the Toy Box.

This quick Mastery Adventure teaches you about a certain category of objects known as Physics Blocks. They are called this because they react according to the laws of physics. There are three main types of these blocks—Glass, Wood, and Steel.

Your first task is to knock down a tower made up of Glass Blocks. Move towards it and press the attack button to destroy individual blocks. As the blocks on top fall to the ground, they also break since they are made of glass.

Now you must take down a tower made of Wooden Blocks. Wooden Blocks break when you attack them or they fall, however they are tougher than Glass Blocks. This time you are going to use objects to do it rather than attack it yourself. Off to one side of the tower, balls are being launched. Open the editor and use Bumpers and Flippers as found in a pinball game to hit the balls into the tower to knock it down. Try placing a bumper in the middle of the grass at the foreground end so the ball will bounce off the side of the bumper and move towards the tower. All it takes is a few hits with some balls and the tower falls.

GAME BASICS

CHARACTERS

POWER DISCS

PLAY SETS

TOY BOX

TOY BOX COLLECTION

ACHIEVEMENTS

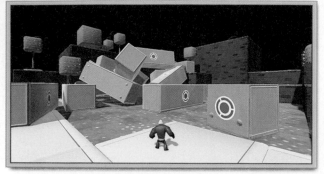

The next task features Steel Blocks. While they will fall like Glass or Wooden Blocks, Steel Blocks are indestructible. As you approach the steel tower, it falls down. Notice that the blocks remain intact however.

To quickly reassemble the steel tower, find the Reset-O-Matic and step on it. This switch is a great way to restore a structure to its original construction.

Now place an Explosive Block into one of the gaps in the steel tower. Explosive Blocks blow up when they are hit by something. This time you are going to use a Slingshot.

After putting the Explosive Block into position, move over to the Slingshot and take control of it. Take aim and follow the directions on the screen to fire the Slingshot. Hit the Explosive Block to knock down the steel tower and complete the Mastery Adventure. For your efforts you are awarded a Mastery Star and a Spin, and you also unlock an Adventure—Castles and Slingshots.

CREATIVI-TOYS MASTERY PART 1

Your Creativi-Toys are the key to making your own games in the Toy Box.

Creativi-Toys are powerful toys that you can use to create actions and reactions within the Toy Box. Start off by moving towards the stadium. Pick up the Wand and then use it to select the Trigger in front of the gate. This will act as a trigger. Choose to connect the Trigger, and then select "Stepped On". This sets the Trigger to send a trigger signal when someone steps on it.

Now select the Stadium Gate to connect it to the Trigger. From the menu, select "Open". This instructs the gate to open when someone steps on the Trigger. You have just completed your first connection. Step on the plate and then move through the now open gate to enter the stadium.

TIP

While you can't do it in the Mastery Adventure now, if you wanted to, you could then use the gate as a new trigger and cause another object to react. For example, when the gate opens, it can then trigger another object by connecting it. In this way, you could create a chain of events that are all started by stepping on a single Trigger.

GAME BASICS

CHARACTERS

POWER DISCS

PLAY SETS

TOY BOX

TOY BOX COLLECTION

ACHIEVEMENTS

Next you need to connect another Trigger. Do the same thing you did before, however this time, connect it to the Boom Box. Now choose the song you want it to play.

Now select the Boom Box again. We are going to use it as a trigger. Select "Started" as the trigger. Then select the Party Cannon to connect it. For the Party Cannon, choose "Confetti" as the behavior.

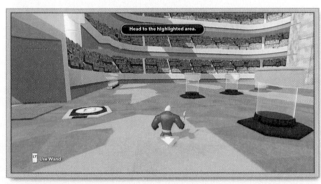

The Adventure then connects several more Party Cannons as well as Time Delay toys together to make an even more impressive show. Walk over to The Teleporter and step on it to travel to another Teleporter outside of the stadium.

Move back through the gate and step on the Trigger. As you do, the Boom Box begins playing and the Party Cannons begin firing in succession.

If you want, you can play around with a number of Creativi-Toys and other objects. Just open the editor to select and place them in the Toy Box, and then try connecting them. When you are done, follow the directions to a second Trigger past the Boom Box and the first Party Cannon to finish the Mastery Adventure. You not only earn a Mastery Star and a Spin, but also unlock the Creativi-Toys Mastery Part 2 Adventure.

CREATIVI-TOYS MASTERY PART 2

Use even more Creativi-Toys to make your own games in the Toy Box.

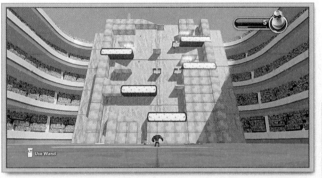

Now that you have learned the basics of placing and assigning orders or behaviors to Creativi-Toys, it is time to see how you can use them to create a game. Phineas and Ferb townspeople have already built the beginnings of a platforming game. They just need you to finish it and then play it.

To get started, pull out your Magic Wand, select the Trigger, and set it to "Stepped On".

Next target the Repeater and turn it on. Now step onto the Teleporter and use it to get to the top of the game.

At the top, you can see a Falling Object Generator. Since you already have the Repeater selected, connect it to the Falling Object Generator and then select the ESPN Bowling Ball. The Trigger now activates the Falling Object Generator and the Repeater causes it to drop a ball every few seconds. Take the Teleporter back down to the ground level.

To help you play this game, you have been given a Star Command Boost Pack. Press the attack button and the Boost Pack will shoot you up into the air. Move to the Trigger in the game to get it started.

TIP

Notice that as soon as the game starts, the camera angle changes to a side scrolling game type. That is because the Mastery Adventure is using a Side-Step Camera behind the scenes that was activated when you stepped on the Trigger. This tool allows you to create your own side scrolling games.

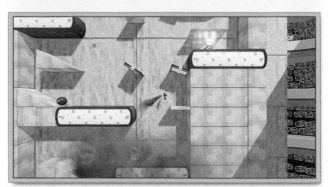

Make your way up through the game while trying to avoid being hit by the bowling balls. The key is to get to the small gray platform on the right. Then from there, boost your way up to the Flipper above. From there, boost up to another small gray platform—but you have to watch out for bowling balls here. Then move on to another Flipper, wait for a bowling ball to pass over your head, and then boost on up to the highest small gray platform to complete the game. At the end, you get a Mastery Star and a Spin.

ADVENTURES

Adventures are like short challenges where you have to put the skills you need to know to succeed in *Disney Infinity* into action. They are unlocked by completing the Mastery Adventures. Each Adventure has three different medals you can earn—Bronze, Silver, and Gold. Each time you earn a medal for the first time in an Adventure, you receive not only Sparks but also a Spin. In addition, you can play all of the Adventures in multiplayer. Two players on the same system can play them together with a split screen, while up to four players can play together over a network connection.

> ### TIP
> Troy Johnson and Jared Bals at Disney Interactive and Avalanche were kind enough to provide some great tips for each of the Adventures and Character Adventures. Since they designed or worked on these, they know how to beat them and get gold medals and are passing their tips along to you.

CASTLES AND SLINGSHOTS

> Try to keep your spheres whole while searching out and destroying the spheres in the other castles.
>
> **Gold:** 3 Spheres
> **Silver:** 2 Spheres
> **Bronze:** 1 Sphere

For this adventure, you have 1 minute to break down the walls of your opponents' castles, find the hidden spheres, and then destroy the spheres. To accomplish this, you have a Slingshot. The Slingshot can be rotated and elevated. Then pull back and release to fire the rocket projectiles.

As you hit the colored walls of the castles, you break them down. Keep firing until you can see one of the spheres and then shoot at it to destroy it. The key to getting a gold medal for this adventure is to immediately start pulling back on the Slingshot as soon as you release. Novices will wait to see where the first projectile hit before pulling back on the Slingshot. By pulling back as soon as you release it, you can have a second shot in the air by the time the first one hits. The faster you can fire, the more blocks you can break down and the more spheres you can destroy.

> ### TIP
> You'll have to improve your skill at using the Slingshot. Always pulling back on the Slingshot, even while you're still tuning your aim, can save you tons of time over the course of the Adventure because you'll always be ready to unleash a shot. The breakable spheres in opponents' castles always appear inside in random locations, so a little luck on your side can make the difference. Just go crazy and destroy as much of the opposing castles as possible in the time limit. In multiplayer, however, there is no time limit—it's simply "last castle standing." Under these circumstances, the winner almost invariably earns a gold medal anyway.

SUMO

> Stay on solid ground as long as possible while the ground disappears out from underneath you.
>
> **Gold:** Survive over 3:00 minutes
> **Silver:** Survive over 2:10 minutes
> **Bronze:** Survive over 1:00 minutes

This is a combat Adventure where you have to fight against several different enemies. However, the blocks on which you are standing randomly disappear. Therefore, you have to keep moving and avoid being knocked off of the blocks. Random tools such as Blasters or balls appear, which you can shoot or throw at enemies to help you keep them away from you.

As the timer progresses, blocks begin to disappear. They turn transparent a second or two before they vanish, so be quick to move to solid ground or risk falling. Also watch out for the Wooden Block with the skulls on it bouncing around. If it hits you, you take damage. Enemies are destroyed when the Wooden Block blows up near them. Shoot at it while it is near enemies to take them out. If you want to get the gold medal, try using Power Discs that increase the damage you inflict so you can more easily defeat the enemies. Also stay away from the edges since some of the enemy's attacks can push you back over the edge and end the adventure for you.

TIP

This is one of the more difficult Adventures to earn a gold medal on...unless you use Randy or Violet. By the time you last long enough to earn silver, the enemies spawn so rapidly that it's difficult to keep track of them all, and you're likely to get hit from behind and knocked off. Randy and Violet, however, have the ability to turn invisible, and enemies do not notice or attack you in this state. You can survive until the final block falls with either of them. Boring, yes, but easier. The Lone Ranger is another solid choice, and if you're using a character with weaker combat capabilities, look for Phineas's baseball gun because it has a great knock-back effect on enemies. In split-screen multiplayer, the other player's camera view can also be helpful. This is especially true if the other camera is in spectator mode because it actually shows most of the arena from a zoomed-out perspective.

GLADIATOR ARENA

Players can use all their packs and tools to survive increasingly difficult waves of enemies in a gladiatorial arena setting.

Gold: Survive 3 enemy waves
Silver: Survive 2 enemy waves
Bronze: Survive 1 enemy wave

Think you are good at combat? Test out your skills in the arena. While it begins with just a single enemy, you then have to take on two, three, four, or even more enemies at a time. A Zurg spaceship flies around and then teleports enemies into the arena, so be sure to keep an eye on the ship once you clear out the latest batch of baddies so you are ready for more. Be sure to use all your character's different attacks.

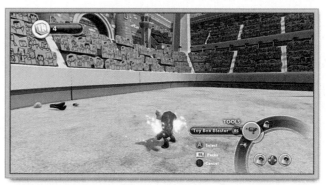

Use Power Discs that increase your damage, increase your health, and/or give you some invincibility. Also don't forget to use the tools and packs you have collected. You should at least have the Toy Box Blaster from the Toy Box Launch. This gives you a ranged attack so you can pick off enemies before they get in close. A few of the enemies have their own ranged attacks, so be sure to keep moving to avoid getting hit.

TIP

Choose a character with awesome offensive capabilities (Violet, Lone Ranger, etc.). Being defeated one time ends the Adventure, so if you start running low on health, do your best to run away until it regenerates, and then re-enter the fray. There are plenty of waves, so your endurance will be put to the test if you want to earn the gold.

DOME DEFENSE

Help! Stop the *Disney Infinity* enemies from smashing through the domes and taking the townspeople inside! One destroyed dome ends the Adventure. Use your packs and tools to keep 'em safe!

Gold: 6 enemy waves
Silver: 4 enemy waves
Bronze: 2 enemy waves

There are three domes with Princess townspeople in them. Each has a number that represents the health of the dome. If the number ever reaches 0, the Adventure is over. Omnidroid enemies come out of the towers and make their way towards the closest dome. Your job is to defeat them before they can break open a dome. Be sure to use Blasters or other tools to attack the enemies, as well as use any Power Discs you have.

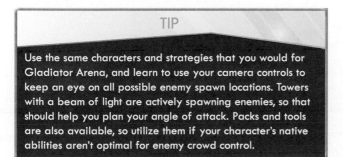

At the start, the enemies come out of the towers at a slower rate. However, as you move on to subsequent waves, they come faster and from different towers. Watch the sky above the towers. A beam of light shines down on the towers that are spawning enemies. Therefore, by looking for the beam, you can set yourself up to hit the enemies as they emerge from the towers.

TIP

Use the same characters and strategies that you would for Gladiator Arena, and learn to use your camera controls to keep an eye on all possible enemy spawn locations. Towers with a beam of light are actively spawning enemies, so that should help you plan your angle of attack. Packs and tools are also available, so utilize them if your character's native abilities aren't optimal for enemy crowd control.

BATTLE RACE

Ready...Get set...Go! Be the fastest in this three-lap race with weapons!

Gold: Finish in under 2:05
Silver: Finish in under 3:00
Bronze: Finish in under 4:30

This is a race where you can use weapons to help you get ahead—or stay in the lead. Pick up weapons by running over the surprise boxes with the "?" on them. To build up turbo, run over the blue gas cans in addition to drifting and doing tricks.

You can fire your weapons forward as well as behind you—so if you have an opponent behind you, open fire to keep them behind you. Also, be sure to look for the shortcut. It can be tough to find in this race and involves jumping up onto a blue and white striped platform to get to a higher track area. It is fairly easy to get a bronze in this race. Silver is a bit tougher. However, if you want to get gold, you need to use the shortcut and drive a perfect race without crashing into anything. While you are racing against other cars, you are also racing against the clock to earn the medals.

TIP

For all of the Battle Race and Lap Race Adventures, the key is driving skill—taking hairpin turns smoothly and finding the single true shortcut on this level (it's the same shortcut route on both regular and reverse versions). Once you pull ahead in the Battle Races, be sure to use your weapons liberally against opponents behind you—they are never too far behind and will use their own weapons on you.

GAME BASICS

CHARACTERS

POWER DISCS

PLAY SETS

TOY BOX

TOY BOX COLLECTION

ACHIEVEMENTS

LAP RACE

Ready...Get set...Go! Be the fastest in this three-lap race!

Gold: Finish in under 2:05
Silver: Finish in under 3:00
Bronze: Finish in under 4:30

This race is on the same track at the Battle Race, but this time you have no weapons. Rapidly press the accelerator button while waiting to start the race to rev up. Then when the race starts, you burst from the starting line with turbo. Drift and do tricks while racing to build up power so you can use turbo on the straightaways.

As you are moving next to another car, nudge the other car off the course and hopefully into a wall or off the edge. Also try combining the Fix-It Felix Repair Power Disc with the Pieces of Eight Power Disc to create the Turbo Charge ability, which provides bonus turbo energy. The Turbo Charge Power Coin Bonus can also be acquired using Fix It Felix's Repair Power and Scrooge McDuck's Lucky Dime.

BATTLE RACE REVERSE

Get set...Go! Be the fastest in this three-lap race with weapons!

Gold: Finish in under 2:05
Silver: Finish in under 3:00
Bronze: Finish in under 4:30

This race takes place on the same track as the Battle Race but in reverse. Pick up weapons and use them freely to slow down the competition.

The shortcut is in the same place as before—you just have to access it from a different spot. Once again, look for the blue and white striped platform.

LAP RACE REVERSE

Get set...Go! Be the fastest in this three-lap race!

Gold: Finish in under 2:05
Silver: Finish in under 3:00
Bronze: Finish in under 4:30

This race takes place on the same track as the Lap Race but in reverse. Hit the shortcut and turbo on the straightaways to get ahead and keep your time low enough to get the gold medal.

OFF ROAD

Sure, the raceway is awesome. But how are your skills on this off-road course?

Gold: Finish in under 0:40
Silver: Finish in under 0:50
Bronze: Finish in under 1:10

The track for this race is short and has weapons you can pick up. However, it is played from a top-down view, making it a bit tougher to play. You can see exactly where your opponents are located, which makes it easier to target them—especially when they are behind you. The key to finishing the race with a good time is to avoid overcorrecting as you go around the turns. Plus when you are going down along the left side of the track, you have to remember that the controls are reversed. If you need to go to the right, you have to turn to the left.

TIP

Even though you don't see the prompt, make sure to rev it during the countdown to get your starting boost. Likewise, you won't be able to see your boost meter or load-outs because the camera is too far away, but they are available. Try to use them where you think they'll be most effective, regardless of what type might fire off.

CHARACTER ADVENTURES

When selecting Adventures, in addition to the common Adventures, there are also Character Adventures. These appear in the Adventures menu, but only for the character you currently have on the Infinity Base. Therefore, if you have Mr. Incredible on the Base, then the "Mr. Incredible, the Hero" Adventure will be available to play. Like the other Adventures, these can be played by yourself or with 1 to 3 other players. You can also earn three levels of medals based on your performance. The more character toys you have, the more Adventures you can play.

MR. INCREDIBLE, THE HERO

You have all your packs and tools to help you smash domes to release the townspeople caught in them before the time runs out.

Gold: Release 3 townspeople
Silver: Release 2 townspeople
Bronze: Release 1 townsperson

After the first dome is smashed, the timer resets and you get 1 minute and 30 seconds to go after the second dome. Follow the green arrow to your next objective. Watch out for turrets that fire at you along the way and try to slow you down. The Omnidroids defending the second dome are tougher. Use Mr. Incredible's alternate attack that creates a line of destruction along the ground. If you line it up correctly, you can destroy enemies and damage the dome at the same time.

Unlike the Dome Defense Adventure, this time you are the one trying to smash the domes. You have only 1 minute to smash as many as possible. However, it will not be easy. Syndrome has positioned Omnidroids around each one. Quickly get to the first dome and then clear out the enemies while attacking the dome as much as possible. More Omnidroids spawn in, so focus on the dome, otherwise you will spend all your time on enemies.

You also have 1 minute and 30 seconds to smash the third dome. This time you must pass by more turrets as well as spike pads to get to it. Don't waste time trying to destroy them. Instead, rush past them and get to the dome. You can climb a Rope or use some Fans to get to the top of a ledge where the dome is located. Here you face lots of Omnidroids in all varieties and the dome is tougher to smash than the previous two. Try to keep moving so the dome is between you and the enemies as much as possible and keep attacking it. Using Power Discs can really help get the gold medal here.

TIP

You don't technically need to destroy any enemies to earn the medals, so focus almost entirely on the domes. Any time you get surrounded by enemies, your attacks will likely auto-target them instead of the domes. So peel away and around to the opposite side of the dome where you'll be more likely to be able to attack without interruption. Also, remember that any tools and packs you've obtained are available to you, so use Blasters to make quick work of the domes.

SULLEY'S PAINTBALL BRAWL

It's time to show your rivals a victory of a different color. Put them in their place before time runs out.

Gold: 35 enemies defeated
Silver: 15 enemies defeated
Bronze: 5 enemies defeated

You have 4 minutes to defeat as many enemies as possible in this Adventure. To accomplish this, you are armed with a Paintball Gun.

At the same time, you have to avoid being beaten, so watch your health. Your Paintball Gun fires several rounds and then must reload. The key to staying in the game is to keep moving—especially while reloading—otherwise you are a sitting duck. Also, when you hit an opponent, he or she is momentarily stunned, so quickly follow up with more shots to defeat the opponent before he or she can return fire. This also applies to you, so if you get hit and stunned, try to move away and get to cover before your opponents follow up with more hits.

There are teleporters along the sides that can be used to quickly get from one side of the arena to the other. A couple of balconies that run the length of the sides of the arena can be accessed by ramps at either end. This gives you a height advantage. However, since the range of the Paintball Guns is not all that long, it is usually better to stay down in the arena.

Power Discs that increase your damage are useful for getting the gold medal since they can reduce the number of hits for defeating opponents and give you more time for going after others. Avoid getting surrounded by opponents or you can get into trouble. If one hits you, others can follow up with additional hits while you are momentarily stunned. That is why it is important to keep moving and use cover to avoid being ganged up on by your opponents.

TIP

Never stop pursuing the enemies. They spawn in waves of 5, so if you have trouble finding one, you're right on the cusp of a new wave of points. This one is all about persistent offense. If you start reloading your Paintball Gun before an enemy is defeated, be sure to use your shoulder charge or other attacks in the meantime.

SPARROW'S FLIGHT

Captain Jack Sparrow is on the run—to collect as much shine as he can before that scurvy time runs out. This calls for all your packs and tools.

Gold: Gather 25 collectibles
Silver: Gather 15 collectibles
Bronze: Gather 5 collectibles

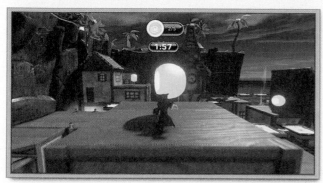

Captain Jack Sparrow finds himself in a small seaside town where he needs to get as many collectibles as he can within 3 minutes. Once you gather the first 5 collectibles, then 5 more appear. Collect those and then another 5 appear. Watch out for several traps on the ground. They can either slow you down or take you out, causing you to wait while your character regenerates.

Many of the collectibles are up on top of buildings or on other elevated positions. Therefore, if you want to get gold, or even silver, having a pack with some type of boost or glide capability is helpful so you can quickly get to the tops of the buildings to grab the goodies.

For the bronze and silver medals, all of the collectibles are within the town or near it. There is no need to climb up the tall cliffs or platforms overlooking the town—that just wastes time. Instead, use the Fans to quickly get up on top of the buildings and jump from building to building to collect the yellow collectibles.

TIP

Learn the layout of the level. There are many possible spawn points for each wave of 5 collectibles, but once you start to learn where they can appear, it becomes easier to understand the quickest route to each location. Also, remember that your packs and tools are available in this Adventure. Boost packs that shoot you into the air can make this one a breeze...sort of.

MRS. INCREDIBLE'S GRAB-IT

Mrs. Incredible to the rescue! Use your elastic arms to take the townspeople to the safe zone and throw the criminals in prison where they belong.

Gold: Earn 40 points
Silver: Earn 20 points
Bronze: Earn 5 points

Mrs. Incredible scores 1 point for getting townspeople to the park in the middle of town and 5 points for throwing criminals into the police station. Some of these people and criminals are on the ground, but many are up on top of buildings. Get as many as you can in 4 minutes and 30 seconds.

While you can climb up the sides of the buildings, it is much quicker to use the Fans and Elevators. There are also Super Cannons to help you get from one building to another. Use Glider packs to soar down to lower buildings or to the streets. The key to earning a lot of points is to throw the citizens off the tops of the buildings towards the park. Don't worry, they have parachutes. Throw the criminals down to the street level as well, then once you have cleared the buildings, go down and throw them into the police station. If you hand deliver every person individually, you will not be able to get even a silver medal.

GAME BASICS

CHARACTERS

POWER DISCS

PLAY SETS

TOY BOX

TOY BOX COLLECTION

ACHIEVEMENTS

If you want to get gold, spend one attempt just exploring the area. Learn where the Super Cannons, Fans, and Elevators are located. Often getting part way up one building will lead to a Cannon that will shoot you up to the top of an another building. Then once you see how all the Cannons are connected, you can quickly move from building to building, throwing people and criminals down below. Make sure you leave enough time to get down to street level to put them all where they need to go.

TIP

It'll take a little practice and learning the layout of the level, but staying on the roofs for most of the Adventure is imperative. Don't hand deliver each citizen and crook one at a time. Toss all the townspeople off the roofs in the general direction of their targets, and then move directly to the next roof. Many of them will parachute down into the goal areas. Drop to the ground and deliver all the others when you have about 45 seconds left.

VIOLET'S STEALTH MISSION

Avoid the Omnidroids and spotlights in Syndrome's maze! Find as many collectibles as you can.

Gold: Gather 25 collectibles
Silver: Gather 15 collectibles
Bronze: Gather 5 collectibles

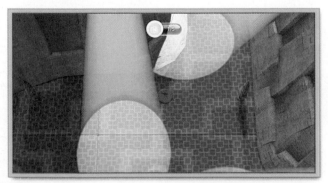

Violet has to avoid spotlights and Omnidroids with lights as she moves through a maze-like canyon while gathering collectibles. There is no time limit on this Adventure, so use caution. Instead, the Adventure ends when a light beam hits you. This Adventure is played from a top-down camera view.

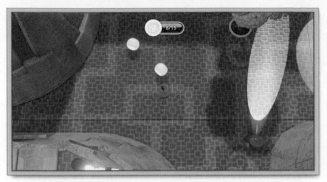

Observe the direction of motion of the spotlights and the patrol patterns of the Omnidroids before rushing into an area. A good tactic is to follow an Omnidroid through an area—just be careful it does not turn around on you. Don't try attacking them if you want to pull of a stealth mission. However you can destroy the Omnidriods before they turn around by holding the attack button while standing behind them.

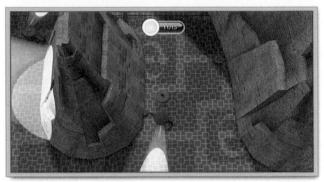

Getting bronze is fairly easy, since you can easily get the first 5 collectibles. However, the next 10 are a bit tougher and those final 10 are downright difficult to get. The best way to earn silver and gold is to play it over and over so you learn the patterns and where the safe spots are.

TIP

There's no timer on this one, so you can remain calm and wait out the searchlights until you're sure of their patterns. However, the lights subtly increase their speed over time, so waiting too long can also get you into trouble eventually. If you're caught between a couple lights closing in on you, a quick dodge roll may be able to squeeze you out of it if you just have a short distance to safety.

DASH'S DATA-DART

Syndrome's at it again! You've got to gather the collectibles while avoiding the blue and red balls.

Gold: Gather 60 collectibles
Silver: Gather 40 collectibles
Bronze: Gather 10 collectibles

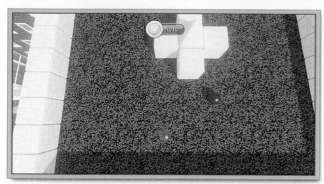

This is another top-down Adventure. While the concept is simple, mastering it is still challenging. You must move around a rooftop while avoiding blue and red balls. The blue balls drop yellow collectibles that you must collect. There is no time limit—the Adventure ends when you get hit by a ball.

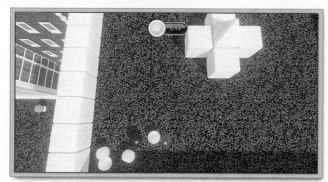

As the Adventure progresses, it gets tougher. It begins with one blue ball and then adds a second and a third. The blue balls bounce around using physics like billiard balls, so you can predict where they will go after a bounce. However, red balls are larger and follow you around, so you have to keep moving.

If this were not tough enough, bumpers spawn and can give the balls some unpredictable bounces. Plus tar traps slow you down—as well as the balls. Try to avoid tar traps if possible, but you will need to walk onto them to get some collectibles. Also, the collectibles disappear after a few seconds, so you have to go after them before they are gone.

TIP

Avoid taking risks. While you have to stay close enough to the dodge balls because they produce the yellow collectibles, you should have plenty of time to let the dodge balls move away before you snag the collectibles. Though you might not notice an effect at first, you can still actually jump in this Adventure, and you can double-jump over the blue dodge balls. (Don't try this with the red ones, though!) Finally, once the pinball bumpers appear, you can actually stand on top of them if you need a little time to compose yourself or wait for the balls to roll away. In split-screen multiplayer, the other player's camera view can also be helpful. This is especially true if the other camera is in spectator mode, because it actually shows most of the arena from a zoomed-out perspective.

SYNDROME'S SORTING SPRINT

You've met your match with this crazy challenge. Fling townspeople to safety with your Zero Point Energy, stop oncoming attacks, and stay alive while being pushed to your doom. Do it all before time runs out.

Gold: Earn 40 points
Silver: Earn 25 points
Bronze: Earn 5 points

This Adventure requires you to pick up townspeople on your roof and throw them onto adjacent rooftops for points. You have 5 minutes to score as many points as possible. You get 1 point for every townsperson thrown to another rooftop. Hit the targets and you score 2 points.

GAME BASICS

CHARACTERS

POWER DISCS

PLAY SETS

TOY BOX

TOY BOX COLLECTION

ACHIEVEMENTS

The rooftop on which you play has several conveyor belts, so you have to be careful you don't fall off the roof. While you will be taken back up to the rooftop, it wastes time. It is important to aim when you throw the townspeople since you want them to at least land on a rooftop. If they miss a roof, no points for you. For long shots, drop kick the townspeople by jumping and then pressing the alternate combat button.

Use Syndrome's Zero Point Energy to pick up and throw townspeople. This lets you grab them from a short distance and gives you a better chance of hitting the targets. As you progress, Omnidroids start appearing. Throw them off the roof with the Zero Point Energy to get them out of your way. If you want to get gold, you need to focus on hitting the targets. Take time to aim before each throw. While it may take a bit more time than just tossing them onto a rooftop, it still takes less time than picking up and throwing two different townspeople.

TIP

Once you've gotten the hang of turning your character and the camera at the same time, you'll be able to find and toss the townspeople quickly. Though it's actually possible to earn gold without using aiming, if you get the hang of that skill, it becomes pretty easy to hit the center of the targets for an extra point per townsperson. That will get you to the gold in no time.

MIKE'S SCARE PIG DASH

It's time for Mike to hog the spotlight. Race on Archie the Scare Pig around campus and collect as many points as you can!

Gold: Earn 200 points
Silver: Earn 120 points
Bronze: Earn 30 points

You have 3 minutes to score as many points as possible by gathering collectibles. Yellow collectibles are worth 1 point each, orange collectibles are 2 points, and red collectibles are 5 points. Since you have a limited amount of time, be sure to make the Scare Pig run throughout this Adventure. If you are content to get bronze, just run around the ground and pick up all of the yellow collectibles.

For those who want a silver medal, you need to get up onto the floating platforms with the orange collectibles. Jump from one platform to another without falling and get those orange collectibles. The red collectibles, which you will need to get in addition to the other colors if you want gold, are very tough to reach. You need to run and double jump to get across to the platforms where they are located or drop down from a platform to get them on your way down.

On the ground level are several scare traps. Avoid them or they will hit you and the Scare Pig and waste your precious time. These are all located near the center of the area. As with several other Adventures, spend some time exploring so you know the lay of the land and look for ways to get those red collectibles.

TIP

Practice. At first, 200 points might seem impossible, but I assure you that it can be done. First off, master controlling Archie while sprinting because that is the only way you'll reach 200. Focus on the upper-level platforms first, because you can earn more points per second up there. Learn the layout of the level, plan your lines, and be sure to explore some of the nooks and crannies for secret launcher pranks that can boost you to some valuable red collectibles.

RANDY'S SCAVENGER HUNT

Race with Randy through the scream tunnels and collect as much as you can before your time drains away.

Gold: Gather 20 collectibles
Silver: Gather 14 collectibles
Bronze: Gather 5 collectibles

While the scream tunnels are not that large, they are patrolled by enemies. Try to avoid them and grab as many yellow collectibles as you can within 3 minutes.

There are two Fear Tech Students that throw things at you down in the tunnels. When they hit, they inflict damage and slow you down a bit by the impact. Luckily you are armed with a Toilet Paper Launcher. It takes two hits to destroy an enemy and your launcher is slow to reload, however. Also, the monsters regenerate after a bit.

Once you get the first 5 collectibles, 14 more spawn in the tunnels. Get those and the final collectible number 20 spawns. Be sure to use the green arrows to help you find the collectibles as quickly as possible so you don't waste time going down tunnels where there is nothing for you to gather.

TIP

Don't worry about the enemies. Only attack them if they're directly in your way as you follow the compass to the nearest collectible. Constantly using your attack roll is actually faster than simply running. Do that and enemies won't be a problem anyway. It might make you a little dizzy, but it's definitely the best approach.

BARBOSSA'S BLOCKADE

There be pirates here, and you'd be wanting to gather as many collectibles as possible and stop your enemies before the time be runnin' out.

Gold: Earn 35 points
Silver: Earn 20 points
Bronze: Earn 5 points

This combat Adventure gives you 6 minutes and 20 seconds to defeat as many enemies as possible and collect the collectibles they leave behind. Follow the red arrows to get to the next enemies. When playing as a pirate, such as Barbossa or one of the others (in Multiplayer, you can be someone other than Barbossa), use your Flintlock to fire at a distance, then move in if your enemies are not defeated by the gun to finish them off with the sword.

There are several items that you can pick up and use, such as Blasters and Cherry Bombs. Or wait for an enemy to get near one of the Explosive Blocks and then shoot the block to defeat the enemy with a blast.

While most enemies only give up a yellow collectible worth 1 point, more powerful enemies give up a red collectible that scores you 4 quick points. Use any special attacks your character may have. Also use Power Discs to increase your damage or help you avoid taking damage. The key to getting gold is to use your ranged weapons to damage enemies as you approach, then get in a series of attacks. Remember to block when you are under attack, then counterattack before the enemies can block.

TIP

Never stop moving and attacking. This is one of the more difficult gold medals to achieve because it takes a while before enough enemies really start spawning with each wave. Once you earn bronze, two enemies spawn from each gate, and once you earn silver, shield-wielding enemies worth 2 points each begin to spawn. The best approach is to find a bomb-type tool, as they deal the most damage and can hit multiple enemies at once. If you still have trouble, here's a little cheat: the number of enemies scales up with the number of players, so add a second player as you start, and just play with one! You'll notice that it's much easier to defeat enough enemies to really get the points rolling in.

DAVY JONES COLLECTS SOULS

Ye'll fear death with this challenge. Defeat yer enemies whilst collectin' their souls so you can send them to the Locker before time runs out.

Gold: Defeat 35 enemies
Silver: Defeat 20 enemies
Bronze: Defeat 5 enemies

This is another combat Adventure. This time you have 4 minutes to defeat as many enemies as possible. The only weapon you have for this Adventure is the Blunderbuss. Don't expect to find anything.

The Turtle pirates like to throw bombs at you. Plus there are some up on the pirate ship, so keep moving or you risk getting hurt by  the bombs they rain down on you.

Each enemy is a bit different, so it is important to know how best to beat them. The skinny Driftwood pirates can be defeated with a single shot of the Blunderbuss. The Clam pirates are a bit tougher and like to block your attacks. Let them come at you, block their attacks, and then counterattack. Turtle pirates are best engaged up close so they can't throw bombs at you. However, their shell lets them take extra damage. If you want a chance at gold, be sure to use some Power Discs to give you an advantage.

GAME BASICS

CHARACTERS

POWER DISCS

PLAY SETS

TOY BOX

TOY BOX COLLECTION

ACHIEVEMENTS

TIP

As with Barbossa's Blockade, never stand still, and fire your Blunderbuss at enemies at every chance you get. With each wave of 5 enemies, there are 2 pirate-bomb-throwing units, 1 tough unit with a Flintlock, and 2 weak/standard units. When possible, focus on the pirate bomb throwers, as they prove to cause the most trouble. The weak units will go down with a single shot from the Blunderbuss, while the other two unit types take one shot and one fully charged strike. If you can get a rhythm down to combo that attack pair together, you should be able to pull this one off. Also, note that the hammerhead shark pirate Maccus is on the upper level of the pirate ship. He's worth 4 points, but if you go after him, be sure to have an attack strategy.

LIGHTNING'S COLLECTOR COURSE

It's ka-chow countdown! How many collectibles can you gather while racing around the stunt arena before time runs out?

Gold: Earn 120 points
Silver: Earn 70 points
Bronze: Earn 20 points

This car Adventure requires you to score points by running into as many collectibles as you can within 3 minutes. Yellow collectibles are worth 1 point, orange collectibles are 2 points, and red collectibles are 3 points. The red and orange are a bit tougher to collect. Right at the start, jump off the ramp and collect a row of red and orange collectibles.

In order to score points, you essentially have to perform stunts. Look for loops that are full of orange collectibles. You can score 30 points within a couple seconds. Make sure you have enough speed to get all the way around.

In order to get gold, you have to go after the red collectibles as well. Build up energy so you can use turbo, and then use ramps and tunnels to get up high enough to get those higher-point collectibles.

TIP

Keep your boost meter up at all times by performing tricks at every opportunity. Many of the collectibles and a few of the areas can only be accessed by boosting off ramps and jumps. There are three key areas that can quickly and dramatically increase your score. The first is the string of collectibles right off the entry jump. Timing your jump correctly here can nab you 18 points in the first few seconds. The second area is the loop-de-loop, which is lined with orange collectibles (and, therefore, LOTS of points). The third area is on the perimeter of the level directly across from the starting line—it is a large ramp up a wall. If you boost and jump off that ramp, you can actually land on another area above that has plenty of collectibles of every color. Other than that, just explore for lines of collectibles in quick succession.

MATER'S TOW'N'GO

Time's a tickin'! Can Tow Mater live up to his name and tow the tourist cars to their destination before time runs out?

Gold: 18 tourist cars
Silver: 10 tourist cars
Bronze: 3 tourist cars

There are several tourist cars stranded outside of Radiator Springs and Mater needs to tow them to the correct locations

within 4 minutes. The green light beacons show you where the cars are located. Once you approach a car, press the tow button to pull it behind you. Then pull it to the beacon with the same color of light.

To save time, you can even throw the tourist cars towards their destination so you can start heading to the next car while the first is on its way. Just drive straight towards the beacon and then press the throw button. However, if you miss, you have to retrieve the car and tow it back again.

Get ready to race for this Adventure. There are three different shortcuts that can help you get the gold medal. The first is when you are driving down a canyon—take a left around a stone pillar so you can then make a right turn into a cave. There are a couple of tight turns in the cave, but this can get you ahead of your opponents.

The key to getting gold on this adventure is to think ahead. Know where the locations for the three colors of cars are located. Then, as soon as you pick up a car, drive towards that location. As you are driving, look for other cars and go after those that are closest to their location or to you first. This saves time. Get good at throwing cars and you can save even more time so you can get 18 cars within the time limit.

The second shortcut can't be accessed if you took the first since the first shortcut puts you past the entrance to the second. After you get through the canyon and have to make a left turn, look for a ramp on the left side. It takes you on a paved course for a short bit and cuts off a bit of time.

TIP

Success on this Adventure comes down to speed and precision. The level is small and easy to memorize, so it just takes practice. A goal of 18 tourist cars delivered is a lofty goal, but it's definitely possible. Practice, practice, practice (and use your tow-to-throw ability to save a few precious seconds when you can).

FRANCESCO'S RUSH

Set on a course filled with challenges and shortcuts, even Francesco will appreciate this race.

Gold: Finish in under 3:00
Silver: Finish in under 4:00
Bronze: Finish in under 6:00

The third shortcut is shortly after the exits to the other two shortcuts. When the road turns to the right, and you can see the castle directly ahead, drive straight ahead, through the barriers, and jump across a gap. Then avoid swinging pendulums as you drive into the castle and out into the lead. For the quickest time, it is best to take the first and third shortcuts—if you can handle the sharp turns in the cave. Even then, you need to race clean and avoid crashes in order to earn that elusive gold medal.

GAME BASICS

CHARACTERS

POWER DISCS

PLAY SETS

TOY BOX

TOY BOX COLLECTION

ACHIEVEMENTS

> **TIP**
>
> Besides skill, shortcuts are the key to success on Francesco's Adventure. They are littered throughout, but in addition to the three mentioned above, there is another near the start that can give you an advantage early on. Just around the first right turn is a left turn. Instead of turning left, drive straight forward and jump up a short ledge and through the left-pointing arrow signs to enter a secret shortcut.

HOLLEY'S C.H.R.O.M.E. COURSE

> Have what it takes to be a C.H.R.O.M.E. Agent? Eliminate the enemy targets in this combat challenge to find out.
>
> **Gold:** 30 enemies defeated
> **Silver:** 22 enemies defeated
> **Bronze:** 10 enemies defeated

This is a combat course more than a race. While driving around an arena, you must defeat as many enemies as possible within 5 minutes. Pick up weapons from the surprise boxes to help you earn medals. The weapons only have a few shots, so you have to constantly drive over the surprise boxes to get more weapons.

The enemies spawn in the four corners of the arena. The green arrow will show you where they are in relation to your vehicle. Use weapons to eliminate them or keep up your speed and crash right into them to destroy most of the enemies.

Since you will be making lots of passes against the enemies who come in groups of three, use the 180-degree turn to quickly turn around and head back towards the enemy. Later in the adventure, the enemies that appear are tougher to defeat and just running into them once may not do the trick. Also, if you don't like the weapon you have, quickly fire it off and pick up another.

> **TIP**
>
> Never stop moving, and always look for the nearest surprise box when you don't have a load-out at the ready. An effective strategy with the missile load-out is to crash into an enemy at the same time that you fire the missile—it's a powerful one-two punch. Finally, don't waste bomb launcher load-outs by dropping them as mines. Search for faraway clusters of enemies and fire off your bombs—the blast radius is great for taking out several enemies at once. However, they might fly farther than you'd expect, so gauge your distance wisely!

LONE RANGER'S JUSTICE RUN

> Pursue the Cavendish Gang through the canyons, deserts, and ghost towns of the Old West and defeat them before they escape. Enemies on horseback are worth more points than enemies on foot.
>
> **Gold:** Earn 100 points
> **Silver:** Earn 65 points
> **Bronze:** Earn 20 points

You have 4 minutes to ride along a course and defeat as many outlaws as possible. You get 2 points per outlaw and 10 points for an outlaw on a horse. The course makes a circuit with the same outlaws appearing during each time around.

Keep your horse riding as fast as possible as you move towards the next group of outlaws. Hit as many as you can by riding towards them until the reticle appears on them, then fire. Plus, you can also defeat an outlaw by running into them while your horse is running fast.

This is another collection Adventure. However, this time you have Tonto and his ability to turn into a Crow. There are colored collectibles spread throughout the area. Yellow collectibles are worth 1 point, orange collectibles are worth 2 points, and red collectibles are worth 3 points. Collect as many as you can within 5 minutes.

Unlike Gliders, you can press the flap button to flap your wings and rise up into the air as you fly. There are several high-value collectibles near where you begin, so grab them quickly.

The key to getting gold is to go after the mounted outlaws. They spawn near the town, so it is important to try to get around the circuit as quickly as possible to go after those outlaws on horseback.

Not all of the collectibles are out in the open—check out the cave as well. If you want to earn gold, you need to play wisely. Gather all the collectibles in your immediate area before moving on to the next area. Flying to the next collectible you can see can waste time since it may be farther away than one closer to you that you cannot readily see.

TIP

Always be firing the Blaster, and go after any mounted enemy that you see, because they're worth 10 points instead of the usual 2. Go fast, and practice accuracy. With each lap that you make around the canyons, a new batch of enemies spawns, and that means a new batch of valuable mounted enemies is in fresh supply each time.

TONTO'S FLIGHT

Race through the desert with the Crow Wing Pack, gathering collectibles before time runs out.

Gold: Earn 35 points
Silver: Earn 20 points
Bronze: Earn 5 points

TIP

Focus on the more valuable orange and red collectibles first. Travel in layers of altitude rather than simply following the compass all the time (which points you to the nearest collectible, even if it could take longer to reach it because terrain is in the way). Each wave of collectibles comes to about 27 or 28 points, so if you're having trouble finding more and your score is around that, you're close to a fresh wave of reds and oranges! Use the crow liberally (obvious, but necessary).

JACK'S NIGHTMARE

Jack is in a fight with his Nightmare creations. How long can you last using all your Packs and Tools against the waves of unpleasant presents?

Gold: 3 Enemy Waves
Silver: 2 Enemy Waves
Bronze: 1 Enemy Wave

As you might guess, each round gets progressively more difficult with more enemies and more time you must survive.

Round 1 is pretty easy with 3 minutes on the clock and basic melee enemies to deal with. The next round is similar, but a gate will open, allowing you access to another area, and projectile foes will appear. The extra room is great if you need to retreat, but the best approach for the first two rounds is to find a place where the enemies funnel in towards you. Jack is more than capable of holding his ground with his exploding jack-o-lanterns. One of the best spots to take on your foes is the raised section in the center of the first area. Enemies are forced to come to you using the ramp, and they can't reach you due to the elevation of this section. If you do get overwhelmed, simply jump off the edge in the back and maneuver until your green health meter recharges.

The third round is a real challenge because you must survive for 5 minutes. The new enemies that spawn are numerous and powerful. Many have projectile weapons, which means you can be outgunned as well as hit from multiple directions and various distances. Look for the Skull block that can be used to destroy all enemies, but overall the best tactic is to use the fully opened map to spread the enemies out and avoid open areas that leave your flank exposed. For example, use long walls around the castle to protect your sides while you do battle and when you need to run around a corner to recharge your health.

BUZZ LIGHTYEAR, SAVE ME!

The townspeople are in trouble! They're stranded on meteors out in space and only Buzz can help. Rescue them before time runs out!

Gold: 25 Points
Silver: 15 Points
Bronze: 4 Points

The first four people to collect are on the section with the IN gated pad. These will be easy to pick up and toss into the pen. However, the following set of townspeople are farther out on various meteors. You have 6 minutes to complete the challenge, and it seems like a long time until you realize how spread out some of the townspeople are. The goal is pretty straightforward, but you have to actually get them into the pen to rescue them. The first thing to master is your throwing distance and aim, as it is easy to overshoot the target or just plain miss it. Failing to get the townsfolk into the octagon means you will waste a lot of time. It is even possible to get these little folks stuck on the top of the gate. Whenever you are flying back to retrieve a person, try to land directly on the target pad to avoid having to stop, aim, and toss the person.

Although there is plenty of time on the clock, you need to fly (using the jetpack) as much as possible to avoid a time-consuming walking pace.

The basic challenge is how to effectively return the townsfolk that are scattered on the meteors at various heights. If they are located at or above the height of the target pad you can fly directly back, but many are purposely placed too low. It goes without saying, but you should always seek higher ground when you try to return. However, many spots are just too low to make it back to the main hub directly. A good choice is to use the ramp to fly right up to the targeted area. The trick is looping around this ramp so you don't slam into the wall rather than fly up the incline.

There are lots of enemies that will spawn on the meteors and you are equipped with the blaster if you need to use it. Still, keep your focus on the rescue mission and ignore all of the Zurgbots as they will only slow you down.

GAME BASICS
CHARACTERS
POWER DISCS
PLAY SETS
TOY BOX
TOY BOX COLLECTION
ACHIEVEMENTS

WOODY'S ROUND UP

> Race around the meteor track three times and show us how fast you are, Cowboy!
>
> **Gold:** Under 3:00
> **Silver:** Under 4:00
> **Bronze:** Under 6:00

The three-lap race is pretty long, and if you want a chance at getting gold you need to sprint as much as possible. A lot of the turns will be tough to navigate at top speeds, however. Run as much of the time as you can and let up only when you are coming into a turn too fast. In this challenge you have a blaster at your disposal, but don't waste time gunning for the Zurgbots. Instead, use the gun just to remove crates and obstacles from your path that might slow you down.

There are plenty of orange arrows to guide you along the way, but it is the yellow gates that you really need to pay attention to. You  must pass through these checkpoints, but that doesn't mean there is only one way to get to them. There are a few alternate paths that can give you an edge as well as let you collect some green capsules. One example is at the very start where you can jump across to a parallel path that is a long straightaway versus the obvious path that curves several times.

The other choice is to take the ramp and seek higher ground to collect some green capsules along the way.

There are several obstacles to deal with, including the fences, but the Purple Goo can also be a problem. Purple pools will shrink you, thus making your ride smaller and slower. On the opposite end, the Green Goo will triple your size, and a giant-sized Bullseye can really ride like the wind.

JESSIE'S CRITTER CORRAL

> The poor lil' critters have all escaped and gotta be corralled before they all get lost!
>
> **Gold:** 24 Critters
> **Silver:** 15 Critters
> **Bronze:** 4 Critters

You have 4 minutes to round up as many critters as you can, but before you try to wrangle any of them, quickly hop on Bullseye to speed up the process. While toys like the jetpack and rocket booster can be very useful, your trusty steed is always available and is ideal for the job of corralling critters. There are plenty of critters around the pen to meet the minimum requirement, but to meet the gold standard you need to venture out farther and herd them back to the pen. Stick close to the pen as long as you can to get all the easy targets and make sure to toss them from a good distance to avoid having to ride all the way up to the corral.

Keep in mind that the smaller critters are easy to carry and won't slow down Bullseye, but the big ones are heavy enough to impact the  horse's speed. Always choose the smaller critters if you can, but if you must go for the larger ones consider using the Goo Shrinker to make them small enough that they become easy to carry.

RAPUNZEL'S RAIL RIDE

> Race along the rails to collect all the lanterns before time runs out.
>
> **Gold:** 70 Lanterns in 3:00
> **Silver:** 50 Lanterns in 3:00
> **Bronze:** 20 Lanterns in 3:00

The first important tip is to keep pressing the directional stick forward to slide faster along the rails on the straight paths. Also, keep

in mind that you can jump to another rail quickly as well as hop off and slide back in the opposite direction.

Many of the lanterns are above the track and will require you to jump while sliding in order to collect them. Try to avoid using

the same rails and work on a flow from one to another to allow you to keep moving, but avoid going in a big circle where you already have tread. As you continue to slide and collect the lanterns, note that many of them require you to leap off the rail and jump or climb. Don't take any long departures from the main rail that will burn your precious time, but it is worth grabbing some lanterns if you can quickly hop back on a rail.

RALPH'S WRECK'N WRANGLE

> Smash, wreck, fight, and jump your way through a mulit-storied building, and see how many of the collectibles you can gather before time is up.
>
> **Gold:** 50 Collectibles
> **Silver:** 30 Collectibles
> **Bronze:** 8 Collectibles

You have 6 minutes to scale this tall building and pick up as many collectibles as you can. There are lots of collectibles hidden in the

stacks of blue squares, and the fastest way to find them is to toss Cherry Bombs like crazy. There is a lot of platforming to master on this level, such as avoiding swinging hammers and hot lava. As you race to the top, keep a look out for the round pads you need to step on to destroy walls in your way, make blocks appear over lava pitfalls, or shift large stone platforms.

The toughest part is the area with long stone platforms that have two switches on each top tier. Triggering the first on the right will move some

of the platforms, but the one on the left will create more blue blocks throughout the entire section. The key to getting through this fast is knowing which of these blue blocks has a collectible. On your first trip through, bust open all of the blue blocks and remember which ones hold a valuable collectible for your next attempt. It is easy to waste a lot of time searching this area, especially if you fall from the top level all the way to the bottom.

The rooftop is a rough area filled with a bunch of conveyor belts and lots of Zurgbots. Normally, you would avoid the enemies, but in

this case they hold the collectibles you need. Stand on the stone part of the roof and toss Cherry Bombs to waste your foes. If any of your enemies gets too close, use your attack to quickly crush them. This spot is very chaotic as many of the enemies can shoot you from a distance and spawn from different areas. Try to destroy the robots as quickly as possible and use jumps to collect the yellow orbs and avoid the pull of the conveyors.

VANELLOPE'S SWEET RIDE

> Vanellope is made for racing and will prove it in this three-lap Race of Awesomeness.
>
> **Gold:** Under 3:45
> **Silver:** Under 4:45
> **Bronze:** Under 7:00

In any of the racing challenges, you must master the essential driving skill of drifting into the turns to increase your turbo meter, and

use those boosts on the straightaway sections. There are a few alternate paths, but you can achieve great times by paying more attention to the actual terrain itself. Along the track there are yellow boost arrows, and you need to ride over them as much as possible while avoiding the brown sections that will slow you down. A good example of this is a section with several boost arrows on the left and brown tiles on the right. If you can hit all the arrows on the left and leap over the upcoming brown tiles, you can really drift into that upcoming turn to keep high speed and raise the turbo meter.

GAME BASICS

CHARACTERS

POWER DISCS

PLAY SETS

TOY BOX

TOY BOX COLLECTION

ACHIEVEMENTS

The other aspect you need to focus on in this race is the three competitors. This is a battle race, and that means that weapons will spawn from the question mark icons. It's best to run through those icons as much as possible to stay stocked with artillery, but the best time to use it is when you have an opponent dead in your sights. You should be able to take first place for most of the race, but keep an eye out for the other racers trying to even the odds with weapons.

ANNA'S CHILLING CHALLENGE

Prove your royal skills in this chilling challenge by collecting the most objects before time runs out.

Gold: 85 Points
Silver: 50 Points
Bronze: 10 Points

This is a pretty large area to work with including lots of ladders to climb and platforms to leap to. The key of course is trying to collect the high-value objects over the lower-point orbs. The point value for each target is as follows: yellow is worth 1 point, orange is worth 2, and red is worth 3. The high-value targets can be found on the top tier, and this is where you should spend most of your time. While it is okay to drop down to grab a few objects, don't chase the compass arrow just to find a few yellow targets. The rocket booster is a great tool to bring you up to the top level quickly, but avoid overusing it, sending you so high in the air that the collectibles below will disappear.

ELSA'S SNOWY SLINGSHOT

Using a slingshot, hit the yellow targets for 1 point or the red ones for 3 points.

Gold: 60 Points
Silver: 35 Points
Bronze: 5 Points

Spend a little time learning the range and arc of the slingshot. It is worth spending your first attempt just practicing your shooting, as it can be tough to judge how far to pull back on the slingshot to determine the trajectory of the actual shot. The best approach is

to always try to pull back on the slingshot when you are moving from target to target to avoid wasting time. You can also pull back too far and overshoot many of these close targets. The red targets are worth triple the points and they represent an obvious incentive. These elusive red ones can move and will even disappear after a little while, flashing before they are gone for good. Keep your eyes peeled for the red ones and try to figure out if they are moving or stationary while picking off neighboring yellow ones. Hitting these red targets is the only way you will get the gold.

MICKEY'S MAGICAL ESCAPE

Brooms have surrounded the castle and it's up to Mickey to find a way out.

Gold: Under 3:00
Silver: Under 4:00
Bronze: Under 8:30

The challenge is easy to complete, but deceptively tricky to do in under 3 minutes. Basically you just follow the path laid out in front of you and shoot a few obstacles in your way. The tough part is there are things like swinging hammers, stomping barriers, and other pitfalls. Ultimately, you always want to take the high road, and if you fall by either missing a jump or getting knocked down, just restart. Because it is a timed event, you don't want to wait too long to try to circumvent any one obstacle, so you need to be brave and jump in fairly quickly. Of course you don't want to get smashed or fall, so it is not worth it to just rush in blindly. A few time-saving measures include pushing forward on the rail slide to get maximum speed and time your leap into the winds of the giants fans. You need to float across an updraft rather then run along the bottom because it takes too much time to climb back up.

If your timing is off on the red plungers, they can crush you and waste a lot of time. Try jumping to the edge of the ledge and hang on if you are not sure of their timing, and then quickly pull yourself up and go. At the stone ramp, take the high road to hop across a few rotating platforms and grab the green capsule at the end of this section. Forget about the enemies and tanks—just sprint along the castle wall, avoiding anything that will slow you down and only stop to shoot the large red blocks that bar your way.

AGENT P & THE INFINITY-INATOR

Dr. Doofenshmirtz has trapped Perry in the Infinity-inator!
Survive the twisted games it creates and search for
collectibles.

Gold: 25 Collectibles
Silver: 20 Collectibles
Bronze: 10 Collectibles

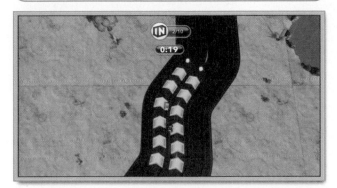

Agent P has an arch nemesis, Dr. Doofenshmirtz, who is an evil
scientist bent on taking over the Tri-State Area. Dr. Doofenshmirtz
is a hapless inventor who creates machines to fulfill his evil plans,
and they all seem to have the suffix "inator". In this challenge,
Agent P must navigate several "games" and destroy the Infinity-
inator while collecting yellow orbs.

Your first challenge is a driving game with 48 seconds on the
clock. Even though this is a timed event, don't be too concerned
with your speed. Instead, take your time to line up along the
yellow arrows on the track to pick up the collectibles. Use the
accelerator between collectible sections to quickly get to the
next pair, but don't go so fast you drive recklessly. The track is
relatively short and can be completed as long as you don't crash
and keep your speed up between collectibles.

This wouldn't be much of a challenge if the track was empty, so
of course it is filled with traffic. Agent P's vehicle is fitted with
machines guns that can wipe out obstacles in his path, but the
guns can't be fired continuously. If the guns are reloading, you
still have the ability to jump over cars if you need to avoid a
head-on collision.

The next game is a sneaking mission where you must avoid
the lights while picking up the collectibles. If you are spotted,
Omnidroids will appear. They are not difficult to deal with, so the
real challenge is that, over time, the collectibles will vanish. With
no time limit on this section, the key is still to take it slow!

Watch the movement pattern of the spotlights before getting
too close. All of the lights can easily be avoided utilizing two
techniques. The first is the ability to jump up to or down from
ledges to change levels quickly. By changing levels, you should be
able to move quickly and avoid lights, allowing you to jump up to
grab a collectible and hastily retreat below.

The other more subtle skill to master is running while holding on
to a ledge. This tricky technique will allow you to run beneath
the spotlights on the level above as well as barely go above the
large circle of light below. This is an essential tool to avoid some
of the toughest spots that may seem impossible to navigate.

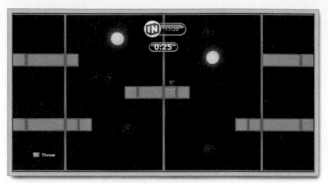

In the third game, you have to collect the yellow balls while avoiding the red and blue ones. There are three sections to this game, and each has two yellow balls you can collect. The best way to tackle this section is to avoid the temptation to run into the grassy area filled with balls. The better option is to follow the stone walls to a section where you can isolate the yellow balls and drop down to collect them.

The fourth game is an old-school 2D platformer that is all about timing and dodging. Chase down the yellow dodge balls using the Boost ability when needed to change levels or to quickly grab a ball above. Continue to change levels boosting up or dropping down to avoid the balls as you search for the collectibles. The balls will bounce off the ledges and each other, but they always move at a constant speed, which should allow you to figure out their path. If you feel like you are getting trapped, remember that you can walk through the walls on each side of the screen to make a quick escape to the opposite side.

Once you enter an open area filled with balls, get the yellow one you were hunting and leap up to the square stone platform to plan your next move. Don't try to chase the yellow collectibles in the open without scouting for them first. That said, you can't wait all day on a stony perch for the perfect chance as you will run out of time. From your high vantage point, spot the yellow targets and get to them quickly.

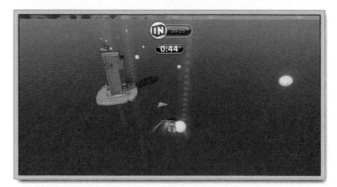

The final challenge is a gliding game. Soar through the air to get to the rooftop of the Doofenshmirtz Evil Incorporated building and destroy that Infinity-inator. There are lots of collectibles floating around and you have 55 seconds to grab them on the way to the rooftop. Don't get too greedy trying to fly around grabbing the yellow orbs or you could risk falling in the water and have to do it all over with less time on the clock. Keep an eye out for the vertical line of blue arrows and pick up the collectibles on your way as you glide from one to another. Each line of up arrows will boost you up high and give you the essential height you need to keep gliding to the roof.

When you finally land on the roof, attack the Infinity-inator and make sure to destroy it to pick up three more yellow collectibles.

PHINEAS' PINBALL MANIA

> It's a giant Pinball Table! Phineas has to keep the balls moving and enemies at bay with his Creativi-Toys.
>
> **Gold:** Under 3:00
> **Silver:** Under 2:15
> **Bronze:** Under 1:00

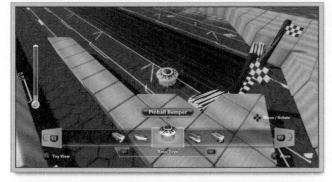

Using the boy genius, put your building skills to the test to construct a giant pinball game that keeps five spawning enemy Omnidroids from going past the final flippers at the bottom of the table. At your disposal are several pinball parts including bumpers, bouncers, and flippers. These can be placed and rotated in a variety of ways, but there are some restrictions. The first is that none of the parts can be placed on the center track, back curve, pinball launch chute, or too close to each other. The other limitation is that you are only allowed 10 pieces to create your game.

Controlling the pinball doesn't mean you can zoom around the table smashing enemies at will. It still takes a clever table design to allow you to quickly move the ball where you need it. The slow speed and sluggish nature of moving a giant-sized ball will require you to use the bouncers, bumpers, and flippers to quickly get the ball where you want. This task is not as simple as putting all the pinball parts on the bottom of the table near the final flippers. While it might seem like a great idea to try to isolate the ball at the bottom to keep any of the robots from escaping, the real goal is to hit the ones near the bottom and quickly and move towards the top to wipe them out as they spawn. If you allow too many enemies to reach the bottom area of the table, it will not be possible to maneuver the ball fast enough to hit them all before they escape.

There are tons of options to actually craft the oversized retro game and it may take a few tries at placing the parts to see how they can work together. You have to decide when it is best to have the pinball bounce and ricochet versus using the flippers to move the ball in a straight line. There really is no single best building option, which leaves the you free to explore any arrangement you want. The best approach is to space out the pinball pieces to use them to move the ball up or down the table. Also avoid putting them too close together so the balls don't get trapped. However, the real secret is not simply to build the best automated pinball table, but to take control of the pinball yourself. You do not have to worry about the game going Tilt, so you are free to help steer the largest ball around the table. Learning to control the ball is the key to victory as it allows you to smash into enemies directly and move the pinball up and down the table when needed. To do this simply move the control stick to guide the ball, but don't expect it to be that responsive. The ball has it's own momentum and can be sluggish to maneuver, but once you master controlling the pinball that gold medal is in the bag.

The goal is to keep five enemies from passing the final set of flippers, and as the time ticks away you should expect them to spawn faster and run down the center lane with haste. Keep an eye on the whole table and move the ball to the bottom whenever you see a robot nearing the bottom of the table. After dealing with their threat, move the ball up the center lane and wipe out any approaching Omnidroids. However, if there are none nearby it might be faster to move the ball past the final flippers into the pinball launcher on the left side to quickly spring the ball to the top of the table. It can be very effective to launch the ball to the top and simply roll straight down the center track smashing enemies when they spawn or rolling straight down toward the bottom. This is technique can be especially useful if you are having difficulty maneuvering the ball.

GAME BASICS

CHARACTERS

POWER DISCS

PLAY SETS

TOY BOX

TOY BOX COLLECTION

ACHIEVEMENTS

HALL OF HEROES

The Hall of Heroes is a part of the game where you can see how your characters have progressed and keep track of all the Power Discs you have collected. At the Disney Infinity Hub, step on the purple button to travel to the Hall of Heroes. You can also access it from the Start menu when you first enter the game.

When you first begin playing *Disney Infinity*, the Hall of Heroes is very empty and consists of only a central area surrounded by pedestals. However, as you progress through the game, you not only fill in the open slots, you also build up the hall itself.

As you collect and use Power Discs, they will appear on the ground as tiles in the Hall of Heroes. The first wave consists of 20 Power Discs. However, another 35 Discs will be released in waves 2 and 3 combined for a total of 55 Power Discs. You can learn about the Power Discs you do not yet have by pressing the button indicated on the screen.

The Hall of Heroes grows as you earn stars in the Play Sets and the Toy Box—the architecture improves and you receive additional decorations. Here is a list of what you get at various levels of stars.

1 Star—Stage 1 adds some details to the flooring
4 Stars—Stage 2 adds some initial walls
9 Stars—Stage 3 gives you some interior planters
16 Stars—Stage 4 provides columns on the outside of the Hall
25 Stars—Stage 5 adds plants to the lower area inside the Hall
37 Stars—Stage 6 gives you inside columns and a ring around the top
52 Stars—Stage 7 puts a dome over the top of the Hall
70 Stars—Stage 8 adds plants outside of the Hall
92 Stars—Stage 9 provides statues on the upper ring
118 Stars—Stage 10 puts some plants on the dome
148 Stars—Stage 11 hangs banners on the lower levels
183 Stars—Stage 12 gives you an outside garden as well as a central tree and a pond
223 Stars—Stage 13 adds an outside garden with Townspeople statues
268 Stars—Stage 14 provides an upper ring as well as some outside plants
318 Stars—The final stage hangs banners on the upper level

Once a character reaches level 1, a bronze statue of that character appears on its pedestal. Get that character to level 5 to change the statue to silver. Continue leveling up your characters to level 10 to get a gold statue. It is fun to return to the Hall of Heroes periodically to see how it is growing and what you have added through your endeavors.

The Hall of Heroes also gets buttons for interactive events as you acquire character statues. When you have 3 statues, you get a fireworks button that sets off fireworks when you step on it. At 10 character statues, a music button appears. Get 18 statues and a button appears that allows you to change the sky. Finally, if you take ownership of all 29 characters and get a bronze statue, a special item will appear in the central fountain's pillar of light, and it will unlock the Ultimate Pack that can be used by all non-car characters.

Feats

While you are in a Toy Box, you can earn Feats. These are small awards that you get for a variety of actions, ranging from building things, to driving, or even defeating enemies. While some are easy to earn, others will take a while. Each time you complete a Feat, you also earn some Sparks. The more difficult the Feat, the more Sparks you collect as a reward.

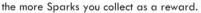

Feat	Requirement
Air Croquet	Fly through an Arch Block
Air Time	Stay up in the air for 3 seconds with one ground vehicle in one try
Backwards	Get 5 seconds of air time in reverse with one ground vehicle in one try
Barriers Not Included	Use your ground vehicle to jump over 100 objects in total
Barriers Not Included 2	Use your ground vehicle to jump over 1,000 objects in total
Bash 'n' Smash	Destroy 500 bashables
Blast Off!	Ride a ground vehicle off of a launch ramp
Blipped!	Destroy 25 Blip Blocks in one session
Bringin' Up Baddies	Use an Enemy Creator
Broken In	Travel a total distance of 100 kilometers on a mount
Clown Car	Ride in a shrunk vehicle while oversized
Crash Course	Drift into 2 bashables in one attempt
Crazy Driver	Do 2 tricks in one try in a ground vehicle
Crazy Driver 2	Do 3 tricks in one attempt.
Creator Extraordinaire	Place 500 blocks in total
Creator Extrordinaire 2	Place 5000 blocks in total.
Daredevil	Do 4 different tricks in one attempt
Destruction Zone	Destroy 5 bashables in under 5 seconds
Dodge Ball	Use a giant ball found in your editor to hit two townspeople in under 2 seconds
Double Dribble	Bounce a giant ball found in your editor off 2 enemies within 5 seconds
Drivin' You Crazy	Do 100 tricks in ground vehicles
Drivin' You Crazy 2	Do 500 tricks in ground vehicles.
Equestrian	Jump over 10 meters with a mount in one attempt
Equestrian 2	Jump over 50 meters with a mount in one attempt
Floatin' Along	Float for over 30 seconds
Frequent Flyin'	Travel a total distance of 25 kilometers in air vehicles
Game Maker	Place 10 Creativi-Toys in one session
Game Maker Extraordinaire	Set up 100 Creativi-Toy connections
Giddy Up!	Destroy 100 enemies while mounted in one session
Go Long!	Throw 100 townspeople
Goal!	Knock a giant ball found in your editor into a soccer goal
Green Thumb	Place 5 plants
Green Thumb 2	Place 50 Plants
Havin' a Bash	Destroy 100 bashables in one session
High Dive	Land in a Splash Pool after travelling 40 meters
High Hoppin'	Jump 12 times in a single Wall Jump attempt
High Score	Score a soccer goal with an air vehicle

Feat	Requirement
Hop and Spin	Jump from one Spinner to another
Hop Over	Jump directly over 10 blocks with a ground vehicle in one attempt
Hot Pursuit	Race around at top speed in your ground vehicle for 5 kilometers total
Hover Happy	Travel between 12 Fans without touching any other toys
It's Alive!	Cause 10 Creativi-Toys to react simultaneously
Just for Kicks	Punt a townsperson
Just for Kicks 2	Punt 50 townspeople
Landscapin'	Place 5 Terrain Blocks
Look Out Below!	Destroy 100 enemies with an air vehicle in one session
Look Ma, No Road!	Spend over 10 minutes in the air in a ground vehicle
Lookin' Good	Place 5 decorations
Master Builder	Place over 100 blocks in one session
Monster Mount	Ride an oversized mount while shrunk
New World	Customize 5 Terrain Blocks while in Spark Mode or with the Magic Wand
Next Floor Please	Ride an Elevator
Nifty Drifter	Drift for over 5 kilometers in total
Nifty Drifter 2	Drift for over 50 kilometers in total
Pest Control	Destroy 100 enemies
Pest Control 2	Destroy 1000 Enemies
Please Stand to the Right	Stay on a Conveyor Belt for over 5 seconds
Prize Collector	Have 5 Gold Statues in your Hall of Heroes
R.O.F.	Do a trick through the Ring of Fire
Rapid Rider	Keep going as fast as you can on your mount for 30 seconds
Rapid Rider 2	Keep going as fast as you can on your mount for 60 seconds
Road Rage	Destroy 100 enemies with a ground vehicle in one session
Saddle Sore	Jump over 100 objects with your mount during the course of play
Sharp Shooter	Shoot 1,000 objects
Sky Driving	Jump over 400 meters in one attempt in your ground vehicle
Slide Swipe	Drift into a townsperson
Speedy Steed	Ride your mount at top speed for 5 kilometers total
Spinning Shot	Shoot an enemy while on a Spinner
Straight Shooter	Shoot 5 enemies in under 5 seconds
Straight Shootin'	Shoot 10 objects in one session
Straight Shootin' 2	Shoot 500 objects in one session
Sunday Driver	Travel a total distance of 100 kilometers in a ground vehicle

Feat	Requirement
Sunday Driver 2	Travel a total distance of 500 kilometers in ground vehicles
Supersonic	Use 2 Super Cannons without hitting the ground
Supersonic 2	Use 5 Super Cannons without hitting the ground.
Track Changin'	Customize a track piece
Trickin'	Do a trick in reverse
Tricky	Do a trick while going boost speed in your ground vehicle
Triple Tricker	Do 3 tricks while going boost speed in your ground vehicle

Feat	Requirement
Turbo Booster	Use 25 boost pads in one session
Turbo Booster 2	Use three boost pads in 3 seconds.
Turbo Charged	Boost in a ground vehicle 100 times
Wrecking Crew	Destroy 25 enemies in one session
Wrecking Machine	Destroy 2 enemies in 10 seconds
Wrecking Machine 2	Destroy 3 enemies in 10 seconds
Wrecking Machine 3	Destroy 5 enemies in 10 seconds

Unlocking Toys for the Toy Box

The Toy Box is the place where you can let your creativity run wild. At the beginning of the game, you start off with only a few toys. However, you can collect many more toys as you play through the game.

UNLOCKING TOYS IN THE PLAY SETS

One of the best ways to unlock toys for the Toy Box is to play through the Play Sets. Each Play Set has a number of types of toys themed to that Play Set that you can then take into the Toy Box once you unlock them. There are several ways to unlock toys. First, as you are playing in a Play Set, look for green capsules—these contain toys for the Toy Box. (The red capsules have toys that remain in the Play Set.) Green capsules are rarer than red capsules, so stay on the lookout for them while in the Play Sets.

Another way to unlock toys is through the Character Chests. These also appear in the Play Set. However, unlike the green capsules, the Character Chests require a specific character to unlock them. A picture of the specific character appears on the chest. Switch to that character to unlock the chest and unlock toys as well.

While exploring a Play Set, be sure to look for large Vaults. These look like large Character Chests, however you need all of the characters from the Play Set in order to open one of these Vaults. For example, in the Pirates of the Caribbean Play Set, you not only need Captain Jack Sparrow, but also Barbossa and Davy Jones. Opening these Vaults unlocks an entire Toy Box world as well as several different toys for all Toy Boxes. As you can see, it is important to have all the characters if you want to get all of the toys.

TIP

If you are missing a character from a Play Set, but your friend has it, you can always borrow your friend's character and use it as a guest to unlock Character Chests and the large Vaults. Just be sure to return the favor.

THE DISNEY INFINITY VAULT

All of the toys unlocked in the Play Sets are themed or related to the specific Play Sets. However, there are also a great number of other toys that can be unlocked from within the Toy Box itself. These can be unlocked at the Disney Infinity Vault, which can be accessed through the Pause menu while In a Toy Box or at the Disney Infinity Hub by stepping on the yellow button. The Vault is like a game of chance. It offers 16 different toys or toy packs. You then spend Spins for a chance to randomly unlock one of the 16. If you don't get what you want, you can spend another Spin to get one of the remaining 15 toys. You can also shuffle the Vault to randomly get a new set of 16 toys to spin for. Some of the toys have a yellow background. That indicates that you not only get the toy shown, but also some bonus toys as well. For packs, select the toy in the Vault to see what the pack contains. Most packs consist of two or more townspeople, or groups of plants or decorations.

Spins are the currency you use in the Vault to unlock the toys. There are several ways to get Spins.

- Collect them in the Toy Box Launch where they are Inside green capsules. Look for these capsules hidden in clusters of crates and barrels.

- Complete the Mastery Adventures. You get a Spin once you complete each of these for the first time.

- Earn medals in the Adventures and Character Adventures. You get a Spin for earning each medal for the first time. Therefore, you can get three Spins for each Adventure—one each for bronze, silver, and gold.

- Level up your characters. Each time you collect enough Sparks to level up a character, you get another Spin. You can level them up in the Toy Box or in the Play Sets. The Spins can only be used in the Toy Box though.

TIP

If you want to ensure you get the toys you want, make sure you have at least 16 Spins before you use the Disney Infinity Vault. Then keep shuffling the Vault until there are several Toys that you want on the same screen of 16. At that point start spending Spins. At the worst, it will cost you 16 Spins—but you are guaranteed to get that toy.

GAME BASICS

CHARACTERS

POWER DISCS

PLAY SETS

TOY BOX

TOY BOX COLLECTION

ACHIEVEMENTS

The Toy Box Worlds

Toy Box and Toy Box Worlds can be confusing. Toy Box is the mode of play in *Disney Infinity* where you can create your own worlds. These worlds are called Toy Boxes or collectively as Toy Box Worlds. Some of them, such as the Toy Box Launch, are available right from the start. Others must be unlocked. This section covers each of these Toy Box Worlds and how to unlock them, if necessary. You can create and use all the toys you have collected or unlocked in each of these Toy Box Worlds.

Captain Jack Sparrow was kind enough to take us on a tour of the Toy Box Worlds along with Dumbo the Flying Elephant (which is one of the rare Power Discs in the first wave).

BASIC TOY BOX WORLDS

These Toy Box Worlds are all created using the Fairytale Kingdom theme and are fairly open, so you can start building right away without too much effort.

EMPTY TOY BOX

This is one of the Toy Box Worlds available right at the start of the game. It is just a square of flat ground. You can use it for a small world or just use it as a starting block for an entire world of your own. The possibilities are endless.

BASIC TOY BOX

To unlock this Toy Box World, you must find a special green capsule in the Toy Box Launch world. It is located down on a small ledge between the castle and the race track. If you do not have an air vehicle, you can drop down to this ledge. Then, since you can't climb back up, go to the Pause menu and select "Reset Gameplay" to return your character to a safe location.

This world is flat and already has edges along with a few plants. This is a good place to start your first world of your own when you only have a limited number of toys with which to begin building. However, as you get more and more toys, you will probably want to use the Empty Toy Box instead, since it is easier to expand.

ROLLING HILLS

Take an air vehicle, or use Spark mode, to get to the small floating island on the side of the mainland near the River Gazebo where the Disney Infinity Hub is located. Once you get the green capsule, you unlock the Rolling Hills world.

Larger than most of the other basic Toy Box Worlds, Rolling Hills has no finished edges and has slopes that raise the land towards the center. Play around in this world to get a feel for how to create hills and other raised terrain so that it looks natural. This is a fun place to build a race track or some caves for others to explore.

WORLD OF WALKWAYS

The green capsule that unlocks this world is on a small floating island high above the Toy Box Launch world on the opposite side of the mainland from the Rolling Hills green capsule. Again, use an air vehicle or Spark mode to get there.

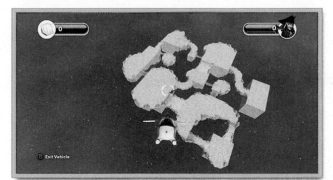

This world contains floating islands connected by walking paths and bridges. Use this world for paintball matches or horse races. It also has some larger islands on which you can easily expand. Again, this is a good place to explore to see how the designers connect larger land masses together.

THE PLAY SET TOY BOX WORLDS

Each Play Set has a Toy Box World that you can unlock. Look for a large Vault in each Play Set. In order to open these Vaults, you need all of the characters for that Play Set. Use each character to open one of the locks. Then when the Vault is opened, you not only are rewarded with lots of toys, but also an entire Toy Box World themed after that Play Set.

In addition to providing pre-built Toy Boxes, these worlds are already themed. Take some time to study how the designers built them by taking a character with a Magic Wand and selecting different features. By studying and exploring these worlds, you can learn a lot about how to make a Toy Box World look really cool so you can impress your friends.

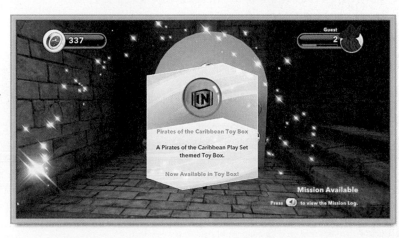

GAME BASICS

CHARACTERS

POWER DISCS

PLAY SETS

TOY BOX

TOY BOX COLLECTION

ACHIEVEMENTS

METROVILLE TOY BOX

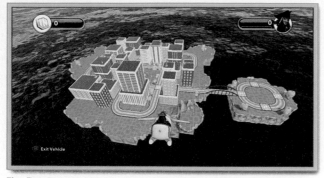

This Toy Box World is themed after The Incredibles Play Set. It features a city with tall buildings and a small island connected to the mainland by a road bridge. Explore it to learn how to build cities or just use the pre-built city for your own world.

MONSTERS UNIVERSITY TOY BOX

Themed after Monsters University, this world has a hedge around its border, a few buildings, and even a clock tower. There is still some open ground on which to build even more.

PIRATES OF THE CARIBBEAN TOY BOX

Ahoy there matey! This tropical island comes complete with a shipwreck, a small town, and even some small islands to which you can build bridges or pathways. Observe how to build waterfalls and streams so they appear natural and try building a treasure grotto under the ground, along with a cave that leads down to the gold and jewels. Maybe even put some pirate enemies to guard the treasure.

RADIATOR SPRINGS TOY BOX

Get ready race fans. This Cars-themed world comes complete with an awesome race track that covers most of the world. This is a good place to see how to build a great race track of your own and then theme it with landmarks and other features to make it aesthetically pleasing—or are they just obstacles you need to avoid hitting while at high speed? Once you unlock this world, be sure to invite your friends over for a race.

COLBY TOY BOX

Themed after the Lone Ranger Play Set, Colby has a southwestern desert feel with tall mesas, canyons, tepee villages, and much more. This world has a lot of possibilities for making shooting games where players ride horses and can use the canyons for cover or to try to lose a pursuer. Or modernize it by building a race track across the tops of the mesas with some half loops that lead down to the desert floor below.

TOY STORY TOY BOX

This outer spaced themed Toy Box is a great area to build adventures about flying around its vast landscape and floating platforms. It also features some fun caverns that are perfect for setting up a race. The truly unique aspect of this Toy Box is the mountain that oozes purple and green Goo. These special pools can shrink or enlarge anything that that they touch, and it can add a whole new physical dimension to your creations.

Creating in the Toy Box

While you can do Adventures and play around in the Toy Box, the main feature of *Disney Infinity* is the ability to create within a Toy Box World a land of your very own that is only limited by your imagination—and the toys you have unlocked. After going to a Toy Box World, your main tool is the Magic Wand. Open up the Tools/Packs menu and select the Magic Wand. It will be your best friend in the Toy Box.

CHANGING THE THEME

Another menu pops up and now you can change the theme of just that one piece of terrain, or all themed terrain in the entire world. Once again, this is a powerful feature and allows you to change the look of a world very easily.

You can change the look of a Toy Box World with just a few steps and not even have to build anything new. The default theme for most of the Pre-Built Toy Box Worlds, with the exception of the Play Set Toy Boxes, is Fairytale Kingdom. This theme affects the ground. To change it, select the ground of any part of the world and then press the button corresponding to the art palette icon. A menu pops up along the bottom and allows you to select from all of the themes you have unlocked. Then you can either change just the theme of the block you have selected, or change the theme for the entire world. One of the ways to get new themes is to unlock them within the Play Sets so you can theme your world like those Play Sets.

The area surrounding the land of your Toy Box World is called the Sky Theme. It is the backdrop or background to your world. It too can be customized to fit your theme. To do this, go into the editor and, within the Basic Toys category, select the Sky Changer. Place it anywhere in the world. When you hit the large button on the side of the Sky Changer, the Sky Theme changes to a different theme. It can change the sky to night or make the Sky Theme look like it something from one of the Play Sets. Keep hitting the button on the Sky Changer to cycle through your choices. Sky Themes are not only visual effects, but also have audio. The background sounds and music change with some Sky Themes, thus adding even more to the experience.

You can also change the theme of some of the decorations. Select a tree or group of terrain with your Magic Wand and, if it is themed terrain, you will have the option of editing the theme.

Another way to change themes is through the use of Power Discs. There are two different types of Power Discs that affect theme. The Terrain Theme changes the ground and themed terrain to the new theme, while the Sky Theme changes the sky to the new theme. For example, if you want to change the theme of your world to *Alice in Wonderland*, you would need two Power Discs— one for the Terrain Theme and one for the Sky Theme. Then if you want to change it back to your original theme, just use the steps above to change the land, the terrain, and the Sky Theme.

TIP

In Series 1 of the Power Discs, there are four different themes you can collect. In addition to *Alice in Wonderland*, there are also themes for Sugar Rush from *Wreck-It Ralph*, the Lantern Sky and textures from *Tangled*, and an underwater theme from *Finding Nemo*. Look for even more themes in Series 2 and Series 3 of Power Discs.

CATEGORIES OF TOYS

Before you start building, it is important to understand that there are several different categories of toys within the Toy Box.

When you first open the editor, you are presented with the "Pick a Toy…" screen. Here you can cycle through every toy that you have unlocked. However, when building in a world, it is easier to use the build view. Switch to this view by pressing the button shown on the screen. As you unlock more and more toys, the "Pick a Toy…" screen can be overwhelming. The build view, on the other hand, organizes the toys into 18 different categories. Let's take a look at each category and what you can expect from them.

TERRAIN

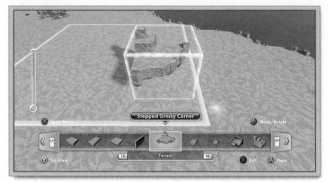

Terrain is the ground for your Toy Box Worlds. You can use it to expand the size of your worlds or to create features on your worlds. Build slopes and hills or even underground caves. When building a world, you usually want to start out with the terrain first, since it is on this terrain that you will build all your structures. Experiment with different levels of terrain to create some interesting features. For example, create a cave system or canyon through which you can have a horse race.

BUILDING SETS

Building sets are unlocked through the Disney Infinity Vault and within the Play Sets. These toys consist of several different parts that can be put together to create one type of building. For example, you can unlock parts to build a Disney-style castle or the Agrabah Palace. There are several different parts for each, so you can really create a custom castle or palace with lots of different features. Use these toys to build stadiums or cities. If you are going to be using Building Sets toys, it is a good idea to start with them, since they can make some very large structures.

BUILDINGS

Buildings are complete structures. You pick one, place it, and you are done. You don't have to assemble a bunch of pieces like the Building Sets. Some are unlocked in the Play Sets—and have the theme of that Play Set—while others are unlocked through the Disney Infinity Vault. They range in size from the very small Hotdog Stand to the large buildings from the Monsters University Play Set.

SET PIECES

Set Pieces, for the most part, are very large toys. Many are from the sets of Disney movies, shows, or theme parks, or they have some type of interactive features. These are fun to use and can add a major talking point to your worlds when you invite your friends. Be sure to show them your very own Pride Rock, Matterhorn, or Dungeon—all right next to each other. Only in *Disney Infinity*.

BASIC TOYS

The Basic Toys contain a variety of different toys such as the Disney Infinity Hub, the Sky Changer, the Enemy Creator, and several other items. Many are interactive in some way and don't necessarily fit into one of the other categories. Be sure to check out these toys, since most can be fun to use in your world no matter what the theme.

ACTION TOYS

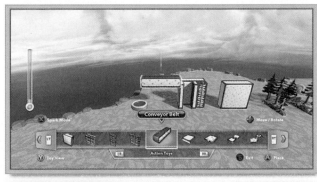

If you think the Basic Toys can be fun, wait until you try out the Action Toys. These all move or do some action—hence the name. Use Action Toys to create your own games or adventures and challenge your friends to visit your worlds and try them out. Set up a series of Action Toys and then try them out. Action Toys work great for platforming-type games. Combine them with Creativi-Toys for even more options and fun.

GAME BASICS

CHARACTERS

POWER DISCS

PLAY SETS

TOY BOX

TOY BOX COLLECTION

ACHIEVEMENTS

CREATIVI-TOYS

Creativi-Toys are the thinking or logic toys of the Toy Box. They can be programmed with functions to be triggers or reactions. You can even link several of these toys in series or parallel so that one action or trigger can result in several different reactions. We have included a section devoted entirely to Creativi-Toys later in this chapter. Be sure to check it out. And the best way to learn about these toys is to put them in your Toy Box Worlds and play with them. Creativi-Toys can be unlocked in the Disney Infinity Vault and by completing Creativi-Toys Mastery Adventures part 1 and 2. Creativi-Toys can interact with some toys in other categories as well.

BLOCKS

Blocks are just that—blocks. They come in very many different shapes and sizes. Use them to build things just like you might with a box of wooden blocks in real life. You can even change the theme of the blocks from their default stone look to a variety of themes that you can unlock. In addition to the standard blocks, there are also blip blocks that are destroyed when you hit them. Physics blocks behave following the laws of physics and some of them, such as the glass and wood ones, can be destroyed. There are even explosive blocks—which blow up when you hit them—and lava blocks.

TRACK PIECES

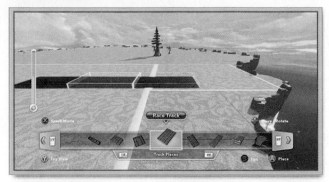

Track Pieces include road track as well as grinding rails and even barriers that you can set up around your tracks. The key to assembling a track is to ensure that each piece connects to the adjacent pieces, otherwise you have trouble racing or grinding on them. Once you have used the pieces to create a track, try changing the theme. While the slot car track is the default, there are several themes that can be unlocked in the Play Sets or the Disney Infinity Vault. You can even make your track look like a running track by using the ESPN Sports theme. Track pieces also include ramps and other toys for doing stunts.

SPORTS TOYS

These toys are great for creating games you can play with other players. Several of the goals can be linked to Creativi-Toys to keep score or do other functions. The balls and puck all react according to the laws of physics. It is a good idea to include some barriers when building with Sports Toys. It is no fun when your soccer ball rolls off the edge of the world.

PLANTS

Your world can always benefit from some green and the Plants category has you covered. Pick from trees, flowers, shrubs, and even some non-organic toys such as light poles to give your world some color and flora. Some of the toys in the Plant category are themed. This can be helpful when you want to change the theme of your entire world. Select one of your plants and edit the theme for all plants and, with one action, every themed Plant toy will change to the new theme. Some plants, such as those unlocked in the Play Sets, cannot change themes.

DECORATIONS

While you have some large toys with which to play, Decorations are much smaller. However, they can be just as important. Decorations fill in empty spaces and provide continuity for your world. Some decorations can be destroyed, while others are static and just stay there.

VEHICLES AND MOUNTS

Your characters need a way to get around the Toy Box Worlds you create. That is where Vehicles and Mounts come in. A Mount is an animal you can ride—usually a horse, mule, or even an elephant. Vehicles come in two types—ground or air. Ground vehicles can drive along the ground and stay on the ground—unless you drive off a cliff or do some stunts. Air vehicles, on the

other hand, can fly through the air. You can use both vehicles and mounts for races as well as transportation. Some vehicles also include weapons, such as the Attack Copter or The Incredicar. You can use these for games where you have to destroy a number of targets or even for getting hits on opponents' vehicles.

ENEMIES

What would a Disney movie be without villains or enemies? Add some spice and conflict to your world by including Enemies. While you start out with only a few, you can unlock lots more in the Play Sets as well as at the Disney Infinity Vault. You can keep a theme for your Enemies, or mix and match them for a battle royale. In a Toy Box World, Enemies will attack any players (unless you use a Creativi-Toy to assign teams). They do this automatically and will actually seek out players as they wander around the world. Of course it is always fun to let loose a few Enemies when visiting a friend's world as well.

CAST MEMBERS

Cast Members are unlocked in the Play Sets. They are the characters in the Play Sets that give you missions to complete. Cast Members will walk around a Play Set on their own. They do not interact with you, do not attack you, and can't be harmed or defeated. They are there to add personalities to your world. Don't be shy about mixing up these toys. It is always fun to see monsters roaming the streets of an Old West town. Remember, this is your world.

TOY BOX TOWNSPEOPLE

These little townspeople like to dress up in costumes from various Disney movies or related features. They will scoot around the world not causing any harm. They are great for populating a town in your world to give it some more personality and life. While they don't attack, you can pick them up and even throw them. Try picking them up and drop kicking them by jumping and then pressing the alternate attack button. You can make a game where you have to punt Townspeople through a goal post. (Only in your Toy Box World. Please do not attempt this in the real world.) These toys can be unlocked from the Disney Infinity Vault.

PLAY SET TOWNSPEOPLE

These Townspeople are just like the Toy Box Townspeople. The only difference is that they are unlocked through the Play Sets rather than spending Spins in the Disney Infinity Vault.

CRITTERS

Critters are just like Townspeople—except they are not people. They are animals. While you may want to put Townspeople near your buildings and towns in your worlds, place Critters out in the forests. You can pick up Critters just like the Townspeople. However, Critters are skittish and tougher to catch. You need to move slow if you want to catch them. Rush at them and they tend to run away.

GETTING STARTED

So you want to try your hand at building in the Toy Box? Here is a sample of the process you might go through with just the basics. You can take this and add a lot more to it, however the basic procedures are the same. Start off with a Pre-Built Toy Box World. For this we chose a blank one. Make sure you have your Wand handy, since it is the tool for building and modifying your Toy Box World. This tiny world is going to be centered around the Matterhorn. Select this toy from the Set Pieces category and place it on the terrain. You can also add some plants to the corners of the land now or later.

If you noticed, the Matterhorn has some grinding rails built into it. These are the tracks for the bobsleds. However, in this world, the characters can take a ride by grinding the rails going through the Matterhorn. Switch to the Track Pieces category and select rails. Be careful that they connect to the existing rails by changing the view so you can check from all angles. Add some bending rails to go down and some curved rails to make turns.

The rails are a bit high for characters to jump onto. Therefore, switch to the Blocks category and put in a couple Long Wedge Blocks to serve as ramps for your characters to get up to the rails.

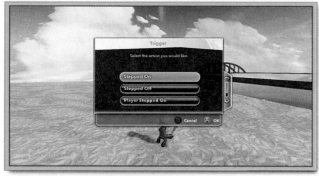

Now that you have completed the rails and ramps, try it out. Walk your character up one of the ramps and jump onto the rail to begin a ride through the scenic Alpine Matterhorn. This was just a simple example of how easy it is to create in the Toy Box Worlds. You can then add more terrain and create a complete theme park of your own. Just remember, the best way to learn about building is to build. Hands-on experience is a great teacher.

USING CREATIVI-TOYS IN THE TOY BOX

Most of the toys are straightforward in their use. You place them in the Toy Box World and there they are. Creativi-Toys, on the other hand, require a bit more effort, since you have to program them in order to make full use of them. The key to understanding these toys is learning their two main functions. First, they can act as a trigger. Remember those "If (or when) and then" logic equations you might have learned in math? The trigger is the "when". For example, when a player steps on this pad. Or it could be something like "when the elevator reaches the top of its path". These triggers set the conditions for another action or behavior. That is the second function of a Creativi-Toy—to cause a behavior effect. This is the "then" part of the equation. It could be something like "then the door opens" or "the pad spawns a blaster". A quick setup uses a Trigger and a Falling Object Generator. Select the Trigger by pressing the connect button and choose a trigger action such as "stepped on". Then select the Falling Object Generator with the connect button and select a behavior such as "ESPN Soccer Ball". Now if your character walks onto the Trigger, a soccer ball will drop from the Falling Object Generator.

Some Creativi-Toys can only be a trigger or an effect and some can be both. Let's take a look at all of the different Creativi-Toys available in the Toy Box.

TRIGGER

The Trigger is a pressure pad and one of the simplest Creativi-Toys. In order for it to have an effect, it must be connected to another toy. There are four different ways you can set the Trigger.

Trigger Action	Description
Stepped On	When the Trigger is stepped on by a player or AI
Stepped Off	When a player or AI steps off of the Trigger
Player Stepped On	When the Trigger is stepped on only by a human player
Player Stepped Off	When only a human player steps off the Trigger

TRIGGER AREA

The Trigger Area acts like a trigger. However, instead of stepping on a pad, it triggers when something walks through an area that is invisible in the Toy Box World (but visible in the editor mode). There are several different ways you can set the Trigger Area, including for specific players. This works great when creating games to play against other players.

Trigger Action	Description
Entered	When a player or AI enters the Trigger Area
Exited	When a player or AI leaves the Trigger Area
Player Entered	When any player enters the Trigger Area
Player Exited	When any player leaves the Trigger Area
Player 1 Entered	When only player 1 enters the Trigger Area
Player 2 Entered	When only player 2 enters the Trigger Area
Player 3 Entered	When only player 3 enters the Trigger Area
Player 4 Entered	When only player 4 enters the Trigger Area
Player 1 Exited	When only player 1 leaves the Trigger Area
Player 2 Exited	When only player 2 leaves the Trigger Area
Player 3 Exited	When only player 3 leaves the Trigger Area
Player 4 Exited	When only player 4 leaves the Trigger Area

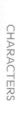

ACTION BUTTON

The Action Button can be a trigger as well as a behavior. You could have another trigger cause the Action Button to be pressed as the behavior, so something else could trigger the Action Button to be pressed.

Trigger Action	Description	Behavior	Description
Pressed	When the Action Button is pressed	Press Button	The Action Button's button to be pressed.

TARGET

This trigger device can be activated several ways including shooting it, throw something at it, or hitting it with a melee attack if it is within reach. This is best utilized in shooting games.

Trigger Action	Description
Hit	When the Target is hit by any weapon or tool

POWER SWITCH

The Power Switch is a toggle. By stepping on the red side you turn it on. Step on the yellow side to turn it off. You can assign different triggers to both the on and off triggers. In addition, you can have it as a behavior in response to another trigger.

Trigger Action	Description	Behavior	Description
On	When the Power Switch gets stepped on and the Power Switch gets turned on (red part of switch is down), the output is supposed to happen	On	The power switch to turn on (red = down)
Off	When the Power Switch gets stepped on and the Power Switch gets turned off (red part of switch is up), the output is supposed to happen	Off	The power switch to turn off (red = up)
Output	When the Power Switch receives an "Input" behavior and the Power Switch is in the on position	Input	The Power Switch to send an "Output" action if it is in the on position

DUAL ACTION TRIGGER

The Dual Action Trigger requires two inputs in order to activate the trigger function. To use it, you would first select two different triggering actions and connect them to the Dual Action Trigger as input 1 and input 2. Then select the Dual Action Trigger and select for what it will act as the trigger. An example of this could be you have to walk through a Trigger Area and hit a Target, then the Dual Action Trigger will cause a light to turn on.

Trigger Action	Description	Behavior	Description
Complete	When the Dual Action Trigger completes both inputs	Input 1	The Dual Action Trigger's input 1 to turn on
		Input 2	The Dual Action Trigger's input 2 to turn on
		Reset	The Dual Action Trigger to reset (both inputs return to off)

RACING GATE

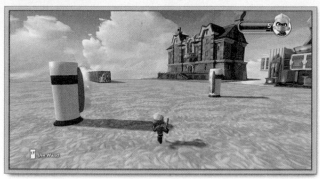

This is similar to a Trigger Area. However, the Racing Gate works better for tracks and is also visible so players can see a visual end or finish line to a race.

Trigger Action	Description
Crossed by Player	When a player runs/drives/flies through the Racing Gate

COLLECTION PEN

This toy acts as a trigger. However, you can distinguish different triggers depending on what you put into the pen. For example, you could cause one counter to advance if an enemy is placed into the Collection Pen and another counter to advance when a friend is put into the pen. This can be a lot of fun for creating your own games.

Trigger Action	Description
Enemy Entered	When an enemy enters the Collection Pen
Friend Entered	When an NPC/Critter enters the Collection Pen
Ball Entered	When a ESPN/Action Toy Ball enters the Collection Pen

CHECKPOINT

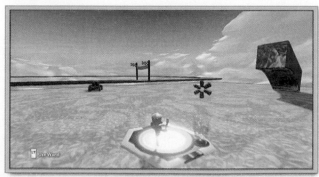

The Checkpoint is a bit different than a Trigger. It keeps track of the fact that it has been triggered and can only be used once.

Use Checkpoints for races or other games where you want a player to go to different spots and so they only get one point for each Checkpoint. Once a Checkpoint is activated, it cannot send out another trigger.

Trigger Action	Description	Behavior	Description
Checkpoint Set	When the Checkpoint is set (stepping on the checkpoint can set the Checkpoint)	Set Checkpoint	The Checkpoint to be set

OBJECT GENERATOR

The Object Generator usually is the behavior as a result of another trigger. You can select from a variety of objects you want to appear on this toy. However, you can also use this as a trigger for when this toy spawns an object or for when an object that is spawned is destroyed. These can be fun for lots of different types of games. (Note: You must have already unlocked an object in order to have it generated by this toy.)

Trigger Action	Description	Behavior	Description
Spawned	When the Object Generator spawns an object	Buzz Lightyear's Jetpack	The Object Generator to spawn a Buzz Lightyear's Jetpack
Killed Spawned Toy	When the spawned object is killed	Star Command Boost Pack	The Object Generator to spawn a Star Command Boost Pack.
		Pirate Bombs	The Object Generator to spawn Pirate Bombs
		Frying Pan	The Object Generator to spawn a Frying Pan
		Mania Blaster	The Object Generator to spawn a Mania Blaster
		Toilet Paper Launcher	The Object Generator to spawn a Toilet Paper Launcher
		Paintball Gun	The Object Generator to spawn a Paintball Gun
		Zero Point Energy Gauntlet	The Object Generator to spawn a Zero Point Energy Gauntlet
		Goo Grower	The Object Generator to spawn a Goo Grower
		Goo Shrinker	The Object Generator to spawn a Goo Shrinker
		Hover Board	The Object Generator to spawn a Hover Board
		Glide Pack	The Object Generator to spawn a Glide Pack
		Surfboard	The Object Generator to spawn a Surfboard
		Flamingo Mallet	The Object Generator to spawn a Flamingo Mallet

GAME BASICS

CHARACTERS

POWER DISCS

PLAY SETS

TOY BOX

TOY BOX COLLECTION

ACHIEVEMENTS

Trigger Action	Description	Behavior	Description
		Blunderbuss	The Object Generator to spawn a Blunderbuss
		Grappling Hook	The Object Generator to spawn a Grappling Hook
		Star Command Blaster	The Object Generator to spawn a Star Command Blaster
		Elasti-Hand	The Object Generator to spawn an Elasti-Hand
		Invisibility Device	The Object Generator to spawn an Invisibility Device
		Medicine Ball	The Object Generator to spawn a Medicine Ball
		Glow Urchin	The Object Generator to spawn a Glow Urchin
		Sword	The Object Generator to spawn a Sword
		Crow Wing Pack	The Object Generator to spawn a Crow Wing Pack
		TNT Pack	The Object Generator to spawn a TNT Pack
		Thundering Hooves Pack	The Object Generator to spawn a Thundering Hooves Pack
		Silent Warrior Pack	The Object Generator to spawn a Silent Warrior Pack
		Kill All	All objects spawned by the Object Generator to be removed

FALLING OBJECT GENERATOR

This toy drops balls or a puck down into your world. You can also set its behavior to destroy all of the objects it spawns as a behavior to a trigger. It can also act as a trigger if one of the objects it drops is killed.

Trigger Action	Description	Behavior	Description
Spawned	When the Falling Object Generator spawns an object	ESPN Bowling Ball	When the Falling Object Generator spawns a Bowling Ball
Killed Spawned Toy	When the spawned object is killed	ESPN Soccer Ball	When the Falling Object Generator spawns a Soccer Ball
		ESPN Basketball	When the Falling Object Generator spawns a Basketball
		ESPN Baseball	When the Falling Object Generator spawns a Baseball

Trigger Action	Description	Behavior	Description
		ESPN Football	When the Falling Object Generator spawns a Football
		ESPN Tennis Ball	When the Falling Object Generator spawns a Tennis Ball
		ESPN Golf Ball	When the Falling Object Generator spawns a Golf Ball
		ESPN Hockey Puck	When the Falling Object Generator spawns a Hockey Puck
		Kill All	All the objects spawned from the Falling Object Generator to be removed

FRIEND GENERATOR

This is similar to the Object Generator except that it spawns friendly toys.

Trigger Action	Description	Behavior	Description
Spawned	When the Friend Generator spawns a Friend	Spawn Bullseye	The Friend Generator to spawn Bullseye
Killed Spawned Toy	When the spawned Friend is killed	Spawn Snow White	The Friend Generator to spawn Snow White
		Spawn Hulk	The Friend Generator to spawn Hulk
		Kill All	All the Friends spawned from the Friend Generator to be removed

ENEMY GENERATOR

This functions just like the Friend Generator, but this spawns Enemies. It also offers lots of options for the types of Enemies you can spawn. Use this toy for combat games.

Trigger Action	Description	Behavior	Description
Spawned	When the Enemy Generator spawns an Enemy	Soldier of Clubs Costume	The Enemy Generator to spawn a Soldier of Clubs Costume
Killed Spawned Toy	When the spawned Enemy is killed	Soldier of Hearts Costume	The Enemy Generator to spawn a Soldier of Hearts Costume
		Sorcerer's Broom Costume	The Enemy Generator to spawn a Sorcerer's Broom Costume
		The King's Guard	The Enemy Generator to spawn a The King's Guard
		Agrabah Guard	The Enemy Generator to spawn an Agrabah Guard
		Rhino Guard	The Enemy Generator to spawn a Rhino Guard
		Omnidroid	The Enemy Generator to spawn an Omnidroid
		Melee Omnidroid	The Enemy Generator to spawn a Melee Omnidroid
		Ranged Omnidroid	The Enemy Generator to spawn a Ranged Omnidroid
		Tank Omnidroid	The Enemy Generator to spawn a Tank Omnidroid
		Mini Zurgbot	The Enemy Generator to spawn a Mini Zurgbot
		Zurgbot	The Enemy Generator to spawn a Zurgbot
		Giant Zurgbot	The Enemy Generator to spawn a Giant Zurgbot
		Mini Blasting Zurgbot	The Enemy Generator to spawn a Mini Blasting Zurgbot
		Blasting Zurgbot	The Enemy Generator to spawn a Blasting Zurgbot
		Giant Blasting Zurgbot	The Enemy Generator to spawn a Giant Blasting Zurgbot
		Goo Bot	The Enemy Generator to spawn a Goo Bot
		Cavendish's Pistol Man	The Enemy Generator to spawn a Cavendish's Pistol Man
		Cavendish's TNT Man	The Enemy Generator to spawn a Cavendish's TNT Man

Trigger Action	Description	Behavior	Description
		Cavendish's Shotgun Man	The Enemy Generator to spawn a Cavendish's Shotgun Man
		Clam Pirate	The Enemy Generator to spawn a Clam Pirate
		Driftwood Pirate	The Enemy Generator to spawn a Driftwood Pirate
		Maccus	The Enemy Generator to spawn a Maccus
		Turtle Pirate	The Enemy Generator to spawn a Turtle Pirate
		Fear Tech Paintball Player 1	The Enemy Generator to spawn a Fear Tech Paintball Player 1
		Fear Tech Paintball Player 2	The Enemy Generator to spawn a Fear Tech Paintball Player 2
		Fear Tech Paintball Player 3	The Enemy Generator to spawn a Fear Tech Paintball Player 3
		Fear Tech Student 1	The Enemy Generator to spawn a Fear Tech Student 1
		Fear Tech Student 2	The Enemy Generator to spawn a Fear Tech Student 2
		Fear Tech Student 3	The Enemy Generator to spawn a Fear Tech Student 3
		Fear Tech Student Patrol 1	The Enemy Generator to spawn a Fear Tech Student Patrol 1
		Fear Tech Student Patrol 2	The Enemy Generator to spawn a Fear Tech Student Patrol 2
		Fear Tech Student Patrol 3	The Enemy Generator to spawn a Fear Tech Student Patrol 3
		Kill All	All the Enemies spawned from the Enemy Generator to be removed

GAME BASICS

CHARACTERS

POWER DISCS

PLAY SETS

TOY BOX

TOY BOX COLLECTION

ACHIEVEMENTS

VEHICLE WEAPON GENERATOR

Similar to the other generator toys, this spawns random vehicle weapons. Place these on your race tracks to add a battle element to races.

Trigger Action	Description	Behavior	Description
Item Collected	When a player collects the Vehicle Weapon	Spawn Item	The Vehicle Weapon Generator to spawn a vehicle weapon
Item Spawned	When a Vehicle Weapon spawns		

PARTY CANNON

The Party Cannon is usually used as a behavior for another toy's trigger. However, you can also use this toy to trigger behaviors in other toys. Set these up at the end of a race or as a victory celebration at the end of a game.

Trigger Action	Description	Behavior	Description
Explode	When the Party Cannon shoots something out	Fireworks	The Party Cannon to shoot Fireworks
		Confetti	The Party Cannon to shoot Confetti
		Grand Finale	The Party Cannon to shoot Grand Finale

SAFETY DOME

The Safety Dome is great to use as an objective to either try to destroy or to try to defend. It can be used as both a trigger and a behavior.

Trigger Action	Description	Behavior	Description
Started	When the Safety Dome starts (need another toy to Start the Safety Dome)	Start	The Safety Dome to start (an NPC spawns in the Dome)
Destroyed	When the Safety Dome is destroyed	End	The Safety Dome to end (the NPC in the Dome disappears)

MARCHING ORDERS

This is a cool toy. It sets up an area. Any NPC or enemy that moves (or is thrown into) the area of the Marching Orders toy will begin walking in the direction the toy is pointing—even after they exit the toy area. You can position several of these toys around a world and set up patrol paths. While Marching Orders is visible in the editor, it can not be seen out in the Toy Box World. This is a fun toy to play around with.

Trigger Action	Description
Entered	When the Marching Orders is entered by an NPC/Enemy
Exited	When an NPC/Enemy leaves the Marching Orders

TELEPORTER

Teleporters require two or more of this type of toy in order to work. They are a quick way to transport players around the Toy Box World. You can program them to go from one to another if you have more than two. Otherwise, they just teleport the player between the two Teleporters.

Trigger Action	Description	Behavior	Description
Teleport (can only go to another teleporter)	When a player steps on the Teleporter	Teleport Here (can only activate from another teleporter)	The player to be teleported from the starting teleporter to this destination

STOPWATCH

The Stopwatch is a toy that when activated will stop all enemies and NPCs. You can hit the button to start and stop it or set is as either a trigger or even a behavior.

Trigger Action	Description	Behavior	Description
Stopwatch Started	When the Stopwatch starts	Start Stopwatch	The Stopwatch to start
Stopwatch Stopped	When the Stopwatch stops	Stop Stopwatch	The Stopwatch to stop

REPLAYER

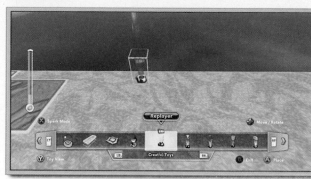

The Replayer is one of the more powerful tools you can use in the Toy Box. An easy way to use it is to connect it to several Triggers that you can then use as your buttons for recording, stopping, and playing back. When the Replayer is recording, it will save all the actions you do in the editor, such as building things. Stop the recording after you exit the editor and then play. You will then see your building efforts appear right before you. The Replayer can be used to actually create a game where the course appears before you as you move. Be sure to play around with it and you will be impressed with what you can do.

Trigger Action	Description	Behavior	Description
Recording Started	When the recording starts	Start Recording	The Replayer to start recording
Recording Stopped	When the recording stops	Stop Recording	The Replayer to stop recording
Clear	When the recording is cleared	Clear	The Replayer to clear everything it has recorded so far
Playback	When the recording is played back	Playback	The Replayer to play back everything that was placed into the world
Reverse Playback	When the recording is played back in reverse	Reverse Playback	The Replayer to play back everything that was placed into the world in reverse
Reset	When the recording is reset	Reset	The Replayer to remove all the objects it has played back into the world

REPEATER

The Repeater is a toy you can use to make another toy do the same thing over and over. For example, connect it to a Falling Object Generator and it will continue to drop objects. You can even adjust the amount of time between each trigger that the Repeater sends out.

Trigger Action	Description	Behavior	Description
On	When the Repeater is turned on (the player can now repeat an action)	On	The Repeater to turn on
Off	When the Repeater is turned off (the player can no longer repeat an action)	Off	The Repeater to turn off
Repeat	Every time the Repeater repeats an action		

TIME DELAY

If you want to create a series of behaviors from one trigger, but do not want them all to occur at the same time, use the Time Delay. It lets you set a delay between the trigger and the behavior. Try this with a row of Party Cannons so they go off one at a time rather than all at once.

Trigger Action	Description	Behavior	Description
Delay Completed	When the amount of time the player set in the Properties to delay an action is completed	Start Delay	The Time Delay to start the delay

TIMER

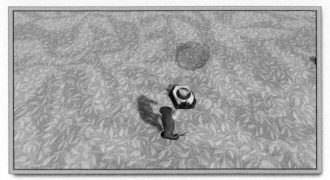

This toy actually creates a timer at the top of the screen when it is activated, so you can time players during a game. Connect it to one Racing Gate to start and another Racing Gate to stop. Or you can even set it to be a countdown timer.

Trigger Action	Description	Behavior	Description
Started	When the Timer starts timing something	Start	The Timer to start timing
Stopped	When the Timer stops timing something	Stop	The Timer to stop timing
Timer Expired	When the amount of time the player sets up in the Properties expires		

COUNTER

Like the Timer, this puts some numbers at the top of the screen. However, this time it counts signals from a trigger as its behavior. Connect this to a goal in the Sports toys to keep track of how many goals you score.

Trigger Action	Description	Behavior	Description
Target Reached	When the Counter reaches the limit the player sets up in the Properties	Reset	The Counter to reset (return to 0)
Zero Reached	When the Counter reaches zero	Increment	The Counter to increase by 1
		Decrement	The Counter to decrease by 1

SCOREBOARD

The Scoreboard is like a bit counter, except instead of counting just one action, it can keep track of scores for four different players.

Trigger Action	Description	Behavior	Description
Increment Score 1	When the scoreboard increases the score for Player 1	Increment Score 1	The Scoreboard to increase by 1
Increment Score 2	When the scoreboard increases the score for Player 2	Increment Score 2	The Scoreboard to increase by 2
Increment Score 3	When the scoreboard increases the score for Player 3	Increment Score 3	The Scoreboard to increase by 3
Increment Score 4	When the scoreboard increases the score for Player 4	Increment Score 4	The Scoreboard to increase by 4
Reset	The Scoreboard to reset the score	Reset	When the Scoreboard is reset to 0
Remove Display	The Scoreboard to remove the score at the top of the screen		
Player 1 Wins	When player 1 is declared the winner		
Player 2 Wins	When player 2 is declared the winner		
Player 3 Wins	When player 3 is declared the winner		
Player 4 Wins	When player 4 is declared the winner		

BIRD'S EYE CAMERA

When activated, the Bird's Eye Camera changes the view of the Toy Box to a top-down angle. This can be great for some types of games you can create to play against your friends.

Trigger Action	Description	Behavior	Description
Started	When the camera first becomes active	Start	The camera to become active
Ended	When the camera ends	End	The camera to stop

SIDE-STEP CAMERA

This functions just like the Bird's Eye Camera, except the view is from this side. Use this when making platforming type games.

Trigger Action	Description	Behavior	Description
Started	When the camera first becomes active	Start	The camera to become active
Ended	When the camera ends	End	The camera to stop

AREA LIGHT

This toy allows you to light up an area. It can be programmed to turn on, off, or toggle in response to a trigger or even be a trigger itself.

Trigger Action	Description	Behavior	Description
Turn On	When the light turns on	Turn Light On	The light to turn on
Turn Off	When the light turns off	Turn Light Off	The light to turn off
Toggle	When the light turns on or off	Toggle Light	The light to toggle to the next state

GAME BASICS

CHARACTERS

POWER DISCS

PLAY SETS

TOY BOX

TOY BOX COLLECTION

ACHIEVEMENTS

SOUND EFFECTS

You can select from a variety of sounds that emanate from this toy as a behavior. For example, connect it to a goal for a sound effect when a player moves a ball into the goal. This just adds more fun to games.

Trigger Action	Description	Behavior	Description
Started	When the sound effects start playing	Alarm	The Sound Effects toy to play an alarm sound
		Horn	The Sound Effects toy to play a horn sound
		Cheering	The Sound Effects toy to play a crowd cheering sound
		Cash Register	The Sound Effects toy to play a cash register sound
		Charge!	The Sound Effects toy to play a trumpet playing the "Charge!" theme
		Countdown	The Sound Effects toy to play the narrator counting down from 3 to 1
		Destruction	The Sound Effects toy to play an explosion sound
		Success	The Sound Effects toy to play the narrator to say "What a performance"
		Awesome!	The Sound Effects toy to play the narrator to say "Awesome!"
		Fantastic!	The Sound Effects toy to play the narrator to say "Fantastic!"

BOOM BOX

This is similar to the Sound Effects toy. However, the Boom Box plays music instead of just sound effects.

Trigger Action	Description	Behavior	Description
Started	When the Boom Box is activated	Off	
Stopped	When the Boom Box becomes inactivate	Mickey Mouse	The Boom Box to play the Mickey Mouse song
		Cinderella's Castle	The Boom Box to play the Cinderella's Castle song
		Peter Pan's Flight	The Boom Box to play the Peter Pan's Flight song
		Alice in Wonderland	The Boom Box to play the Alice in Wonderland song
		Tangled	The Boom Box to play the Tangled song
		Sugar Rush	The Boom Box to play the Sugar Rush song
		Vanellope	The Boom Box to play Vanellope's song
		Jessie	The Boom Box to play Jessie's song
		Alien Emperor Zurg	The Boom Box to play the Alien Emperor Zurg song
		Metroville	The Boom Box to play the Metroville song
		Finding Nemo	The Boom Box to play the Finding Nemo song
		WALL-E	The Boom Box to play the WALL-E song
		The Nightmare Before Christmas	The Boom Box to play The Nightmare Before Christmas song
		Frankenweenie	The Boom Box to play the Frankenweenie song
		Phineas and Ferb	The Boom Box to play the Phineas and Ferb song
		Recognizer	The Boom Box to play the Recognizer song
		Tron	The Boom Box to play the Tron song
		Condorman	The Boom Box to play the Condorman song

INVULNERABILITY BEACON

Normally your characters in the Toy Box Worlds are invulnerable. However, this toy can turn on a health bar that shows how much damage a character is taking and allows them to be defeated. This can be good for combat games where a kill or defeat can be used for scoring or another reason.

Trigger Action	Description	Behavior	Description
Health Bar On	When the health bar is turned on, on the small screen	Health Bar on	The Health Bar on the screen to turn on
Health Bar Off	When the health bar is turned off, on the small screen	Health Bar off	The Health Bar on the screen to turn off

KILL SWITCH

The Kill Switch is a way to get rid of something in the game. It can be a trigger, but its main function is a behavior. For example, you could set it to when a player enters a Target Area over a lava block, the player dies.

Trigger Action	Description	Behavior	Description
Killed	When something is killed by the Kill Switch	Kill	The Kill Switch to kill the entity that triggered this behavior (i.e., step on a button that tells the Kill Switch to kill whatever just stepped on the button)

BLUE AND ORANGE TEAM ACTIVATORS

These two toys are a lot of fun. They can set players and enemies into two teams. Set Marching Orders toys to move

enemies into these team activators and create team fighting games. If you have also walked through the activator, you will have a color as well. Enemies on your team will not attack you. Instead they will attack players and other enemies on the opposing team. This is a lot of fun to try out.

Trigger Action	Description
Team Set	When an entity is set to the blue (or orange) team

VICTORY TRACKER

While this toy can seem complex, it is just a trigger that is activated by players being killed, killing other players, killing enemies, or getting hit by something. You will usually connect this to a Scoreboard or Counter to keep track of the score.

Trigger Action	Description
Player 1 was Killed	When player 1 is killed
Player 2 was Killed	When player 2 is killed
Player 3 was Killed	When player 3 is killed
Player 4 was Killed	When player 4 is killed
Player 1 Killed Enemy	When player 1 kills an enemy
Player 2 Killed Enemy	When player 2 kills an enemy
Player 3 Killed Enemy	When player 3 kills an enemy
Player 4 Killed Enemy	When player 4 kills an enemy
Player 1 Killed Player	When player 1 kills another player
Player 2 Killed Player	When player 2 kills another player
Player 3 Killed Player	When player 3 kills another player
Player 4 Killed Player	When player 4 kills another player
Player 1 was Hit	When player 1 gets hit by something
Player 2 was Hit	When player 2 gets hit by something
Player 3 was Hit	When player 3 gets hit by something
Player 4 was Hit	When player 4 gets hit by something

GAME BASICS

CHARACTERS

POWER DISCS

PLAY SETS

TOY BOX

TOY BOX COLLECTION

ACHIEVEMENTS

OTHER TOYS THAT INTERACT

In addition to the Creativi-Toys, there are also several other different toys that can be used as a trigger or a behavior. The following is a list of these toys and the trigger and/or behaviors for which they can be connected.

Toy	Trigger Action	Description	Behavior	Description
Automatic Door	Opened	When the Automatic Door opens	Open	The Automatic Door to open
	Closed	When the Automatic Door closes	Close	The Automatic Door to close
			Query	The Automatic Door to send an output based on the door's current state (opened if currently open and closed if currently closed)
Automatic Double Door	Opened	When the Automatic Double Door opens	Open	The Automatic Double Door to open
	Closed	When the Automatic Double Door closes	Close	The Automatic Double Door to close
			Query	The Automatic Double Door to send an output based on the door's current state (opened if currently open and closed if currently closed)
The Big Spinner	Off	When The Big Spinner turns off	Off	The Big Spinner to turn off
	On	When The Big Spinner turns on	On	The Big Spinner to turn on
	Speed Up	When The Big Spinner speeds up	Speed Up	The Big Spinner to start spinning faster
	Slow Down	When The Big Spinner slows down	Slow Down	The Big Spinner to start spinning slower
Boost Pad	Used	When the player drives over the Boost Pad	On	When something causes the Boost Pad to turn on
			Off	When something causes the Boost Pad to turn off
Cars	Entered	When the Car is entered	None	
	Exited	When the Car is exited		
	Boost	When boost is activated in the car		
	Trick Completed	When a trick is completed with a Car		
Elevator Platform	Off	When the Elevator Platform turns off	Off	The Elevator Platform to turn off
	On	When the Elevator Platform turns on	On	The Elevator Platform to turn on
	At Top	When the Elevator Platform reaches the top of the path	Move Up	The Elevator Platform to move up
	At Bottom	When the Elevator Platform reaches the bottom of the path	Move Down	The Elevator Platform to move down
Exploding Mine	Exploded	When the Exploding Mine explodes	Reset	The Exploding Mine to return to its initial state (mine is not exploded)
Fan	Stopped	When the Fan stops	Off	The Fan to turn off
	Started	When the Fan starts	On	The Fan to turn on
	Entered	When a player enters the Fan		
The Flipper	Started	When The Flipper gets started	On	The Flipper to turn on
	Stopped	When The Flipper gets stopped	Off	The Flipper to turn off
Floor Spikes	Spikes Engaged	When the Floor Spikes pop out of the pad	Activate Spikes	The Floor Spikes to pop out of the pad
	Spikes Retracted	When the Floor Spikes return to the pad		
	Killed Player	When the Floor Spikes kill a player		
Helicopters	Entered	When the Helicopter is entered	None	
	Exited	When the Helicopter is exited		
Hop Over Gate	Broken	When a player breaks the Hop Over Gate	Reset	The Hop Over Gate to return to its initial state (unbroken)
	Cleared	When a player jumps over the Hop Over Gate		
Invisinator	Invised	When the player turns invisible	Off	The Invisinator to turn off (standing on the Invisinator will not turn the player invisible)
	Expired	When the invisible turns visible	On	The Invisinator to turn on (standing on the Invisinator will turn the player invisible)
Masher	Triggered	When the Masher's stamping mechanism slams down	Action	The Masher's stamping mechanism to slam down
	Reset	When the Masher's stamping mechanism returns to the Masher		
	Killed Player	When the Masher's stamping mechanism kills a player		
Mounts	Mounted	When the player gets on the Mount	None	
	Dismounted	When the player gets off the Mount		
	Sprint	When the player uses sprint while on the Mount		

GAME BASICS

CHARACTERS

POWER DISCS

PLAY SETS

TOY BOX

TOY BOX COLLECTION

ACHIEVEMENTS

Toy	Trigger Action	Description	Behavior	Descritption
	Jump	When the player jumps while on the Mount		
Moving Wall	Off	When the Moving Wall gets turned off	Off	The Moving Wall to turn off
	On	When the Moving Wall gets turned on	On	The Moving Wall to turn on
Pendulum	Off	When the Pendulum stops swinging	Off	The Pendulum to stop swinging
	On	When the Pendulum starts swinging	On	The Pendulum to start swinging
Pop Up Turret	Activated	When the Pop Up Turret pops up and shoots	Off	The Pop Up Turret to turn off (the turret will not shoot at the player when standing near it)
	Deactivated	When the Pop Up Turret goes down and stops shooting	On	The Pop Up Turret to turn on (the turret will shoot at the player when standing near it)
Reset-o-Matic	Reset	When the toy is reset	Reset	The Reset-o-Matic to reset physics toys
	Start	When the toy starts its action	Start	The Reset-o-Matic to start
Ring of Fire	Go Through	When something goes through the ring	Stop Spinning	The Ring of Fire to stop spinning
			Start Spinning	The Ring of Fire to start spinning
The Spinner	Off	When The Spinner turns off	Off	The Spinner to turn off
	On	When The Spinner turns on	On	The Spinner to turn on
Splash Pool	Entered	When a player enters the Splash Pool	N/A	
Super Cannon	Tilted Complete	When the Super Cannon finishes a tilt	Turn Off	The Super Cannon to turn off
	Launched	When a player gets launched from the Super Cannon	Turn On	The Super Cannon to turn on
			Tilt	The Super Cannon's angle to tilt
Tall Automatic Door	Opened	When the Tall Automatic Door Opens	Open	The Tall Automatic Door to open
	Closed	When the Tall Automatic Door Closes	Close	The Tall Automatic Door to close
Tar Trap	Player Entered	When a player enters the Tar Trap	N/A	
	Player Exited	When a player leaves the Tar Trap		
	Object Entered	When on object enters the Tar Trap		
	Object Exited	When an object enters the Tar Trap		
Tripwire	Tripped	When a player trips on the Tripwire	On	The tripwire to turn on (be able to trip a player)
			Off	The tripwire to turn off (not be able to trip a player)

Tips for Designing Worlds and Games in the Toy Box

There are a lot of different things you can do in your Toy Box Worlds. This section is designed to give you some quick tips to help you create your own worlds from scratch as well as games you can play against your friends. These focus on the basics of design to help you get started with some of the more difficult aspects of creating in the Toy Box. However, once you have mastered these tips, feel free to continue adding to your world to make them even more cool and exciting.

> ## TIP
>
> Be sure to keep track of the thermometer-like meter on the left side of the screen that appears when you are in the editor. It keeps track of how much you can add to your world. Once the meter is full, nothing else can be added to the Toy Box. Lots of things in your Toy Box can also affect multiplayer games. So if you want to invite other players over to your world, be sure to not push the meter all the way to the top, since it can slow down playing. In fact for worlds you are building for games, keep the meter in the green so there is less lag and fewer connection problems.

OPEN WORLD BUILDER

This part covers the steps for building in an open world and helps you avoid some pitfalls and mistakes made by new players.

1. THE TERRAIN

When you are starting from scratch in a world of your own, you must first be sure you have enough land on which to build and that there are no obstacles in your way. Depending on which prebuilt world you choose, you may need to add more large terrain blocks to make it large enough or clear out hills and plants that might be in your way.

2. STRUCTURES

Next, start building your buildings. The Building Sets and Set Pieces are usually the largest toys, and you want to place them down on your world before adding anything else. Some of them are very large and you need to be sure you have space. Once you have the big structures in place, add other buildings.

3. TRACK PIECES

After you get your structures in place, put in any track pieces you want. Remember that with a Magic Wand in the hand of your character, you can change the theme of the track pieces. While they default as the slot track, you can change that to any of the themes you have already unlocked to make your track look like roads or trails. Roads are important for cities and towns since they add to the look and feel of these types of worlds.

4. PLANTS AND DECORATIONS

Now that you have the main part of the world completed, go in and fill it out with lots of plants and decorations. These may be small—or large in some cases—but they really add to a world. They are the details that help complete the look. In addition, you may also want to use some more terrain to finish off the land. Rather than leaving your world with square corners at the edge of the landmass, put in some edge pieces to soften the borders of your land and accent them with more plants and decorations. Adding some slopes or higher levels of terrain at the edges can give the illusion that the land goes on further but you can't see it because of the higher terrain.

5. POPULATE THE WORLD

The final step is to populate the world you have created. You can use enemies, townspeople, and cast members. Don't forget to throw in some vehicles or mounts for helping players get around the world quickly. This final step is another important part of a world. By adding people, you will feel like you are in a realistic world where people are going about their business instead of having players feel like they are all alone. Now that you have completed your world, play in it and have fun. Don't forget to invite some friends over to see the efforts of your labor.

RACING GAME

Do you want to create the most awesome race track in the world? If so, you have come to the right place. Racing games are really quite easy to make. Just follow the step-by-step instructions included here.

1. GET THE RACE TRACK START TOY

If you want to create a racing game, you have to have the Race Track Start track piece. It is the key to starting a race. It can be found in the Disney Infinity Vault. Save up at least 16 Spins before visiting the vault. Then shuffle the selections until you see the Race Track Start toy (and hopefully some other track pieces as well) as one of the 16. Start spending your Spins without shuffling again until you get it.

2. LAY DOWN SOME TRACK

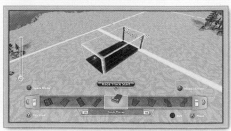

Place the Race Track Start toy down on your world. Then select other track pieces and begin connecting them.

It is important that you line up the ends of the track pieces so they fit together exactly. Change the angle of your view around so you can see the track pieces from all sides to ensure they are connected. Add loops, curves, and ramps to make your track as easy or challenging as you want. You can even add some shortcuts.

3. COMPLETE THE CIRCUIT

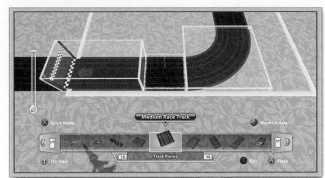

As your track continues to grow, make sure you end up at the opposite side of the Race Track Start. Again, be sure to line up the track carefully. Only when you have made a complete circuit of track connecting the two ends of the Race Track Start toy can you have a race on your track. If you added shortcuts, make sure your main track is a complete circuit.

4. ADD BARRIERS OR DECORATIONS

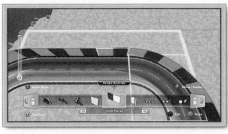

While the track is completed, add some barriers to the turns to prevent cars from driving off the road if you want and place some plants and decorations to make the race track more exciting and visually pleasing. If you want to turn this race into a battle race, be sure to include Vehicle Weapon Generators to the track to add some firepower. Try to place objects or decorations on the track that are destructible to hide or disguise your shortcuts.

5. START YOUR ENGINES

When you are ready, drive a vehicle or ride a mount up onto the Race Track Start and a button will appear. Follow the on-screen instructions to start a race. Three opponents will automatically be provided and a three-lap race is ready to begin.

GAME BASICS · CHARACTERS · POWER DISCS · PLAY SETS · TOY BOX · TOY BOX COLLECTION · ACHIEVEMENTS

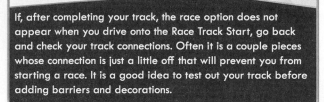

ACTION AND PLATFORMER GAMES

There are lots of action toys you can use to create some fun games. Be sure to use different cameras to provide different effects for the game.

1. PLANNING

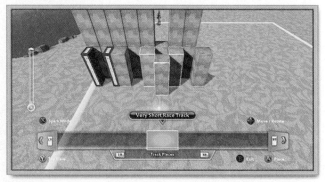

The first step in creating this type of game is planning out what you want to do. Figure out where you want to start, where you want to end, and what you want players to accomplish along the way.

2. BUILD THE COURSE

Once you know what you want to do, start putting together the course. Use blocks or action toys to create the level and then add more action toys as obstacles or challenges that players must get past. As you are building it, use your character to try it out and make sure it is possible to jump across gaps or up to higher blocks.

3. SET UP A TIMER

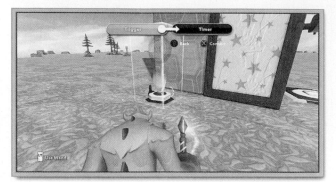

Place Triggers or Trigger Areas at the start and finish of the course. Connect them to a Timer so that the Timer starts when the player goes through the starting trigger and ends when he or she passes through the end trigger. You can also connect other toys such as Party Cannons to shoot out fireworks when the player gets to the end. Try setting Triggers along the way and connect them to Sound Effects to help cheer the player on in the middle of the game.

4. CAMERAS

Depending on the type of game, you may want to include a specific camera angle. For example, when making a platform game, put a Side-Step Camera to the side of the course and position it so it is facing the course. Program it to follow the player. Connect it to the start and end triggers so the camera starts up as the game starts. Or you may even want to have a starting trigger somewhere before the start so the player can get used to the camera angle before the game and timer begins.

5. TEST IT

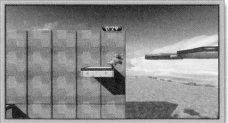

As with any games, once you are done, test it out. If something is not working correctly, whip out the Magic Wand and make some corrections.

Keep trying and fixing until you have everything working perfectly.

SPORTS GAMES

Sports games are a lot of fun—especially in the Toy Box Worlds. There are several different types of balls and goals that you can use to re-create real sports games or create games of your own.

1. DETERMINE THE TYPE OF GAME

The entire design of a sports game depends on what type of game you want to do. Do you want players to try to push a soccer ball into a goal, shoot basketballs, or put a football through the goal post? There is even a hockey puck. Don't feel constrained to re-create a real sport. This is your world so you can come up with the most outrageous sports you can think of.

2. BUILD THE STADIUM

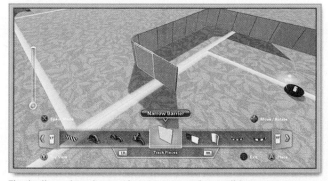

The balls and puck are physics toys, so they will keep moving for a bit after you push or run into them. Therefore, it is usually a good idea to build some boundaries for your game. You can build a stadium with the Building Sets toys or just use some barriers from the Track Pieces. The goal is to keep the ball or puck in play.

> ### TIP
>
> If you find your ball or puck leaving the play area or falling off the world at times, put in a Falling Object Generator that releases a new ball or puck if the ball or puck in play leaves the world. Therefore, If It goes "out of bounds" you get a new ball or puck.

3. GOALS

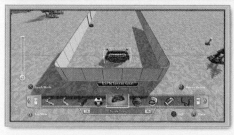

Once the stadium or playing area is set up, you need to place goals. The ESPN Soccer Goal works great for soccer or hockey. If you are using the ESPN Basketball Hoop or ESPN Goal Post, you will also need to provide a way to get the ball up into or through the goals.

Try placing a Super Cannon on the field in line with the goals so players can move the balls to the cannon, which then launches them up into the air. Or you can even put several Toy Box Townspeople in the world and then drop kick them over the goals to score points.

4. SCORING

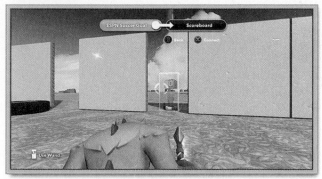

You can't have a sports game with a score. Place a Scoreboard toy from the Creativi-Toy category. Then link it to one of the goals (with the goal as the trigger and the Scoreboard as the behavior) and determine which of four possible teams gets the score. Under Properties in the Scoreboard menu, you can choose the victory requirements for the game.

5. EFFECTS

Finally, to make the game more exciting, link a Sound Effects toy to the goal so that you get cheering or other sounds when a goal is scored. Then link a Boom Box and/or Party Cannons to the Scoreboard. Use the Scoreboard as a trigger when one of the players wins to set off music or effects to show the end of the game. Once you have everything in place, be sure to test out your game to make sure it works how you want it to.

COMBAT OR FIGHTING GAMES

Combat games can be a lot of fun. It is easy to create one that even sets teams so you can have several enemies on your team to fight against your opponent and his or her team of enemies.

1. BUILD THE ARENA

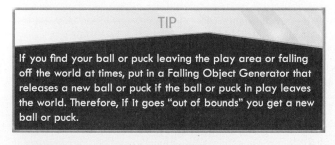

While you can just fight out in the open world, it is usually more fun to have some type of battle arena. Again, you can use the stadium toys to create a large stadium complete with a crowd or you can make your own area out of blocks. Place blocks or other objects in the arena to provide cover or to add to the challenge—especially if you will be using Blasters or other ranged weapons.

2. WEAPONS

If you want to use weapons, place some Object Generators around the arena and set them to spawn the tools or packs of your choice. It is a good idea to have a variety of weapon types unless you want to focus on a single type. For example, if you want a paintball match, only have the Object Generators spawn Paintball Guns.

3. ENEMIES

If you want to play a game where you have to defeat enemies, then you will need an Enemy Generator. Set these to spawn a specific type of enemy. You can even have several different triggers connected to one Enemy Generator to spawn different types of enemies depending on the triggering action. If playing a two-player team combat match, you can even set the enemies spawned to either a blue or orange team in the properties. Be sure to place Orange and Blue Team Activators that players can move through to designate their team color. Then enemies of your same color will not attack you, but attack other players and enemies of the opposing team's color.

4. KEEPING SCORE

Since combat games do not have physical goals like sports games, you need to use a Victory Tracker. This acts as a trigger that you can set for a variety of actions, such as defeating an enemy, defeating another player, being defeated, or taking a hit. Connect the Victory Tracker to a Scoreboard to then keep track of the score.

5. EFFECTS

Once you have the combat game all set up, then it is time to add the effects. As with other games, you can set sounds, music, or visual effects to occur for various aspects of the game to add more flavor and fun.

> **TIP**
>
> Try making combat games with different camera angles for a challenge. The Bird's Eye Camera provides a top-down view that can be fun. However, try combining platforming with combat with a Side-Step Camera.

MULTIPLAYER GAMES

Any type of game you create can be played multiplayer. You can play split screen on a single console or invite up to three other friends to join you in your world and challenge them to try out the games you have created. It is usually a good idea to create a separate world for each game so that you do not have too many toys in one world, which can slow down your connection to other players. Play through the Adventures and Character Adventures to get a feel for the various types of games you can create for multiplayer games, since all of those can be played against other players.

> **TIP**
>
> While this section provides some tips and ideas to help you get started, there are many more types of games you can create. The key is to experiment and try out different combinations. The Creativi-Toys are very powerful toys that can allow you to do many different things in games in addition to keeping score and providing effects. Let your imagination run wild and be sure to share your creations with others and look at those worlds that have been built by other players to get some new ideas.

Online/Multiplayer

While there is a lot to do solo in the *Disney Infinity* Toy Box, it is even more fun to play with others and show off your hard work. There are two main ways you can interact with other players online. The first is to invite them into your worlds to explore, play games you have created, or challenge them to play the Adventures and Character Adventures with you. The second is to use the Toy Box Share to upload Toy Box Worlds that you have created.

WELCOME TO MY TOY BOX

Join up with your friends by inviting them to play with you in one of your Toy Box Worlds, or join another player's game to visit his or her worlds. Use Xbox Live, the PlayStation Network, or whatever online network you have for your gaming system. You can have a total of four players in one world at a time. Take some time to show your friends around the world that you have created.

Any player can choose to start an Adventure from those that player has unlocked. In addition, a player can also start a Character Adventure for the character they are currently playing as. To change characters, just replace the Disney Infinity Figure on your Disney Infinity Base. For example, if you are playing as Mr. Incredible, you can invite your friends to play the "Mr. Incredible, the Hero" Adventure. While you play as Mr. Incredible, your friends play as whichever character they currently have selected.

Once everyone had joined, the game is on. While you are competing against your opponents for points or to finish first with the best time, you are also competing against yourself to earn medals, if you have not already earned them during solo play. Some medals are easier to earn during multiplayer games since there may be more point earning opportunities. Multiplayer versions of some Adventures and Character Adventures have more collectibles. So if you are trying for the elusive gold, get on with some friends and have them go after low-point collectibles while you focus on the higher value ones. Then when you and your friends have gathered them all, more collectibles will appear in a second batch.

SHARE WITH THE WORLD

While you can invite three friends over to one of your Toy Box Worlds to check it out, you can also submit your worlds for the entire planet to enjoy and explore. To do this, open the Pause menu and then select Online/Multiplayer. Next select Toy Box Share. Follow the on-screen directions for uploading one of your saved Toy Box Worlds. Disney will review your submission and may feature it on their collection of user-created Toy Box Worlds for other people to try out.

DISNEY'S TOY BOXES

Several lucky people will be selected to share their Toy Box creations with the entire world in Disney's Toy Boxes. It is a lot of fun to see what other people have designed and to explore how they were able to do it. This is especially true for worlds with lots of Creativi-toys linked together. Who knows what you might find when you take millions of players' imaginations to the power of Infinity.

In addition to submitting your Toy Box Worlds, you can also download featured Toy Box Worlds from Disney's collection. New Toy Boxes are usually released in groups of five and appear periodically throughout each month. This means that as new characters, toys, and gadgets are released, newly inspired Toy Boxes will be created with these items to continue to keep the Toy Boxes current and full of fresh content. Here is a list of the vast number of Toy Boxes that are currently available, with new ones being added all the time!

- Rapunzel's Rumble
- Hidden Worlds
- Tangled Hair
- Maximus Speed
- A Tangled Race
- EpicPirateCombat
- Man the Cannons!
- Blast and Seek
- TreasureHuntRace
- Blackbeard's Map
- Ralph vs Turbo
- Mirror Mirror
- Olympus Coliseum
- King of the Hill
- Save the City!
- Frozen Hunt
- Frozen Adventure
- Anna's Quest
- Let it Go!
- Olaf's Race
- North Pole Racer
- Castle Fireworks
- Frozen Challenge
- BlastFromThePast
- Paris Fireworks
- COUNTDOWN
- Sydney Fireworks
- Fireworks Blast
- NorthHoleMiniGolf
- Saving Christmas
- Winter Express
- Santa's Workshop
- Christmas Town
- Litwak's Arcade
- Game On!
- Helping Felix Jr.
- Dig-it-Ralph!
- Wreck-It-Hunt
- Saving Scrooge
- Scrooge'd
- McDuck in Danger
- Safe Cracking
- Mega Gizmoduck
- Toy Story Claw

- Big Thunder
- Sky Gauntlet II
- Toy Story Race
- Zurgiving Day
- The Big Room
- Capture Zurg!
- Woody's Roundup
- Saving Mr. Rex
- The City Dump
- Halloweentown
- 100 Acre Wood
- Tangled Hunt
- Fantasia
- Swiss Family
- Jack in the Box
- Trick or Treat
- Adventure Maze
- Frozen Cave Maze
- Wonderland
- Giant Castle
- Disney Kingdom
- GOOD vs EVIL
- Paintball World
- Aladdin's Race
- Western Race
- E.A. Sea Race
- MonsterTruckFun
- Super Fun Track
- Tron Highway
- Sugar Mania
- CosmicPlatformer
- It's a Trap!
- 8 in 1 Arena
- Blue Breakout
- Jungle Cruise
- Trench Run
- Sky Gauntlet
- Wrestling Arena
- Cave of Wonders
- Hot Lava
- Medieval Arena
- Tron Sugar Rush
- Disneyland

The Collection

There are over a thousand toys that you can collect and use in the Toy Box. Some are available right from the start. Others can be unlocked by spending Spins in the Disney Infinity Vault. Finally, others are collected in the Play Sets. As new Play Sets and characters are released in the future, there will be even more toys for you to use.

The following table includes information on all the toys available at the release of *Disney Infinity*. It contains the names, the type of toy, and how it is unlocked. Plus we have included a check box so you can keep track of the toys you have in your collection and what you still need to get.

The function of a toy refers to how it interacts with characters or other toys. Here is a key for these attributes:

Air Vehicle: These vehicles can fly through the air and move off the edges of the land in Toy Box Worlds.

Blip Block: These blocks can be destroyed when they are hit by characters or projectiles.

Breakable: This toy can be destroyed by attacking it or hitting it with projectiles or vehicles.

Critter: These are animals that can't be destroyed, but you can still pick them up.

Custom: This toy can be connected with other toys for interaction.

Enemy: Watch out for these toys. They can attack you.

Flying Critter: These critter toys can fly around and are not stuck on the ground.

Ground Vehicle: These toys can be driven by characters, but stay on land—unless you drive off a cliff or jump.

Mission Givers: These are non-player characters that provide missions in the Play Sets but they can also be brought in to the Toy Box just for fun.

Mount: These animal toys can be ridden by characters.

Pack: This toy is carried on the back of a character and activated by pressing the attack button.

Physics Ball: This ball moves and bounces according to the laws of physics.

Physics Block: These blocks obey the laws of physics. They fall and some can break.

Rail Grind: Characters, even Cars characters, can grind on these toys. Connect them together for long periods of grinding.

Static: These toys just sit there. Come back later, they are still there. They can't be destroyed.

Tool: This is a toy that can be carried by a character and activated by pressing the alternate attack button.

Towable: These toys can be towed by a Cars character.

Townspeople: These small people can be picked up, thrown, and even drop kicked. They do not attack nor can they be destroyed.

Track: Connect these toys together to create a race track.

> ### NOTE
>
> Themed Terrain can be changed when you use a Magic Wand to customize it. The default is Fantasy Terrain in the editor. However, by selecting a themed terrain toy, you can change the theme to any that you have unlocked. This terrain also changes when you place a Terrain Theme Power Disc on the Disney Infinity Base.

Got It?	Icon	Toy Name	Category	Function	Unlock
✓		Abu the Elephant	Vehicle/Mount	Mount	Power Disc
✓		Action Button	Creativi-Toys	Custom	Disney Infinity Vault
✓		Admiral's Daughter	Play Set Townspeople	Townspeople	Play Set (Pirates)
✓		Agrabah Guard	Enemy	Enemy	Disney Infinity Vault
✓		Agrabah Palace Base	Building Sets	Static	Disney Infinity Vault
✓		Agrabah Palace Columns	Building Sets	Static	Disney Infinity Vault
✓		Agrabah Palace Entrance	Building Sets	Static	Disney Infinity Vault
✓		Agrabah Palace Front	Building Sets	Static	Disney Infinity Vault
✓		Agrabah Palace Ramp	Building Sets	Static	Disney Infinity Vault

Got It?	Icon	Toy Name	Category	Function	Unlock
✓		Agrabah Palace Tower 1	Building Sets	Static	Disney Infinity Vault
✓		Agrabah Palace Tower 2	Building Sets	Static	Disney Infinity Vault
✓		Agrabah Palace Tower 3	Building Sets	Static	Disney Infinity Vault
✓		Agrabah Palace Tower 4	Building Sets	Static	Disney Infinity Vault
✓		Agrabah Palace Wall	Building Sets	Static	Disney Infinity Vault
✓		Agrabah Palace Wall Corner	Building Sets	Static	Disney Infinity Vault
✓		Agrabah Palace Wall Long	Building Sets	Static	Disney Infinity Vault
✓		Agrabah Palace Wall Lookout	Building Sets	Static	Disney Infinity Vault
✓		Air Conditioning Unit	Decoration	Static	Play Set (Incredibles)
✓		Alien	Play Set Townspeople	NPC	Play Set (Toy Story)
✓		Alien Bo Peep	Play Set Townspeople	NPC	Play Set (Toy Story)
✓		Alien Bullseye	Play Set Townspeople	NPC	Play Set (Toy Story)
✓		Alien Buttercup	Play Set Townspeople	NPC	Play Set (Toy Story)
✓		Alien Chuckles	Play Set Townspeople	NPC	Play Set (Toy Story)
✓		Alien Chunk	Play Set Townspeople	NPC	Play Set (Toy Story)
✓		Alien Doctor	Play Set Townspeople	NPC	Play Set (Toy Story)
✓		Alien Dolly	Play Set Townspeople	NPC	Play Set (Toy Story)
✓		Alien Emperor Zurg	Play Set Townspeople	NPC	Play Set (Toy Story)
✓		Alien Hamm	Play Set Townspeople	NPC	Play Set (Toy Story)
✓		Alien Horse	Vehicle/Mount	Mount	Play Set (Toy Story)
✓		Alien Jessie	Play Set Townspeople	NPC	Play Set (Toy Story)
✓		Alien Lotso	Play Set Townspeople	NPC	Play Set (Toy Story)
✓		Alien Mechanic	Play Set Townspeople	NPC	Play Set (Toy Story)
✓		Alien Mr. Pricklepants	Play Set Townspeople	NPC	Play Set (Toy Story)
✓		Alien Researcher	Play Set Townspeople	NPC	Play Set (Toy Story)
✓		Alien Rex	Play Set Townspeople	NPC	Play Set (Toy Story)
✓		Alien Sarge	Play Set Townspeople	NPC	Play Set (Toy Story)
✓		Alien Slinky	Play Set Townspeople	NPC	Play Set (Toy Story)
✓		Alien Stinky Pete	Play Set Townspeople	NPC	Play Set (Toy Story)
✓		Alien Stretch	Play Set Townspeople	NPC	Play Set (Toy Story)
✓		Alien Tourist	Play Set Townspeople	NPC	Play Set (Toy Story)
✓		Alien Trixie	Play Set Townspeople	NPC	Play Set (Toy Story)

Got It?	Icon	Toy Name	Category	Function	Unlock
✓		Alien Twitch	Play Set Townspeople	NPC	Play Set (Toy Story)
✓		Alien Woody	Play Set Townspeople	NPC	Play Set (Toy Story)
✓		Andy's Wagon	Decoration	Breakable	Play Set (Toy Story)
✓		Angered Tiki Monument	Decoration	Static	Disney Infinity Vault
✓		Angus	Vehicle/Mount	Mount	Power Disc
✓		Animal Costume	Toy Box Townspeople	Townspeople	Disney Infinity Vault
✓		Anna Costume	Toy Box Townspeople	NPC	Avatar (Anna)
✓		Announcer Speakers	Decoration	Breakable	Play Set (Cars)
✓		Apogee	Play Set Townspeople	Townspeople	Play Set (Incredibles)
✓		Arch Blip Block	Block	Blip Block	Disney Infinity Vault
✓		Arch Block	Block	Static	Disney Infinity Vault
✓		Arched Race Track Ramp	Track Piece	Track	Disney Infinity Vault
✓		Archie the Scare Pig	Vehicle/Mount	Mount	Play Set (Monsters)
✓		Area Light	Creativi-Toys	Custom	Disney Infinity Vault
✓		Ariel Costume	Toy Box Townspeople	Townspeople	Disney Infinity Vault
✓		Armadillo	Critter	Critter	Play Set (Lone Ranger)
✓		Armorer	Play Set Townspeople	Townspeople	Play Set (Pirates)
✓		Art	Cast Member	Mission Giver	Play Set (Monsters)
✓		Astro Blasters Space Cruiser	Vehicle/Mount	Vehicle	Power Disc
✓		Atlas Blade	Tool/Pack	Pack	Play Set (Pirates)
✓		Attack Copter	Vehicle/Mount	Air Vehicle	Disney Infinity Vault
✓		Automatic Door	Action Toy	Custom	Disney Infinity Vault
✓		Automatic Double Door	Action Toy	Custom	Disney Infinity Vault
✓		Autopia Car	Vehicle/Mount	Vehicle	Disney Infinity Vault
✓		Awning	Building Sets	Static	Play Set (Pirates)
✓		Balcony (Block)	Block	Static	Disney Infinity Vault
✓		Balcony (Pirates)	Building Sets	Static	Play Set (Pirates)
✓		Banked Curve	Terrain	Static	Disney Infinity Vault
✓		Banked Race Track Curve	Track Piece	Track	Disney Infinity Vault
✓		Banked Race Track Turn	Track Piece	Track	Disney Infinity Vault
✓		Baron Von Ruthless	Play Set Townspeople	Townspeople	Play Set (Incredibles)
✓		Barrel	Decoration	Breakable	Disney Infinity Vault

Got It?	Icon	Toy Name	Category	Function	Unlock
✓		Barrel Costume	Enemy	Enemy	Disney Infinity Vault
✓		Barricade Post	Decoration	Static	Disney Infinity Vault
✓		Barrier Corner	Track Piece	Static	Disney Infinity Vault
✓		Barriers 1	Decoration	Static	Play Set (Monsters)
✓		Barriers 2	Decoration	Static	Play Set (Monsters)
✓		Barriers 3	Decoration	Static	Play Set (Monsters)
✓		Barriers and Barrel 1	Decoration	Static	Play Set (Monsters)
✓		Barriers and Barrel 2	Decoration	Static	Play Set (Monsters)
✓		Barriers and Barrel 3	Decoration	Static	Play Set (Monsters)
✓		Baseball Shooter	Tool/Pack	Tool	Avatar (Phineas)
✓		Bayou Beauty	Play Set Townspeople	Townspeople	Play Set (Pirates)
✓		Bayou Raftman	Play Set Townspeople	Townspeople	Play Set (Pirates)
✓		Bayou Rascal	Play Set Townspeople	Townspeople	Play Set (Pirates)
✓		Beach Ball	Basic Toy	Physics Ball	Starting Toy
✓		Beagle Boy Costume	Enemy	Enemy	Disney Infinity Vault
✓		Beaked Mask	Play Set Townspeople	Townspeople	Play Set (Lone Ranger)
✓		Bear	Critter	Critter	Disney Infinity Vault
✓		Bear Topiary	Plants	Static	Disney Infinity Vault
✓		Bearded Lady	Play Set Townspeople	Townspeople	Play Set (Lone Ranger)
✓		Bee Hive	Decoration	Breakable	Disney Infinity Vault
✓		Belle Costume	Toy Box Townspeople	Townspeople	Disney Infinity Vault
✓		Bench (Incredibles)	Decoration	Static	Play Set (Incredibles)
✓		Bench (Monsters)	Decoration	Static	Play Set (Monsters)
✓		Bending Rail	Track Piece	Rail Grind	Disney Infinity Vault
✓		Bevel Beast	Critter	Critter	Play Set (Monsters)
✓		Bird	Critter	Critter	Disney Infinity Vault
✓		Bird's Eye Camera	Creativi-Toys	Custom	Disney Infinity Vault
✓		Bison Head	Play Set Townspeople	Townspeople	Play Set (Lone Ranger)
✓		Black Horse	Vehicle/Mount	Mount	Play Set (Lone Ranger)
✓		Black Pinto	Vehicle/Mount	Mount	Play Set (Lone Ranger)
✓		Blasting Zurgbot	Enemy	Enemy	Play Set (Toy Story)
✓		Blue Crystals	Decoration	Breakable	Play Set (Toy Story)

Got It?	Icon	Toy Name	Category	Function	Unlock
✓		Blue Mailbox	Decoration	Breakable	Play Set (Cars)
✓		Blue Plane	Critter	Flying Critter	Play Set (Cars)
✓		Blue Shipwreck	Set Piece	Static	Play Set (Pirates)
✓		Bluff	Terrain	Static	Starting Toy
✓		Blunderbuss	Tool/Pack	Tool	Play Set (Pirates)
✓		Boatswain	Play Set Townspeople	Townspeople	Play Set (Pirates)
✓		Bone Chime	Decoration	Breakable	Play Set (Pirates)
✓		Bonny Lass	Play Set Townspeople	Townspeople	Play Set (Pirates)
✓		Boom Box	Creativi-Toys	Custom	Disney Infinity Vault
✓		Boomeroid	Critter	Critter	Play Set (Toy Story)
✓		Boost Pad	Track Piece	Static	Disney Infinity Vault
✓		Boulder	Basic Toy	Physics Ball	Disney Infinity Vault
✓		Bounty Hunter	Play Set Townspeople	Townspeople	Play Set (Pirates)
✓		Bowed Race Track Ramp	Track Piece	Track	Disney Infinity Vault
✓		Box o' Fireworks	Decoration	Breakable	Disney Infinity Vault
✓		Box Topiary	Plants	Static	Disney Infinity Vault
✓		Boxy Monacle Monster	Critter	Critter	Play Set (Monsters)
✓		Breaking News Ender	Decoration	Custom	Play Set (Monsters)
✓		Brick Building	Building Sets	Static	Play Set (Incredibles)
✓		Broken Cement Barrier	Decoration	Breakable	Play Set (Incredibles)
✓		Broken Dinoco Crate	Decoration	Breakable	Play Set (Cars)
✓		Brontosaurus Topiary	Plants	Static	Disney Infinity Vault
✓		Brown Hair Tiki Totem	Decoration	Static	Disney Infinity Vault
✓		Brown Pinto	Vehicle/Mount	Mount	Play Set (Lone Ranger)
✓		Buck	Critter	Critter	Disney Infinity Vault
✓		Building Base Corner	Building Sets	Static	Play Set (Pirates)
✓		Building Base Ground Corner	Building Sets	Static	Play Set (Pirates)
✓		Building Base with Arch	Building Sets	Static	Play Set (Pirates)
✓		Building Nook	Building Sets	Static	Play Set (Pirates)
✓		Bulletin Board	Decoration	Breakable	Play Set (Monsters)
✓		Bullseye	Vehicle/Mount	Mount	Play Set (Toy Story)
✓		Buzz Lightyear Alien	Play Set Townspeople	NPC	Play Set (Toy Story)

Got It?	Icon	Toy Name	Category	Function	Unlock
✓		Buzz Lightyear Costume	Toy Box Townspeople	NPC	Play Set (Toy Story)
✓		Buzz Lightyear's Jetpack	Tool/Pack	Pack	Play Set (Toy Story)
✓		Bump Rail	Track Piece	Rail Grind	Disney Infinity Vault
✓		Business Man	Play Set Townspeople	Townspeople	Play Set (Incredibles)
✓		Business Woman	Play Set Townspeople	Townspeople	Play Set (Incredibles)
✓		Cabin Boy	Play Set Townspeople	Townspeople	Play Set (Pirates)
✓		Candace Costume	Toy Box Townspeople	NPC	Disney Infinity Vault
✓		Cannon Base	Basic Toy	Custom	Disney Infinity Vault
✓		Cannon Bunker	Decoration	Breakable	Play Set (Toy Story)
✓		Canyon Bend	Terrain	Static	Disney Infinity Vault
✓		Canyon Curve	Terrain	Static	Disney Infinity Vault
✓		Canyon Divide	Terrain	Static	Disney Infinity Vault
✓		Canyon End	Terrain	Static	Disney Infinity Vault
✓		Canyon Gulley	Terrain	Static	Disney Infinity Vault
✓		Canyon Outer Curve	Terrain	Static	Disney Infinity Vault
✓		Canyon Split	Terrain	Static	Disney Infinity Vault
✓		Canyon Wall	Terrain	Static	Disney Infinity Vault
✓		Capsule Creator	Basic Toy	Custom	Starting Toy
✓		Captain	Play Set Townspeople	Townspeople	Play Set (Pirates)
✓		Captain Hook Costume	Toy Box Townspeople	Townspeople	Disney Infinity Vault
✓		Captain Hook's Ship	Vehicle/Mount	Helicopter	Power Disc
✓		Captured Baron von Ruthless	Decoration	Breakable	Play Set (Incredibles)
✓		Captured Snoring Gloria	Decoration	Breakable	Play Set (Incredibles)
✓		Captured The Hoarder	Decoration	Breakable	Play Set (Incredibles)
✓		Cardboard Box	Decoration	Breakable	Disney Infinity Vault
✓		Carl Fredricksen's Cane	Tool/Pack	Pack	Power Disc
✓		Carl Fredricksen's House	Set Piece	Static	Disney Infinity Vault
✓		Carpenter	Play Set Townspeople	Townspeople	Play Set (Pirates)
✓		Cars Crossing Sign	Decoration	Breakable	Play Set (Cars)
✓		Castle Bridge	Building Sets	Static	Disney Infinity Vault
✓		Castle Floor	Building Sets	Static	Disney Infinity Vault
✓		Castle Front Entrance	Building Sets	Static	Disney Infinity Vault

Got It?	Icon	Toy Name	Category	Function	Unlock
✓		Castle Front Full	Building Sets	Static	Disney Infinity Vault
✓		Castle Ladder Wall	Building Sets	Static	Disney Infinity Vault
✓		Castle Ramp	Building Sets	Static	Disney Infinity Vault
✓		Castle Rope Wall	Building Sets	Static	Disney Infinity Vault
✓		Castle Spire 1	Building Sets	Static	Disney Infinity Vault
✓		Castle Spire 2	Building Sets	Static	Disney Infinity Vault
✓		Castle Stairs	Building Sets	Static	Disney Infinity Vault
✓		Castle Top Archway	Building Sets	Static	Disney Infinity Vault
✓		Castle Tower 1	Building Sets	Static	Disney Infinity Vault
✓		Castle Tower 2	Building Sets	Static	Disney Infinity Vault
✓		Castle Tower 3	Building Sets	Static	Disney Infinity Vault
✓		Castle Tower Base	Building Sets	Static	Disney Infinity Vault
✓		Castle Tower Corner 1	Building Sets	Static	Disney Infinity Vault
✓		Castle Tower Corner 2	Building Sets	Static	Disney Infinity Vault
✓		Castle Tower Top	Building Sets	Static	Disney Infinity Vault
✓		Castle Wall	Building Sets	Static	Disney Infinity Vault
✓		Castle Wall and Bridge	Building Sets	Static	Disney Infinity Vault
✓		Castle Wall and Tower 1	Building Sets	Static	Disney Infinity Vault
✓		Castle Wall and Tower 2	Building Sets	Static	Disney Infinity Vault
✓		Castle Wall Angled Corner	Building Sets	Static	Disney Infinity Vault
✓		Castle Wall Corner	Building Sets	Static	Disney Infinity Vault
✓		Castle Wall Inside Corner	Building Sets	Static	Disney Infinity Vault
✓		Castle Wall Lookout	Building Sets	Static	Disney Infinity Vault
✓		Castle Wall Overhang	Building Sets	Static	Disney Infinity Vault
✓		Cauldron	Decoration	Breakable	Play Set (Pirates)
✓		Cave	Terrain	Static	Disney Infinity Vault
✓		Cave and Well	Terrain	Static	Disney Infinity Vault
✓		Cave Bend	Terrain	Static	Disney Infinity Vault
✓		Cave Cliff	Terrain	Static	Disney Infinity Vault
✓		Cave End	Terrain	Static	Disney Infinity Vault
✓		Cave Fort	Terrain	Static	Disney Infinity Vault
✓		Cave Fort Block	Terrain	Static	Disney Infinity Vault

GAME BASICS
CHARACTERS
POWER DISCS
PLAY SETS
TOY BOX
TOY BOX COLLECTION
ACHIEVEMENTS

Got It?	Icon	Toy Name	Category	Function	Unlock
✓		Cave Intersection	Terrain	Static	Disney Infinity Vault
✓		Cave of Wonders	Set Piece	Static	Disney Infinity Vault
✓		Cave Tunnel	Terrain	Static	Disney Infinity Vault
✓		Cave Waterfall	Terrain	Static	Disney Infinity Vault
✓		Cavendish's Pistol Man	Enemy	Enemy	Play Set (Lone Ranger)
✓		Cavendish's Shotgun Man	Enemy	Enemy	Play Set (Lone Ranger)
✓		Cavendish's TNT Man	Enemy	Enemy	Play Set (Lone Ranger)
✓		Cement Barrier	Decoration	Breakable	Play Set (Incredibles)
✓		Chair	Decoration	Static	Disney Infinity Vault
✓		Checkered Flags	Decoration	Breakable	Play Set (Cars)
✓		Checkpoint	Creativi-Toys	Custom	Disney Infinity Vault
✓		Chestnut Horse	Vehicle/Mount	Mount	Play Set (Lone Ranger)
✓		Chicane	Track Piece	Static	Disney Infinity Vault
✓		Chicane Base	Track Piece	Static	Disney Infinity Vault
✓		Chicane End	Track Piece	Static	Disney Infinity Vault
✓		Chicane Hop Over	Track Piece	Static	Disney Infinity Vault
✓		Chick Hicks	Cast Member	Mission Giver	Play Set (Cars)
✓		Chicken Coop	Decoration	Breakable	Disney Infinity Vault
✓		Cinderella Costume	Toy Box Townspeople	Townspeople	Disney Infinity Vault
✓		Cinderella's Castle	Set Piece	Static	Starting Toy
✓		Cinderella's Coach	Vehicle/Mount	Ground Vehicle	Power Disc
✓		Clam Pirate	Enemy	Enemy	Play Set (Pirates)
✓		Cliff	Terrain	Static	Disney Infinity Vault
✓		Cliff Corner	Terrain	Static	Disney Infinity Vault
✓		Cliff Ledge	Terrain	Static	Disney Infinity Vault
✓		Cliff Slope 1	Terrain	Static	Disney Infinity Vault
✓		Cliff Slope 2	Terrain	Static	Disney Infinity Vault
✓		Climbing Cliff	Terrain	Static	Disney Infinity Vault
✓		Climbing Hook	Tool/Pack	Tool	Avatar (Anna)
✓		Climbing Ledge Wall	Terrain	Static	Disney Infinity Vault
✓		Clock Tower	Set Piece	Static	Play Set (Pirates)
✓		Clothing Store	Building	Static	Play Set (Toy Story)

Got It?	Icon	Toy Name	Category	Function	Unlock
✓		Colby Bush 1	Plants	Static	Play Set (Lone Ranger)
✓		Colby Cactus 1	Plants	Static	Play Set (Lone Ranger)
✓		Colby Cactus 2	Plants	Static	Play Set (Lone Ranger)
✓		Colby Cactus 3	Plants	Static	Play Set (Lone Ranger)
✓		Colby Cactus 4	Plants	Static	Play Set (Lone Ranger)
✓		Colby Terrain 1	Themed Terrain	Static	Play Set (Lone Ranger)
✓		Colby Terrain 2	Themed Terrain	Static	Play Set (Lone Ranger)
✓		Colby Terrain 3	Themed Terrain	Static	Play Set (Lone Ranger)
✓		Colby Terrain 4	Themed Terrain	Static	Play Set (Lone Ranger)
✓		Colby Terrain 5	Themed Terrain	Static	Play Set (Lone Ranger)
✓		Colby Terrain Corner 1	Themed Terrain	Static	Play Set (Lone Ranger)
✓		Colby Terrain Corner 2	Themed Terrain	Static	Play Set (Lone Ranger)
✓		Colby Terrain Strip 1	Themed Terrain	Static	Play Set (Lone Ranger)
✓		Colby Terrain Strip 2	Themed Terrain	Static	Play Set (Lone Ranger)
✓		Colby Train Station	Building	Static	Play Set (Lone Ranger)
✓		Colby Tree	Plants	Static	Play Set (Lone Ranger)
✓		Colby's General Store	Building	Static	Play Set (Lone Ranger)
✓		Colby's Hardware Store	Building	Static	Play Set (Lone Ranger)
✓		Colby's Rooming House	Building	Static	Play Set (Lone Ranger)
✓		Colby's Saddler	Building	Static	Play Set (Lone Ranger)
✓		Colby's Stable	Building	Static	Play Set (Lone Ranger)
✓		Colby's Undertaker	Building	Static	Play Set (Lone Ranger)
✓		Colby's Wash House	Building	Static	Play Set (Lone Ranger)
✓		Collection Pen	Creativi-Toys	Custom	Disney Infinity Vault
✓		Column	Block	Static	Disney Infinity Vault
✓		Comanche Warrior	Play Set Townspeople	Townspeople	Play Set (Lone Ranger)
✓		Combat Simulator	Building	Static	Play Set (Toy Story)
✓		Combover Classmate	Play Set Townspeople	Townspeople	Play Set (Monsters)
✓		Concerned Tiki Monument	Decoration	Static	Disney Infinity Vault
✓		Condorman Glider	Tool/Pack	Pack	Power Disc
✓		Cone Topiary	Plants	Static	Disney Infinity Vault
✓		Construction Pylon	Decoration	Breakable	Play Set (Cars)

Got It?	Icon	Toy Name	Category	Function	Unlock
✓		Construction Pylon with Reflector	Decoration	Breakable	Play Set (Cars)
✓		Construction Terrain 1	Themed Terrain	Static	Starting Toy
✓		Construction Terrain 2	Themed Terrain	Static	Starting Toy
✓		Construction Terrain 3	Themed Terrain	Static	Starting Toy
✓		Construction Terrain 4	Themed Terrain	Static	Starting Toy
✓		Construction Terrain 5	Themed Terrain	Static	Starting Toy
✓		Construction Terrain Corner 1	Themed Terrain	Static	Starting Toy
✓		Construction Terrain Corner 2	Themed Terrain	Static	Starting Toy
✓		Construction Terrain Strip 1	Themed Terrain	Static	Starting Toy
✓		Construction Terrain Strip 2	Themed Terrain	Static	Starting Toy
✓		Construction Worker	Play Set Townspeople	Townspeople	Play Set (Incredibles)
✓		Conveyor Belt	Action Toy	Custom	Disney Infinity Vault
✓		Cook	Play Set Townspeople	Townspeople	Play Set (Pirates)
✓		Corner Block with Ramps	Terrain	Static	Starting Toy
✓		Corner Hill	Terrain	Static	Starting Toy
✓		Corner Slope	Terrain	Static	Starting Toy
✓		Corporal	Play Set Townspeople	Townspeople	Play Set (Pirates)
✓		Couch	Decoration	Static	Disney Infinity Vault
✓		Counter	Creativi-Toys	Custom	Disney Infinity Vault
✓		Covered Walkway	Building Sets	Static	Play Set (Toy Story)
✓		Cow Boss	Play Set Townspeople	Townspeople	Play Set (Lone Ranger)
✓		Cowboy	Play Set Townspeople	Townspeople	Play Set (Lone Ranger)
✓		Cowman	Play Set Townspeople	Townspeople	Play Set (Lone Ranger)
✓		Cozy Cone Motel	Building	Static	Play Set (Cars)
✓		Cracklin' Backpack	Tool/Pack	Pack	Play Set (Monsters)
✓		Crate	Decoration	Breakable	Starting Toy
✓		Crow Wing Pack	Tool/Pack	Pack	Play Set (Lone Ranger)
✓		Cruella De Vil Costume	Toy Box Townspeople	Townspeople	Disney Infinity Vault
✓		Crystal Cavern	Terrain	Static	Disney Infinity Vault
✓		Cube Topiary	Plants	Static	Disney Infinity Vault
✓		Curved Barrier	Track Piece	Static	Disney Infinity Vault
✓		Curved Blip Block	Block	Blip Block	Disney Infinity Vault

Got It?	Icon	Toy Name	Category	Function	Unlock
✓		Curved Block	Block	Static	Disney Infinity Vault
✓		Curved Fence Corner	Decoration	Static	Disney Infinity Vault
✓		Curved Floating Bridge	Terrain	Static	Disney Infinity Vault
✓		Curved Rail	Track Piece	Rail Grind	Disney Infinity Vault
✓		Curved Stadium	Building Sets	Static	Disney Infinity Vault
✓		Curved Tire Fence	Track Piece	Static	Disney Infinity Vault
✓		Damaged Wood Crate	Decoration	Breakable	Play Set (Pirates)
✓		Dash Costume	Toy Box Townspeople	Townspeople	Play Set (Incredibles)
✓		Dash Statue	Decoration	Breakable	Play Set (Incredibles)
✓		Davy Jones Costume	Toy Box Townspeople	Townspeople	Play Set (PIrates)
✓		Decoration Center	Building	Static	Play Set (Toy Story)
✓		Deer	Critter	Critter	Disney Infinity Vault
✓		Devil Mask	Play Set Townspeople	Townspeople	Play Set (Lone Ranger)
✓		Dinosaur Eggs	Decoration	Breakable	Play Set (Toy Story)
✓		Dip Beam	Block	Static	Disney Infinity Vault
✓		Dipped Rail	Track Piece	Rail Grind	Disney Infinity Vault
✓		Disney Dragon Terrain 1	Plants	Static	Power Disc
✓		Disney Dragon Terrain 2	Plants	Static	Power Disc
✓		Disney Dragon Terrain 3	Plants	Static	Power Disc
✓		Disney Dragon Terrain 4	Plants	Static	Power Disc
✓		Disney Dragon Terrain 5	Plants	Static	Power Disc
✓		Disney Dragon Terrain Corner 1	Plants	Static	Power Disc
✓		Disney Dragon Terrain Corner 2	Plants	Static	Power Disc
✓		Disney Dragon Terrain Strip 1	Plants	Static	Power Disc
✓		Disney Dragon Terrain Strip 2	Plants	Static	Power Disc
✓		Disney Infinity Bush 1	Plants	Static	Disney Infinity Vault
✓		Disney Infinity Bush 2	Plants	Static	Disney Infinity Vault
✓		Disney Infinity Flowers 1	Plants	Static	Starting Toy
✓		Disney Infinity Flowers 2	Plants	Static	Starting Toy
✓		Disney Infinity Flowers 3	Plants	Static	Starting Toy
✓		Disney Infinity Hub	Basic Toy	Custom	Starting Toy
✓		Disney Infinity Leaf Patch	Plants	Static	Starting Toy

GAME BASICS

CHARACTERS

POWER DISCS

PLAY SETS

TOY BOX

TOY BOX COLLECTION

ACHIEVEMENTS

Got It?	Icon	Toy Name	Category	Function	Unlock
✓		Disney Infinity Pine Tree	Plants	Static	Starting Toy
✓		Disney Infinity Spruce Tree	Plants	Breakable	Starting Toy
✓		Disney Infinity Tree 1	Plants	Static	Disney Infinity Vault
✓		Disney Infinity Tree 2	Plants	Static	Disney Infinity Vault
✓		Dock	Building Sets	Static	Play Set (Pirates)
✓		Dock Balcony Corner	Building Sets	Static	Play Set (Pirates)
✓		Dock Stairs	Building Sets	Static	Play Set (Pirates)
✓		Dolly's Sunflowers	Decoration	Breakable	Play Set (Toy Story)
✓		Don Carlton	Cast Member	Mission Giver	Play Set (Monsters)
✓		Dopey Costume	Toy Box Townspeople	Townspeople	Disney Infinity Vault
✓		Dr. Doofenshmirtz Costume	Toy Box Townspeople	NPC	Disney Infinity Vault
✓		Dragon Gate	Basic Toy	Custom	Parks Keychain
✓		Dragon Woman	Play Set Townspeople	Townspeople	Play Set (Pirates)
✓		Driftwood Pirate	Enemy	Enemy	Play Set (Pirates)
✓		Driving Loop	Track Piece	Track	Disney Infinity Vault
✓		Dual Action Trigger	Creativi-Toys	Custom	Disney Infinity Vault
✓		Dual Street Light	Decoration	Static	Play Set (Incredibles)
✓		Dumbo the Flying Elephant	Vehicle/Mount	Air Vehicle	Power Disc
✓		Dumpster	Decoration	Breakable	Play Set (Incredibles)
✓		Dungeon	Set Piece	Static	Disney Infinity Vault
✓		Dynaguy	Play Set Townspeople	Townspeople	Play Set (Incredibles)
✓		Edna Mode	Cast Member	Mission Giver	Play Set (Incredibles)
✓		Edna's Costume Shop	Building	Static	Play Set (Incredibles)
✓		Egg	Basic Toy	Custom	Disney Infinity Vault
✓		EKO House	Building	Static	Play Set (Monsters)
✓		Elasti-Hand	Tool/Pack	Tool	Play Set (Incredibles)
✓		Electrical Box	Decoration	Breakable	Play Set (Incredibles)
✓		Elephant (Critter)	Critter	Critter	Play Set (Incredibles)
✓		Elephant (Lone Ranger)	Vehicle/Mount	Mount	Play Set (Lone Ranger)
✓		Elephant Topiary	Plants	Static	Disney Infinity Vault
✓		Elevator Platform	Action Toy	Custom	Disney Infinity Vault
✓		Elliott Costume	Toy Box Townspeople	Townspeople	Disney Infinity Vault

Got It?	Icon	Toy Name	Category	Function	Unlock
✓		Elsa Costume	Toy Box Townspeople	NPC	Avatar (Elsa)
✓		Enemy Creator	Basic Toy	Custom	Starting Toy
✓		Enemy Generator	Creativi-Toys	Custom	Disney Infinity Vault
✓		Engineer	Cast Member	Mission Giver	Play Set (Lone Ranger)
✓		Epcot's Spaceship Earth	Set Piece	Static	Disney Infinity Vault
✓		ESPN Award Podium	Sports Toy	Static	Disney Infinity Vault
✓		ESPN Banner	Sports Toy	Static	Disney Infinity Vault
✓		ESPN Baseball	Sports Toy	Physics Ball	Disney Infinity Vault
✓		ESPN Basketball	Sports Toy	Physics Ball	Disney Infinity Vault
✓		ESPN Basketball Hoop	Sports Toy	Custom	Disney Infinity Vault
✓		ESPN Bench	Sports Toy	Static	Disney Infinity Vault
✓		ESPN Bowling Ball	Sports Toy	Physics Ball	Disney Infinity Vault
✓		ESPN Corner Track Railing	Sports Toy	Static	Disney Infinity Vault
✓		ESPN Curved Track Railing	Sports Toy	Static	Disney Infinity Vault
✓		ESPN Double Banner	Sports Toy	Static	Disney Infinity Vault
✓		ESPN Flag	Sports Toy	Static	Disney Infinity Vault
✓		ESPN Football	Sports Toy	Physics Ball	Disney Infinity Vault
✓		ESPN Goal Post	Sports Toy	Custom	Disney Infinity Vault
✓		ESPN Golf Ball	Sports Toy	Physics Ball	Disney Infinity Vault
✓		ESPN Hockey Puck	Sports Toy	Physics Ball	Disney Infinity Vault
✓		ESPN Pylon	Sports Toy	Static	Disney Infinity Vault
✓		ESPN Scrolling Sign	Sports Toy	Static	Disney Infinity Vault
✓		ESPN Soccer Ball	Sports Toy	Physics Ball	Disney Infinity Vault
✓		ESPN Soccer Goal	Sports Toy	Custom	Disney Infinity Vault
✓		ESPN Stadium Lights	Sports Toy	Static	Disney Infinity Vault
✓		ESPN Tennis Ball	Sports Toy	Physics Ball	Disney Infinity Vault
✓		ESPN Track Railing	Sports Toy	Static	Disney Infinity Vault
✓		Evil Queen Costume	Toy Box Townspeople	Townspeople	Disney Infinity Vault
✓		Exploding Mine	Action Toy	Custom	Disney Infinity Vault
✓		Explosive Block	Block	Physics Block	Disney Infinity Vault
✓		Explosive Crate	Decoration	Breakable	Play Set (Cars)
✓		Extended Castle Wall Corner	Building Sets	Static	Disney Infinity Vault

GAME BASICS

CHARACTERS

POWER DISCS

PLAY SETS

TOY BOX

TOY BOX COLLECTION

ACHIEVEMENTS

Got It?	Icon	Toy Name	Category	Function	Unlock
✓		Extra Wide Canyon Wall	Terrain	Static	Disney Infinity Vault
✓		Fairy Godmother Costume	Toy Box Townspeople	Townspeople	Disney Infinity Vault
✓		Falling Object Generator	Creativi-Toys	Custom	Disney Infinity Vault
✓		Fan	Action Toy	Custom	Disney Infinity Vault
✓		Fantasy Terrain 1	Plants	Static	Starting Toy
✓		Fantasy Terrain 2	Plants	Static	Starting Toy
✓		Fantasy Terrain 3	Plants	Static	Starting Toy
✓		Fantasy Terrain 4	Plants	Static	Starting Toy
✓		Fantasy Terrain 5	Plants	Static	Starting Toy
✓		Fantasy Terrain Corner 1	Plants	Static	Starting Toy
✓		Fantasy Terrain Corner 2	Plants	Static	Starting Toy
✓		Fantasy Terrain Strip 1	Plants	Static	Starting Toy
✓		Fantasy Terrain Strip 2	Plants	Static	Starting Toy
✓		Fear Tech Fraternity Brother	Play Set Townspeople	Townspeople	Play Set (Monsters)
✓		Fear Tech Freshman	Play Set Townspeople	Townspeople	Play Set (Monsters)
✓		Fear Tech Junior	Play Set Townspeople	Townspeople	Play Set (Monsters)
✓		Fear Tech Paintball Player 1	Enemy	Enemy	Play Set (Monsters)
✓		Fear Tech Paintball Player 2	Enemy	Enemy	Play Set (Monsters)
✓		Fear Tech Paintball Player 3	Enemy	Enemy	Play Set (Monsters)
✓		Fear Tech Senior	Play Set Townspeople	Townspeople	Play Set (Monsters)
✓		Fear Tech Sophomore	Play Set Townspeople	Townspeople	Play Set (Monsters)
✓		Fear Tech Student 1	Enemy	Enemy	Play Set (Monsters)
✓		Fear Tech Student 2	Enemy	Enemy	Play Set (Monsters)
✓		Fear Tech Student 3	Enemy	Enemy	Play Set (Monsters)
✓		Fear Tech Student Patrol 1	Enemy	Enemy	Play Set (Monsters)
✓		Fear Tech Student Patrol 2	Enemy	Enemy	Play Set (Monsters)
✓		Fear Tech Student Patrol 3	Enemy	Enemy	Play Set (Monsters)
✓		Fence Corner	Decoration	Static	Disney Infinity Vault
✓		Fenced Glass Sidewalk	Building Sets	Static	Play Set (Toy Story)
✓		Fenced Solid Sidewalk	Building Sets	Static	Play Set (Toy Story)
✓		Ferocious Freshman	Play Set Townspeople	Townspeople	Play Set (Monsters)
✓		Fillmore	Cast Member	Mission Giver	Play Set (Cars)

Got It?	Icon	Toy Name	Category	Function	Unlock
✓		Fillmore's Organic Fuels	Building	Static	Play Set (Cars)
✓		Fin Fan Freshman	Play Set Townspeople	Townspeople	Play Set (Monsters)
✓		Finn McMissile	Cast Member	Mission Giver	Play Set (Cars)
✓		Finn McMissile Paint Job	Toy Box Townspeople	Townspeople	Play Set (Cars)
✓		Fire Escape	Decoration	Static	Play Set (Incredibles)
✓		Fire Hydrant	Decoration	Breakable	Play Set (Incredibles)
✓		Fix-It Felix, Jr. Costume	Toy Box Townspeople	Townspeople	Disney Infinity Vault
✓		Flagpole	Decoration	Static	Play Set (Toy Story)
✓		Flamingo Croquet Mallet	Tool/Pack	Pack	Power Disc
✓		Flapping Freshman	Play Set Townspeople	Townspeople	Play Set (Monsters)
✓		Flat Race Track Ramp	Track Piece	Track	Disney Infinity Vault
✓		Flat Terrain Block	Terrain	Static	Disney Infinity Vault
✓		Flintlock	Tool/Pack	Tool	Play Set (Pirates)
✓		Flo	Cast Member	Mission Giver	Play Set (Cars)
✓		Flo's Mailbox	Decoration	Breakable	Play Set (Cars)
✓		Floating Bridge Hill	Terrain	Static	Disney Infinity Vault
✓		Floating Rope Cliff	Terrain	Static	Starting Toy
✓		Floating Waterfall	Terrain	Static	Starting Toy
✓		Floor Spikes	Action Toy	Custom	Disney Infinity Vault
✓		Flo's V8 Café	Building	Static	Play Set (Cars)
✓		Flower Power	Decoration	Breakable	Play Set (Cars)
✓		Flowerbed 1	Decoration	Breakable	Play Set (Toy Story)
✓		Flowerbed 2	Decoration	Breakable	Play Set (Toy Story)
✓		Fly Swatter Launcher	Decoration	Custom	Play Set (Monsters)
✓		Folding Construction Barrier	Decoration	Breakable	Play Set (Cars)
✓		Foot Locker	Decoration	Breakable	Play Set (Monsters)
✓		Football Player Costume	Toy Box Townspeople	Townspeople	Disney Infinity Vault
✓		Fortune Teller	Play Set Townspeople	Townspeople	Play Set (Lone Ranger)
✓		Francesco Bernoulli Paint Job	Toy Box Townspeople	Townspeople	Play Set (Cars)
✓		Friend Generator	Creativi-Toys	Custom	Disney Infinity Vault
✓		Frog	Critter	Critter	Starting Toy
✓		Frozen Terrain 1	Cluster Customization	Static	Power Disc

Got It?	Icon	Toy Name	Category	Function	Unlock
✓		Frozen Terrain 2	Cluster Customization	Static	Power Disc
✓		Frozen Terrain 3	Cluster Customization	Static	Power Disc
✓		Frozen Terrain 4	Cluster Customization	Static	Power Disc
✓		Frozen Terrain 5	Cluster Customization	Static	Power Disc
✓		Frozen Terrain Corner 1	Cluster Customization	Static	Power Disc
✓		Frozen Terrain Corner 2	Cluster Customization	Static	Power Disc
✓		Frozen Terrain Strip 1	Cluster Customization	Static	Power Disc
✓		Frozen Terrain Strip 2	Cluster Customization	Static	Power Disc
✓		Fuel Barrel Pile	Decoration	Breakable	Play Set (Cars)
✓		Fuel Barrel Pyramid	Decoration	Breakable	Play Set (Cars)
✓		Fuel Barrel Stack	Decoration	Breakable	Play Set (Cars)
✓		Fuel Barrel Tower	Decoration	Breakable	Play Set (Cars)
✓		Fuel Barrels	Decoration	Breakable	Play Set (Cars)
✓		Full Dome	Block	Static	Disney Infinity Vault
✓		Gal	Play Set Townspeople	Townspeople	Play Set (Lone Ranger)
✓		Garbage Can	Decoration	Static	Play Set (Incredibles)
✓		Gargoyle 1	Decoration	Static	Play Set (Monsters)
✓		Gargoyle 2	Decoration	Static	Play Set (Monsters)
✓		Gaston Costume	Toy Box Townspeople	Townspeople	Disney Infinity Vault
✓		Gator Goon Costume	Enemy	Enemy	Disney Infinity Vault
✓		Gazerbeam	Play Set Townspeople	Townspeople	Play Set (Incredibles)
✓		Genie Costume	Toy Box Townspeople	Townspeople	Disney Infinity Vault
✓		Giant Blasting Zurgbot	Enemy	Enemy	Play Set (Toy Story)
✓		Giant Snowball	Basic Toy	Physics Ball	Avatar (Snow Queen)
✓		Giant Zurgbot	Enemy	Enemy	Play Set (Toy Story)
✓		Giraffe	Critter	Critter	Play Set (Incredibles)
✓		Giraffe Topiary	Plants	Static	Disney Infinity Vault
✓		Give 'em a Hand Launcher	Decoration	Custom	Play Set (Monsters)
✓		Glass Block	Block	Physics Block	Disney Infinity Vault
✓		Glass Sidewalk	Building Sets	Static	Play Set (Toy Story)
✓		Glass Tower	Building Sets	Static	Play Set (Incredibles)
✓		Glide Pack	Tool/Pack	Pack	Play Set (Incredibles)

Got It?	Icon	Toy Name	Category	Function	Unlock
✓		Glow Urchin	Tool/Pack	Tool	Play Set (Monsters)
✓		Gold Crate	Decoration	Breakable	Play Set (Toy Story)
✓		Gold Parking Meter	Decoration	Breakable	Play Set (Cars)
✓		Golden Horse	Vehicle/Mount	Mount	Play Set (Lone Ranger)
✓		Goo Bot	Enemy	Enemy	Play Set (Toy Story)
✓		Goo Grower	Tool/Pack	Tool	Play Set (Toy Story)
✓		Goo Shrinker	Tool/Pack	Tool	Play Set (Toy Story)
✓		Goo Volcano	Set Piece	Custom	Play Set (Toy Story)
✓		Gopher	Critter	Critter	Disney Infinity Vault
✓		Gopher (Lone Ranger)	Critter	Critter	Play Set (Lone Ranger)
✓		Graduating Growler	Play Set Townspeople	Townspeople	Play Set (Monsters)
✓		Grand Duke Costume	Toy Box Townspeople	Townspeople	Disney Infinity Vault
✓		Granny	Play Set Townspeople	Townspeople	Play Set (Lone Ranger)
✓		Grappling Hook	Tool/Pack	Tool	Play Set (Pirates)
✓		Grassy Bridge	Terrain	Static	Disney Infinity Vault
✓		Green Basketball Jersey Costume	Toy Box Townspeople	Townspeople	Disney Infinity Vault
✓		Green Hair Tiki Totem	Decoration	Static	Disney Infinity Vault
✓		Green Plane	Critter	Flying Critter	Play Set (Cars)
✓		Ground Vehicle Weapon Generator	Creativi-Toys	Custom	Disney Infinity Vault
✓		Grow Panel	Action Toy	Custom	Disney Infinity Vault
✓		Grumbling Tiki Monument	Decoration	Static	Disney Infinity Vault
✓		Grumpy Costume	Toy Box Townspeople	Townspeople	Disney Infinity Vault
✓		Guido	Cast Member	Mission Giver	Play Set (Cars)
✓		Guido at Work Sign	Decoration	Breakable	Play Set (Cars)
✓		Gummboid	Critter	Critter	Play Set (Toy Story)
✓		Gunner	Play Set Townspeople	Townspeople	Play Set (Pirates)
✓		Hades Costume	Toy Box Townspeople	Townspeople	Disney Infinity Vault
✓		Half Dome	Block	Static	Disney Infinity Vault
✓		Half Loop	Track Piece	Track	Disney Infinity Vault
✓		Halloween Town Gate	Set Piece	Custom	Avatar (Skellington)
✓		Halloween Town Jack−O−Lanterns	Tool/Pack	Tool	Avatar (Skellington)
✓		Halloween Town Terrain 1	Cluster Customization	Static	Power Disc

GAME BASICS

CHARACTERS

POWER DISCS

PLAY SETS

TOY BOX

TOY BOX COLLECTION

ACHIEVEMENTS

Got It?	Icon	Toy Name	Category	Function	Unlock
✓		Halloween Town Terrain 2	Cluster Customization	Static	Power Disc
✓		Halloween Town Terrain 3	Cluster Customization	Static	Power Disc
✓		Halloween Town Terrain 4	Cluster Customization	Static	Power Disc
✓		Halloween Town Terrain 5	Cluster Customization	Static	Power Disc
✓		Halloween Town Terrain Corner 1	Cluster Customization	Static	Power Disc
✓		Halloween Town Terrain Corner 2	Cluster Customization	Static	Power Disc
✓		Halloween Town Terrain Strip 1	Cluster Customization	Static	Power Disc
✓		Halloween Town Terrain Strip 2	Cluster Customization	Static	Power Disc
✓		Hamm	Cast Member	Mision Giver	Play Set (Toy Story)
✓		Hangin' Ten Stitch with Surfboard	Tool/Pack	Pack	Power Disc
✓		Hangin' Tire	Decoration	Breakable	Play Set (Cars)
✓		Hanging Rope Cliff	Terrain	Static	Disney Infinity Vault
✓		Hatchery	Building	Static	Play Set (Toy Story)
✓		Haunted Mansion	Set Piece	Static	Disney Infinity Vault
✓		Have a Nice Trip Launcher	Decoration	Custom	Play Set (Monsters)
✓		Hay Bale	Decoration	Breakable	Play Set (Cars)
✓		Hazard Fence	Decoration	Breakable	Play Set (Cars)
✓		Headless Horseman's Horse	Vehicle/Mount	Mount	Power Disc
✓		Hector Barbossa Costume	Toy Box Townspeople	Townspeople	Play Set (Pirates)
✓		Hedge Arch	Plants	Static	Disney Infinity Vault
✓		Hedge Corner	Plants	Static	Disney Infinity Vault
✓		Hedge Wall	Plants	Static	Disney Infinity Vault
✓		Hillside Block	Terrain	Static	Disney Infinity Vault
✓		Hockey Player Costume	Toy Box Townspeople	Townspeople	Disney Infinity Vault
✓		Holley Shiftwell Paint Job	Toy Box Townspeople	Townspeople	Play Set (Cars)
✓		Holley's Hubcap Pinwheel	Decoration	Breakable	Play Set (Cars)
✓		Hop Over Gate	Action Toy	Custom	Disney Infinity Vault
✓		Horned Mask	Play Set Townspeople	Townspeople	Play Set (Lone Ranger)
✓		Hospital	Building	Static	Play Set (Toy Story)
✓		Hotdog Stand	Building	Static	Play Set (Incredibles)
✓		Hover Board	Tool/Pack	Pack	Play Set (Incredibles)
✓		HQ Research Station	Building	Static	Play Set (Incredibles)

Got It?	Icon	Toy Name	Category	Function	Unlock
✓		HSS House	Building	Static	Play Set (Monsters)
✓		Identity Disc	Tool/Pack	Pack	Disney Infinity Vault
✓		Incoming Call Ender	Decoration	Custom	Play Set (Monsters)
✓		Incredibles Antenna	Decoration	Static	Play Set (Incredibles)
✓		Inflatable Guido Balloon	Decoration	Static	Play Set (Cars)
✓		Insect Car	Critter	Flying Critter	Play Set (Cars)
✓		Insurance Sales Woman	Play Set Townspeople	Townspeople	Play Set (Incredibles)
✓		Interstate Sign	Decoration	Static	Play Set (Cars)
✓		Invisibility Device	Tool/Pack	Tool	Play Set (Incredibles)
✓		Invisinator	Action Toy	Custom	Disney Infinity Vault
✓		Invulnerability Beacon	Creativi-Toys	Custom	Disney Infinity Vault
✓		Jack Skellington Costume	Toy Box Townspeople	NPC	Avatar (Skellington)
✓		Jack Sparrow Costume	Toy Box Townspeople	Townspeople	Disney Infinity Vault
✓		Jack-O-Lantern	Decoration	Breakable	Disney Infinity Vault
✓		Jack-O-Lantern in the Box Costume	Enemy	Enemy	Disney Infinity Vault
✓		Jafar Costume	Toy Box Townspeople	Townspeople	Disney Infinity Vault
✓		Jaunty Junior	Play Set Townspeople	Townspeople	Play Set (Monsters)
✓		Jessie Costume	Toy Box Townspeople	NPC	Play Set (Toy Story)
✓		Jiminy Cricket Costume	Toy Box Townspeople	Townspeople	Disney Infinity Vault
✓		Job Hunter	Play Set Townspeople	Townspeople	Play Set (Incredibles)
✓		Jovial Junior	Play Set Townspeople	Townspeople	Play Set (Monsters)
✓		JOX House	Building	Static	Play Set (Monsters)
✓		Joyful Junior	Play Set Townspeople	Townspeople	Play Set (Monsters)
✓		Jutting Ledge	Terrain	Static	Disney Infinity Vault
✓		Kahn	Vehicle/Mount	Mount	Power Disc
✓		Kermit the Frog Costume	Toy Box Townspeople	Townspeople	Disney Infinity Vault
✓		Key to the City	Decoration	Breakable	Play Set (Toy Story)
✓		Kill Switch	Creativi-Toys	Custom	Disney Infinity Vault
✓		King Candy's Royal Racer	Vehicle/Mount	Vehicle	Disney Infinity Vault
✓		King Costume	Toy Box Townspeople	Townspeople	Disney Infinity Vault
✓		Knight Costume	Toy Box Townspeople	Townspeople	Disney Infinity Vault
✓		Lady (Incredibles)	Play Set Townspeople	Townspeople	Play Set (Incredibles)

Got It?	Icon	Toy Name	Category	Function	Unlock
✓		Lady (Lone Ranger)	Play Set Townspeople	Townspeople	Play Set (Lone Ranger)
✓		Lady Buccaneer	Play Set Townspeople	Townspeople	Play Set (Pirates)
✓		Lake	Terrain	Static	Disney Infinity Vault
✓		Lamp Post	Decoration	Static	Starting Toy
✓		Lantern Pole	Decoration	Static	Play Set (Lone Ranger)
✓		Large Brick Building	Building Sets	Static	Play Set (Incredibles)
✓		Large Canyon Curve	Terrain	Static	Disney Infinity Vault
✓		Large Canyon Outer Curve	Terrain	Static	Disney Infinity Vault
✓		Large Castle Floor	Building Sets	Static	Disney Infinity Vault
✓		Large Cliff	Terrain	Static	Disney Infinity Vault
✓		Large Cliff Ledge	Terrain	Static	Disney Infinity Vault
✓		Large Colby Tree	Plants	Static	Play Set (Lone Ranger)
✓		Large Curved Barrier	Track Piece	Static	Disney Infinity Vault
✓		Large Disney Infinity Pine Tree	Plants	Static	Starting Toy
✓		Large Flat Terrain Block	Terrain	Static	Disney Infinity Vault
✓		Large Floor	Block	Static	Disney Infinity Vault
✓		Large Lava Block	Block	Custom	Disney Infinity Vault
✓		Large Metroville Tree	Plants	Static	Play Set (Incredibles)
✓		Large Monster Tree	Plants	Static	Play Set (Monsters)
✓		Large Nose Mask	Play Set Townspeople	Townspeople	Play Set (Lone Ranger)
✓		Large Radiator Springs Bush	Plants	Static	Play Set (Cars)
✓		Large Radiator Springs Cactus	Plants	Static	Play Set (Cars)
✓		Large Roof Vent	Decoration	Static	Play Set (Incredibles)
✓		Large Rounded Cliff	Terrain	Static	Starting Toy
✓		Large Slope	Terrain	Static	Starting Toy
✓		Large Stone Wall	Block	Static	Disney Infinity Vault
✓		Large Terrain Block	Terrain	Static	Disney Infinity Vault
✓		Large Toy Story Bush	Plants	Static	Play Set (Toy Story)
✓		Large Toy Story Tree	Plants	Static	Play Set (Toy Story)
✓		Lass	Play Set Townspeople	Townspeople	Play Set (Lone Ranger)
✓		Launching Ramp	Track Piece	Static	Disney Infinity Vault
✓		Lava Block	Block	Custom	Disney Infinity Vault

Got It?	Icon	Toy Name	Category	Function	Unlock
✓		Leaf Mask	Play Set Townspeople	Townspeople	Play Set (Lone Ranger)
✓		Leafoid	Critter	Critter	Play Set (Toy Story)
✓		Ledge Block	Block	Static	Disney Infinity Vault
✓		Left Pinball Flipper	Basic Toy	Custom	Disney Infinity Vault
✓		Left Rail	Track Piece	Rail Grind	Disney Infinity Vault
✓		Left Upward Curving Rail	Track Piece	Rail Grind	Disney Infinity Vault
✓		Light Runner	Vehicle/Mount	Ground Vehicle	Disney Infinity Vault
✓		Lightning McQueen Paint Job	Toy Box Townspeople	Townspeople	Play Set (Cars)
✓		Lion	Critter	Critter	Play Set (Incredibles)
✓		Little Boy	Play Set Townspeople	Townspeople	Play Set (Incredibles)
✓		Little Girl	Play Set Townspeople	Townspeople	Play Set (Incredibles)
✓		Little Kid	Play Set Townspeople	Townspeople	Play Set (Incredibles)
✓		Little Mad Tiki Monument	Decoration	Static	Disney Infinity Vault
✓		Little Sad Tiki Monument	Decoration	Static	Disney Infinity Vault
✓		Lizard	Critter	Critter	Play Set (Lone Ranger)
✓		Lock Costume	Enemy	Enemy	Disney Infinity Vault
✓		Log	Decoration	Static	Starting Toy
✓		Lone Ranger Costume	Toy Box Townspeople	Townspeople	Play Set (Lone Ranger)
✓		Long Awning	Building Sets	Static	Play Set (Pirates)
✓		Long Barricade	Decoration	Static	Disney Infinity Vault
✓		Long Blip Block	Block	Blip Block	Disney Infinity Vault
✓		Long Block	Block	Static	Disney Infinity Vault
✓		Long Castle Top Archway	Building Sets	Static	Disney Infinity Vault
✓		Long Flat Terrain Block	Terrain	Static	Disney Infinity Vault
✓		Long Glass Block	Block	Physics Block	Disney Infinity Vault
✓		Long Glass Sidewalk	Building Sets	Static	Play Set (Toy Story)
✓		Long Metal Block	Block	Physics Block	Disney Infinity Vault
✓		Long Race Track	Track Piece	Track	Starting Toy
✓		Long Race Track Ramp	Track Piece	Track	Starting Toy
✓		Long Roof	Building Sets	Static	Play Set (Pirates)
✓		Long Solid Sidewalk	Building Sets	Static	Play Set (Toy Story)
✓		Long Support Arch	Block	Static	Disney Infinity Vault

Got It?	Icon	Toy Name	Category	Function	Unlock
✓		Long Tiny Terrain Block	Terrain	Static	Disney Infinity Vault
✓		Long Walkway	Building Sets	Static	Play Set (Toy Story)
✓		Long Wedge Blip Block	Block	Blip Block	Disney Infinity Vault
✓		Long Wedge Block	Block	Static	Disney Infinity Vault
✓		Long Wooden Block	Block	Physics Block	Disney Infinity Vault
✓		Long Wooden Bridge	Decoration	Static	Disney Infinity Vault
✓		Long Wooden Ladder	Decoration	Static	Disney Infinity Vault
✓		Long-Necked Critter	Critter	Critter	Play Set (Monsters)
✓		Luigi	Cast Member	Mission Giver	Play Set (Cars)
✓		Luigi's Casa Della Tires	Building	Static	Play Set (Cars)
✓		M.U. Clock Tower	Set Piece	Static	Play Set (Monsters)
✓		M.U. Dorm	Building	Static	Play Set (Monsters)
✓		M.U. Entrance Gate	Set Piece	Static	Play Set (Monsters)
✓		M.U. Founder's Fountain	Set Piece	Static	Play Set (Monsters)
✓		M.U. Groundskeeper	Play Set Townspeople	Townspeople	Play Set (Monsters)
✓		M.U. Library	Building	Static	Play Set (Monsters)
✓		M.U. Registration Hall	Building	Static	Play Set (Monsters)
✓		M.U. School of Scaring	Building	Static	Play Set (Monsters)
✓		M.U. University Hall	Building	Static	Play Set (Monsters)
✓		Maccus	Enemy	Enemy	Play Set (Pirates)
✓		Mad Hatter Costume	Toy Box Townspeople	Townspeople	Disney Infinity Vault
✓		Mad Scientist	Play Set Townspeople	Townspeople	Play Set (Incredibles)
✓		Magic Wand	Tool/Pack	Tool	Starting Toy
✓		Mail Box	Decoration	Breakable	Play Set (Incredibles)
✓		Maleficent Costume	Toy Box Townspeople	Townspeople	Disney Infinity Vault
✓		Man About Town	Play Set Townspeople	Townspeople	Play Set (Incredibles)
✓		Man on the Street	Play Set Townspeople	Townspeople	Play Set (Incredibles)
✓		Marching Orders	Creativi-Toys	Custom	Disney Infinity Vault
✓		Masher	Action Toy	Custom	Disney Infinity Vault
✓		Massive Rounded Cliff	Terrain	Static	Starting Toy
✓		Massive Terrain Block	Terrain	Static	Disney Infinity Vault
✓		Mater Paint Job	Toy Box Townspeople	Townspeople	Play Set (Cars)

Got It?	Icon	Toy Name	Category	Function	Unlock
✓		Matterhorn Yeti Costume	Toy Box Townspeople	Townspeople	Disney Infinity Vault
✓		Maximus	Vehicle/Mount	Mount	Power Disc
✓		Medicine Ball	Tool/Pack	Tool	Play Set (Toy Story)
✓		Medium Canyon Outer Curve	Terrain	Static	Disney Infinity Vault
✓		Medium Cliff Ledge	Terrain	Static	Disney Infinity Vault
✓		Medium Fence	Decoration	Breakable	Play Set (Cars)
✓		Medium Race Track	Track Piece	Track	Starting Toy
✓		Medium Waterfall	Terrain	Static	Disney Infinity Vault
✓		Mega Pixar Ball	Tool/Pack	Tool	Play Set (Toy Story)
✓		Melancholy Tiki Monument	Decoration	Static	Disney Infinity Vault
✓		Melee Omnidroid	Enemy	Enemy	Play Set (Incredibles)
✓		Merlin Costume	Toy Box Townspeople	Townspeople	Disney Infinity Vault
✓		Metal Block	Block	Physics Block	Disney Infinity Vault
✓		Metroville Bush	Plants	Static	Play Set (Incredibles)
✓		Metroville Business Office	Building Sets	Static	Play Set (Incredibles)
✓		Metroville Center	Building Sets	Static	Play Set (Incredibles)
✓		Metroville Deli	Building Sets	Static	Play Set (Incredibles)
✓		Metroville Fireman	Play Set Townspeople	Townspeople	Play Set (Incredibles)
✓		Metroville Manor	Building Sets	Static	Play Set (Incredibles)
✓		Metroville Mart	Building Sets	Static	Play Set (Incredibles)
✓		Metroville Police Officer	Play Set Townspeople	Townspeople	Play Set (Incredibles)
✓		Metroville Shop	Building Sets	Static	Play Set (Incredibles)
✓		Metroville Street Light	Themed Terrain	Static	Play Set (Incredibles)
✓		Metroville Terrain 1	Themed Terrain	Static	Play Set (Incredibles)
✓		Metroville Terrain 2	Themed Terrain	Static	Play Set (Incredibles)
✓		Metroville Terrain 3	Themed Terrain	Static	Play Set (Incredibles)
✓		Metroville Terrain 4	Themed Terrain	Static	Play Set (Incredibles)
✓		Metroville Terrain Corner 1	Themed Terrain	Static	Play Set (Incredibles)
✓		Metroville Terrain Corner 2	Themed Terrain	Static	Play Set (Incredibles)
✓		Metroville Terrain Strip 1	Themed Terrain	Static	Play Set (Incredibles)
✓		Metroville Terrain Strip 2	Themed Terrain	Static	Play Set (Incredibles)
✓		Metroville Tree	Plants	Static	Play Set (Incredibles)

Got It?	Icon	Toy Name	Category	Function	Unlock
✓		Metroville Storefront	Building Sets	Static	Play Set (Incredibles)
✓		Metroville's Woman of the Year	Play Set Townspeople	Townspeople	Play Set (Incredibles)
✓		Mickey Topiary	Plants	Static	Disney Infinity Vault
✓		Mickey's Car	Vehicle/Mount	Ground Vehicle	Power Disc
✓		Mike's New Car	Vehicle/Mount	Vehicle	Power Disc
✓		Mike Wazowski Costume	Toy Box Townspeople	Townspeople	Disney Infinity Vault
✓		Miner	Play Set Townspeople	Townspeople	Play Set (Lone Ranger)
✓		Mini Blasting Zurgbot	Enemy	Enemy	Play Set (Toy Story)
✓		Mini Zurgbot	Enemy	Enemy	Play Set (Toy Story)
✓		Mining Tunnel	Terrain	Static	Disney Infinity Vault
✓		Mirage	Cast Member	Mission Giver	Play Set (Incredibles)
✓		Miss	Play Set Townspeople	Townspeople	Play Set (Lone Ranger)
✓		Miss Piggy Costume	Toy Box Townspeople	Townspeople	Disney Infinity Vault
✓		Modern Air Conditioning Unit	Decoration	Static	Play Set (Incredibles)
✓		Monkey	Critter	Critter	Play Set (Incredibles)
✓		Monster Flowers 1	Plants	Static	Play Set (Monsters)
✓		Monster Flowers 2	Plants	Static	Play Set (Monsters)
✓		Monster Flowers 3	Plants	Static	Play Set (Monsters)
✓		Monster Tree	Plants	Static	Play Set (Monsters)
✓		Monsters University Light Post	Decoration	Static	Play Set (Monsters)
✓		Monsters University Terrain 1	Themed Terrain	Static	Play Set (Monsters)
✓		Monsters University Terrain 2	Themed Terrain	Static	Play Set (Monsters)
✓		Monsters University Terrain 3	Themed Terrain	Static	Play Set (Monsters)
✓		Monsters University Terrain 4	Themed Terrain	Static	Play Set (Monsters)
✓		Monsters University Terrain 5	Themed Terrain	Static	Plays Set (Monsters)
✓		Monsters University Terrain Corner 1	Themed Terrain	Static	Play Set (Monsters)
✓		Monsters University Terrain Corner 2	Themed Terrain	Static	Play Set (Monsters)
✓		Monsters University Terrain Strip 1	Themed Terrain	Static	Play Set (Monsters)
✓		Monsters University Terrain Strip 2	Themed Terrain	Static	Play Set (Monsters)
✓		Monstro the Whale	Set Piece	Static	Disney Infinity Vault
✓		Monstrous Citizen	Play Set Townspeople	Townspeople	Play Set (Incredibles)
✓		Monument of Heroes	Set Piece	Static	Play Set (Incredibles)

Got It?	Icon	Toy Name	Category	Function	Unlock
✓		Monument of Heroes	Building	Static	Play Set (Toy Story)
✓		Monument to Zurg's Defeat	Decoration	Breakable	Play Set (Toy Story)
✓		Moose Topiary	Plants	Static	Disney Infinity Vault
✓		Morning Edition Launcher	Decoration	Custom	Play Set (Monsters)
✓		Motorin' Topiary	Decoration	Breakable	Play Set (Cars)
✓		Mountain Cave	Terrain	Static	Disney Infinity Vault
✓		Mountain Tunnel	Terrain	Static	Disney Infinity Vault
✓		Moving Wall	Action Toy	Custom	Disney Infinity Vault
✓		Mr. Gibbs	Cast Member	Mission Giver	Play Set (Pirates)
✓		Mr. Incredible Costume	Toy Box Townspeople	Townspeople	Play Set (Incredibles)
✓		Mr. Incredible Defeats Syndrome	Decoration	Breakable	Play Set (Incredibles)
✓		Mr. Incredible Statue	Decoration	Breakable	Play Set (Incredibles)
✓		Mr. Incredible's Sports Car	Vehicle/Mount	Ground Vehicle	Play Set (Incredibles)
✓		Mrs. Incredible Costume	Toy Box Townspeople	Townspeople	Play Set (Incredibles)
✓		Mrs. Incredible Statue	Decoration	Breakable	Play Set (Incredibles)
✓		Mrs. Incredible vs. Syndrome Statue	Decoration	Breakable	Play Set (Incredibles)
✓		Mule	Vehicle/Mount	Mount	Play Set (Lone Ranger)
✓		Multi-Layer Walkway	Building Sets	Static	Play Set (Toy Story)
✓		Nanny Costume	Toy Box Townspeople	Townspeople	Disney Infinity Vault
✓		Narrow Barrier	Track Piece	Static	Disney Infinity Vault
✓		Narrow Canyon Wall	Terrain	Static	Disney Infinity Vault
✓		Narrow Cliff Ledge	Terrain	Static	Disney Infinity Vault
✓		Narrow Floating Cliff	Terrain	Static	Starting Toy
✓		Narrowing Walkway	Building Sets	Static	Play Set (Toy Story)
✓		Navigator	Play Set Townspeople	Townspeople	Play Set (Pirates)
✓		Nemo's Reef Terrain 1	Themed Terrain	Static	Power Disc
✓		Nemo's Reef Terrain 2	Themed Terrain	Static	Power Disc
✓		Nemo's Reef Terrain 3	Themed Terrain	Static	Power Disc
✓		Nemo's Reef Terrain 4	Themed Terrain	Static	Power Disc
✓		Nemo's Reef Terrain 5	Themed Terrain	Static	Power Disc
✓		Nemo's Reef Terrain Corner 1	Themed Terrain	Static	Power Disc
✓		Nemo's Reef Terrain Corner 2	Themed Terrain	Static	Power Disc

Got It?	Icon	Toy Name	Category	Function	Unlock
✓		Nemo's Reef Terrain Strip 1	Themed Terrain	Static	Power Disc
✓		Nemo's Reef Terrain Strip 2	Themed Terrain	Static	Power Disc
✓		New Holland Lawn Flamingo	Cluster Customization	Static	Power Disc
✓		New Holland Plant Edge 2	Cluster Customization	Static	Power Disc
✓		New Holland Terrain 1	Cluster Customization	Static	Power Disc
✓		New Holland Terrain 2	Cluster Customization	Static	Power Disc
✓		New Holland Terrain 3	Cluster Customization	Static	Power Disc
✓		New Holland Terrain Corner 1	Cluster Customization	Static	Power Disc
✓		New Holland Terrain Corner 2	Cluster Customization	Static	Power Disc
✓		New Holland Terrain Strip 1	Cluster Customization	Static	Power Disc
✓		New Holland Terrain Strip 2	Cluster Customization	Static	Power Disc
✓		New Holland Windmill	Set Piece	Static	Disney Infinity Vault
✓		Newspaper Stand	Building	Static	Play Set (Incredibles)
✓		Newsstand	Decoration	Breakable	Play Set (Monsters)
✓		Niceland Terrain 1	Cluster Customization	Static	Power Disc
✓		Niceland Terrain 2	Cluster Customization	Static	Power Disc
✓		Niceland Terrain 3	Cluster Customization	Static	Power Disc
✓		Niceland Terrain 4	Cluster Customization	Static	Power Disc
✓		Niceland Terrain 5	Cluster Customization	Static	Power Disc
✓		Niceland Terrain Corner 1	Cluster Customization	Static	Power Disc
✓		Niceland Terrain Corner 2	Cluster Customization	Static	Power Disc
✓		Niceland Terrain Strip 1	Cluster Customization	Static	Power Disc
✓		Niceland Terrain Strip 2	Cluster Customization	Static	Power Disc
✓		Nicelander's Apartment Complex	Set Piece	Static	Avatar (Ralph)
✓		Nostrilloid	Critter	Critter	Play Set (Toy Story)
✓		Nurse	Play Set Townspeople	Townspeople	Play Set (Incredibles)
✓		Obelisk	Block	Static	Disney Infinity Vault
✓		Object Generator	Creativi-Toys	Custom	Disney Infinity Vault
✓		Octoid	Critter	Critter	Play Set (Toy Story)
✓		Office Building	Building Sets	Static	Play Set (Incredibles)
✓		Office Tower	Building Sets	Static	Play Set (Incredibles)
✓		Officer	Play Set Townspeople	Townspeople	Play Set (Pirates)

Got It?	Icon	Toy Name	Category	Function	Unlock	
✓		Olaf Costume	Toy Box Townspeople	Townspeople	Disney Infinity Vault	**GAME BASICS**
✓		Old Barrel	Decoration	Static	Play Set (Monsters)	
✓		Old Timer	Play Set Townspeople	Townspeople	Play Set (Lone Ranger)	
✓		Old Woman	Play Set Townspeople	Townspeople	Play Set (Incredibles)	
✓		Omnidroid	Enemy	Enemy	Play Set (Incredibles)	**CHARACTERS**
✓		Onion Dome	Block	Static	Disney Infinity Vault	
✓		Oogie Boogie Costume	Enemy	Enemy	Disney Infinity Vault	
✓		Orange Bat-Winged Pest Bush	Plants	Custom	Play Set (Monsters)	
✓		Orange Crate	Decoration	Breakable	Play Set (Toy Story)	
✓		Overhanging Corner	Terrain	Static	Disney Infinity Vault	**POWER DISCS**
✓		Overhanging Ledge	Terrain	Static	Disney Infinity Vault	
✓		Paintball Gun	Tool/Pack	Tool	Play Set (Monsters)	
✓		Palomino	Vehicle/Mount	Mount	Play Set (Lone Ranger)	
✓		Panda	Critter	Critter	Play Set (Incredibles)	
✓		Parking Meter	Decoration	Breakable	Play Set (Cars)	**PLAY SETS**
✓		Party Cannon	Creativi-Toys	Custom	Disney Infinity Vault	
✓		Pendulum	Action Toy	Custom	Disney Infinity Vault	
✓		Penguin	Critter	Critter	Play Set (Incredibles)	
✓		Peter Pan Costume	Toy Box Townspeople	Townspeople	Disney Infinity Vault	**TOY BOX**
✓		Phone Booth (Incredibles)	Decoration	Breakable	Play Set (Incredibles)	
✓		Phone Booth (Monsters)	Decoration	Breakable	Play Set (Monsters)	
✓		Picket Fence	Decoration	Static	Disney Infinity Vault	
✓		Pig Goon Costume	Enemy	Enemy	Disney Infinity Vault	
✓		Pillar Blip Block	Block	Blip Block	Disney Infinity Vault	
✓		Pillar Block	Block	Static	Disney Infinity Vault	**TOY BOX COLLECTION**
✓		Pinball Bouncer	Basic Toy	Custom	Disney Infinity Vault	
✓		Pinball Bumper	Basic Toy	Custom	Disney Infinity Vault	
✓		Pinchoid	Critter	Critter	Play Set (Toy Story)	
✓		Pink Flamingo 1	Decoration	Breakable	Play Set (Cars)	
✓		Pink Flamingo 2	Decoration	Breakable	Play Set (Cars)	**ACHIEVEMENTS**
✓		Pink Toy Story Horse	Vehicle/Mount	Mount	Play Set (Toy Story)	
✓		Pinocchio Costume	Toy Box Townspeople	Townspeople	Disney Infinity Vault	

Got It?	Icon	Toy Name	Category	Function	Unlock
✓		Pintel	Cast Member	Mission Giver	Play Set (Pirates)
✓		Pipe Climb Block	Action Toy	Static	Disney Infinity Vault
✓		Pirate Bombs	Tool/Pack	Tool	Play Set (Pirates)
✓		Pirate Flag	Decoration	Static	Play Set (Pirates)
✓		Pirate Sign 1	Decoration	Static	Play Set (Pirates)
✓		Pirate Sign 2	Decoration	Static	Play Set (Pirates)
✓		Pirates Bush 1	Plants	Static	Play Set (Pirates)
✓		Pirates Bush 2	Plants	Static	Play Set (Pirates)
✓		Pirates Bush 3	Plants	Static	Play Set (Pirates)
✓		Pirates Bush 4	Plants	Static	Play Set (Pirates)
✓		Pirates Bush 5	Plants	Static	Play Set (Pirates)
✓		Pirates Dock	Decoration	Static	Play Set (Pirates)
✓		Pirates Plant Edge	Themed Terrain	Static	Play Set (Pirates)
✓		Pirates Plants Palm 1	Plants	Static	Play Set (Pirates)
✓		Pirates Plants Palm 2	Plants	Static	Play Set (Pirates)
✓		Pirates Street Lamp 1	Decoration	Static	Play Set (Pirates)
✓		Pirates Street Lamp 2	Decoration	Static	Play Set (Pirates)
✓		Pirates Terrain 1	Themed Terrain	Static	Play Set (Pirates)
✓		Pirates Terrain 2	Themed Terrain	Static	Play Set (Pirates)
✓		Pirates Terrain 3	Themed Terrain	Static	Play Set (Pirates)
✓		Pirates Terrain 4	Themed Terrain	Static	Play Set (Pirates)
✓		Pirates Terrain Corner 1	Themed Terrain	Static	Play Set (Pirates)
✓		Pirates Terrain Corner 2	Themed Terrain	Static	Play Set (Pirates)
✓		Pirates Terrain Strip 1	Themed Terrain	Static	Play Set (Pirates)
✓		Pirates Terrain Strip 2	Themed Terrain	Static	Play Set (Pirates)
✓		Pirates Tree	Plants	Static	Play Set (Pirates)
✓		Pixar Ball	Tool/Pack	Tool	Play Set (Toy Story)
✓		Pixar Lamp	Decoration	Breakable	Play Set (Toy Story)
✓		Pizza Planet Delivery Truck	Vehicle/Mount	Vehicle	Power Disc
✓		Plasmabolt	Play Set Townspeople	Townspeople	Play Set (Incredibles)
✓		Plateau Block with Ramp	Terrain	Static	Disney Infinity Vault
✓		Plated Slug	Critter	Critter	Play Set (Monsters)

Got It?	Icon	Toy Name	Category	Function	Unlock
✓		Platform	Building Sets	Static	Play Set (Pirates)
✓		Plush Flowers	Decoration	Breakable	Play Set (Toy Story)
✓		Plush Hearts	Decoration	Breakable	Play Set (Toy Story)
✓		PNK House	Building	Static	Play Set (Monsters)
✓		Pokey Pest	Critter	Critter	Play Set (Monsters)
✓		Police Barricade	Decoration	Breakable	Play Set (Incredibles)
✓		Pond	Terrain	Static	Starting Toy
✓		Pop Up Turret	Action Toy	Custom	Disney Infinity Vault
✓		Powder Monkey	Play Set Townspeople	Townspeople	Play Set (Pirates)
✓		Power Switch	Creativi-Toys	Custom	Disney Infinity Vault
✓		Powerful Tiki Monument	Decoration	Static	Disney Infinity Vault
✓		Pride Rock	Set Piece	Static	Disney Infinity Vault
✓		Prince Charming Costume	Toy Box Townspeople	Townspeople	Disney Infinity Vault
✓		Princess Jasmine Costume	Toy Box Townspeople	Townspeople	Disney Infinity Vault
✓		Privateer	Play Set Townspeople	Townspeople	Play Set (Pirates)
✓		Puppet Theatre	Decoration	Breakable	Play Set (Toy Story)
✓		Purple Bat-Winged Pest Bush	Plants	Custom	Play Set (Monsters)
✓		Quackoid	Critter	Critter	Play Set (Toy Story)
✓		Quarter Pipe Ramp	Track Piece	Static	Disney Infinity Vault
✓		Quartermaster	Play Set Townspeople	Townspeople	Play Set (Pirates)
✓		Rabbit	Critter	Critter	Disney Infinity Vault
✓		Rabbit (Lone Ranger)	Critter	Critter	Play Set (Lone Ranger)
✓		Rabbitoid	Critter	Critter	Play Set (Toy Story)
✓		Race Track	Track Piece	Track	Disney Infinity Vault
✓		Race Track Bridge	Track Piece	Track	Disney Infinity Vault
✓		Race Track Curve	Track Piece	Track	Starting Toy
✓		Race Track Intersection	Track Piece	Track	Disney Infinity Vault
✓		Race Track Junction	Track Piece	Track	Disney Infinity Vault
✓		Race Track Left	Track Piece	Track	Disney Infinity Vault
✓		Race Track Right	Track Piece	Track	Disney Infinity Vault
✓		Race Track Split	Track Piece	Track	Disney Infinity Vault
✓		Race Track Start	Track Piece	Track	Disney Infinity Vault

Got It?	Icon	Toy Name	Category	Function	Unlock
✓		Racing Gate	Creativi-Toys	Custom	Disney Infinity Vault
✓		Radiator Springs Bush	Plants	Static	Play Set (Cars)
✓		Radiator Springs Cactus	Plants	Breakable	Play Set (Cars)
✓		Radiator Springs Courthouse	Building	Static	Play Set (Cars)
✓		Radiator Springs Curios	Building	Static	Play Set (Cars)
✓		Radiator Springs Farmhouse	Building	Static	Play Set (Cars)
✓		Radiator Springs Terrain 1	Themed Terrain	Static	Play Set (Cars)
✓		Radiator Springs Terrain 2	Themed Terrain	Static	Play Set (Cars)
✓		Radiator Springs Terrain 3	Themed Terrain	Static	Play Set (Cars)
✓		Radiator Springs Terrain 4	Themed Terrain	Static	Play Set (Cars)
✓		Radiator Springs Terrain 5	Themed Terrain	Static	Play Set (Cars)
✓		Radiator Springs Terrain Corner 1	Themed Terrain	Static	Play Set (Cars)
✓		Radiator Springs Terrain Corner 2	Themed Terrain	Static	Play Set (Cars)
✓		Radiator Springs Terrain Strip 1	Themed Terrain	Static	Play Set (Cars)
✓		Radiator Springs Terrain Strip 2	Themed Terrain	Static	Play Set (Cars)
✓		Radiator Springs Tree	Plants	Static	Play Set (Cars)
✓		Ragetti	Cast Member	Mission Giver	Play Set (Pirates)
✓		Railroad Camp Foreman	Play Set Townspeople	Townspeople	Play Set (Lone Ranger)
✓		Railroad Worker	Play Set Townspeople	Townspeople	Play Set (Lone Ranger)
✓		Ralph's Wrecking Truck	Vehicle/Mount	Vehicle	Disney Infinity Vault
✓		Rapunzel Costume	Toy Box Townspeople	NPC	Avatar (Rapunzel)
✓		Rapunzel's Tower	Set Piece	Static	Avatar (Rapunzel)
✓		Recognizer	Vehicle/Mount	Helicopter	Disney Infinity Vault
✓		Research Station	Building	Static	Play Set (Toy Story)
✓		Rex	Cast Member	Misison Giver	Play Set (Toy Story)
✓		Ramone	Cast Member	Mission Giver	Play Set (Cars)
✓		Ramone's House of Body Art	Building	Static	Play Set (Cars)
✓		Ramp Cliff	Terrain	Static	Disney Infinity Vault
✓		Ramp Rail	Track Piece	Rail Grind	Disney Infinity Vault
✓		Ramp Vertical	Block	Static	Disney Infinity Vault
✓		Rancher	Play Set Townspeople	Townspeople	Play Set (Lone Ranger)
✓		Randy Costume	Toy Box Townspeople	Townspeople	Play Set (Monsters)

Got It?	Icon	Toy Name	Category	Function	Unlock
✓		Ranged Omnidroid	Enemy	Enemy	Play Set (Incredibles)
✓		Rat	Critter	Critter	Disney Infinity Vault
✓		Recognizer	Vehicle/Mount	Air Vehicle	Disney Infinity Vault
✓		Red Harrington	Cast Member	Mission Giver	Play Set (Lone Ranger)
✓		Red Mailbox	Decoration	Breakable	Play Set (Cars)
✓		Red Shipwreck	Set Piece	Static	Play Set (Pirates)
✓		Referee Costume	Toy Box Townspeople	Townspeople	Disney Infinity Vault
✓		Reformed Thug	Play Set Townspeople	Townspeople	Play Set (Incredibles)
✓		Repeater	Creativi-Toys	Custom	Disney Infinity Vault
✓		Replayer	Creativi-Toys	Custom	Disney Infinity Vault
✓		Reset-O-Matic	Basic Toy	Custom	Disney Infinity Vault
✓		Retro TV	Decoration	Breakable	Disney Infinity Vault
✓		Rhino Guard	Enemy	Enemy	Disney Infinity Vault
✓		Rhino Topiary	Plants	Static	Disney Infinity Vault
✓		Rick Dicker	Cast Member	Mission Giver	Play Set (Incredibles)
✓		Right Pinball Flipper	Basic Toy	Custom	Disney Infinity Vault
✓		Right Rail	Track Piece	Rail Grind	Disney Infinity Vault
✓		Right Upward Curving Rail	Track Piece	Rail Grind	Disney Infinity Vault
✓		Ring of Fire	Track Piece	Static	Disney Infinity Vault
✓		Ringmaster	Play Set Townspeople	Townspeople	Play Set (Lone Ranger)
✓		River	Terrain	Static	Starting Toy
✓		River Gazebo	Set Piece	Static	Starting Toy
✓		Riverbend	Terrain	Static	Disney Infinity Vault
✓		Road Closed Barrier	Decoration	Breakable	Play Set (Cars)
✓		Robin Hood Costume	Toy Box Townspeople	Townspeople	Disney Infinity Vault
✓		Rocky Climbing Block	Terrain	Static	Disney Infinity Vault
✓		Rocky Layered Block	Terrain	Static	Starting Toy
✓		Rocky Ramp Block	Terrain	Static	Disney Infinity Vault
✓		Rocky Terrain Block	Terrain	Static	Starting Toy
✓		Rocky Wall Jump Block	Terrain	Static	Disney Infinity Vault
✓		Roof	Building Sets	Static	Play Set (Pirates)
✓		Roof Vent	Decoration	Static	Play Set (Incredibles)

Got It?	Icon	Toy Name	Category	Function	Unlock
✓		Roof Wedge	Building Sets	Static	Play Set (Pirates)
✓		Roof Wedge Corner	Building Sets	Static	Play Set (Pirates)
✓		Rooftop Door	Decoration	Static	Play Set (Incredibles)
✓		Rope Bridge	Decoration	Static	Disney Infinity Vault
✓		ROR House	Building	Static	Play Set (Monsters)
✓		ROR Pledge	Play Set Townspeople	Townspeople	Play Set (Monsters)
✓		Rounded Ledge Block	Block	Static	Disney Infinity Vault
✓		Rounded Topiary	Plants	Static	Disney Infinity Vault
✓		Safety Dome	Creativi-Toys	Custom	Disney Infinity Vault
✓		Sally Costume	Toy Box Townspeople	Townspeople	Disney Infinity Vault
✓		Sandbag Barricade	Decoration	Breakable	Play Set (Cars)
✓		Sandstone Building	Building Sets	Static	Play Set (Incredibles)
✓		Sarge's Antique Cannon	Decoration	Breakable	Play Set (Cars)
✓		Sarge's Surplus Hut	Building	Static	Play Set (Cars)
✓		Satellite Dish	Decoration	Static	Play Set (Incredibles)
✓		School Colors Ender	Decoration	Custom	Play Set (Monsters)
✓		Scoreboard	Creativi-Toys	Custom	Disney Infinity Vault
✓		Scottish Stone Circle	Set Piece	Static	Disney Infinity Vault
✓		Scout	Vehicle/Mount	Mount	Play Set (Lone Ranger)
✓		Scream Energy Launcher	Decoration	Custom	Play Set (Monsters)
✓		Scream Tunnel Cover	Decoration	Breakable	Play Set (Monsters)
✓		Scream Tunnel Sludge Ender	Decoration	Custom	Play Set (Monsters)
✓		Scrooge McDuck Costume	Toy Box Townspeople	Townspeople	Disney Infinity Vault
✓		Scrooge's Money Bin	Set Piece	Custom	Disney Infinity Vault
✓		Sea Dog	Play Set Townspeople	Townspeople	Play Set (Pirates)
✓		Sharp Shooter	Play Set Townspeople	Townspeople	Play Set (Lone Ranger)
✓		Shed	Building Sets	Static	Play Set (Pirates)
✓		Sheriff's Badge	Decoration	Breakable	Play Set (Toy Story)
✓		Sheriff	Cast Member	Mission Giver	Play Set (Lone Ranger)
✓		Shield Tower	Building	Static	Play Set (Toy Story)
✓		Shipping Crate	Decoration	Breakable	Play Set (Incredibles)
✓		Shock Costume	Enemy	Enemy	Disney Infinity Vault

Got It?	Icon	Toy Name	Category	Function	Unlock
✓		Shopkeeper	Play Set Townspeople	Townspeople	Play Set (Lone Ranger)
✓		Short Barricade	Decoration	Static	Disney Infinity Vault
✓		Short Castle Ladder Wall	Building Sets	Static	Disney Infinity Vault
✓		Short Castle Rope Wall	Building Sets	Static	Disney Infinity Vault
✓		Short Castle Top Archway	Building Sets	Static	Disney Infinity Vault
✓		Short Castle Wall	Building Sets	Static	Disney Infinity Vault
✓		Short Castle Wall Angled Corner	Building Sets	Static	Disney Infinity Vault
✓		Short Castle Wall Corner	Building Sets	Static	Disney Infinity Vault
✓		Short Castle Wall Double Arch	Building Sets	Static	Disney Infinity Vault
✓		Short Castle Wall Inside Corner	Building Sets	Static	Disney Infinity Vault
✓		Short Cave Block	Terrain	Static	Disney Infinity Vault
✓		Short Fenced Glass Sidewalk	Building Sets	Static	Play Set (Toy Story)
✓		Short Fenced Solid Sidewalk	Building Sets	Static	Play Set (Toy Story)
✓		Short Glass Sidewalk	Building Sets	Static	Play Set (Toy Story)
✓		Short Race Track	Track Piece	Track	Disney Infinity Vault
✓		Short Race Track Curve	Track Piece	Track	Starting Toy
✓		Short Sandstone Building	Building Sets	Static	Play Set (Incredibles)
✓		Short Solid Sidewalk	Building Sets	Static	Play Set (Toy Story)
✓		Short Straight Rail	Track Piece	Rail Grind	Disney Infinity Vault
✓		Short Support Arch	Block	Static	Disney Infinity Vault
✓		Short Tiki Torch	Decoration	Static	Disney Infinity Vault
✓		Short Wooden Bridge	Decoration	Static	Disney Infinity Vault
✓		Short Wooden Ladder	Decoration	Static	Disney Infinity Vault
✓		Shovel	Tool/Pack	Pack	Avatar (Anna)
✓		Shrink Panel	Action Toy	Custom	Disney Infinity Vault
✓		Side-Step Camera	Creativi-Toys	Custom	Disney Infinity Vault
✓		Sidewalk Corner Piece	Decoration	Static	Play Set (Incredibles)
✓		Sidewalk Piece	Decoration	Static	Play Set (Incredibles)
✓		Sidewalk Ramp	Building Sets	Static	Play Set (Toy Story)
✓		Sight Crawler	Critter	Critter	Play Set (Monsters)
✓		Silent Warrior Pack	Tool/Pack	Pack	Play Set (Lone Ranger)
✓		Silver	Vehicle/Mount	Mount	Play Set (Lone Ranger)

GAME BASICS

CHARACTERS

POWER DISCS

PLAY SETS

TOY BOX

TOY BOX COLLECTION

ACHIEVEMENTS

Got It?	Icon	Toy Name	Category	Function	Unlock
✓		Simple Topiary	Plants	Static	Disney Infinity Vault
✓		Single Tire Fence	Track Piece	Static	Disney Infinity Vault
✓		Six Shooter	Tool/Pack	Tool	Play Set (Lone Ranger)
✓		Skittery Critter	Critter	Critter	Play Set (Monsters)
✓		Skull Idol	Decoration	Breakable	Play Set (Pirates)
✓		Skunk	Critter	Critter	Play Set (Lone Ranger)
✓		Sky Changer	Basic Toy	Custom	Starting Toy
✓		Slingshot	Basic Toy	Custom	Disney Infinity Vault
✓		Slinky	Cast Member	Mision Giver	Play Set (Toy Story)
✓		Slithering Senior	Play Set Townspeople	Townspeople	Play Set (Monsters)
✓		Slope	Terrain	Static	Disney Infinity Vault
✓		Sloping Hill	Terrain	Static	Disney Infinity Vault
✓		Small Bridge Cliff	Terrain	Static	Starting Toy
✓		Small Canyon Curve	Terrain	Static	Disney Infinity Vault
✓		Small Canyon Outer Curve	Terrain	Static	Disney Infinity Vault
✓		Small Castle Floor	Building Sets	Static	Disney Infinity Vault
✓		Small Cliff Ledge	Terrain	Static	Disney Infinity Vault
✓		Small Curved Barrier	Track Piece	Static	Disney Infinity Vault
✓		Small Disney Infinity Pine Tree	Plants	Static	Starting Toy
✓		Small Disney Infinity Spruce Tree	Plants	Breakable	Starting Toy
✓		Small Fence	Decoration	Breakable	Play Set (Cars)
✓		Small Flat Terrain Block	Terrain	Static	Disney Infinity Vault
✓		Small Floating Cliff	Terrain	Static	Disney Infinity Vault
✓		Small Floor	Block	Static	Disney Infinity Vault
✓		Small Jutting Ledge	Terrain	Static	Disney Infinity Vault
✓		Small Monster Tree 1	Plants	Static	Play Set (Monsters)
✓		Small Monster Tree 2	Plants	Static	Play Set (Monsters)
✓		Small Radiator Springs Cactus	Plants	Static	Play Set (Cars)
✓		Small Ramp Cliff	Terrain	Static	Disney Infinity Vault
✓		Small Rocky Terrain Block 1	Terrain	Static	Starting Toy
✓		Small Rocky Terrain Block 2	Terrain	Static	Disney Infinity Vault
✓		Small Rocky Terrain Block 3	Terrain	Static	Disney Infinity Vault

Got It?	Icon	Toy Name	Category	Function	Unlock
✓		Small Slope	Terrain	Static	Disney Infinity Vault
✓		Small Terrain Block	Terrain	Static	Disney Infinity Vault
✓		Snailian	Critter	Critter	Play Set (Toy Story)
✓		Snake In My Boot	Decoration	Breakable	Play Set (Toy Story)
✓		Snake Lady	Play Set Townspeople	Townspeople	Play Set (Lone Ranger)
✓		Sneaking Sophomore	Play Set Townspeople	Townspeople	Play Set (Monsters)
✓		Snoring Gloria	Play Set Townspeople	Townspeople	Play Set (Incredibles)
✓		Snoutoid	Critter	Critter	Play Set (Toy Story)
✓		Snow White Costume	Toy Box Townspeople	Townspeople	Disney Infinity Vault
✓		Soaring Senior	Play Set Townspeople	Townspeople	Play Set (Monsters)
✓		Soldier of Clubs Costume	Enemy	Enemy	Starting Toy
✓		Soldier of Hearts Costume	Enemy	Enemy	Starting Toy
✓		Solid Sidewalk	Building Sets	Static	Play Set (Toy Story)
✓		Sorcerer's Apprentice Mickey Costume	Toy Box Townspeople	Townspeople	Disney Infinity Vault
✓		Sorcerer's Broom Costume	Enemy	Enemy	Disney Infinity Vault
✓		Sound Effects	Creativi-Toys	Custom	Disney Infinity Vault
✓		Spare Parts Windmill	Decoration	Breakable	Play Set (Cars)
✓		Spare Tire	Basic Toy	Towable	Disney Infinity Vault
✓		Speed Bump	Track Piece	Static	Disney Infinity Vault
✓		Spiral Topiary	Plants	Static	Disney Infinity Vault
✓		Spirited Sophomore	Play Set Townspeople	Townspeople	Play Set (Monsters)
✓		Splash Pool	Action Toy	Custom	Disney Infinity Vault
✓		Sports Car Topiary	Decoration	Breakable	Play Set (Cars)
✓		Sports Fan Senior	Play Set Townspeople	Townspeople	Play Set (Monsters)
✓		Square Blip Block	Block	Blip Block	Disney Infinity Vault
✓		Square Block	Block	Static	Disney Infinity Vault
✓		Square Castle Tower	Building Sets	Static	Disney Infinity Vault
✓		Square Rocky Terrain Block	Terrain	Static	Disney Infinity Vault
✓		Squid-Legged Sophomore	Play Set Townspeople	Townspeople	Play Set (Monsters)
✓		Squishy	Cast Member	Mission Giver	Play Set (Monsters)
✓		Stacked Boxes	Decoration	Breakable	Play Set (Cars)
✓		Stacked Cube Topiary	Plants	Static	Disney Infinity Vault

GAME BASICS

CHARACTERS

POWER DISCS

PLAY SETS

TOY BOX

TOY BOX COLLECTION

ACHIEVEMENTS

Got It?	Icon	Toy Name	Category	Function	Unlock
✓		Stadium	Building Sets	Static	Disney Infinity Vault
✓		Stadium Gate	Building Sets	Static	Disney Infinity Vault
✓		Stage Coach	Vehicle/Mount	Ground Vehicle	Play Set (Lone Ranger)
✓		Stairs	Block	Static	Disney Infinity Vault
✓		Star Command Blaster	Tool/Pack	Tool	Play Set (Toy Story)
✓		Star Command Boost Pack	Tool/Pack	Pack	Play Set (Toy Story)
✓		Star Command Crate	Decoration	Breakable	Play Set (Toy Story)
✓		Starting Gate Lights	Decoration	Breakable	Play Set (Cars)
✓		Stately Metroville Tower	Building Sets	Static	Play Set (Incredibles)
✓		Steep Arched Race Track Ramp	Track Piece	Track	Disney Infinity Vault
✓		Steep Bending Rail	Track Piece	Rail Grind	Disney Infinity Vault
✓		Steep Bowed Race Track Ramp	Track Piece	Track	Disney Infinity Vault
✓		Steep Flat Race Track Ramp	Track Piece	Track	Disney Infinity Vault
✓		Steep Ramp Rail	Track Piece	Rail Grind	Disney Infinity Vault
✓		Step Cliff	Terrain	Static	Starting Toy
✓		Stepped Grassy Corner	Terrain	Static	Starting Toy
✓		Stitch's Blaster	Tool/Pack	Tool	Power Disc
✓		Stone Arch Fort	Set Piece	Static	Play Set (Pirates)
✓		Stone Wall	Block	Static	Disney Infinity Vault
✓		Stone Wall Corner	Block	Static	Disney Infinity Vault
✓		Stopwatch	Creativi-Toys	Custom	Disney Infinity Vault
✓		Straight Dock Balcony	Building Sets	Static	Play Set (Pirates)
✓		Straight Rail	Track Piece	Rail Grind	Disney Infinity Vault
✓		Straight Tire Fence	Track Piece	Static	Disney Infinity Vault
✓		Street Light (Incredibles)	Decoration	Static	Play Set (Incredibles)
✓		Street Light (Cars)	Decoration	Static	Play Set (Cars)
✓		Street Rubble	Decoration	Breakable	Play Set (Incredibles)
✓		Street Thug	Play Set Townspeople	Townspeople	Play Set (Incredibles)
✓		Stunt Buggy	Vehicle/Mount	Ground Vehicle	Disney Infinity Vault
✓		Stunt Park Clover Pool	Track Piece	Static	Play Set (Cars)
✓		Stunt Park Hill	Track Piece	Static	Play Set (Cars)
✓		Stunt Park Ridge Ramp	Track Piece	Static	Play Set (Cars)

Got It?	Icon	Toy Name	Category	Function	Unlock
✓		Sugar Rush Terrain 1	Themed Terrain	Static	Power Disc
✓		Sugar Rush Terrain 2	Themed Terrain	Static	Power Disc
✓		Sugar Rush Terrain 3	Themed Terrain	Static	Power Disc
✓		Sugar Rush Terrain 4	Themed Terrain	Static	Power Disc
✓		Sugar Rush Terrain 5	Themed Terrain	Static	Power Disc
✓		Sugar Rush Terrain Corner 1	Themed Terrain	Static	Power Disc
✓		Sugar Rush Terrain Corner 2	Themed Terrain	Static	Power Disc
✓		Sugar Rush Terrain Strip 1	Themed Terrain	Static	Power Disc
✓		Sugar Rush Terrain Strip 2	Themed Terrain	Static	Power Disc
✓		Sulley Costume	Toy Box Townspeople	Townspeople	Disney Infinity Vault
✓		Super Cannon	Action Toy	Custom	Disney Infinity Vault
✓		Super Pipe	Track Piece	Static	Play Set (Cars)
✓		SuperMax Prison	Building	Static	Play Set (Incredibles)
✓		Surgeon	Play Set Townspeople	Townspeople	Play Set (Incredibles)
✓		Swabbie	Play Set Townspeople	Townspeople	Play Set (Pirates)
✓		Sword	Tool/Pack	Pack	Play Set (Pirates)
✓		Syndrome Costume	Toy Box Townspeople	Townspeople	Play Set (Incredibles)
✓		Syndrome Statue	Decoration	Breakable	Play Set (Incredibles)
✓		Tail Light Flower Planter	Plants	Static	Play Set (Cars)
✓		Tail Light Flowers	Plants	Static	Play Set (Cars)
✓		Tall Automatic Door	Action Toy	Custom	Disney Infinity Vault
✓		Tall Blip Block	Block	Blip Block	Disney Infinity Vault
✓		Tall Block	Block	Static	Disney Infinity Vault
✓		Tall Building Base	Building Sets	Static	Play Set (Pirates)
✓		Tall Fence	Decoration	Breakable	Play Set (Cars)
✓		Tall Glass Block	Block	Physics Block	Disney Infinity Vault
✓		Tall Metal Block	Block	Physics Block	Disney Infinity Vault
✓		Tall Monster Tree	Plants	Static	Play Set (Monsters)
✓		Tall Narrow Terrain Block	Terrain	Static	Disney Infinity Vault
✓		Tall Terrain Block	Terrain	Static	Disney Infinity Vault
✓		Tall Tiki Torch	Decoration	Static	Disney Infinity Vault
✓		Tall Vaulted Platform	Block	Static	Disney Infinity Vault

GAME BASICS

CHARACTERS

POWER DISCS

PLAY SETS

TOY BOX

TOY BOX COLLECTION

ACHIEVEMENTS

Got It?	Icon	Toy Name	Category	Function	Unlock
✓		Tall Wooden Block	Block	Physics Block	Disney Infinity Vault
✓		Tangled Terrain 1	Themed Terrain	Static	Power Disc
✓		Tangled Terrain 2	Themed Terrain	Static	Power Disc
✓		Tangled Terrain 3	Themed Terrain	Static	Power Disc
✓		Tangled Terrain 4	Themed Terrain	Static	Power Disc
✓		Tangled Terrain 5	Themed Terrain	Static	Power Disc
✓		Tangled Terrain Corner 1	Themed Terrain	Static	Power Disc
✓		Tangled Terrain Corner 2	Themed Terrain	Static	Power Disc
✓		Tangled Terrain Strip 1	Themed Terrain	Static	Power Disc
✓		Tangled Terrain Strip 2	Themed Terrain	Static	Power Disc
✓		Tank Omnidroid	Enemy	Enemy	Play Set (Incredibles)
✓		Tantor	Vehicle/Mount	Mount	Power Disc
✓		Tar Trap	Action Toy	Custom	Disney Infinity Vault
✓		Target	Creativi-Toys	Custom	Disney Infinity Vault
✓		Team 1 Base	Creativi-Toys	Custom	Disney Infinity Vault
✓		Team 2 Base	Creativi-Toys	Custom	Disney Infinity Vault
✓		Tear Drop Topiary	Plants	Static	Disney Infinity Vault
✓		TeePee	Decoration	Static	Play Set (Lone Ranger)
✓		Teleporter	Creativi-Toys	Custom	Disney Infinity Vault
✓		Teleporter Dish	Building	Static	Play Set (Toy Story)
✓		Tennis Player Costume	Toy Box Townspeople	Townspeople	Disney Infinity Vault
✓		Tent	Decoration	Static	Play Set (Lone Ranger)
✓		Terrain Block	Terrain	Static	Starting Toy
✓		Terry and Terri Perry	Cast Member	Mission Giver	Play Set (Monsters)
✓		The Big Spinner	Action Toy	Custom	Disney Infinity Vault
✓		The Boss	Play Set Townspeople	Townspeople	Play Set (Incredibles)
✓		The CEO	Play Set Townspeople	Townspeople	Play Set (Incredibles)
✓		The Colby Bank	Building	Static	Play Set (Lone Ranger)
✓		The Colby Jail	Building	Static	Play Set (Lone Ranger)
✓		The Colby Saloon	Building	Static	Play Set (Lone Ranger)
✓		The Electric Mayhem Bus	Vehicle/Mount	Vehicle	Power Disc
✓		The Flipper	Action Toy	Custom	Disney Infinity Vault

Got It?	Icon	Toy Name	Category	Function	Unlock
✓		The Hoarder	Play Set Townspeople	Townspeople	Play Set (Incredibles)
✓		The Incredicar	Vehicle/Mount	Ground Vehicle	Play Set (Incredibles)
✓		The Incredicopter	Vehicle/Mount	Air Vehicle	Play Set (Incredibles)
✓		The King's Guard	Enemy	Enemy	Disney Infinity Vault
✓		The Matterhorn	Terrain	Static	Disney Infinity Vault
✓		The Mayor of Metroville	Play Set Townspeople	Townspeople	Play Set (Incredibles)
✓		The Radiator Cap	Set Piece	Static	Play Set (Cars)
✓		The Ranch	Building	Static	Play Set (Lone Ranger)
✓		The Spinner	Action Toy	Custom	Disney Infinity Vault
✓		The Sword in the Stone	Set Piece	Custom	Disney Infinity Vault
✓		Thin Metroville Tree	Plants	Static	Play Set (Incredibles)
✓		Thin Radiator Springs Tree	Plants	Static	Play Set (Cars)
✓		Thunderhead	Play Set Townspeople	Townspeople	Play Set (Incredibles)
✓		Thundering Hooves Pack	Tool/Pack	Pack	Play Set (Lone Ranger)
✓		Thundering Stallion	Vehicle/Mount	Mount	Play Set (Lone Ranger)
✓		Tia Dalma	Cast Member	Mission Giver	Play Set (Pirates)
✓		Tigger Costume	Toy Box Townspeople	Townspeople	Disney Infinity Vault
✓		Tiki Torch	Decoration	Static	Disney Infinity Vault
✓		Time Delayer	Creativi-Toys	Custom	Disney Infinity Vault
✓		Timer	Creativi-Toys	Custom	Disney Infinity Vault
✓		Tinker Bell Costume	Toy Box Townspeople	Townspeople	Disney Infinity Vault
✓		Tiny Slope	Terrain	Static	Disney Infinity Vault
✓		Tiny Tall Terrain Block	Terrain	Static	Disney Infinity Vault
✓		Tiny Terrain Block	Terrain	Static	Starting Toy
✓		Tire Shrub	Decoration	Breakable	Play Set (Cars)
✓		Tire Stack 1	Decoration	Static	Play Set (Cars)
✓		Tire Stack 2	Decoration	Static	Play Set (Cars)
✓		Tire Tree	Decoration	Breakable	Play Set (Cars)
✓		TNT Pack	Tool/Pack	Pack	Play Set (Lone Ranger)
✓		Toilet Paper Launcher	Tool/Pack	Tool	Play Set (Monsters)
✓		Tomahawk	Tool/Pack	Tool	Play Set (Lone Ranger)
✓		Tonto Costume	Toy Box Townspeople	Townspeople	Play Set (Lone Ranger)

GAME BASICS

CHARACTERS

POWER DISCS

PLAY SETS

TOY BOX

TOY BOX COLLECTION

ACHIEVEMENTS

Got It?	Icon	Toy Name	Category	Function	Unlock
✓		Torus Topiary	Plants	Static	Disney Infinity Vault
✓		Tourist Sedan	Play Set Townspeople	Townspeople	Play Set (Cars)
✓		Tourist Truck	Play Set Townspeople	Townspeople	Play Set (Cars)
✓		Tourist Van	Play Set Townspeople	Townspeople	Play Set (Cars)
✓		Tow Mater Impound Lot	Building	Static	Play Set (Cars)
✓		Towable Ramp	Basic Toy	Towable	Play Set (Cars)
✓		Towable Wrecking Ball	Basic Toy	Towable	Play Set (Cars)
✓		Tower	Building Sets	Static	Play Set (Pirates)
✓		Tower Fort	Set Piece	Static	Disney Infinity Vault
✓		Toy Box Blaster	Tool/Pack	Tool	Starting Toy
✓		Toy Story Bush	Plants	Breakable	Play Set (Toy Story)
✓		Toy Story Plant 1	Plants	Static	Play Set (Toy Story)
✓		Toy Story Plant 2	Plants	Static	Play Set (Toy Story)
✓		Toy Story Terrain 1	Cluster Customization	Static	Play Set (Toy Story)
✓		Toy Story Terrain 2	Cluster Customization	Static	Play Set (Toy Story)
✓		Toy Story Terrain 3	Cluster Customization	Static	Play Set (Toy Story)
✓		Toy Story Terrain 4	Cluster Customization	Static	Play Set (Toy Story)
✓		Toy Story Terrain Corner 1	Cluster Customization	Static	Play Set (Toy Story)
✓		Toy Story Terrain Corner 2	Cluster Customization	Static	Play Set (Toy Story)
✓		Toy Story Terrain Strip 1	Cluster Customization	Static	Play Set (Toy Story)
✓		Toy Story Terrain Strip 2	Cluster Customization	Static	Play Set (Toy Story)
✓		Toy Story Terrain Strip 3	Cluster Customization	Static	Play Set (Toy Story)
✓		Toy Story Tree	Plants	Static	Play Set (Toy Story)
✓		Toy Story Zebra	Vehicle/Mount	Mount	Play Set (Toy Story)
✓		Tractor	Play Set Townspeople	Townspeople	Play Set (Cars)
✓		Tractor Crossing Sign	Decoration	Breakable	Play Set (Cars)
✓		Traffic Barrel	Decoration	Breakable	Play Set (Incredibles)
✓		Traffic Cone (Incredibles)	Decoration	Breakable	Play Set (Incredibles)
✓		Traffic Cone (Cars)	Decoration	Breakable	Play Set (Cars)
✓		Traffic Light	Decoration	Static	Play Set (Incredibles)
✓		Traffic Sign 1	Decoration	Static	Play Set (Cars)
✓		Traffic Sign 2	Decoration	Static	Play Set (Cars)

Got It?	Icon	Toy Name	Category	Function	Unlock
✓		Train Engine	Vehicle/Mount	Ground Vehicle	Play Set (Lone Ranger)
✓		Training Facility	Building	Static	Play Set (Incredibles)
✓		Trash Pile	Decoration	Breakable	Play Set (Incredibles)
✓		Trash Receptacle	Decoration	Breakable	Play Set (Incredibles)
✓		Treasure Grotto	Terrain	Static	Disney Infinity Vault
✓		Triangle Blip Block	Block	Blip Block	Disney Infinity Vault
✓		Triangle Block	Block	Static	Disney Infinity Vault
✓		Tri-Eye	Critter	Critter	Play Set (Monsters)
✓		Trigger	Creativi-Toys	Custom	Disney Infinity Vault
✓		Trigger Area	Creativi-Toys	Custom	Disney Infinity Vault
✓		Trim	Block	Static	Disney Infinity Vault
✓		Triple Barriers	Decoration	Static	Play Set (Monsters)
✓		Tripwire	Action Toy	Custom	Disney Infinity Vault
✓		TRON Costume	Toy Box Townspeople	Townspeople	Disney Infinity Vault
✓		TRON Terrain 1	Cluster Customization	Static	Power Disc
✓		TRON Terrain 2	Cluster Customization	Static	Power Disc
✓		TRON Terrain 3	Cluster Customization	Static	Power Disc
✓		TRON Terrain 4	Cluster Customization	Static	Power Disc
✓		TRON Terrain Corner 1	Cluster Customization	Static	Power Disc
✓		TRON Terrain Corner 2	Cluster Customization	Static	Power Disc
✓		TRON Terrain Strip 1	Cluster Customization	Static	Power Disc
✓		TRON Terrain Strip 2	Cluster Customization	Static	Power Disc
✓		TRON Terrain Strip 3	Cluster Customization	Static	Power Disc
✓		Trunk	Decoration	Static	Disney Infinity Vault
✓		T-Shaped Barriers	Decoration	Static	Play Set (Monsters)
✓		Turtle Pirate	Enemy	Enemy	Play Set (Pirates)
✓		Twitchoid	Critter	Critter	Play Set (Toy Story)
✓		Underground Pipe Bend	Terrain	Static	Disney Infinity Vault
✓		Underground Pipe Branch	Terrain	Static	Disney Infinity Vault
✓		Underground Pipe End	Terrain	Static	Disney Infinity Vault
✓		Underground Pipe Entrance/Exit	Terrain	Static	Disney Infinity Vault
✓		Underground Pipe Intersection	Terrain	Static	Disney Infinity Vault

GAME BASICS

CHARACTERS

POWER DISCS

PLAY SETS

TOY BOX

TOY BOX COLLECTION

ACHIEVEMENTS

Got It?	Icon	Toy Name	Category	Function	Unlock
✓		Underground Pipe Tunnel	Terrain	Static	Disney Infinity Vault
✓		Unicoid	Critter	Critter	Play Set (Toy Story)
✓		Vampire Teddy Costume	Enemy	Enemy	Disney Infinity Vault
✓		Vanellope Von Schweetz Costume	Toy Box Townspeople	NPC	Avatar (Vanellope)
✓		Vanellope's Candy Cart	Vehicle/Mount	Vehicle	Disney Infinity Vault
✓		Vanellope's Cherry Bomb	Tool/Pack	Tool	Avatar (Vanellope)
✓		Vaulted Platform	Block	Static	Disney Infinity Vault
✓		Very Long Race Track	Track Piece	Track	Disney Infinity Vault
✓		Very Short Race Track	Track Piece	Track	Disney Infinity Vault
✓		Victory Tracker	Creativi-Toys	Custom	Disney Infinity Vault
✓		Violet Costume	Toy Box Townspeople	Townspeople	Play Set (Incredibles)
✓		Violet Statue	Decoration	Breakable	Play Set (Incredibles)
✓		Volcano Trophy	Decoration	Breakable	Play Set (Toy Story)
✓		Volleyball Player Costume	Toy Box Townspeople	Townspeople	Disney Infinity Vault
✓		Vulture	Critter	Flying Critter	Play Set (Lone Ranger)
✓		Vulture Goon Costume	Enemy	Enemy	Disney Infinity Vault
✓		Wagon	Decoration	Static	Play Set (Lone Ranger)
✓		Wall Jump Block	Action Toy	Static	Disney Infinity Vault
✓		Walkway 2-Way Connector	Building Sets	Static	Play Set (Toy Story)
✓		Walkway 3-Way Connector	Building Sets	Static	Play Set (Toy Story)
✓		Walkway 4-Way Connector	Building Sets	Static	Play Set (Toy Story)
✓		Walkway Connector	Building Sets	Static	Play Set (Toy Story)
✓		Walkway Corner	Building Sets	Static	Play Set (Toy Story)
✓		Walkway End	Building Sets	Static	Play Set (Toy Story)
✓		Walkway Ending	Building Sets	Static	Play Set (Toy Story)
✓		Walkway Ramp	Building Sets	Static	Play Set (Toy Story)
✓		Walkway Section 1	Building Sets	Static	Play Set (Toy Story)
✓		Walkway Section 2	Building Sets	Static	Play Set (Toy Story)
✓		Wart's Sword	Tool/Pack	Pack	Avatar (Infinite)
✓		Water Fountain	Decoration	Breakable	Play Set (Toy Story)
✓		Water Tower	Decoration	Static	Play Set (Incredibles)
✓		Waterfall	Terrain	Static	Disney Infinity Vault

Got It?	Icon	Toy Name	Category	Function	Unlock	
✓		Weasel Costume	Enemy	Enemy	Disney Infinity Vault	GAME BASICS
✓		Wedge Blip Block	Block	Blip Block	Disney Infinity Vault	
✓		Wedge Block	Block	Static	Disney Infinity Vault	
✓		Wedgoid	Critter	Critter	Play Set (Toy Story)	
✓		Which Way Sign	Decoration	Breakable	Play Set (Cars)	CHARACTERS
✓		Wide Barrier	Track Piece	Static	Disney Infinity Vault	
✓		Wide Building Base	Building Sets	Static	Play Set (Pirates)	
✓		Wide Canyon Wall	Terrain	Static	Disney Infinity Vault	
✓		Wide Castle Wall and Tower	Building Sets	Static	Disney Infinity Vault	
✓		Wide Floating Bridge Hill	Terrain	Static	Disney Infinity Vault	POWER DISCS
✓		Wide Floating Cliff	Terrain	Static	Starting Toy	
✓		Wide Rope Bridge	Decoration	Static	Disney Infinity Vault	
✓		Willy's Butte	Set Piece	Static	Play Set (Cars)	
✓		Wind Chime	Decoration	Breakable	Play Set (Cars)	PLAY SETS
✓		Winding Floating Bridge 1	Terrain	Static	Disney Infinity Vault	
✓		Winding Floating Bridge 2	Terrain	Static	Disney Infinity Vault	
✓		Winner's Circle	Decoration	Breakable	Play Set (Cars)	
✓		Winnie the Pooh Costume	Toy Box Townspeople	Townspeople	Disney Infinity Vault	TOY BOX
✓		Wolf	Critter	Critter	Disney Infinity Vault	
✓		Woman	Play Set Townspeople	Townspeople	Play Set (Lone Ranger)	
✓		Wonderland Terrain 1	Themed Terrain	Static	Power Disc	
✓		Wonderland Terrain 2	Themed Terrain	Static	Power Disc	
✓		Wonderland Terrain 3	Themed Terrain	Static	Power Disc	TOY BOX COLLECTION
✓		Wonderland Terrain 4	Themed Terrain	Static	Power Disc	
✓		Wonderland Terrain 5	Themed Terrain	Static	Power Disc	
✓		Wonderland Terrain Corner 1	Themed Terrain	Static	Power Disc	
✓		Wonderland Terrain Corner 2	Themed Terrain	Static	Power Disc	
✓		Wonderland Terrain Strip 1	Themed Terrain	Static	Power Disc	
✓		Wonderland Terrain Strip 2	Themed Terrain	Static	Power Disc	ACHIEVEMENTS
✓		Wood Crate	Decoration	Breakable	Play Set (Pirates)	
✓		Wooden Barrel	Decoration	Breakable	Play Set (Pirates)	
✓		Wooden Block	Block	Physics Block	Disney Infinity Vault	

Got It?	Icon	Toy Name	Category	Function	Unlock
✓		Wooden Bridge	Decoration	Static	Disney Infinity Vault
✓		Wooden Bridge Platform	Decoration	Static	Disney Infinity Vault
✓		Wooden Ladder	Decoration	Static	Disney Infinity Vault
✓		Woody Costume	Toy Box Townspeople	NPC	Play Set (Toy Story)
✓		Woody's Roundup Critters	Decoration	Breakable	Play Set (Toy Story)
✓		Wrangler	Play Set Townspeople	Townspeople	Play Set (Lone Ranger)
✓		Wreck-It Ralph Costume	Toy Box Townspeople	NPC	Avatar (Ralph)
✓		Wreck-It Ralph's Cherry Bomb	Tool/Pack	Tool	Avatar (Ralph)
✓		Yellow Crystals	Decoration	Breakable	Play Set (Toy Story)
✓		X Games Barrier	Sports Toy	Static	Disney Infinity Vault
✓		X Games Rolling Stunt Ramp	Track Piece	Static	Disney Infinity Vault
✓		X Games Stunt Pipe Corner	Track Piece	Static	Disney Infinity Vault
✓		X Games Stunt Platform	Track Piece	Static	Disney Infinity Vault
✓		X Games Stunt Quarter Pipe	Track Piece	Static	Disney Infinity Vault
✓		X Games Stunt Ramp	Track Piece	Static	Disney Infinity Vault
✓		Yellow Basketball Jersey Costume	Toy Box Townspeople	Townspeople	Disney Infinity Vault
✓		Zero Point Energy Gauntlet	Tool/Pack	Tool	Play Set (Incredibles)
✓		Zurg Statue	Decoration	Breakable	Play Set (Toy Story)
✓		Zurgbot	Enemy	Enemy	Play Set (Toy Story)

The Toy Box for Wii

The Toy Box is a bit different for the Wii version of *Disney Infinity*. First off, there are no Play Set-themed Toy Box Worlds, nor can you use the buildings from the Play Sets in the Wii worlds. The Wii version also does not contain all the toys in the other versions of the game.

> **NOTE**
>
> This section applies only to the Wii. The standard information in the guide applies to the Wii U.

When you enter the Wii Toy Box, you have your choice of seven themed worlds. When you unlock a toy in the Disney Infinity Vault, it will only be unlocked for some of the worlds. The Vault will let you know in which worlds your toys will be available. Now let's take a look at those seven worlds.

TOY BOX LAUNCH

This world is where you begin *Disney Infinity*. It has the Disney Infinity Hub, which you can use to get to the other worlds and places in the game. There is also the castle, a vehicle, and character chests that you can open to unlock new toys. Look around for Spins in this world to unlock more toys. While you can explore, you can't edit this world nor can you place toys into it. It is mainly the hub to explore and access other places.

> **NOTE**
>
> Not all toys are available in every Toy Box World. Instead, each Toy Box World has a set number of toys that can be unlocked.

BUILDING TOY BOX

This Toy Box World is designed to let you build with blocks, building sets, terrain, and plants, and then populate it with Townspeople. The following is a list of the toys available in this world.

Got It?	Icon	Toy Name	Category
✓		Sky Changer	Basic Toy
✓		Arch Block	Block
✓		Balcony	Block
✓		Column	Block
✓		Curved Block	Block
✓		Dip Beam	Block
✓		Full Dome	Block
✓		Half Dome	Block
✓		Large Floor	Block
✓		Large Stone Wall	Block
✓		Ledge Block	Block
✓		Long Block	Block
✓		Long Support Arch	Block
✓		Long Wedge Block	Block
✓		Obelisk	Block
✓		Onion Dome	Block
✓		Pillar Block	Block
✓		Ramp Vertical	Block
✓		Rounded Ledge Block	Block
✓		Short Support Arch	Block
✓		Small Floor	Block
✓		Square Block	Block

Got It?	Icon	Toy Name	Category
✓		Stairs	Block
✓		Stone Wall	Block
✓		Stone Wall Corner	Block
✓		Tall Block	Block
✓		Tall Vaulted Platform	Block
✓		Triangle Block	Block
✓		Trim	Block
✓		Vaulted Platform	Block
✓		Wedge Block	Block
✓		Agrabah Palace Base	Building Sets
✓		Agrabah Palace Columns	Building Sets
✓		Agrabah Palace Entrance	Building Sets
✓		Agrabah Palace Front	Building Sets
✓		Agrabah Palace Ramp	Building Sets
✓		Agrabah Palace Tower 1	Building Sets
✓		Agrabah Palace Tower 2	Building Sets
✓		Agrabah Palace Tower 3	Building Sets
✓		Agrabah Palace Tower 4	Building Sets
✓		Agrabah Palace Wall	Building Sets
✓		Agrabah Palace Wall Corner	Building Sets
✓		Agrabah Palace Wall Long	Building Sets
✓		Agrabah Palace Wall Lookout	Building Sets
✓		Awning	Building Sets
✓		Balcony	Building Sets
✓		Brick Building	Building Sets
✓		Building Base Corner	Building Sets
✓		Building Base Ground Corner	Building Sets
✓		Building Base with Arch	Building Sets
✓		Building Nook	Building Sets

Got It?	Icon	Toy Name	Category
✓		Castle Bridge	Building Sets
✓		Castle Floor	Building Sets
✓		Castle Front Entrance	Building Sets
✓		Castle Front Full	Building Sets
✓		Castle Ladder Wall	Building Sets
✓		Castle Ramp	Building Sets
✓		Castle Rope Wall	Building Sets
✓		Castle Spire 1	Building Sets
✓		Castle Spire 2	Building Sets
✓		Castle Stairs	Building Sets
✓		Castle Top Archway	Building Sets
✓		Castle Tower 1	Building Sets
✓		Castle Tower 2	Building Sets
✓		Castle Tower 3	Building Sets
✓		Castle Tower Base	Building Sets
✓		Castle Tower Corner 1	Building Sets
✓		Castle Tower Corner 2	Building Sets
✓		Castle Tower Top	Building Sets
✓		Castle Wall	Building Sets
✓		Castle Wall and Bridge	Building Sets
✓		Castle Wall and Tower 1	Building Sets
✓		Castle Wall and Tower 2	Building Sets
✓		Castle Wall Angled Corner	Building Sets
✓		Castle Wall Corner	Building Sets
✓		Castle Wall Inside Corner	Building Sets
✓		Castle Wall Lookout	Building Sets
✓		Castle Wall Overhang	Building Sets
✓		Dock	Building Sets
✓		Dock Balcony Corner	Building Sets

Got It?	Icon	Toy Name	Category
✓		Dock Stairs	Building Sets
✓		Extended Castle Wall Corner	Building Sets
✓		Glass Tower	Building Sets
✓		Large Brick Building	Building Sets
✓		Large Castle Floor	Building Sets
✓		Long Awning	Building Sets
✓		Long Castle Top Archway	Building Sets
✓		Long Roof	Building Sets
✓		Metroville Business Office	Building Sets
✓		Metroville Center	Building Sets
✓		Metroville Deli	Building Sets
✓		Metroville Manor	Building Sets
✓		Metroville Mart	Building Sets
✓		Metroville Shop	Building Sets
✓		Metroville Storefront	Building Sets
✓		Office Building	Building Sets
✓		Office Tower	Building Sets
✓		Platform	Building Sets
✓		Roof	Building Sets
✓		Roof Wedge	Building Sets
✓		Roof Wedge Corner	Building Sets
✓		Sandstone Building	Building Sets
✓		Shed	Building Sets
✓		Short Castle Ladder Wall	Building Sets
✓		Short Castle Rope Wall	Building Sets
✓		Short Castle Top Archway	Building Sets
✓		Short Castle Wall	Building Sets
✓		Short Castle Wall Angled Corner	Building Sets
✓		Short Castle Wall Corner	Building Sets

Got It?	Icon	Toy Name	Category
✓		Short Castle Wall Double Arch	Building Sets
✓		Short Castle Wall Inside Corner	Building Sets
✓		Short Sandstone Building	Building Sets
✓		Small Castle Floor	Building Sets
✓		Square Castle Tower	Building Sets
✓		Stately Metroville Tower	Building Sets
✓		Straight Dock Balcony	Building Sets
✓		Tall Building Base	Building Sets
✓		Tower	Building Sets
✓		Wide Building Base	Building Sets
✓		Wide Castle Wall and Tower	Building Sets
✓		Art	Cast Member
✓		Chick Hicks	Cast Member
✓		Don Carlton	Cast Member
✓		Edna Mode	Cast Member
✓		Engineer	Cast Member
✓		Fillmore	Cast Member
✓		Finn McMissile	Cast Member
✓		Flo	Cast Member
✓		Guido	Cast Member
✓		Hamm	Cast Member
✓		Luigi	Cast Member
✓		Mirage	Cast Member
✓		Mr. Gibbs	Cast Member
✓		Pintel	Cast Member
✓		Ragetti	Cast Member
✓		Ramone	Cast Member
✓		Red Harrington	Cast Member
✓		Rex	Cast Member

Got It?	Icon	Toy Name	Category
✓		Rick Dicker	Cast Member
✓		Sheriff	Cast Member
✓		Slinky	Cast Member
✓		Squishy	Cast Member
✓		Terry and Terri Perry	Cast Member
✓		Tia Dalma	Cast Member
✓		Bear	Critter
✓		Bird	Critter
✓		Buck	Critter
✓		Deer	Critter
✓		Frog	Critter
✓		Gopher	Critter
✓		Rabbit	Critter
✓		Rat	Critter
✓		Wolf	Critter
✓		Angered Tiki Monument	Decoration
✓		Barrel	Decoration
✓		Barricade Post	Decoration
✓		Bee Hive	Decoration
✓		Box o' Fireworks	Decoration
✓		Cardboard Box	Decoration
✓		Chicken Coop	Decoration
✓		Concerned Tiki Monument	Decoration
✓		Crate	Decoration
✓		Curved Fence Corner	Decoration
✓		Fence Corner	Decoration
✓		Jack-O-Lantern	Decoration
✓		Lamp Post	Decoration
✓		Little Mad Tiki Monument	Decoration

Got It?	Icon	Toy Name	Category
✓		Little Sad Tiki Monument	Decoration
✓		Log	Decoration
✓		Long Barricade	Decoration
✓		Long Wooden Bridge	Decoration
✓		Long Wooden Ladder	Decoration
✓		Melancholy Tiki Monument	Decoration
✓		Picket Fence	Decoration
✓		Retro TV	Decoration
✓		Rope Bridge	Decoration
✓		Short Barricade	Decoration
✓		Short Wooden Bridge	Decoration
✓		Short Wooden Ladder	Decoration
✓		Wide Rope Bridge	Decoration
✓		Wooden Bridge	Decoration
✓		Wooden Bridge Platform	Decoration
✓		Wooden Ladder	Decoration
✓		Bear Topiary	Plants
✓		Box Topiary	Plants
✓		Brontosaurus Topiary	Plants
✓		Cone Topiary	Plants
✓		Cube Topiary	Plants
✓		Disney Infinity Bush 1	Plants
✓		Disney Infinity Bush 2	Plants
✓		Disney Infinity Flowers 1	Plants
✓		Disney Infinity Flowers 2	Plants
✓		Disney Infinity Flowers 3	Plants
✓		Disney Infinity Leaf Patch	Plants
✓		Disney Infinity Pine Tree	Plants
✓		Disney Infinity Spruce Tree	Plants

Got It?	Icon	Toy Name	Category
✓		Disney Infinity Tree 1	Plants
✓		Disney Infinity Tree 2	Plants
✓		Elephant Topiary	Plants
✓		Fantasy Terrain 3	Plants
✓		Fantasy Terrain 4	Plants
✓		Fantasy Terrain Corner 2	Plants
✓		Fantasy Terrain Strip 1	Plants
✓		Giraffe Topiary	Plants
✓		Hedge Arch	Plants
✓		Hedge Corner	Plants
✓		Hedge Wall	Plants
✓		Large Disney Infinity Pine Tree	Plants
✓		Mickey Topiary	Plants
✓		Moose Topiary	Plants
✓		Pirates Plants Palm 1	Plants
✓		Pirates Plants Palm 2	Plants
✓		Rhino Topiary	Plants
✓		Rounded Topiary	Plants
✓		Simple Topiary	Plants
✓		Small Disney Infinity Pine Tree	Plants
✓		Small Disney Infinity Spruce Tree	Plants
✓		Spiral Topiary	Plants
✓		Stacked Cube Topiary	Plants
✓		Tear Drop Topiary	Plants
✓		Torus Topiary	Plants
✓		Carl Fredricksen's House	Set Piece
✓		Cave of Wonders	Set Piece
✓		Clock Tower	Set Piece
✓		Doofenshmirtz Evil Incorporated	Set Piece

Got It?	Icon	Toy Name	Category
✓		Dungeon	Set Piece
✓		Epcot's Spaceship Earth	Set Piece
✓		Goo Volcano	Set Piece
✓		Halloween Town Gate	Set Piece
✓		Haunted Mansion	Set Piece
✓		M.U. Entrance Gate	Set Piece
✓		M.U. Founder's Fountain	Set Piece
✓		Monstro the Whale	Set Piece
✓		Monument of Heroes	Set Piece
✓		New Holland Windmill	Set Piece
✓		Nicelander's Apartment Complex	Set Piece
✓		Phineas and Ferb's Water Slide	Set Piece
✓		Pride Rock	Set Piece
✓		Rapunzel's Tower	Set Piece
✓		Scottish Stone Circle	Set Piece
✓		Scrooge's Money Bin	Set Piece
✓		Stone Arch Fort	Set Piece
✓		The Radiator Cap	Set Piece
✓		The Sword in the Stone	Set Piece
✓		Willy's Butte	Set Piece
✓		Bluff	Terrain
✓		Canyon Curve	Terrain
✓		Canyon Outer Curve	Terrain
✓		Canyon Wall	Terrain
✓		Cave	Terrain
✓		Cave and Well	Terrain
✓		Cave Bend	Terrain
✓		Cave End	Terrain
✓		Cave Fort	Terrain

GAME BASICS

CHARACTERS

POWER DISCS

PLAY SETS

TOY BOX

TOY BOX COLLECTION

ACHIEVEMENTS

Got It?	Icon	Toy Name	Category
✓		Cave Fort Block	Terrain
✓		Cave Intersection	Terrain
✓		Cave Tunnel	Terrain
✓		Climbing Ledge Wall	Terrain
✓		Corner Block with Ramps	Terrain
✓		Corner Hill	Terrain
✓		Corner Slope	Terrain
✓		Crystal Cavern	Terrain
✓		Floating Bridge Hill	Terrain
✓		Floating Rope Cliff	Terrain
✓		Grassy Bridge	Terrain
✓		Hanging Rope Cliff	Terrain
✓		Large Canyon Curve	Terrain
✓		Large Canyon Outer Curve	Terrain
✓		Large Rounded Cliff	Terrain
✓		Large Slope	Terrain
✓		Large Terrain Block	Terrain
✓		Long Tiny Terrain Block	Terrain
✓		Massive Rounded Cliff	Terrain
✓		Medium Canyon Outer Curve	Terrain
✓		Medium Cliff Ledge	Terrain
✓		Mining Tunnel	Terrain
✓		Mountain Tunnel	Terrain
✓		Narrow Canyon Wall	Terrain
✓		Narrow Floating Cliff	Terrain
✓		Plateau Block with Ramp	Terrain
✓		Ramp Cliff	Terrain
✓		Rocky Layered Block	Terrain
✓		Rocky Ramp Block	Terrain

Got It?	Icon	Toy Name	Category
✓		Rocky Wall Jump Block	Terrain
✓		Short Cave Block	Terrain
✓		Slope	Terrain
✓		Sloping Hill	Terrain
✓		Small Bridge Cliff	Terrain
✓		Small Canyon Curve	Terrain
✓		Small Canyon Outer Curve	Terrain
✓		Small Floating Cliff	Terrain
✓		Small Jutting Ledge	Terrain
✓		Small Rocky Terrain Block 2	Terrain
✓		Small Rocky Terrain Block 3	Terrain
✓		Small Slope	Terrain
✓		Small Terrain Block	Terrain
✓		Square Rocky Terrain Block	Terrain
✓		Step Cliff	Terrain
✓		Stepped Grassy Corner	Terrain
✓		Tall Terrain Block	Terrain
✓		Terrain Block	Terrain
✓		The Matterhorn	Terrain
✓		Tiny Slope	Terrain
✓		Tiny Tall Terrain Block	Terrain
✓		Tiny Terrain Block	Terrain
✓		Treasure Grotto	Terrain
✓		Underground Pipe Bend	Terrain
✓		Underground Pipe Branch	Terrain
✓		Underground Pipe End	Terrain
✓		Underground Pipe Entrance/Exit	Terrain
✓		Underground Pipe Intersection	Terrain
✓		Underground Pipe Tunnel	Terrain

Got it?	Icon	Toy Name	Category
✓		Wide Canyon Wall	Terrain
✓		Wide Floating Bridge Hill	Terrain
✓		Wide Floating Cliff	Terrain
✓		Agent P Costume	Toy Box Townspeople
✓		Animal Costume	Toy Box Townspeople
✓		Anna Costume	Toy Box Townspeople
✓		Ariel Costume	Toy Box Townspeople
✓		Belle Costume	Toy Box Townspeople
✓		Buzz Lightyear Costume	Toy Box Townspeople
✓		Candace Costume	Toy Box Townspeople
✓		Captain Hook Costume	Toy Box Townspeople
✓		Cinderella Costume	Toy Box Townspeople
✓		Cruella De Vil Costume	Toy Box Townspeople
✓		Dash Costume	Toy Box Townspeople
✓		Davy Jones Costume	Toy Box Townspeople
✓		Dopey Costume	Toy Box Townspeople
✓		Dr. Doofenshmirtz Costume	Toy Box Townspeople
✓		Elliott Costume	Toy Box Townspeople
✓		Elsa Costume	Toy Box Townspeople
✓		Evil Queen Costume	Toy Box Townspeople
✓		Fairy Godmother Costume	Toy Box Townspeople
✓		Ferb Costume	Toy Box Townspeople
✓		Finn McMissile Paint Job	Toy Box Townspeople
✓		Fix-It Felix, Jr. Costume	Toy Box Townspeople
✓		Francesco Bernoulli Paint Job	Toy Box Townspeople
✓		Gaston Costume	Toy Box Townspeople
✓		Genie Costume	Toy Box Townspeople
✓		Grand Duke Costume	Toy Box Townspeople
✓		Grumpy Costume	Toy Box Townspeople

Got it?	Icon	Toy Name	Category
✓		Hades Costume	Toy Box Townspeople
✓		Hector Barbossa Costume	Toy Box Townspeople
✓		Holley Shiftwell Paint Job	Toy Box Townspeople
✓		Jack Skellington Costume	Toy Box Townspeople
✓		Jack Sparrow Costume	Toy Box Townspeople
✓		Jafar Costume	Toy Box Townspeople
✓		Jessie Costume	Toy Box Townspeople
✓		Jiminy Cricket Costume	Toy Box Townspeople
✓		Kermit the Frog Costume	Toy Box Townspeople
✓		King Costume	Toy Box Townspeople
✓		Knight Costume	Toy Box Townspeople
✓		Lightning McQueen Paint Job	Toy Box Townspeople
✓		Lone Ranger Costume	Toy Box Townspeople
✓		Mad Hatter Costume	Toy Box Townspeople
✓		Maleficent Costume	Toy Box Townspeople
✓		Mater Paint Job	Toy Box Townspeople
✓		Matterhorn Yeti Costume	Toy Box Townspeople
✓		Merlin Costume	Toy Box Townspeople
✓		Mike Wazowski Costume	Toy Box Townspeople
✓		Miss Piggy Costume	Toy Box Townspeople
✓		Mr. Incredible Costume	Toy Box Townspeople
✓		Mrs. Incredible Costume	Toy Box Townspeople
✓		Nanny Costume	Toy Box Townspeople
✓		Norm Costume	Toy Box Townspeople
✓		Olaf Costume	Toy Box Townspeople
✓		Peter Pan Costume	Toy Box Townspeople
✓		Phineas Costume	Toy Box Townspeople
✓		Pinocchio Costume	Toy Box Townspeople
✓		Prince Charming Costume	Toy Box Townspeople

GAME BASICS
CHARACTERS
POWER DISCS
PLAY SETS
TOY BOX
TOY BOX COLLECTION
ACHIEVEMENTS

Got It?	Icon	Toy Name	Category
✓		Princess Jasmine Costume	Toy Box Townspeople
✓		Randy Costume	Toy Box Townspeople
✓		Rapunzel Costume	Toy Box Townspeople
✓		Robin Hood Costume	Toy Box Townspeople
✓		Sally Costume	Toy Box Townspeople
✓		Scrooge McDuck Costume	Toy Box Townspeople
✓		Snow White Costume	Toy Box Townspeople
✓		Sorcerer's Apprentice Mickey Costume	Toy Box Townspeople
✓		Sulley Costume	Toy Box Townspeople
✓		Syndrome Costume	Toy Box Townspeople
✓		Tigger Costume	Toy Box Townspeople
✓		Tinker Bell Costume	Toy Box Townspeople
✓		Tonto Costume	Toy Box Townspeople
✓		TRON Costume	Toy Box Townspeople
✓		Vanellope Von Schweetz Costume	Toy Box Townspeople
✓		Violet Costume	Toy Box Townspeople
✓		Winnie the Pooh Costume	Toy Box Townspeople
✓		Woody Costume	Toy Box Townspeople
✓		Wreck-It Ralph Costume	Toy Box Townspeople

DRIVING TOY BOX

In addition to terrain and blocks, you also get lots of track pieces as well as mounts and vehicles so you can create your own racetracks and then see if you can beat the competition. Check out the list of the toys available in this world.

Got It?	Icon	Toy Name	Category
✓		Sky Changer	Basic Toy
✓		Spare Tire	Basic Toy
✓		Towable Ramp	Basic Toy
✓		Towable Wrecking Ball	Basic Toy
✓		Arch Block	Block
✓		Balcony	Block
✓		Column	Block
✓		Curved Block	Block
✓		Dip Beam	Block
✓		Full Dome	Block
✓		Half Dome	Block
✓		Large Floor	Block
✓		Large Stone Wall	Block
✓		Ledge Block	Block
✓		Long Block	Block
✓		Long Support Arch	Block
✓		Long Wedge Block	Block
✓		Obelisk	Block
✓		Onion Dome	Block
✓		Pillar Block	Block
✓		Ramp Vertical	Block
✓		Rounded Ledge Block	Block
✓		Short Support Arch	Block
✓		Small Floor	Block
✓		Square Block	Block
✓		Stairs	Block
✓		Stone Wall	Block
✓		Stone Wall Corner	Block
✓		Tall Block	Block

Got It?	Icon	Toy Name	Category
✓		Tall Vaulted Platform	Block
✓		Triangle Block	Block
✓		Trim	Block
✓		Vaulted Platform	Block
✓		Wedge Block	Block
✓		Fantasy Terrain 3	Plants
✓		Fantasy Terrain 4	Plants
✓		Fantasy Terrain Corner 2	Plants
✓		Fantasy Terrain Strip 1	Plants
✓		Bluff	Terrain
✓		Canyon Curve	Terrain
✓		Canyon Outer Curve	Terrain
✓		Canyon Wall	Terrain
✓		Cave	Terrain
✓		Cave and Well	Terrain
✓		Cave Bend	Terrain
✓		Cave End	Terrain
✓		Cave Fort	Terrain
✓		Cave Fort Block	Terrain
✓		Cave Intersection	Terrain
✓		Cave Tunnel	Terrain
✓		Climbing Ledge Wall	Terrain
✓		Corner Block with Ramps	Terrain
✓		Corner Hill	Terrain
✓		Corner Slope	Terrain
✓		Crystal Cavern	Terrain
✓		Floating Bridge Hill	Terrain
✓		Floating Rope Cliff	Terrain
✓		Grassy Bridge	Terrain

Got It?	Icon	Toy Name	Category
✓		Hanging Rope Cliff	Terrain
✓		Large Canyon Curve	Terrain
✓		Large Canyon Outer Curve	Terrain
✓		Large Rounded Cliff	Terrain
✓		Large Slope	Terrain
✓		Large Terrain Block	Terrain
✓		Long Tiny Terrain Block	Terrain
✓		Massive Rounded Cliff	Terrain
✓		Medium Canyon Outer Curve	Terrain
✓		Medium Cliff Ledge	Terrain
✓		Mining Tunnel	Terrain
✓		Mountain Tunnel	Terrain
✓		Narrow Canyon Wall	Terrain
✓		Narrow Floating Cliff	Terrain
✓		Plateau Block with Ramp	Terrain
✓		Ramp Cliff	Terrain
✓		Rocky Layered Block	Terrain
✓		Rocky Ramp Block	Terrain
✓		Rocky Wall Jump Block	Terrain
✓		Short Cave Block	Terrain
✓		Slope	Terrain
✓		Sloping Hill	Terrain
✓		Small Bridge Cliff	Terrain
✓		Small Canyon Curve	Terrain
✓		Small Canyon Outer Curve	Terrain
✓		Small Floating Cliff	Terrain
✓		Small Jutting Ledge	Terrain
✓		Small Rocky Terrain Block 2	Terrain
✓		Small Rocky Terrain Block 3	Terrain

Got It?	Icon	Toy Name	Category
✓		Small Slope	Terrain
✓		Small Terrain Block	Terrain
✓		Square Rocky Terrain Block	Terrain
✓		Step Cliff	Terrain
✓		Stepped Grassy Corner	Terrain
✓		Tall Terrain Block	Terrain
✓		Terrain Block	Terrain
✓		The Matterhorn	Terrain
✓		Tiny Slope	Terrain
✓		Tiny Tall Terrain Block	Terrain
✓		Tiny Terrain Block	Terrain
✓		Treasure Grotto	Terrain
✓		Underground Pipe Bend	Terrain
✓		Underground Pipe Branch	Terrain
✓		Underground Pipe End	Terrain
✓		Underground Pipe Entrance/Exit	Terrain
✓		Underground Pipe Intersection	Terrain
✓		Underground Pipe Tunnel	Terrain
✓		Wide Canyon Wall	Terrain
✓		Wide Floating Bridge Hill	Terrain
✓		Wide Floating Cliff	Terrain
✓		Banked Race Track Curve	Track Piece
✓		Banked Race Track Turn	Track Piece
✓		Barrier Corner	Track Piece
✓		Boost Pad	Track Piece
✓		Chicane	Track Piece
✓		Chicane Base	Track Piece
✓		Chicane End	Track Piece
✓		Chicane Hop Over	Track Piece

Got It?	Icon	Toy Name	Category
✓		Curved Barrier	Track Piece
✓		Curved Tire Fence	Track Piece
✓		Driving Loop	Track Piece
✓		Half Loop	Track Piece
✓		Large Curved Barrier	Track Piece
✓		Launching Ramp	Track Piece
✓		Long Race Track	Track Piece
✓		Long Race Track Ramp	Track Piece
✓		Medium Race Track	Track Piece
✓		Narrow Barrier	Track Piece
✓		Quarter Pipe Ramp	Track Piece
✓		Race Track	Track Piece
✓		Race Track Bridge	Track Piece
✓		Race Track Curve	Track Piece
✓		Race Track Intersection	Track Piece
✓		Race Track Junction	Track Piece
✓		Race Track Left	Track Piece
✓		Race Track Right	Track Piece
✓		Race Track Split	Track Piece
✓		Ring of Fire	Track Piece
✓		Short Race Track	Track Piece
✓		Short Race Track Curve	Track Piece
✓		Single Tire Fence	Track Piece
✓		Small Curved Barrier	Track Piece
✓		Speed Bump	Track Piece
✓		Steep Arched Race Track Ramp	Track Piece
✓		Steep Bowed Race Track Ramp	Track Piece
✓		Steep Flat Race Track Ramp	Track Piece
✓		Straight Tire Fence	Track Piece
✓		Stunt Park Clover Pool	Track Piece

Got It?	Icon	Toy Name	Category
✓		Stunt Park Hill	Track Piece
✓		Stunt Park Ridge Ramp	Track Piece
✓		Super Pipe	Track Piece
✓		Very Long Race Track	Track Piece
✓		Very Short Race Track	Track Piece
✓		Wide Barrier	Track Piece
✓		X Games Rolling Stunt Ramp	Track Piece
✓		X Games Stunt Pipe Corner	Track Piece
✓		X Games Stunt Platform	Track Piece
✓		X Games Stunt Quarter Pipe	Track Piece
✓		X Games Stunt Ramp	Track Piece
✓		Alien Horse	Vehicle/Mount
✓		Archie the Scare Pig	Vehicle/Mount
✓		Autopia Car	Vehicle/Mount
✓		Black Horse	Vehicle/Mount
✓		Black Pinto	Vehicle/Mount
✓		Brown Pinto	Vehicle/Mount
✓		Bullseye	Vehicle/Mount
✓		Chestnut Horse	Vehicle/Mount
✓		Elephant	Vehicle/Mount
✓		Golden Horse	Vehicle/Mount
✓		King Candy's Royal Racer	Vehicle/Mount
✓		Light Runner	Vehicle/Mount
✓		Mr. Incredible's Sports Car	Vehicle/Mount
✓		Mule	Vehicle/Mount
✓		Palomino	Vehicle/Mount
✓		Pink Toy Story Horse	Vehicle/Mount
✓		Ralph's Wrecking Truck	Vehicle/Mount
✓		Scout	Vehicle/Mount
✓		Silver	Vehicle/Mount

Got It?	Icon	Toy Name	Category
✓		Stage Coach	Vehicle/Mount
✓		Stunt Buggy	Vehicle/Mount
✓		Thundering Stallion	Vehicle/Mount
✓		Toy Story Zebra	Vehicle/Mount
✓		Train Engine	Vehicle/Mount
✓		Vanellope's Candy Cart	Vehicle/Mount

COMBAT TOY BOX

Build a battlefield or combat arena, then populate it with enemies to fight. Here is a list of the toys available in this world.

Got It?	Icon	Toy Name	Category
✓		Exploding Mine	Action Toy
✓		Floor Spikes	Action Toy
✓		Grow Panel	Action Toy
✓		Masher	Action Toy
✓		Shrink Panel	Action Toy
✓		Tar Trap	Action Toy
✓		Cannon Base	Basic Toy
✓		Sky Changer	Basic Toy
✓		Arch Block	Block
✓		Balcony	Block
✓		Column	Block
✓		Curved Block	Block
✓		Dip Beam	Block
✓		Full Dome	Block

INFINITY

Got It?	Icon	Toy Name	Category
✓		Half Dome	Block
✓		Large Floor	Block
✓		Large Stone Wall	Block
✓		Ledge Block	Block
✓		Long Block	Block
✓		Long Support Arch	Block
✓		Long Wedge Block	Block
✓		Obelisk	Block
✓		Onion Dome	Block
✓		Pillar Block	Block
✓		Ramp Vertical	Block
✓		Rounded Ledge Block	Block
✓		Short Support Arch	Block
✓		Small Floor	Block
✓		Square Block	Block
✓		Stairs	Block
✓		Stone Wall	Block
✓		Stone Wall Corner	Block
✓		Tall Block	Block
✓		Tall Vaulted Platform	Block
✓		Triangle Block	Block
✓		Trim	Block
✓		Vaulted Platform	Block
✓		Wedge Block	Block
✓		Barriers 1	Decoration
✓		Barriers 2	Decoration
✓		Barriers 3	Decoration
✓		Barriers and Barrel 1	Decoration
✓		Barriers and Barrel 2	Decoration

Got It?	Icon	Toy Name	Category
✓		Barriers and Barrel 3	Decoration
✓		Bulletin Board	Decoration
✓		Foot Locker	Decoration
✓		Give 'em a Hand Launcher	Decoration
✓		Have a Nice Trip Launcher	Decoration
✓		Old Barrel	Decoration
✓		School Colors Ender	Decoration
✓		Scream Energy Launcher	Decoration
✓		Scream Tunnel Cover	Decoration
✓		Scream Tunnel Sludge Ender	Decoration
✓		Triple Barriers	Decoration
✓		T-Shaped Barriers	Decoration
✓		Agrabah Guard	Enemy
✓		Barrel Costume	Enemy
✓		Beagle Boy Costume	Enemy
✓		Gator Goon Costume	Enemy
✓		Jack-O-Lantern in the Box Costume	Enemy
✓		Lock Costume	Enemy
✓		Oogie Boogie Costume	Enemy
✓		Pig Goon Costume	Enemy
✓		Rhino Guard	Enemy
✓		Shock Costume	Enemy
✓		Soldier of Clubs Costume	Enemy
✓		Soldier of Hearts Costume	Enemy
✓		Sorcerer's Broom Costume	Enemy
✓		The King's Guard	Enemy
✓		Vampire Teddy Costume	Enemy
✓		Vulture Goon Costume	Enemy
✓		Weasel Costume	Enemy
✓		Fantasy Terrain 3	Plants

Got It?	Icon	Toy Name	Category
✓		Fantasy Terrain 4	Plants
✓		Fantasy Terrain Corner 2	Plants
✓		Fantasy Terrain Strip 1	Plants
✓		Blue Shipwreck	Set Piece
✓		Red Shipwreck	Set Piece
✓		Bluff	Terrain
✓		Canyon Curve	Terrain
✓		Canyon Outer Curve	Terrain
✓		Canyon Wall	Terrain
✓		Cave	Terrain
✓		Cave and Well	Terrain
✓		Cave Bend	Terrain
✓		Cave End	Terrain
✓		Cave Fort	Terrain
✓		Cave Fort Block	Terrain
✓		Cave Intersection	Terrain
✓		Cave Tunnel	Terrain
✓		Climbing Ledge Wall	Terrain
✓		Corner Block with Ramps	Terrain
✓		Corner Hill	Terrain
✓		Corner Slope	Terrain
✓		Crystal Cavern	Terrain
✓		Floating Bridge Hill	Terrain
✓		Floating Rope Cliff	Terrain
✓		Grassy Bridge	Terrain
✓		Hanging Rope Cliff	Terrain
✓		Large Canyon Curve	Terrain
✓		Large Canyon Outer Curve	Terrain
✓		Large Rounded Cliff	Terrain
✓		Large Slope	Terrain

Got It?	Icon	Toy Name	Category
✓		Large Terrain Block	Terrain
✓		Long Tiny Terrain Block	Terrain
✓		Massive Rounded Cliff	Terrain
✓		Medium Canyon Outer Curve	Terrain
✓		Medium Cliff Ledge	Terrain
✓		Mining Tunnel	Terrain
✓		Mountain Tunnel	Terrain
✓		Narrow Canyon Wall	Terrain
✓		Narrow Floating Cliff	Terrain
✓		Plateau Block with Ramp	Terrain
✓		Ramp Cliff	Terrain
✓		Rocky Layered Block	Terrain
✓		Rocky Ramp Block	Terrain
✓		Rocky Wall Jump Block	Terrain
✓		Short Cave Block	Terrain
✓		Slope	Terrain
✓		Sloping Hill	Terrain
✓		Small Bridge Cliff	Terrain
✓		Small Canyon Curve	Terrain
✓		Small Canyon Outer Curve	Terrain
✓		Small Floating Cliff	Terrain
✓		Small Jutting Ledge	Terrain
✓		Small Rocky Terrain Block 2	Terrain
✓		Small Rocky Terrain Block 3	Terrain
✓		Small Slope	Terrain
✓		Small Terrain Block	Terrain
✓		Square Rocky Terrain Block	Terrain
✓		Step Cliff	Terrain
✓		Stepped Grassy Corner	Terrain

Got It?	Icon	Toy Name	Category
✓		Tall Terrain Block	Terrain
✓		Terrain Block	Terrain
✓		The Matterhorn	Terrain
✓		Tiny Slope	Terrain
✓		Tiny Tall Terrain Block	Terrain
✓		Tiny Terrain Block	Terrain
✓		Treasure Grotto	Terrain
✓		Underground Pipe Bend	Terrain
✓		Underground Pipe Branch	Terrain
✓		Underground Pipe End	Terrain
✓		Underground Pipe Entrance/Exit	Terrain
✓		Underground Pipe Intersection	Terrain
✓		Underground Pipe Tunnel	Terrain
✓		Wide Canyon Wall	Terrain
✓		Wide Floating Bridge Hill	Terrain
✓		Wide Floating Cliff	Terrain
✓		Attack Copter	Vehicle/Mount
✓		Recognizer	Vehicle/Mount
✓		The Incredicopter	Vehicle/Mount

DYNAMICS TOY BOX

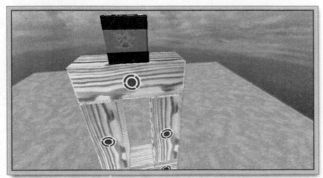

This Toy Box has the physics toys, such as breakable blocks that will fall if unsupported and can even be blown up with the explosive blocks. The following is a list of the toys available in this world.

Got It?	Icon	Toy Name	Category
✓		Beach Ball	Basic Toy
✓		Boulder	Basic Toy
✓		Egg	Basic Toy
✓		Giant Snowball	Basic Toy
✓		Left Pinball Flipper	Basic Toy
✓		Pinball Bouncer	Basic Toy
✓		Pinball Bumper	Basic Toy
✓		Reset-O-Matic	Basic Toy
✓		Right Pinball Flipper	Basic Toy
✓		Sky Changer	Basic Toy
✓		Slingshot	Basic Toy
✓		Arch Block	Block
✓		Balcony	Block
✓		Column	Block
✓		Curved Block	Block
✓		Dip Beam	Block
✓		Explosive Block	Block
✓		Full Dome	Block
✓		Glass Block	Block
✓		Half Dome	Block
✓		Large Floor	Block
✓		Large Stone Wall	Block
✓		Ledge Block	Block
✓		Long Block	Block
✓		Long Glass Block	Block
✓		Long Metal Block	Block
✓		Long Support Arch	Block
✓		Long Wedge Block	Block
✓		Long Wooden Block	Block

Got It?	Icon	Toy Name	Category
✓		Metal Block	Block
✓		Obelisk	Block
✓		Onion Dome	Block
✓		Pillar Block	Block
✓		Ramp Vertical	Block
✓		Rounded Ledge Block	Block
✓		Short Support Arch	Block
✓		Small Floor	Block
✓		Square Block	Block
✓		Stairs	Block
✓		Stone Wall	Block
✓		Stone Wall Corner	Block
✓		Tall Block	Block
✓		Tall Glass Block	Block
✓		Tall Metal Block	Block
✓		Tall Vaulted Platform	Block
✓		Tall Wooden Block	Block
✓		Triangle Block	Block
✓		Trim	Block
✓		Vaulted Platform	Block
✓		Wedge Block	Block
✓		Wooden Block	Block
✓		Fantasy Terrain 3	Plants
✓		Fantasy Terrain 4	Plants
✓		Fantasy Terrain Corner 2	Plants
✓		Fantasy Terrain Strip 1	Plants
✓		Bluff	Terrain
✓		Canyon Curve	Terrain
✓		Canyon Outer Curve	Terrain

Got It?	Icon	Toy Name	Category
✓		Canyon Wall	Terrain
✓		Cave	Terrain
✓		Cave and Well	Terrain
✓		Cave Bend	Terrain
✓		Cave End	Terrain
✓		Cave Fort	Terrain
✓		Cave Fort Block	Terrain
✓		Cave Intersection	Terrain
✓		Cave Tunnel	Terrain
✓		Climbing Ledge Wall	Terrain
✓		Corner Block with Ramps	Terrain
✓		Corner Hill	Terrain
✓		Corner Slope	Terrain
✓		Crystal Cavern	Terrain
✓		Floating Bridge Hill	Terrain
✓		Floating Rope Cliff	Terrain
✓		Grassy Bridge	Terrain
✓		Hanging Rope Cliff	Terrain
✓		Large Canyon Curve	Terrain
✓		Large Canyon Outer Curve	Terrain
✓		Large Rounded Cliff	Terrain
✓		Large Slope	Terrain
✓		Large Terrain Block	Terrain
✓		Long Tiny Terrain Block	Terrain
✓		Massive Rounded Cliff	Terrain
✓		Medium Canyon Outer Curve	Terrain
✓		Medium Cliff Ledge	Terrain
✓		Mining Tunnel	Terrain
✓		Mountain Tunnel	Terrain

GAME BASICS

CHARACTERS

POWER DISCS

PLAY SETS

TOY BOX

TOY BOX COLLECTION

ACHIEVEMENTS

Got It?	Icon	Toy Name	Category
✓		Narrow Canyon Wall	Terrain
✓		Narrow Floating Cliff	Terrain
✓		Plateau Block with Ramp	Terrain
✓		Ramp Cliff	Terrain
✓		Rocky Layered Block	Terrain
✓		Rocky Ramp Block	Terrain
✓		Rocky Wall Jump Block	Terrain
✓		Short Cave Block	Terrain
✓		Slope	Terrain
✓		Sloping Hill	Terrain
✓		Small Bridge Cliff	Terrain
✓		Small Canyon Curve	Terrain
✓		Small Canyon Outer Curve	Terrain
✓		Small Floating Cliff	Terrain
✓		Small Jutting Ledge	Terrain
✓		Small Rocky Terrain Block 2	Terrain
✓		Small Rocky Terrain Block 3	Terrain
✓		Small Slope	Terrain
✓		Small Terrain Block	Terrain
✓		Square Rocky Terrain Block	Terrain
✓		Step Cliff	Terrain
✓		Stepped Grassy Corner	Terrain
✓		Tall Terrain Block	Terrain
✓		Terrain Block	Terrain
✓		The Matterhorn	Terrain
✓		Tiny Slope	Terrain
✓		Tiny Tall Terrain Block	Terrain
✓		Tiny Terrain Block	Terrain
✓		Treasure Grotto	Terrain

Got It?	Icon	Toy Name	Category
✓		Underground Pipe Bend	Terrain
✓		Underground Pipe Branch	Terrain
✓		Underground Pipe End	Terrain
✓		Underground Pipe Entrance/Exit	Terrain
✓		Underground Pipe Intersection	Terrain
✓		Underground Pipe Tunnel	Terrain
✓		Wide Canyon Wall	Terrain
✓		Wide Floating Bridge Hill	Terrain
✓		Wide Floating Cliff	Terrain

PLATFORMING TOY BOX

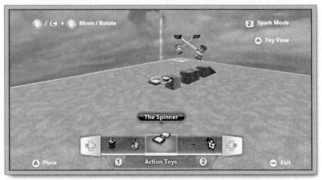

This toy box has lots of action toys as well as Creativi-Toys so you can create your own games. Here is a list of the toys available in this world.

Got It?	Icon	Toy Name	Category
✓		Automatic Door	Action Toy
✓		Automatic Double Door	Action Toy
✓		Conveyor Belt	Action Toy
✓		Elevator Platform	Action Toy
✓		Exploding Mine	Action Toy
✓		Fan	Action Toy
✓		Floor Spikes	Action Toy
✓		Hop Over Gate	Action Toy
✓		Invisinator	Action Toy
✓		Masher	Action Toy
✓		Moving Wall	Action Toy

PRIMA Official Game Guide

Got It?	Icon	Toy Name	Category
✓		Pendulum	Action Toy
✓		Pipe Climb Block	Action Toy
✓		Splash Pool	Action Toy
✓		Super Cannon	Action Toy
✓		Tall Automatic Door	Action Toy
✓		Tar Trap	Action Toy
✓		The Big Spinner	Action Toy
✓		The Flipper	Action Toy
✓		The Spinner	Action Toy
✓		Tripwire	Action Toy
✓		Wall Jump Block	Action Toy
✓		Sky Changer	Basic Toy
✓		Arch Blip Block	Block
✓		Arch Block	Block
✓		Balcony	Block
✓		Column	Block
✓		Curved Blip Block	Block
✓		Curved Block	Block
✓		Dip Beam	Block
✓		Full Dome	Block
✓		Half Dome	Block
✓		Large Floor	Block
✓		Large Lava Block	Block
✓		Large Stone Wall	Block
✓		Lava Block	Block
✓		Ledge Block	Block
✓		Long Blip Block	Block
✓		Long Block	Block
✓		Long Support Arch	Block

Got It?	Icon	Toy Name	Category
✓		Long Wedge Blip Block	Block
✓		Long Wedge Block	Block
✓		Obelisk	Block
✓		Onion Dome	Block
✓		Pillar Blip Block	Block
✓		Pillar Block	Block
✓		Ramp Vertical	Block
✓		Rounded Ledge Block	Block
✓		Short Support Arch	Block
✓		Small Floor	Block
✓		Square Blip Block	Block
✓		Square Block	Block
✓		Stairs	Block
✓		Stone Wall	Block
✓		Stone Wall Corner	Block
✓		Tall Blip Block	Block
✓		Tall Block	Block
✓		Tall Vaulted Platform	Block
✓		Triangle Blip Block	Block
✓		Triangle Block	Block
✓		Trim	Block
✓		Vaulted Platform	Block
✓		Wedge Blip Block	Block
✓		Wedge Block	Block
✓		Bird's Eye Camera	Creativi-Toy
✓		Boom Box	Creativi-Toy
✓		Checkpoint	Creativi-Toy
✓		Collection Pen	Creativi-Toy
✓		Counter	Creativi-Toy

Got It?	Icon	Toy Name	Category
✓		Dual Action Trigger	Creativi-Toy
✓		Invulnerability Beacon	Creativi-Toy
✓		Kill Switch	Creativi-Toy
✓		Marching Orders	Creativi-Toy
✓		Racing Gate	Creativi-Toy
✓		Scoreboard	Creativi-Toy
✓		Side-Step Camera	Creativi-Toy
✓		Target	Creativi-Toy
✓		Team 1 Base	Creativi-Toy
✓		Team 2 Base	Creativi-Toy
✓		Teleporter	Creativi-Toy
✓		Time Delayer	Creativi-Toy
✓		Timer	Creativi-Toy
✓		Trigger	Creativi-Toy
✓		Trigger Area	Creativi-Toy
✓		Vehicle Weapon Generator	Creativi-Toy
✓		Victory Tracker	Creativi-Toy
✓		Bulletin Board	Decoration
✓		Foot Locker	Decoration
✓		Give 'em a Hand Launcher	Decoration
✓		Have a Nice Trip Launcher	Decoration
✓		School Colors Ender	Decoration
✓		Scream Energy Launcher	Decoration
✓		Scream Tunnel Cover	Decoration
✓		Scream Tunnel Sludge Ender	Decoration
✓		Fantasy Terrain 3	Plants
✓		Fantasy Terrain 4	Plants
✓		Fantasy Terrain Corner 2	Plants
✓		Fantasy Terrain Strip 1	Plants

Got It?	Icon	Toy Name	Category
✓		Bluff	Terrain
✓		Canyon Curve	Terrain
✓		Canyon Outer Curve	Terrain
✓		Canyon Wall	Terrain
✓		Cave	Terrain
✓		Cave and Well	Terrain
✓		Cave Bend	Terrain
✓		Cave End	Terrain
✓		Cave Fort	Terrain
✓		Cave Fort Block	Terrain
✓		Cave Intersection	Terrain
✓		Cave Tunnel	Terrain
✓		Climbing Ledge Wall	Terrain
✓		Corner Block with Ramps	Terrain
✓		Corner Hill	Terrain
✓		Corner Slope	Terrain
✓		Crystal Cavern	Terrain
✓		Floating Bridge Hill	Terrain
✓		Floating Rope Cliff	Terrain
✓		Grassy Bridge	Terrain
✓		Hanging Rope Cliff	Terrain
✓		Large Canyon Curve	Terrain
✓		Large Canyon Outer Curve	Terrain
✓		Large Rounded Cliff	Terrain
✓		Large Slope	Terrain
✓		Large Terrain Block	Terrain
✓		Long Tiny Terrain Block	Terrain
✓		Massive Rounded Cliff	Terrain
✓		Medium Canyon Outer Curve	Terrain

Got It?	Icon	Toy Name	Category
✓		Medium Cliff Ledge	Terrain
✓		Mining Tunnel	Terrain
✓		Mountain Tunnel	Terrain
✓		Narrow Canyon Wall	Terrain
✓		Narrow Floating Cliff	Terrain
✓		Plateau Block with Ramp	Terrain
✓		Ramp Cliff	Terrain
✓		Rocky Layered Block	Terrain
✓		Rocky Ramp Block	Terrain
✓		Rocky Wall Jump Block	Terrain
✓		Short Cave Block	Terrain
✓		Slope	Terrain
✓		Sloping Hill	Terrain
✓		Small Bridge Cliff	Terrain
✓		Small Canyon Curve	Terrain
✓		Small Canyon Outer Curve	Terrain
✓		Small Floating Cliff	Terrain
✓		Small Jutting Ledge	Terrain
✓		Small Rocky Terrain Block 2	Terrain
✓		Small Rocky Terrain Block 3	Terrain
✓		Small Slope	Terrain
✓		Small Terrain Block	Terrain
✓		Square Rocky Terrain Block	Terrain
✓		Step Cliff	Terrain
✓		Stepped Grassy Corner	Terrain
✓		Tall Terrain Block	Terrain
✓		Terrain Block	Terrain
✓		The Matterhorn	Terrain
✓		Tiny Slope	Terrain

Got It?	Icon	Toy Name	Category
✓		Tiny Tall Terrain Block	Terrain
✓		Tiny Terrain Block	Terrain
✓		Treasure Grotto	Terrain
✓		Underground Pipe Bend	Terrain
✓		Underground Pipe Branch	Terrain
✓		Underground Pipe End	Terrain
✓		Underground Pipe Entrance/Exit	Terrain
✓		Underground Pipe Intersection	Terrain
✓		Underground Pipe Tunnel	Terrain
✓		Wide Canyon Wall	Terrain
✓		Wide Floating Bridge Hill	Terrain
✓		Wide Floating Cliff	Terrain
✓		Bending Rail	Track Piece
✓		Bump Rail	Track Piece
✓		Curved Rail	Track Piece
✓		Dipped Rail	Track Piece
✓		Left Rail	Track Piece
✓		Left Upward Curving Rail	Track Piece
✓		Ramp Rail	Track Piece
✓		Right Rail	Track Piece
✓		Right Upward Curving Rail	Track Piece
✓		Short Straight Rail	Track Piece
✓		Steep Bending Rail	Track Piece
✓		Steep Ramp Rail	Track Piece
✓		Straight Rail	Track Piece

GAME BASICS

CHARACTERS

POWER DISCS

PLAY SETS

TOY BOX

TOY BOX COLLECTION

ACHIEVEMENTS

SPORTS TOY BOX

Use the sports toys to create sports games to play with your friends. Check out the toys available in this world.

Got It?	Icon	Toy Name	Category
✓		Sky Changer	Basic Toy
✓		Arch Block	Block
✓		Balcony	Block
✓		Column	Block
✓		Curved Block	Block
✓		Dip Beam	Block
✓		Full Dome	Block
✓		Half Dome	Block
✓		Large Floor	Block
✓		Large Stone Wall	Block
✓		Ledge Block	Block
✓		Long Block	Block
✓		Long Support Arch	Block
✓		Long Wedge Block	Block
✓		Obelisk	Block
✓		Onion Dome	Block
✓		Pillar Block	Block
✓		Ramp Vertical	Block
✓		Rounded Ledge Block	Block
✓		Short Support Arch	Block
✓		Small Floor	Block

Got It?	Icon	Toy Name	Category
✓		Square Block	Block
✓		Stairs	Block
✓		Stone Wall	Block
✓		Stone Wall Corner	Block
✓		Tall Block	Block
✓		Tall Vaulted Platform	Block
✓		Triangle Block	Block
✓		Trim	Block
✓		Vaulted Platform	Block
✓		Wedge Block	Block
✓		Curved Stadium	Building Sets
✓		Stadium	Building Sets
✓		Stadium Gate	Building Sets
✓		Bird's Eye Camera	Creativi-Toy
✓		Boom Box	Creativi-Toy
✓		Checkpoint	Creativi-Toy
✓		Collection Pen	Creativi-Toy
✓		Counter	Creativi-Toy
✓		Dual Action Trigger	Creativi-Toy
✓		Invulnerability Beacon	Creativi-Toy
✓		Kill Switch	Creativi-Toy
✓		Marching Orders	Creativi-Toy
✓		Racing Gate	Creativi-Toy
✓		Scoreboard	Creativi-Toy
✓		Side-Step Camera	Creativi-Toy
✓		Target	Creativi-Toy
✓		Team 1 Base	Creativi-Toy
✓		Team 2 Base	Creativi-Toy
✓		Teleporter	Creativi-Toy

Got It?	Icon	Toy Name	Category
✓		Time Delayer	Creativi-Toy
✓		Timer	Creativi-Toy
✓		Trigger	Creativi-Toy
✓		Trigger Area	Creativi-Toy
✓		Vehicle Weapon Generator	Creativi-Toy
✓		Victory Tracker	Creativi-Toy
✓		Fantasy Terrain 3	Plants
✓		Fantasy Terrain 4	Plants
✓		Fantasy Terrain Corner 2	Plants
✓		Fantasy Terrain Strip 1	Plants
✓		ESPN Award Podium	Sports Toy
✓		ESPN Banner	Sports Toy
✓		ESPN Baseball	Sports Toy
✓		ESPN Basketball	Sports Toy
✓		ESPN Basketball Hoop	Sports Toy
✓		ESPN Bench	Sports Toy
✓		ESPN Bowling Ball	Sports Toy
✓		ESPN Corner Track Railing	Sports Toy
✓		ESPN Curved Track Railing	Sports Toy
✓		ESPN Double Banner	Sports Toy
✓		ESPN Flag	Sports Toy
✓		ESPN Football	Sports Toy
✓		ESPN Goal Post	Sports Toy
✓		ESPN Golf Ball	Sports Toy
✓		ESPN Hockey Puck	Sports Toy
✓		ESPN Pylon	Sports Toy
✓		ESPN Scrolling Sign	Sports Toy
✓		ESPN Soccer Ball	Sports Toy
✓		ESPN Soccer Goal	Sports Toy

Got It?	Icon	Toy Name	Category
✓		ESPN Stadium Lights	Sports Toy
✓		ESPN Tennis Ball	Sports Toy
✓		ESPN Track Railing	Sports Toy
✓		X Games Barrier	Sports Toy
✓		Bluff	Terrain
✓		Canyon Curve	Terrain
✓		Canyon Outer Curve	Terrain
✓		Canyon Wall	Terrain
✓		Cave	Terrain
✓		Cave and Well	Terrain
✓		Cave Bend	Terrain
✓		Cave End	Terrain
✓		Cave Fort	Terrain
✓		Cave Fort Block	Terrain
✓		Cave Intersection	Terrain
✓		Cave Tunnel	Terrain
✓		Climbing Ledge Wall	Terrain
✓		Corner Block with Ramps	Terrain
✓		Corner Hill	Terrain
✓		Corner Slope	Terrain
✓		Crystal Cavern	Terrain
✓		Floating Bridge Hill	Terrain
✓		Floating Rope Cliff	Terrain
✓		Grassy Bridge	Terrain
✓		Hanging Rope Cliff	Terrain
✓		Large Canyon Curve	Terrain
✓		Large Canyon Outer Curve	Terrain
✓		Large Rounded Cliff	Terrain
✓		Large Slope	Terrain

Got It?	Icon	Toy Name	Category
✓		Large Terrain Block	Terrain
✓		Long Tiny Terrain Block	Terrain
✓		Massive Rounded Cliff	Terrain
✓		Medium Canyon Outer Curve	Terrain
✓		Medium Cliff Ledge	Terrain
✓		Mining Tunnel	Terrain
✓		Mountain Tunnel	Terrain
✓		Narrow Canyon Wall	Terrain
✓		Narrow Floating Cliff	Terrain
✓		Plateau Block with Ramp	Terrain
✓		Ramp Cliff	Terrain
✓		Rocky Layered Block	Terrain
✓		Rocky Ramp Block	Terrain
✓		Rocky Wall Jump Block	Terrain
✓		Short Cave Block	Terrain
✓		Slope	Terrain
✓		Sloping Hill	Terrain
✓		Small Bridge Cliff	Terrain
✓		Small Canyon Curve	Terrain
✓		Small Canyon Outer Curve	Terrain
✓		Small Floating Cliff	Terrain
✓		Small Jutting Ledge	Terrain
✓		Small Rocky Terrain Block 2	Terrain
✓		Small Rocky Terrain Block 3	Terrain
✓		Small Slope	Terrain
✓		Small Terrain Block	Terrain
✓		Square Rocky Terrain Block	Terrain
✓		Step Cliff	Terrain
✓		Stepped Grassy Corner	Terrain

Got It?	Icon	Toy Name	Category
✓		Tall Terrain Block	Terrain
✓		Terrain Block	Terrain
✓		The Matterhorn	Terrain
✓		Tiny Slope	Terrain
✓		Tiny Tall Terrain Block	Terrain
✓		Tiny Terrain Block	Terrain
✓		Treasure Grotto	Terrain
✓		Underground Pipe Bend	Terrain
✓		Underground Pipe Branch	Terrain
✓		Underground Pipe End	Terrain
✓		Underground Pipe Entrance/Exit	Terrain
✓		Underground Pipe Intersection	Terrain
✓		Underground Pipe Tunnel	Terrain
✓		Wide Canyon Wall	Terrain
✓		Wide Floating Bridge Hill	Terrain
✓		Wide Floating Cliff	Terrain
✓		Football Player Costume	Toy Box Townspeople
✓		Green Basketball Jersey Costume	Toy Box Townspeople
✓		Hockey Player Costume	Toy Box Townspeople
✓		Referee Costume	Toy Box Townspeople
✓		Tennis Player Costume	Toy Box Townspeople
✓		Volleyball Player Costume	Toy Box Townspeople
✓		Yellow Basketball Jersey Costume	Toy Box Townspeople

Achievements & Trophies

Got It?	#	Name	Location	Category	Criteria	Xbox 360 Achievements	PS3 Trophies
✓	1	Star Extractor	Global	Stars	Collect 15 stars in a Play Set	5	Bronze (15)
✓	2	1 More to Go	Global	Stars	Collect 15 stars in 2 Play Sets	10	Bronze (15)
✓	3	All Star	Global	Stars	Collect 15 stars in 3 Play Sets	25	Bronze (15)
✓	4	It's a Start	Global	Stars	Collect 50 stars	10	Bronze (15)
✓	5	Wish Upon a Star	Global	Stars	Collect 70 stars in the Disney Infinity Starter Pack	100	Gold (90)
✓	6	New Friends	Global	In Game Progression	Play a 2-player game using two different characters	10	Bronze (15)
✓	7	Character Plunder	Global	In Game Progression	Unlock 3 Character Chests	4	Bronze (15)
✓	8	Character Elite Force	Global	In Game Progression	Level up 3 Characters to level 15	100	Gold (90)
✓	9	Character Elite Set	Global	In Game Progression	Level up 2 Characters to level 15	25	Bronze (15)
✓	10	Character Elite	Global	In Game Progression	Level up 1 Character to level 15	10	Bronze (15)
✓	11	Visit the Hall	Global	General	Visit the Hall of Heroes	4	Bronze (15)
✓	12	Infinity and Beyond	Global	General	Play 3 Play Sets and the Toy Box	10	Bronze (15)
✓	13	All Modes	Global	General	Drive a car, pilot a helicopter, and ride a mount	10	Bronze (15)
✓	14	Power Up!	Global	Toys	Place one Power Disc on the Disney Infinity Base	4	Bronze (15)
✓	15	Great Communicator	Global	A.I. Interactions	Talk to mission givers 20 times throughout Disney Infinity	10	Bronze (15)
✓	16	Defender of the Universe	Global	A.I. Interactions	Defeat 100 enemies throughout Disney Infinity	10	Bronze (15)
✓	17	It's a Party	Toy Box	Multiplayer	Play a 4-player game	10	Bronze (15)
✓	18	Sorry?	Toy Box	Multiplayer	Defeat another player's Character	4	Bronze (15)
✓	19	Not Sorry?	Toy Box	Multiplayer	Defeat 40 player Characters	10	Bronze (15)
✓	20	Acrobat	Toy Box	Multiplayer	Stand on top of a stack of 4 Characters	5	Bronze (15)
✓	21	The Champion	Toy Box	Multiplayer	Win First Place in a Multiplayer Adventure	10	Bronze (15)
✓	22	Creator	Toy Box	General	Save 4 different Toy Box worlds	5	Bronze (15)
✓	23	Graduate	Toy Box	General	Complete all Mastery Adventures	10	Bronze (15)
✓	24	Import Master	Toy Box	General	Place a toy from a Play Set in a Toy Box you are hosting	10	Bronze (15)
✓	25	Spin Start	Toy Box	Disney Infinity Vault	Take 10 turns in the Disney Infinity Vault	10	Bronze (15)
✓	26	Spin Master	Toy Box	Disney Infinity Vault	Take 20 turns in the Disney Infinity Vault	15	Bronze (15)
✓	27	Bonus Bank	Toy Box	Disney Infinity Vault	Win 5 bonuses in the Disney Infinity Vault	10	Bronze (15)
✓	28	Disney Infinity Vault Extreme	Toy Box	Disney Infinity Vault	Take 30 turns in the Disney Infinity Vault	15	Silver (30)
✓	29	Star Hunter	Toy Box	Stars	Get 18 stars from Adventures	10	Bronze (15)
✓	30	Feat Novice	Toy Box	Feats	Complete 25 feats	10	Bronze (15)
✓	31	Feat Master	Toy Box	Feats	Complete 75 feats	15	Bronze (15)
✓	32	Not Last!	Toy Box	Adventures	Complete 3 Adventures to bronze standard	10	Bronze (15)
✓	33	Almost There	Toy Box	Adventures	Complete 3 Adventures to silver standard	25	Silver (30)
✓	34	It's All Gold!	Toy Box	Adventures	Complete 3 Adventures to gold standard	100	Silver (30)
✓	35	Team Work	Play Sets	Multiplayer	Complete a Story Mission in a multiplayer game	5	Bronze (15)
✓	36	Getting It Started	Play Sets	Story Missions	Complete a Story Mission	4	Bronze (15)
✓	37	Journey Complete	Play Sets	Story Missions	Complete the story in a Play Set	10	Bronze (15)
✓	38	Another Happy Outcome	Play Sets	Story Missions	Complete the story in 2 Play Sets	25	Bronze (15)
✓	39	There Is No "End" in Infinity!	Play Sets	Story Missions	Complete the story in 3 Play Sets	100	Gold (90)
✓	40	Full of Toys	Play Sets	PS Specific Toys	Unlock 10 toys from Play Sets	10	Bronze (15)
✓	41	Power Pack!	Play Sets	PS Specific Toys	Buy 2 Packs from one Play Set	10	Bronze (15)
✓	42	Multi-Tool!	Play Sets	PS Specific Toys	Buy 2 Tools from one Play Set	10	Bronze (15)
✓	43	City Planner	Play Sets	PS Specific Toys	Buy 4 Play Set buildings and place them in the Toy Box	10	Bronze (15)
✓	44	Doesn't This Look Better?	Play Sets	PS Specific Toys	Customize 6 buildings in the Play Sets	10	Bronze (15)
✓	45	Challenger	Play Sets	Challenges	Complete the "Easy" level on all Challenges in a single Play Set	5	Bronze (15)
✓	46	Challenging	Play Sets	Challenges	Complete the "Medium" level on all Challenges in a single Play Set	10	Bronze (15)
✓	47	Challenges Conquered	Play Sets	Challenges	Complete the "Hard" level on all Challenges in a single Play Set	25	Silver (30)
✓	48	That Was Easy	Play Sets	Challenges	Complete 5 Challenges on Easy	10	Bronze (15)
✓	49	That Was Rough	Play Sets	Challenges	Complete 5 Challenges on Medium	25	Bronze (15)
✓	50	That Was a Challenge	Play Sets	Challenges	Complete 5 Challenges on Hard	100	Silver (30)
✓		Platinum Challenge	Global (PS3 only)	PS3	Complete all Trophies		Platinum

INF(IN)ITY

PRIMA Official Game Guide

Written by:
Howard Grossman & Michael Knight

Prima Games
An Imprint of Random House, Inc.
3000 Lava Ridge Court, Suite 100
Roseville, CA 95661
www.primagames.com/2014DI

The Prima Games logo is a registered trademark of Random House LLC, registered in the United States and other countries. Primagames.com is a registered trademark of Random House LLC, registered in the United States.

Prima Games is an imprint of Random House LLC, New York, a Penguin Random House Company.

© Disney. © Disney/Pixar. All Rights Reserved.

THE LONE RANGER . © Disney Enterprises, Inc. and Jerry Bruckheimer, Inc. The LONE RANGER property is owned by and TM & © Classic Media, Inc., an Entertainment Rights group company. Used by permission.

The term Omnidroid used by permission of Lucasfilm Ltd.

Plymouth Superbird is a trademark of DaimlerChrysler Corporation

Slinky® Dog © Poof-Slinky

Sarge's rank insignia design used with the approval of the U.S. Army

Volkswagen trademarks, design patents and copyrights are used with the approval of the owner Volkswagen AG

Petty marks used by permission of Petty Marketing LLC

Hudson Hornet is a trademark of DaimlerChrysler Corporation

FIAT is a trademark of FIAT S.p.A.

Chevrolet Impala is a trademark of General Motors

Cadillac Range background inspired by the Cadillac Ranch by Ant Farm (Lord, Michels and Marquez) © 1974.

The ESPN Logo and X Games Logo are registered trademarks of ESPN, Inc. Used with permission of ESPN, Inc.

Senior Product Marketing Manager: Donato Tica
Design and Layout: Ryan Zagar, Jody Seltzer & In Color Design
Copyeditor: Julia Mascardo
Gameplay/Maps Dude: Josef Frech
Special Thanks: Connor Knight and Tanner Knight

IMPORTANT:

ISBN: 978-0804-16273-9/978-0804-16274-6/978-0804-16320-0
Printed in the United States of America

Prima Games would like to thank the following people for their support:

Michael Schneider, Mathew Solie, Greg Hayes, Cyril Bornette, Phil Knight, Manfred Neber, Chad Liddell, David White, Troy Johnson, Troy Leavitt, Mark McArther, Kevin Pulley, Mike Thompson, Jeff Byers, Vince Bracken, John Blackburn, John Vignocchi, Kristin Yee, Aaron King, Stephanie Martinelli, Stephen Lewis, Vince Griffin, Rick Gusa, Mary Galligan, Disney Interactive QA team, The team at Avalanche Software.